The OLD TESTAMENT
Teacher's Wraparound Edition

ave maria press  Notre Dame, Indiana

Scripture texts in this work are taken from the *New American Bible with Revised New Testament and Revised Psalms* © 1991, 1986, 1970 Confraternity of Christian Doctrine, Washington, D.C. and are used by permission of the copyright owner. All Rights Reserved. No part of the *New American Bible* may be reproduced without permission in writing from the copyright owner.

English translation of the *Catechism of the Catholic Church* for the United States of America copyright © 1994, United States Catholic Conference, Inc.— Libreria Editrice Vaticana. Used with permission.

Other references cited as End Notes with each chapter.

Theological Consultant:
Hugh R. Page, Jr., Ph.D.
Associate Dean and Director of Undergraduate Studies in the College of Arts and Letters
University of Notre Dame

© 2005 by Ave Maria Press, Inc.

All rights reserved. No part of this book may be used or reproduced in any manner whatsoever except in the case of reprints in the context of reviews, without written permission from Ave Maria Press®, Inc., P.O. Box 428, Notre Dame, IN 46556.

www.avemariapress.com

International Standard Book Number: 0-87793-604-8

Teacher Manual Author: Janie Gustafson, Ph.D.

Project Editor: Michael Amodei

Cover and text design by Brian C. Conley

Printed and bound in the United States of America.

The OLD TESTAMENT
Teacher's Wraparound Edition

our call to faith & justice

Daniel Smith-Christopher
TWE author Janie Gustafson, Ph.D.

Contents

Introduction to the Teacher's Wraparound Edition 6

1 Preparing for the Journey: Basic Information 16
2 Maps for the Journey: Geographical, Historical, and Literary Context 36
3 Stories for the Journey: Creation and the Founding of a People 62
4 The Journey to the Promised Land Begins: The Exodus and the Sinai Covenant 90
5 The Journey Takes New Shape: A People at Home 114
6 The Monarchy: The Journey Takes a New Direction 134
7 God's Prophets: At the Heart of the Journey 158
8 Turning Point in the Journey: The Destruction of Judah, Exile, and Return 178
9 A Spiritual Journey: A Look at Wisdom and Apocalyptic Literature 204
10 The Journey Leads to the Time of Jesus and Beyond 228

Epilogue 253
Resource Section 259

Introduction to the Teacher's Wraparound Edition

Course Objectives and Theology

The Second Vatican Council described the Church as a "pilgrim people" (see *Lumen Gentium*, Chapter VII). The Church is the People of God moving toward, and helping to build, the kingdom of God. We are on a spiritual journey, to be sure. But we are also on a physical journey in time and space. We travel together with Jesus Christ, who became human so that we might "know God's love" (*CCC*, 458) and enter into "the perfect unity of the Blessed Trinity" (*CCC*, 260). In Jesus, our physical journey through life in this world and our spiritual journey toward God have become one. Our journey's destination is no less than a new creation: assuming the mind and heart of Jesus, who "became human so that we might become God" (St. Athanasius).

A real journey is much more than a theoretical exercise or looking at images on a computer monitor. A real journey involves our whole being—minds, hearts, and hands. We are immersed in the experience, caught up in each event. We truly have to "be there" each step along the way in order to reach our destination.

Think about the journeys you have taken in your own life. There was likely a period of preparation in which you mapped out the route, made reservations if needed, and gathered the necessary provisions. You packed your bags, and you made sure someone would pick up your mail, feed the pets, and water the houseplants. The actual journey may have gone smoothly; more likely, little things went wrong. You may have had a flat tire, been lost, had an argument with family members, or taken an unplanned detour. Or, if you were traveling by air, there may have been long lines, delayed flights, extra security inspections, or other inconveniences. It was only by actually dealing with these experiences that you eventually reached your intended destination.

When we read the Old Testament, it is important to realize that it contains the writings of people who were on a journey—both physical and spiritual—over many centuries. At times along the way, these people got lost and made detours. Sometimes they ran out of provisions, and often times they wondered if they would ever really reach the Promised Land to which God called them. The journey challenged them; it also changed them. It changed their *minds*—their thoughts about God and their relationship with him. It changed their *hearts*—how they felt about God, their identity as a people, and the world around them. And it changed their *hands*—what they did and how they behaved as individuals and as a nation.

Studying the Old Testament today is also a journey. Instead of being an academic pursuit *about* a long-ago journey of strangers, it invites us to embark on a journey of our own with family members of faith. As we learn about the plights and predicaments of the people of Israel, we recognize situations in our own faith journey. We are challenged to grow in our understanding of God, ourselves, and other people. Father Basil Moreau, founder of the Congregation of the Holy Cross, once said, "An education that is complete is one in which the hands and heart are engaged as much as the mind." These words form the foundation of this course.

The Old Testament: Our Call to Faith and Justice aims to tell the journey of God's People for Catholic teenagers in such a way that they will progress on their own journey of friendship with God, discipleship to Christ, and Catholic identity. Furthermore, the text hopes to motivate students to continue looking to their past as they continue forward in their own personal faith journey.

The author of the Student Text, Dr. Daniel Smith-Christopher, is a professor of theology specializing in the Old Testament at Loyola Marymount University in Los Angeles. The Student Text contains the fruit of his own years of study and personal reflection with the Scriptures. His core thesis is that the Old Testament is God's sacred words calling us to total relationship with him. The course teaches that there is no separation between faith and justice. If we truly believe in God, then we will act justly in all our relationships—with our families, with our communities, with other nations, and with the environment. In particular, we will do our best to help the poor who are often described as the widow, orphan, and alien in the Old Testament.

Jesus himself emphasized the integral connection between faith and justice. "I was hungry and you gave me drink, a stranger and you welcomed me, naked and you clothed me, ill and you cared for me, in prison and you visited me. . . . Whatever you did for one of these least brothers of mine, you did for me" (Mt 25:35–36, 40). For Jesus, justice is not an "extra" or optional addendum to faith in God; rather, it is to be an integral part of our identity and behavior. To live as disciples of Jesus in the twenty-first century, we must *really* be people of peace and justice.

While the New Testament *fulfills* the Old Testament in the person and teachings of Jesus, it does not *replace* the Old Testament. Indeed, truly knowing the Old Testament adds immeasurable dimension to our understanding of the Gospels. It helps us perceive new depths of meaning in the words of Jesus and what it means to follow him. As St. Paul writes, "All scripture is inspired by God and is useful for teaching, for refutation, for correction, and for training in righteousness, so that one who belongs to God may be competent, equipped for every good work" (2 Tm 3:16–17).

It is our hope that this course on the Old Testament will enliven your own Christian faith and discipleship. May it empower you to bring the message of peace and justice to all your students. And may they, in turn, grow to be a true "light of the world" and "salt of the earth" (Mt 5:14, 13).

About the Course

The Old Testament: Our Call to Faith and Justice consists of the following components:
- Student Text
- Teacher's Wraparound Edition
- Text Files at avemariapress.com

Student Text Overview

The Student Text is divided into ten chapters and an appendix. Each chapter describes a portion of the Israelites' journey as found in certain books of the Old Testament. The material reflects on the Old Testament from a Catholic perspective.

- Chapter 1 explains the differences between the Catholic, Protestant, and Jewish Scripture. It presents the classification and arrangement of the Old Testament books. It shows why knowledge of the original languages of the Bible, the various translations, other ancient writings, and the science of archaeology is so important to Bible study.
- Chapter 2 presents the writings of the Old Testament in a geographical, historical, and religious context. It also discusses what archaeological finds have revealed about the peoples of the Biblical period.
- Chapter 3 contains an overview of the stories (creation, first sin, flood, tower of Babel) found in the book of Genesis. It also presents the lives and challenges of the Israelite patriarchs: Abraham, Isaac, Jacob, and Joseph.
- Chapter 4 covers the central covenant of the Old Testament: the Sinai Covenant given to Moses. It also covers the call of Moses, the ten plagues, and the exodus. The book of reference is the book of Exodus.
- Chapter 5 focuses on the Biblical books known as the Deuteronomic History (books based on the book of Deuteronomy). These books are Joshua, Judges, 1 and 2 Samuel, 1 and 2 Kings, as well as the book of Ruth. Primarily, the chapter deals with Joshua and Judges, books that describe Israelite history from the conquest of Jericho to the time of the kings.
- Chapter 6 discusses the books of 1 and 2 Samuel and 1 and 2 Kings. Specifically, the chapter focuses on the period of the united monarchy in Israel and presents the stories of Kings Saul, David, and Solomon.
- Chapter 7 introduces the prophetic literature found in the Old Testament. Specifically the chapter deals with the prophets of the northern kingdom Israel in the ninth and eighth centuries B.C.: Elijah, Elisha, Hosea, and Amos.
- Chapter 8 deals with some of the events leading to the destruction of Jerusalem by Babylon in 587 B.C. Among these events are the exile of the people of Judah to Babylon and their eventual return to Palestine with the help of King Cyrus of Persia. In addition, the chapter deals with several important prophets of this time: Isaiah of Jerusalem, Micah, Ezekiel, Jeremiah, Deutero-Isaiah, and Third Isaiah.
- Chapter 9 discusses Biblical Wisdom literature—the books of Job, Psalms, Proverbs, Ecclesiastes, Song of Songs, Sirach, and Wisdom.
- Chapter 10 covers the last six hundred years of Israel's history before the birth of Christ. During this time, the Jews lived under successive foreign rule: the Babylonians, the Persians, the Greeks, and the Romans. Stories from this period—from the books of Daniel, Tobit, Esther, and Judith—contain messages about how the Jews are to survive under foreign rule.
- The Appendix contains a Catholic Handbook for Faith—prayers, teachings, creeds, Church history, sacraments, and practices.

Student Text Organization

In addition to the regular text, each chapter includes the following elements:
- **Overview** Gives a brief introduction about the chapter contents.
- **Features** This material gives more in-depth information about some topic discussed in the student text.
- **Vocabulary Words** The definitions of faith-based words found in the text are given in the margin.
- **Review and Reflection** These objective questions help the students learn the major points presented in the main chapter sections and thus prepare for the Chapter Tests.
- **Journal Assignment** These affective projects help the students internalize what the text has discussed and apply what they have learned to their own lives.
- **"Mind" Exercise** These cognitive exercises and projects are designed to strengthen the students' knowledge of the Old Testament and are designated by this icon.

- **"Heart" Exercise** These presentations and activities promote prayerful study of the Scripture and connect the students to the Church's liturgy and are designated by this icon.

- **"Hands" Exercise** These practical applications encourage the students to become involved in service and ministry and are designated by this icon.

- **Learn by Doing** These end-of-the chapter activities offer a chance for the students to utilize the material they have covered.
- **Called to Prayer** These prayers, quotations, or reflections—based on the chapter content—may be used in communal or individual prayer.

Scope of the Course

By studying the Pentateuch, historical books, Wisdom literature, and prophetic books of the Bible, the students learn about the history of the Israelites from the time of Abraham to the time of Christ. In addition to learning history, the students will be introduced to the geography, politics, and social milieu of the Ancient Near East. More important are the religious lessons of Scripture. The Old Testament is God's Word. The students will learn about the evolution of the Israelites' belief in one God and how they developed into a people of faith. The students will see how this faith shaped the Israelites' identity as God's People and gradually led them to understand the importance of justice in all relationships.

Course Sequence

The Old Testament offers a "prefiguration" of what God did in the fullness of time in the person of his son, Jesus Christ. Catholics read the Old Testament "in the light of Christ crucified and risen" (see *CCC*, 128–129). This unity between the Old Testament and New Testament is based on typology. The listing by chapters indicates the major treatment of the following subjects under this typological approach:

Chapter 1: Preparing for the Journey: Basic Information
- The Catholic canon of the Old Testament includes forty-six books.
- All the books found in the canon of the Old Testament are the inspired word of God.
- The Holy Spirit inspired the authors of the biblical books to write only what God wanted to be written.

Chapter 2: Maps for the Journey: Geographical, Historical, and Literary Context
- Understanding the geography, history, and religious background of the Israelites helps us to understand the content, message, and importance of Scripture.
- The Old Testament is inspired by God and is the true Word of God.
- Ultimately, the Old Testament prepares us for the coming of Jesus Christ, Messiah and Son of God.

Chapter 3: Stories for the Journey: Creation and the Founding of a People
- God alone made the universe out of love. All creation is good. God loves all that he created and continually cares for it.
- Through free will, humans brought sin into the world.
- God made a promise to save humanity from sin.
- God chooses unlikely candidates to lead his people and makes a covenant with them.
- God can work with family relationships that are far from perfect and can bring good out of conflict and evil.

Chapter 4: The Journey to the Promised Land Begins: The Exodus and the Sinai Covenant
- God keeps his promises to his people.
- God is a God of liberation, not enslavement.
- God made a covenant with the ancient Israelites to be his People.
- The Old Law is the first stage of revealed law. Its moral prescriptions are summed up in the Ten Commandments.

Chapter 5: The Journey Takes New Shape: A People at Home
- Fidelity to God ensures victory or success. Trust in one's own prowess is fruitless; in fact, it usually ends in disaster.
- Yahweh is a God of peace rather than warfare.
- Like the ancient Israelites who frequently lapsed back into idolatry, we too are in need of continual conversion.
- We are called to place our trust firmly and solely in God.

Chapter 6: The Monarchy: The Journey Takes a New Direction
- Political authority has its limits; rulers rule with God's consent and must obey God's laws.
- When we obey the commandments and act with justice toward others, God is present to us both as individuals and as a nation.
- Jesus is a descendant of David. He is the new King of Kings. He rules, not with oppressive power and taxing authority, but with the attitude of a servant. He ushers in God's kingdom of justice and peace for all people, not just the wealthy.

Chapter 7: God's Prophets: At the Heart of the Journey
- Social justice is at the core of the Bible's message. God sides with the poor—especially the orphan, the widow, and the alien resident.
- God judges us, not by our elaborate worship ceremonies but by the way we treat others.
- Jesus himself confirms the prophets' vision. When the kingdom of God comes, the Son of Man will judge people according to their just and loving treatment of others. God will reward those who give shelter to the homeless, feed the hungry, and care for the sick. Likewise, God will punish those who oppress others.
- We too are to be prophets for today—applying Biblical principles to modern-day topics such as abortion, the death penalty, genetic research, warfare, poverty, the environment, and so forth.

Chapter 8: Turning Point in the Journey: The Destruction of Judah, Exile, and Return
- God can be found and worshiped everywhere, even outside the Temple in Jerusalem.
- God is present in our times of suffering. Suffering itself has a purpose, even if we don't understand what it is. Suffering can help to strengthen our faith, to purify our attitudes and behaviors.
- God is not only just; God is also compassionate and merciful.

Chapter 9: A Spiritual Journey: A Look at Wisdom and Apocalyptic Literature
- God is present in all human experience. We find God through our day-to-day challenges, not in addition to them. Our relationship with God is the beginning of all wisdom.
- God's Spirit helps us discern meaning and find happiness in the midst of our experiences.
- God is always in control despite "evidence" or fears to the contrary.

Chapter 10: The Journey Leads to the Time of Jesus and Beyond
- In order to understand fully the New Testament, it is important to have a solid background in Old Testament study.
- Our faith calls us to be people of peace and justice.
- When there is a conflict between God's law and human-made laws, it is more important to obey our conscience and follow spiritual values than to obey political authority.

Teacher Wraparound Edition

The Teacher Wraparound Edition provides suggestions for teaching the course, including lesson ideas for every page of the Student Text.

Chapter Organization

Each chapter includes the following regular elements:

Introducing the Chapter. A brief overview of the chapter highlighting its central points.

Background Notes for the Teacher. Provides further theological and doctrinal information on the material to be covered in the chapter.

Resources. Includes a list of films, videos, music, magazine articles, and the like that can be used to extend the lessons. *Printed resources* are referenced by page numbers within the book or article. These readings are mainly intended to provide teachers with further historical and theological references. Some of these readings can occasionally be assigned as student reading or read aloud to the entire class. *Audiovisual Materials* is primarily a list of videos suitable for play as part of a class lesson. Publishers are listed with the titles. Often diocesan or Catholic school offices sponsor a library with many of these videos. The total play time for each video is also listed. Several *Internet Links* are provided as teacher support. Several links may also be appropriate to refer students to for assignments and projects. Citations with the text of *Church Documents* provide reference points for Church teaching on the particular topics being covered. Refer to these when answering difficult questions asked by the students. The *Music Suggestions* are primarily intended to support the end of chapter Prayer Services. These songs can also be played as background music when the students enter the classroom or for when working on individual or group classroom assignments.

Chapter Outline. Gives an overview of the chapter in outline form.

Advance Preparation. Introduces any long-term assignments that may be required of the students throughout the chapter.

Chapter Objectives. Lists the major goals the chapter hopes to accomplish with the students. These objectives may be both objective and affective.

Lesson Plan. Each lesson plan includes:
- *Bell-Ringers.* These are arrival activities, assignments, discussion questions, and the like for students. The purpose is to introduce the day's material, to serve as an icebreaker, or to review homework or previous class assignments.
- *Teacher Approaches.* This is the main element of the lesson plan. It offers several specific, creative approaches for teaching the material, page by page. Included may be Background Information to share with the students, notes on Handouts or Overheads, activities for re-teaching previously covered material and for teaching new material, Review Questions Answers and Bible study activities, and optional suggestions for extending the lesson. Each class session ends with a homework assignment.
- *Overheads.* These pages may be duplicated onto transparencies for use as teaching aids in the classroom. They can be accessed at avemariapress.com. See the "Religious Education" area of the website for information on special teacher privileges.
- *Handouts.* These pages may be copied onto blackline masters or simply reproduced to put in the hands of the students. Handouts include information, activities, discussion questions, and prayer services to enhance material found in the student text. Online versions of these materials are available at **avemariapress.com**.

Testing Program. Tests with both objective and subjective questions follow each chapter. They can be accessed at **avemariapress.com**. See the "Relgious Education" area of the website for information on special teacher privileges. The answers to the tests are included with the material for the particular chapter.

Tips for Teaching Adolescents

Educational experts all agree that no student learns in exactly the same way as other students. Research on multiple intelligences shows that each student has a primary way of learning. That way may be visual, or auditory, or hands-on experiential. Some students are more spatially oriented. Others need reflection and a quiet environment. The Teacher Wraparound Edition for *The Old Testament: Our Call to Faith and Justice* has included many different teaching methods in its suggested activities to accommodate the students' various needs. Some of these teaching methods are described in the succeeding sections.

Individual and Group Activities

Some activities require research and a more in-depth exploration of a chapter topic. Students are encouraged to conduct their research via the Bible, Internet, library books, or personal interviews. Other activities—skits, role-playing, artistic creations, games, competitions, and class presentations require more imagination and physical participation. The Teacher Wraparound Edition contains a variety of different activities, based on multiple intelligence learning. Among these activities are:

Intelligence Type	Activities
Bodily/Kinesthetic	dance, gesture, movement, drama, clowning, mime, puppetry
Interpersonal/Relational	games, competitions, discussions
Intrapersonal/Introspective	reflection questions, prayer, journal writing
Logical/Mathematical	games, research, constructing scale models
Musical/Rhythmic	singing, music, raps, poetry
Naturalist	architecture, photography
Verbal/Linguistic	oral presentations
Visual/Spatial	art projects, working with textiles

Projects and Assignments Using Multiple Intelligences Learning Styles

Multiple Intelligences is a term used to describe the ways people learn. Developed by Howard Gardner, a professor at the Harvard Graduate School of Education, the multiple intelligences allow for eight ways for a student to learn in ways that fit his or her preferred "learning style." Though people learn using all eight learning styles, each person has preferred ways of acquiring and processing information. The best learning takes place when teaching methods offer processes, assignments, and projects for all eight learning styles with opportunities for students to access their preferred learning styles and proceed from their chosen strengths.

This section offers (1) a brief description of Gardner's eight multiple intelligences, (2) information about which methods students who learn in each of these styles prefer, and (3) two semester-long assignments for each learning style.

It is suggested that you allow the students to choose and complete one or two of these assignments over the course of the semester. The assignments are intended to provide a broad scope of their study of the Old Testament.

Bodily/Kinesthetic Intelligence

The Bodily/Kinesthetic Intelligence involves the capacity to use one's whole body to express ideas and feelings. It specifically involves using one's hands to create things or to skillfully manipulate objects. A concrete way to think of people who learn in this style is that they must be active and engaged in a "learning by doing" assignment or project. Methods include:

- developing and performing role plays
- participating in a theatre arts performance
- creating and/or demonstrating a use of a relevant tool, instrument, or utensil
- exercising or competing in athletics

Student Assignments

- Produce a dramatization of the call of Samuel (1 Sm 3:1–21). If you work with others, include characters for Samuel, Eli, and Yahweh. If you work alone, create a soliloquy of Samuel in which he hears and ultimately responds to Yahweh's call.
- Research and create a clay vessel representative of a period in Old Testament history. Note Isaiah 41:25 which describes a potter treading clay with his feet! Search the Internet using key phrases: e.g., "pottery in the Bible."

Interpersonal/Relational Intelligence

This intelligence involves the ability to perceive and appreciate the feelings, moods, intentions, and motivations of other people. These types of learners flourish well working in groups, teams, or with a partner. Learning methods include:

- brainstorming ideas
- playing cooperative games
- dialoguing with others
- working on a group project

Student Assignments
- Work with a group of students to write fifty questions that have answers that can be found in the Old Testament. Print the questions on flash cards. Then brainstorm several games you could teach the class for using the flash cards (e.g., competing in teams, cooperatively learning in pairs). Agree to one or two games. Share your game instructions with the class. Allow them to play.
- Invite a Jewish teenager to your class. Prepare a panel discussion where a group of students in your class dialogue with the Jewish teen about religious and other contemporary issues including Sabbath worship, family traditions, use of Scripture for prayer and study.

Intrapersonal/Introspective Intelligence

Intrapersonal/Introspective Intelligence is the ability to base one's actions on self-understanding. Being in touch with one's dreams, feelings, moods, intentions, motivations, and spirituality is a key aspect of this intelligence. People who learn best in this intelligence usually prefer to work alone on self-directed assignments. Examples of learning methods are:
- writing reports or research papers
- keeping a journal
- explaining the personal connection of some given information
- identifying with characters in a story

Student Assignments
- Develop a thesis and work to prove it. For example, "the tomb of King David is located in modern Jerusalem." Cite references to support your claim.
- Imagine you were a Hebrew pilgrim who left Egypt at the Exodus. Write a journal with several entries that chronicles your experience in the desert. As much as possible, related your entries to events chronicled in the book of Exodus.

Logical/Mathematical Intelligence

Logical/Mathematical Intelligence includes the skill to work well with numbers and to use reason to solve problems. Persons who learn well in this style are apt at categorizing and exploring relationships within a set of data. They tend to find it difficult to function in an environment that is chaotic or one in which the goals are not clearly defined. Methods that work well in this learning style are:
- categorizing names, places, and events
- outlining bodies of material
- exploring patterns and relationships
- problem solving

Student Assignments
- Involve yourself in several calculations involving geography in distance. For example, estimate the amount of time to walk from Egypt to Palestine.
- Research several statistics involving both ancient and contemporary nations that have made their home in Palestine. Include data that is both similar (rainfall, average temperature) and different (average life expectancy, income) to both lists.

Musical/Rhythmic Intelligence

The ability to distinguish rhythm, pitch, and melody is a characteristic of this intelligence. People who prefer to learn in this style often express themselves in musical forms. They enjoy being surrounded by sound and rhythm and understand these as learning tools. Some methods preferred by learners in this style are:
- making and playing instruments
- setting stories to music
- creating and/or performing in a musical
- writing new lyrics for familiar tunes

Student Assignments
- Set some lyrical passages from the Old Testament to music (e.g., the song of Moses and the Israelites at the time of Exodus from Exodus 15:1-17 or a favorite psalm). Perform the song for your classmates.
- Audition for a part in a play based on an Old Testament story (e.g., *Joseph and the Amazing Technicolor Dreamcoat*) in a school, parish, or community production. Invite your classmates to your performance.

Naturalist Intelligence

A person with preference for a Naturalist Intelligence is at home in the natural environment. He or she appreciates the joys of nature, is comfortable raising and caring for plants and animals. This person would also enjoy events in the lines of camping, hiking, and many other outdoor activities. A person with a preference for learning in the Naturalist Intelligence learning style appreciates methods like:
- experimenting in a lab setting
- classifying elements in the natural world
- "digging" or any simulation of an archaeological experience
- demonstrating proper procedure and care for gardens or animals

Student Assignments
- Develop a zoological chart tracing one of today's common animals to its ancestors from the beginning of time.
- Collect meaningful and symbolic items from each of your classmates and place them in a large fifteen gallon water jug. Arrange for a burying ceremony in which this time capsule is preserved for future generations of archaeologists. Write what you think could be gleaned about this generation from the items that are collected.

Verbal/Linguistic Intelligence

A Verbal/Linguistic Intelligence involves aptitude with both the spoken and written word. A person who learns best with this intelligence appreciates being able to see things in print, hear spoken words, and say things aloud. Memorization is also key learning method. Other methods preferred by this type of learner are:
- debating
- reading and summarizing the material
- memorizing and repeating aloud many facts
- writing essays

Student Assignments
- Peruse the book of Proverbs. Memorize and share ten of your favorite proverbs. Also, rewrite these proverbs to fit modern situations. Share your rewrites as well.
- As a summary of the Old Testament course, write a minimum 500-word essay entitled "Israel: God's Chosen People."

Visual/Spatial Intelligence

This intelligence caters to people who learn by visualizing and dreaming about concepts and ideas. Learners in this style incorporate both sight as well as mental images. Whereas printed materials may frustrate these learners, visuals in the forms of charts, pictures, graphs, and maps help them to grasp a topic. Other methods that work well for learners in this style include:
- drawing, painting, and sculpting
- creating collages, posters, and murals
- designing maps and graphs
- producing video

Student Assignments
- Produce a video which captures the beauty of God's creation. Intersperse an instrumental musical background with Scripture reading from the creation stories in Genesis and some of the pslams.
- Paint or sculpt a caricature of a favorite Old Testament hero.

Small Group and Whole Class Discussion Questions

These questions provide an opportunity to evaluate how well lesson objectives are being met. Moreover, discussion builds community among the students and often is a gateway for real faith sharing.

Reading and Summary

Students are assigned readings from the text and asked to summarize the reading through discussion or written assignments.

Hands-On Scripture Exploration

The Teacher Wraparound Edition includes many assignments in which the students are invited to read, reflect on, and apply to their own lives certain Scripture passages.

Journal Assignments

Journal keeping is an effective way for the students to make applications of the lessons for their own lives. Also, it is an effective method of prayer and an opportunity for faith formation.

Prayer

Each chapter concludes with a brief Prayer Service that can be lengthened by added shared reflection, by singing, or by the sharing of student meditations taken from their journal entries.

Service Involvement

Many of the exercises with the "hands" logo encourage the students to become involved in service projects in their local community. Such projects are designed to help the students grow in their own faith and justice, as well as be of help to other people.

Scheduling the Course

The Old Testament: Our Call to Faith and Justice fits well into several different programming models. Before teaching the course, sit down with your planner. Determine how many class sessions you will have in which to teach and give exams. Also take into account the length of the class period itself. A semester course usually covers 16 weeks; a year course usually covers thirty-two weeks. In a school setting, you may teach three to five sessions per week. Typically, these daily sessions are forty to sixty minutes long. In a religious education setting, you will probably only teach one session per week that lasts from ninety minutes to three hours.

The Teacher Wraparound Edition has divided the course material into class sessions lasting approximately one hour in length. Overall, there will be 81 sessions. If you wish to follow the this model exactly, the schedule will look like this:

Course Material	Teaching Sessions	Exam Session	Total Sessions
Chapter 1	6	1	7
Chapter 2	6	1	7
Chapter 3	9	1	10
Chapter 4	9	1	10
Chapter 5	6	1	7
Chapter 6	6	1	7
Chapter 7	6	1	7
Chapter 8	7	1	8
Chapter 9	8	1	9
Chapter 10	8	1	9

If you are teaching the course over a semester and are meeting five times a week for 16 weeks, spend one day on each session. If you are teaching the course over a year and are meeting five times a week for 32 weeks, spend two days teaching each session in the Teacher Wraparound Edition. Your planner would follow this chart:

Course Material	Semester Course	Year Course
Chapter 1	7 days	14 days
Chapter 2	7 days	14 days
Chapter 3	10 days	20 days
Chapter 4	10 days	20 days
Chapter 5	7 days	14 days
Chapter 6	7 days	14 days
Chapter 7	7 days	14 days
Chapter 8	8 days	16 days
Chapter 9	9 days	18 days
Chapter 10	9 days	18 days

The Teacher Wraparound Edition provides many different types of activities, exercises, discussion questions, and suggestions for audiovisual materials. Feel free to select the activities best suited for your students and your time situation.

Scheduling for Parish Religious Education

The Old Testament: Our Call to Faith and Justice is suitable for use in parish religious education programs. The entire text can be covered in ten two-hour sessions or twenty one-hour sessions.

Religious Education Lesson Adaptations are included for each chapter and can be accessed online at **avemariapress.com**. See the "Religious Education" area of the website for catechist information. For each lesson, the students are required to read the chapter to be covered in advance of the session.

The Lesson Adaptations include the following elements:
- **Warm-up** Suggestions for introducing the chapter, pointing out central themes, and reviewing material from previous classes are offered. Also provided are questions to use as discussion starters.
- **Part I: Lesson** This is a lesson of approximately thirty minutes covering the first half of the chapter. References to the Student Text are provided. Several opportunities are built in for student participation, including panel discussion, role plays, and one-to-one sharing.
- **Break/Writing Exercise** This provides approximately fifteen minutes for a short stretch break. Also, this time may be used for individual journal writing.

- **Part II: Lesson** This is a second thirty-minute lesson covering the last half of the chapter. References to the Student Text are provided. Suggestions for teacher summaries and student assignments are included.
- **Prayer Experience** This component is an opportunity for the students to pray communally. These experiences often suggest music and video accompaniment. A special prayer space is preferred.
- **Conclusion** Assignments for the next session are given prior to dismissal.

For courses meeting ten times (two hours per session), use the entire Lesson Plan Adaptation above. For courses meeting twenty times (one hour per session), use the Warm-up and Part I Lesson for the first session. Use the Part II Lesson, Prayer Experience, and Conclusion for the second lesson.

Introducing Chapter 1

Catholics, Protestants, Orthodox Christians, and Jews share most of the same Old Testament, with minor differences. The Jewish portion of the Old Testament is called the Hebrew Scriptures because thirty-nine of the books were originally written in Hebrew. Protestants and Orthodox Christians also have thirty-nine books in their Old Testament—the same as the Hebrew Scriptures. Catholics have forty-six books in their Old Testament—books written Aramaic and Greek besides those written in Hebrew. Protestants recognize the extra material of the Catholic Old Testament in a separate section called the *apocrypha* ("secret" or "hidden").

The books of the Old Testament were written over the course of a millennium (between 1000 B.C. and 150 B.C.) and tell the story of God and his Chosen People, the Israelites. There are several names for God in the Old Testament. The most common name is *Yahweh*, which means "I am." Basically, the Old Testament is about the relationship between Yahweh and the Israelite people, descendants of Abraham through Jacob. Despite the many times the Israelites were unfaithful to Yahweh, Yahweh continued to keep his promises to them. He remained steadfast, merciful, and loving.

Chapter 1 introduces the students to various skills required for serious Bible study. Among such skills are knowledge of the original languages of the Bible, knowledge of the various translations of the Bible, knowledge of other ancient writings and how they compare to the biblical text, and familiarity with archaeology and the various ways to read the material, especially from a religious sense.

Students will learn that the arrangement of the books of the Old Testament does not necessarily follow a chronological order of history. Some events are recorded twice in the Bible; indicating more than one oral tradition as the source for the material. Students will also learn that many of the books have been edited, perhaps in post-Exilic times.

An overall history of the Israelites can be found in the Old Testament. God made a *covenant* ("agreement") with the Patriarch Abraham and the Israelites to be his people. Their descendants were known as the twelve tribes of Israel. For a time, the Israelites were slaves in Egypt. Then God freed them and led them to Canaan, where they settled in the hill country. At first, the Israelites were a loose confederacy, ruled by military leaders and judges. Eventually, all the tribes were united under a single king. After the time of Solomon, the kingdom was divided into two separate kingdoms: Israel in the north and Judah in the south. Neighboring countries overran both kingdoms and took the people away in exile. The prophets of Israel reminded the people to be faithful to Yahweh who would restore them to Jerusalem.

The books found in the canon of the Old Testament are the inspired word of God. What this means is that the Holy Spirit inspired the authors of the Biblical books to write only what God wanted to be written. These authors used various literary styles to get across God's message. Among these literary styles were poetry, fables, myths, history, speeches, letters, songs, and fictional narrative. The books of the Bible are categorized in four sections: the Pentateuch (the first five books of the Bible), the Historical Books, the Wisdom Books, and Prophetic Books. Finally, it is important to keep in mind that when we read the Old Testament, we are reading the Scriptures that Jesus knew and read. The Old Testament is "a light for our path" preparing us for the coming of Jesus.

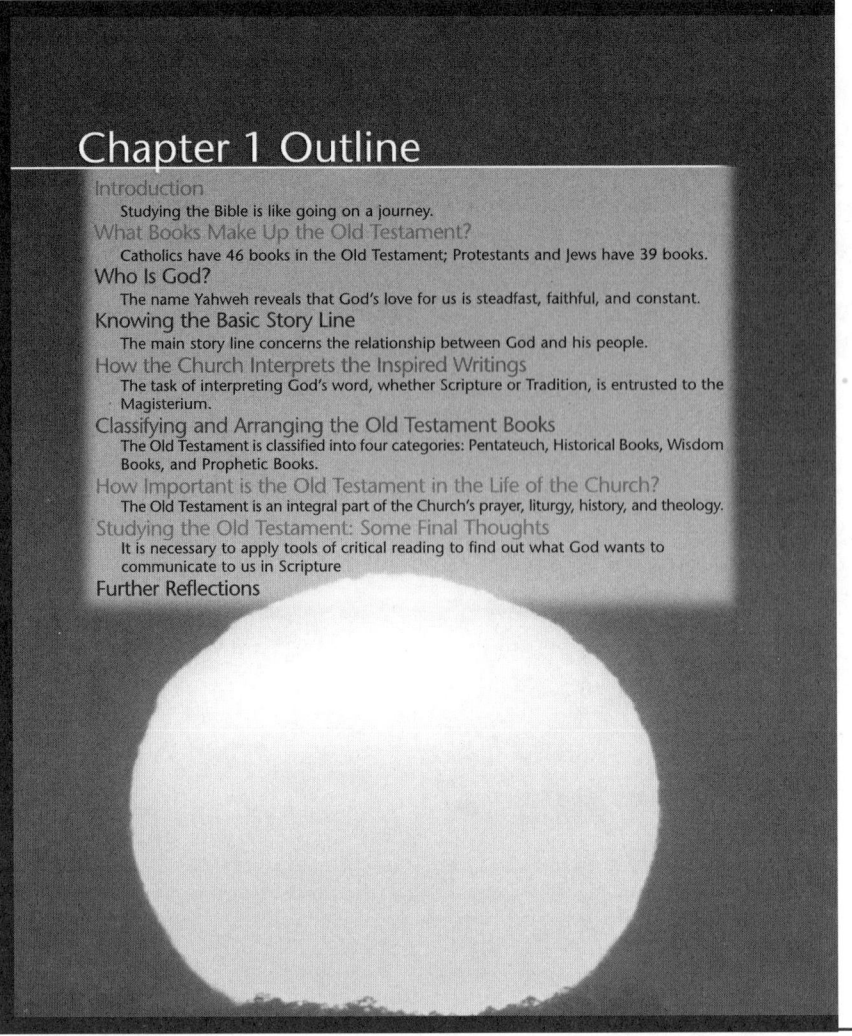

Chapter 1 Outline

Introduction
 Studying the Bible is like going on a journey.
What Books Make Up the Old Testament?
 Catholics have 46 books in the Old Testament; Protestants and Jews have 39 books.
Who Is God?
 The name Yahweh reveals that God's love for us is steadfast, faithful, and constant.
Knowing the Basic Story Line
 The main story line concerns the relationship between God and his people.
How the Church Interprets the Inspired Writings
 The task of interpreting God's word, whether Scripture or Tradition, is entrusted to the Magisterium.
Classifying and Arranging the Old Testament Books
 The Old Testament is classified into four categories: Pentateuch, Historical Books, Wisdom Books, and Prophetic Books.
How Important is the Old Testament in the Life of the Church?
 The Old Testament is an integral part of the Church's prayer, liturgy, history, and theology.
Studying the Old Testament: Some Final Thoughts
 It is necessary to apply tools of critical reading to find out what God wants to communicate to us in Scripture
Further Reflections

Resources
Music Suggestions: see page 18
Printed Materials: see page 24
Audiovisual Materials: see page 26
Internet Links: see page 29

CHAPTER 1
PREPARING FOR THE JOURNEY
Basic Information

Background Notes for the Teacher

The Catholic canon of the Old Testament includes forty-six books. The word *canon* means "reed" or "instrument of measure." A canonical book is a book recognized by the Church to be inspired by God and to be a source of true revelation. In addition to the Hebrew Scriptures, the church at Alexandria included additional books written in Greek. These books are 1 and 2 Maccabees, Tobit, Judith, Baruch, Sirach, and Wisdom, and additional passages in Esther and Daniel. At, the Council of Trent (1546), the Church officially accepted both the Hebrew and the Greek books as canonical.

Advance Preparations
- Check the Resources for materials you may wish to provide for the students to use.
- Make copies of the handouts needed for these sessions.
- Transfer the overhead outlines to transparent acetate (see avemariapress.com).
- Supply drawing paper, markers, glue, magazines, and scissors for the exercise suggested on page 21 of the TWE.
- *Optional:* Arrange for someone who has visited the Holy Land to speak to the students about the trip. If this person is able to provide a visual presentation (e.g., slides), encourage him or her to do so. Have the students prepare questions for the speaker prior to the presentation. Allow time for question and answer follow-up.

Relevant Teachings from Church Documents
- God has revealed himself fully by sending his own Son, in whom he has established his covenant forever. The Son is his Father's definitive Word; so there will be no further Revelation after him (*CCC*, 73).
- *God is the author of Sacred Scripture* (*CCC*, 105).
- God inspired the human authors of the sacred books (*CCC*, 106).
- The inspired books teach the truth (*CCC*, 107).
- *Read the Scripture within "the living Tradition of the whole Church"* (*CCC*, 113).
- It was through apostolic Tradition that the Church discerned which writings are to be included in the list of the sacred books (*CCC*, 120).
- Holy Mother Church, relying on the belief of the apostles, holds that the books of both the Old and New Testament in their entirety, with all their parts, are sacred and canonical because, having been written under the inspiration of the Holy Spirit (cf. Jn. 20:31; 2 Tm 3:16; 2 Pet. 1:19–21; 3:15–16) they have God as their author and have been handed on as such to the Church herself. In composing the sacred books, God chose men and while employed by Him they made use of their powers and abilities, so that with Him acting in them and through them, they, as true authors, consigned to writing everything and only those things which He wanted (*Dogmatic Constitution on Divine Revelation*, 11).

Chapter Objectives
The students will be able to:
- understand the differences between Catholic, Protestant, and Jewish Bibles.
- obtain an overview of the basic story line in the Old Testament.
- realize why knowledge of the original languages of the Bible, the various translations, other ancient writings, and the science of archaeology is important to Bible study.
- classify and arrange the Old Testament books.
- value the Old Testament as the inspired Word of God.
- appreciate the Old Testament as an integral part of the Church's prayer, liturgy, history, and theology.

CHAPTER 1

INTRODUCTION
WHAT BOOKS MAKE UP THE OLD TESTAMENT?

Bell-Ringers

1. Introduce yourself to the students and briefly explain some of the things you hope to accomplish in this course.

2. Go around the room and have the students introduce themselves. In addition to telling their names, students could be asked to share one thing they know about the Old Testament or one question they have about the Old Testament. Record their responses.

3. Divide the class into groups of four. Ask the students to discuss the following questions with their group:
   - Suppose you and your friends are going on a week-long camping trip. What information would you need to know before going on the trip?
   - What supplies would you need to gather before going? Make a list.

4. Allow time in class for the groups to work. Then call for class sharing. Relate this discussion to things a person might do to prepare to study the Old Testament. For example: purchase a Bible, enroll in a course, read background information on the Bible, talk with others who have previously studied the Old Testament.

Teaching Approaches

1. Direct the students to read the Introduction on page 14. Point out that this course will not teach them *everything* there is to know about the Bible. True Bible study is a lifelong journey. We grow in our understanding of the Bible as we mature and have new experiences. There is always something new to learn and appreciate about the Bible.

2. Next, assign pages 14–15, "What Books Make Up the Old Testament?" Then have the students open their Bibles to the table of contents. Point out the books of the Old Testament that are included in the Catholic Bible but not the Jewish or Protestant Bibles. Paraphrase the following information about the inspired books unique to the Catholic Bible. Print the boldface words on the board or overhead.
   - **The book of Judith** is a heroic tale about a woman who rescued her people by beheading the enemy leader. The message is that God works through human means to save his people. (Mozart and Beethoven wrote music for the story of Judith, and countless painters have portrayed her on canvas.)

THE OLD TESTAMENT

canon—An official list of books belonging to the Bible, both the Old Testament and New Testament.

deuterocanonical—A term meaning "second canon." Books included in the Catholic Old Testament but not in the Hebrew Bible. These additions are 1 and 2 Maccabees, Judith, Tobit, Baruch, Sirach, Wisdom, and parts of Esther and Daniel.

apocrypha—Another name for the deuterocanonical books and verses. The word "apocrypha" means "hidden."

Introduction

An ancient Chinese philosopher named Lao Tzu once said, "A journey of a thousand miles begins with a single step." This wise saying applies to any journey we make in life. It also applies to every course we study. In order to complete the journey successfully, we need to know basic information at the onset. We need to prepare, to gather all the supplies we need.

Similarly, it is important to prepare before we delve into a serious study of the Bible. Before we can actually start, there are many questions that need answers. If these questions are not answered at least briefly, it is hard to keep our minds on the task. The questions will only keep nagging us! Furthermore, if we don't approach Bible study with the appropriate background information, we may easily get overwhelmed or sidetracked. We may give up and never complete our journey. Most importantly, we must always keep in mind that the Bible is different than any other book. Since the Bible is the inspired word of God, it "must be read and interpreted in the light of the same Spirit by whom it was written" (*Dei Verbum*, 12 § 3).

So let's begin with some basic preparation and background information. If you have additional questions about the Bible, record them in a notebook or journal.

What Books Make Up the Old Testament?

This may seem like a simple question. But actually, it's not. Catholics and other Christians call the first part of their Bible the "Old Testament" in relation to the "New Testament" which has as its central object, Jesus Christ (CCC, 124). Jews prefer the term "Hebrew Bible" because they do not use the New Testament.

When Jews refer to the "Hebrew Bible" and Christians refer to the "Old Testament" they are basically talking about the same thing; however, there are differences. Catholics include 46 books of the Old Testament (45 if Jeremiah and Lamentations are counted as one book) and 27 books of the New Testament as part of the **canon** of Scripture.

The Old Testament is really a *collection* of books written over the course of a millennium, roughly between 1000 B.C. and 150 B.C. The books were written predominantly in the Hebrew language. The early Church, however, differed with early Judaism in the decision about the canon of the Old Testament. The Church included seven books (1 and 2 Maccabees, Judith, Tobit, Baruch, Sirach, and Wisdom) not included in the Hebrew Bible that were mostly written in Greek after 300 B.C. These seven books are referred to as **deuterocanonical**—"second canon"—to show that they are not accepted in the Jewish canon. Some of the deuterocanonical books also include additional chapters added to older Hebrew books like Daniel and Esther.

At the time of the Protestant Reformation, Martin Luther decided to include only books in the Hebrew Bible. Most Protestant Bibles do print these seven books, but they include them in a separate section and call them the **apocrypha**, which means

14

Resources
Music Suggestions

"Celtic Alleluia" by Fintan O'Carroll and Christopher Walker from *Gather* (GIA) or *Music Issue* (OCP).

"Fill Us with Your Word" by David Haas from *Breaking Bread* (OCP).

"Happy Those Who Hear the Word of God" by Gregory Norbet from *That There May Be Bread* (Weston) or *Glory & Praise 3* (OCP [NALR]).

"If Today You Hear God's Voice" by David Haas from *Gather* (GIA).

"Psalm 19: Lord, You have the Words" by David Haas from *Gather* (GIA).

"Remember Your Love" by Darryl Ducote and Gary Daigle from *Remember Your Love* or *Glory & Praise 2* (NALR); *Gather* (GIA); *Breaking Bread* (OCP).

"The Word is in Your Heart" by Bob Moore in *Gather* (GIA).

"hidden." And, most Protestants read the apocrypha with great interest, and all Christian scholars study them. Nevertheless, to this day, you may hear people speak of "Catholic Bibles" and "Protestant Bibles" because of this very issue.

Who Is God?

In the Old Testament, the God of the Hebrew people has many names. But the most common name is "Yahweh," the name that Moses first heard when he was called to be the liberator of God's people in Egypt (Ex 3). Yahweh is a name constructed from the basic Hebrew verb, "is."

Yahweh is usually translated as "I am," but it could also be "I am the God who is" or "I am and will be." Parts of this name Yahweh are in many Hebrew personal names like the "iah" in "Isaiah" or "Jeremiah." If these Hebrew names were translated into English, they would sound like Native American names: Isaiah literally means "Yahweh saves" or "Yahweh is salvation!" and Jeremiah means "Yahweh has established."

The non-Hebrew people in the ancient world had their own gods under many different names as well. Baal was the most popular god of the nearby Canaanites. Baal is mentioned in several places in the Old Testament. (More on this later in the journey.)

In some Jewish traditions, the name Yahweh is itself considered too sacred to actually pronounce out loud. When reading the Bible, these Jews use "Adonai" (ah-dō-nī) as a replacement. Adonai simply means "Lord." In order to help Jewish readers, most modern Hebrew Bibles have taken the vowel letters from the word "Adonai" and overlaid them on the consonants for Yahweh. This strange combination was supposed to remind the reader to say "Adonai." However, when some early Christians read this in centuries past, they did not know about the tradition, and thought it was a real word—which they pronounced "Jehovah." Jehovah is actually a mistaken reading of the name Yahweh. Sometimes when very Orthodox Jews write about God, they even write "G*d" to remind them of the mystery of the sacred name.

Catholics have no custom of not saying the name Yahweh out loud. The Church holds that the name "Yahweh" expresses God's faithfulness: "despite the faithlessness of men's sin and the punishment it deserves, he keeps 'steadfast love for thousands'" (CCC, 211). Church **Tradition** also teaches that the name Yahweh reveals that God is "the fullness of Being and of every perfection, without origin and without end" (CCC, 213). As revealed to the Hebrews, God's love for us is steadfast, faithful, and constant.

One way to think about the Old Testament is that it contains books about the Hebrew people learning about Yahweh over hundreds of years. In other words, God reveals himself through the words of the Old Testament precisely because he

SHARING THE FAITH

Write a thank-you letter to a person who has taught you about God and faith.

Tradition—The process and content of the transmission of official Church beliefs, doctrines, rituals, Scripture, and the like.

PREPARING FOR THE JOURNEY

- **The book of Tobit** is about a young man who goes on a journey to find medicine for his blind father. The story reminds people how they should respect all family members—the elderly as well as the young, the sick as well as the healthy, women as well as men.
- **The first and second books of Maccabees** tell about a family who led a rebellion of Jews against the Greeks. The books remind people that God can perform miracles, that the weak can prevail against strong enemies. The books also exhort people to remain faithful to the ways of Judaism despite pressure from other religious beliefs.
- **The book of Baruch** reminds the Jews that God can be found anywhere, even in foreign territory. The book helps displaced people to focus on their faith and remain true to their religious beliefs.
- **The book of Sirach** contains a collection of proverbs that are arranged to form short essays. The book teaches people how to be wise.
- **The book of Wisdom** was written for Jews who were being pressured into accepting Greek philosophy, religion, and culture as their own. The book encourages Jews to practice justice and to remain faithful to the Israelite tradition. Just as God rescued the Israelites from slavery in Egypt, so he will rescue them from oppressive foreign domination.

3. Distribute copies of Handout 1A, "Old Testament Themes" (page 262 of TWE). Explain that these themes form the underlying message of each book of the Old Testament. Offer definition and perspective citing your own personal examples. Also, allow the students to suggest personal reflections for each theme.

4. **Homework Assignment**:
   - Read "Who Is God?" (pages 15–16) and "Knowing the Basic Story Line" (pages 16–17).
   - Complete the exercise "Sharing the Faith" (page 15).

WHO IS GOD?
KNOWING THE BASIC STORY LINE

Bell-Ringers

1. Recount a story about someone who taught you about God and was an influence in your faith development. Then ask volunteers to share the same type of experiences.

2. Allow time for students to share their thank-you letters (see page 15) with partners.

Chapter 1

Teaching Approaches

1. **Re-teach:** Review the homework reading assignment. Choose a person to be "on the spot" and come before the class. Ask the student the following questions:
   - Who does the Bible say that God is? (Yahweh, the God who is; the one, true God; the God of steadfast love and mercy.)
   - How did the name "Jehovah" come about? (It was a misinterpretation of the Hebrew tradition of writing "Adonai" and "Yahweh" together to remind Jews not to say the name of God aloud.)
   - Do you think Christians should say the name of God out loud? Does this custom affect our tendency to swear or take the Lord's name in vain? Give reasons for your opinion. (Accept all reasonable opinions.)
   - Choose several other students to be "on the spot" to share their own answers to these questions.

2. On the board or overhead, write **relationship** and have the students offer their own definitions of the term in their own words. (Accept all suitable definitions.) Write down their ideas. Make sure they realize that there are many types of relationships (e.g., platonic, sexual, parental, childlike, sibling, friendship, coworker, etc.). Say that all of our relationships reflect something about our relationships with God. Then write on the board **"God is . . . relational."** Ask the students to discuss why this statement is so revolutionary. (God doesn't really need us, but he chooses to be in relationship with us. God initiates the relationship. God never abandons us.)

3. Assign the reading of Hosea 2 and Proverbs 3:13–18 in their Bibles. Explain that Baal is the name of a Canaanite god of fertility thought to be responsible for the rain. Instead of being faithful to God, the Israelites were often tempted to worship Baal and other false gods. Ask:
   - What is similar between the readings? (Both passages say that fidelity to God leads to peace, life, and happiness. To be wise means to obey God.)
   - What kind of relationship does God want with us? (A one-on-one personal relationship that never ends.)

THE OLD TESTAMENT

sin—An offense against God. Sin is a deliberate thought, word, deed, or omission against the eternal law of God.

PRIME ADVICE
The book of Deuteronomy records these instructions of the Lord:

Keep these words that I am commanding you today in your heart. Recite them to your children and talk about them when you are at home and when you are away, when you lie down and when you rise. Bind them as a sign on your hand, fix them as an emblem on your forehead, and write them on the doorposts of your house and on your gates (Dt 6:6–9 NRSV).

Read Deuteronomy 6:4–5. What is the subject of the Lord's instructions? Make a sign illustrating the heart of the Lord's instruction. After sharing your sign in class, hang it in your room at home to remind you of your ongoing relationship with God.

---

intends and wants to be known by humans—there are no secret "codes" or hidden tricks. God's very being is Truth and Love. For the ancient Hebrews, they summed up what they knew of God with the name "Yahweh." Catholics, too, affirm that part of studying the Bible is remembering that the God of our faith has revealed himself as Yahweh, the God who is. In the fullness of time God revealed himself completely in the sending of his Son, Jesus Christ.

Knowing the Basic Story Line

Unlike most books, the Old Testament is not one continuous plot divided into episodes or chapters. Instead, what is central to the Old Testament is one relationship—a loving relationship through history between a people and their God.

It's easy to understand from a human perspective why relationship would be so important throughout the Old Testament. God created man out of love and calls us all to love. "To love" is the fundamental vocation of being human. This offer of God's love to man can be understood in the context of Christian marriage where the mutual love between a husband and wife "becomes an image of the absolute and unfailing love with which God loves man" (CCC, 1604).

Yet, there are ups and downs in any relationship to go along with the wonderful times. Readers of the Old Testament discover that man's relationship with God is not always amiable. The story of the fall of man (Gn 3:1–24) tells of man's disobedience of God. This first **sin** would effect man's relationship with God from that time on. Some first-time readers of the Old Testament are often surprised how the authors of Scripture describe the level of anger that God is said to feel in return to man, especially as expressed through his special messengers called "prophets" (more on them later).

Like all relationships, this divine-human one described in the Old Testament has its dramatic episodes of jealousy and angry disappointment, but perhaps most impressive, the Old Testament also exemplifies moments of moving intimacy, love, compassion, and forgiveness. Yahweh, according to the ancient Hebrews, had very human-like qualities. That's not so odd when you think about it. After all, how else can we picture a living God? Our words are never sufficient to entirely portray God, but words are necessary to communicate and to even think about God. The Hebrews wanted to talk to God! They wanted a *relationship*.

Perhaps part of the spell that the Old Testament casts on all those who study it is thus not unlike the fascination of being in love, with all the wonders provided by the occasional surprises, disappointments, and great joys of romantic relationships. It comes as no surprise, then, that the study of Scripture, too, is compared to "being in love" with "Lady Wisdom" (Prv 3:13–18).

Have you ever received a letter from a loved one? Perhaps a new boyfriend or girlfriend? If so, you take your love letter home and read it and re-read it. You wanted to "hear" the words of love and affection again and again. For modern Bible study, and our relationship with God, it is as necessary to re-read the previous words spoken between us, as it is to continue to find new words to speak, and new skills for listening to God today. In short, it is essential to return to the source, which is Scripture.

REVIEW & REFLECTION

1. What is the difference between the Hebrew Bible and the Catholic Old Testament?
2. What does the name "Yahweh" mean?
3. What is the basic story line of the Old Testament?

JOURNAL ASSIGNMENT

- In what ways has God's love for you been steadfast, faithful, and constant? Write a short testimony of your faith to someone younger than you (e.g., a younger sibling, someone in a religious education class, or a scout) in a letter.

How the Church Interprets the Inspired Writings

The Catholic understanding of inspiration is that the Bible was written by human authors deeply moved by God. The Church has accepted their writings because through the same wisdom of the Holy Spirit that inspired the original authors, the Church leaders—the pope and bishops—have also been inspired.

The written Scriptures along with the oral preaching of the Apostles are handed on in the Church through apostolic succession. The living transmission of the message of the Gospel of the Church, accomplished in the Holy Spirit, is called Tradition. The Sacred Scripture and Sacred Tradition are bound closely together, and communicate with one another. Likewise, the task of interpreting God's Word, whether in the form of Scripture or Tradition, is entrusted to the **Magisterium**. This means that it is the bishops, in communion with the pope, who can interpret God's Word for each generation. The Church relies equally on Scripture *and* its living Tradition to enrich all people with God's Word. "Both Scripture and Tradition must be accepted and honored with equal sentiments of devotion and reverence" (*Dei Verbum*, 9).

The particular writings of the Bible are valuable and powerful helps in our learning about God and learning how God builds up his Church. The judgment that

Magisterium—The teaching authority of the Church concerning issues of faith and morals. The Magisterium consists of the pope and the college of bishops acting together.

PREPARING FOR THE JOURNEY

4. Assign the exercise "Prime Advice" (page 16). Make available drawing paper, markers, glue, magazines, and scissors for each student to make a sign. Allow sufficient time for the students to work on their signs. Then have the students display and share their signs.

5. **Homework Assignment**:
   - Complete Review and Reflection questions 1–3 on page 17.
   - Complete the Journal Assignment. Encourage the students to think of a younger person and address their testimonies to those individuals personally.
   - Read "How the Church Interprets the Inspired Writings" (pages 17–21) including the separate feature, "What Inspiration Means."

HOW THE CHURCH INTERPRETS THE INSPIRED WRITINGS

Bell-Ringers

1. Play a simple game of charades with the class using events from the Old Testament (e.g., Moses parting the Red Sea, manna falling from heaven, Ezekiel bringing to life the dry bones). When the game is done, compare the way that students "inspired" one another to give the correct answer to God's inspiration of authors to write the books of Scripture.

2. Call on volunteers to read the testimonial letters they wrote to younger children. Comment as necessary. Remind the students that a relationship with God is ongoing and continual. Even if we turn away from God, he is still there, inviting us back.

Review and Reflection Answers

1. The Hebrew Bible has thirty-nine books, which were originally written in Hebrew. The Catholic Old Testament has forty-six books. These forty-six books consist of the Hebrew Scriptures and the books of 1 and 2 Maccabees, Wisdom, Sirach, Baruch, Judith, and Tobit. Also included are passages from Esther and Daniel. These additional books, known as *apocrypha* or *deuterocanonical*, were originally written in Greek.

2. The name *Yahweh* means "I am," "I am the God who is" or "I am and will be." The Jews consider this name too sacred to pronounce aloud.

3. The basic story line of the Old Testament is the ongoing relationship through history between the Israelites and God. This relationship expresses all the emotions found in human relationships, but is mostly marked with intimacy, love, compassion, and forgiveness.

Chapter 1

Teaching Approaches

1. Focus on the Catholic understanding of Biblical inspiration from the Student Text, pages 18–19. Highlight these points (write on the board):

- **The Scriptures were written by human authors who were inspired by God.**
- **The Scriptures are handed on to the Church through apostolic succession.**
- **Sacred Scripture and Sacred Tradition are both equally accepted and honored by the Church.**
- **In order to interpret Scripture, we must pay attention to both what the human author wanted to say and what God wanted to communicate.**

2. Ask the students to name the three criteria for interpreting Scripture (1. Look at the content and unity. 2. Read Scripture within the Tradition of the Church. 3. Be attentive to the analogy of faith.)

THE OLD TESTAMENT

WHAT INSPIRATION MEANS

God is the author of the Sacred Scripture. But what exactly does that mean? The Bible was not literally "penned" by God. It did not "fall from the sky." Inspiration involves God's inspiring human authors to write the sacred words. Another Christian viewpoint is more literal, holding that the words themselves are inspired. For the sake of understanding, examine critically both points of view.

If it is the *authors* who are inspired, then how can we be sure that the person fully and adequately wrote down what should have been written?

If it is merely the *words* that are inspired, then the author's importance diminishes: anybody could have recorded inspired words accurately—even a young child could have done it! Doesn't it matter that the writer was a spiritual person, deeply in tune with the inspiration of the Holy Spirit? Would we be satisfied to say that they acted like a robot, and just copied words "whispered in their ear" by the Holy Spirit?

- Form small groups to debate the meaning of inspiration. Share the conclusions of your group's debate with the rest of the class.

these writings are inspired comes from the experience of the Church with these writings. They did not come to the Church pre-packaged and pre-marked "These are the inspired books." Instead, the Church leaders (Magisterium) read and studied them and came to realize that they were inspired. The Pontifical Biblical Commission wrote: "What characterizes Catholic exegesis is that it deliberately places itself within the living tradition of the Church. . . ."

All Catholics can join in the process of understanding the meaning of the Scripture. It is an ongoing process of prayerful dialogue and study. Each succeeding generation raises questions about the Scriptures and keep the dialogue going. The Preface to the Pontifical Biblical Commission states that the study of the Bible ". . . is never finished; each age must in its own way newly seek to understand the sacred books."

In order for us to interpret Scripture correctly, we must pay attention to both what the human author wanted to say and what the Holy Spirit intended to communicate. To find out the human author's intentions, we should take into account the time and culture, the literary forms of the time, and the manner of speaking and thinking that was current then. Since the Scripture is inspired, they "must be read and interpreted in the light by the same Spirit by whom it was written" (*Dei Verbum*, 12 § 3). The Second Vatican Council offered three criteria for interpreting Scripture in the light of the Holy Spirit:

1. Look closely at the content and unity of the whole Scripture.
2. Read the Scripture within "the living Tradition of the whole Church."
3. Be attentive to the analogy of faith. This means the unity of the truths of faith among themselves and within the whole context of God's revelation.

Our understanding and wisdom of the Scriptures increases over time. And a compassionate God has not abandoned us *only* to the words in the Scriptures. The Holy Spirit continues to lead us through the Church. The Church teaches that there are two senses of Scripture: the literal and the spiritual.

The *literal sense* of Scripture is foundational. It refers to what the actual words directly mean, either in a precise sense (e.g., the narrative of the Passion) or in a figurative sense (e.g., a metaphor or parable).

The *spiritual sense* refers to how the words of Scripture can be signs of something more profound. Understanding the Bible in this way is important for a student of the Old Testament. The spiritual sense has three parts. The allegorical sense helps us understand how some of the events of the Old Testament prefigure Christ, for example, the crossing of the Red Sea symbolizes Christ's victory over death. The moral sense teaches us how to act in a right way, for example, that Abraham's faith obliges us to believe in Christ. The anagogical sense (from a Greek word for "leading") helps us to relate what

18

Background Information

Dead Sea Scrolls

Recent translations of the Bible have been greatly helped by the discovery of the Dead Sea Scrolls. These are the oldest known copies of books from the Old Testament. These scrolls were discovered in 1947 in eleven caves near Qumran. The caves contained the remains of over 600 manuscripts written on ten complete scrolls and fragments of others. One-fourth of these manuscripts are biblical. Today, scholars think there was a religious community at Qumran that devoted itself to prayer and to transcriptions of the Old Testament. The community was destroyed by fire and earthquake and rebuilt after a thirty to forty year interval. It is believed that the community continued until 68 A.D.

Pontifical Biblical Commission

The Pontifical Biblical Commission was established by Pope Leo XIII in 1902 in order that the text of Sacred Scripture "will find here and from every quarter the most thorough interpretation which is demanded by our times and be shielded, not only from every breath of error, but also from every temerarious opinion" (*Enchiridion Biblicum*, 139). The members of the Commission were given as a goal "that Catholics should not admit the malignant principle of granting more than is due to the opinion of heterodox writers, and of thinking that the true understanding of the Scriptures should be sought first of all in the researches which the erudition of unbelievers has arrived at" (*EB*, 141). At the same time the Pope allowed that "there may arise an occasion when the Catholic interpreter may find some assistance in authors outside the Church, especially in matters of criticism, but here there is need of prudence and discernment" (*EB*, 142).

the events of Scripture have to do with our final destiny—heaven.

It is the task of those who study the Bible to work according to these rules toward a better understanding and explanation of Scripture. The Magisterium of the Church is ultimately responsible for "watching over and interpreting the Word of God" (*Dei Verbum* § 3).

Learning Some Necessary Skills

Working from the rules listed above, there are several skills that further help to study the Bible. Among these skills is a basic understanding of the original languages in which the Old Testament was written. Many languages were spoken and written in the Ancient Near East during the time of the writing of the Old Testament. Most of the Old Testament was written in Hebrew, but parts were written in Aramaic (a language very close to Hebrew, but more widely spoken among ancient peoples) and some of the later writings were written in Greek. Hebrew and Aramaic are known as "Semitic" languages. There remain a few modern Semitic languages spoken today, including Arabic or Maltese.

The grammar and vocabulary of Hebrew and Semitic languages are similar. Many of the words sound and mean the same thing. For example, the word "peace" is "shalom" in Hebrew and "salaam" in Arabic. Knowing that these languages are related ("cognate") can help us to understand the culture, context, and wider political and social setting of ancient Hebrew history. In fact, serious students of the Bible learn to read Hebrew, Aramaic, and Greek in order to study the Bible in its original languages.

Of course, most of us do not speak or read these original Biblical languages. We rely on translators to bring the words of the Bible to us. Today there are many different English translations of the Bible. How accurate are they? To understand the answer to this question, you need to ask yourself some analogous questions. For example, Why can't scientist No. 1 announce that he has discovered the cure for cancer one day and immediately sell the cure for money the next day? Or, why couldn't scientist No. 2 claim that that there is another planet in our solar system that is beyond Pluto and have her claim immediately accepted? The answer, of course, is that any scientist would have to *prove* their announcement to lots of other scientists! A discovery isn't "real" until *many* people confirm it.

Translation of the Bible is similar. Hundreds of translators work with the original languages of the Bible. And there are literally hundreds of ancient manuscripts of the Bible in Greek, Hebrew, and many other ancient languages, that these translators use to compare to each other. A translation into English is never based on one or two texts in Greek and Hebrew—but *dozens and dozens* of them! It is usually pretty easy to spot single mistakes from one ancient scribe when you have over a hundred other texts of the same passage to compare.

So, not only are there many texts to work with, there are lots of people working on them simultaneously. Biblical scholars—Jewish, Catholic, and Protestant—meet regularly in conferences, compare notes, argue about their ideas, and suggest new ideas. Bible translations that we use today are the results of years and years of scholarship and learning, debate and checking. We are learning more all the time, and new discoveries give us more confidence about our translations. The discovery of the Dead Sea Scrolls in 1947–1950, for example, helped Biblical scholars and all Christians tremendously because these scrolls were Hebrew writings of the Bible that were almost 1,000 years *older* than the Hebrew texts we had previously. The Dead Sea Scrolls helped to confirm the previous translations.

The details of Biblical translations are debated. But it would be virtually impossible for someone to suggest a wild translation and get it past all the other translators who are also working on these texts. Take, for example, the *New American Bible*, which is the translation

---

PREPARING FOR THE JOURNEY

3. Examine the two senses of Scripture (literal and spiritual). Choose a Bible story (e.g., the crossing of the Red Sea by the Israelites) and have the students briefly summarize the three parts of the spiritual sense of this story.

4. Move on to a contextual understanding of Scripture. Have the students form small groups. Distribute one copy of the same sports page from a recent newspaper to each group. Ask each group to find five headings that could be confusing to someone who may know basic English but doesn't know the context for certain sports phrases. (For example, "Padres Smash Diamondbacks" taken literally sounds like Spanish priests killing poisonous snakes instead of one baseball team defeating another in a game.) Allow sufficient time for the groups to work. Then call for class sharing. Explain that understanding the Bible likewise means understanding the correct context of words and phrases. Not only do we need to know what the words mean; we need to be able to interpret them in the proper context.

5. Point out that different scholars who know these original languages will still translate the Bible somewhat differently. Distribute copies of Handout 1B, "Comparing Translations of Psalm 13" (page 263 of the TWE). Have the students work in small groups to note how the translations of Psalm 13 are similar but also different. Ask: Do the different translations convey a different message or offer clarification? Note the meaning of the psalm: Oppressed by enemies, the psalmist laments his condition and prays for God's help.

CHAPTER 1

6. Address another skill needed for Bible study, comparing the Bible texts to non-Biblical texts of the same era. These non-Biblical texts are called *Pseudepigrapha*. Their titles may say "Gospel of (name)" or "Acts of (name)" but the Church has determined that these books are not canonical. Many of these texts are "gnostic," which means that they espouse a certain philosophy of "knowing hidden things about God."

7. Introduce information about the *Pontifical Biblical Commission*, which was established in 1902. This commission is responsible for promoting biblical studies and for protecting the conclusions of such studies from error.

8. Assign as a small group activity "What Inspiration Means" (page 18). Direct the students to discuss the meaning of inspiration. After allowing sufficient time for the groups to work, call for each group to summarize the meaning of inspiration by sharing an original example.

THE OLD TESTAMENT

Psuedepigrapha— Ancient books from the same time frame as the books of the Bible, especially the New Testament. The Church decided these books were not inspired by God and could not be included in the canon of the Bible.

quoted in this text. In 1943, Pope Pius XII issued an encyclical on Scripture studies. He wrote:

> We ought to explain the original text which was written by the inspired author himself and has more authority and greater weight than any, even the very best, translation whether ancient or modern. This can be done all the more easily and fruitfully if the knowledge of languages be joined to a real skill in literary criticism of the same text (*Divino afflante Spiritu*).

The text of the *New American Bible* is a completely new translation taken from the original and the oldest available sacred texts (see Preface to the *New American Bible*, Old Testament). Again, it's important to remember also that the Pope and college of bishops are ultimately responsible for not only determining the validity of a translation, but also of interpreting its words.

Another skill for serious Bible study is a knowledge of other ancient writings and how they compare to the Biblical text. A large number of books have survived from before the time of Jesus, mostly from the Hellenistic and Roman Periods (e.g., 333 B.C. through about A.D. 250). known as the **Pseudepigrapha**. Many such books were discovered in 1945 near Nag Hammadi, in Egypt, and in 1948 by the Dead Sea in Israel. These books are of considerable historical, literary, and religious interest for the study of the late Old Testament era and early Christianity. They have long been translated into English and are readily available, and often provide us with an excellent idea of the great diversity in religious thinking in these times.

While there is nothing dangerous or secret about them (although some of them are a bit odd) the Church long ago determined that these writings were not inspired by God and could not be included in either the Old Testament or New Testament canon. It's a good idea to have a strong grounding in the Bible before launching into reading these non-Biblical materials—particularly if you want to appreciate how these other books use Biblical ideas and then go in different directions. As interesting as some of these "other books" are, they aren't nearly as interesting as the Bible itself. If you become a serious student of the Bible in college, this will be the time to read and analyze them.

The books that are in the canon of the Old Testament and New Testament are historically considered the inspired books of the Bible. To be inspired means that what is written in them is what God wanted to be communicated to mankind. Any interpretation of the Bible must be attentive above all to what God wants to reveal through the sacred authors. What comes from the Spirit is not fully understood except by the Spirit's action. Reading the Bible, in short, is not simply an intellectual exercise, but a prayerful one as well. As the *Catechism*, quoting Luke 24:45, reminds us:

> If the Scriptures are not to remain a dead letter, Christ, the eternal Word of the living God, must through the Holy Spirit "open [our] minds to understand the Scriptures" (CCC,108).

Resources

Printed Materials

"Bible," "Inspiration and Inerrancy," "Interpretation, History of," and "Translations" in *The Oxford Companion to the Bible*, ed. by Bruce M. Metzger and Michael D. Coogan. (New York, NY: Oxford University Press, 1993), pp. 78–80, 302–324, 749–778.

"Bible," "Inspiration," "Interpretation," and "Text" in *Dictionary of the Bible*, ed. by John L. McKenzie, S.J. (New York, NY: Macmillan Publishing Co., Inc., 1965), pp. 95–96, 389–395, 880–881.

Barton, John. "Reading and Interpreting the Bible" in *Harper's Bible Commentary*, ed. by James L. Mays. (San Francisco, CA: Harper & Row Publishers, 1988), pp. 2–13.

Bergant, Diane, C.S.A. "Introduction to the Bible" in *The Collegeville Bible Commentary*, ed. by Dianne Bergant, C.S.A. and Robert J. Karris, O.F.M. (Collegeville, MN: The Liturgical Press, 1989), pp. 3–34.

Brown, Raymond, S.S., and Raymond F. Collins. "Canonicity" in *The New Jerome Biblical Comm*entary, ed. by Raymond E. Brown, S.S., Joseph A. Fitzmyer, S.J., and Roland E. Murphy, O.Carm. (Englewood Cliffs, NJ: Prentice Hall, 1990), pp. 1034–1054

Brown, Raymond, S.S., D. W. Johnson, S.J., and Kevin G. O'Connell, S.J. "Text and Versions" in *The New Jerome Biblical Comm*entary, ed. by Raymond E. Brown, S.S., Joseph A. Fitzmyer, S.J., and Roland E. Murphy, O.Carm. (Englewood Cliffs, NJ: Prentice Hall, 1990), pp. 1083–1112.

Collins, Raymond F. "Inspiration" in *The New Jerome Biblical Comm*entary, ed. by Raymond E. Brown, S.S., Joseph A. Fitzmyer, S.J., and Roland E. Murphy, O.Carm. (Englewood Cliffs, NJ: Prentice Hall, 1990), pp. 1023–1054.

Finally, for serious study of the Bible, **archaeology** is also of importance. Archaeology is both a science and an art. Imagine digging the remains of a village from Biblical times. What would you find? The lines of the foundations, perhaps some remnants of building material, perhaps some gravesites, and maybe a trash dump with remnants of old broken jars and containers. That is the science part—because that is what you actually see.

What can we learn from this kind of evidence? Here is where science meets art—or in other words, where evidence meets intuition. Sometimes it is difficult to reconstruct (in our minds) what the buildings actually looked like, how the people lived, and what they did. Also, when the ancient foundation of a village is dug up, for example, archaeologists have many problems trying to identify the name of this particular village. They must search for clues.

In the Ancient Near East, it is possible that the name of the village may be found on clay tablets or papyrus scrolls. Or, the Bible can help if it refers to a particular village that was in the area of the excavation. Sometimes modern local traditions may help.

Sometimes names are found on **artifacts**. A discovery in Northern Israel (from the early 1990s), for example, mentioned "The House of David" and an Assyrian royal carving found many decades ago famously pictures Omri, a king of Northern Israel who is mentioned in 1 Kings and 1 Chronicles. Archaeological discoveries that mention Biblical persons or places can confirm their existences, though not everything about the context of the persons or places. Archaeology and Biblical study, therefore, must always be in dialogue because archaeological discoveries must be "interpreted" as much as Biblical texts.

archaeology—The science of studying material remains of past human life and activities.

artifact—Something created by past humans, usually for a specific purpose (tools, pottery, clothing, etc.).

REVIEW & REFLECTION

1. How do Sacred Scripture and Sacred Tradition function together in transmitting God's word?
2. Explain the literal sense and scriptural sense for understanding Scripture.
3. What does it mean to say a Biblical book is inspired?
4. What is the ideal relationship between archaeology and Biblical study?

JOURNAL ASSIGNMENT

- How has a passage from the Old Testament inspired you in your relationship with God? In other words, what do you think God wished to communicate to you through this Bible passage?

PREPARING FOR THE JOURNEY

9. Briefly discuss archaeology and its role in Bible study. Explain that this science complements the study of the Bible. It often helps us to understand certain Bible passages and events better and put them into the context of history and geography.

10. **Homework Assignment:**
    - Assign the students to read an article from the *Pontifical Biblical Commission* website (see page 29 of the TWE) and report on one of the articles or findings of the Commission.
    - Complete in writing Review and Reflection questions 1–4.
    - Write your response to the Journal Assignment. Be prepared to share what you have written (or a summary of it) with your classmates. Remind the students to look for the three parts of the spiritual sense of this passage (see page 18).
    - Assign "Classifying and Arranging the Old Testament Books" including the timeline under the heading "Ancient Hebrew History: A Basic Outline" (pages 22–26).

Review and Reflection Answers

1. The Sacred Scripture and Sacred Tradition are bound closely together and communicate with one another. The task of interpreting Scripture and Tradition is entrusted to the Magisterium.
2. The literal sense of Scripture refers to what the actual words directly mean, either precisely or figuratively. The spiritual sense refers to how the words of Scripture can be signs of something more profound.
3. Inspiration means that the Holy Spirit guided or inspired authors of the Bible to write only what God wanted written in order to convey his message of love and salvation.
4. The ideal relationship between archaeology and Bible study is dialogue. Archaeologists benefit from the findings of Bible study, and Bible study can benefit from the findings of archaeologists.

CHAPTER 1

CLASSIFYING AND ARRANGING THE OLD TESTAMENT BOOKS

Bell-Ringer
1. Have the students form small groups to share their journal assignment responses. Allow sufficient time for the groups to talk.

Teaching Approaches
1. **Re-teach:** Use "Organization of the Hebrew Bible" (Overhead 1A online) to review how the books of the Bible are arranged. Make the following points:

- 1 and 2 Samuel, 1 and 2 Kings, and 1 and 2 Chronicles are each combined as one book.
- The historical books are classified together with prophetic writing in the "Prophets" column. Explain the underlying reason for that grouping: both the prophets and the history of Israel call people to be faithful to the Torah.
- The distinction "major" prophets and "minor" prophets refers to the length of the books in this category, not a prophet's relative importance. Major prophets refer to long books. Minor prophets refer to shorter books.
- The "Writings" category contains reflections on how to live the Torah. Essentially, Jews consider the Torah to be the source from which all the other books flow.
- Point out that Canticle of Canticles (see page 22) is another name for the book Song of Songs (on the overhead).

THE OLD TESTAMENT

Classifying and Arranging the Old Testament Books

The Jews traditionally divided the books of the Hebrew Bible into three distinct sections:
1. Law (in Hebrew, "Torah")
2. Prophets (in Hebrew, "Neviim")
3. Writings (in Hebrew, "Ktuvim")

The Law consists of the first five books of the Bible—Genesis, Exodus, Leviticus, Numbers, and Deuteronomy. The Prophets are subdivided into the Former Prophets (Joshua, Judges, 1 and 2 Samuel, and 1 and 2 Kings), the Latter Prophets (Isaiah, Jeremiah, Ezekiel), and the Minor Prophets. The Writings included eleven books: Psalms, Proverbs, Job, Canticle of Canticles, Ruth, Lamentations, Ecclesiastes, Esther, Daniel, Ezra/Nehemiah, and Chronicles. If you put together the first letter of the three words in Hebrew, you get the acronym "TaNaK," which is the term often used as a short-hand by modern Jews to refer to the Hebrew Bible.

The Old Testament in the *New American Bible* is arranged slightly differently, under *Pentateuch* (Greek for "five books"), *Historical Books*, *Wisdom Books*, and *Prophetic Books*. The books of the Old Testament are arranged in these categories as follows (with abbreviations):

The Pentateuch		The Historical Books	
Genesis	Gn	Joshua	Jos
Exodus	Ex	Judges	Jgs
Leviticus	Lv	Ruth	Ru
Numbers	Nm	1 Samuel	1 Sm
Deuteronomy	Dt	2 Samuel	2 Sm
		1 Kings	1 Kgs
The Prophetic Books		2 Kings	2 Kgs
Isaiah	Is	1 Chronicles	1 Chr
Jeremiah	Jer	2 Chronicles	2 Chr
Lamentations	Lam	Ezra	Ezr
Baruch	Bar	Nehemiah	Neh
Ezekiel	Ez	Tobit	Tb
Daniel	Dn	Judith	Jdt
Hosea	Hos	Esther	Est
Joel	Jl	1 Maccabees	1 Mc
Amos	Am	2 Maccabees	2 Mc
Obadiah	Ob		
Jonah	Jon	**The Wisdom Books**	
Micah	Mi	Job	Jb
Nahum	Na	Psalms	Ps(s)
Habakkuk	Hb	Proverbs	Prv
Zephaniah	Zep	Ecclesiastes	Eccl
Haggai	Hg	Song of Songs	Sg
Zechariah	Zec	Wisdom	Wis
Malachi	Mal	Sirach	Si

Resources

Audiovisual Materials

A Firm Foundation: Introduction to the Old Testament (Ecufilm)—22 minutes

This video gives an overview of the Old Testament and an understanding of the context in which certain parts of the Bible were written. It also discusses the question, "Why is the Old Testament important to Christians?"

Enigma of the Dead Sea Scrolls (A&E Production)—50 minutes

This video explains the discovery and significance of the Dead Sea scrolls and how they contribute to our understanding of the Bible.

Faith and Reason: The Authority of the Bible (Ecufilm)—25 minutes

Questions discussed include: What does it mean to say the Bible is true? Is everything in the Bible literally true? How do faith and reason play a part in how we interpret the Bible?

Scriptures Alive! Dead Sea Scrolls: Fact or Fiction (Ecufilm)—30 minutes

The video examines the relationship between today's Christian beliefs and the Dead Sea Scrolls, some of the Bible's oldest texts.

The Bible under Fire (Ecufilm)—49 minutes

This video presents the political and cultural conflicts surrounding the publishing of the *Revised Standard Version* of the Bible in 1952. The video also shows how this translation cleared the way for the many Bible translations available today.

Understanding the Bible (St. Anthony Messenger)—2 videos, 90 minutes each

These videos explore six major themes of the Bible: God's word, law and worship, priests, kings and prophets, God's word in God's Church, God's word in human words, and light in our darkness.

Understanding the Bible (Iowa Religious Media Services)—28 minutes

Viewers learn about the development of the written Bible, the formation of the canon, the need for Bible translations, and aids that can help us understand the Bible.

The most important things to keep in mind about the arrangement of the books, however, is that the Bible is *not* in chronological order. The first books are *not* necessarily the *oldest* books, and the final books are *not* necessarily the most recently written. Nor is it true that events recorded in the first books all took place before the events in the next books. For example, Leviticus and Deuteronomy both include details about Moses receiving the Ten Commandments. A reader needs to learn about history and the text in order to have a good sense of when a book was written. But there is also the certainty that many books were edited at a later time, or were combinations of other books. For example, the psalms were probably once in shorter collections before being put together to form the large collection that is the book of Psalms today. (Catholics and Protestants have 150 Psalms; Orthodox Christians have 151 Psalms.)

Some Biblical books even quote books that are not in the Old Testament canon—for example, the "Book of the Kings of Israel" (e.g., 1 Kgs 14:19;15:31) or the "Book of Jashar" (e.g., Jos 10:13; 2 Sm 1:18). These were likely ancient books that the Biblical authors had in front of them as they were writing their text.

So when, in fact, were the books of the Old Testament written? The earliest of the Biblical books were based on oral traditions that were first written down either during the time of Solomon (around 950 B.C.) or perhaps between 900–700 B.C. The latest books (especially many of the deuterocanonical books) were written, probably in Greek, around 150–100 B.C.

The reason that the time of Solomon is usually cited is because it is believed that Solomon would have been the first king of Israel who actually had scribes to do some of the writing. Another school of thought is that most of the early writings come from later on—the eighth or seventh centuries B.C.—when there is more evidence of widespread literacy, and more evidence of royal administrations that would have kept such written records. Ancient writing required institutions—a scribal class—not merely a few literate persons.

Most certainly, a large portion of the Bible was edited after the fall of Jerusalem in 587 B.C. The idea of books being "edited" often upsets new students of the Bible—it sounds like the writings were tampered with in some way. But why can't an editor be just as inspired by God as a writer? Remember, inspiration refers to what God *wanted* recorded in the Bible, including clarifying that message by editors.

Sometimes editing means that someone thought of something really important to add—or experienced a profound insight into the meaning of an older phrase or teaching, and simply added their insight to the work. Instead of being nervous about the idea of "editing" perhaps we should be thankful that editors added their inspired insights about God and their understanding of him so that we benefit from *their* experiences as well as those of the original authors.

To summarize, it continues to be debatable as to when different books of the Bible were actually written, edited, and began to take on the form that we have today. Of course, since many Biblical books were found among the Dead Sea Scrolls, we know that much of the Bible was already in its present form by 100–200 years before the time of Jesus.

PREPARING FOR THE JOURNEY

2. On the board write the words: **oral tradition—written form—edited versions**. Explain that the Old Testament books came about as the result of a centuries-long process. For centuries, the stories of the Old Testament were told orally. Some tribes of Israelites emphasized certain parts of the stories, or had slightly different details. In the days of the monarchy, scribes began to collect and write down the stories. Later, probably in post-Exilic times, editors refined the original writings.

3. **Game:** Divide the class into two teams for a game and have them stand. Call out the name of an Old Testament book and ask a member of each team to put it into one of the categories listed on page 22. If a student gets the answer right, he or she may continue standing. If a student gets the answer wrong, he or she has to sit down. The team with the last member(s) standing wins.

Chapter 1

4. Review the timeline, "Ancient Hebrew History: A Basic Outline" (pages 24–25). Refer the students to the introductions of several books of the Old Testament. Call on students to tell the approximate year for the main events of the book. *Optional:* Show the video *A Firm Foundation: Introduction to the Old Testament* (Ecufilm)—22 minutes.

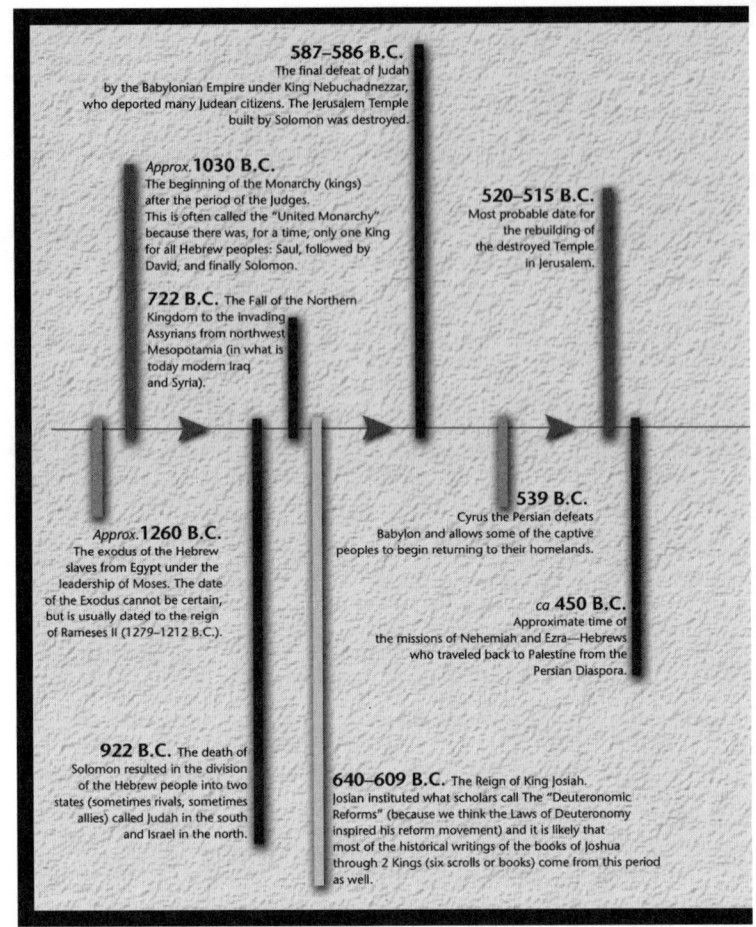

PREPARING FOR THE JOURNEY

ANCIENT HEBREW HISTORY: A Basic Outline

The following dates represent important milestones in the history of the Hebrew people. These are especially important to introductory students of the Old Testament as they will allow you to relate specific books of the Old Testament to specific events and time periods.

ca 6–4 B.C.
The birth of Jesus.

A.D. 70
The destruction of the Temple by the Romans and the scattering of the Jerusalem Christians mostly eastward.

ca 64 B.C.
Palestine comes under direct Roman control, although the Romans had been watching events in Palestine for some time before, and occasionally involved themselves in local disputes.

167 B.C.
Antiochus IV (Epiphanes) attempts to unite his territory through forced Hellenism. There was serious oppression of many Jews during this time. As a direct result, the Maccabean resistance breaks out, as described in the Books of Maccabees.

333 B.C.
Alexander the Great's invasions of Palestine and the Near East—the beginning of the influence of Hellenism (Greek Culture).

5. **Homework Assignment:**
   - Write answers to the Review and Reflection Questions 1–3, page 26.
   - Read the book of Tobit and write your response to the Journal Assignment, page 26. (The book of Tobit is often considered a bridge between historical and wisdom books in the Old Testament.)
   - Read "How Important is the Old Testament in the Life of the Church?" "Jesus' Bible," "Studying the Old Testament: Some Final Thoughts," and "Further Reflections," pages 26–31.
   - Write three questions you have about the Old Testament that have not been answered so far in this course. See the Learn by Doing exercise on page 30. Be prepared to exchange these questions with another student at the next class session and play the game suggested.

Resources
Internet Links

www.bible.org
This site is sponsored by the Biblical Studies Foundation. It includes software, and study resources.

www.ccel.org
An online Bible connected to the *Encyclopedia of Christianity*. The site organizes Scripture versions, commentaries, sermons, study guides, and book references.

www.bibles.net
Provides various translations of the Bible, as well as cross-references between the translations.

www.scborromeo.org/bible.htm
This site offers Biblical study based on the Church's liturgical calendar.

www.vatican.va/roman_curia/congregations/cfaith/pcb_index.htm
The website for the Pontifical Biblical Commission referred to on page 18 of the Student Text and page 25 of the TWE.

CHAPTER 1

HOW IMPORTANT IS THE OLD TESTAMENT IN THE LIFE OF THE CHURCH?
STUDYING THE OLD TESTAMENT: SOME FINAL THOUGHTS
FURTHER REFLECTIONS

Bell-Ringers

1. Start class by asking the students to discuss their reflections from the book of Tobit regarding relationships. Summarize the students' comments on the board.

2. Have the students form teams of four and play the game described in the Learn by Doing exercise, page 30. Consider making the game more competitive by developing a bracket of preliminary round games, quarterfinals, semifinals, and finals. Also, work out a consolation bracket so that teams that lose can continue playing.

THE OLD TESTAMENT

REVIEW & REFLECTION

1. How have the Jews traditionally classified the books of the Hebrew Scriptures?
2. How does the *New American Bible* classify the books of the Old Testament?
3. Why is it so difficult to pinpoint when a specific Old Testament book was written?

JOURNAL ASSIGNMENT

- Read the book of Tobit. What message do you think God is giving us regarding relationships (e.g., children and parents, husbands and wives, self and God)? How does the setting of the story influence your interpretation?

How Important Is the Old Testament In the Life of the Church?

This is a very important question for your study of the Old Testament in the context of your course in a Catholic high school. The Church considers the Old Testament "an indispensable part of the Sacred Scripture" (*CCC*, 121). The Old Testament is the true Word of God. The Church has always rejected any idea that the Old Testament was voided by the New Testament. All of the books of the Old Testament are inspired by God and contain a great amount of teachings on God, wisdom on human life, a treasury of prayers, and a glimpse of the mystery of salvation. The Old Testament offers a "prefiguration" of what God did in the fullness of time in the person of his son, Jesus Christ. This means that Christians also read the Old Testament "in the light of Christ crucified and risen" (see *CCC*, 128–129). This unity between the Old Testament and New Testament is based on **typology**.

As Church Father, St. Augustine, put it: "The New Testament lies hidden in the Old and the Old Testament is unveiled in the New." Christians read the Old Testament in light of Christ crucified and risen, but also remember that the Old Testament has "its own intrinsic value as Revelation reaffirmed by our Lord himself" (*CCC*, 129). When asked which was the first of all the commandments, Jesus taught those he learned from the Hebrew Scripture (see Mk 12:28–34).

The *Catechism of the Catholic Church* summarizes the importance of the Old Testament to the Church as taught by the Second Vatican Council:

typology—The study of types of writing that have common traits. Typology in Scripture study involves reading the Old Testament in light of Christ crucified and risen.

26

Review and Reflection Answers

1. Traditionally, the Jews have classified the books of the Hebrew Scriptures into three sections: the Pentateuch, the Prophets, and the Writings.
2. The *New American Bible* classifies the books of the Old Testament into four sections: the Pentateuch, the Prophets, the Historical Books, and the Wisdom Books.
3. Many of the Old Testament books were written over centuries derived from oral tradition. They may also have been edited before reaching their final form.

Preparing for the Journey

Indeed, "the economy of the Old Testament was deliberately so oriented that it should prepare for and declare in prophecy the coming of Christ, redeemer of all men" (CCC, 122 quoting *Dei Verbum*).

As the Church itself was foreshadowed from the beginning of creation, the Church "was prepared for in a remarkable way throughout the history of the people of Israel and by means of the Old Covenant" (*Lumen Gentium*, 2).

Jesus' Bible

It is important to remember that when we read the Old Testament we are sharing this book with another living faith, Judaism. The faith of the Jews is a viable and living response to God's revelation in the Old Testament. The Church does not believe, as some Christians unfortunately and wrongly think, that the Jews have been "rejected" or even "cursed" by God. Judaism has a unique relationship to Christianity and Christians ought to affirm Jewish response to God and indeed, learn from it as a means of enriching our own faith response to God.

Jesus and most of the earliest Christians in the first generation of the Church were all Jews. As you study the Old Testament, remember that you are in effect studying "Jesus' Bible"—it was the Scripture used by Jesus. We have the benefits of books later written about Jesus and quoting Jesus. But for Jesus himself and his first followers, their "Bible" is what we study in this course.

Preparing for the Journey

Teaching Approaches

1. Assign Mark 12:28–34 (referenced on page 26). Direct student attention to the footnote regarding this passage. It tells them to go to the note for Matthew 22:34–40. Then have them read all the footnotes pertaining to the Matthew passage. Ask: "What Old Testament passages are quoted in Jesus' answer?" (Leviticus 19:18 and Deuteronomy 6:4–5). Have the students read these two Old Testament passages. Explain that all the books of the New Testament quote or have parallels to the Old Testament. The Church teaches that the New Testament fulfills the Old Testament, but does not render it void. Share the following passage with the students to emphasize this point:

> All scripture inspired by God and is useful for teaching, for refutation, for correction, and for training in righteousness, so that one who belongs to God may be competent, equipped for every good work (2 Tm 3:16–17).

Chapter 1

2. Introduce a definition of anti-Semitism at this point. Explain that anti-Semitism is discrimination against people because they are Jews. Throughout history some Christians have discriminated against Jews because they held Jews responsible for the death of Christ. The Church has spoken against the misguided belief, pointing out that the main culpability for Christ's death is on each of us as sinners. Today, the Church teaches that anti-Semitism is a moral wrong. We are not to blame the Jews for killing Christ. The Church promotes respect for the Jewish people and acknowledges our common spiritual heritage.

3. Note the definition of "critical reading" on page 28 (a method of studying the Bible to find out what God is communicating.) Using "Methods of Critical Reading" (Overhead 1B online), explain some of the different types of critical reading. Also explain that while this course on the Old Testament does not get into the intricacies of these methods, it does provide students with a basic introduction to reading and interpreting the Old Testament. Basically, we must read the Bible from the perspective of faith, tempered by Church-approved scholarship. The Old Testament is truly the Word of God, an important part of liturgy, a sourcebook for prayer, and a powerful witness to God's challenge to live in justice and compassion.

Studying the Old Testament: Some Final Thoughts

A final question to pose as we begin a detailed study of the Old Testament has to do with the

critical reading—A number of methods of studying the Bible that aim to discover what God is communicating—both to the people of the Bible and to people today.

nature of the study itself. A first truth must be acknowledged: The books of the Bible have been written under the inspiration of the Holy Spirit. This means that, while God chose men as their author, he also instructed them in "writing everything and only those things which he wanted" (*Dei Verbum*, 11).

Therefore, because the authors were inspired by the Holy Spirit, the books of the Bible "must be acknowledged as teaching firmly, faithfully, and without error that truth which God wanted put into the sacred writings for the sake of our salvation" (*Dei Verbum*, 11).

Nevertheless, since God speaks in the Scripture through human authors, it is necessary to apply tools of **critical reading** to find out what God wants to communicate with us. What do we mean by "critical" reading of the Bible? First, critical reading does *not* mean "finding faults, picking apart, or making disparaging remarks." Rather, in Biblical studies, critical reading simply means very careful examination of all the information that is at hand and thinking it through carefully. To understand the Scriptures, we must try to figure out what the authors wanted to say and what God wanted to reveal in those writings. This means paying special attention to the historical time and the culture in which the writing took place and to the literary styles the author used.

To think "critically" about the Bible, however, is by no means an easy task. This is a book that is not merely a typical human writing. The Bible is the word of God. The Church teaches that the word of God is "a light for our path" (a quote from Psalm 119:105), and we must study in faith and prayer to put it in practice. The Scriptures actually guide our sense of conscience and morality. The ability to deal with difficult questions raised by careful analysis is a mark of a mature belief in God—even if it means living with open questions or difficult problems. Be willing to live with questions that you are wondering about—this is a part of becoming a serious student.

If, when you begin to read the Bible, you wonder whether the Adam and Eve stories were religious parables rather than literal history, this is not an "evil" question. It is not necessary, for example, to believe in *historical* people named Adam and Eve in order to have a deep and abiding faith that God is the author of all creation and that the story is intended to teach profound truth.

The Old Testament remains a primary source for our faith—and Catholics do well to take seriously the God who liberates slaves, unseats kings, speaks through radical prophets, and acts within history. At this stage of your learning, let's concentrate on learning what the Bible is actually talking about rather than whether or not a Biblical character can be verified historically or not.

A serious study of the Old Testament will deepen your understanding of God and how he revealed himself over time to mankind. As the fathers of the Second Vatican Council taught:

> And such is the force and power of the Word of God that it can serve the Church as her support and vigor and the children of the Church as strength for their faith, food for the soul, and a pure and lasting font of spiritual life (*Dei Verbum*, 22).

REVIEW & REFLECTION

1. How would you describe the relationship between the Old Testament and the New Testament?
2. What is critical reading of the Bible? What is the purpose of critical reading?
3. What are four reasons teens today should study the Bible?

JOURNAL ASSIGNMENT

- Read one of the following passages from the Old Testament: Psalm 42:1–12, Sirach 2:1–11, Psalm 139:1–24, or Isaiah 43:1–7. Spend some time in silence, reflecting on the meaning of the passage. Then write your own prayer based on the passage. You will have an opportunity to share your prayer with the class.

PREPARING FOR THE JOURNEY

4. **Homework Assignment:**
   - Answer the Review and Reflection questions 1–3, page 29. Answer question 3 from both your own perspective and that of your friends.
   - Complete the Journal Assignment on page 29. (You will have a chance to share your prayer at the prayer service.)
   - Dialogue with your parents or other family members. Ask them to share any questions they have about the Old Testament. Research and provide answers to their questions.

Review and Reflection Answers

1. The Old Testament prepares for the New Testament. The New Testament fulfills the Old Testament. Both the Old and the New Testaments are the inspired word of God.
2. Critical reading of the Bible means a careful examination of all the information obtained from scholars and archaeologists and thinking it through. We pay special attention to the historical time and the culture in which the writing took place and to the literary styles the author used. The purpose of critical reading is to find out what God wants to communicate to us.
3. Teens today should study the Bible for these four reasons: 1) The books are divinely inspired. 2) The Old Testament is important for the Church's liturgy. 3) The Old Testament contains many beautiful prayers and can be used in personal prayer. 4) The Old Testament is a powerful witness to God's challenge to live in justice and compassion.

CHAPTER 1

REVIEW PERIOD

🔔 Bell-Ringer

1. Ask the students to share questions their parents or other family members had about the Old Testament and how they went about providing answers.

🍎 Teaching Approaches

1. Quiz the students on the vocabulary words highlighted in this chapter. For example, randomly choose three words. Have the students write definitions for each word. *Options:* Have the students check answers with a partner. Or, collect the definitions. Grade and award one bonus point on the upcoming test for each correct answer.

2. Provide plenty of time for the students to study for the Chapter 1 Test. Allow the students to work in small groups, with a partner, or individually to review the contents of the chapter. The Review and Reflection questions offer a basic outline of the main content that will be covered on the Chapter 1 Test.

3. **Prayer Service:** Lead the students in prayer. Say: "Let us quiet ourselves and remember that we are in the Lord's presence. Play an opening song from one of the suggested musical options on page 18 of the TWE. Choose four readers. In between the following Scripture readings, invite volunteers to share the prayers they wrote for the Journal Assignment on page 29:
   - Psalm 42:1–2
   - Sirach 1–11
   - Psalm 139:1–24
   - Isaiah 43: 1–7

4. Conclude by having the students recite aloud the prayer, "For Insight" on page 31.

5. **Homework Assignment:**
   - Study for the Chapter 1 Test.

Further Reflections

The Old Testament has great value for Christians. The books of the Old Testament should be received and read with reverence. As the fathers of the Second Vatican Council teach:

> Now the books of the Old Testament, in accordance with the state of mankind before the time of salvation established by Christ, reveal to all men the knowledge of God and of man and the ways in which God, just and merciful, deals with men. These books, though they also contain some things which are incomplete and temporary, nevertheless show us true divine pedagogy. These same books, then, give expression to a lively sense of God, contain a store of sublime teachings about God, sound wisdom about human life, and a wonderful treasury of prayers, and in them the mystery of our salvation is present in a hidden way. Christians should receive them with reverence (*Dei Verbum*, 15).

As to your study of the Old Testament, in summary, there are several important reasons to pursue it:

First, the books are divinely inspired.
The Old Testament is an important part of the liturgy.
It contains many beautiful prayers.
It is a powerful witness to God's challenge to live in justice and compassion.

The books of the Old Testament are a testimony to the entire story of our salvation, including a prophecy of the coming of Jesus Christ, our Redeemer, and an indication of the revolutionary meaning of his coming. The Old Testament is *essential* to a full comprehension of who Jesus is, what he taught, and what he meant in his teachings. For example, the power of Jesus' teaching on justice is highlighted by understanding the relationship of the prophets to Jesus.

● *Learn by Doing*

Write three questions you have about the Old Testament not asked and answered in this chapter. Exchange your questions with another student in class. Research and write answers to each other's questions and share what you discover.

Form teams of four. Use all twelve questions and answers to compete in quiz contests against other teams. Take turns asking questions to each team. Team members can take three minutes to discuss possible answers. Award five points for a partial correct answer and ten points for a complete correct answer. Compete to a given amount of total points (e.g., 50) or until all questions have been asked by both teams.

● Called to Prayer
For Insight

May the Lord Jesus touch our eyes,
    as he did those of the blind.
Then we shall begin to see
    in visible things those which are invisible.
May he open our eyes to gaze,
    not on present realities, but on the blessings to come.
May he open the eyes of our heart
    to contemplate God in Spirit, through Jesus Christ the Lord,
        to whom belong power and glory through all eternity.
                  —Origen of Alexandria

CHAPTER 1 TEST

 **Teaching Approaches**

1. Administer the Chapter 1 Test (online at **avemariapress.com**).

2. *Optional:* If there is time after the test, allow the students to peruse Chapter 2. Or, review some of the lessons from the Catholic Handbook of Faith (pages 259–280 of the Student Text).

Chapter 1 Test Answers

Part 1: Matching: 1. C; 2. D; 3. G; 4. F; 5. A; 6. H; 7 E; 8. B.

Part 2: Chronology: 9. 1; 10. 3; 11. 7; 12. 2; 13. 4; 14. 6; 15. 5.

Part 3: Fill-in-the blank: 16. Torah; 17. Prophets; 18. Writings; 19. The Pentateuch; 20. The Historical Books; 21. The Wisdom Books; 22. The Prophetic Books.

Part 4: Short Answers: 23-25. One understanding is that God inspired the authors to write sacred words. Another understanding is that the words themselves are inspired. The Catholic understanding of inspiration is that the Bible was written by human authors deeply moved by God.

Chapter 1 Parish Religious Education Adaptation

- See pages 14–15 from the Introduction of this Teacher's Wraparound Edition for an explanation for teaching each chapter in a parish religious education setting.
- "Chapter 1 Parish Religious Education Adaptation" (online at **avemariapress.com**) is a lesson plan for Chapter 1 suitable for use in a one- to two-hour religious education period.

Note: Completing the lesson for Chapter 1 presumes that the students will be assigned to read Chapter 1: Preparing for the Journey: Basic Information (pages 12–31) and complete the Review and Reflection questions on page 17 of the text prior to coming to class.

Introducing Chapter 2

Putting Scripture into context helps us to understand its meaning. The context explored in this chapter includes three facets: the geography of the Near East, the history of the region, and the religious beliefs of the peoples in the area.

Archaeology tells more about the ancient Near East. The discovery and subsequent deciphering of the Rosetta Stone has allowed scholars to learn about Egyptian religion and life and also to compare Egyptian writing to Biblical writing. The Merneptah Stele contains a thirteenth-century B.C. reference to the people called "Israel." Other artifacts discovered in digs at Jericho and Ain Ghazal give further insight into life in ancient Canaan.

The geography of the Near East also played an important role in Israelite history. The Promised Land is situated in the Fertile Crescent, an ancient trade route between Egypt and Mesopotamia. Although the Israelites chose to settle in the hill country of Canaan rather than in the more fertile valley, they were continually exposed to stronger neighbors who sought the land for its agricultural possibilities. The desirability of the land accounts for the numerous wars found through the Old Testament. It also accounts for the Israelites' understanding of Yahweh as a powerful warrior who would protect them from foreign invaders.

Most likely, some of the Israelites who left slavery in Egypt to settle in Canaan intermarried with the local Canaanites. These Canaanites were converted by marriage to the Israelite belief in Yahweh. Others remained true to El, his wife Asherah, the rain god Baal, and numerous other gods. It is interesting to note the similarities and differences between the Israelites' understanding of Yahweh and the Canaanites' understanding of their gods. A comparison between ancient Canaanite literature from Ugarit with the Old Testament reveals interesting parallels.

The chapter continues by giving the students an overview of the literature found in the Old Testament. Primarily, the types of literature include the Pentateuch (the first five books of the Bible), the Historical Books, the Wisdom Books, and the Prophetic Books. Students will also get a brief introduction to the meaning of "prophet" and Biblical apocalyptic literature.

As the students will see, understanding the geography, history, and religious background of the Israelites helps us to understand the Bible's importance. We understand better how the Old Testament is inspired by God and is the true Word of God. Ultimately, the Old Testament prepares us for the coming of Jesus Christ, Messiah and Son of God.

Chapter 2 Outline

Introduction
The Old Testament must be read in the context of the religious, historical, and geographical experiences of the Hebrew people.

Archaeology and Biblical Studies
Archaeological evidence is a modern activity that explores prehistoric civilizations in the context of the Israelites and the Biblical period.

The Land of Canaan: At the Center of Civilization
Canaan—later known as Palestine—was to be home to God's People and the center of the great ancient civilizations.

Tracing the History of the Israelites From the Old Testament
The history of the Israelites in the Old Testament officially begins at the time of the Exodus and spans to the century before Christ.

Background On Literature Styles of the Bible
The Old Testament is made up of religious literature arranged as the Pentateuch, Historical Books, Prophetic Books, and Wisdom Books.

Further Reflections

Resources
Music Suggestions: see page 38
Printed Materials: see page 42
Audiovisual Materials: see page 45
Internet Links: see page 47

CHAPTER 2
MAPS FOR THE JOURNEY
Geographical, Historical, and Literary Context

Background Notes for the Teacher

Archaeology—far from being the glamorous adventure of Indiana Jones movies—is actually a tedious, backbreaking science. Often, the members of a dig must endure scorching heat, scorpions, snakes, dysentery, not to mention campsite food. Still, the thrill of finding even one artifact that reveals something new about ancient peoples makes the effort exceedingly worthwhile.

Most modern digs in the Holy Land consist of a joint effort between archaeologists, zoologists, geologists, physical and cultural anthropologists, hydrologists, ethnographers, and paleoethnobotanists. Aerial photography, along with a study of Biblical name places and modern land surveys, can give scholars an idea of where to start digging. While ancient peoples often built new structures on the ruins of old ones, there is no uniform measurement of how deep the scholars must dig to reach the desired Biblical time period.

Clay is by far the most widespread ancient building material that can be dug up today. In addition to its use in buildings, clay was often used by ancient peoples to make cooking utensils and pottery. Broken shards of pottery have proved to be a reliable method of dating—to within fifty years of the exact date.

To give the students an idea of what archaeology involves, make use of the Internet resources and audiovisuals listed on pages 45 and 47. Also consult a local archaeology society. If there is a dig being conducted in your local area, you may wish to arrange for the students to visit the site and talk to the archaeologists about what they hope to find.

Relevant Teachings from Church Documents

- In Sacred Scripture, God speaks to man in a human way. To interpret Scripture correctly, the reader must be attentive to what the human authors truly wanted to affirm and to what God wanted to reveal to us by their words (*CCC*, 109).
- In other words, to discover the sacred authors' intention, the reader must take into account the conditions of their time and culture, the literary genres in use at that time, and the modes of feeling, speaking, and narrating then current (*CCC*, 110).
- Let those who cultivate biblical studies . . . neglect none of those discoveries, whether in the domain of archaeology or in ancient history or literature, which serve to make better known the mentality of the ancient writers, as well as their manner and art of reasoning, narrating and writing. In this connection Catholic laymen should consider that they will not only further profane science, but moreover will render a conspicuous service to the Christian cause if they devote themselves with all due diligence and application to the exploration and investigation of the monuments of antiquity and contribute, according to their abilities, to the solution of questions hitherto obscure (Pope Pius XII, *Divino Afflante Spiritu*, 40).

Advance Preparations

- Prepare any handouts and overhead transparencies (see avemariapress.com) you plan to use for all sessions.
- Obtain and view any videos or Internet resources you wish to include in your lesson plan.
- Provide magazines, scissors, glue, and poster board for the assignment on page 38 of the TWE.
- Arrange for the students to have necessary art supplies for the exercise "One, True, Living, God" (page 45) if it is to be completed during class time.
- Plan to have complete sets of the daily newspaper for the Bell Ringer activity described on page 55 of the TWE.
- If possible, arrange for an archaeologist or geologist to speak to the students about what we can learn about history from various artifacts.

Chapter Objectives

The students will be able to:

- put the writings of the Old Testament in a geographical, historical, and religious context.
- discover what archaeological finds have revealed about the peoples of the Biblical period.
- see how the geography of Canaan contributed to the frequency of war in ancient Israelite life.
- understand why Canaan became the center of great civilizations and was so important to surrounding countries such as Egypt and Mesopotamia.
- trace the history of the Israelites from the time of the Exodus to the century before Christ.
- study the major types of religious literature that make up the Old Testament.
- appreciate why we consider the Old Testament, along with the New Testament, to be God's Word.

CHAPTER 2

INTRODUCTION
ARCHAEOLOGY AND BIBLICAL STUDIES

Bell-Ringers

1. **Re-teach:** Note the chapter objectives from Chapter 1 and use them to review the main content from the chapter. Also, return the graded Chapter 1 Tests to the students.

2. Show a 10 to 15 minutes segment of the film *Raiders of the Lost Ark* (see note on page 45 of the TWE.) Explain that in the film Indiana Jones is looking for the lost Ark of the Covenant that the Israelites carried with them to remind them of Yahweh's presence and protection. Focus on a scene that depicts an archaeological site. Point out the value of archaeology in helping to learn about people from the past.

Teaching Approaches

1. Print the word **context** on the board. Review its meaning as defined in the Introduction, page 34 (e.g., the setting, or environment, that surrounds an object). Explain that archaeologists are often detectives. When they discover something at a dig, they have to interpret it according to its context—what else they find around it.

2. **Assignment:** Demonstrate the meaning of *context*. Have the students work in groups. Provide each group with a sheet of poster board, several magazines, scissors, and glue. Have them create a scene where people are "out of context." For example, the face of a famous person can be glued on a different body. Or, an athlete can be placed in a non-athletic setting. Have the groups share their work. Explain that unless we know the story in the correct context, it's hard to understand its importance.

THE OLD TESTAMENT

context—The historical, cultural, social, or political circumstances surrounding an event or record.

Introduction

To analyze something by its *context* involves looking at the circumstances in which it occurs. One of the best ways to understand more about the Old Testament is to put the origins, uses, and interpretations of the books *into context*. For example, Moses' reception of the Ten Commandments must first be understood in the context of the Hebrews' Exodus from Egypt, God's great liberating event that is at the heart of the Old Testament.

Putting the Old Testament into context equates with providing both geographical and historical "maps" for our journey. With the historical context, we can also include the cultural and social factors of the day. For example: What was life like in Palestine in the ancient world? Which groups of people lived in Palestine before the Israelites? What were the important characteristics of the cultures of other people in the Near East? The purpose of this chapter is to shed some light on these kinds of questions.

What is considered the "Old Testament" Biblical era runs from the decline of the Egyptian and Hittite Empires[1] in roughly 1300-1100 B.C. until just after the time of Alexander the Great's conquests in the entire region (ca. 333 B.C. to 64 B.C.). The Exodus of the Israelites from Egypt is typically dated to approximately 1270 B.C. As we will see in the chapters that follow, while there is some question about *when* the Bible actually started to be written down, the events that the Bible describes are almost entirely confined to roughly this time period: 1300–100 B.C. Historically, this is a fairly short period of time. In studying this period of history, it is helpful to examine what happened in Palestine just prior to this time as well.

Archaeology and Biblical Studies

Imagine that you are living hundreds of years in the future. Your house (or what is left of it after being buried in dust and mud over the centuries) has just been uncovered by a group of teenagers studying a unit in archaeology. As they dig in the remains, they stumble upon your room. What will they find? More importantly, what might they be able to tell about you on the basis of what they find? Remember, they will only find those kinds of things that would last for hundreds of years; they will not find paper or clothing, and they will probably not discover many wood products either.

This kind of problem faces archaeologists who are studying the Ancient Near East today. They discover little written material and precious little of anything else.

However, today's archaeologists do have models to emulate. The ancient Israelites were also interested in a kind of archaeology.[2] For example, the Biblical authors presumed that their first readers knew of some interesting locations where events were said to have occurred many years, perhaps even centuries, before the time the books

34

Resources

Music Suggestions

"Glory and Praise to Our God" by Dan Schutte from *A Dwelling Place* or *Glory & Praise 1* (OCP [NALR]); *Gather* (GIA); *Music Issue* or *Breaking Bread* (OCP).

"How Beautiful" by Daniel Consiglio from *Lord of Field and Vine* (OCP [NALR}) and *Glory and Praise* (OCP [NALR]).

"Jerusalem, My Destiny" by Rory Cooney from *Gather* (GIA).

"Jerusalem, My Happy Home" by Joseph Bromehead from *Gather* (GIA).

"On Holy Ground" by Donna Pena in *Gather* (GIA).

"Psalm 122: I Was Glad" by David Haas in *Gather* (GIA).

"Psalm 25: To You, O Lord" by Marty Haugen from *Gather* (GIA).

"Psalm 27: The Lord Is My Light" by David Haas from *Gather* (GIA).

"Shepherd Me, O God" by Marty Haugen from *Shepherd Me, O God* or *Gather* (GIA); *Breaking Bread* (OCP).

were written. In the book of Joshua, for example, there is a brief discussion of the destruction of the village Ai. Joshua 8:28 refers to a village in a heap of ruins, adding, "as it remains to this day." At the time the passage was written, it was already a ruin, a site where destroyed remnants were considered to be "evidence" of previous events.

So, in a sense, archaeology is an ancient activity. By the seventeenth century, archaeology had become a romantic endeavor in the mode of the Indiana Jones movies with archaeologists unearthing dramatic discoveries. In the twenty-first century, however, archaeology has become more of an exact science, and the *context* of each find is as important as the find. In fact, an artifact is almost totally useless if we don't know the context of its discovery—that is, the approximate level of the dig, other artifacts associated with it, and its location.

Archaeologists can provide clues about the land of Palestine before the arrival of the Israelites. There is very little written about Palestine (also known as "Canaan"), and most of the information comes from digging among the ancient ruins of village locations. When ancient writings *are* discovered they must be translated. This is one of the major tasks of the modern archaeologist, especially if it is an unknown language. In these cases, translators must be "decoders."

Decoding Ancient Writing

Most scholars date the origins of Ancient Near East writing systems to 3500–3000 B.C. Writing emerged in Egypt and Mesopotamia (modern Iraq) at about the same time. It is likely that the earliest forms of writing were **pictograms**. These pictures then evolved slowly to conventional symbols. It wasn't until relatively very late in human history that the Phoenicians (Canaanites) invented a new system of organizing symbols—a designated number of symbols that were used as an alphabet.

Before alphabets were invented **scribes** needed to learn literally hundreds of signs and symbols. That is one reason why literacy was not widespread. A scribe had to train from youth to learn all the signs! Also, early on, only the wealthy could afford to hire scribes. It follows that most of the earliest documents that we have preserved tend to be royal documents (the kings could certainly afford scribes), business documents, and occasionally military documents. When archaeologists are lucky, they discover a wealthy temple that could afford to have its religious ideas written down. In those cases, the next task is for the archaeologist to decipher the writings. Archaeologists with an interesst in the Bible then try to determine how many of them actually mention the events or the people of the Bible or religious ideas that may shed light on the Bible in addition to their inherent historical significance in and of themselves.

As mentioned, by the seventeenth century many Western explorers were traveling to the Holy Land. By the nineteenth

pictograms—The earliest form of writing in which pictures represented words or ideas.

scribes—People trained to write using the earliest forms of writing before literacy was widespread.

3. Point out the first paragraph under "Archaeology and Biblical Studies" (page 34). Have them write their responses to the questions posed in the paragraph and share what they wrote with a partner.

4. Distribute copies of Handout 2A, "Secret Codes" (page 264 of the TWE). Challenge the students to write a verse from the Old Testament using one of the codes. Or have the students make up their own code and then use it to write a Bible passage. Have the students exchange their messages with a partner and "decode" each other's secret message.

5. **Homework Assignment**:
   - Finish reading the section "Archaeology and Biblical Studies" (pages 34–39) including the subsections "Decoding Ancient Writing" and "Other Archaeological Evidence" and the separate feature "Dating the Ages" in the text.
   - Prepare for a group discussion on the questions from "Personal Archaeology" (page 36).
   - Bring in one item that represents your life (e.g., trading card, old jewelry, worn article of clothing).

Chapter 2

ARCHAEOLOGY AND BIBLICAL STUDIES

Bell-Ringer

1. Assign triads to answer the questions proposed in "Personal Archaeology" (page 36). Call on a representative from each group to share their ideas with the class.

2. Collect the items that the students brought in to represent their lives. Put them in a multi-gallon plastic container. Leave it in the classroom as a symbolic time capsule of their shared experiences.

THE OLD TESTAMENT

hieroglyphic writing—An ancient form of Egyptian writing, more stylized than pictograms but not based on an alphabet.

The Rosetta Stone

century, there were several books with illustrations (sometimes photos, often drawings) of the Holy Land that sold very well to European Christian readers who were anxious to know more about the "context" of the Bible. These readers wanted to know what places like Jerusalem and Bethlehem looked like.

Luckily, some of these early Western explorers were also serious scientists and scholars. The famous **hieroglyphic writing** of ancient Egypt was finally deciphered in 1822, after Napoleon's invasion of Egypt and the recovery of the Rosetta Stone. The Rosetta Stone featured the same text in two Egyptian languages, including hieroglyphic, and also Greek, allowing Greek readers to work out the Egyptian translation. From that time on archaeologists could read ancient Egyptian writings—on stone, on the walls of tombs, from rooms in pyramids—and learn about Egyptian religion and life. Biblical scholars could then compare Egyptian writing with Biblical writings.

By 1846, all of the major ancient languages of the Eastern part of the Near East (Mesopotamia, or modern Iran and Iraq) were finally translated. Thus, by the middle of the nineteenth century the two most dominant civilizations of the Biblical era, Egypt and Mesopotamia, were beginning to be understood on a level never previously known.

Another ancient writing that has been deciphered is known as the "Mesha Inscription," discovered in 1868. This inscription comes from Moab, one of the rival states of Israel just across the Jordan River. The writing mentions an Israelite king, Omri, albeit in a negative light since Israel and Moab were enemies at the time. However, the reference is but another piece of evidence in piecing together the world in which the Old Testament was created. In the Mesha Inscription, the king of Moab claimed that Moab's God, Chemosh, gave him victory over Israel. Religion and war, sadly, are *both* ancient activities.

Finally, Sir Flanders Petrie made a discovery of an inscription known as the "Merneptah Stele." It was first published in 1897. In the writing, an Egyptian Pharaoh, Merneptah, brags that he successfully defeated a "people" called "Israel" in a writing that can be dated to roughly 1207 B.C. This writing is, in fact, the oldest reference to the Israelites in existence. It doesn't say much, but at least

PERSONAL ARCHAEOLOGY

Go back to thinking about the students digging in the remains of your house hundreds of years from now. What would they learn by digging in houses nearby? houses in a nearby town? a nearby state? How would that information help them learn about you and your room?

36

we have a written testimony to a people called Israel. Furthermore, we know that Merneptah was wrong; after all, he claimed to have wiped out the "seed of Israel." Apparently, political exaggeration is not an exclusively modern practice!

You may be wondering if these few references to the Israelites are the only historical evidence outside of the Bible to corroborate their existence. Although there are hundreds of texts that have been translated, and many more that are not yet published, the fact remains that there is *not* a great deal of information about Israel in these vast amounts of writings found among non-Hebrew peoples. These ancient texts tell us about the life and beliefs of the people surrounding the Hebrews, and in some cases, it is easy to see how these other peoples may have influenced the Hebrews (see page 45).

Fortunately, writing is not the only source of information about Biblical times—ruins and artifacts are another major source. What can this kind of evidence tell us?

Other Archaeological Evidence

Modern, scientifically excavated archaeological evidence tells us a great deal about civilizations in the context of the Israelites and the Biblical period.

Archaeological evidence (mostly stone tools) shows that humans have lived in the Palestinian region for over a million years (from the early Paleolithic era). Scientific study revealed that with the end of the final Ice Age in about 10,000 B.C., the climate became more hospitable to human existence. The evidence suggests that humans began to live in groups. By 9,000 B.C. they were engaged in food production.

Good food production requires water and flat, easily plowed and workable land. Food production allows humans to stay in one location rather than constantly moving to hunt, so it is obviously an important building block for the foundations of a civilization. Large settlements were established near the Tigris and Euphrates rivers in Mesopotamia and the Nile in Egypt. Settlement also creates the conditions for leaving artifacts in one place, which assists archaeologists in making more educated guesses about what life would have been like in those years and in a single location or area.

Two of the most important sites for discovering **prehistoric**[3] artifacts in this part of the world are Jericho, in modern Palestine; and Ain Ghazal, north of Amman, Jordan. In Ain Ghazal, burials have been discovered under the floors of dwellings and human-like and animal figurines suggest a religious life of some kind. Special treatment of skulls at both Jericho and Ain Ghazal also suggest the possibility of some sort of religious practices or observances associated with these burials.[4] Artifacts from other parts of the Near Eastern world were found in Ain Gahzal, suggesting a trading network. Finally, Ain Ghazal reveals the development of pottery that can be dated there to roughly 5,000 B.C. In

prehistoric—Refers to events or objects that date to a time before writing developed and written records exist.

MAPS FOR THE JOURNEY

Teaching Approaches

1. **Re-teach:** Ask these questions:
   - Before there were alphabets, how did people record ideas? (pictograms and hieroglyphics)
   - What is the difference between the two? (Hieroglyphics are more detailed.)
   - What discovery enabled scholars to decipher the hieroglyphs of Egypt? (the Rosetta Stone)

2. Use the Resource suggestions (from this chapter) and the Background Information below to prepare a short presentation on the Rosetta Stone. Share with the class.

3. Use "Israel in Merneptah Stele" (Overhead 2A online at **avemariapress.com**) to show the students the earliest known pictogram or hieroglyphic of the word "Israel," from the Merneptah Stele. Explain that the word is read from right to left. The two palm fronds stand for the letter "i," the door bolt represents the letter "s," the open mouth is "r," the stylized hawk is "a," the eye for seeing combined with the following symbols mean "in desolation." The translation: "Israel is desolated." The stele says, "Israel is desolated, his seed is not. Palestine has become a widow for Egypt. All lands are united, they are pacified, everyone that is turbulent is bound by King Merneptah, life like Re, every day."

Background Information

Rosetta Stone

The Rosetta Stone was carved in 196 B.C. on basalt. It was found in 1799 by French soldiers near the town of Rosette in Egypt (modern-day Raschid), located on the western delta of the Nile. The Rosetta Stone was written in three different scripts—all in use at the time in ancient Egypt. These scripts were written in hieroglyphics (used for important or religious documents), demotic (the common script of Egypt), and Greek. It was written by a group of Egyptian priests from Memphis to honor Ptolemaios V, the Pharaoh of the time. It was written in all three scripts so that priests, government officials, and rulers of Egypt could read what it said. The Stone lists all the good things Pharaoh has done for the priests and for the people. The text was finally deciphered in 1822 by Jean-Francois Champollion. Today the Rosetta Stone is in the British Museum in London.

Chapter 2

4. Explain that people tend to rebuild on the places where they or their ancestors have previously lived. Throughout history, people built new structures on top of ruins (which acted as land-fill). Gradually, the elevation of the land in populated areas became higher. Archaeologists can learn about ancient peoples by digging. The further down they dig, the older is the human settlement they find.

5. Distribute copies of the chart "Archaeological Time Periods and the Old Testament" (Handout 2B, page 265 of the TWE). Explain that archaeological time periods are based roughly on the main type of metal used to make weapons and tools. Explain that if "ground level" is at the top of the chart, the deeper down you go, the farther back you go in history. The oldest known tools were made of stone (hence, this time period is called the Stone Age). The next metal to be used was copper. Then bronze. Then iron. Help the students have an overall idea of when events in the Bible happened in relation to the designations of these historical periods.

DATING THE AGES

Some historians still use the terms "Stone Age," "Bronze Age" (which is divided into early, middle, and late), and "Iron Age" to classify prehistoric artifacts according to successive stages of technological development. The original idea was that metal could be used as a general indicator of human technological innovation, and thus a reliable way to date sites. However, many modern archaeologists have reminded us that this is not a precise science, as older types of materials coexisted with certain new metals—for example, wood plows were used at the same time as bronze or iron plow tips because some of the new metals were perhaps too expensive, or difficult to make for the larger population.

Also, an "Iron Age" doesn't mean *everyone* was using iron, anymore than the beginning of a "computer age" means that all families have a PC in their homes. Note, for example, that the Old Testament suggests that there was a time when the Israelites did not know how to make iron implements (swords or plows), even though the Philistines had this technology.

---

fact, pottery styles are among the most important clues to help archaeologists determine specific dates of finds. In short, human beings lived in this part of the world literally centuries before the first writings of the Bible.

One of the most important things the tools of the early Israelites can teach us is that the Israelites seemed to have settled in the hills of Palestine, rather than on the coastal plains where larger cities were located. In these terraced hillside villages, they worked with cisterns that kept water available throughout the year. They also used a typically Canaanite form of a collared-rim jar for storage. They lived in a four pillared house—that is, a typical structure with a second floor (built on beams laid across stone or wood pillars). The people lived on the second floor, but would cook on the ground, and sometimes keep animals on the ground floor as well—especially in cold weather.

Hill country of Palestine

In the Near East, civilization began to take other major steps during the fourth millennium B.C. Large territories in Egypt and Mesopotamia merged toward common forms of pottery and artifacts, suggesting larger production of materials and populations that were in contact.[5] Cities began to form. These larger urban areas, controlling even larger surrounding territories, were the basis for increased agricultural production and trade and provided the social basis for the beginning of writing.

The largest motivation for writing was not spiritual or religious, but business and military. Most of the writing samples besides

---

Resources
Printed Materials

"Archaeology and the Bible," and "Geography of Palestine" in *The Oxford Companion to the Bible*, ed. by Bruce M. Metzger and Michael D. Coogan. (New York, NY: Oxford University Press, 1993), pp. 46–54, 250–252.

"Archaeology," in *Dictionary of the Bible*, ed. by John L. McKenzie, S.J. (New York, NY: Macmillan Publishing Co., Inc., 1965), pp. 51–52.

Brown, Raymond, S.S., and Robert North, S.J. " Biblical Geography" in *The New Jerome Biblical Comm*entary, ed. by Raymond E. Brown, S.S., Joseph A. Fitzmyer, S.J., and Roland E. Murphy, O.Carm. (Englewood Cliffs, NJ: Prentice Hall, 1990), pp. 1175–1195.

North, Robert, S.J., and Philip J. King "Biblical Archaeology" in *The New Jerome Biblical Comm*entary, ed. by Raymond E. Brown, S.S., Joseph A. Fitzmyer, S.J., and Roland E. Murphy, O.Carm. (Englewood Cliffs, NJ: Prentice Hall, 1990), pp. 1196–1218.

Maps for the Journey

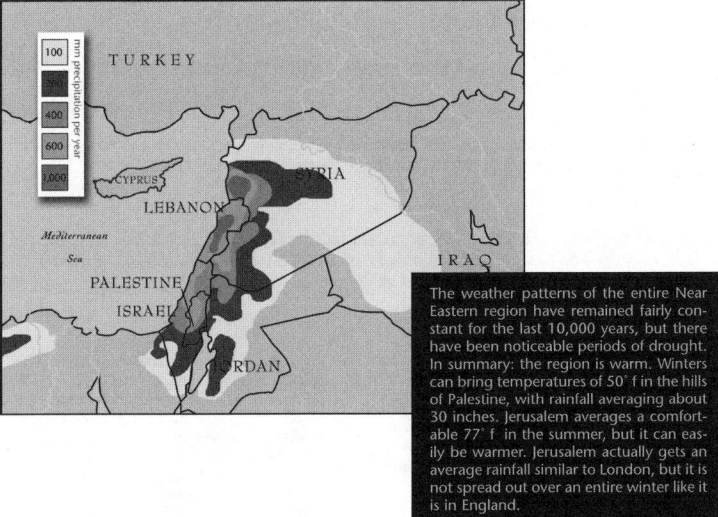

The weather patterns of the entire Near Eastern region have remained fairly constant for the last 10,000 years, but there have been noticeable periods of drought. In summary: the region is warm. Winters can bring temperatures of 50° f in the hills of Palestine, with rainfall averaging about 30 inches. Jerusalem averages a comfortable 77° f in the summer, but it can easily be warmer. Jerusalem actually gets an average rainfall similar to London, but it is not spread out over an entire winter like it is in England.

royal documents, tended to be business documents or military-related documents. In both Egypt and Mesopotamia, the dominant political systems that arose were centralized monarchies that formed powerful, military states. These empires have been described as "giant vacuum cleaners" whose intent was to "suck in" resources by military conquest as far as they could manage, and send them to the elite at the centers of power.

Military states, conquest, and political control were occurrences that had gone on for thousands of years by the time the Israelites began to form a nation. Even the "creation myths" of some of these empires reflected domination and control (more information in Chapter 3). Often, these myths suggested that the gods once had to do the work of the fields, but they created human beings to work for them![6] This idea is very different from the creation story told by the Israelites of the one God, Yahweh, who is loving and compassionate toward his people.

6. **Homework Assignment:**
   Writes answers to the Review and Reflection questions 1–3, page 40.
   - Complete the Journal Assignment, page 40. *Optional*: Bring an item from your list to class and tell a story about why it will still be valuable in 1,000 years.
   - Read the entire section "The Land of Canaan: At the Center of Civilization" (pages 40–46), including the features.
   - Begin work on the essay assigned in Learn by Doing, page 57. (Refer the students to some of the Resource references, pages 42 and 47 of the TWE).

Chapter 2

THE LAND OF CANAAN: AT THE CENTER OF CIVILIZATION

Bell-Ringers

1. **Re-teach:** Check the student's knowledge of the homework reading assignment. Print the following questions on the board. Have the students write answers and exchange papers for grading.

- **What is the Fertile Crescent?** (a crescent-shaped area of farmable land in the Middle East)
- **What was the name of this area in Biblical times?** (Canaan)
- **Why was Canaan important in Biblical times?** (It was situated between Egypt and Mesopotamia who both fought for control of it. Thus, Canaan was often the site of battles. Canaan was also important because the culture and religion of its people became intertwined with the culture and religion of the Israelites.)

THE OLD TESTAMENT

REVIEW & REFLECTION

1. What years are considered the Old Testament Biblical era? Make a simple timeline covering these dates.
2. What is the importance of the Rosetta Stone?
3. List the archaeological discoveries that have been made at Jericho and Ain Ghazal. What do these findings suggest about the people who lived there?

JOURNAL ASSIGNMENT

- Make a list of five things in your room at home that archaeologists might find interesting 1,000 years from now. Tell why.

The Land of Canaan: At the Center of Civilization

The land of Canaan (later known as Palestine) sat on the coast line between two great centers of ancient civilization—Egypt and Mesopotamia. It was Canaan that God had chosen as a homeland for the Israelites. If you look on a map (see page 41), you can see that Canaan was really a land bridge between Egypt and Mesopotamia. What do you think it meant for the Israelite nation to arise in a land surrounded by two mighty empires?

Egypt—on the south end of the land bridge—was called a "gift of the Nile" by the Greeks. The agricultural and farming economies of Egypt grew to create vast surpluses. That allowed the Egyptian pharaohs to grow into mighty overlords mastering vast territories and fashioning weapons for huge armies for conquest and plunder. For example, Egypt was famous for perfecting the chariot and equipping vast armies of chariots and infantry. Also, don't forget that the great cultural achievements of the ancient Egyptians—the pyramids, monuments, and temples—were paid for by the masses of people who were forced into labor to make these accomplishments possible—laborers who were both Egyptians and enslaved foreigners.

At the other end of the land bridge east of the Israelites was another fertile land fed by the waters of the Euphrates and Tigris rivers. The land between and around these rivers was known as Mesopotamia ("between the rivers"). Here again, the plentiful supply of fresh water allowed for rich agricultural production, and vast empires arose in Mesopotamia—including the Assyrians and Babylonians. The Persian Empire developed further east.

So, between Egypt to the South and West and Mesopotamia to the North and East lay a narrowly habitable land known in Old Testament times as Canaan. We now know this land as Syro-Palestine or Palestine. It includes the territories of Syria, Lebanon, Israel, and Palestine. A closer examination of Palestine reveals more information about the people who lived there in Biblical times.

Review and Reflection Answers

1. The Old Testament Biblical era runs from the decline of the Egyptian and Hittite Empires in roughly 1300–1100 B.C. until just after the time of Alexander the Great's conquests in the entire region (c. 333 B.C.–70 B.C.). Accept all reasonable timeline drawings.

2. The Rosetta Stone, which was written in ancient hieroglyphics, another Egyptian language, and Greek, enabled scholars to translate or "decode" the hieroglyphics. From that time on, archaeologists could read ancient Egyptian writings and learn about Egyptian religion and life. Biblical scholars could then compare Egyptian writings with Biblical writings.

3. In Ain Ghazal, burials under the floors of dwellings and humanlike and animal figurines suggest a religious life of some kind. Other artifacts from Ain Ghazal and Jericho include skulls and pottery. These artifacts suggest some sort of religious practices or observances associated with burials, as well as a trading network.

Maps for the Journey

Maps for the Journey

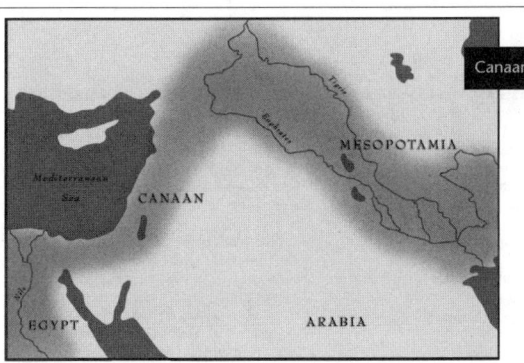
Canaan in Old Testament times

The geography of Palestine runs in zones or strips from North to South. If you flew over Palestine from the Mediterranean Sea (flying from the west and heading east) you would move from the beach toward the inland areas and see below you the following strips or zones:

- the *coastal plains*, which narrow toward the north of Palestine (near modern Haifa);
- the *hill country*, which runs like a spine up the "back" of Palestine, and into modern Lebanon, where the hills actually become mountains;
- the *Jordan Valley* – a "rift" in the earth that extends all the way from Turkey to Africa. This "rift" is actually the meeting place of the two continental plates of Africa and Asia, and thus is somewhat unstable, which accounts for the frequency of serious earthquakes in Palestine
- the *Transjordanian Plateau*. This was perhaps the best known regional zone in the ancient period as it contained the "King's Highway," the major North-South trade route of the ancient world.

Finally, after passing over the major geographical zones listed above, you would encounter a vast desert, largely uninhabited—sometimes called the *Syrian Desert*. The Syrian Desert extends all the way to Arabia and down to Yemen on the southern coast. Modern archaeologists have learned that there were occasional settlements, and even cities, in these vast areas, at one time.

Most of the larger ancient cities that were active prior to the founding of the Israelites were located on

HEADING TO THE HILLS

In American history, the relationship between the Hopi and Navajo peoples parallels the relationship between the Israelites and the Philistines. The Navajos were once the dominant tribe of the American Southwest, living in the lowlands of what is now Arizona and New Mexico. The Hopi people, more peaceful, made their dwellings high in the plateaus or "mesas" of that region where they could avoid fighting the Navajos for the more valuable land. The principle the Hopis followed appears to be similar to that of the Israelites—head to the hills for less desirable but more easily protected settlements.

Both the Israelites and Hopis had to be innovative in figuring out how to make a living and raise crops, which they did by terracing their land.

Hopi dwelling

2. Locate the Fertile Crescent on a modern map. Point out the location to the students.

Resources
Audiovisual Materials

Mysteries of the Bible: The Bible's Greatest Secrets (Videos with Values)—50 minutes
This video deals with the many archaeologists who are trying to unlock the mysteries of the Bible by sifting through the sands in the Holy Land today. Viewers learn how the science of archaeology can shed light on Scripture and provide us with clues about Biblical times.

Religions of the Book: Holy Places and Pilgrimage (Films for the Humanities and Sciences)—29 minutes
This video takes us to the Holy Land and explores the holy places of Judaism, Christianity, and Islam. The video also discusses the importance of pilgrimages to people of faith.

Scripture from Scratch II: On the Road Again, Geography in the Hebrew Scriptures (St. Anthony Messenger Press)—2 videos, 25 minutes each
Virginia Smith and Elizabeth McNamer discuss the importance of geography in understanding the Old Testament. Locales, distances, topography, and climatic conditions of Canaan, Mesopotamia, and Egypt all affect the Biblical story.

Scripture from Scratch II: Piecing It Together, What Archaeology Can Tell Us (St. Anthony Messenger Press)—50 minutes
This video presents archaeological sites and artifact to show how people lived in biblical times.

The Philistines: Archenemy (A & E Old Testament Collection)—50 minutes
Archaeologists search for clues about the Philistines, the archenemy of the Israelites. We learn more about life in Old Testament times.

Note: The chapter mentions the Indiana Jones movies. To date, there are three movies in the series: *Raiders of the Lost Ark*, *The Temple of Doom*, and *The Last Crusade*. These three movies have been combined into one DVD entitled *The Adventures of Indiana Jones*. Some excerpts from these films are appropriate to whet the students' appetite for the field of archaeology.

CHAPTER 2

Teaching Approaches

1. Provide more information about the land of Canaan in Biblical times (see below). Consider showing all or part of the video, *Scripture from Scratch II: On the Road Again, Geography in the Hebrew Scriptures* (see page 45 of the TWE).

---

the coastal plains. Travel and farming was easier on the largely level grounds there. The oceans are close to this area, and there were some useable ports for shipping. The Jordan River Valley was another populated region with access to water and rich soil for farming.

When the Israelites finally settled in Canaan they likely chose neither of these strips or zones. Instead, the Israelites took up residence in the hill country of Palestine because there was little competition for this land. The hill country also afforded natural protection against enemies. A major difficulty to overcome in the hill country was its lack of suitability for farming. The Israelites definitely had to be innovative and resourceful to survive there.

In spite of the willingness of the hill-dwelling peoples to avoid the settlers on the coastal plain and in the Jordan Valley, they were nevertheless still viewed as competition by the older civilizations. This was the case even when the militarily strong Philistines settled in the coastal plains shortly before Israel came to Canaan. (In fact, the name Palestine derives from "Philistine.") The Philistines established cities such as Ekron, Ashdod, and Askelon on the coastal plains. When the Israelites did arrive they settled in the hills, perhaps to avoid a battle or simply to establish themselves apart from the other civilizations that were already in place. (One of the questions that will be considered as we proceed is whether or not the Israelites were really such "latecomers" to Canaan. After all, the Bible tells of Abraham and his family living in this region at the time of the founding of his people.)

The Fertile Crescent: Corridor of Conflict

It is rather clear when you examine a map of Canaan that there is actually a very narrow corridor of arable land that runs along the Mediterranean coastline and connects the ancient civilizations of Egypt and Mesopotamia. This land bridge between the two great civilizations is part of what is known as the "fertile crescent."

Taking note of this piece of valuable land is a critically important point in Biblical studies. Knowing that the coast road is a major trade route for the ancient world, you begin to see the geographical explanation for the horrendous violence of the Biblical period: *The people of Israel took up residence in the middle of the "land bridge" that connected two great centers of human civilization.* They did not live in a quiet or remote territory, but in the middle of the ancient highways of trade and military transportation. The little area of Palestine that the Israelite tribes settled was blessed with good grapes and olives, but cursed to be the main thoroughfare for ancient armies marching north and south, back and forth, as the Egyptian and Mesopotamian empires struggled for control of this critical passageway, and for control of each other. Israel was literally "caught in the middle."

Many new students of the Old Testament are disturbed by the level of violence in these books. Understanding the position of the Israelites in Canaan is helpful in understanding why the Old Testament contains many examples of warfare and retribution. Warfare was all around the Israelites.

Such understanding also helps to explain the Israelites' portrayal of their God Yahweh as a warrior. Since the Israelites were not capable of doing much military damage, they held to the belief that their God was a powerful warrior who would protect them. The Israelite peoples would have been intimately familiar with the bottom of every boot that marched through Palestine over the centuries. It is not that the vast empires were all that interested in controlling the Israelites; rather it was the passageway that they lived on that interested Israel's enemies. To summarize: Geography matters. Context matters. Next, the focus will be on some of the history of the people who lived in the land of Canaan itself.

Background Information
The Land of Canaan

The land of Canaan was already occupied when the Israelites arrived from Egypt. One of the important Canaanite cities at the time was Ugarit, located about 1000 meters from the Mediterranean Sea. Archaeological digs have found that Ugarit was a very ancient city, originally built around 6000 B.C. The Egyptians dominated Ugarit through 1400 B.C. When the Israelites arrived in the twelfth century B.C., Ugarit had a population between 7,000 and 8,000 people.

Archaeological digs have revealed ancient tablets from Ugarit, which blended an alphabetic script (like Hebrew) and cuneiform (like Akkadian). The Ugaritic literature has proved very important in studying the Bible for three reasons: 1) a number of Hebrew Psalms were adapted from previous Ugaritic psalms, so we can learn the meaning of individual archaic words; 2) the story of the flood in Genesis is almost the same as a flood story found in Ugarit, thus indicating a common literary heritage; 3) the religion of Ugarit had a profound impact on the Hebrews. Ugaritic religious poetry is very similar to Biblical poetry and is therefore useful in interpreting difficult passages.

Maps for the Journey

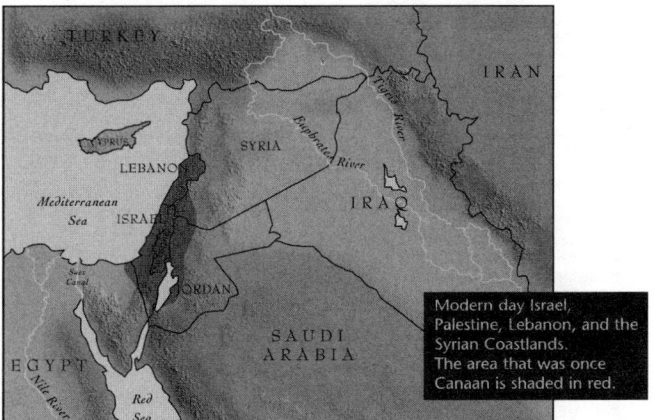

Modern day Israel, Palestine, Lebanon, and the Syrian Coastlands. The area that was once Canaan is shaded in red.

2. Write the names of some of the gods of Ugarit on the board:
   - El (the chief god)
   - El Shaddai, El Elyon, and El Berith (other gods)
   - Asherah, (the consort or wife of El)
   - Baal (the god of rain)
   - Yam (the god of the sea)
   - Mot (the god of death)
   - **Assignment**: Point out references to these false gods in Scripture. Have the students look up and note the context of two Scripture references to Baal and one Scripture reference to another false god.

Before Israel: The Canaanites

Israel arose in the land known to history as *Canaan*. This name is used to designate a territory that includes much of modern Israel and Palestine, Lebanon, and the Syrian coastlands, all the way to the beginning of the Sinai peninsula in the south (see map above). There was a civilization in this land for thousands of years before the ancient Israelites formed their state there.

From about 2000 B.C. to the time of the formation of Israel in 1300–1100 B.C., Egypt considered Canaan part of its territory, crucial to Egypt's interests. A major Egyptian trading route ran through Canaan, and the Egyptians also used the seaport in Byblos (now Beirut in Lebanon). However, there were native people living in Canaan, the Canaanites.

The relationship between the Egyptians and the Canaanites was stormy. Canaan was considered a rough and unruly land by the Egyptians. They often engaged in military activities to maintain their control of Canaanite cities and would bring prisoners-of-war back to Egypt to engage them in forced labor. At other times, Canaanites would migrate into the northeastern region of Egypt to find water, better land, and work when rainfall was scarce in Canaan or when military threats forced them south.

For a period of time from roughly 1650–1550 B.C., a substantial number of the Canaanites invaded and briefly controlled Egypt. This is known as the *Hyksos Period* because the Egyptians called the foreigners "Hyksos." When the Hyksos were eventually defeated and Egyptians were restored to power, oppression of the Canaanites followed. Some historians suggest that retribution associated with the Hyksos Period provides a possible background to the eventual oppression of the Israelites by the Egyptians. This assumes that the later Israelites had some ancestors from among the "Hyksos."

What else is known of the Canaanites? For one, the Canaanites established a strong civilization of their own. Many Caananite cities

Resources

Internet Links

www.bibleplaces.com
Beautiful, high-resolution images of archaeological sites in Israel.

www.questia.com
Dozens of books and journal articles on Biblical archaeology

www.imj.org.il
View objects in the permanent exhibit "Archaeology of Israel" in the Israel Museum, Jerusalem.

http://orion.mscc.huji.ac.il/
Visit the Orion Center for the Study of the Dead Sea Scrolls. Go on a virtual cave tour and view a site map.

www.mysteries-megasite.com/main/bigsearch/dead-sea.html
Site provides over 300 links to the Dead Sea Scrolls.

Chapter 2

3. Assign the exercise "One, True, Living God," (page 45). Provide various art supplies. Allow the students to display their finished work around the classroom.

---

were quite impressive and powerful, as represented by *Ugarit*, a city located on what is today the Syrian coast, near the modern village of Ras Shamra. The ancient city of Ugarit was apparently destroyed by the Philistines, perhaps even before the tribes of Israel settled in the land of Canaan further south.

At Ugarit, a number of tablets were discovered that shed light on the religious ideas of the Canaanites. The Canaanites worshipped a variety of gods, including a main god, *El*, who they believed had a wife known as *Asherah*. (Asherah is the goddess named in 2 Kings 23:4–7 as one of the pagan gods that the Israelites were not supposed to worship. She was also referred to as the "queen of heaven" in Jeremiah 44:17–25.)

But the most popular god of the Canaanites was the god who brought rain and thus provided for fertile grounds. This god was known as *Baal*. All of the peoples surrounding the Israelites in Canaan worshipped Baal. In the Bible, Baal is often referred to as the most significant rival to Yahweh. The most serious warnings in the Old Testament against worshiping other gods were directed at the worship of Baal. The descriptions of Elijah leading the struggle against the worship of Baal in 1 Kings 17–19 (especially chapter 18) represent how serious was the interaction and debate between the Canaanites and Israelites regarding religion—and how competitive that debate was.

The Canaanites worshipped their gods in temples administered by various kinds of priests. In fact, the design of these Canaanite temples was exactly the same as the great Temple of Solomon in Jerusalem that was built later. It seems likely that Solomon borrowed from the design of some of the Canaanite temples. The Canaanites offered animal sacrifices to their gods and would sing songs and poems. They would also tell stories of their gods. Some of these stories have survived, found at places such as Ugarit. They tell the tales of Baal in his wars against other gods such as *Mot* the god of death and *Yam* the god of the sea.

Because the Israelites lived in such close proximity in time and space with the Canaanites (and some ancestors of the Israelites may have actually been Canaanites), it is understandable that the Bible mentions their myths, poems, and legends. Several of the expressions in Psalm 29 are also found in Canaanite texts written in the fifteenth century B.C. at Ugarit. For example the text in Psalm 29:7 describes Yahweh as a storm God, which is also what Baal was. Consider the thunder and lightning images here:

> The voice of the Lord strikes fiery flames;
> the voice of the Lord shakes the desert, the Lord shakes the wilderness of Kadesh (29:7).

The Canaanite religion was also a religion that supported the dominance of the rich and powerful over the majority who were agricultural peasants who did not own land. The story of a Canaanite princess, Jezebel (1 Kings 21), who used her influence to steal the land of an Israelite named Naboth contrasts the justice and equality of Yahweh with the privilege and power of the Canaanite gods. For the Israelites to be a member of God's Chosen People meant a commitment to a way of life that emphasized justice and care for others. In fact, many Canaanites converted to the religion of Yahweh and called themselves "Israelites" to make it clear they no longer worshipped Baal and Asherah.

Maps for the Journey

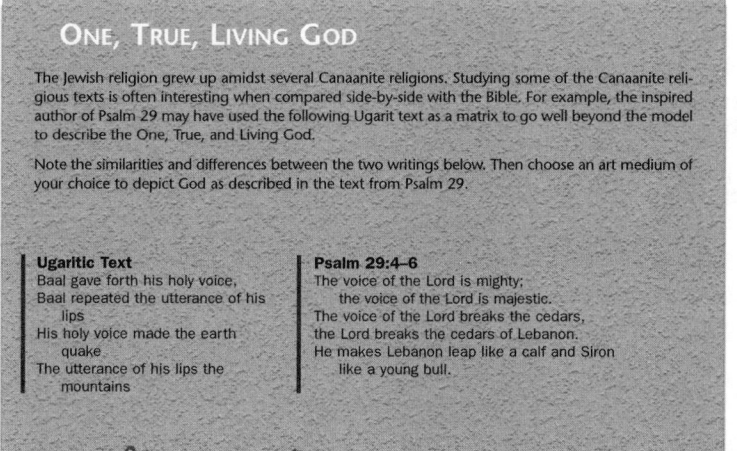

ONE, TRUE, LIVING GOD

The Jewish religion grew up amidst several Canaanite religions. Studying some of the Canaanite religious texts is often interesting when compared side-by-side with the Bible. For example, the inspired author of Psalm 29 may have used the following Ugarit text as a matrix to go well beyond the model to describe the One, True, and Living God.

Note the similarities and differences between the two writings below. Then choose an art medium of your choice to depict God as described in the text from Psalm 29.

Ugaritic Text
Baal gave forth his holy voice,
Baal repeated the utterance of his lips
His holy voice made the earth quake
The utterance of his lips the mountains

Psalm 29:4–6
The voice of the Lord is mighty;
   the voice of the Lord is majestic.
The voice of the Lord breaks the cedars,
   the Lord breaks the cedars of Lebanon.
He makes Lebanon leap like a calf and Sirion
   like a young bull.

ONE, TRUE, LIVING GOD
In your journal, write your own prayer of praise to the One, True, Living God.

4. Have the students read 1 Kings 17–19 and note the following from the passage:
   - How Yahweh is portrayed as different from Baal.
   - Why Canaanites and Israelites worship Yahweh rather than Baal?
   - Point out that Yahweh, the one, true, living God, is portrayed as much more compassionate and merciful than Baal. What emerged in Israelite belief was an understanding that Yahweh is a God of love, forgiveness, compassion, and understanding. The Journal Assignment (page 46) extends this theme.

5. **Homework Assignment:**
   - Write answers to the Review and Reflection questions 1–3, page 46.
   - Finish working on the Learn by Doing essay. page 57. (Due at the next class session.)
   - Read "Tracing the History of the Israelites from the Old Testament" through the subsection, "Israelite Monarchy" (pages 46–49).

CHAPTER 2

TRACING THE HISTORY OF THE ISRAELITES FROM THE OLD TESTAMENT

Bell-Ringer

1. Call on volunteers to summarize their Learn by Doing essay, page 57. Point out that while the Israelites did not invent great machines or new technology, they contributed greatly to the advancement of religious beliefs. The Israelites came to believe in the one, true God, a God of love and compassion.

THE OLD TESTAMENT

REVIEW & REFLECTION

1. Describe the geography of Canaan (now Palestine) including the four North-South strips (or zones) that divide the region.
2. What two important civilizations bordered Canaan to the north and to the south?
3. What were the names of the major gods of the Canaanites? Which was most likely to have appealed to the Israelites? Why?

JOURNAL ASSIGNMENT

- Look through the book of Psalms and list descriptions of a compassionate God.

Tracing the History of the Israelites From the Old Testament

Learning about the geography and history of Canaan or Palestine provides us with a large sense of the context of the experience of the Israelites. The nation of Israel arose in a time of great empires among people with their own ancient traditions and civilization, especially the Canaanites. The history of the Israelites parallels much of the Canaanite experience. The Old Testament provides us with another kind of map for our journey, an historical summary of the origins and development of God's Chosen People, the Israelites, and a chance to analyze the literary styles of the Old Testament to learn more about them.

The book of Genesis traces the origins of the Israelite patriarchs—beginning with Abraham—but not until chapter 12 of the book. The first twelve chapters contain stories about the origins of the world, humans, and varying cultures, often described as the *primeval history*.

The primeval history is followed by descriptions of the first Israelites, including Abraham, Sarah, Isaac, Rebekah, and Jacob and his sons (including Joseph). It is difficult to trace a reliable history of the Israelites using Genesis, as the book was written many years after the events described. It seems best to treat Genesis as a religiously motivated story of the origin of the Hebrew people and their arrangement in "clans" that are named for figures discussed in Genesis (e.g. the "twelve tribes" named for the twelve sons of Jacob).

The Genesis stories about the origins of mankind and the Israelite people provided a unifying history for those Canaanites of 1200–1000 B.C. who converted to the worship of Yahweh. The patriarchal accounts also carry the theme of God's persistent attention to his people,

primeval history– Stories or myths about the origins of the earth, humans, other creatures, languages, and cultures.

46

Review and Reflection Answers

1. The geography of Canaan runs in zones or strips from North to South. These strips are:
- coastal plains that narrow toward the north of Palestine (new modern Kaifa);
- hill country that runs like a spine up the "back" of Palestine;
- the Jordan Valley, a "rift" in the earth that extends all the way from Turkey to Africa; and
- the Transjordanian Plateau, which contained a major North-South trade route in the ancient world.

2. Egypt bordered Canaan to the south and Mesopotamia bordered Canaan to the north. These two civilizations often fought over control of Canaan.

3. The major gods of the Canaanites included a main god, El, and his consort Asherah, as well as Baal, the rain or fertility god; Mot, the god of death, and Yam, the god of the sea. The god that appealed most to the Israelites was Baal because they were dependent on rain to make their crops grow.

despite the constant failures of the humans represented in these incidents. Genesis will be analyzed in greater depth in Chapter 3.

It is the book of Exodus that formally introduces the Chosen People. However, the precise date and circumstances of the Exodus from Egypt are difficult to determine from the Old Testament. For example, Exodus 10:28–29 ends by suggesting an "escape" from Egypt, while Exodus 11–12 supports the idea of an "expulsion" of the Jews after a tenth and final "plague" of the death of all Egyptian first-born children.

The book of Exodus blends the two differing circumstances by portraying Pharaoh as changing his mind and chasing away the Israelites, giving rise to the traditions of the delivery of the Israelites by the sea. But here again, there are two traditions—one that portrays the Israelites as escaping across slightly muddy marshland that rendered the Egyptian chariots useless (a more natural explanation), and the later editing that turned the episode into a miraculous parting of a large body of water likely intended to magnify the theological importance of Yahweh's assistance of the Israelites in times of trouble. (These somewhat differing views show that there were slightly different traditions that were brought together to form the current book of Exodus.)

It is likely that a group of former slaves from Egypt arrived in Canaan about 1250–1230 B.C. with a religion based in the experience of a God who liberated them from Egyptian slavery. This religion, in its early form, is closely associated with Moses. Early Israelite faith was based on:
- a relationship with a God by the name of "Yahweh."
- worship in a movable shrine or tent;
- basic moral expectations ("laws");

The main feature of this religion was the fact that Yahweh was a God who liberated slaves, and was thus a God who spoke to their condition. This religion had an explosive impact upon its arrival in Canaan, and a good number of people who became part of the "Twelve Tribes of Israel" were probably Canaanites who converted to the new religion though they had never been in Egypt with the group that arrived as former slaves.

The conversion to the religion of Yahweh, however, was uneven, with a persistent problem of mixing Canaanite and Yahwist religious ideas throughout the era of the Kings of Israel and Judah, from about 1000 B.C. to the Deuteronomic Reforms of 640–609 B.C. There have been a number of recent archaeological discoveries that reveal the extent of the *syncretism* in this era. For example, prayers inscribed on pieces of clay were found in a small shrine near the Sinai desert that addressed "Yahweh" and "his consort/wife Asherah." Such a prayer gives evidence that people were mixing Israelite and Canaanite religious ideas.

The Bible's condemnation of many of the Israelite and Judean kings who abandoned pure

syncretism — a blending of two or more religious traditions.

47

MAPS FOR THE JOURNEY

Teaching Approaches

1. **Re-teach**: Print the following questions on the board. Have the students write answers, exchange with partners, and grade. Collect and record.
- **What is syncretism?** (the blending of two or more religious traditions.)
- **Why do you think the Israelites and their kings were often tempted to worship the Canaanite gods?** (Answer should compare and contrast characteristics of Canaanite gods (e.g., warlike, bloodthirsty, vengeful, angry) with those of Yahweh (e.g., compassionate, merciful, loving, kind, concerned). Explain that our belief in the one, true, and living God requires us to be like the God we worship. Most people find it easier to be warlike, bloodthirsty, vengeful, and angry than to be kind, loving, and compassionate. The new beliefs about Yahweh challenged the Israelites to be better moral people.)
- **Who were the main kings of Israel?** (Saul, David, and Solomon)

Chapter 2

2. Assign the exercise "Just Treatment of Workers" page 49. Provide the link for the complete text of *Rerum Novarum*: http://www.vatican.va/holy_father/leo_xiii/encyclicals/documents/hf_lxiii_enc_15051891_rerum-novarum_en.html. Encourage the students to provide examples from contemporary work situations that speak to both just and unjust treatment of workers.

Yahweh worship reveals that the kings often found the conservatism of Canaanite religion more to their liking than the reformist zeal of Yahweh worship with its laws of compassionate and equal treatment for all, including care of the poor and the sharing of resources. These kings were severely criticized by the advocates of the worship of Yahweh, the prophets. At least two assumptions can be made at this point:

1. Worship and living by the laws of Yahweh began as a religion among former Egyptian slaves and converted Canaanites.
2. This religious movement eventually gained ascendancy late in the monarchy (especially in Josiah's reign). By this time, however, the economic and political fate of the independent nations of Judah and Israel was sealed as subordinate to other nations (e.g., first the Assyrians, next the Babylonians). This religion would lead to the Judaism practiced at the time of Jesus that relied heavily on the belief that God would provide, that God would save the people from their enemies, and that faith meant obedience to God wherever they lived throughout the region.

Israelite Monarchy

Israelite kings ruled beginning about 1020 B.C. Although tradition holds that Saul was the first king, David was the most significant early leader who managed to unite a diversified people against the immediate threat of the coastal invaders known as Philistines. David also established a capital city, Jerusalem, and extended Israelite political influence across the Jordan into the territories of Ammon, Moab, Edom (in what is largely today the country of Jordan) and northward into Syria.

The son who eventually succeeded David, Solomon, engaged in further campaigns of consolidation, including the construction of a national Temple modeled on Canaanite temple architecture. But despite Solomon's reputation for diplomacy and "wisdom," the human toll of his building campaigns was considered oppressive by the Hebrew tribal leaders and peoples, especially in the northern territory.

Canaan was not a homogeneous environment, and agricultural differences led to social differences that were exacerbated by both labor and taxes—the requirements for Solomon's construction. When Solomon died, the northern peoples broke from the Jerusalem dynasty (a revolt that involved people and territory from ten of the twelve tribes), and established a new Israelite state in 922 B.C. The Old Testament refers to the northern state as *Israel* and the southern state as *Judah*. People in Judah later came to be called "Judeans" or "Jews" for short.

Judah continued with leaders who were descendants of King David. Israel was ruled by a succession of monarchs, none of whom was ultimately able to establish a family that could rival the dynasty of King David. It therefore appears that the northern state was more unstable. One certain reason for this was because the prophets in the north (Elisha, for example) would occasionally lead coups by proclaiming that God had chosen a new king—while the old king still sat on the throne! The prophets were constantly involved in politics.

Assyrian and Babylonian Exiles

In the latter half of the eighth century B.C., the northern kingdom, Israel, joined a coalition of states in an attempt to resist the increasing pressure of the Assyrian Empire. When Ahaz, the southern king of Judah, refused to join the coalition, the coalition members were determined to force Ahaz's hand and initiated a war. In response, Ahaz called on the massive Assyrian Empire with its brutal legions of soldiers for assistance. Assyria responded with a crushing invasion in the west. The coalition, including the northern state of Israel, was destroyed by the invading Assyrians in 722 B.C.

The Assyrian Empire practiced a military technique that guaranteed conquered territories would never again be able to offer resistance. This technique involved deporting large numbers of the newly conquered population (especially leaders and landowners) and exchanging this body of people with a group taken from another part of the empire. This exile involved some of the people of the northern kingdom, especially the elite upper classes who might have tried to resist Assyrian authority.

The Assyrian Empire was eventually defeated by the rise of a rival Mesopotamian power based in the southern part of the Tigris-Euphrates basin, the "Babylonians" (so-called because they based themselves in the ancient religious capital of Babylon, near modern-day Baghdad, Iraq).

Between 640–609 B.C., that is, between the decline of the Assyrian Empire and the Babylonian ascendancy, Josiah reigned as the king of Judah. Josiah is credited with initiating a major reform among the Hebrews in Judah, centralizing all worship in Jerusalem (thus ending worship in local shrines, which may have contributed to syncretism with Canaanite religious practices) and restoring a purer form of Yahweh worship, probably in league with some of the prophets. His reforms were based on the laws contained in the book of Deuteronomy, and therefore are referred to as the "Deuteronomic Reform." This reform also inspired further literary production. After the tragic death of Josiah in a campaign against the Egyptians (609 B.C.), the *Deuteronomic History* was written, beginning with accounts in the book of Joshua and carrying on to the Babylonian conquest described at the end of 2 Kings.

The Babylonians eventually defeated the Assyrian armies in 609 B.C. Next, the Babylonian king Nebuchadnezzar led the Babylonians further south on the Canaanite coastlands, consolidating his control of the area as a buffer zone against the Egyptians. In 597 B.C., the young king of Judah, Jehoiachin, surrendered to Nebuchadnezzar. Judah became a vassal state of the Babylonians.

Nebuchadnezzar placed a puppet ruler of his own choosing in Jerusalem. Nebuchadnezzar renamed this man "Zedekiah"

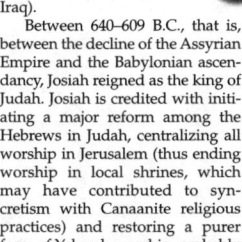

JUST TREATMENT OF WORKERS

Read and compare 1 Kings 9:22 with 1 Kings 5:27, 1 Kings 11:28, and 1 Kings 12. What clues can you find that Solomon's treatment of workers was oppressive? Next, read the following passage from *Rerum Novarum* (On the Condition of Workers) by Pope Leo XIII (1891):

> Workers are not to be treated as slaves, justice demands that the dignity of human personality be respected in them . . . gainful occupations are not a mark of shame to man, but rather of respect, as they provide him with an honorable means of supporting life. It is shameful and inhuman, however, to use men as things for gain and to put no more value on them than what they are worth in muscle and energy (#31).

Contrast this view of workers with Solomon's view.

Also, write a journal entry describing what you believe to be the dignity and value of work.

3. **On the Spot**: Choose a volunteer to come before the class and tell what it means to have religious ancestors. Next, ask the person to explain how the Israelites are our religious ancestors. Then, ask other students to be "on the spot" and respond to the same issues.

Chapter 2

4. **Homework Assignment:**
   - Answer the Review and Reflection questions 1–3, page 51. (The Babylonian and Assyrian Exiles will be covered later in the text. For now, remind the students to answer Question 3 based only on information gleaned so far in the course.)
   - Write a prayer of praise as requested in the Journal Assignment, page 51. Read several psalms from the book of Psalms to get the idea of a format or style you may use.
   - Go to www.bibleplaces.com. Write a review of five places from the Holy Land that you visited online.
   - Read "Background on Literature Styles of the Bible" (pages 51–56).

(name-changing often symbolized political control), placed him on the throne, and then returned to Babylon with a number of Jewish exiles, including King Jehoiachin. These actions were the beginning of the *Babylonian Exile*, which apparently involved not only the upper classes of Jewish society, but anyone who might pose an immediate threat to the rule of Babylon—royalty, landowners, military leaders, and even many priests.

In Zedekiah's ten years as token ruler of Judah, he became more ambitious about ruling Judah as an independent state. Zedekiah was encouraged in this bold folly by promises of the neighboring Egyptians for assistance. The prophet Jeremiah bitterly condemned the idea that Egypt would provide any credible assistance in a bid for Jewish independence. When Zedekiah ceased paying taxes to the Babylonians, this was tantamount to a declaration of independence, and it wasn't long before Nebuchadnezzar arrived back in the west with his armies to reassert control.

Jerusalem was destroyed in 587–586 B.C. after a long siege. Zedekiah's sons were killed. Zedekiah himself was tortured and taken to Babylon. The Temple was destroyed, and Temple furnishings were removed. Large numbers of the population were killed, fled as refugees, or were taken captive. This exile was more wide-spread than ten years before, involving a significant percentage of the population. Estimates vary from 20,000 to over 70,000 inhabitants of Judah, but the smaller numbers are more likely. Still, 20,000 is a large number of people to forcibly resettle in a foreign land.

The Babylonian Exile represents one of the most decisive changes of destiny for the Jewish people. Perhaps most remarkable of all was that the Judeans not only survived in exile, they reconstructed their faith. When the Persians finally conquered Babylon in 539, the Persian emperor Cyrus allowed many Judeans to return to Palestine. Although a sizable Jewish community remained in Babylon, various groups of Judeans returning to Palestine (described in the book of Ezra) continued to reconstruct the faith, their community, and Temple worship.

Post-Exilic Judean Society

We know very little about post-Exilic Judean society. There are only a few books that are confidently dated to this era, such as the prophetic books Haggai, Zechariah, and Malachi, and the historical books, Ezra and Nehemiah. Notice, also, how short these books are. This lack of information continues to the Hellenistic (Greek) Period, post-333 B.C., when we once again begin to have historical literary sources such as the first book of Maccabees, though even it is clearly a partisan perspective on history.

What we can surmise about the post-Exilic period is that the Judeans formed a strong communal and faith identity under the leadership of priests, who emerged as the primary leaders in place of the kings who were descendants of King David. Hopes for a new king from the family of David became the hope for a future age, occasionally inspiring nationalist activity among some Jews in Palestine.

At this time many Jews were still living in a *Diaspora*, that is, in lands other than Palestine that extended from Egypt far into the east beyond Babylon and into Persian territory. For Jews in the Diaspora, their faith was no longer associated with national existence, but with spiritual identity, family practices and diet, and with their ability to resist cultural assimilation. Biblical stories of faithful Jews in foreign lands, such as Daniel, Esther, and Tobit derive from experiences of the Jews in the Diaspora.

From the time of the Babylonian Exile until the twentieth century and the founding of the nation of Israel, with the exception of only a relatively brief time before the Roman occupation in 64 B.C., the Jewish people were to remain politically and economically subordinate to non-Jews. This means that both Judaism and Christianity are religions whose roots are to be found in people who either lived in the Diaspora or in their own land under the military and political control of outsiders. How does this impact the Bible?

In the Bible, Yahweh is the God of the powerless and separated. He is the God who judges the rich and powerful. For the Diaspora or any occupied people, you can understand why these ideas would have considerable meaning. If you keep in mind that virtually all of the Old Testament was written, edited, and arranged by a politically powerless people, then its text takes on a different tone. The focus certainly is not on a vengeful, warring God as many Christians often feel.

Diaspora — A group migration or flight away from the homeland into one or more other countries. The word can also refer to people who have maintained their separate identity (often religious, but occasionally ethnic, racial, or cultural) while living in those other countries after the migration.

REVIEW & REFLECTION

1. Name three basic features of the faith of the early Israelites.
2. Give an example of the blending of Canaanite and Yahwist religions.
3. From what information you have now, which seemed to have the greatest impact on Jewish faith: the Assyrian Exile or the Babylonian Exile? Why?

JOURNAL ASSIGNMENT

- Write your own prayer of praise to the one, true, living God.

Background on Literature Styles of the Bible

If it is true that writing history is never merely a description of events, the recording of Jewish history is surely an excellent example of history written with a clear motive and goal in mind. The main task of the historical writers of ancient Israel was to illustrate their understanding of God and how he was involved in their lives. In short, the Old Testament is written primarily as religious literature. It is never simply a historical or royal record.

A survey of the various types of literature of the Old Testament offer a good companion to the historical study of Old Testament times, and reveals further clues about the God of mercy, compassion, and love.

BACKGROUND ON LITERATURE STYLES IN THE BIBLE

Bell-Ringers

1. Call on volunteers to share their reviews of Holy Land sites (see Homework Assignment, page 54 of the TWE). Then play all or part of a video depicting the Holy Land (e.g., *Religions of the Book: Holy Places and Pilgrimage*).

2. Distribute complete sets of the daily newspapers. Have the students work in small groups to discover different types of writing in a newspaper. Then list the students' findings on the board. (Among the types of writing will be: news stories, sports articles, editorials, letters, human interest stories, historical events, speeches, lists of upcoming events, poems, recipes, prayers, jokes, etc.) Point out that the Bible is similar to a newspaper in that it contains many different styles of writing.

Review and Reflection Answers

1. The faith of the early Israelites had these three qualities:
   - a relationship with a God named "Yahweh,"
   - worship in a movable shrine or tent, and
   - basic moral expectations or laws.

2. An example of *syncretism* (a blending of the Canaanite and the Israelite religions) is the prayer inscribed on clay at a small shrine near the Sinai desert that addressed "Yahweh and his consort Asherah."

3. The Assyrians destroyed the northern state of Israel in 722 B.C. The Babylonians conquered the southern state of Judah in 587 B.C. Of the two invasions and subsequent exiles, the Babylonian Exile was the worst. It was much more widespread, involving a significant percentage of the population. Furthermore, the Temple was destroyed and the people were separated from Jerusalem, the seat of God's house.

Chapter 2

Teaching Approaches

1. **Re-teach**: Ask the students to write their answers to the following questions based on the reading assignment. Grading is optional.
   - **What do we mean when we say that God is the author of the Bible?** (God inspired the authors to write the message he wanted to convey.)
   - **What are the major types of literature found in the Old Testament?** (The Pentateuch, Historical Books, Wisdom Literature, Prophetic Literature and Apocalyptic Literature)

2. Distribute copies of "Types of Literature in the Old Testament" (Handout 2C, page 266 of the TWE). Review the list with the students. Call on volunteers to look up and read some of the examples. Provide definitions of the following terms as needed:
   - saga—story that takes place in a specific time or place; usually used in the Bible to teach or explain something.
   - legend—exaggerated story about a sanctuary, a cultic object, a religious person, a prophet, or a martyr.
   - parable—story that has a parallel religious or moral meaning
   - anecdote—short story of an interesting, amusing, or curious incident.

3. Distribute Handout 2D, "Categorizing the Old Testament Books," (page 267 of the TWE) to help summarize the homework reading assignment. Explain that different types of literature may be found in each book, but that the overall book may be categorized in this general way. Have the students keep the handout in front of them for the next re-teaching activity.

THE OLD TESTAMENT

GOD AS THE AUTHOR OF THE BIBLE

It is accurate to say that God is the author of the Bible, but that is not as simple as it sounds. First, what the statement does not mean: God did not magically pen the scriptures and then rain the texts down on earth. Nor did God whisper into the ears of the Biblical authors word for word, punctuation and all.

Rather, God *inspired* the authors of Scripture. The authors had the freedom to choose the words they wrote, including the stories and incidents they chose to share. As the Second Vatican Council explained, God chose the authors of the Bible:

> who all the while he employed them in this task, made full use of their own faculties and powers so that, though he acted in them and by them, it was as true authors that they consigned to writing whatever he wanted written, and no more" (*Dei Verbum*).

Related to this understanding of inspiration is another fact: the Jews of Biblical times, up to and including Jesus, were great storytellers. In reading the Old Testament, we must understand the difference between a story intended to teach a lesson and the description of a historical event, all the while remembering that the text is inspired. God intended for us to read it—both history *and* stories.

For example, the proper response to the fall of mankind and the flood narrative of the book of Genesis is to appreciate the religious lessons of moral responsibility, God's care for mankind, and mankind's stubborn resistance. Joining an expedition to find pieces of the "authentic" ark of Noah on Mount Ararat in modern Turkey (to cite one popular example of people who supposedly take the Bible "seriously" by insisting on a literal flood) is not the most appropriate response to the Biblical texts because it misses their central message and attempts to make some of these texts into something that they often are not—literal history. Sometimes we must use our best judgment to determine the differences between history and story, while some passages are more obvious.

Much of this religion textbook is devoted to looking at the religious meaning of the Old Testament, while providing some brief background on the context of a particular book.

The Pentateuch

The core of the Old Testament is the Pentateuch, which means "five books." In the Hebrew Bible, these books are called the "Torah," a Hebrew word for "Law." Law is the most prominent feature of the Pentateuch. Virtually all of the religious laws, civil laws, and moral principles of ancient Israel are codified in three collections of laws contained in the first five books.

The earliest of these collections, known as the "Covenant Code," is contained in the book of Exodus (the laws are roughly chapters 19–24). The Covenant Code was supplemented by the "Deuteronomic Code" of the seventh century B.C. and included in the book of Deuteronomy. (Deuteronomy means "second law.") The third collection of laws consists mainly of priestly or religious laws that were added by the Jewish priests in the post-Exilic period. These laws can be found mainly in Leviticus. One of the oldest layers of this priestly law is in Leviticus 17–26 (sometimes called the "Holiness Code"). Later commentary and additional laws are found in other parts of Leviticus and Numbers.

The frequent repetition of laws (e.g., the fact that the Ten Commandments are listed twice) is explained by this practice of adding later legal material to the laws from different eras. Interestingly, the supplementation of texts allows modern students to do comparative work on the development of several facets of Jewish life.

Take the development of the treatment of "slaves" or technically what we call "indentured servants." Much can be learned from looking at the different versions of the laws. Note, for example, the progression of the status of slaves between Exodus 21 (the Covenant Code) and Deuteronomy 15:12–18 (the Deuteronomic Code). While both passages prohibit perpetual slavery, only the latter code specifically delineates the provisions to be provided to released slaves whose debts were paid after seven years, and furthermore prohibits the return of escaped slaves to masters (Dt 23:16). Most impressive of all, perhaps, is the expectation of social justice provided by the priests in Leviticus 25, where the "Jubilee Year" was to provide for the return of all purchased land to the original tribal owners, thus preventing a growing rift between the rich and poor by redistributing the land every fifty years. Law, in ancient Israel, was clearly both normative and prescriptive, and tended toward what we would call "distributive justice." There was to be a fair distribution of basic necessities!

Historical Books

Following the Pentateuch, the historical books tell about the history of Israel first as a collection of tribes (the books of Joshua and Judges) and then eventually moving toward existence as a royal state led by a king (1, 2 Samuel, and 1, 2 Kings, much of which is repeated in 1, 2 Chronicles. The number 1 or 2 before the name of the book is to be read "first book of . . ." or "second book of . . . ").

Later historical books tell of the breakup of the kingdom—the disobedience of the kings, the disasters preceding the exiles, and the exiles themselves. The first and second books of Maccabees were written in approximately 100 B.C. and provide two different views of the Jewish revolt against the Seleucid ruler Antiochus IV and the Hellenistic Greek culture that was imposed during his reign.

Wisdom Books and Psalms

The "Wisdom Books" is a category of the Old Testament that includes the books of Job, Psalms, Proverbs, Ecclesiastes, Song of Songs, Wisdom, and Sirach (Ecclesiasticus). The wisdom books consist of poetic religious hymns, stories, and wise advice.

The books of wisdom literature are intended to guide people in learning the lessons of human life. Wisdom literature is not unique to the Bible. In fact, part of the book of Proverbs is drawn directly from Egyptian wisdom literature (e.g., Prv 22:17–24:22). This is surely because the main themes of wisdom literature—relationships, diplomacy, watching one's tongue, money and frugality, the dangers of adultery or of strong drink, and the gaining of knowledge—are basic human issues. Wisdom literature includes many observations of the human condition and is an indication of God's respect for human thought in the reality of faith.

The largest body of religious poetry in the Bible is the book of Psalms. Ever popular as devotional literature, the psalms were written over a large span of Jewish history. As for the content of the book of Psalms, there are many different subjects. Some psalms have their origin in the enthronement ceremonies of a king or the celebration of the new year (e.g., Ps 2, 72, 89, and 110). Others, clearly referring to the events of the Exile, reveal a very late origin (e.g., Ps 126, 137). The religious messages of the psalms make it a very popular work.

4. **Re-teach:** Have the students form teams for a quiz game on the reading for this lesson. Give five points for each correct answer, three points if the person needs help from a teammate, and two points if the entire team helps with the answer.

Questions
- What does the word *Pentateuch* mean? (five books)
- What books make up the Pentateuch? (Genesis, Exodus, Leviticus, Numbers, and Deuteronomy)
- What is the most prominent feature of the Pentateuch? (Law)
- How many collections the Law are found in the Pentateuch? (three)
- What do we call the earliest collection of laws in the Bible? (Covenant Code)
- Where do we find the second collection of laws in the Bible? (Deuteronomy)
- Where do we find the third collection of laws in the Bible? (Leviticus)
- How many times are the Ten Commandments listed? (two)
- According to the Deuteronomic Code, when were slaves supposed to be released? (after seven years)
- When was all purchased land supposed to be returned to the original tribal owners? (The Jubilee Year, once every 49 or 50 years)
- The books of Joshua and Judges are primarily what literary style? (historical)
- The books of Job and Proverbs are primarily what literary style? (wisdom)
- What is the largest body of religious poetry in the Bible? (the book of Psalms)
- What literary style in the Old Testament has the most number of books? (Prophetic)
- True or false: In the Bible, prophets predict the future. (false)
- What do we call traveling bands of prophets who spoke out of a trance? (charismatics)
- What is the shortest book in the Bible? (Obadiah)
- Who was the earliest writing prophet? (Amos)
- Which prophet used intimate and romanticized images to describe God? (Hosea)
- What image does Isaiah use to describe the Israelite exiles? (the Suffering Servant)
- Which prophet was active among the Babylonian exiles? (Ezekiel)
- Which two prophets wrote to the post-exilic community? (Haggai and Zechariah)
- What do we call Biblical writing that contains strange, bizarre, and highly symbolic visions? (apocalyptic literature)

Chapter 2

5. **Homework Assignment:**
   - Answer Review and Reflection questions 1–3, page 56. For question 1, cite the book of the Bible where the particular style of writing occurs.
   - Complete the Journal Assignment on page 56. Remember, a prophet's task is to comment on the situation, not to write a prediction for future events.
   - Read the section "Further Reflections" (page 57).

Prophetic Books

While several of the historical books mention prophets, the largest collection of books of the Old Testament is arranged under a separate category—Prophetic Books—that lists books by the so-called "writing prophets."

It is unfortunate that popular ideas about the prophets tend to focus on the notion that prophets "predict the future." In fact, the main activities of the prophets were:

1. to be *messengers* of God, delivering messages very much like a royal emissary or message runner;
2. to be *God's prosecutor*, that is, delivering judgment on sinful acts that were considered to have violated God's laws given through the tradition of Moses;
3. to act as tireless *advocates* for the less fortunate of Israelite society—summarized by Jeremiah as "the widow, the orphan, and the foreigner" but called by Amos and Isaiah simply, "the poor."

Any suggestions by the prophets about future events were always in the prior context of these other main activities. The prophets' words were intended mainly for their own time and represented God's continual involvement in history. To suggest that the words of the prophets were for a distant future not only removes the prophets from history (thus misrepresenting the main point of God's involvement in the history of the people), but also invites irresponsible attempts to "interpret" the prophets words "for the modern times" as if they are hidden predictions.

The prophets' words were feared, not because they were cryptic messages for future times, but because they were understood only too well and spoke of real events in the lives of the kings and people who first heard them, and who often did *not* like what they heard.

The prophets of ancient Israel were mysterious and charismatic men and women (yes, there were female prophets, too) who were feared as well as respected. From occasional references in 1 and 2 Samuel, it appears that prophecy had its origins in traveling bands of *charismatics* who would speak out of a self-imposed, trance-like state (see 1 Sm 10:9ff). In time, however, great prophets became individually noted, and traditions and/or legends sprung up around them. Bands of disciples often were associated with these more noteworthy figures. The best examples of this later development are the accounts of Elijah and Elisha in the historical books (1 Kgs 17–21; 2 Kgs 2–13). Eventually later prophets were remembered as teachers and their sayings were written down.

Each of the prophets is a unique figure with an interesting difference in outlook and perspective, although in the case of some of the shorter books it is hard to determine a perspective on the basis of so little material. The book of Obadiah, for example, is only 21 verses long; Nahum and Malachi are each only three chapters.

The earliest writing prophet was Amos, himself a somewhat mysterious man, whose prophecies consisted of unrelenting judgment against many nations—not simply Israel and Judah. In fact, some scholars believe that the final few verses of the book of Amos, which offer some hope, may not have been his words because they sound so uncharacteristically hopeful.

In contrast to Amos, the prophet Hosea used intimate and romanticized images to describe God as a lover and a parent of the people of Israel and to describe his sadness at Israel's disobedience (which Hosea compared to adultery or to rejecting a parent). Hosea even carried his message to the point of giving his children names that were symbolic of God's anger at the people (for example, *Lo-Ammi* means "you are not my people").

About the same time that Hosea and Amos were active in the northern kingdom of Israel, the traditions surrounding the prophet Isaiah began in the south. The book of Isaiah is a good example of the continued tradition that major prophetic figures can inaugurate. The prophet himself was active from about 740 B.C., and his words are largely recalled in chapters 1 to 39 of the present book of Isaiah. Chapters 40–55, however, are attributed to an unidentified prophet active toward the end of the Babylonian Exile because of the references to Cyrus the Persian (see Is 45:1). This part of the text is sometimes called "Deutero-Isaiah" or "Second Isaiah."

One of the most important images of Deutero-Isaiah is the "Suffering Servant." The Suffering Servant passages were deeply influential among early Christians in their struggle for ways to interpret the events and meaning of the life, death, and resurrection of Jesus (see especially Is 42:1–4; 49:1–6; 50:4–9 and 52:13–53:12). Christ himself explained the meaning of his life and death in relation to God's Suffering Servant: "The Son of Man did not come to be served but to serve and give his life as ransom for many" (Mt 20:28) The final chapters, 56–66, are often called "Trito-Isaiah" and consist of collections of sayings, perhaps by disciples of the prophet Deutero-Isaiah.

Less openly hopeful, the prophet Jeremiah was a prophet who felt the tragic duty to proclaim to Israel that the Babylonian exile was ordained by God. Jeremiah shared the general Deuteronomic perspective that the exilic events were punishment for the rejection of the laws of God during the period of the monarchy. The book of Jeremiah is composed in two main sections—the poetic sayings of Jeremiah himself, and prose sections of biographical information about Jeremiah. Both are attributed to Baruch, a scribe who was a companion to Jeremiah.

Ezekiel was a prophet active among the Babylonian exiles. He was given to

occasionally bizarre acts to illustrate his prophetic messages. His main concern was to function as the mediator of the exiles' spiritual well-being. In his great vision (Ez 40–48), the prophet had hopes for a fresh start for the Jews back in Palestine, where land would be divided equally, and the "princes" (he never used the word "King") would have only a fair allotment and never oppress their people again.

Prophetic books continued to be produced in the post-Exilic community as well. The prophet Haggai, for example, was concerned mainly with the restoration of religious life in the post-Exilic community, particularly the importance of rebuilding the Temple. Similarly, Zechariah dealt with issues of faith and practice in the post-Exilic community. The prophets, as will be covered in succeeding chapters of this text, have many surprises in store not only for their first audience but for you, the modern reader, as well.

MAPS FOR THE JOURNEY

REVIEW PERIOD

Bell-Ringer

1. Assign the following Suffering Servant passages: Isaiah 42:1–4; 49:1–6; 50:4–9; 52:12–53:12. Have the students list ways that the Suffering Servant passages are fulfilled in Jesus. List responses on the board as a follow up.

Teaching Approaches

1. Use the Chapter 2 Review and Reflection questions to help the students prepare for the Chapter 2 Test. Have the students work in pairs to review the chapter material by quizzing each other back and forth using the the Review and Reflection questions as well as other questions they glean from the text.

2. Also, use Chapter 2 Review Puzzle (Handout 2E, page 268 of the TWE) to help the students prepare for the test. Allow time for them to work on the puzzle in class and to complete it for homework.

Review Puzzle Answer Key

DOWN	ACROSS
1 Isaiah	2 Rosetta
3 scribes	4 pictograms
4 prophet	6 visions
5 Mesopotamia	7 Diaspora
10 artifacts	8 Israel
13 David	9 Pentateuch
14 Solomon	11 Merneptah
15 syncretism	12 Judah
16 Yahweh	17 hieroglyphic
18 Saul	19 Abraham
22 Canaan	20 Amos
24 Asherah	21 law
28 Egypt	23 primeval
29 psalm	25 Exodus
30 hills	26 Babylon
31 Cyrus	27 Mesha
33 myth	30 Hyksos
	32 wisdom
	34 Torah
	35 context
	36 Baal
	37 Hosea

Chapter 2

3. **Prayer Service:** Recite with the students the words of the traditional Jewish song (Called to Prayer, page 57):
   Wherever I go, only you!
   Wherever I stand, only you!
   Only you, again you
   Always you!

- Ask the students to spend a few minutes in silence, thinking about how God continually calls us to his friendship. Then choose several students to share the prayers they wrote as part of the Journal Assignment on page 51. Conclude by playing or singing one of the song selections from page 38 of the TWE.

4. **Homework Assignment:**
   - Complete the Chapter 2 Review Puzzle.
   - Study for the Chapter 2 Test.

Review and Reflection Answers

1. The five major writing styles in the Old Testament are:
   - Pentateuch (Genesis, Exodus, Leviticus, Numbers, and Deuteronomy),
   - Historical Books (Joshua, Judges, Ruth, 1 Samuel, 2 Samuel, 1 Kings, 2 Kings, 1 Chronicles, 2 Chronicles, Ezra, Nehemiah, Tobit, Judith, Esther, 1 Maccabees, 2 Maccabees),
   - Wisdom literature (Job, Psalms, Proverbs, Ecclesiastes, Song of Songs, Wisdom, Sirach),
   - Prophetic Books (Isaiah, Jeremiah, Lamentations, Baruch, Ezekiel, Daniel, Hosea, Joel, Amos, Obadiah, Jonah, Micah, Nahum, Habakkuk, Zephaniah, Haggai, Zechariah, Malachi), and
   - Apocalyptic literature (the book of Daniel).
2. The main focus of the Pentateuch is the law. There were three main categories of laws: the Covenant Code, the Deuteronomic Code, and the Levitical (or Priestly) Code.
3. The three main activities of the prophets were: 1) to be messengers of God, delivering messages very much like a royal emissary or message runner; 2) to be God's prosecutor, that is, delivering judgment on sinful acts that were considered to have violated God's laws given through the tradition of Moses; and 3) to act as tireless advocates for the less fortunate of Israelite society (the poor).

What About Apocalyptic Literature?

Apocalyptic literature is a bit of a wildcard in Biblical literature. It is literature often described as strange, bizarre, and involving highly symbolic visions. The visions are usually described in graphic detail and are accompanied by the narration of an angel or heavenly figure.

Apocalyptic literature became very popular in the Hellenistic (Greek) period and continued to be influential in the Roman period among both Jews and early Christians. Although there are only two major examples of apocalyptic literature in the Bible (Daniel 7–12 and the book of Revelation in the New Testament), many examples of non-Biblical apocalyptic writings have survived from this period. It was obviously a highly popular form of writing.

Apocalyptic literature focused on contemporary events of the day. Apocalyptic visionaries described symbolic visions from God, references to the coming judgment on the oppressive rulers and events of their times. By envisioning God's intervention on behalf of the oppressed, Jewish apocalyptic literature called for an activism of resistance to Greek and Roman culture and rule. The visions of Daniel are attached to stories of Jewish figures in foreign courts who are vindicated for their faithful persistence or, in other words, their spiritual resistance. Indeed, after three months of reading the Bible in a South African jail, Mahatma Gandhi emerged proclaiming Daniel to be "one of the greatest nonviolent resistors in history."

Apocalyptic literature, then, illustrates a central concern of post-Exilic Hebrew faith—maintaining faith and identity in circumstances of powerlessness and even oppression.

REVIEW & REFLECTION

1. List the five major writing styles in the Old Testament. Cite at least one example of each kind of writing.
2. What is the main focus of the five books in the Pentateuch?
3. Describe three main activities of the prophets.

JOURNAL ASSIGNMENT

- Choose a current issue at your school, in your local community, or in the national news. Write a "prophetic" paragraph about it.

Chapter 2 Parish Religious Education Adaptation

- See pages 14–15 from the Introduction of this Teacher's Wraparound Edition for an explanation for teaching each chapter in a parish religious education setting.
- "Chapter 2 Parish Religious Education Adaptation" (online at **avemariapress.com**) is a lesson plan for Chapter 2 suitable for use in a one- to two-hour religious education period.

Note: The students should complete the assignment listed under "Student Preparation" on the lesson plan prior to coming to class.

Further Reflections

This chapter has presented a sense of the geography and historical context of Canaan, later called Palestine, a quick survey of the history of the Israelite people (later called Jews), and a quick overview of the various kinds of Biblical literature. Learning to put the Old Testament in these areas of context helps us to dig deeper into God's Word and to further apply the lessons of these texts to our faith.

For example, our faith tells us that God is the author of Sacred Scripture.

The Bible should be read—not as merely human words—but as the word of God. As St. Paul wrote to the Thessalonians:

> . . . you received not a human word but, as it truly is, the word of God, which is now at work in you who believe (1 Thes 2:13).

God inspired the human authors of the Bible. The human authors had the freedom to choose the words they wrote, and also the discretion of the stories and the incidences that they would include in their texts. Remember, *stories* can be inspired as well as history or poetry.

The Old Testament was written over a period of many years. The Hebrew scriptures are contained in the Old Testament.

The Old Testament is oriented to prepare for and declare in prophecy the coming of Jesus Christ.

In no way has the Old Testament been rendered void by the New Testament. The "Old Covenant has never been revoked" (*CCC*, 121).

Christians hold the Old Testament as the true Word of God.

Learn by Doing

Read and note at least two major discoveries and contributions by each of the following ancient civilizations: Egyptians, Babylonians, Phoenicians, Greeks, and Romans. When completed, write a short essay describing Israel's major "discovery and contribution" to world history.

Called to Prayer

Wherever I go, only you!
Wherever I stand, only you!
Only you, again you
Always you!
　　—from a traditional Jewish song

Notes

1. The Hittite Empire was in what is today the country of Turkey. It is sometimes called "Asia Minor" by classical historians
2. J. Maxwell Miller, "The Ancient Near East and Archaeology," Ch. 15, in *Old Testament Interpretation: Past, Present, and Future*, p. 245–260.
3. Prehistoric technically means "before writing."
4. p. 13–15, in M. Coogan, "In the Beginning," Prologue to *The Oxford History of the Biblical World*, ed. M. Coogan, Oxford University Press: New York, Oxford, 1998: 3–32.
5. p. 22–23, Coogan.
6. p. 27, Coogan.

MAPS FOR THE JOURNEY

CHAPTER 2 TEST

Teaching Approaches

1. Administer the Chapter 2 Test (online at **avemariapress.com**). Allow the students to use separate paper to write their responses to the short answer question.

2. If you were not able to include the prayer service at the last class, do so after the students have finished the test.

3. *Optional:* If there is time after the test, allow the students to peruse Chapter 3. Or, review some of the lessons from the Catholic Handbook of Faith (pages 259–280 of the student text).

Chapter 2 Test Answers

Part 1: Matching: 1. H; 2. B; 3. F; 4. E; 5. A; 6. I; 7. G; 8. D; 9. C.

Part 2: Map: 10–17 on map.

Part 3: List: 18. Popular as religious devotional literature, the largest body of poetry is in the book of Psalms; 19. There were writing prophets (e.g., Amos, Isaiah, Jeremiah, and Ezekiel) distinct from prophets like Elijah and Elisha who do not have books named for them in the Old Testament; 20. Highly symbolic visions that are accompanied by the narration of an angel of heavenly figure (e.g. the books of Daniel and Revelation); 21. Law is the most prominent feature of the Pentateuch. Virtually all religious laws, civil laws, and moral principles of ancient Israel are codified in the Pentateuch. 22. The historical books tell about Israel, first as a collection of tribes, then moving toward a royal state. These books fall after the Pentateuch (e.g., Joshua, 1 and 2 Samuel, 1 and 2 Kings).

Part 4: Short Answer: 23. By taking up residence in the middle of the "land bridge" that connected two great centers of civilization, the Israelites were caught in the middle of several conflicts.
24. The prophets' main activities were to be messengers of God, God's prosecutors, and advocates for the less fortunate. These three activities are expanded on pages 54–55.

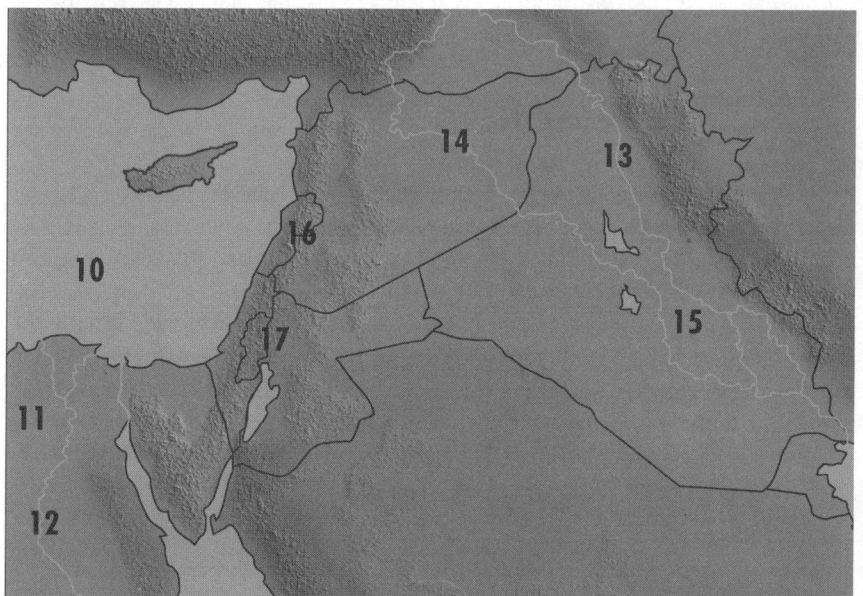

Introducing Chapter 3

We can learn a great deal about the culture and values of a nation by studying its traditional stories. We can especially learn about the ancient Israelites by studying the stories found in Genesis. What is most important is not, "Did the story really happen word for word?" but rather "What can we learn from this story?"

The primeval history events in Genesis tells us how the Israelites believed that God created the entire world. The first creation story tells how God created everything in six days and then rested on day seven. The second creation story tells how God first created Adam and then created Eve from one of Adam's ribs. The story of the fall of Adam and Eve (and consequently all mankind) is an attempt to explain the cause of sin and death in the created world. The flood story in Genesis explains how God saved the righteous Noah and his family and made a covenant with all humanity through them. The story about the Tower of Babel explains the origin of the many different languages in the world. We learn from these stories that God loves creation and cares for it. God also expects humans to care for everyone and everything in the created environment.

Further ancestor stories in Genesis tell us about the patriarchs of our faith: Abraham, Isaac, Jacob, Joseph. The occasional duplication in these stories are clues that they came from two different sources—the Yahweh (J) source and the Elohist (E) source. At some point in Israelite history these two sources were edited together in the book we now know as Genesis.

Chapter 3 Outline

Introduction
The stories told by the Hebrews reveal much of their identity and purpose.

God's Creation
The two creation stories in the book of Genesis tell about the nature of God as Creator and answer other questions about the origins of the world and mankind.

Original Justice and the Fall of Man
The first humans were given the gift of original justice which was lost due to their disobedience.

Renewal of Life
The Hebrew flood story teaches that God made an everlasting covenant with Noah and mankind.

Ancestors of Faith
The accounts of Abraham and the patriarchs set the foundation for God's full revelation in the coming of Jesus Christ.

Abraham: Father of Faith
Abraham is known as the "father of faith," not only for Judaism but also Christianity and Islam.

The Blessing of Jacob
The deception leading to Jacob's blessing by his father Isaac is the prelude to this cycle of stories.

Joseph In Egypt: Foreshadowing the Exodus
The extended story of Joseph previews the formation of the people of Israel at the time of the Exodus.

Further Reflections

Background Notes for the Teacher

The book of Genesis recounts the Israelites' understanding of how the world came to be. The stories in Genesis elaborate on mankind's relationship to God, as well as God's abiding justice and fidelity. The book of Genesis consists of four main parts: the primeval stories of creation and the beginning of human civilization (Gn 1–11), the Abraham cycle (Gn 12–25), the Jacob cycle (Gn 25–36), and the Joseph story (Gn 37–50). The entire book has three sources: J (Yahwist), P (Priestly), and E (Elohist).

- The creation stories include the sin of Adam and Eve (the *original sin* accounting for the presence of sin and death in the world), Cain's murder of Abel, the descendants of Cain and the invention of culture, the flood and Noah's deliverance, and the Tower of Babel.
- The second part of Genesis finds the call of Abram, the evolution of God's covenant with Abraham, and stories about Sarah, Lot, Hagar and Ishmael. There is also the account of the birth of Isaac and Abraham's initial plan to sacrifice his son to God.
- The third part of Genesis includes the birth of the twins Esau and Jacob, the plots of Rebecca to trick Isaac into giving Jacob the inheritance, Jacob's marriages to Leah and Rachel, Jacob's life of trickery and deception, his twelve sons, and his eventual reunion with Esau.
- The final part deals with the story of Joseph, the oldest son of Jacob by Rachel. We learn how Joseph's brothers sold him into slavery in Egypt, how Joseph managed to rise to power in the Egyptian government, and how his brothers eventually came to him for food.

The main themes of Genesis include God's promise to save humanity (the implied promise to send a savior), his blessings in the midst of struggle, the election of unlikely candidates to lead his people, and God's ability to work with family relationships that are far from perfect. The narratives found in Genesis are not literal history or exact science. Rather, they inspired narratives that express religious truth—the Israelites' basic belief and trust in God's providence and plan. As the Israelites learn repeatedly from these stories, God's ways are not our ways. God can bring good out of conflict and evil.

Resources

Music Suggestions: see page 64
Printed Materials: see page 65
Audiovisual Materials: see page 68
Internet Links: see page 73

CHAPTER 3
STORIES FOR THE JOURNEY
Creation and the Founding of a People

Advance Preparations
- Preview the Resources for materials and media that you may wish to use for the lessons of this chapter.
- Bell-Ringer 2 for the first lesson ("Introduction") asks the students to bring an item for home that symbolizes something about their life.
- The lesson suggestion on page 69 of the TWE requires art media.
- The Learn by Doing assignment (pages 84-85 of the Student Text) suggests several things for the students to do that will require extra preparation and time. Consider introducing this assignment early in the chapter.
- Rent a copy of the musical *Joseph and the Amazing Technicolor Dream Coat* from a local video store. Have this on hand for the class session on Joseph.
- Make copies of the handouts needed for these sessions (see pages 269-271 of the TWE).
- Transfer the overhead outlines to transparent acetate (see **avemariapress.com**).

Chapter Objectives
The students will be able to:
- name the stories found in the book of Genesis.
- learn more about the two creation stories and how they teach religious truth.
- appreciate that humans are made in the image of God and are called by God to have a personal relationship with him.
- understand how the original justice given to mankind was lost due to their disobedience at the time of the original sin.
- explore the significance of the Great Flood as well as the story of the tower of Babel.
- study the lives and challenges of the ancestors of Israel, beginning with Abraham.
- understand how God remains faithful to his covenant through the stories of Jacob and Joseph.

Relevant Teachings from Church Documents
- Beyond the witness to himself that God gives in created things, he manifested himself to our first parents, spoke to them and, after the fall, promised them salvation (cf. Gen 3:15) and offered them his covenant. (*CCC*, 70)
- God made an everlasting covenant with Noah and with all living beings (cf. Gen 9:16). It will remain in force as long as the world lasts. (*CCC*, 71)
- Catechesis on creation is of major importance. (*CCC*, 282)
- Among all the Scriptural texts about creation, the first three chapters of Genesis occupy a unique place. From a literary standpoint, these texts may have had diverse sources. The inspired authors have placed them at the beginning of Scripture to express in their solemn language the truths of creation—its origin and its end in God, its order and goodness, the vocation of man, and finally the drama of sin and the hope of salvation. Read in the light of Christ, within the unity of Sacred Scripture and in the living Tradition of the Church, these texts remain the principal source for catechesis on the mysteries of the "beginning": creation, fall, and promise of salvation. (*CCC*, 289)
- By his sin Adam, as the first man, lost the original holiness and justice he had received from God, not only for himself but for all human beings. (*CCC*, 416)

CHAPTER 3

INTRODUCTION

Bell-Ringers

1. **Re-teach:** Print the vocabulary words from Chapter 2 on the board. Ask the students to write definitions for each word on scrap paper. Have them exchange with a partner and correct using the following definitions:

context—the historical, cultural, social, or political circumstances surrounding an event or record.

Diaspora—a group migration or flight away from the homeland into one or more other countries. The word can also refer to people who have maintained their separate identity (often religious, but occasionally ethnic, racial, or cultural) while living in those other countries after the migration.

hieroglyphic writing—an ancient form of Egyptian writing, more stylized than pictograms but not based on an alphabet.

pictograms—the earliest form of writing in which pictures represented words or ideas.

prehistoric—refers to events or objects that date to a time before writing developed and written records exist.

primeval history—stories or myths about the origins of the earth, humans, other creatures, languages, and cultures.

scribes—people trained to write using the earliest forms of writing before literacy was widespread.

syncretism—a blending of two or more religious traditions.

2. Call on students to share an item that symbolizes an important interest, quality, or skill they possess (e.g., baseball glove, music book, photo of a favorite place). Allow each student a chance to tell why the item is important to him or her. The discussion can be done with a partner or in small groups. Call on some volunteers to share their items and stories before the whole class.

3. Introduce the importance of remembering and sharing stories about who we are as individuals, families, and society. While the students are still in their groups, distribute one copy of "The Value of Stories" (Handout 3A, page 269 of the TWE) to each group. Assign the students to discuss the material and come to agreement on one book, movie, and television show. One person should record the group's information. Another person should summarize the group's discussion for the entire class.

THE OLD TESTAMENT

Introduction

Learning about the history of a people is not only about facts and dates. If you think this isn't true, imagine what a future historian might learn about you from the facts of your permanent record:
- date of birth
- place of birth
- schools attended, grades, and dates of graduation
- traffic offenses and any other legal matters

The longer you live, the more facts about your life will become available for public record. But would this information really tell about who you are—the essence of your life? Certainly there would be much more to know about you.

How would a historian find out more about you? How would a historian find out more about your generation and its culture? As an exercise, think, for example, what a future historian might learn about you and your generation and culture from the current movies and television shows produced as well as fiction books and stories.

The point is that to learn about the history of individuals and societies, we need to listen carefully to their stories. The book of Genesis contains stories about the founding of God's People, the Israelites, beginning with the patriarchy of Abraham. But the first eleven chapters of Genesis go beyond the founding of the Israelites; they present stories of creation.

The stories of Genesis 1–11 are not historical in the sense that they include verifiable names, facts, and dates. The first eleven chapters contain stories about the origins of the world, humans, the fall of man, and varying cultures, often described as the primeval history.

The first three chapters of Genesis express the truths of creation. From a literary standpoint, these stories may have borrowed from several sources, including **myths** from the ancient Near East. The Israelites—under the inspiration of the Holy Spirit—adapted these stories to tell how God was working in history in a radical way.

The book of Genesis also bridges primeval history with information about important people in our religious history. From Genesis 11:27–50:26, we read of our **ancestors** of faith, including Abraham (Gn 12–23, 25), Isaac (Gn 24, 25–27), Jacob (Gn 28–35, 49), and Joseph (Gn 37–48, 50).

The ancient Hebrews loved to tell stories. For hundreds of years these stories were preserved through *oral traditions*. Writing was difficult during these early times, and most people did not read. For centuries legends, myths, songs, laws, and stories were passed on orally. Eventually the stories began to be written down. Some of the Old Testament was written in the tenth century B.C. And some of the book of Genesis may not have been written until the sixth century B.C.

The tradition of storytelling was continued by Jesus. He was the master storyteller. Many of his stories are so widely known that people of all faiths can and do refer to them. Sometimes people don't even realize they are quoting Jesus. For example,
- a person who does a good deed for another may be called a "good Samaritan";

myths—Symbolic stories that express a spiritual truth or a basic belief about God.

ancestor—Any person to whom you are related by blood who comes before you on a family tree.

Resources
Music Suggestions

"All Creatures of Our God and King" by St. Francis of Assisi from *Gather* (GIA).

"As Jacob with Travel Was Weary One Day" (English Folk Song) in *Worship II* (GIA).

"Canticle of the Sun" by Marty Haugen from *With Open Hands* or *Gather* (GIA); *Music Issue* or *Breaking Bread* (OCP).

"For the Beauty of the Earth" by Folliot S. Peirpoint in *Gather* (GIA).

"How Great Thou Art" by Stuart Hine from *Music Issue* or *Breaking Bread* (OCP); *Gather* (GIA).

"In Adam We Have All Been One" by Martin Franzmann in *Worship II* (GIA).

"Morning Has Broken" by Eleanor Farjeon from *Even the Sparrow* (Maranatha! Music); *Celebrate, Worship,* or *Gather* (GIA); *Breaking Bread* or *Spirit Song* (OCP).

"We Are Climbing Jacob's Ladder" (Afro-American Spiritual) in *Lead Me, Guide Me* (GIA) and *Gather* (GIA).

- the visit of a relative who comes home after a long absence may be referred to as the "return of the prodigal son"; and
- good people are commonly called "the salt of the Earth."

All of these common phrases are taken directly from the stories of Jesus. They have become a part of our day-to-day culture. Stories are powerful and lasting. This chapter offers a tour of the book of Genesis—stories that tell us about creation and our ancestors of faith.

REVIEW & REFLECTION

1. What kinds of information can we learn about a culture even from stories that are not simply historical reports?
2. What two groups of stories appear in the book of Genesis? List examples of each.

JOURNAL ASSIGNMENT

- Think of two or three things you believe to be true about God and write a short story about your ancestors that reveals those truths.

God's Creation

Human beings are created with a desire to know their origins, from their personal beginnings or the beginnings of the entire human race. Everyone wants to know how things got started. So did the ancient peoples, including the ancient Hebrews. The book of Genesis includes *two* creation stories, not one. The first story is the familiar "seven-day creation" story which runs from Genesis 1:1 through 2:4a (the "a" after the number 4 means the first *half* of verse 4). In this story, creation takes place in six days before God rests on the seventh day, the Sabbath. Also, note that the material God uses for creation is water:

> In the beginning when God created the heavens and the earth, the earth was a formless wasteland, and darkness covered the abyss, while a mighty wind swept over the waters (Gn 1:1–2).

Also, note, that in this first creation story, humanity is created *at the same time, in the same moment* as male and female. Both man and woman are created in the image of God:

> Then God said: "Let us make mankind in our image, after our likeness. Let them have dominion over the fish of the sea, the birds of the air, and the cattle, and over all the wild animals and all the creatures that crawl on the ground."
>
> God created man in his image;
> in the divine image he created him;
> male and female he created them (Gn 1:26–27).

In the second creation story in the book of Genesis (2:4b–25) God's handiwork does not begin out of water, but from the land:

> At the time when the Lord God made the earth and the heavens—while as yet there was no field shrub on earth and no

STORIES FOR THE JOURNEY

Teaching Approaches

1. Assign the Introduction text, pages 60–61.

2. Have the students scan the Genesis passages suggested on page 60 describing Abraham, Isaac, Jacob, and Joseph and write down one or two passages that stand out about each person in their journals or on paper. Allow time for them to share why they found the passage meaningful.

3. Make sure the students are aware of the meaning of the Scripture references quoted on page 60. Ask:
   - What is a good Samaritan? (If the students are unfamiliar with this parable, refer them to Luke 10:29–37).
   - Summarize the parable of the prodigal son. (Refer the students to the story in Luke 15:11–32.)
   - What does it mean to call someone "the salt of the earth?" (If necessary, refer the students to Matthew 5:13).

Resources
Printed Materials:

"Genesis, The Book of" in *The Oxford Companion to the Bible*, ed. by Bruce M. Metzger and Michael D. Coogan. (New York, NY: Oxford University Press, 1993), pp. 245–249.

"Genesis," "Creation," "Deluge," "Fall," "Patriarchs," and "Pentateuch" in *Dictionary of the Bible*, ed. by John L. McKenzie, S.J. (New York, NY: Macmillan Publishing Co., Inc., 1965), pp. 301–302, 157–160, 188–190, 271–273, 646–648.

Clifford, Richard J., S.J. and Murphy, Roland E. " Genesis" in *The New Jerome Biblical Commentary*, ed. by Raymond E. Brown, S.S., Joseph A. Fitzmyer, S.J., and Roland E. Murphy, O.Carm. (Englewood Cliffs, NJ: Prentice Hall, 1990), pp. 8–43.

Kselman, John S. "Genesis" in *Harper's Bible Commentary*, ed. by James L. Mays. (San Francisco, CA: Harper & Row Publishers, 1988), pp. 85–128.

Murphy, Roland E., O. Carm. "Introduction to the Pentateuch" in *The New Jerome Biblical Comm*entary, ed. by Raymond E. Brown, S.S., Joseph A. Fitzmyer, S.J., and Roland E. Murphy, O.Carm. (Englewood Cliffs, NJ: Prentice Hall, 1990), pp. 3–7.

Viviano, Pauline A. "Genesis" in *The Collegeville Bible Commentary*, ed. by Dianne Bergant, C.S.A. and Robert J. Karris, O.F.M. (Collegeville, MN: The Liturgical Press, 1989, pp. 35–78.

# Chapter 3

4. Use "The Book of Genesis" (Overhead 3A online) to introduce the material. Explain that Genesis is a collection of stories that were passed down orally from one generation to the next. Inspired authors and editors from some time after the Exile (approximately the fifth century B.C.) wrote down the stories and arranged them in a somewhat logical order. Use the outline to explain the following information:
   - The first part of Genesis includes two stories of creation, the sin of Adam and Eve (accounting for the presence of sin and death in the world), Cain's murder of Abel, the descendants of Cain and the invention of culture, the flood and Noah's deliverance, and the Tower of Babel.
   - In the second part, we find the call of Abram, the evolution of God's covenant with Abram/Abraham, stories about Sarah, Lot, Hagar, and Ishmael. There is also the account of the birth of Isaac and Abraham's initial commitment to sacrifice his son to God.
   - In the third part, we read about the birth of the twins Esau and Jacob, how Rebecca plots to trick Isaac into giving Jacob the inheritance, Jacob's marriages to Leah and Rachel, Jacob's life of trickery and deception, his twelve sons, and his eventual reunion with Esau.
   - The last part deals with the story of Joseph, the oldest son of Jacob by Rachel. We learn how Joseph's brothers sold him into slavery in Egypt, how Joseph managed to rise to power in the Egyptian government, and how his brothers eventually came to him for food.

5. **Homework Assignment:**
   - Write answers to Review and Reflection questions 1–2 on page 61. Use complete sentences.
   - Respond to the Journal Assignment, page 61. Be prepared to share your short story at the next class session.
   - Read "God's Creation," pages 61–65.

GOD'S CREATION

Bell-Ringers:
1. Ask the students to name "things they believe to be true about God" (see Journal Assignment, page 61). Then call on some volunteers to read their short stories that reveal these truths through the lives of their ancestors.

THE OLD TESTAMENT

grass of the field had sprouted, for the Lord God had sent no rain upon the earth and there was no man to till the soil . . . (Gn 2:4b–6).

In this version, the order of creation is different (man, then plants, then animals, whereas in the first story it starts with plants, then animals, then finally man). The second account portrays God as more of a craftsman than did the first creation story: God makes the man out of mud, and actually "breathes life" into him. Life is a rare gift from God—something God did not do with any other part of creation.

The second creation story also mentions:
- Adam and Eve as the names of the first humans,
- the story of the temptation of eating the fruit of the tree, and
- the continued population of the world.

So there are two different creation stories, and thus different sets of ideas, about the beginning of the world in the Old Testament—similar, but not exactly the same. Some who study the Bible believe that the Hebrews had different versions of these events (rather like having more than one version of the life of Jesus in the different Gospels in the New Testament) and included more than one because important things are said in each version.

The Truths of Creation

We can learn much about the nature of God and his intentions for man through the stories of creation. The Genesis stories provide clear answers to other related and perpetual questions (*CCC*, 282): Where do we come from? Where are we going? What is our origin? What is our end? Where does everything that exists come from and where is it going?

In more recent times, scientific discoveries have cast more specific light on the details of creation, including the **evolution** of mankind and attempts to pinpoint when and where the first humans appeared on earth. Human intelligence is certainly already capable of finding an accurate answer to these questions. These studies only enhance our appreciation for God, the Creator, whose existence can be known by human reason alone. St. Paul wrote that denial of God is inexcusable because of the light of human reason:

> The wrath of God is indeed being revealed from heaven against every impiety and wickedness of those who suppress the truth by their wickedness. For what can be known about God is evident to them, because God made it evident to them. Ever since the creation of the world, his invisible attributes of eternal power and divinity have been able to be understood and perceived in what he has made (Rom 1:18–20).

In fact, the questions about creation are so important for human life that God wants to reveal everything that is good about it. This knowledge is revealed by God to individuals as the mystery of creation was revealed progressively to Israel

evolution—The scientific theory which proposes that current forms of life developed gradually out of earlier ones.

62

Review and Reflection Answers

1. Nonfactual stories can teach us about the culture and its values: what people think is important, valuable, and good.

2. The two groups of stories that appear in Genesis are primeval stories and ancestor stories. Examples of primeval stories include the two creation accounts, the fall of Adam and Eve, the story of Cain and Abel, Noah and the flood, and the Tower of Babel. Examples of ancestor stories include the stories of Abraham, Sarah, and Hagar, Isaac and Rebekah, Jacob, Leaf, and Rachel, and Joseph and Asenath.

(CCC, 287). The creation of the world and the creation of man and woman was Yahweh's first step at forging a **covenant** with Israel. It is easy to understand why the Hebrew Biblical authors addressed creation with two stories and why these stories come first in the Bible. As the *Catechism* teaches:

> The inspired authors have placed them at the beginning of Scripture to express in their solemn language the truths of creation—its origins and its end in God, its order and goodness, the vocation of man, and finally the drama or sin and the hope of salvation (CCC, 289).

God's creative actions also reveal several other important truths about him, including:

- God began everything that exists outside of himself, he alone is the Creator, and everything that exists in the world depends on God who gives it being (see Gn 1:1).
- God created everything through the eternal Word, his begotten Son, Jesus (see Col 1:16–17).
- Creation is the common work of the Holy Trinity. God the Father made all things "by the Son and the Spirit" (CCC, 292 quoting St. Irenaeus). The prologue to the Gospel of John likewise teaches that the Father created everything by his eternal Word, his beloved Son (see Jn 1:1–5, page 64). The Church also professes the Spirit's role as the "giver of life" (see CCC, 291). The image of wind ("a mighty wind swept over the waters") in Genesis 1:2 attests to the presence of the Holy Spirit at creation.

God created the world to show his glory and to communicate it. God's perfection is shown through the gifts he offers us, his creations. Human beings are unique because we are made in the image and likeness of God. We are called to share "by knowledge and love" (CCC, 356) in God's own life.

The first story of creation also reveals a great deal about the human person. We have been

The Creation of Adam by Michelangelo

covenant—A binding and solemn agreement between human beings or between God and his people, holding each to a particular course of action.

Background Information
Enuma Elish

Other Ancient Near East cultures had creation stories. One of the most famous were the Babylonian stories, *Enuma Elish*. Austin Henry Layard from the British Museum discovered the Enuma Elish stories in 1849. These stories were written on baked tablets thirty inches high. The stories were written approximately 1100 B.C. and told about the creation of the world by Marduk, the god of Babylon. The Babylonian story is full of battles, wars, and bloody duels. The Hebrew stories of creation, in contrast, are peaceful and calm: God creates the world out of love, rather than the desire for conquest or revenge.

STORIES FOR THE JOURNEY

2. Introduce the lesson. Begin with the commonly asked questions about the origins of the world (page 62, "The Truths of Creation"). Assign the Journal Assignment (page 65) to introduce the lesson. Then call on students to share some of their questions. Choose volunteers to come before the class, be "on the spot," and attempt to answer these questions.

Teaching Approaches
1. Direct the students to read the two creation stories from Genesis 1:1–2:4 and Genesis 2:4b–25. Compare and contrast the two accounts. Explain that the first story (Gn 1:1–2:4a) is thought to be from a priestly source. In this story creation takes place in six days with God resting on the seventh day, the Sabbath. In the second creation story, God's creation is from the land, concluding with the creation of man. Ask the students to tell why there may have been two different creation stories (see the paragraph beginning with "So, there are at least two different creation stories" (page 62). Explain that the second creation story probably came from the Yahwist, or J source. It is much older than the first creation story, and reads like a folk tale. The focus of the story is the relationship of friendship between God and humans, between male and female, between humans and the rest of the creation. The nakedness of Adam and Eve is a symbol of innocence and right relationship with God. Emphasize that both accounts reveal several unique things about God. Summarize by printing the following on the board or overhead (also on page 63):

- **God began everything that exists outside of himself, he alone is the Creator, and everything that exists in the world depends on God who gives it being (see Gn 1:1).**
- **God created everything through the eternal Word, his begotten Son, Jesus (see Col 1:16–17).**
- **Creation is the common work of the Holy Trinity.**

2. Address God's creation of the Sabbath. Explain that a day of rest would have been unheard of for the Israelites when they were slaves in Egypt. Taking a day of rest is a sign of dignity and respect. It helps to give value to the human person. Distribute "The Sabbath or Shabbat" (Handout 3B, page 270 of the TWE). After explaining the material, discuss with the students ways for keeping the Sabbath holy.

Chapter 3

3. Point out the separate feature "What Else Does the Bible Say About Creation?" (page 64). Ask the students to name how the roles of Father, Son, and Holy Spirit are explicitly referred to in the two passages (Psalm 104 and the prologue of the gospel of John.)

4. Discuss the term *revelation*. Ask: "Why do you think God's revelation was a gradual one throughout history?" Direct the discussion to a comparison with individual human growth and development. For example, a parent does not "reveal" everything there is to know about family history, faith, sexuality, etc. when a child is young. These subjects and others must be revealed through time.

5. **Homework Assignment:**
   - Write answers to the Review and Reflection questions 1–3 (page 65).
   - Read Genesis 2:4–3:24 and Genesis 4:1–6.
   - Read "Original Justice and the Fall of Man" (pages 65–67) and Genesis 2:4–3:24.

---

created by God with both a body and soul. The "soul" refers to the entire human person. It also refers to the innermost, spiritual aspect of man. The human body, too, shares in the image of God because it is intended to be the temple of the Holy Spirit. Also, we are to regard the human body as good and to honor it, since God has created it and will raise it on the last day.

What Else does the Bible Say About Creation?

There are other discussions of Creation in the Bible besides the book of Genesis. For example, Psalm 104 praises God the Creator, saying in part:

> How manifold are your works, O Lord!
>   In wisdom you have wrought them all— (vs. 24).

The wisdom of Solomon praises God for giving the gift of understanding of the details of creation:

> For he gave me sound knowledge of existing things,
>   that I might know the organization
>   of the universe and its elements,
> The beginning and the end and the midpoints of times,
>   the changes in the sun's course and
>   the variations of the seasons;
> Cycles of years, positions of the stars,
> natures of animals, tempers of beasts,
> Powers of winds and thoughts of men
>   uses of plants, and virtues of roots—
> Such things as are hidden I learned,
>   and such as are plain;
> for Wisdom, the artificer of all,
>   taught me (Wis 7:17–22).

The prologue of the gospel of John (1:1–5) also addresses creation:

> In the beginning was the Word,
>   and the Word was with God,
>   and the Word was God.
> He was in the beginning with God.
> All things came to be through him,
>   and without him nothing came to be.
> What came to be through him was life,
>   and the life was the light of the human race;
> the light shines in the darkness,
>   and the darkness has not overcome it.

Resources

Audiovisual Materials

Abraham (available from Vision Video)—150 minutes
Abraham and Sarah respond to God by beginning a difficult journey through the desert to the Promised Land.

Creation or Evolution (available from Vision Video)—58 minutes
This video discusses the controversial debate between the creation story in Genesis and the scientific theory of evolution.

Genesis (available from Vision Video)—60 minutes
This video, part of four in a set entitled *The Bible*, is shot on location in the Holy Land and dramatizes the stories of Genesis.

Jacob (available from Vision Video)—94 minutes
Jacob works seven years to marry Rachel, only to be deceived into marrying her sister. He agrees to work another seven years in order to marry Rachel.

Joseph (available from Vision Video)—185 minutes
Joseph's brothers sell him into slavery. Despite numerous setbacks in Egypt, Joseph gradually rises to a powerful position in the government.

Mysteries of the Bible: Cain and Abel (available from Videos with Values)—50 minutes
Viewers explore possible reasons that compelled Cain to kill his brother. We see how scripture scholars study this story in Genesis to search for clues regarding its faith message.

Mysteries of the Bible: Joseph, Master of Dreams (available from Videos with Values)—50 minutes
Archaeologists dig for clues in Egypt that may tell us more about Joseph, one of the patriarchs of God's people.

Testament, Bible and History: As It was in the Beginning (Films for the Humanities and Sciences)—52 minutes
John Romer, writer and archaeologist, traces Abraham's journey from Ur to Canaan. He explains how the great civilizations of Mesopotamia contribute to many Old Testament ideas.

The Wonders of God's Creation (available from Vision Video)—3 videos, 193 minutes total
Spectacular photography presents the beauty of God's creation. Part 1 focuses on planet Earth as a sanctuary of life. Part 2 focuses on the animal kingdom. Part 3 explores human life.

The Beginning of God's Revelation

In the person and mission of Jesus Christ, God has fully been revealed. But this revelation was a gradual one through history. The beginning of God's revelation to man came when he made himself known to our first parents.

God invited Adam and Eve to an "intimate communion with himself and clothed them with resplendent grace and justice" (CCC, 54). When Adam and Eve sinned (see page 66), God did not withdraw the revelation of himself. Rather, he encouraged mankind with the hope of salvation and the promise of redemption.

God continued to offer a covenant to mankind. The first covenant was made with Noah. God also chose Abraham and formed his people, Israel. After the time of the patriarchs, God freed Israel from slavery in Egypt and established with them the covenant of Mount Sinai, and through Moses, gave them his Law so that they would know and worship him as they awaited the Messiah who would save them from their sins. This ongoing revelation is the subject of the Old Testament. It serves as a prelude to the New Testament and God's full revelation in Christ. Though God's revelation is complete, it is not explicit. It remains the task of the Church, and our own task, to understand its significance over the course of centuries.

REVIEW & REFLECTION

1. What is the most important question addressed by the two creation stories in the book of Genesis? What answer do these stories provide?
2. List some of the differences between the two creation stories.
3. What do God's creative actions reveal about him?

JOURNAL ASSIGNMENT

- Write a list of some of the puzzling questions you have about the origins of life and the origins of evil in the world.

Original Justice and the Fall of Man

Read Genesis 2:4–3:24

The second creation story teaches us that the first man was created "in friendship with his Creator and in harmony with himself and with the creation around him" (CCC, 374). The Church also teaches that Adam and Eve were created in a state of grace known as "original justice." The benefits of original justice were wonderful, surpassed only by the glory of new creation in Christ. As long as man remained in friendship with God, the gifts of original justice would remain, for example:

- There would be no suffering or death.
- Man would be at peace with himself.
- There would be harmony between man and woman.
- There would be peace between Adam and Eve, the first couple, and all of creation.

STORIES FOR THE JOURNEY

ORIGINAL JUSTICE AND THE FALL OF MAN

Bell-Ringer

1. Play all or part of the video *Creation or Evolution* (see page 68 of the TWE). Continue the discussion on the Catholic view of evolution, especially God's providence over the evolutionary chain of events and the existence of the soul.

Teaching Approaches

1. Distribute art media (paper, colored pencils, etc.). Allow some time for the students to draw their ideas about the world as it was first created in harmony with the Creator and creation. Other students may wish to write a paragraph or two on the same topic (see Journal Assignment, page 67). Allow time for sharing.

2. Discuss each of the gifts of original justice. Call for a panel of students to address each example (e.g., "There would be no suffering or death.") and how they would imagine the world in such a state. Allow responses and questions from students not on the panel.

Review and Reflection Answers

1. The most important question the two creation stories in Genesis answer concerns the nature of God as Creator. God is loving and seeks a relationship with human beings. The creation of the world and the creation of men and women were Yahweh's first two steps at forging a covenant with Israel.
2. The differences between the two creation stories include:
   - In the first story, creation begins out of water; in the second story: creation begins out of the land.
   - In the first story, all creation takes place in six days; no time for creation is specified in the second story.
   - In the first story, God creates men and women at the same moment; in the second story God creates man first, then creates woman out of Adam's rib.
   - In the first story, the order of creation is plants, animals, then mankind; in the second story the order of creation is humans, then plants, then animals.
3. God's creative action reveals that:
   - God is the source of everything that exists outside of himself, he alone is the Creator, and everything that exists in the world depends on God who gives it being (see Gn 1:1).
   - God created everything through the eternal Word, his begotten Son, Jesus (see Col 1:16–17).
   - Creation is the common work of the Holy Trinity.

Chapter 3

3. Point out the difference between original sin and personal sin. All people are born with original sin because we are all members of the human race. We have a "built in" weakness for sin, simply through our human nature. Personal sin, however, is sin that we choose to commit of our own free will. Cain's murder of Abel is an example of personal sin (see Gn 4:1–16).

4. Repeat this statement to the students: "Without the doctrine of original sin, the mystery of Christ is undermined." Ask the students to write a sentence on a piece of scrap paper explaining why this is true (see Review and Reflection question 3, page 67). Have them exchange papers. Make sure that they understand that the doctrine of original sin teaches that we come into the world as sinners. Because we are sinners, we need the salvation that was won for us by Jesus Christ.

5. **Homework Assignment:**
   - Complete the Review and Reflection questions 1–3, page 67.
   - Complete the Journal Assignment if not finished in class.
   - Read "Renewal of Life (pages 67–70)." Read Genesis 6:5–9:17 and Genesis 11:1–9.
   - Bring photos or news articles of devastation caused by a recent flood somewhere in the world.

THE OLD TESTAMENT

At the time of creation, our first parents were blessed with the

Cain murders his brother Abel

gifts of "self mastery," meaning they had power over lustful desires of the body and covetousness for earthly goods. This deep friendship with God at the time of creation is such that he placed man in a garden (see Gn 2:8). At the time, work was not a burden for man; rather, it was a collaboration with God to bring perfection to all of creation.

The second creation story in Genesis describes another reality: the sin of Adam and Eve. With their sin, the harmony of original justice intended for mankind would be lost.

Original Sin

As with other events in primeval history, the fall of man described in Genesis 3 uses figurative language but describes an actual "deed that took place *at the beginning of the history of man*" (CCC, 390) that reveals with the certainty of faith that all human history is marred by an original, voluntary sin committed by our first parents.

The basic root of sin is man's rejection of God and opposition to his will. The second creation story describes how this first happened. Adam and Eve were tempted to sin by a serpent, a fallen **angel** who was "Satan" or the "devil."

What was the original sin? Essentially, it was an abuse of man's freedom. Tempted by the devil, Adam disobeyed God and lacked trust in God's goodness. The book of Genesis describes the sin as Adam and Eve eating fruit from the forbidden "tree of the knowledge of good and bad" (Gn 2:17, 3:6). All sin, including this original sin, is rooted in disobedience of God. The original sin, in essence, is that man *preferred* himself to God. Man was created to be like God in all glory, but instead he chose to be like God but "without God, before God, and not in accordance with God" (CCC, 398 quoting St. Maximus the Confessor).

The original sin has consequences for all of humanity. Adam and Eve immediately lost the graces of original holiness. The harmony of original justice is destroyed: human nature is weakened and inclined to sin, man's spiritual control over his body is lost, tensions between men and women are introduced, and the rest of creation (e.g., animals, climate) becomes hostile to mankind. Moreover, "death makes its entrance into human history" (CCC, 400).

angel—A spiritual, personal, and immortal creature, with intelligence and free will, who glorifies God and serves as God's messenger. Satan was at first a good angel, but along with other devils, they became evil through their own choices.

Background Information

More Text From the Exultant At the Easter Vigil

This is the night when Jesus Christ broke the chains of death and rose triumphant from the grave.

Father, how wonderful you care for us! How boundless your merciful love! To ransom a slave you gave away your Son.

O happy fault, O necessary sin of Adam, which gained for us so great a Redeemer!

The power of this holy night dispels all evil, washes guilt away, restores lost innocence, brings mourners joy.

Night truly blessed when heaven is wedded to earth and man is reconciled with God!

Stories for the Journey

Yet it is important to note that even after the sin of Adam and Eve, God immediately offered his mercy and the first promise of a Redeemer for the fallen mankind. God said to the serpent:

> I will put enmity between you and the woman
> and between your offspring and hers;
> He will strike at your head,
> while you strike at his heal
> (Gn 3:15)

The woman's offspring is Jesus Christ. The first letter of John teaches: "Indeed, the Son of God was revealed to destroy the works of the devil" (1 Jn 3:8).

Still, sin spread quickly after Adam and Eve. Cain's murder of his brother Abel is a personal sin, which arose from the shared original sin of humanity. After the incident (see Gn 4:1–16), God asks Cain to explain himself and tell where his brother is. Cain responds by saying, "I do not know. Am I my brother's keeper?" Sin has caused him to abdicate his responsibility for others, a practice that continues on through each generation.

The doctrine of original sin is an essential truth of the faith. Without the doctrine of original sin, the mystery of Christ is undermined. We come into the world as sinners and need the salvation that is offered to all through Christ. As the exultant at the Easter vigil proclaims:

> O happy, fault, O necessary sin of Adam,
> which gained for us so great a Redeemer!

REVIEW & REFLECTION

1. What is original justice?
2. Define original sin.
3. Why is the doctrine of original sin essential for understanding the mystery of Christ?

JOURNAL ASSIGNMENT

- Describe life in the garden before Adam and Eve sinned.

Renewal of Life

Read Genesis 6:5–9:17

God's revelation was not broken off by the sin of Adam and Eve. In fact, after the fall, God immediately offered the hope of salvation by promising redemption. At Mass, we hear this reminder:

> Even when he disobeyed you and lost your friendship you did not abandon him to the power of death.... Again and again you offered a covenant to man (*Roman Missal*, Eucharistic Prayer IV, 118).

The covenant God made with Noah is part of the next stage of his revelation. Noah became the new ancestor for mankind. God blessed him and his sons and said to them: "Be fertile and multiply and fill the earth" (Gn 9:1). The covenant with Noah revealed the basic

67

Review and Reflection Answers

1. Original justice is the state of grace in which Adam and Eve were created by God.

2. Original sin is the sin of Adam and Eve, the original abuse of man's freedom. In essence, this sin is that man preferred himself to God.

3. Due to original sin, we come into the world as sinners. Because we are sinners we need the salvation that is offered to all through Christ.

STORIES FOR THE JOURNEY

RENEWAL OF LIFE

Bell-Ringers

1. Bring to class pictures of devastation caused by a recent flood somewhere in the world. Also, ask students who have been caught in a flood situation to share their experiences.

2. Review the fall of mankind and the original sin of Adam and Eve. Read Genesis 2:14–19. Ask the students to identify the passages that tell how God immediately offered the hope of salvation even after Adam and Eve had sinned (see Gn 3:15).

Teaching Approaches

1. Check the student's detailed reading of the flood story from Genesis 6:5–9:17. Ask these questions:

- How many animals did Noah take onto the ark? (Most students will answer that Noah took a pair of each species onto the ark. Direct them to Genesis 7:2–3. There, God tells Noah to bring seven pairs of "clean animals and a single pair of "unclean" creatures. Explain that the terms "clean" and "unclean" come from dietary laws found in Leviticus and Deuteronomy.)
- How long did the flood last? (Most students will answer that the flood lasted forty days and forty nights. Direct them to Genesis 7:24, which says the flood crested after 150 days.)

Explain that a close reading of the Noah story reveals many duplications throughout the story. These differences and duplications are probably the result of editing, of compiling material from two different sources, J and P.

Chapter 3

2. Next, review Genesis 9:8–17. Then ask:
   - What covenant did God make? (God promised never to send another flood to destroy all the earth.)
   - With whom did God make this covenant? (Noah and his descendants, and every living creature on the ark.) Point out that the passage tells us of God's eternal care, not just for people, but for all plants, animals, birds, fish, and more.

3. Also call on volunteers to discuss what implications the Noah story has on today's environmental issues. (Accept all reasonable answers.) Read excerpts from the *Catechism of the Catholic Church*, 2415–2418, on the "respect for the integrity of creation."

4. Summarize the text feature "Why So Many Flood Stories?" (page 69). Present some information to the students on the end of the Ice Age. Allow them to form their own thesis to the query suggested at the bottom of the feature. See, for example, a *National Geographic* article that suggests the collapse of a large Antarctica ice sheet was the beginning of the end of the Ice Age: http://news.nationalgeographic.com/news/2003/03/0317_030317_iceshelf.html

---

The Old Testament

paganism—The profession of no religion.

precepts of the law and combated **paganism**, a combination of idol worship (idolatry) and worship of many gods (polytheism). This covenant also called all people—including Gentiles—to relationship with God and remains in force "until the universal proclamation of the Gospel" (*CCC*, 58).

The Literary Nature of the Noah Covenant

The story of Noah and the great flood is the last great story of Genesis 1–11 that details events of primeval history.

The ancient peoples surrounding the Hebrews also had flood legends. One of the most famous is part of the great myth cycle of a Mesopotamian poem known as "The Epic of Gilgamesh." Many copies of Gilgamesh have been found by archaeologists, from as early as 2000 B.C. in some places and as late as the sixth century B.C. in other locations. It was obviously an ancient story that was widely known and very popular throughout the region. The Hebrews, too, would have known the story.

While there are similarities between the flood story of the Epic of Gilgamesh and the inspired text of Scripture, the Hebrew story shares how God reveals himself to man and a hint to man's eventual destiny. Here are some of the unique teachings of the Hebrew version:

♦ Humanity is to be destroyed because they are evil and constantly doing violence to each other.
♦ Noah is saved because he is a righteous man.
♦ The Gilgamesh hero takes money on the ark. Noah only takes animals.
♦ The Hebrew version represents a "second creation story." Noah takes the place of a new "Adam."

Now we understand the wisdom of the Church's interpretation and understanding of elements of this story. The story says that God made an everlasting covenant with Noah and mankind. God intervenes in history and offers his salvation. This will be an ongoing occurrence through the Old Testament, leading to God's ultimate intervention in history, the incarnation of his son, Jesus Christ, who offers salvation to all.

68

Background Information

More on The Epic of Gilgamesh

The Epic of Gilgamesh is divided into twelve tablets. It is named after the hero, Gilgamesh, who is "two-thirds god" and one-third man." The similarities in the flood portion of the Epic with the Hebrew account of the flood include facets like:
- the flood is decided on by the divine
- one man and his family are to be saved
- the details of the construction of the ark are decided by the divine
- animals are taken aboard the ark
- the end of the flood is determined by a bird
- the ark rests on the mountain
- an acceptable sacrifice ends the story.

WHY SO MANY FLOOD STORIES?

The Epic of Gilgamesh is one of many flood stories from the ancient world. There are some Biblical scholars who believe that the reason for the many flood stories (including the Genesis story of the Great Flood) relates specifically to an ancient historic event.

One theory of the preponderance of flood legends according to Columbia University geologists is that as the Ice Age ended and glaciers melted and a wall of seawater surged from the Mediterranean into the Black Sea. During the Ice Age, the geologists argue, the Black Sea was an isolated freshwater lake surrounded by farmland.

Then, according to the theory, about 12,000 years ago, toward the end of the Ice Age, the Earth began growing warmer. Vast sheets of ice that sprawled over the Northern Hemisphere began to melt. Oceans and seas grew deeper as a result. About 7,000 years ago even the Mediterranean Sea swelled. Seawater pushed northward, slicing through what is now Turkey. Funneled through the narrow Bosporus, the water hit the Black Sea with two hundred times the force of Niagara Falls. Each day the Black Sea rose about six inches and coastal farms were flooded. Settlements were discovered in what is today submerged former shorelines of the Black Sea.

Seared into the memories of terrified survivors, the story of the flood was passed down through the generations and eventually became the basis for some of the ancient flood stories.[1]

This is a relatively recent theory, and lots of materials are available online and in recent books to assemble more information. Ruins of civilizations are being explored along what is supposed to be the ancient shoreline of the Black Sea to find out if these were the original villages and cities of the flood victims.

* Research and read more information on the end of the Ice Age and its connection to worldwide flooding. Write a summary of your findings.

The Tower of Babel: More Hope for the World
Read Genesis 11:1–9

The last of the primeval history events of Genesis 1–11 details how the sin of pride, brought into the world by the sin of Adam, has now increased as an entire city tries to make itself God. The short nine-verse story also has a secondary motive: to show in an imaginative way how the many different languages of the world came to be. This of itself is a hopeful gesture to mankind (see below).

Notice *where* this is taking place. The place is called "Shinar" (vs. 2). This is an ancient term that the Bible often uses for "Babylon" (and thus the play on the name "Babel"). Why is Babylon important? Remember that Babylon was the great Empire that conquered Jerusalem and destroyed Solomon's Temple in 587 B.C. This powerful memory of the Hebrews was so great, that "Babylon" passed into history as a symbol for *any* oppressive Empire or state. The New Testament uses Babylon to refer to the Roman Empire (e.g., 1 Pt 5:13; Rv 16:19; 18:2,10, & 21).[2]

Next, consider the second part of the story. One interpretation of the diversity of languages is that God is punishing the people for their sins. However, the unification of all humanity under one language, and putting them all to work to build a great city and tower, would have been good only for the

5. Point out that the main point of the Tower of Babel story is that we should not put our faith entirely in human achievements, that God is still God, the one in control. Also show how the story tells how human sin always leads to alienation, the inability to communicate, and the loss of unity with others.

Resources
Internet Links

www.dur.ac.uk/oriental.museum
Tour the Oriental Museum at the University of Durham, England, to view artifacts from excavations in Ur, the home of Abraham.

www.concentric.net
Discusses recent discoveries in Biblical archaeology, including the Dead Sea scrolls, Noah's ark, and other sites.

www.bible-archaeology.com
View cities of ancient Israel, the homes of Abraham and the Patriarchs.

www.thebritishmuseum.ac.uk/ane/anehome.html
Visit the Department of Ancient Near East Antiquities at the British Museum in London.

www.blmj.org
Features a virtual tour of the Bible Lands Museum in Jerusalem. The permanent exhibit includes artifacts from Genesis 14 and the Age of the Patriarchs.

CHAPTER 3

6. Put the summary list of teachings about God gleaned from the primeval history stories of Genesis on the board or overhead. Allow students time to refer back through Genesis 1–11 to find citations that support each of these points. Allow for sharing and discussion. Then have the students complete the Journal Assignment (page 70). When completed, allow them to share some surprising discoveries with a partner.

7. **Homework Assignment:**
   - Write answers to the Review and Reflection questions 1–2, page 70.
   - Read "Ancestors of Faith" (pages 71–75.)

THE OLD TESTAMENT

rulers. The scattering of the peoples into different languages would really have been God's *liberation* for most of the people of "Shinar."

Therefore, dividing into different peoples and languages was not punishment, but freedom. Consider the parallel story in Acts

2:5–13. We now can appreciate that each person gathered in Jerusalem at the Pentecost feast heard Peter *in their own language*, also a positive development. The Church teaches that God willed the diversity of his creatures and their own particular goodness, their interdependence, and their order. This diversity is deeply celebrated in the liberation of God at the story of the Tower of Babel.

The primeval history stories of Genesis tell us much about the Hebrew people—including what they value about life and their beliefs about Yahweh. Here is a summary of some of the things these stories teach us about God and his will:

- God's will is to create a people in his image—both male and female.
- God's will is peace, not violence. Violence is considered sinful in these stories. God creates in peace—it is humans that bring on violence. The Flood story suggests that God was so sickened by human violence that God regretted making humanity.
- God's will is trust and truthfulness—not the lies and deceptions of human beings in their society.
- God's will is care for creation—not destruction and exploitation.
- God's will is joyful diversity—not forced unification.
- God is not impressed with how great our human material accomplishments are, but with how we care for each other and also how we care for the created environment.

REVIEW & REFLECTION

1. What are some of the unique religious truths expressed in the Hebrew story of Noah and the Flood?
2. What important historical experiences of the Hebrew people help you to understand the story of the Tower of Babel?

JOURNAL ASSIGNMENT

- What surprised you the most in the stories you read from the beginning of the Bible? What new information caused you to think differently about human nature or about God?

Review and Reflection Answers

1. The flood story teaches these unique religious truths:
   - God destroys people because they do evil things, and are constantly doing violence to each other.
   - God saves Noah because he is a righteous man.
   - Noah takes animals, rather than money, on the ark.
   - The flood is really a second creation story. Noah takes the place of Adam.
   - God intervenes in human history and offers his salvation.
   - God made an everlasting covenant with humans through Noah.

2. The Promised Land was situated in the middle of important trade routes in the Near East. The Hebrews would have been exposed to people of many different nations, speaking many different languages. The story of the Tower of Babel explains why humans are divided into so many language groups. God's will is joyful diversity, not forced unification. Also, God is not impressed with human accomplishments but rather with how we care for each other, and care for the created environment.

Ancestors of Faith

The structure of Genesis changes with the introduction of the Patriarch Abraham in Genesis 11:27 and continues in the same way through the rest of the book with accounts of other **patriarchs**, Isaac and Jacob, and narrative surrounding Jacob's son, Joseph. While the accounts of the patriarchs are not counted as history in the strict sense, people and events from the time of Abraham onward can be placed in the historical and social setting of the Near East from between 2000–1700 B.C.

Abraham is the father of the Chosen People who were called to prepare the way for Christ. At Christ's coming, the Chosen People would be the "root onto which the Gentiles would be grafted, once they came to believe" (see Rom 11:17–18, 24). Abraham, then, is also the "father of all believers."

Why are these accounts of our ancestors of faith important? Why were they included in the Bible? Why would you tell stories of individual family members as a way of learning about your history? These are only a few of the many interesting questions that we must ask when we begin to read the stories of the patriarchs of ancient Israel.

The first thing to notice about Genesis 12–50, besides the fact that it covers a great deal of material, is that this really reads like a collection of short stories. Each of these sections has a clear beginning and a clear ending. When the Bible was divided into chapters and verses (much later than the original manuscripts, of course, which have no such numbers) it was easy to divide Genesis into chapters because the stories easily divide into units.

This is the reason stories about the main characters in Genesis are often referred to as "cycles" of stories: they read very much like a series of short stories all based around prominent central characters which were gathered together into one cycle. When Genesis is looked at in this way, an interesting aspect of the book becomes surprisingly clear. Look at the chapters in which the main characters of Genesis appear. The total chapters are in parenthesis:

- Abraham—Chapters 12–23, 25 **(13)**
- Isaac—Chapters 24, 26–27 **(3)**
- Jacob—Chapters 28–35, 49 **(9)**
- Joseph—Chapters 37–48, 50 **(12)**

Who are the dominant people in the book of Genesis? Abraham, certainly, but second to him is Joseph, followed by Jacob. Isaac is more like a transitional figure without a great deal of tradition surrounding his life and adventure. This section of the text focuses the most attention on the patriarchs that the authors of Genesis wrote the most about.

It is also important to look at the roles women play in these **story cycles**. Women play a much more significant role in these ancestor stories than they do in many other later portions of the Old Testament.

Dating Ancestor Stories

One way those who closely study the Bible know that the book of Genesis was written much later

patriarchs—Male rulers, elders, or leaders. The patriarchs of faith of Israel are Abraham, Isaac, and Jacob.

story cycles—The series of short stories in Genesis that are centered around a particular character or group of characters. These cycles are collections of different stories which sometimes duplicate one another.

STORIES FOR THE JOURNEY

ANCESTORS OF FAITH

Bell-Ringers

1. Ask the students to share one brief story about one of their ancestors with a partner. Call on two or three students to share their stories in front of the entire class.

2. Quiz the students on their reading. Ask the following questions:
   - Why do we tell stories of ancestors? (Accept all reasonable answers.)
   - Why would you tell stories of individual family members as a way of thinking about your history? (Accept all reasonable answers.)
   - Which two patriarchs appear most in the book of Genesis? (Abraham and Joseph)
   - What literary devices are used to show that the events in Genesis were written about much later than they happened? (The phrase "to this day" and other such phrases are used.)
   - What name does the (J) source use for God? (Yahweh)
   - What name does the (E) source use for God? (Elohim)

CHAPTER 3

Teaching Approaches

1. Arrange to display several books that the students might easily be able to date to the approximate year based on their content. For example, a book about United States' presidents through Ronald Reagan's presidency. Or, a book about the pro football Super Bowls through a certain past season. Call on volunteers to guess the date of the book. *Optional*: Play video samples of motion pictures. Have the students try to date the story being told based on current events mentioned, the type of technology displayed (e.g. rotary phones).

2. Connect the previous exercise with how those who study the Bible are able to date the stories of Genesis.

3. Cover the next two subsections—Duplication of Ancestor Stories and Formation and Arrangement of Ancestor Stories—together. Point out that some of the differences between two accounts of the same story may simply be due to a different literary style. The more detailed response is that there are two different collections of stories preserved in Genesis. Explain more about the "J" (Jahweh) and "E" (Elohim) sources. Then have the students identify the following passages either from a J source or from an E source.
   - Genesis 12:10–20 (J)
   - Genesis 20:1–13 (E)
   - Genesis 16:1–14 (J)
   - Genesis 21:8–21 (E)

Help the students to understand how to identify these passages based on their different names for God.

---

than the events it describes is by the phrase "of today" or "to this day" that is included after several of its short lessons. For example:
- He is the ancestor of the Moabites *of today* (Gn 19:37).
- He called it Shibah; hence the name of the city, Beersheba, *to this day* (Gn 27:33).
- That is why, *to this day*, the Israelites do not eat the sciatic muscle that is on the hip socket, inasmuch as Jacob's hip socket was struck at the sciatic muscle (Gn 32:32).

This type of phrase is not entirely unique to Genesis. For instance, the book of Joshua includes similar references, including:
- . . . [they] piled a great heap of stones over him, which remains *to the present day* (Jos 7:25b-26).

The phrase "to this day" or something similar indicates that the writer of these words is living at a time much later than the time the stories themselves occurred. The way these stories read, it is almost as if the author is sharing the incident with listeners and then pointing to a heap of stones, or a tree, or to a group of people and explaining how the story relates to what they see.

There are other interesting phrases in Genesis that suggest that these stories were written down much later than the events they describe. For example, look at these two verses, paying special attention to the parts in italic writing:

Abram passed through the land as far as the sacred place at Sheckhem, by the terebinth of Moreh. *(The Canaanites were then in the land.)* (Gn 12:6)

The following are the kings who reigned in the land of Edom *before any king reigned over the Israelites* (Gn 36:31).

These verses sound like they were written long after the events they are describing. In fact, Genesis 36:31 could not have been written before the first king in Israel, and therefore can be no older than roughly 1020 B.C. which is hundreds of years (if not a thousand) *after* the times that Abraham may have lived.

Duplication of Ancestor Stories

The ancestor stories provide many clues as to how the authors arranged the particular stories and why certain information was included in the stories.

First of all, we mentioned that they come to us in cycles of short stories. Second, there are a number of these stories that are told twice—in almost the same way. Note, for example, that Abraham tells Sarah to "Tell them you are my sister" once in Genesis 12:13 and again in Genesis 20:12. The same story is used by Isaac regarding his wife Rebekah in Genesis 26:7–11. In another duplication of stories, Abraham sends Hagar into the desert, not only in Genesis 16:5–14, but again in 21:8–21.

Sometimes, however, the stories offer differing facts or explanations. One famous example occurs in Genesis 21:31 and 26:33 where there are two *different* explanations for how the village of Beer-Sheba received it's name. In the first it was because Abimelech and Abraham took an oath there. In the latter, the naming had to do with the discovery of water at the location.

What might account for these "double appearances" of stories, or apparent contradictions between them? Simply a literary style? Or did the ancient writers simply not pay that much attention to such editorial discrepancies? Actually, there is even more to it that that.

Formation and Arrangement of Ancestor Stories

There is strong evidence that these stories were told and re-told over a long period of time. Some of them contain a little explanation as to why a city remains so named or a pile of stones is still in place "to this day" (at least on "the day" that the author told the story). Biblical scholarship

has concluded that these were originally oral stories, which were probably passed on by word of mouth long before they were ever written down in the form in which we have them today. This understanding leads us to at least two obvious questions:
- ◆ Why have these particular stories been preserved?
- ◆ What is important in each of these stories?

Furthermore, these stories were then gathered up in groups which became the cycles or sections in Genesis 12–50. But was there originally more than one group of these stories? There is another mysterious detail about these stories—especially the stories told twice—to consider.

When there are two versions of the same story, the two different versions always use a different name for God. This is somewhat difficult to spot in some English translations of the Bible, but in most good translations, the name for God—"Yahweh"—will be translated consistently as either "Lord" or "Lord God."

Meanwhile, another tradition used a more generic name for Israel's God—*Elohim*—which is usually translated simply "God." Go back and look through those two Abraham stories that are repeated (Gn 12:10–20 and Gn 20:12; Gn 16:5–14 and Gn 21:8–21) and notice that the "Lord" is in one of the two versions, while "God" is always in the one.

This famous clue involving the use of different words for God, combined with many of the other observations that we have pointed out, has led to a popular theory about the origins of the Bible. The basic idea is that there were originally *two* different "collections" of early stories and traditions. One version of these stories consistently used "Yahweh" as the name for God. It is often suggested that this is the older of the two collections. This material was called the "*J*" *source* or "*J*" *document* because the letter "J" is used for "Jahweh," the German spelling of Yahweh (German scholars first proposed the theory). The other collection of stories used "Elohim" as the name for God. The Elohim material was designated the "*E*" *source* or "*E*" *document*.

At some point in Israelite history these two sources were brought together (either as written sources, or as oral traditions that were remembered in different ways in different places) and when they were brought together, some of the stories were repeated.

It is an interesting question, however, to ask why these ancient editors and writers decided to keep both versions of some of these stories in the collection. Why *two* versions of the Creation? Why *two* versions of Abraham telling Sarah, "Tell them you are my sister!"? There is no clear answer to this good question, but two possibilities strongly suggest themselves.

First, all of these stories in the book of Genesis must have been treasured stories among the people who told them and knew them. It would be hard to give up a story that is traditional, and told in a way that people were used to. When stories were brought together to form a common tradition, different groups of people would probably be rather insistent that *their* version be included. Furthermore, sometimes the separate versions of the same story have slightly different messages—and perhaps both messages were considered to be significant and important.

However, a more popular theory is that the "E" source was actually added to the "J" source as a kind of commentary—perhaps working out some perceived difficulties of the "J" versions. Notice, for example, that Abraham is much nicer to Hagar in Genesis 21, the "E" version, than he is in Genesis 16, the older "J" version. Perhaps the editors added the second version so that we don't have such a negative, uncaring picture of

73

STORIES FOR THE JOURNEY

4. Expand on the exercise above. Have the students begin on the Journal Assignment on page 75. Call on students to explain why they think the two stories they have chosen were each included in the Bible.

5. Point out the Learn by Doing activity on pages 84–85, and have the students determine which one they will do. Provide the following website addresses that may help the students in researching information about their families:
- www.ancestry.com
- www.onegreatfamilytree.com
- www.allvitalrecords.com
- www.genealogy.com

Explain that this assignment will be due at the time of the Chapter Test.

Background Information
Names for God in Scripture
God has no personal name. The following are three ways God is referred to in Scripture:
- *El, Elhoim* Originally the Canaanites had a god named El, the source of all other gods and creatures. Elhoim is the pural form of El.
- *El Shaddai* In Genesis, God is often designated as El Shaddai, or "God Almighty." The term "Shaddai" may have meant "God of the mountain" or "God of the open wastes." Refer to Genesis 17:1, 28:3, 35:11, 43:14, 48:3, and 49:25.
- *Yahweh* The "J" author in Genesis used Yahweh to address God. In Scripture, the word appears as "YHWH." In Hebrew, the word probably is some form of "to be."

Chapter 3

4. **Homework Assignment**:
   - Write answers to the Review and Reflection questions, page 74.
   - Complete the Journal Assignment that was assigned during class time.
   - Read "Abraham: Father of Faith" (pages 75–79).
   - Begin work on two assignments from this section, "Abraham's Travels" (page 76) and "God and Abraham" (page 78).
   - Continue working on the Learn by Doing activity (pages 84–85).

Abraham, the great father of the Israelites.

But we also realize that the "final form" of the text—as we have it now—is also important. So we must acknowledge that because of their inclusion in the Bible, *all* of these stories were considered to be important and *all* of these stories are inspired. As the fathers of the Second Vatican Council taught:

> But, since holy Scripture must be read and interpreted according to the same Spirit by whom it was written, no less serious attention must be given to the content and unity of the whole of Scripture, if the meaning of the sacred texts is to be correctly brought to light (*Dei Verbum*, 12).

The theories about sources or versions being combined is an attempt to understand how the present books of the Bible came about, or evolved.

The Importance of Ancestor Stories

Have you ever done any research into your family history? If not, would you like to someday? Why do you think research of this kind might be interesting? What is it about researching our "roots" that seems so fascinating for many people? Some people find that studying their family history helps them get a better idea of who they are. A follow-up point is this: If we understand more about ourselves, perhaps we can know a little more about how we should live, and the kind of people that we should try to be.

However, family history can include *both* positive and negative experiences. Sometimes we hear family stories and think, "That is a powerful story. My great grandparents worked hard so that their descendents would have a better life. I should work to improve my life too." But you might also discover some things you don't like: "My great-uncle made some of the same mistakes I am making. I want to learn from his mistakes and not repeat them." It seems clear to us that we should read the ancestor stories of Israel in both ways—to learn from the positive experiences, and remember the hard lessons from negative experiences!

Keeping in mind this information on why the ancestor stories were included in the book of Genesis, it is time to move on to the principals of these stories, the patriarchs of the Jewish faith.

REVIEW & REFLECTION

1. Which of the main characters in Genesis are most important? What evidence is there that the authors considered those characters most important?
2. How have Biblical scholars concluded that there were two sources for many of the stories that appear in Genesis?

Review and Reflection Answers

1. The most important characters in Genesis are Abraham, then Joseph, followed by Jacob. Isaac is less important. We know this because the authors of Genesis devoted more space, or attention to the major characters. They appear in more chapters.

2. We know that there are at least two sources because a number of stories are told twice, in almost the same way. Other stories flatly contradict one another.

Journal Assignment

- Choose a pair of stories from the book of Genesis that are versions of each other. Identify which story is from the J source and which is from the E source. Consider the similarities and differences between them and explain why you think both versions of the story would have been included in the Bible.

Abraham: Father of Faith

Abraham is the first patriarch of the Jewish faith. With his wife, Sarah, his descendants make up a nation of people from whom God would bring salvation. When he is first mentioned in the Bible, Abraham goes by the name Abram.

Abraham the Wanderer

Abraham is known as the "father of faith," not only for Judaism but also for Christianity and Islam. Interestingly, he is not a mighty general, a great king or ruler, or an influential leader of any kind. Rather, he is a herdsman and a wanderer.

Abraham was not native to the land of Palestine. The tradition states that Abraham was born in the ancient city of Ur in Mesopotamia and that God called him to go with his family from this familiar land "to a land that I will show you" (Gn 12:1).

Abraham's travel itinerary is anything but direct. He travels up the Tigris and Euphrates valleys to Haran, and then crosses over to the coast and travels to southern Palestine and the Negev desert, where Beer-Sheva is located. He and his family finally venture into Egypt and back again.

The Genesis account seems intent on showing that Abraham wandered throughout all of the known world. His journey

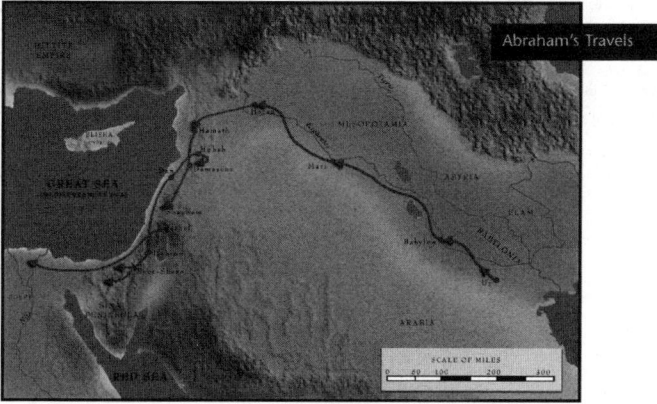

Abraham's Travels

STORIES FOR THE JOURNEY

ABRAHAM: FATHER OF FAITH

Bell-Ringer

1. Allow some arrival time for the students to complete two assignments from this section, "Abraham's Travels" (see Background Information, below) and the "God and Abraham" essay. Encourage the students to cite examples from Genesis for each element of the essay: Abraham's call by God, his faith in God, and his friendship with God. Allow time for students to share their essays with a partner. Collect and record each assignment.

Background Information
Nomads

Abraham's nomadic lifestyle was likely pastoral; that is, he and his family probably traveled with flocks of sheep and herds of goats. Donkeys were likely the form of transportation. People wandered in search of both food and water. However, Abram and his clan were not purely nomadic, as they were easily able to settle at Canaan in a more urban as well as agricultural setting. Abraham, like other nomadic people, would have traveled with his extended family. They took their entire flock with them, and any remaining family members would have been left without food and water.

CHAPTER 3

Teaching Approaches

1. Read Genesis 12:1-4. God's call of Abram blesses him and promises him that a great nation will emerge from him and his descendants. Point out that Abram heard God's call, believed it, and obeyed. Ask students to share if they have ever felt similarly "called" by God and how they responded.

2. Explain that what is extraordinary about Abraham is that he had faith in the midst of doubts. He may not have truly understood how God could make the covenant promises come true. But he chose to live as God's chosen one anyway. In this, Abraham is a good role model for us today. We, too, often have many doubts and questions. Choosing to believe in a loving, ever-present God can be quite a challenge.

THE OLD TESTAMENT

circumcision—The surgical removal of the male foreskin; it was the physical sign of the covenant between God and Abraham.

ABRAHAM'S TRAVELS

Abraham and his family lived a semi-nomadic lifestyle prevalent in the Ancient Near East. Research the following information on nomadic life during the time and place of Abraham:

- How large was a family group?
- Would more than one family group travel together?
- What distances were covered in one day on average?
- Did people walk? ride animals? use carts?
- What special arrangement for food and water would be needed for travel in arid regions?
- What common dangers did travelers face?

"Semi-nomadism" means that travelers would never travel too far from towns or off trade routes.

foreshadows the one that the Hebrew people will later make in various stages of their history. For example, his return from Egypt is a preview of the Hebrews' journey out of Egypt following the Exodus that will form the people of Israel in the stories of Moses.

Abraham's descendants also eventually journeyed far and wide in the Jewish Diaspora. And, St. Paul, another spiritual descendant of Abraham, traveled all over his known world—the Roman Empire—to share the good news of Jesus Christ, who was himself a travelling preacher teaching *all* people. God's message always "travels."

Covenant with Abraham

One of the most important elements of the Abraham traditions is the covenant God establishes with Abraham. Recall that a covenant is a solemn agreement between human beings or between God and people and that a number of such agreements are struck between important Biblical figures and God. The most important covenant in the Old Testament is God's covenant with Moses that includes the giving of the Law. There is also the covenant with Noah as mentioned on pages 67–68. God also established a covenant with King David. The *terms* of God's covenant with Abraham are laid out in Genesis 12:1–3. First, God tells what he requires of Abraham:

"Go forth from the land of your kinsfolk and from your father's house to a land that I will show you" (Gn 12:1).

God's part of the agreement comes next:

"I will make of you a great nation,
 and I will bless you;
I will make your name great,
 so that you will be a blessing.
I will bless those who bless you
 and curse those who curse you.
All the communities of the earth
 shall find blessing in you"
(Gn 12:2–3).

Besides the terms, there is typically a *sign* or *symbol* of Biblical covenants. With Moses, for example, the sign is the giving of the laws themselves. With Abraham, there are two such signs. First, his name is changed from Abram to Abraham.[3] His wife's name is changed from Sarai to Sarah. More importantly, there is the sign of **circumcision**. The tradition of practicing circumcision on all males who are Hebrews is attributed to Abraham himself. Since Abraham's heirs were to come from Abraham's own natural child (and not an adopted child, as Abraham apparently thought at first, see Genesis 15) then it seems obvious that this sign would somehow be connected to the idea of descendents or offspring. Thus, the sign was circumcision—a physical symbol on the male genital—since God's part of the covenant deals with offspring and descendents (Gn 17:1–10).

Understanding the promise made to Abraham is a crucial element for gaining a modern Christian understanding of the Bible. The Church teaches, for example, that God chose Abraham and made a covenant with him and his descendants and that by the covenant God formed his people. Abraham's faith in God's promises is considered an act of righteousness; that is the "right" attitude a person should have toward God. As St. Paul pointed out, "For what does the scripture say? Abraham believed in God, and it was credited to him as righteousness" (Rom 4:3). The Church is an extension of the covenant with Abraham, part of God's people. As the *Catechism of the Catholic Church* explains:

> The people descended from Abraham would be the trustees of the promise made to the patriarchs, the chosen people, called to prepare for that day when God would gather all his children into the unity of the Church. They would be the root onto which the Gentiles would be grafted, once they came to believe (CCC, 61).

Blessing and Threats

Another important theme in the early ancestor stories of Abraham is "blessings," which have been promised to him and his descendants by God. It is God who is the source of the blessings. But in conjunction with the blessings are related "threats," which are not of God's doing, but attributed to human weakness and doubt.

In other words, in many of these stories, even though God has blessed and made a promise, there are also threats to that promise—possibilities that the promise will not be kept. For example, Abraham is promised heirs through his wife Sarah, but she doubts that she will be able to have children because of her age. Later, Abraham himself feels threatened. Will he have to sacrifice his child? These twists in the plot and drama also serve to make the lessons learned even more memorable. The sub-sections below look at a few more of these.

External Threats to Sarah: Genesis 12:10–20 and 20

Already in Genesis 12:10–20, the future of Abraham is threatened. Sarah is taken into the household of Pharaoh. The details of this brief story are so minimal that it does not answer many questions that we have, but the fact that Sarah experiences the "captivity" of Pharaoh, and thus anticipates the later oppression of the Hebrews is surely a central idea in this brief story. But the threat is also very clear. How can Sarah bear the promised descendents of Abraham if she is in the harem of the Pharaoh? In 12:17 "the Lord struck Pharaoh and his household with severe plagues" (another reference to the later Exodus story?) so that he releases Sarah, and they are both asked to leave Egypt.

There is another example of this "external threat" in Genesis 20. There, the story is repeated with a ruler who is local in Palestine, and not from Egypt. Some of the other details are different. For example, the ruler in this version is warned by God (Gn 20:3) and therefore is able to avoid the sin of marrying a woman who is already married. Both versions of this story, however, represent "external" threats to God's promise.

Internal Threats to Sarah: Genesis 16, 21:1–21

Unlike external threats from the Egyptian Pharaoh or a local ruler, Abimelech, in two stories, in Genesis 16 and again in Genesis 21:1–21, Sarah has doubts that she is really going to be the bearer of the promised descendents of Israel. The internal threat is her own lack of faith.

In Genesis 16 she is so doubtful that she will be able to become pregnant that she asks Abraham to have a son through Hagar, an Egyptian servant of Sarah. (Hagar's son Ishmael is honored as the father of another great people, the later "Ishmaelites," who are often thought to be the Arab peoples in later popular tradition.) Then, in Genesis 21:1–21, Sarah does herself produce a son—Isaac—who is the answer to God's promise.

3. Distribute "The Faith of Abraham" (Handout 3C, page 271). The students may work individually or with a partner. Call on volunteers to summarize each passage and explain their answers.

Handout 3C Answers

TRUST	DOUBT
Genesis 12:1–9	Genesis 12:10–20
Genesis 14:1–24	Genesis 13:1–8
Genesis 15:1–21	Genesis 16:1–14
Genesis 17:1–27	Genesis 18:1–15
Genesis 18:16–33	Genesis 20:1–18
Genesis 21:1–20	
Genesis 21:21–33	
Genesis 22:1–14	
Genesis 23:1–20	

4. Review the stories of Abraham and Sarah having a child (Isaac) and read about the potential threat to Isaac (pages 78–79). Make sure that the students understand that while God provides the blessings in these situations, human weakness led to the internal and external threats. Read from the book of Genesis to highlight these blessings and threats. As a follow-up, have the students begin the Journal Assignment on page 79.

Background Information

Births and Heirs

Genesis 15:1–6 makes a significant point of Abraham's advanced age and Sarah's barrenness. Miraculous birth stories are literary devices used frequently in the Bible to indicate that the person being born will be someone important. In the days of Abraham, there were several ways that a man could have heirs. First, he could adopt one of his servants and give his possessions to that man at his death. Second, he could conceive children by his wife's servants, who acted as "surrogate wives" but whom he never married. The children of these unions would then be his heirs. And finally, the man could have children with his wife.

Chapter 3

5. **Homework Assignment:**
   - Write answers to the Review and Reflection questions 1–3, page 79.
   - Complete the Journal Assignment on page 79.
   - Continue work on the "Learn by Doing" activity.
   - Read "The Blessing of Jacob" (pages 79-81) along with the main passages dealing with Jacob's story, beginning in Genesis 27.

THE OLD TESTAMENT

GOD AND ABRAHAM

Write an essay on Abraham's relationship with God, addressing each of these ideas: his call by God, his faith in God, and his friendship with God.

But the image of Sarah's character is called into question in both stories. First, because of her doubts about God's promise (see Gn 16), and secondly because of her jealousy of Hagar and her son even though he is also an heir to Abraham. When Sarah notices Isaac playing with Ishmael, she demands that Abraham "drive out that slave and her son" (Gn 21:10). This seems very unfair. After all, Hagar had Ishmael only because Sarah suggested the plan.

What lessons could God have intended with these inspired writings? A key lesson involves Hagar herself. Hagar is a woman, a servant girl, and a foreigner, and yet the Bible shows how God's compassion extends beyond the central character of Abraham and his wife Sarah. In both Genesis 16 and Genesis 21, she is seriously mistreated, and yet God "hears her cries" and takes care of both her and Ishmael. The later Mosaic laws, and the prophet Jeremiah, will teach that God demands care for "the widow, the orphan, and the foreigner" (e.g., Dt 27:19; Jer 7:6, 22:3). The story of Hagar clearly illustrates this "justice of God." She and Ishmael *are* a "widow, orphan, and foreigner" when they are sent away by Abraham.

Threat to the Heir: Genesis 22:1–19

Another incident that clearly follows the theme of promised blessing and threat is one of the most troubling in the entire Bible. It is the recounting of Abraham's near sacrifice of Isaac in Genesis 22:1–19. What a horrible threat this story seems to be. Could God actually have asked for a *human* sacrifice? Notably, there was human sacrifice in Canaanite religious practice, and in many other religious traditions surrounding the Israelites. That an Ancient Near Eastern deity asks for human sacrifice would not have been unprecedented. It is possible that Abraham would have been sad, but not shocked, with this request so common in other religions all around him.

However, the author of Genesis presents this challenge as a "test" of human character (much in the same way Job's character is tested in the book of Job). The climax of the incident is that God provides another sacrifice—the ram dies in place of Isaac—and thus saves the child. Child sacrifice is, in the story, finally not accepted. This is one of the lessons of the story: Hebrews do not sacrifice humans to their God. Others believe that the story is about Abraham's trust that God would somehow provide a way through this test.

Christians can read the passage in yet another way. It is a profound anticipation of another "Father" who is anguished at the *human* demand that he "sacrifice a son" on the cross. God was faithful in affirming the promise—both at the mountain of Moriah in Genesis 22, and the mountain of Golgotha (see, for example, Mk 15:22). When God demanded a sacrifice in Genesis 22, he provided an alternative to the loss of Abraham's son. When the crowds that had gathered before Jesus cried, "Crucify him!"—crowds that represent all human rejections of God's plan for our lives—we were not so generous.

There are several possible explanations for the contrast between blessings and threats in these incidents. Part of this interesting interplay is probably the inspired author's art. All good stories involve a twist to the plot—a danger that the hero must overcome—in order for the story to be dramatic. There is another more important message we must consider as we try and understand God's intentions. These stories of the patriarchs teach us to trust God as the giver of all blessings, and to continue to trust him even when things seem difficult. A good story should surprise, upset, teach, and comfort. Genesis certainly does all of these and more.

REVIEW & REFLECTION

1. Use the scale and map on page 75 to estimate the distances Abraham and his family traveled before they settled in Canaan.
2. What were the terms of the covenant God made with Abraham? What signs were given as evidence of the covenant?
3. What was the significance of the covenant for the Hebrew people? What does the covenant mean to the Church today?

JOURNAL ASSIGNMENT

- Make a list of three blessings God has given you in your life. Then discuss the external and internal threats you have faced or are facing in connection with those blessings. What part of the stories of Abraham and Sarah helps to give you hope that God will overcome the threats you face?

The Blessing of Jacob

Isaac's role in the book of Genesis is smaller than that of Abraham, Jacob, and Joseph. Isaac is a transitional character between the Abraham and Jacob stories.

Rebekah loves her younger son, Jacob, while Isaac seems to prefer his first-born, Esau. In order to secure Isaac's blessing on Jacob, Rebekah instructs him to deceive his father and take his older brother's place. Isaac is fooled and Jacob gets his blessing, but then he must flee.

The familiar story of Genesis 27 begins the stories of Jacob, all of which involve one form of trickery or another. In a sense, then, the figure of Rebekah and the deception she introduces really sets up the incidents involving Jacob.

Jacob and Laban: Trickery and Social Justice

Genesis 27–28 tells of Jacob's travels to the family of Laban, the brother of Rebekah. When Jacob meets Laban's daughter Rachel in Genesis 29, he promptly falls in love. Seeing an opportunity here (apparently living by clever strategy *was* common in Rebekah's family!), Laban hires Jacob as a worker in order to help Jacob pay the bride-price to marry Rachel. After seven years of labor as a Hebrew

STORIES FOR THE JOURNEY

THE BLESSING OF JACOB

Bell-Ringers

1. Have the students work in small groups of four or five and develop a short skit that depicts a common (good-natured) trick that peers play on one another. For example, putting a funny sign on someone's back, getting someone to mistake salt for sugar, or giving a new player phony directions on team rules. After a short time to practice, call on the groups to present their skits before the class.

2. Continue on the theme of trickery. Ask:
   - How did Rebecca and Jacob trick Isaac? (They tricked him into giving Jacob, the younger son, the blessing intended for Esau.)
   - How does Jacob get what he deserves by being tricked himself? (Laban tricks him into marrying Leah, the older daughter, and then working another seven years for Rachel, the woman he loves.)
   - How does Laban get what he deserves by being tricked? (Jacob and Rachel leave, taking with them many sheep and goats as well as stolen household items.)
   - What lesson do you think we are to learn from these stories of trickery? (Help the students see that honesty is better than trickery. What goes around, comes around. Also, God continues to carry out his covenant promise despite human faults and sins. God doesn't call perfect people; he calls sinners. Despite the obstacles we put up, God can always find a way to accomplish what is best for us.)

Review and Reflection Answers

1. Approximately 1400 miles.

2. God promises to make Abram a great nation and bless him. Abram promises to go to the land God will show him. Abraham's descendants and the circumcision of males are signs of this covenant.

3. Abraham's covenant with God meant that the Hebrews, the descendants of Abraham, had a covenant with God also. They were God's chosen people. Today, the Church is an extension of the covenant with Abraham. We are the new people of God.

Chapter 3

Teaching Approaches

1. Summarize the text section "Jacob and Laban: Trickery and Social Justice" (pages 79–80). Have the students re-read Genesis 31:38–42. Ask the students to describe what they think is the religious message here. Should the reader admire or be embarrassed by the series of tricks and subtle plays in this story?

2. Continue the discussion. Direct the students to read Genesis 33:4–9. Point out the importance of forgiveness in the Jacob stories. Isaac is challenged to forgive Rebecca and Jacob for deceiving him. Esau is challenged to forgive Jacob for stealing his inheritance. Jacob is challenged to forgive Laban for tricking him. And in the end, Laban is challenged to forgive Jacob for outsmarting him. Ask:
   - Why was forgiveness and reconciliation important in family relationships in the Old Testament? (People lived in family groups and depended on one another for survival.)
   - Why is forgiveness so important in family relationships today? (Accept all reasonable answers.)

THE OLD TESTAMENT

"slave" (remember the laws regarding the freeing of slaves in Exodus 21 and Deuteronomy 15), Laban allows Jacob to marry Rachel. But at the night time wedding, his bride is covered with a wedding veil, and Jacob does not realize until the next morning the trick that Laban had played on him involving Rachel's older sister Leah:

> In the morning Jacob was amazed: it was Leah! So he cried out to Laban: "How could you do this to me! Was it not for Rachel that I served you? Why did you dupe me?" "It is not the custom in our country," Laban replied, "to marry off a younger daughter before an older one. Finish the bridal week for this one, and then I will give you the other too, in return for another seven years of service with me" (Gn 29:25–27).

But the trickery visited upon Jacob comes back to haunt Laban. After the second seven year stint to earn again the price of marrying Rachel,[4] Jacob thought up a few tricks of his own. He agrees to yet another seven year period of service to Laban, taking as his wages only the speckled, spotted, or streaked sheep and goats in Laban's flock at the end of that time (see Gn 30). Laban thinks that this is terrific arrangement, and to further ensure his success in the deal, he immediately removes all but the solid-colored sheep and goats to prevent the imperfectly colored ones from breeding and reproducing more like themselves and thus become sheep that would go to Jacob. But Jacob works some interesting "magic" in Genesis 30:37–40 showing striped sticks to the sheep as they mate and thus causing them to produce striped or speckled young (obviously modern readers aren't intended to press the science of this story too hard!).

At the end of six years working for the flocks, Jacob's flock of "speckled" sheep and goats is huge, and he is a wealthy man. He has served Laban for fourteen years and is ready to return home, especially as Laban's sons are not pleased at the success Jacob has had in increasing his flocks from among their father's. Finally, when Jacob, Rachel, and Leah decide that it is time to make a quick getaway from the house of Laban, Rachel steals some valuables to add to the humiliation. When Laban confronts Jacob about his rapid departure and the theft, the speech that follows indicates that Jacob considered his own trickery to be justice for Laban's foul play (*Read Genesis 31:38–42*). As readers, we are left to wonder whether or not we should admire or be embarrassed by the series of tricks and subtle plays in the stories of Rebekah, Jacob, Rachel, and Leah. Meanwhile, Jacob takes his large family of wives, children, and possessions and begins his return to Canaan.

Jacob's Return to Canaan

The next stories about Jacob concern his reconciliation with his own family. After leaving the land of Laban, Jacob must travel through the lands of Esau, and he is terribly afraid that his brother still harbors great anger at being betrayed when they were young men. He even has dreams of conflict in Genesis 32:22–32, an unusual story of Jacob's "wrestling with God" at Jabbok with a messenger of God who is in the form of a man.

Rachel

Background Information

Inheritance Customs

Inheritance customs in Old Testament times stated that all of a father's possessions would pass on to his oldest son. The man's daughters and younger sons would not receive anything, although it would be the oldest son's responsibility to look after them. Although Jacob had one daughter, named Dinah, she never is considered one of the twelve tribes of Israel. There are several possible reasons for this custom. First, by passing on the entire inheritance to one son, the father ensured that wealth remained in the family. The next generation would not have to start over. Second, the father ensured that family members would continue to relate to one another and rely on one another after his death. It was a way to keep family members dependent on one another and close together.

The Name "Israel"

In the course of Jacob's struggle with a messenger of God in Genesis 32:22–32, Jacob is given a new name, as Abraham before him was given a new name.

When Jacob had subdued the messenger, the man asked him his name:

He answered, "Jacob." Then the man said, "You shall no longer be spoken of as Jacob, but as Israel, because you have contended with divine and human beings and prevailed" (Gn 32:28–29).

The origins of **Israel** are related to the verb **sara** ("struggle") and the first syllable of **Elohim**, that is, "God."

To prepare for the meeting with Esau, Jacob sends gifts to his brother to appease his expected anger. In the end, however, Jacob's gifts are more than matched by Esau's forgiveness. Their reconciliation is one of the most striking examples of reconciliation and peacemaking in the Bible.

Read Genesis 33:4–9.

Jacob had stolen the blessing intended for the firstborn, his brother Esau. When Jacob acknowledges his debt by sending gifts, Jacob finally says that he gives Esau a "blessing." Justice was done. Esau had cause to be angry, but Jacob repents and bows to his brother. Jacob's willingness to engage in the traditional forms of peacemaking leads to reconciliation with Esau, who lives in Seir. Jacob is able to remain in Canaan.

It could be argued that these stories represent the hope that Israel can at times live in peace with their neighbors, especially the Edomites, who are traditionally seen as descended from Esau. Edom was a nation across the Jordan River, and in the southern part of what is today the country of Jordan. The Edomites are often portrayed in the Bible as a people at war with Israel.[5] In this case, Jacob is able to humble himself, ask for forgiveness, and even offer compensation for past injustices, all in the name of making peace. Part of the power of this story is to suggest that if Jacob and Esau can reconcile, even peace between nations is possible.

REVIEW & REFLECTION

1. How did Rebekah and Isaac serve to introduce the more important figure of Jacob in Genesis 25:19 and Genesis 27?
2. What possible religious message is there in the stories of Rebekah's, Jacob's, and Laban's trickery?

JOURNAL ASSIGNMENT

- What are aspects of the relationships between the characters in these stories that remind you of your own family or of families that you know? What lessons about family relationships can you draw from these stories?
- Put yourself in Esau's place. What is it that convinces you to be reconciled with your brother?

---

3. Ask the students to summarize what happened when Esau and Jacob finally met after many years of separation. Include in the discussion the importance of the sacrament of Penance for Catholics today (see *CCC*, 1385, 1395, 1446, 1484).

4. **Homework Assignment**:
   - Write answers to Review and Reflection questions 1–2, page 81.
   - Complete both Journal Assignments on page 81. For the second entry, you may wish to write a first person account in Esau's voice.
   - Read "Joseph in Egypt: Foreshadowing the Exodus" (pages 82–84). Read Genesis 37–50.
   - Continue to work on the Learn by Doing exercise. Make sure to make arrangements with your teacher if your presentation will involve any extra time or details (e.g., a presentation given by a grandparent).

Review and Reflection Answers

1. Rebekah and Isaac were the parents of Jacob. Rebekah favored Jacob, even though he was the younger brother. So she tricked Isaac into giving him his blessing (which should have gone to Esau.) Rebekah and Isaac are transitional characters. Their story explains why the genealogy of the Israelites continued through Jacob rather than Esau.

2. A possible message is that God's will prevails; God's plan is carried out despite human foibles and trickery. God is the one in charge, not people.

CHAPTER 3

JOSEPH IN EGYPT: FORESHADOWING THE EXODUS

Bell-Ringer

1. Play one or two musical selections from video or DVD recording of the musical *Joseph and the Amazing Technicolor Dream Coat*. Ask the students to concentrate on the lyrics of the song(s).

2. From their reading of Genesis 37–50, ask them to brainstorm several adjectives to describe Joseph (e.g., creative, witty, conniving, callous, merciful, compassionate, etc.). Record their suggestions on the board or overhead. Then, ask: "What are some ways you identify with Joseph?"

Teaching Approaches

1. Choose five to ten volunteers to stand in a line across the front of the classroom. Begin a summary of the Joseph story from Genesis 37. Introduce Joseph as the preferred son of Jacob. Retell the story of Joseph through his dream about his brothers (Gn 37:5–8). Then, have the first person in line continue telling the story of Joseph from where you left off. At a certain point, have the next person in line continue the story. Keep going until the entire Joseph story (Gn 37–50) is told.

2. Offer teaching on the historically verifiable parts of the Joseph story (see pages 82–83).

3. Refer to the separate feature, "Parallels Between Joseph & Other Biblical Stories" (page 82). Have the students meet in pairs and compare Daniel 2–3; 6 with Genesis 39–40. Ask:
   - What religious message is being conveyed?" (God is always with us, helping us face diversity and trial.)

   Next, have the students work alone or with a partner to graphically and colorfully illustrate one or more of their favorite verses in the canticle of the three young men in Daniel 3:52–90.

4. With this lesson, the students conclude their in-depth study of the book of Genesis. Refer to the feature "Genesis in Context" (page 83) to help summarize the lessons in this chapter.

5. Have the students work on the Journal Assignment (page 84) in class. Point out the difference between the two reconciliations. Jacob, who offended Esau, seeks his brother's compassion and forgiveness. Joseph was the one offended by his brothers (sold into slavery), yet it is he who initiates the reconciliation.

weather changes than was the more fragile agricultural economy of Palestine.

Furthermore, there is little indication that there was much concern for the general well-being of the wider population, beyond the Pharaoh's religious responsibility to maintain good relations with the Egyptian gods, thereby "guaranteeing" the productivity of the land. It is hard to know, frankly, whether the Joseph narrative is based on an ancient Hebrew admiration for the achievements of Egypt, or resentment of Egyptian dominance (and frequent interference) in the affairs of the Palestine economy. One question to consider is whether we are meant to admire Joseph's role in Egyptian dominance, or like Jacob's trickery, question his judgment.

Finally, however, the Joseph stories set the stage for the main event of the Old Testament: the formation of the people of Israel by their Exodus experience and their efforts to carve out a life for themselves in Canaan. The book of Genesis concludes with these words and a request made by Joseph to his brothers:

"I am about to die. God will surely take care of you and lead you out of this land to the land that he promised on oath to Abraham, Isaac and Jacob." Then, putting the sons of Israel under oath, he continued, "When God thus takes care of you, you must bring my bones up with you from this place" (Gn 50:24–25).

These verses and words of Joseph lead the journey to the study of the book of Exodus.

Genesis in Context

The stories of the patriarchs Abraham, Isaac, and Jacob, as well as the long narrative of Jacob's son, Joseph, are important because they were so relevant to the Jews who told and read them years later. For example, imagine how the Joseph stories (and also the book of Daniel) provided hope and consolation to the Jews living as a minority in the Babylonian, Persian, Hellenistic, or Roman empires from 587 B.C. to the time of Christ.

Also, imagine how Jews living in exile would understand the famous tricks and deceitfulness of Jacob or the chicanery of the other characters in these stories—Rebekah and her daughters-in-law Rachel and Leah. If the clever strategies of Jacob and the others were read in the context of being a Hebrew living in Babylon (book of Daniel), Susa (book of Esther), or Nineveh (book of Tobit), then Jacob's behavior takes on a different meaning. In the context of the oppressive political and social conditions of living as a minority in a dominant empire, perhaps Jacob's strategies were taken as clever ploys of an oppressed people who were trying to survive. Stories read in different settings sometimes sound very different indeed.

REVIEW & REFLECTION

1. How are the Genesis chapters about Joseph different from the preceding story cycles of Abraham and Sarah; and Jacob, Leah, and Rachel?
2. What historical evidence is there to support the Biblical story of Joseph?

6. As time allows, have the students offer their presentations assigned in the Learn by Doing exercise. Allow three to five minutes for each oral summary of their work.

7. **Homework Assignment**:
   - Answer Review and Reflection questions 1–2, page 83.
   - Complete the Journal Assignment. (See note on the Journal Assignment in no. 5, above).
   - Read "Further Reflections," page 84.
   - Complete the Learn by Doing assignment.

Review and Reflection Answers

1. Instead of a series of short stories, Joseph is really an extended single story with drama and character development.

2. At this time in history, the Hyksos invaded Egypt and became the country's leaders. These foreign rulers would have been open to Joseph and his family, and would have allowed him to advance in political power.

Chapter 3

REVIEW PERIOD

Bell-Ringer

1. Remind the students that in the Old Testament, God gradually reveals himself to mankind. Ask students to share several examples of how God has gradually revealed himself in their own personal lives.

Teaching Approaches

1. Summarize with the students what the book of Genesis teaches us about creation. Print the summary on the board or overhead. For example:
   - **God created and loves all things.**
   - **God created all things good.**
   - **We have a responsibility to take care of the earth and one another.**
   - **Humans, while not perfect, have dignity because they are made in God's image.**

2. Call on the remaining students to present their Learn by Doing projects to the class. (Make sure to schedule presentations by grandparents and other relatives at a convenient time.)

3. Offer a practice quiz on the chapter material by asking the students to define the vocabulary words (listed below) and by dictating to them some or all of the Review Questions from this chapter.

Vocabulary Words

ancestor—any person to whom you are related by blood who comes before you on a family tree.

angel—a spiritual, personal, and immortal creature, with intelligence and free will, who glorifies God and serves as God's messenger. Satan was at first a good angel, but along with other devils, they became evil through their own choices.

circumcision—the surgical removal of foreskin; it was the physical sign of the covenant between God and Abraham.

evolution—the scientific theory which proposes that current forms of life developed gradually out of earlier ones.

covenant—a binding and solemn agreement between human beings or between God and his people, holding each to a particular course of action.

myths—symbolic stories that express a spiritual truth or a basic belief about God.

paganism—the profession of no religion.

THE OLD TESTAMENT

JOURNAL ASSIGNMENT

- When Joseph reveals his identity to his brothers in Egypt, he attempts to reassure them that he does not intend to seek revenge on them. Read his explanation in Genesis 45:4–13. How is this moment of reconciliation different from Jacob's reconciliation with Esau?

Further Reflections

In the beginning, God created the heavens and the earth. God gave a beginning to all that exists. He alone is the Creator. All of creation depends on God who gives it being.

Creation reveals the common creative action of the Son and the Holy Spirit, inseparably one with the Father. The first creation story describes a "mighty wind" that swept over the created waters.

There is great mystery in God's creation, revealed in the creation stories of Genesis.

For example, he creates by wisdom and love. God did not need to create. Nor was the world created from blind chance or fate. Creation stems from God's free will—he wanted to share his wisdom, being, and goodness with his creation.

Also, God creates "out of nothing." God was able to make his light shine in the darkness (see Gn 1:3).

God creates an ordered and good world. Human beings are made in the "image of God" and are called to enjoy a personal relationship with God:

God created man in his image;
in the divine image he created him;
male and female he created them
(Gn 1:27).

God is infinitely greater than his works of creation. Yet, God is present to each part of his creation in the deepest and most intimate way. God never abandons his creation. Rather, he "at every moment, upholds and sustains them in being, enables them to act and brings them to their final end" (CCC, 301).

Though God created man in his image and friendship, man's freedom opened the door to the possibility of his turning from God and being mastered by sin. The eating of the forbidden fruit by Adam and Eve was the original sin of humanity.

Besides the stories of creation, the book of Genesis tells of the famous ancestors of the People of God, Israel, including Abraham and his wife Sarah. The Israelites will come together as a people based on their experience of the Exodus from Egypt. The story of Joseph in Egypt previews the Exodus experience.

Finally, God reveals himself in many ways. As all humans are ordered to God and destined to life in God, the Hebrews shared in the revelations of their God from their surrounding neighbors in the land of Canaan.

When the Hebrews return to Canaan after the Exodus from Egypt, a shared allegiance is maintained with the Canaanites, though God's covenant with Israel will ultimately make them God's Chosen People.

Learn by Doing

Christians are descendants of Abraham. The patriarchs of faith prepared for the time when "God would gather all his children into the unity of the Church" (CCC, 60). Spend some time learning about your own ancestors of Christian faith. Do one or more of the following:
- Locate the baptismal records of your grandparents by contacting (via Internet, mail, or phone) the parish where they were baptized. Record information like date, place, name, and godparents.

Chapter 3
Parish Religious Education Adaptation

- A one- to two-hour lesson plan for covering Chapter 3 in a parish religious education setting is offered at **avemariapress.com**. See pages 14–15 of the Introduction for explanation on how to organize the plan to fit your schedule.
- The lesson plan requires the students to read Chapter 3 prior to coming to class and to do the Chapter 2 Review Puzzle, page 268 of the TWE.

- Write a report on how the Christian faith originally came to the nation(s) of your ancestors.
- Write a short essay or produce an audio or video presentation that shares what you learned about God and faith from one of your relatives.
- Trace your family's history on an ancestry site on the World Wide Web.
- Develop a display with religious artifacts that are important to your family. Tell why they are so.
- Arrange for a relative to tell his or her "story of faith" in a presentation to your classmates.

Called to Prayer

How wonderful, O Lord, are the works of your hands!
The heavens declare your glory,
    the arch of the sky displays your handiwork
In your love you have given us the power
    to behold the beauty of your world robed in all its splendor.
The sun and the stars, the valleys and the hills,
    the rivers and the lakes all disclose your presence.
The roaring breakers of the sea tell of your awesome might,
    the beast of the field and the birds of the air bespeak
        your wondrous will.
In your goodness you have made us able to hear
    the music of the world.
The voices of the loved ones reveal to us that You are in our midst.
A divine voice sings through all creation.
                —Traditional Jewish Prayer

Notes

1. http://www.nationalgeographic.com/blacksea/ax/frame.html
2. Some modern Christians in parts of the Developing World still use "Babylon" to refer to powerful or oppressive governments (e.g. in Reggae music from Jamaica this is a common theme).
3. There is lots of speculation about the meaning of the actual words Abraham and Sarah. Does the extra syllable from "Abram" to "Abra-ham" derive from a word that refers to the sounds of many peoples, a multitude—thus the "sounds" of his many descendants? In any case, name changing was clearly a sign of submission to one who is more powerful (note how Nebuchadnezzar changes Mattaniah's name in 2 Kings 24:17).
4. Polygamy was still practiced in the time of the Patriarchs, though God's forming of an exclusive covenant with Israel prepared the Chosen People for the exclusiveness and indissolubility of married love (see CCC, 1609–1611).
5. The prophet Amos, for example, has little good to say about the Edomites (Am 1–2) who were apparently slave traders. Also, Psalm 139 expresses anger at Edomite participation in the destruction of Jerusalem. There may be a political purpose to the story of Jacob's reconciliation with Esau.

---

patriarchs—male rulers, elders, or leaders. The patriarchs of faith of Israel are Abraham, Isaac, and Jacob.

story cycles—the series of short stories in Genesis that are centered around a particular character or group of characters. These cycles are collections of different stories which sometimes duplicate one another.

4. **Prayer Service:** Play a song that praises God in its lyrics and music (e.g., "Canticle of the Son" by Marty Haugen). Call on students to offer spontaneous prayers of thanks for the blessings in their lives. Conclude by praying together the Jewish prayer of praise under Called to Prayer (page 85).

5. **Homework Assignment:**
   - Study for the Chapter 3 Test.

CHAPTER 3 TEST

Teaching Approaches

1. Administer the Chapter 3 Test (online at **avemariapress.com**). Allow the students to use separate paper or the back of the test paper to write their responses to the short answer essay.

2. If there is time after the test, consider playing one of the videos (see page 68 of the TWE) related to the material in this chapter.

3. Ask the students to preview Chapter 4. Or, review some of the lessons from the Catholic Handbook of Faith (pages 259–280 of the Student Text).

Chapter 3 Test Answers

Part 1: Fill-in-the-blanks: 1. The "father of faith" for Judaism, Islam, and Christianity, __(Abraham)__ was the spouse of __(Sarah)__, and the father of __(Ishmael)__ and __(Isaac)__; 2. Rachel was the daughter of __(Laban)__, the sister of __(Leah)__, the wife of __(Jacob)__, and the mother of __(Joseph)__; 3. __(Jacob)__ was the younger twin of __(Esau)__; he was his mother, __(Rebekah)__'s, favorite; he married __(Leah)__ first and then her sister, __(Rachel)__, and had twelve sons whose descendants were the twelve tribes of Israel; 4. Although she was not Abraham's wife, __(Hagar)__ was the mother of his first son, __(Ishmael)__.

Part 2: True or False: 5. 0; 6. +; 7. +; 8. 0; 9. +; 10. 0; 11. 0; 12. +; 13. +; 14. 0;
Part 3: Matching: 15. c, g; 16. a, f; 17. i; 18. b, h; 19. d, e;
Part 4: Short Answer: 20. Answers should include an explanation of the different names for God in the J and E sources, the need to satisfy different groups of people when stories were combined, the significance and importance of slightly different messages in repeated stories, the possibility that the E material was added as a commentary on the J material.

Introducing Chapter 4

The Exodus event is an important step in God's divine plan; it moves humanity closer to the time when God will "be everything to everyone" (1 Cor 15:28). The word *exodus* comes from a word that means "exit" or "departure." The book of Exodus covers the Israelites' slavery in Egypt and ends with their journey— during the reign of Rameses II (1279–1212 B.C.)—to independence in a new land.

Exodus opens with an account of Moses' birth, infancy, and childhood—a literary device indicating that his life will be one of great importance. The next significant event is Moses' meeting with God at the burning bush (cf. Ex. 3). God shares his name with Moses: "I Am who Am," from which comes the Biblical name "Yahweh."

As further reading of Exodus teaches, what is most important to people of faith is not just knowing the name of God, but rather *how* God is known and *what* God has done and will do. The reader of Exodus learns the *how* and *what* beginning in Exodus 5 and the ten plague stories and how they lead to the Israelites' expulsion from Egypt. From these stories, two basic religious points are made: 1) God keeps his promises to his people, and 2) God is a God of liberation, not enslavement.

Exodus reinforces these two teachings by recounting other key events: the wandering of the Israelites in the desert wilderness, God's provision of food (manna) and water, and the revelation on Mount Sinai in which the Israelites receive the directions (laws) about how to live as God's People. These laws include both the Ten Commandments and the laws of Moses. As Chapter 4 explains, the laws of Moses have three sources: 1) the Covenant Code, 2) the Deuteronomic Code, and 3) the Levitical or "Priestly" Code. All three of these codes contain civil and religious laws.

The chapter also examines ways that Catholics can live according to the Ten Commandments and the laws of Moses in a modern context. One way is to practice the Beatitudes preached by Jesus in the Sermon on the Mount (cf. Mt. 5–7) as an expression of the "New Law" of the Gospel.

Chapter 4 Outline

Introduction
The book of Exodus, collected and edited at the time of the Babylonian exile, includes the miraculous release of the Hebrews from Egypt, the call of Moses, and the reception of the Law.

The Call of Moses
Yahweh reveals himself to Moses and commissions him to lead the Exodus from Egypt to the Promised Land.

The Exodus: Confrontation Followed by Escape
The Hebrews release from Egyptian captivity follows a series of ten plagues.

The Wandering of the People In the Wilderness
Exodus 15–18 features a series of the Israelite's "murmurings" or complaints against God.

The Reception of the Law at Mount Sinai
At Mount Sinai the most important covenant of the Old Testament was established with obligations for both the Israelites and Yahweh.

Three Collections of the Law
There are three different collections of the Law in the books of Moses: the Covenant Code, the Deuteronomic Code, and the Levitical ("Priestly") Code.

The Approach to the Promised Land
At the conclusion of the Torah, the Israelites approach Canaan and lead to the sequence of books known as the historical books.

Further Reflections

Background Notes for the Teacher

Exodus is the second book of the Pentateuch. Although its authorship has been traditionally ascribed to Moses, it was more likely compiled and edited in the sixth century B.C. by a priestly writer. As with the other books of the Pentateuch, the Exodus compilation consists of four ancient sources: the Yahwistic (J), Elohistic (E), Deuteronomic (D), and Priestly (P).

This book serves as an important archetype of New Testament themes. In Exodus, God leads the Israelites from slavery in Egypt to freedom; in the New Testament, Jesus leads God's People from the slavery of sin to the freedom of living as children of God. Just as Moses leads the people and becomes a great lawgiver, so Jesus leads us to God's Kingdom and gives us the new law of love. Just as the Ten Commandments and laws of Moses are ways to live as God's People, so Jesus' New Law summarizes the Mosaic law and enables us to be faithful to God's covenant with us.

The book of Exodus has two main parts: the rescue of the Israelites from Pharaoh in Egypt (Ex 1:1–15:21) and the journey from Egypt to Mount Sinai (Ex 12:37–40:38). The narrative shows us how Yahweh keeps his promises to his people and rescues them from slavery. God sustains the people throughout their wilderness trials and brings them to the sacred mountain where they receive four gifts that identify them as God's people: a leader (Moses), a law (the Ten Commandments), a temple (the desert tabernacle with its ministers and ritual), and land.

Resources

Music Suggestions: see page 99
Printed Materials: see page 95
Audiovisual Materials: see page 100
Internet Links: see page 104

CHAPTER 4

THE JOURNEY TO THE PROMISED LAND BEGINS
The Exodus and the Sinai Covenant

Relevant Teachings from Church Documents
- By the covenant God formed his people and revealed his law to them through Moses. (*CCC*, 72)
- The Old Law is the first stage of revealed law. Its moral prescriptions are summed up in the Ten Commandments. (*CCC*, 1980)
- The Law of Moses contains many truths naturally accessible to reason. God has revealed them because men did not read them in their hearts. (*CCC*, 1981)
- The Decalogue contains a privileged expression of the natural law. It is made known to us by divine revelation and by human reason. (*CCC*, 2080)
- By his covenant with Abraham (see Gn 15:18) and, through Moses, with the race of Israel (see Ex 24:8), [God] acquired a people for himself, and to them he revealed himself in words and deeds as the one, true, living God. (Vatican II, *Dogmatic Constitution on Divine Revelation*, 14)
- After the era of the patriarchs, [God] taught [Israel], through Moses and the prophets, to recognize him as the only living and true God, as a provident Father and just judge. (Vatican II, *Dogmatic Constitution on Divine Revelation*, 3)

Advance Preparations
- Prepare any handouts and overhead transparencies you plan to use with the class and obtain and view any videos or Internet resources you wish to include in your lesson plans.
- Obtain a recording of any music you wish to include in the Prayer Service (see page 113 of the TWE) or at any other point during a lesson. See Music Suggestions on page 99
- Arrange for a student, parent, or school staff person to show some home movies of his or her infancy while then describing how these formative years contributed to the kind of person he or she is now (see Bell Ringer on page 93 of the TWE).
- Arrange for a rabbi or practicing Jew to speak to the students on the symbols and practice of the Passover celebration.
- Gather together the supplies the students will need to make collages: magazines, scissors, drawing paper, and glue (see Enrichment on page 111 of the TWE).
- Have large pieces of butcher paper available for the students to do the map suggested in the Learn By Doing activity (page 109 of the Student Text).

Chapter Objectives
The students will be able to:
- summarize the chronology of the book of Exodus.
- learn about Moses through stories of his birth and childhood.
- understand more about the name and nature of God.
- explore ways to understand the ten plagues described in the book of Exodus.
- see what the "murmuring stories" tell us about the Israelites.
- understand the central importance of the Sinai Covenant in the Old Testament.
- examine ways to apply the Ten Commandments to their own lives
- differentiate between the three collections of the Law in "the books of Moses."
- appreciate how the events of the Exodus are made present in Jewish Passover celebrations and in the Eucharist.

CHAPTER 4

INTRODUCTION

Bell-Ringers

1. **Re-teach**: Print this question on the board: **What do the primeval history stories teach us about God and his will?** Have the students record their answers. Consider awarding one bonus point to the Chapter 3 Test for each correct answer.

Answers
- God's will is to create a people in his image—both male and female.
- God's will is peace, not violence. Violence is considered sinful in these stories. God creates in peace—it is humans that bring violence. The flood story suggests that God was so sickened by human violence that God regretted making humanity.
- God's will is trust and truthfulness—not the lies and deceptions of human beings in their society.
- God's will is care for creation—not destruction and exploitation.
- God's will is joyful diversity—not forced unification
- God is not impressed with how great our human material accomplishments are, but with how we care for each other, and also how we care for the created environment.

2. Introduce more of the theme of journey present in Chapter 4 in the Israelites' journey from slavery to freedom. Ask the students to think about an important journey they have made and discuss in a triad:
   - How long did the journey last?
   - Where did they go?
   - What happened first?
   - What supplies or equipment did they need to take with them?

Choose one person from each triad to summarize for the entire class the "journeys" that were discussed.

Teaching Approaches

1. Introduce the book of Exodus. You may wish to have the students turn to the introduction to Exodus in their Bibles. Highlight the principal divisions of the book outlined in the introduction. Compare this outline with the major steps offered on page 88 of the Student Text.

2. Explain how Exodus 1 is a transitional chapter that bridges the story of Joseph to Moses. Call on several good readers to read Exodus 1 aloud as the others follow along in their Bibles.

3. Refer to the stories of journeys that were shared by the students and explain further how Exodus covers an important journey made by the Israelites. The

---

THE OLD TESTAMENT

Introduction

The book of Exodus continues the story of Joseph and his brothers in Egypt where the book of Genesis leaves off. As time passed, according to the introduction in Exodus, the positive accomplishments of Joseph were forgotten. When the Israelites "became so numerous and strong that the land was filled with them" (Ex 1:7) the Egyptian leaders were concerned about them siding with Egypt's enemies. This concern is given as the reason for the enslavement of the Hebrews.

As with the other books of the Torah, the stories of Exodus were collected and edited at the time of the Babylonian Exile, about seven hundred years after the events took place. The people exiled in Babylon would certainly have understood what it was like to be held in slavery and they would have been comforted and encouraged by stories that celebrated the liberation of slaves.

Exodus is just such a recounting of events, telling of the miraculous release of the Israelites from Egypt and their journey across the Red Sea to Mount Sinai where they entered into a special covenant with God. At Mount Sinai, through Moses, God gave the Israelites the Law—the moral, civil, and worship regulations which allowed them to become a holy people.

The Ten Commandments are at the heart of the Sinai Covenant.

Hyksos—A group of non-Egyptians who came to power in Egypt between 1650 and 1500 B.C.

The *Catechism* teaches: "The 'ten words' sum up and proclaim God's law" (CCC, 2058). These are basic moral laws given by God to his people. The book of Deuteronomy quotes Moses explaining the significance of the Ten Commandments:

> These words, and nothing more, the Lord spoke with a loud voice to your entire assembly on the mountain from the midst of the fire and the dense cloud. He wrote them upon two tablets of stone and gave them to me (Dt 5:22).

The origins of the Ten Commandments and their meaning for people today will be covered in this chapter in the context of the book of Exodus. The book of Exodus follows a clear pattern. The major steps of the story are:

- The Call of Moses
- The Exodus: Confrontation Followed by Escape
- The Wandering of the People In the Wilderness
- The Reception of the Law at Mount Sinai
- The Approach to the Promised Land

Read Exodus 1
The first chapter of Exodus is largely transitional material, bridging the gap from Joseph, the last major figure in the book of Genesis, to Moses, the central figure of the book of Exodus, and in fact the entire Old Testament.

Background Information

Records of Slaves

Slavery of foreign laborers is recorded in the ancient papyri of Egypt. Among these slaves were Syrians and Canaanites (the Israelites). These slaves were involved in building projects at Pithom and Rameses. The Israelites were most likely slaves in Egypt during the New Kingdom (1550–1970 B.C.). Ramesses II reigned from 1279–1212 B.C., the time that the Exodus reportedly began. The Exodus journey took approximately forty years to complete.

THE HYKSOS—FOREIGN RULERS IN EGYPT

The Joseph stories may have been situated in a brief period of foreign rule in Egypt that occurred between 1650 and 1500 B.C. Egyptian records from that time do make reference to the rule of a people called the "**Hyksos**"—an Egyptian term for "foreigner." The Hyksos were probably not people of a distinct race, but probably the rulers among the non-Egyptian population of the time. It would have been possible for a Hebrew like Joseph to rise to a high position among the Hyksos and perhaps that explains the later enslavement of the Hebrews. All those who served and benefited from the Hyksos rule may have been punished once the Egyptian rulers regained power.

REVIEW & REFLECTION

1. When were the stories of Exodus collected and edited into the form we have today? What connection was there between the stories of Exodus and the lives of the Jews at that time?
2. What connection might there have been between the imposition of slavery on the Hebrew people in Egypt and the period of "Hyksos" rule in Egypt between 1650 and 1500 B.C.?
3. Why are the Ten Commandments the centerpiece of the Sinai Covenant?

JOURNAL ASSIGNMENT

- Ask your parents to tell you what they remember about your birth or your infant and toddler years. Try to find a story that seems indicative of the sort of person you are becoming, or that you want to be. Write the story, embellishing it a bit, if you like, until you think it tells something significant about you.

The Call of Moses

Read Exodus 2:1–10

Birth stories are rare in the Bible, but when they do occur they are usually a strong indication that the person born is going to be someone important. The book of Genesis included stories about Isaac's birth, Jacob's and Esau's, and Joseph's too. Their births were significant because of who they grew up to be.

Like people of other traditions, the Hebrews told birth stories of famous people—especially stories of previously barren women miraculously giving birth to great figures like Samson and Samuel. Such storytelling was a way of honoring the memory of a famous person, much in the same way that traditions have arisen in the United States surrounding the youth of its founding fathers; for example, George Washington ("never told a lie") and Abraham Lincoln ("read book after book by firelight").

The book of Exodus begins with the story of Moses' birth, the threat to his life from the

---

Review and Reflection Answers

1. The stories of Exodus were probably collected and edited at the time of the Babylonian exile, about seven hundred years after the events took place. The Israelites in captivity in Babylon would have identified with their ancestors who were slaves in Egypt. Just as God freed the slaves, so they could hope that God would free them and restore them to the land of Israel.
2. While the Hyksos were in power in Egypt, the Israelites would have been welcomed by the government. They could even aspire to positions of power, as did Joseph. When the Egyptians regained power and exiled the Hyksos, they would have turned against the Israelites, even making them slaves.
3. The Ten Commandments are the basic moral laws given by God to his people. These "ten words," as they are known, sum up and proclaim God's law.

THE JOURNEY TO THE PROMISED LAND BEGINS

journey starts in northeastern Egypt and ends in Canaan, the site of modern-day Israel and Palestine. Use "The Exodus Journey" (Overhead 4A, online at **avemariapress.com**) to help trace the path of the Israelites' journey from Egypt to Canaan.

4. Choose and play a video that details the geography of northeastern Egypt and the Nile (e.g., see Internet link to *National Geographic's Treasures of Egypt*).

5. Allow class time for the students to read the Introduction and short feature, "The Hyksos—Foreign Rules in Egypt" (pages 88–89). Explain further that the Hyksos pharaohs resided in Memphis and Avaris (or Tanis) from 1720–1552 B.C. They opened the borders to non-Egyptians, and allowed these non-Egyptians to rise to power in their governments. (This may be the time of Joseph's rise to power in Egypt.) In 1552 B.C., two native Egyptians from the south—Kamose and Ahmose—drove the Hyksos back to Syria-Palestine. When they became the new pharaohs, they degraded the social status of all Semites in Egypt to that of slaves.

6. **Re-teach:** Have the students read and compare Genesis 47:1–6 to Exodus 1:8–14 and note the difference in the attitudes of the pharaohs to the Hebrews in each of these passages.

7. Point out the paragraphs in the Introduction that share the significance of the Ten Commandments for people today. Explain that while many of the individual laws from the Old Testament are dietary laws, the Ten Commandments are based in the natural law and have significance for all of mankind.

8. **Homework Assignment**:
   - Write answers to the Review and Reflection questions 1–3, page 89.
   - Work on the story of your birth or early childhood. Especially focus on how this story tells what kind of person you are and are becoming. (See Journal Assignment, page 89).
   - Read "The Call of Moses" (pages 89–91) including the passages in the book of Exodus that are assigned in the text.

THE CALL OF MOSES

Bell-Ringer

1. Arrange for a student, parent, or other person known to the students (e.g., staff members) to show "home movies" of their infant years. Then have the person talk about how his or her birth and the first formative years went.

Chapter 4

2. Call on volunteers to share the stories they wrote as part of the Journal Assignment.

Teaching Approaches

1. Choose a good reader to read aloud Exodus 2:1–10. Have the other students follow along in their Bibles.

2. Distribute "Biblical Birth Stories" (Handout 4A, page 272). Organize the class in groups of five. Each student should read and summarize one of the listed scripture birth stories. Allow time. Then have the students share summaries of their stories with the group. Each person should record the others' summaries on their paper. Next, have the students compare these birth stories to the stories of Moses' birth (Ex 2:1–10). Finally, lead a brief class discussion that summarizes the groups' findings (see Background Information, below).

Enrichment: Research at least five other rules or facts about the Hebrew language. Use the Internet (www.jewfaq.org/alphabet.htm) and other sources.

---

edict of the Pharaoh, and his mother's attempts to protect him. The story of the infant Moses floating down the Nile River in a basket most likely had a long oral tradition. It is the only story that survives from his youth, but its existence in Scripture is enough to inform us that Moses' role will be an important one.

The Hebrew authors claim that Moses' name derived from the Hebrew verb *masha*—"to draw out" (Ex 2:10) though it is also strongly related to the names of Egyptian pharaohs "Thut<u>mosis</u>" or "Ah<u>mose</u>" meaning simply, "son of" or "progeny of." The special attention paid in Exodus 2:10 to the Hebrew root of the name Moses has important significance. This was the only point made in verse 10. It serves to establish Moses' Hebrew identity, despite his Egyptian upbringing, and refers both to his own being "drawn out" of the River Nile and to his efforts to draw the Hebrew people out of Egypt. At that point, the story abruptly ends, and an entirely different time in the life of Moses begins at Exodus 2:11.

View of the Nile River

Read Exodus 2:11–22

With this next episode, Moses is an adult, confronting for the first time one of the main themes of the entire Moses tradition—the slavery of the Hebrew people. While there are doubts about the exact historical details of the Moses stories, the slave economy of Egypt is quite clearly historically accurate, and is often referred to in Egyptian documents from that time. There are even ancient Egyptian writings that refer to the escape of slaves, although not in great numbers.

When Moses intervenes in two fights between Hebrew slaves and Egyptian slave masters, he immediately gets into trouble. In the first fight, Moses kills an Egyptian slave master to prevent him from beating a Hebrew slave. In the second, he is condemned by two Hebrews (who are fighting amongst themselves) for assuming that he has anything to teach them and it becomes obvious that he has been recognized as the one who killed the Egyptian in the first fight. After these episodes, he lives for years among a desert-dwelling people called the Midianites, where he marries and learns to shepherd his father-in-law's flock. It is while he is living in the desert that he receives his amazing call to be the liberator of God's people.

This short introduction to Moses suggests that violence is not going to be the way of success for him. He will not defeat the Pharaoh in a great battle, nor free the slaves by force of arms. The inspired message of these early chapters of Exodus is that a power much greater than Moses' own human attempts is necessary to settle the issue of the Hebrew's slavery. God himself must liberate his people, though Moses will be the instrument he chooses to bring this about.

Background Information

Moses' Ark

The basket in which baby Moses was put is sometimes referred to as an "ark." An ark is simply a chest or box. In this case, it was covered with tar, or pitch, to prevent water from seeping through. The story connects with other stories in the Bible. For example:

- The story of Noah's ark. (Both Noah and Moses are saved through water.)
- The story of the ark of the Covenant, a portable box the Israelites carried with them from Mount Sinai until the days of the monarchy. This ark symbolized God's protection and presence.
- The story of Jesus' baptism and the sacrament of Baptism—in which salvation comes to us through water.

The Journey to the Promised Land Begins

"I Am the One Who Is"
Read Exodus 2:23–3:23

In Exodus 3, God calls Moses to his mission. Moses meets God in a fiery bush in the desert, a bush that at first attracts Moses' attention because it does not burn though it is engulfed in flames. In Exodus 3:14, God shares his name with Moses. It is a mysterious name, translated into English as "I am who I am"—but actually built on the basic Hebrew verb "is" from which the Biblical name "Yahweh" derives. "It is a mysterious name because God is mysterious" (CCC, 206). Although Orthodox Jews do not pronounce this name (believing it to be so sacred that they must not speak it) Christians have never observed this practice, believing instead that what God has revealed is intended for our use and understanding. But that doesn't mean that there haven't been mistakes in what is to be understood (see "Does God Have A Name?" below).

What is important in the Moses tradition is not necessarily the *name* of God, but rather *how* God is known and *what* God has done and will do: "God, who reveals himself as 'I AM,' reveals himself as the God who is always there, present to his people in order to save them" (CCC, 207).

Exodus 3:15–17 presents an interesting summary of who God is by mentioning the ancestors of Israel (Abraham, Isaac, and Jacob) as well as the events that will take place—liberation from Egypt and entry into the Promised Land. This is what is really important to the Hebrews—God is known by what he does, not by special names or words.

Interestingly, even the name of Jesus communicates this fact. The name "Jesus" literally means "Yahweh Saves." Even the name of the Messiah communicates that God is known by what he *does*, not primarily by what he is *called*.

Does God Have a Name?

In Hebrew, after the tradition arose among the Jews that one should not speak Yahweh, the holy name of God, the Jewish scribes came up with a little trick to remind readers not to pronounce it by accident—especially in *public* reading of the scriptures.

In order to understand this trick, remember that Hebrew is written with consonants only, and not vowels (which are indicated, instead, by little signs above and below the consonants). What the scribes did was to take the vowel signs from the word Adonai ("Lord") and artificially put them on the consonants of "YHWH." It was not really supposed to be pronounced. Rather, it was supposed to remind the reader to say "Adonai" not "Yahweh."

At some point, the tradition was forgotten among Christians, and the word was misread, taking the consonants *and* the added vowels. This new word came out "Jehovah." This means that, contrary to what some Christians believe, "Jehovah" is *not* the "true" name of God. In fact, the opposite is true; it is a historically mistaken reading.

The traditional name for God is "Yahweh" (usually pronounced "Yah-way," but even this is partly an assumed pronunciation). Parts of this name are heard in Hebrew personal names like "YAH-shua"=Joshua/Jesus, or "Jerem-e-YAH"=Jeremiah. Also Elohim is a name for God that was widely used in the Bible, depending on the geographic region. Elohim was often thought to be more typical of northern Israelite, and Yahweh more common in southern Israel. Elohim appears in Hebrew names like "Mich-EL," "Dan-i-EL," and "Ari-EL."

---

3. Re-read Exodus 2:11–22 as needed. Point out that the surrounding cultures in the Old Testament era often thought of the gods as violent. Moses' revelation that violence is not the will of God was extremely significant. Ask the students to share examples from the news today of people who do or do not consider violence to be a part of God's will.

4. Refer to the subsection "I Am the One Who Is." Direct the students to read Exodus 2:23–3:23. Note that this title used for God is the source of the word Yahweh. Point out the feature "Does God Have a Name?" (page 91).

5. Conclude the lesson by reminding the students that the importance of God's name is overshadowed by *how* God is known and *what* Go has done and will do. This point is emphasized in Exodus 3:15–17.

6. **Homework Assignment**:
   - Begin planning and work on an assignment that come later in the chapter: the research report based on the quote of Frederick Douglass (page 98).
   - Arrage to view one of these videos: *The Ten Commandments* with Charlton Heston (or, alternatively the Disney film *The Prince of Egypt*). Think about how accurately you think the movie portrays Moses. Be prepared to share your findings at the next class session.
   - Read the "Who Does God Call?" section in the text (page 92).

Resources

Printed Materials

"Exodus, The" and "Exodus, The Book of" in *The Oxford Companion to the Bible*, ed. by Bruce M. Metzger and Michael D. Coogan. (New York, NY: Oxford University Press, 1993), pp. 209–217.

"Exodus" and "Exodus, Book of" in *Dictionary of the Bible*, ed. by John L. McKenzie, S.J. (New York, NY: Macmillan Publishing Co., Inc., 1965), pp. 255–258.

Clifford, Richard J., S.J. "Exodus" in *The New Jerome Biblical Comm*entary, ed. by Raymond E. Brown, S.S., Joseph A. Fitzmyer, S.J., and Roland E. Murphy, O.Carm. (Englewood Cliffs, NJ: Prentice Hall, 1990), pp. 44–60.

Craghan, John F. "Exodus" in *The Collegeville Bible Commentary*, ed. by Dianne Bergant, C.S.A. and Robert J. Karris, O.F.M. (Collegeville, MN: The Liturgical Press, 1989), pp. 79–114.

McCarter, P. Kyle, Jr. "Exodus" in *Harper's Bible Commentary*, ed. by James L. Mays. (San Francisco, CA: Harper & Row Publishers, 1988), pp. 129–156.

CHAPTER 4

Who Does God Call?

Bell-Ringers

1. Choose to play parts of both films assigned for homework—*The Ten Commandments* and *The Prince of Egypt*. Play the same scene (e.g., Moses' reception of the Law) from both films. Note the differences.

2. Have the students write their impressions of how Moses was portrayed in one or both films compared to how he was described in Scripture. Call on volunteers to share their impressions. Record a summary of their responses on the board or overhead.

3. Call on students to share the meaning of their last name or the names of some of their family members. Ask if any of these names actually describe the person's character.

4. Call on students who did the Enrichment assignment (page 94 of the TWE) to report their findings about the Hebrew language.

Teaching Approaches

1. **Re-teach:** Call on students to answer these questions:
   - Is Jehovah a true name of God? Why or why not? (No, Jehovah was a misread form of Yahweh.)
   - What is the meaning of the name *Jesus*? (Jesus literally means "Yahweh saves.")

2. Refer to the assigned text reading. Also, allow time for the students to read Exodus 3–4. Point out God's power in transforming what first appeared to be a flawed man into a great leader. Also point out that in the history of our nation, we, too, have had unlikely leaders. Franklin Delano Roosevelt was crippled from polio, and yet he led the United States through its worst depression and served as president for four terms. Ask the students to name leaders from their peer groups, teams, or school who have overcome impediments or flaws to become good leaders.

3. Allow time in class for the students complete the Journal Assignment (page 93). As an alternative, you may wish to allow them to use any art medium to depict the Israelite's relationship with Yahweh while on pilgrimage in the desert.

4. **Homework Assignment**:
   - Write answers to the Review and Reflection questions 1–3, page 93.
   - Read Exodus 5–11. Memorize the ten plagues and plan to review them in class.
   - Read "The Exodus: Confrontation Followed by Escape" in the text (pages 93–95).
   - Continue working on the essay previously assigned.

THE OLD TESTAMENT

Who Does God Call?

The movies love to portray great and mighty heroes. Consider the impressive figure of actor Charlton Heston playing Moses in the great film classic, *The Ten Commandments*. Even for children, Moses is portrayed as powerful and mighty, as in the animated film, *The Prince of Egypt*. How accurate are these portrayals of Moses?

Charlton Heston as Moses in *The Ten Commandments*

In fact, Exodus 3 and 4 present a very reluctant hero. Moses has four objections to being chosen. First, he wonders "who am I?" to go about rescuing an enslaved people (Ex 3:11). When God reassures him that it will be God, not Moses, doing the rescuing, Moses asks, essentially, "who are you?" (Ex 3:13). After hearing God's answer to this, Moses worries that the Israelites will not believe him, so God gives him a staff and shows him miracles that Moses can perform to convince the Israelites that God is with him (Ex 4:1-9). When Moses continues his objections, saying that he is not a good speaker, God promises to tell him everything he needs to say. At this point, Moses is running out of objections so he simply begs God to "send someone else!" (Ex 4:13). To this point, though it seems like we do not have a flattering portrait of Moses, actually we are learning much about the power of God and the value of prayer, that is, "the requesting of good things from God" (St. John Damascene as quoted in *CCC*, 2559). The *Catechism* points out:

> But in the dialogue in which God confides in him, Moses also learns how to pray: he balks, makes excuses, above all questions: and it is in response to his question that the Lord confides his ineffable name, which will be revealed through his mighty deeds (CCC, 2575).

What else can we learn from this? Who does God call? The brave and the mighty? The great generals or the powerful leaders? No. God calls the simple and timid, the questioning and the doubtful, and often the weak and the few. God calling a man like Moses reminds us of Jesus calling men like Peter and Thomas despite their weakness and doubt. Moses is the classic "anti-hero" in the sense that he does not exhibit many qualities associated with human greatness. Yet, he is *the* hero of the Old Testament!

God, it seems, does not need the mighty—only the willing. Moses finally goes, clutching a staff in his hand as a reminder that he does not go alone. The story of God's people continues in a powerful and dramatic way.

REVIEW & REFLECTION

1. Why did the original editors of the book of Exodus include the story about Moses' birth and adoption by one of Pharoah's daughters?
2. Why do the Hebrew authors have Pharoah's daughter give Moses a Hebrew name? What is the significance of the Hebrew meaning of the name "Moses?"
3. What four objections did Moses have to being sent to Egypt to free the Israelites from slavery?

JOURNAL ASSIGNMENT

- Have you ever been asked to do something that you weren't sure you could do, even though the person asking thought you could? How did you feel about being asked? How did you respond?

The Exodus: Confrontation Followed by Escape

Read Exodus 5–11

There are many interesting elements to the great story of God's conflict with Pharaoh, and the horrific events that lead up to the final release of the Hebrews from Egyptian bondage. There are also a number of interesting understandings about how these stories—which include the ten plagues—are to be read.

One common understanding of the ten plagues is that each is directed against a specific Egyptian god. But trying to match up all the plagues with known deities and their images presents problems. Consider the following:

	Plague	Egyptian God
1.	Nile turned to blood	Khnum or Hapi (god of water or the River Nile)
2.	Frogs	Heket (goddess of childbirth portrayed as frog)
3.	Lice/gnats	?
4.	Flies	?
5.	Pestilence	Hathor (god portrayed as a bull)
6.	Boils	?
7.	Hail	Seth (god of wind and storms)
8.	Locusts	Min (goddess of fertility and vegetation)
9.	Darkness	Amon-Re (Sun god)
10.	Death of Firstborn	Osiris (god of judgment or death)

Review and Reflection Answers

1. Biblical authors often told amazing birth and infancy stories about important people. Because Moses was important, it was fitting that there was some mention in the Bible about his miraculous deliverance from death as a baby.
2. The name Moses is derived from a Hebrew word that means "to draw out." But Moses is also related to the names of Egyptian pharaohs. "Mosis" means "son of." The Pharaoh's daughter may have given Moses his name to show that he, though adopted, was also a son of Pharaoh. Furthermore, the name establishes Moses' Hebrew identity and prefigures his leadership in drawing out the Hebrew people from Egypt.
3. Moses had these four objections: 1) He worried that he was the wrong person to rescue the enslaved people. 2) He did not know the name of the voice who was speaking to him. 3) He worried that the Israelites will not believe him. 4) He did not have speaking skills to get the job done.

THE JOURNEY TO THE PROMISED LAND BEGINS

THE EXODUS: CONFRONTATION FOLLOWED BY ESCAPE

Bell-Ringer

1. Call on ten students to line up before the class. Ask them to recite in order the ten plagues from Exodus 5–11. If a person misses one of the plagues, replace him or her with another student who stands in the same place. Then have the group begin again. Continue until all ten plagues are named in order.

2. Share with the students a recent news item that is weather-related (a flood, drought, earthquake, wildfire caused by lightning, hurricane, tornado, frost, etc.). Then form a panel of students (four or five) and ask them the following questions. Also allow for the other students to offer their feedback:
   - What do you think is the relationship between God and these natural disasters? Where is God when these events occur?
   - Does God send these disasters to punish certain people?
   - Does God have no power to stop these disasters?
   - Does God really care what happens to the victims of such disasters?

   Then say that the next part of the Exodus story deals with nature and what the Israelites came to believe was its relationship to God.

Teaching Approaches

1. Explain more about the use of the divine infliction of plagues as a literary device in the Bible. In fact it is used in other places of the Bible outside Exodus. For example, when the Philistines were victorious in battle against the Israelites and stole the Ark of the Covenant, God inflicted punishment in the form of mice and tumors (cf. 1 Sm 4–6). When King David angered God by taking a national census, God retaliated by sending a plague that decimated the country (cf. 2 Sm 24). The plague literary device points out God's justice and his mercy toward the victims of injustice.

2. Allow the students to work in triads to complete Handout 4B (page 273 of the TWE), "The Plagues Against Egypt." The handout asks the students to compare the number and order of plagues from three sources: the Exodus 7:8–13:16, Psalms 78: 23–38, and Psalms 105:40–55. Then, as a class, discuss how these three accounts are similar or different. How many plagues are listed in each biblical source? Ask the students to give possible explanations about why the Bible seems to contradict itself. (Most likely, the

CHAPTER 4

stories of the plagues were passed down orally throughout the centuries. Different tribes developed different details to the stories.)

Handout 4B Answers

Exodus	Psalm 78	Psalm 105
1. blood	1. blood	1. darkness
2. frogs	2. flies	2. blood
3. gnats	3. frogs	3. frogs
4. flies	4. caterpillars/locust	4. flies/gnats
5. cattle	5. hail/frost	5. hail
6. boils	6. cattle	6. locusts
7. hail	7. firstborn	7. firstborn
8. locusts		
9. darkness		
10. firstborn		

3. Explain that the *number* of plagues is not nearly as important as believing something disastrous happened to make Pharaoh change his mind. Also point out that it is not important whether or not the plagues literally happened. What is important is that God is faithful to his promises to the descendants of Abraham and Jacob. God is with them and will help them to become a great nation in their own land.

4. Ask the students to summarize what we can learn from the story of the ten plagues. Write these ideas on the board and call on the students to elaborate each point:
   - **God acts to save his people.**
   - **God wills the liberation of slaves.**
   - **God remains faithful to his ancient promises to make the Israelites his people.**

   Summarize the discussion by re-reading the final paragraph before the subsection "The Release from Egypt" (page 95).

5. Brainstorm a list of who or what might enslave people today (see Journal Assignment, page 97). Have the students take note of the list prior to completing the journal entry.

6. **Homework Assignment**:
   - Complete the Journal Assignment on page 97. Use the list of people and things that cause enslavement.
   - Read Exodus 12. Note the rules for Passover leading up to the departure of the Hebrews from Egypt.
   - Read "The Release from Egypt" (pages 95–97).
   - Complete most of the work on the "Passover Today" assignment (page 96). View the "Judaism 101" website and/or other resources (also use Handout 4C,

---

Not only does this theory fail to account for the three plagues that *cannot* be associated with any known gods, but some of the gods are associated to the plague by their image (i.e., Heket and Hathor), others by the area over which they were understood to have influence (i.e., Seth, Min, Amon-Re, and Osiris), and some of these gods were never

The eighth plague was a swarm of locusts.

"worshipped" by the Egyptians at all (i.e., Khnum or Hapi). The idea that each plague was directed against a specific Egyptian deity is a clever argument, but ultimately must be set aside as contrary to what we know both of Biblical texts and Egyptian history and culture. In fact, the Biblical portrayal presents these plagues as directed against Pharaoh himself. He was, after all, considered a divine figure in Egypt whose responsibilities included the well-being of Egypt itself.

Similar questions must be raised about another popular theory that these plagues were actually naturally-occurring circumstances. Perhaps, for example, red algae of some kind turned the Nile red and made the water undrinkable (the first plague). Perhaps excessive flooding of the Nile River Valley left pools of standing water for mosquitoes (the third plague). Perhaps there was an outbreak of anthrax among the livestock of Egypt, infecting cattle and even making the people sick (the fifth and tenth plagues). Hail storms and locusts are obviously both naturally occurring phenomenon (the seventh and eighth plagues). And so on.

Such an explanation starts out to prove that the story of the Israelite's escape from the Pharaoh is possible, that it can be believed because the plagues can be explained rationally. But others take that explanation one step further and argue that if that the plagues are not miraculous at all, if they are merely "natural events," then Moses, Pharaoh, and all the people were entirely fooled into thinking that some "God" was behind these merely freakish events of nature. In truth, no matter what way the story is examined, God was the initiator of these events. It was in the Exodus that "God formed Israel as his people by freeing them from slavery in Egypt" (*CCC*, 61).

The first nine plagues follow an arrangement of three sets of plagues, which are indicated by the special way that each set is introduced. Each set includes three different plagues:
Set A (plagues 1, 4, and 7)
   ◆ Introduced with a phrase instructing Moses to go to the Pharaoh in the morning.
Set B (plagues 2, 5, and 8)
   ◆ Introduced with the phrase: "The Lord said to Moses, 'Go to Pharaoh. . . .'"
Set C (plagues 3, 6, and 9)
   ◆ Introduced by instruction from God to Moses or Aaron to perform an act.

Plague	Introductory Phrase	Set
1. Nile turned to blood	Exodus 7:15	A
2. Frogs	Exodus 8:1	B
3. Lice/Gnats	Exodus 8:12	C
4. Flies	Exodus 8:20	A
5. Pestilence (cattle dying)	Exodus 9:1	B
6. Boils	Exodus 9:8	C
7. Hail	Exodus 9:13	A
8. Locusts	Exodus 10:1	B
9. Darkness	Exodus 10:21	C

The arrangement of the plagues into three sets by introductory phrases was an interesting literary technique. The purpose of the stories of the plagues is not only to show God's power over Pharaoh or even that he can work miracles, but that God's will is for liberation of slaves and the creation of a people out of the enslaved and oppressed. What is important is that God revealed his will to the Israelites and they understood their history as a people in light of that revelation. These stories teach us about God and the formation of his people, the Israelites. They teach that God chooses slaves—that God liberates the oppressed. They teach that earthly powers, such as Pharaoh, cannot maintain oppression when God wills liberation. They also teach that with liberation comes responsibility.

The Release from Egypt
It appears most likely that, once again, two different oral traditions have been woven together in the book of Exodus to tell the story of how the Israelites left Egypt. In the conclusion of the nine plagues in Exodus 10:28, Pharaoh and Moses have the following exchange:

"Leave my presence," Pharaoh said to him, "and see to it that you do not appear before me again! The day you appear before me you shall die!" Moses replied, "Well said! I will never appear before you again."

But look at the words of the Lord to Moses that begin chapter 11:

Then the Lord told Moses, "One more plague will I bring upon Pharaoh and upon Egypt. After that he will let you depart. In fact, he will not merely let you go; he will drive you away" (Ex 11:1).

Exodus 10 ended with Moses saying that the Israelites were leaving, yet Exodus 11 opens with God calling for another plague. A

Resources

Music Suggestions

"Be Not Afraid" by Bob Dufford, S.J. from *Earthen Vessels*, *Glory & Praise 1*, or *Young People's Glory & Praise* (OCP [NALR]); *Celebrate or Gather* (GIA); *Breaking Bread* (OCP).

"Come to the Water" by John Foley, S.J., from *Wood Hath Hope* or *Glory & Praise 2* (OCP [NALR]); *Gather* (GIA); *Breaking Bread* (OCP).

"Go Down, Moses" (African-American Spiritual) from *Lead Me, Guide Me* or *Gather* (GIA).

"Here I Am, Lord" by Dan Schutte from *Lord of Light* or *Glory & Praise 3* (OCP [NALR]); *Celebrate* or *Gather* (GIA); *Spirit Song* or *Breaking Bread* (OCP).

"Lift Up Your Hearts" by Roc O'Connor, S.J., from *Lord of Light* or *Glory & Praise 3* (OCP [NALR]); *Gather* (GIA); *Breaking Bread* (OCP).

"Psalm 95: If Today You Hear God's Voice" by David Haas from *Gather* (GIA).

"Shepherd of Souls" by James Montgomery from *Worship II* or *Gather* (GIA); *Breaking Bread* (OCP).

"Song at the Sea/Exodus 15" by Niamh O'Kelly-Fischer in *Gather* (GIA).

"Unless A Grain of Wheat" by Bob Hurd from *Breaking Bread* (OCP); *Gather* (GIA).

"Wade in the Water" (African-American Spiritual) in *Lead Me, Guide Me* or *Gather* (GIA).

"You Are All We Have" by Francis Patrick O'Brien in *Gather* (GIA).

THE JOURNEY TO THE PROMISED LAND BEGINS

"Seder Food Symbols" on page 274 of the TWE) to help with background information on how Passover is celebrated today (www.jewfaq.org/holidaya.htm). You will have some more time to finish the assignment in the next class period.

The Release from Egypt

Bell-Ringer

1. Ask volunteers to share more of their lists of addictions from the Journal Assignment. Write them on the board. Note that any form of addiction is a type of slavery. Addictions can be sinful because they degrade human dignity and liberty. Follow-up this part of the discussion by having the students comment on how God offers freedom from addition. *Optional:* Invite a person who has overcome an addiction and returned to a life of faith to speak briefly about this conversion.

Teaching Approaches

1. Summarize the text section, "The Release from Egypt." Help the students to understand the possible explanations for how the two oral traditions were woven together. The Passover tradition is included in Exodus 10:26 as Moses speaks of a sacrifice that will be offered to the Lord. Then the entire Passover tradition is included in Exodus 12. Ask the students to explain how the Passover story would have evolved if included directly after the killing of the Hebrew boys at the time of Moses' birth (Ex 1:15–16). Finally, point out again that the key points of the text are that 1) God keeps his promises to his people and 2) God is a liberator not a God who enslaves.

2. Connect the Jewish experience of Passover with the Church's celebration of Eucharist. Point out that deeper meaning of Eucharist as explained in the *Catechism of the Catholic Church*, 1364.

Chapter 4

3. **Guest Speaker:** Allow at least 15–20 minutes for your guest speaker (rabbi or practicing Jew) to speak to the students on Passover celebrations today. Encourage students to take notes to help in completing the "Passover Today" assignment on page 96.

4. Allow time for the students to work in pairs or small groups to complete the "Passover Today" assignment. Call on some students to share their list of foods with meal directions. Others can share answers to the four questions asked of younger children at the Seder Meal. Two others can retell the story of the Exodus in their own words.

5. **Homework Assignment:**
   - Write answers to the Review and Reflection questions 1–3 on page 97. Note Scripture references from Exodus 12 to support your answer to question 3.
   - Read Exodus 15–18.
   - Read "The Wandering of the People in the Wilderness" including the separate feature "Book of Numbers: Organizing a People" (pages 97–99).
   - Complete the report on slavery from page 98.

Enrichment: Work with other classmates to organize and plan a Seder Meal for the class to share in the final class period before the Chapter Test.

THE OLD TESTAMENT

PASSOVER TODAY

Write a script outlining the significant elements of a Passover celebration today. Include:
- Food and Table preparation. Write a grocery list of foods for the meal and directions for food preparation and table setting.
- Write and answer the four questions asked of younger children at the Seder Meal.
- Retell the story of the Exodus in your own words.

discriminating reader will wonder why.

The usual answer is that the end of Exodus 10 and the beginning of Exodus 11 is a rather awkward transition between *two originally different traditions about how the people of Israel left Egypt.* Chapters 7 to 10 of Exodus represent the "nine plagues" tradition and chapter 11 is the story of the Israelites leaving Egypt following the first Passover. By weaving in the beginning of the Passover tradition at the end of Exodus 10, it becomes the "tenth" plague. But, perhaps it was once an entirely unique story about how the people left Egypt after one horrendous event—the death of the firstborn of Egypt.

Furthermore, by adding the Passover tradition to the tradition of the nine plagues, the text obscures a connection that would otherwise be more obvious—that the "Passover" event is directly related to the *beginning* of the story of Moses. Without the intervening chapters that relate the nine plagues, it is possible to connect the killing of the first-born Egyptian children (Ex 12:29–30) to the edict of the Egyptian Pharoah to kill the Hebrew boys at the time of Moses' birth (Ex 1:15–16). Rather than being merely cruel or even horrendous, the Passover event can be understood as punishment on the Egyptian people for the Pharoah's original decree. Violence leads to violence.

The two traditions of the release of the Hebrews from Egypt may blur an exact understanding of how the Exodus actually took place in history.[1] But there was a distinct religious purpose to editing these materials together to form the story as it is now included in the Old Testament, mainly that

    God keeps his promises to his people and
    God is a God of liberation and not enslavement.

Another important teaching to keep in mind is that as Jews celebrate Passover today[2], they commemorate the saving actions of God and give thanks for them. The "Exodus events are made present to the memory of believers so that they may conform their lives to them" (CCC, 1363). In the Church's liturgy, the memorial takes on a new, deeper meaning and the saving events actually become present: "When the Church celebrates the Eucharist, she commemorates Christ's Passover, and it is made present: the sacrifice Christ offered once for all on the cross remains ever present" (CCC, 1364).

96

Resources

Audiovisual Materials

A & E Old Testament Video Collection: Moses (British Broadcasting Corporation)—50 minutes
Shows the call of Moses and the Exodus event. Produced in 1996.

Exodus: Volume 1 (Cokesbury)—80 minutes
Dr. Maxine Dunnam covers the first seven chapters of Exodus, including a discussion of Moses' birth, the burning bush, and Pharaoh's stubbornness.

Exodus: Volume 2 (Cokesbury)—80 minutes
Dr. Maxine Dunnam discusses Exodus 8–20: the ten plagues, crossing the Red Sea, wandering in the desert, and the Ten Commandments.

Exodus: Volume 3 (Cokesbury)—80 minutes
Dr. Maxine Dunnam covers Exodus chapters 21–40, discussing the ark of the covenant, the tabernacle, and the mercy seat.

Moses (available from Vision Video)—184 minutes
After God appears to him in a burning bush, Moses becomes the leader and spokesman for the Israelite people who are slaves in Egypt. Eventually, he is able to lead his people to freedom across the Red Sea.

Power Tools: Ten Commandments (Concordia)—33 minutes
This presentation teaches the facts about the Ten Commandments and then uses "power tools" to help students apply the Ten Commandments to their own lives.

The Ten Commandments (Mass Media)—219 minutes
This classic movie, starring Charleton Heston, covers the events in the life of Moses. Included are his birth, his rise to leadership, and his successful liberation of his people.

The Journey to the Promised Land Begins

REVIEW & REFLECTION

1. Why is the explanation of the plagues as evidence of God's superiority over the gods of the Egyptians insufficient?
2. What is the religious message that is conveyed through the story of Moses' confrontation with Pharaoh and the Israelites' release from Egypt?
3. Explain the origin of the celebration of Passover as it is described in Exodus 12.

JOURNAL ASSIGNMENT

- What does it mean that "God is a God of liberation and not enslavement?" What or who might enslave people today? How can God help you to stay or to get free?

The Wandering of the People In the Wilderness

Read Exodus 15–18

After a canticle sung by Moses and the Israelites celebrating God's saving power (Ex 15:1–17), Exodus continues with another story cycle containing traditional stories about the life of the Israelites during the time they were wandering in the wilderness (Ex 15–18). Sometimes these episodes are referred to as **"murmurings"** as they are primarily a series of complaints from the people against the leadership of Moses, and eventually, against God himself.

These chapters depict an unruly and restive people who have left Egypt, unsure of their future. They complain about food (Ex 16:1–4) and water (Ex 17:1–3), and they face serious dangers from desert peoples who are considerably less than hospitable (Ex 17:8–16). Finally, Moses' father-in-law, Jethro, suggests that Moses select some helpers from among the people to assist in organizing the group (Ex18). This story provides a plausible explanation of the leadership of **elders** among the Hebrews, although this is not a particularly unusual social system for agrarian societies.

How many people wandered in the wilderness with Moses? The traditional number, 600,000 (Ex 12:37), seems unacceptably high. Not only is this number quite likely larger than the entire population of whole sections of Palestine, it would represent a massive number of people trying to survive in the Sinai deserts. The problem is typically solved by pointing out that the Hebrew term usually

"murmurings"—The stories in the book of Exodus of the complaints of the Israelites in the desert against Moses and against God.

elders—Mature, usually male, members of the Israelite community who met regularly to rule on specific disputes within the community.

THE JOURNEY TO THE PROMISED LAND BEGINS

THE WANDERING OF THE PEOPLE IN THE WILDERNESS

Bell-Ringers

1. Bring a "crate" to class with some items that you treasure and would want to take with you if you were told to move immediately and would only be able to take a few things. Continue by having the students work in pairs to do the "Relocation" activity on page 98. Allow time for them to share their lists with a partner.

2. Introduce the lesson of a wandering people who wound up complaining about their time in the desert. Ask these questions for general discussion:
   - Is it normal for people to complain no matter how good their situation may be? Give examples for your opinion."
   - What are some popular complaints teens have today? How legitimate are these complaints?
   - What were the complaints of the Israelites in the desert? Do you think these complaints were legitimate? Why or why not?"

Teaching Approaches

1. Play approximately ten minutes of a film of Moses, including the time of wandering in the desert. (See the presentation from the A & E Old Testament Video Collection on Moses on page 100 of the TWE.)

2. Highlight some of the important events from the desert from Scripture, including:
   - The Quail and Manna (Ex 16:4–15)
   - Water from the Rock (Ex 17: 1–7)
   - Battle with Amalek (Ex 17: 8–16)
   - Origins of Elders, Tribes of Israel (Ex 18:17–27)

Review and Reflection Answers

1. Not every plague corresponds to an Egyptian god. Furthermore, some of the gods were never worshipped by the Egyptians at all.
2. The message: God wills the liberation of slaves and the creation of a people out of the enslaved and oppressed. God chooses slaves and makes them his people.
3. The Israelites celebrate a ritual meal and spread the blood of the lamb on their lintels. The angel of death, which kills the firstborn sons of the Egyptians, sees the blood and spares the sons of the Israelites. Since that time, the Israelites celebrate the Passover meal, recounting how the angel passed over them, how God saved them.

Chapter 4

3. Continue with an explanation of the twelve tribes. Refer to the separate feature, "Book of Numbers: Organizing A People." From Overhead 4B (online at **avemariapress.com**), "The Israelite Tribes in the Promised Land" call on students to locate the tribes on the map. Mention that the descendants of the two sons of Joseph were each given a portion of land, whereas the descendants of Levi were given no land, because their heritage as priests was thought to be God himself.

4. Call on students to share part or all of their reports on slavery based on the quotation from Frederick Douglass. The Religious Tolerance website offers some background information on the issue. See www.religioustolerance.org/chr_slav.htm.

5. **Homework Assignment**:
   - Answer the Review and Reflection questions 1–2, page 99.
   - Complete the Journal Assignment, page 99. Try to write the entry in narrative form rather than just making a list of several random times God has been present to you as well as times when you have "murmured" against God.
   - Memorize the Ten Commandments as listed on page 270 of the Catholic Handbook for Faith in the Student Text.
   - Read "The Reception of the Law at Mount Sinai," "Hebrew Understanding of Covenant," and "The Ten Commandments" in the text (pages 99–102).

THE OLD TESTAMENT

RELOCATION
Imagine you *have* to move immediately from your home and relocate to a land a great distance away. You are given only one wooden crate that you may fill with ten personal treasures: possessions, heirlooms, symbols of your life that will remind you of yours and your family's past. Write the ten things you will take with you.

How many of the ten items involved a memory of a time when you or your family reached out to others? Explain.

translated "thousands," can also be translated "family group" or "village group." So, if there were six hundred "family groups" that left Egypt, a more reasonable number would be no more than 6,000 (and perhaps much less)—certainly not over half a million people! We should also keep in mind that the Bible mentions that some Egyptians and possibly other foreigners left with the Hebrews (Ex 12:38)—so it was a group of mixed ancestry long before Israel is formed as a nation in the Promised Land.

BOOK OF NUMBERS: ORGANIZING A PEOPLE

The book of Numbers also tells the story of the Israelites' journey, begun with the Exodus and continuing for thirty-eight years from their time at Mount Sinai to their arrival at the border of Canaan, the Promised Land.

Numbers gets its name from two censuses of the Hebrew people, one taken at the beginning of their desert journey (Nm 1) and the other near the end (Nm 26). The "numbers" of the Hebrews reported in each of the censuses may be exaggerated and interpreted in the same way as the numbers of people in the Exodus were. The book does explain the social organization of Israel into twelve tribes.

Two common themes from the book of Exodus are also prevalent in the book of Numbers. The first is Yahweh's care for the Israelites. He leads them by day with a cloud and by night with fire. He provides food, water, and protection for their needs. The second theme involves Israel's "murmurings." As in Exodus, the people complain both about Moses and Yahweh himself.

Frederick Douglass

Greatness does not come on flowery beds of ease to any people. We must fight to win the prize. No people to whom liberty is given, can hold it as firmly and wear it as grandly as those who wrench liberty from the iron hand of the tyrant. The hardships and dangers involved in the struggle give strength and toughness to the character, and enable it to stand firm in storm as well as in sunshine.

—FREDERICK DOUGLASS

Research and report on one or more of the following:
- ways in which former African American slaves identified with the Israelites in their quest for freedom;
- how Christianity was introduced to slaves and former slaves;
- how abolitionist texts relied on the Bible to support an end to slavery.

Background Information
Twelve Tribes of Israel

The twelve tribes of Israel are all descendants of Abraham. They were headed by ten sons and two grandsons of Jacob who became Israel:
- Reuben— by his first wife Leah (Ex 29:32)
- Simeon— by his first wife Leah (Ex 29:33)
- Levi— by his first wife Leah (Ex 29:34)
- Judah— by his first wife Leah (Ex 29:35)
- Dan—by Bilhah, the maidservant of his second wife Rachel (Ex 30:3–6)
- Naphtali—by Bilhah, the maidservant of his second wife Rachel (Ex 30:7–8)
- Gad—by Zilpah, the maidservant of his first wife Leah (Ex 30:9–11)
- Asher—by Zilpah, the maidservant of his first wife Leah (Ex30:12–13)
- Issachar—by his first wife Leah (Ex 30:16–18)
- Zebulun—by his first wife Leah (Ex 30:19–20)
- Joseph—by his second wife Rachel (Ex30:22–24)
- his sons = Ephraim and Manesseh
- Benjamin—by his second wife Rachel (Ex 35:16–18)

REVIEW & REFLECTION

1. What are the two prominent themes of the stories of the Israelites' time spent in the wilderness?
2. How might the number of people who escaped Egypt actually be less than the 600,000 cited in the book of Exodus?

JOURNAL ASSIGNMENT

- Think about how the two themes of the wilderness stories are present in your relationship with God. What needs of yours has God met throughout your life? When have you "murmured," or doubted God's care or the care of those God put in your life to care for you?

The Reception of the Law at Mount Sinai

The release of the Israelites from Egypt leads ultimately to their gathering at the foot of Mount Sinai and their reception of the "Law": the religious, civil, and ritual statute from God by which they were to become a holy people. In fact, it is only when the Israelites make an agreement with God at Mount Sinai that they fully become a people in whom the promise of a Savior for mankind would be fulfilled. Their liberation was only part of the agreement—learning and keeping their responsibilities as required by the Law was the other part. It is the Ten Commandments that summarize the obligations of all who love God.

This agreement between God and the Chosen People is often referred to as the "Sinai Covenant." With the covenant comes the Law of Moses, often called "The Torah." The Law given to Moses is an expression of what man knows in his own soul to be right or wrong, the **natural law**. The basic principles of natural law extend to the entire human race. Natural law corresponds to three basic human drives and needs: 1) preserving life; 2) developing as individuals and communities; and 3) sharing life with others. The Ten Commandments provide the principal commandments of the natural law.

natural law—The participation of man in God's eternal law that reveals what he intends us to do and avoid according to his wise and loving plan.

Hebrew Understanding of Covenant

Recall again that a covenant is an agreement between God and people. At Mount Sinai the most important covenant of the Old Testament is established. Essentially, it is a two-way agreement, with obligations for *both* parties involved. God agrees to be the God of this

---

THE JOURNEY TO THE PROMISED LAND BEGINS

THE RECEPTION OF THE LAW AT MOUNT SINAI

Bell-Ringer
1. Call on students to recite the Ten Commandments in order. Or, make a game of it with each student asked to recite one commandment, moving in order around the room. If there is an incorrect response, start over again with the first commandment and the next student.

Teaching Approaches
1. **Review:** Check the students' comprehension of the reading assignment. Print the following questions on the board or overhead. Have the students write their answers and either exchange with a partner for correction or hand in.
- What is another name for the Law of Moses? (The Torah)
- What is a covenant? (an agreement between God and people)
- What was God's obligation in the Sinai covenant? (to be the God of his people)
- What was the Israelites' obligation in the Sinai covenant? (to obey the law and to worship God.)
- What is the centerpiece of ancient Biblical law? (the Ten Commandments)
- What are the three different collections of laws in the books of Moses? (The Covenant Code—Exodus 20–23, the Deuteronomic Code—Dt. 5–28, and the Levitical Code—book of Leviticus.)

Review and Reflection Answers
1. Two prominent themes are: (1) Yahweh cares for Israel. He leads them by day and night. He also provides food, water, and protection for their needs. (2) The Israelites are not grateful for what God is doing. They complain about Moses and about God himself.
2. The number 600,000 is close to the entire population of ancient Palestine. A more reasonable number is 600 family groups, or 6,000 people. The Hebrew word for "thousands" can also mean "family group" or "village group."

Chapter 4

2. Review the basic principles of natural law. Explain that the Ten Commandments provide the principal commandments of natural law (see page 99).

---

people—"I, the Lord, am your God" (Ex 20:2)—but this is immediately followed by the "stipulations" of the agreement for the people—the Ten Commandments. Note that these commandments are made special in the book of Exodus because *all* the people heard God speak these commandments, whereas only Moses heard the remainder of the laws after Exodus 20:18, and then passed them on to the people.

In order to understand the central essence of Hebrew religion, we must understand that the basic covenant between God and the people obligates the people to obedience to the Law. Therefore, the very center of the relationship between God and the people in the Hebrew tradition is not focused on what the people *think about God*. Rather, it is concerned with *how they live their life*. Understanding that obedience to the Law is of primary importance to the Israelites helps us to understand the *entire* Old Testament, especially in the tradition of the Prophets.

The Ten Commandments

If anyone knows anything about ancient Biblical law, it is usually that the Ten Commandments are the centerpiece. They are reproduced in two of the law collections, in Exodus 20 and again in Deuteronomy 5. A summary of the laws as listed in the Old Testament follows:

1. Israelites are to worship no other god but Yahweh.
2. Israelites are to fashion no image (idol) to represent God.
3. Israelites are not to use the name of God in any oaths, or in magical rites or incantations, as if they can control the power of God. (Swearing is more than merely using "bad" language.)
4. Israelites are to observe and honor the Sabbath (Friday night, through Saturday until sundown) as a rest from work.
5. Israelites are to honor their parents.
6. Murder is forbidden.
7. Adultery is forbidden.
8. Stealing another person's property is forbidden.
9. Falsely accusing another Israelite of a crime is forbidden.
10. Acting on desires for neighbors' position or possessions is forbidden.

Because these Ten Commandments were spoken directly to the Israelite people, the tradition arose late in Hebrew history, and into the period of Christianity, that these ten laws were central laws of the Old Testament. Jesus, himself, acknowledged them: "If you wish to enter into life, keep the commandments" (Mt 19:17). Since the time of St. Augustine in the fourth century, the Ten Commandments have been a source for teaching baptismal candidates. As such, the "the tradition of the Church has acknowledged the primordial importance and significance" of the Ten Commandments (CCC, 2064).

The Ten Commandments state clearly what is required in the law of love of God and neighbor and Catholics (and all Christians) in every generation are obliged to keep them. The next subsections explain more about what that obligation entails for Catholics for each commandment.

I. I, the Lord am your God: you shall not have other gods besides me.

To *worship* God means we accept God as our Creator and ourselves as made in his image. To understand what it is to worship, think of some sins against the first commandment: idolatry (false worship of many gods), atheism (denial of God's existence), agnosticism (saying no one knows for sure whether God exists). Oppositely, the first commandment asks us to practice the virtues of faith, hope, and love. Practicing our religion also helps us to keep the first commandment.

II. You shall not take the name of the Lord, your God, in vain.

We must respect God's name and never use the name of God, Jesus, Mary, or the saints

---

Resources

Internet Links

www.magma.nationalgeographic.com/ngm/egypt
National Geographics Treasures of Egypt *includes many photos of Egypt and video presentation that can be ordered.*

www.memphis.edu/egypt
Presents a tour the Institute of Egyptian Art and Archaeology at the University of Memphis to see over 150 objects from 3500 B.C.–A.D. 700. The collection includes mummies, religious and funerary items, and jewelry.

www.egyptianmuseum.org
Offers a virtual tour of the Rosicrucian Egyptian Museum in San Jose, California. In addition to thumbnail images of some of the museum's artifacts, see a full-scale replica of an ancient Egyptian tomb.

http://mv.vatican.va/3_EN/pages/MEZ/MEZ_Main.html
See virtual images from the Gregorian Egyptian Museum, part of the Vatican Museum.

www.khan-al-khalil.com/egyptology.html
Provides many links to sites that feature ancient Egyptian culture, including a link to the Egyptian Museum at Cairo.

www.ancientegypt.co.uk/menu.html
Tour through ancient Egyptian artifacts in the British Museum, London.

www.ancientnile.co.uk/site.html
Resources and information on geographical documentaries on the Nile.

www.jewfaq.org/index.htm
This site presents rules or facts about the Hebrew language, in addition to other facts about Judaism.

in an improper way. This means that when we take an oath or make a promise in God's name, we must be true to it. We should also respect our own name and strive for holiness. God made us and knew us from the beginning of time. Our name will be with us into eternity. This commandment forbids *blasphemy*, a sin that involves hateful words against God, Jesus, or even the Church. Cursing is also a violation against this commandment.

III. Remember to keep holy the Sabbath day.

The Sabbath was set aside by God, to remind us of the time at creation when God rested on the seventh day. It is a day intended for people to rest from their work and to praise God for his works of salvation.

Sunday, the day of Christ's resurrection, replaces the Sabbath for Christians. Sunday is linked with the Paschal mystery, the passion, death, and resurrection of Jesus, commemorated in Eucharist. Catholics are required by Church law to participate in Sunday Mass or its Saturday vigil. To deliberately miss Sunday Mass is mortally sinful. We also make Sunday holy by spending time with our families, visiting our other relatives, helping the poor, or doing other charitable acts.

IV. Honor your father and your mother.

The fourth commandment begins the second part of the Ten Commandments having to do with love for neighbor. This is appropriate, for love truly begins at home. How can you be loving to your friends and teachers at school, when you lambasted your mom or were rude to a sibling on the ride to school? You owe your parents (and other family members) respect and obedience for as long as you live at home. When you are older, you still must respect your parents and care for them when they are old, ill, or lonely. Teachers, civil authorities, religious leaders, and other adults are also owed your respect according to this commandment.

V. You shall not kill.

All human life is of immense value. This statement applies to human life from the first moment of conception until natural death. For this reason, this commandment forbids abortion (the killing of an unborn baby) and euthanasia (mercy killing of the aged or sick).

The Church traditionaly teaches that there are times when killing is morally permissible; for example, in self-defense or when protecting the life of another. Killing in war may be morally permissible if a nation is defending itself against aggressors. Also, the traditional teaching of the Church does not exclude the use of the death penalty, if this is the only way to defend innocent lives against an unjust killer. However, the Church continues to teach that today there are very few, if any, situations in which execution of a person is necessary. Held in a secure prison, the offending person is kept away from society and has the chance to seek redemption and conversion.

This commandment also asks us not to "kill" our own bodies, and requires us to live healthy lives of exercise, wholesome eating, and rest, and to avoid harmful addictions like alcohol and drugs.

VI. You shall not commit adultery.

The sixth commandment encompasses the whole of human sexuality. In the Old Testament, the offense of this commandment primarily involved a husband having sexual intercourse with a married woman other than his wife. Jesus took the command further saying that "everyone who looks at a woman with lust" (Mt 5:28) has already committed adultery.

For people of any age or state in life, keeping this commandment involves practicing the virtue of chastity. Chastity involves a self-mastery over one's sexuality, rejects lust (inordinate enjoyment of sexual pleasure), masturbation (deliberate stimulation of genital organs to derive sexual pleasure), fornication (sex between unmarried persons), pornography (displaying sexual acts for a third party to see), prostitution (selling of sexual acts), rape (forcing another into sexual intimacy), and homosexual acts (sexual activity between persons of the same gender).

THE JOURNEY TO THE PROMISED LAND BEGINS

3. Conduct a detailed presentation helping the students apply the Ten Commandments to their own lives. Refer to the applications suggested on pages 100–102. Print the following questions on the board or overhead. Tell the students to choose two of the questions to respond to in their journals. Allow time for writing. Then, read each question one at a time. Call on volunteers who responded to the question to share their answers. Continue through the list calling on other volunteers.

Questions

- **How do the Ten Commandments play a part in your moral decision-making? Give an example.**
- **What are some other gods you have worshipped in your life?**
- **How do you respond when someone around you uses God's name in vain?**
- **Describe behavior you consider appropriate and inappropriate for Sunday.**
- **How do you honor your parents now? How do you think you will honor them when you are an adult?**
- **How strong is the commitment to save sex until marriage among your peers?**
- **How does society promote an attitude of disrespect for the body and of sexual behavior?**
- **Have you ever told a lie that did damage to another person? How did you repair that damage?**
- **What does it mean to dress modestly?**
- **How is cheating in school an offense against the seventh commandment?**
- **How can you practice loyalty and commitment in relationships now to help you prepare for the same when and if you are married?**

Chapter 4

4. **Homework Assignment:**
   - Write answers to the Review and Reflection questions 1–2, page 102.
   - Complete the Journal Assignment on page 102. Plan to share your "positive" statements of the commandments in class.
   - Read "Three Collections of the Law" including the separate feature "Sacrament of Reconciliation" on pages 103–107.

Rather, this commandment teaches us that sexual love must only be shared in the intimacy of a loving marriage, where sexual intercourse strengthens the unity of the marriage and results in the procreation of children.

VII. You shall not steal.
The seventh commandment forbids *theft*, which is the taking of another's property against his or her will. This is a matter of justice as we must respect the property rights of others.

Stealing, however, is more encompassing than just the unlawful taking of someone else's things. Stealing also includes cheating (e.g., on taxes or on a test), doing shoddy work on the job, and vandalism.

VIII. You shall not bear false witness against your neighbor.
We are to be truthful in our words and actions. Any misrepresentation of the truth is a violation of this commandment. This would include deliberately withholding information in order to prevent someone from knowing the truth and also sins called *detraction* (telling a person's faults for no good reason) and *calumny* (gossiping about another person).

IX. You shall not covet your neighbor's wife.
The word *covet* means to "desire something that is not one's own." In this case, like the sixth commandment, it is directly referring to the covenant of marriage.

Jesus restored God's original intent that marriage be indissoluble by forbidding divorce. Other sins against marriage are polygamy (having more than one spouse), incest (having sexual relations with relatives), sexual abuse of children, and living together before marriage.

X. You shall not covet your neighbor's goods.
Similar to the seventh commandment, the tenth commandment is opposed to greed, envy, and avarice (the seeking of riches and the power that comes with them).

The tenth commandment makes it clear that we desire things that give us pleasure. These desires are morally permissible as long as they do not lead us to crave things that belong to others.

REVIEW & REFLECTION

1. Why are the Ten Commandments made special in the book of Exodus?
2. What did Jesus say to acknowledge the Ten Commandments?

JOURNAL ASSIGNMENT

- Rewrite the Ten Commandments in your own words. Write them as positive statements of "what you will do" rather than "what you will not do."

Review and Reflection Answers

1. All of the people heard the Ten Commandments spoken by God, whereas only Moses heard the remainder of the laws after Exodus 20:18.
2. Jesus said: "If you wish to enter into life, keep the commandments" (Mt 19:17).

Three Collections of the Law

In studying the Law in a Scripture course, it is also important to examine the Law from the perspective of those who first heard it, the people of Israel. For centuries, it has been noted that there are differences between the two "versions" of the Law of Moses that most resemble one another—namely the laws in the book of Exodus and the laws in the book of Deuteronomy. For example, although the Ten Commandments occur in both Exodus 20:1–17 and Deuteronomy 5:6–21 they are not identical in the two books. Although the laws themselves are almost the same, the reasons given for some of these laws differ. Finally, a third source of laws from the book of Leviticus represents quite a different collection of laws altogether. So, it is generally held that there are *three different collections* of the Law in the "books of Moses." They are:

1. The Covenant Code (contained in Exodus 20–23)
2. The Deuteronomic Code (contained in Deuteronomy 5–28)
3. The Levitical ("Priestly") Code (contained in the book of Leviticus)

All three of these collections or codes contain **civil laws** (dealing with day to day issues of living in an agricultural society) and **religious laws** (especially Leviticus). A survey of these laws provides further insight into what was valued in the early life of Israel: family integrity, property, and animals.

Also note that the emphasis of Biblical laws is not on guilt and punishment, but on restoration of the community and the maintenance of social life. There is no mention of law enforcement (police) or prisons. In a small-scale agricultural society such as early Israel, laws and traditions were maintained by everybody together, but especially by the elders of the villages and towns. The elders met on a regular basis to determine specific cases based on traditional laws and values. When compensation was involved, it was not **punitive justice**, but rather **restorative justice** as much as possible. The idea was to *restore* the life of the community as much as possible, because these people had to continue to live together after each case was settled. It was partly the pressure of *personal honor* and the shame of violating themselves and their families that kept the Israelite society functioning.

civil laws—Laws dealing with the day to day issues that arise between people living, in the case of the Israelites, in an agrarian community such as the consequences when one person's animal injures another person, or when borders between properties are disputed.

religious laws—Laws which govern the actions of the priests, the regulations for sacrifice, and the building and maintenance of the Temple.

punitive justice—Laws that rely on punishment as a deterrent to criminal activity.

restorative justice—Laws that are concerned primarily with restoring community after an offense has occurred. The goal is to keep the community together, as the survival of the society depended on everyone fulfilling his or her role.

SACRAMENT OF RECONCILIATION

A sacrament that brings a restoration of relationship between a sinner, God, and the Church is the sacrament of Penance and Reconciliation.

The sacrament is called "Reconciliation" because it offers to the sinner the love of God who reconciles. "Reconciliation with God is thus the purpose and effect of this sacrament" (*CCC*, 1468). The person who is reconciled to God is likewise ready to be reconciled with his or her neighbor. Jesus said:

> Therefore, if you bring your gift to the altar, and there recall that your brother has anything against you, leave your gift there at the altar, go first and be reconciled with your brother, and then come and offer your gift (Mt 5:24).

THE JOURNEY TO THE PROMISED LAND BEGINS

THREE COLLECTIONS OF THE LAW

Bell-Ringer

1. Call on students to share one or more of their positive re-writes of the Ten Commandments (see Journal Assignment, page 102).

2. Connect the study of laws and justice with the bountiful mercy and forgiveness offered by God and celebrated in the sacrament of Penance. Read or summarize the separate feature "Sacrament of Reconciliation" (page 103). Also, review the steps for going to confession (see "How to Go to Confession," page 273). If possible, plan for an opportunity for the class to celebrate the sacrament.

Teaching Approaches

1. Introduce the different collections of the Law of Moses. Write on the board:

1. The Covenant Code (contained in Exodus 20–23)
2. The Deuteronomic Code (contained Deuteronomy 5–28)
3. The Levitical ("Priestly") Code (contained in the book of Leviticus)

To help show the differences, have the students read and compare Exodus 20:1–17 and Deuteronomy 5:6–21. (Note that there are different reasons given for some of these laws.)

Chapter 4

2. Explain that all totaled, there are 611 laws of Moses that Jews were expected to obey. Many of these laws are found in the books of Deuteronomy and Leviticus. Deuteronomy was probably written by many people during the post-exilic period. The same is true for Leviticus. Deuteronomy contains more narrative than Leviticus, including an account of the death of Moses. Both books call the Israelites to a high standard of ethical living, appropriate for God's People. They are to be a holy people, a people who practice justice.

3. Read the Beatitudes (Mt 5:3–12). Point out how the Beatitudes reflect a sense of restorative justice, rather than punitive justice. Much of keeping the Beatitudes demands a change of heart. Ask the students to recall examples of restorative justice they have witnessed.

The practice of laws in ancient agrarian Israel seems dramatically different from the way law functions in modern urban life. Today we hardly know our immediate neighbors, much less the entire town or city. In our legal system, "restoring community" is not considered as important as punishing the guilty. The punishment is intended to be a deterrent for those who might break the law in the future. Also, the person who "wins" a case in a modern court, will probably never see the other party again. Hardly a thought is given to what will happen to either party after a legal decision is rendered. In ancient Israel this was not the case, so law had to restore honor and society. Two parties facing off in a legal case would most likely continue to be involved with one another the rest of their lives. Hopefully you can begin to understand how it is different for ancient Hebrews and modern Christians to follow the Law of Moses.

Catholics today are not obliged to follow too many of the specific laws (e.g., laws regarding clean and unclean food) of the three collections in Exodus, Deuteronomy, or Leviticus. It is the Ten Commandments that contains a "privileged expression of the natural law" (CCC, 2070). We can and do capture the spirit of justice expressed in the Mosaic Law—especially as that spirit is strengthened with the coming of Jesus Christ and the preaching of the gospel. For example, it is precisely the spirit of *justice* and *community* in the Mosaic Law that are embraced by Jesus in the Beatitudes preached in the Sermon on the Mount (see Mt 5:3–12). One way of speaking of the Sermon on the Mount is to see it as an expression of the "New Law" of the Gospel. It fulfills the Law of Moses, focusing on bettering relationships in the community, especially with the poor. The *Catechism of the Catholic Church* explains:

> The Lord's Sermon on the Mount, far from abolishing or devaluing the moral prescriptions of the Old Law, releases their hidden potential and has new demands arise from them: it reveals their entire divine and human truth. It does not add new external precepts, but proceeds to reform the heart, the root of human acts, where man chooses between the pure and the impure, where faith, hope, and charity are formed and with them the other virtues (CCC, 1968).

Comparing the Collections of Laws

An interesting way to compare the *Covenant Code*, considered to be much older, with the *Deuteronomic Code* is to contrast the two versions of the same legal issue. Consider, for example, the issue of what the Hebrews most frequently called *slavery* but which was actually *indentured servitude*.[3]

- In the Covenant Code, read Exodus 21:1–11. Compare this to passages from the Deuteronomic Code (Dt 15:12–18; 23:16–17) on the same subject.

The point is not to debate the issue of slavery per se. We know that the slaveholders of pre-Civil War America tried to justify slavery on the basis of the Bible. (Of course, they hoped that people would not read too carefully, because what the Bible calls "slavery" is clearly not the same thing that African-Americans sadly suffered in American history.) But there is more to be seen in these two laws, from different time periods, on the subject of indentured servitude. What do we notice in our comparison between the two? It is often suggested that Deuteronomy represents further moral development from the older Covenant Code, a humanizing of the laws of slavery.

Whether or not the Covenant Code is older than Deuteronomy, there is clearly a difference in the approach. Deuteronomy seems to reflect the time of the prophets (see Dt 24) during which interests in social justice were prevalent. Even the language of Deuteronomy seems similar to the language of the prophets—for example, Deuteronomy's

The Journey to the Promised Land Begins

famous interest in the poor and weak of society, especially the widow, the orphan, and often including the foreigner or stranger.

- ♦ Read and compare the Deuteronomy passages (10:11–18, 24:19–21, and 27:19) with those of the prophets (Is 1:17, Jer 7:6–7, Jer 22:3, Ez 22:7, Zec 7:10, and Mal 3:5) on the subject of widows and orphans. How are they alike? How are they different?

The most unusual law code of the three, of course, is the *Levitical Code*. This code covers mainly priestly laws and traditions—for example, what the priests should wear, what the high priest is to do, how the tabernacle is to be built and maintained, and how sacrifices are to be classified and performed. The book of Leviticus also includes laws dealing with concerns about purity and maintaining a sense of "being clean" which applied to the entire community. Purity laws are very interesting, although they may seem, again, a bit unusual for those outside the modern traditions that still practice forms of purity laws (Orthodox and Conservative Judaism and Islam practice forms of purity laws, but most forms of Christianity do not). Highlighted below are three areas of laws from the Levitical Code that are of most interest to modern Christians: laws of sacrifice, purity, and **Jubilee**.

Laws of Sacrifice: Leviticus 1–6:7

There were many different kinds of sacrifices made by ancient Hebrews, depending on the reasons for the sacrifice. For example, there were *whole offerings*, that is, "wholly burned" sacrifices in which an entire animal except its hide was consumed in fire on the altar. Its purpose was to give glory and praise to God. There were *cereal offerings*, consisting of grains like barley. Also, there were *peace offerings* in which the meat of the sacrificed animal was partially eaten by priests and those who offered the sacrifice. Also in some temples of other ancient people, and perhaps also in the Hebrew Temple, some of the leftover meat not consumed by the priests was actually sold. Thus ancient temples often doubled as the local butcher shop.

There is debate, however, about what the sacrifices mentioned in Leviticus were actually intended to accomplish. One explanation is that the person who brought a sacrifice offered the animal as a replacement for himself—he identified with the sacrificial victim and thus expressed his repentance. Another interpretation is that the sacrifice was intended to remove the sin from the holy Temple and its altar.

In other words, the Hebrews believed that *two* things happened when people sinned. First, they were guilty themselves and must be forgiven. This personal guilt was taken care of by the act of bringing the animals to the priests at the Temple. The gift represented repentance and sorrow, and served as the symbolic act of asking God for forgiveness. The acts of sacrificing the animals and

Jubilee—Every seventh sabbatical year (i.e., every forty-ninth year). In a year of Jubilee all debts were to be forgiven, and land that had been sold to pay a debt was to be returned to the original family. In this way, the wealth of the entire community was to be redistributed among the poor, preventing unrelieved poverty and large gaps between the rich and the poor.

4. Compare the three collections of the Law of Moses by having the students work through the in-text exercises on pages 104–105. Handout 4D, "Comparing Ancient Israelite Laws" (page 275 of the TWE) offers a worksheet for the students to complete both exercises (see page 104 and 105).

Handout 4D Answers
1. The book of Deuteronomy not only mandates that slaves should be freed after six years, but it also calls for giving them gifts or payment for their service. Furthermore, Deuteronomy calls for the protection of runaway slaves.

2. Both the Deuteronomy passages and the prophets say that society has a duty to protect and take care of its weakest members—widows, orphans, and resident aliens. The Israelites are to do this because God took care of them in their days of weakness in Egypt and in the wilderness.

5. Present an overview of the three areas from the Levitical Code covered on pages 105–107: laws of sacrifice, purity, and Jubilee.

Background Information

Law

The following types of laws need to be considered when making moral decisions:
- **Natural law** God's law written into the nature of things, the way things are made. Note how natural law corresponds to three basic human drives and needs (see page 99 of the Student Text).
- **Civil law** This is the particular application of natural law for a society. Many civil laws help apply the natural law for the protection of human life.
- **Divine law** The Ten Commandments and Beatitudes are examples of divine law, that is law revealed by God.
- **Church law** Church law is the particular application of divine law for Catholics. For example, the Church teaches Catholics must go to Mass on Sunday. This is an application of the third commandment.

Chapter 4

6. Refer to the assignment "Advantages for Keeping God's Law" (page 106). Call on a good reader to read Deuteronomy 4:1–8 aloud. Remind students that Moses says that wisdom and intelligence are the fruits of keeping the Law. Call on students to recall occasions when they have benefited from keeping one of the commandments.

7. **Re-teach:** Ask these questions by way of checking the student's reading of the material and reviewing the lesson:
   - What is the difference between civil law and religious law? (Civil laws deal with day-to-day issues of living. Religious laws deal with ways to worship God and practice one's religion.)
   - Why is there no mention of police or prisons in Biblical laws? (The emphasis of the law was on restoration of the community and the maintenance of social life [restorative justice], not on guilt and punishment [punitive justice].)
   - What are three areas of law found in the Levitical Code? (sacrifice, purity, and jubilee)
   - What kinds of sacrifice are found in Leviticus? (whole offerings, cereal offerings, and peace offerings)
   - What were the two purposes of these sacrifices? (to ask God's forgiveness for personal sin, and to cleanse the Temple from the "pollution" caused by the sins of the people.)
   - In what ways are the Old Testament sacrifices like the sacrifice of Jesus Christ on the cross? How are they different? (Accept all reasonable answers.)
   - What is the Jubilee Year? (the 49th or 50th year)
   - What is supposed to happen during this year? (Debts are to be forgiven; the land is to be given back to its original owners.)

The Old Testament

ADVANTAGES FOR KEEPING GOD'S LAW

Read Deuteronomy 4:1–8. Moses tells the people what they will gain if they keep God's Law. What is it that they will gain? How have you benefited from these gifts for keeping God's Law?

sprinkling their blood on the altar took care of the *second issue*— the "pollution" of the Temple itself from the sins of the people. The actual killing of the animals and then the handling of blood, therefore, seemed to be a kind of religious "cleansing agent" which was mainly for the *purification of the Temple*, and not for "forgiving" the person who offered the animal.

Clearly, coming to an understanding of what was intended in the sacrificial system has interesting implications for our Christian understanding of the death of Jesus—since it is often compared to the sacrifices made by the ancient Hebrews.

Purity Laws: Leviticus 11

One of the most interesting chapters of the "purity laws" in Leviticus is the section dealing with laws of clean and unclean animals. Consider Leviticus 11. The first section of the chapter is rather neatly divided into "classes" of animal—some of which are used for food:

Leviticus 11:2-8—land animals
Leviticus 11:9-12—sea animals (fish)
Leviticus 11:13-19—air animals (birds)
Leviticus 11:20-23—winged insects

It has often been suggested that these "food laws" are based on some primitive form of hygiene; that is, the laws were given to protect the people from foods that are frequently dangerous (especially in an era before bacterial infection was understood) such as shellfish (which are easily infected) or pork (which contains parasites if not properly cooked).

However, the explanation that these laws are based mainly on hygiene does not explain all of Leviticus 11, nor many other purity regulations in the rest of Leviticus. Another suggestion was that purity laws, and laws that reflect a fear of contamination from various things, represented the Israelites' social fears of contamination from the "outside."[4] The point is strengthened by the fact that many of the purity laws of Leviticus were particularly significant during the exilic period after the destruction of Jerusalem in 587 B.C. In other words, the purity laws reflected a minority society that was concerned about the threats from assimilation with foreign cultures. This would parallel concerns about mixed marriages, for example, which one Biblical priest called "pollution" (Ezr 9).

"Clean" animals in this theory are animals that *stay in their categories*, rather than violate "borders" between certain traits (e.g. fish that do not have both scales and fins, like shellfish or amphibians) or animals that do not chew cud and have cloven hoofs (like camels and pigs).[5] Purity laws that reflected concerns of animals staying in their categories could be carried over to encourage people to stay in *their* categories in a multi-religious society like the Babylonian, Persian, and Hellenistic Empires which ruled over the Hebrew people. In short, "purity" can be one way of insuring that people maintain a unique identity.

The Journey to the Promised Land Begins

Laws of Jubilee: Leviticus 25

The laws of Jubilee are the last of the Levitical laws highlighted here. The name "Jubilee" comes from the Hebrew name for "horn" as the beginning of each year was proclaimed by the blast of a horn. According to the laws of Jubilee, after forty-nine years each man was free to return to his own homeland.

How did this understanding of a Jubilee Year develop? The priests were obviously fascinated with the number seven. There are seven days to the week, and every seventh year was proclaimed a "sabbatical year." This is when all the slaves (i.e., indentured servants) were released from their debts, and various parcels of land were allowed to "rest," along with farm animals. But the most impressive of these cycles of seven was the seventh sabbatical year—a kind of "super sabbatical" that was called the "Jubilee Year."

During the Jubilee Year, all the tribal land that had been leased, lost to debt, or bought up by unscrupulous landlords (e.g., Is 5:8) was to be returned to the original tribal families. It was to be one massive redistribution of land! It was similar to the prophet Ezekiel's plan to equally redistribute land, which was probably a version of the Jubilee distribution (see Ez 45).

The laws of Jubilee show a radical concern for social justice. They also reflect a concern not only to deal with fair distribution of resources once, but to revisit the issue of fair distribution on a regular basis. While we have little evidence that the laws of Jubilee were ever actually practiced on a regular basis, they at least offer a laudable ambition on the part of the Hebrew priests to reorient a society on the basis of a socially and economically just distribution.

Comparing Moses and Jesus

Look up the following passages and note the implied comparisons between Jesus and Moses:
- Exodus 2:1–10 and Matthew 2:13–15
- Exodus 20:1–17 and Matthew 5:1–12
- Exodus 14:21–22 and Matthew 14:25–33
- Exodus 16:4–15 and Matthew 14:13–21
- Exodus 1:2–5 and Matthew 1:1–5
- Exodus 12:1–27 and Matthew 26:26–29

The New Moses

The Gospel of Matthew treats Jesus as the New Moses. The twelve apostles are often thought of as the New Israel. The gospel retells scriptural events to help explain and interpret events in the life of Jesus. The focus on the connections between Jesus and Moses came about because Matthew's gospel was originally intended for a Jewish Christian audience.

Like Moses, the infant Jesus faced extermination by a foreign king, Herod. Like Moses, Jesus escapes this threat by going to Egypt (see Mt 2:13–15). Also, in Matthew's gospel, Jesus' body of ethical teachings—the Beatitudes and Sermon—are given on a mountaintop just as Moses received the Law on Mount Sinai, (Compare Matthew 5–7 with Luke 6:20–49). In Luke, the sermon is given on a "plain" not a mountain.) Matthew is trying to tell us about the importance of Jesus by comparing him to Moses. This is another illustration of how much deeper our understanding of the gospels can be with a good foundational knowledge of the Old Testament.

8. **Homework Assignment:**
   - Read the feature, "The New Moses" (page 107). Then complete the "Comparing Moses and Jesus" exercise on page 107.
   - Write answers to the Review and Reflection questions 1–3, page 108.
   - Complete the Journal Assignment, page 108. Develop a story based on a real-life occurrence.
   - Read "The Approach to the Promised Land" and "Further Reflections" in the text.
   - Look up the places and record the route and sequence of stops for the Israelites' desert journey from the Learn by Doing activity (page 109). This is ideal preparation for making the map suggested at the next class session.

Enrichment: Make a collage with photos that represent each beatitude. Or, find a newspaper story for each beatitude. Write a sentence explaining the connection between the story and the beatitude.

Enrichment: Research the following topics: 1) How Leviticus 11 compares to present-day Jewish Dietary Laws. 2) How the Jubilee-Year practice affects agriculture and the environment.

Background Information

Jewish Dietary Laws

The "Kashrut" is the body of laws dealing with what foods Jews can and cannot eat and how these foods must be prepared. The word "kosher" comes from Kashrut. It means "fit, proper, or correct." Here are the basic Jewish dietary laws:

- Do not eat certain animals (camel, rock badger, hare, pig, lobsters, oysters, shrimp, clams, crabs, rodents, reptiles, amphibians, insects, etc.). Do not eat the flesh, organs, eggs, or meat of the forbidden animals.
- Kill the allowed animals according to Jewish law.
- Drain all blood from the allowed meat before eating it.
- Do not eat certain parts of allowed animals.
- Do not eat meat with dairy.
- Use separate utensils for meat and dairy. Utensils that have come in contact with one of these foods may not be used for the other.
- Do not eat/drink grape products made by non-Jews.

Jubilee Year Today

Many farmers today rotate their crops or let certain fields lay fallow so that they may replenish themselves of nutrients. Also, Pope John Paul II declared 2000 a Jubilee Year. Pope John Paul II encouraged government leaders to forgive criminals and release them from prison. He specifically prodded the Italian government to release his would-be assassin from prison and it was done.

CHAPTER 4

THE APPROACH TO THE PROMISED LAND
FURTHER REFLECTIONS

Bell-Ringers

1. **Re-teach:** Review ways the gospel of Matthew treats Jesus as the new Moses. Check the students answers to the "Comparing Moses and Jesus" exercise (page 107).

Answers:

- Ex 2: 1–10 and Mt 2:13–15 (Moses and Jesus were each threatened from the time of their births.)
- Ex 20: 1–17 and Mt 5:1–12 (Moses gave the old Law to his people, Jesus offered the New Law of Love in the Beatitudes.)
- Ex 14: 21–22 and Mt 14:25–33 (Both walked over bodies of water.)
- Ex 16:4–15 and Mt 14:13–21 (Moses fed the people with manna, Jesus fed the people with bread miraculously taken from five loaves and two fish.)
- Ex 1:2–5 and Mt 1:1–5 (Moses and Jesus share the same ancestors.)
- Ex 12:1–27 and Mt 26:26–29 (Moses initiated the Passover ritual, Jesus the Eucharist.)

2. Allow students who worked on any of the enrichment exercises assigned at the end of the previous lesson to share their work. Display the Beatitude collages or art projects around the room. Add details to the reports on Jewish dietary laws and the Jubilee Year (see Background Information, page 111 of the TWE).

Teaching Approaches

1. Discuss the Learn by Doing activity on page 109. Pass out butcher paper and markers. Have the students work in pairs to draw a map of the Israelites' pilgrimage through the desert. Have them include the following places:

   Rameses (Ex 12:37)
   Succoth (Ex 13:20)
   Red Sea (Ex 14:22)
   Desert of Shur (Ex 15:22)
   Marah (Ex 15:23)
   Elim (Ex 15:27)
   Desert of Sin (Ex 16:1)
   Rephidim (Ex 17:1)
   Mount Sinai (Ex 19:18)
   Kadesh (Nm 20:1)
   Mount Hor (Nm 20:22)
   Plains of Moab (Nm 33:50)
   From Shittim to the River Jordan (Jos 3:1)

Point out the passage in Exodus 13:17 that explains that God did not lead the Israelites on the shortest route to help them avoid the land of the Philistines.

Review and Reflection Answers

1. The Law of Moses consists of the Covenant Code (contained in Exodus 20–23), the Deuteronomical Code (Deuteronomy 5–28), and the Levitical (Priestly) Code (book of Leviticus).
2. Our urban society is oriented to punitive justice—punishing those who commit crimes. The agrarian society of ancient Israel was mainly interested in restorative justice, righting the wrong and then restoring the life of the community as much as possible. The rationale for restorative justice rather than punitive justice was that the people had to continue to live together in order to survive and function.
3. The purpose of the purity laws was to encourage the Israelites to stay among and to marry among themselves even though they lived in areas populated with Babylonians, Persians, and Greeks.

Chapter 4 Parish Religious Education Adaptation

- The Chapter 4 Parish Religious Education Adaptation (online at **avemariapress.com**) offers a two-hour lesson with suggestions for covering all of Chapter 4. The lesson is broken into parts to allow for various time-frames.
- The lesson plan requires the students to read Chapter 4 in the text and to do selected Review and Reflection questions from Chapter 3 prior to the class.

Moses, gave them his law so that they would recognize him and serve him as the one living and true God, the provident Father and just judge, and so that they would look for the promised Savior (CCC, 62).

A covenant is a solemn agreement between human beings or between God and human beings. The covenant with Moses is the primary covenant of the Old Testament. In this covenant, God revealed his Law through Moses in preparation for salvation through the prophets, and ultimately the New Covenant established by Christ. The Ten Commandments are central to the Sinai Covenant.

For Jews, the events of the Exodus are not simply *recalled* in celebrations today. Rather, in every Passover, the Exodus events are made present and real so that Jews can conform their lives to these events. In the New Testament, the memorial takes on a new meaning. When the Church celebrates Eucharist, Christ's Passover is made present. The sacrifice of Christ on the cross is made present once and for all.

Learn by Doing

Create a hand-drawn map that traces some of the places on the route of the Exodus. Include places mentioned in the following scripture passages:

Exodus 12:37
Exodus 13:20
Exodus 14:22
Exodus 15:22
Exodus 15:23
Exodus 15:27
Exodus 16:1
Exodus 17:1
Exodus 19:18
Numbers 20:1
Numbers 20:22
Numbers 33:50
Joshua 3:1

Note other geographic elements on your map. Finally, explain why the Israelites did not choose the shortest route from Canaan to Egypt (see Ex 13:17).

Called to Prayer

O let us all from bondage flee
Let my people go!
And let us all in Christ be free
Let my people go!

Go down, Moses,
Way down in Egypt's land.
Tell old Pharoah
To let my people go!
—from an African American Spiritual

Notes

1. One other point of difference: At the end of the nine plagues (Ex 10:28–29), the people leave because Pharaoh tells them to go. In the Passover tradition, it is suggested that the Israelites have to leave Egypt quickly (Ex 12). The Israelites *exodus*, or departure, from Egypt is described in Exodus 13:17–14:31. It includes the story of the miraculous crossing of the Reed Sea or Sea of Reeds. The Israelites are able to cross, but the Egyptians drown.
2. If any of your Jewish friends invite you to a Passover celebration, don't miss it. It is a wonderful tradition to learn about and enjoy.
3. Indentured servitude describes an agreement in which a contract binds one person in service of another for a specific amount of time. At the end of the contract, the servant would be released from his or her duties. In the Mosaic Law, it was a way to pay debts, and the term was traditionally seven years.
4. This famous argument was made by anthropologist Mary Douglas in a 1966 book titled *Purity and Danger*.
5. Note that animals with one category, but not both, are excluded as "unclean" (e.g., the rock badger and hare of Lv 11:5–6).

Chapter 4 Test Answers

Part 1: Matching: 1. d; 2. b; 3. g; 4. a; 5. c; 6. f; 7. e.

Part 2: Multiple Choice: 8. b; 9. a; 10. b; 11. d; 12. c; 13. d; 14. a.

Part 3: Short Fill-ins: 15–16. Any two of the following: "who am I" to go about rescuing people, "who are you" that I should do as you ask, the Israelites will not believe him, and isn't there someone else God could send? 17. the death of the first-born of the Egyptians; 18. murmurings; 19. elders; 20. Jubilee; 21–23. The infant Jesus was threatened by a foreign king; he escaped by going to Egypt; Jesus' law, the Beatitudes, was given on a mountaintop.

Part 4: Short Answer: 24. Answers should include specifically the idea that the death of the first-born of the Egyptians can be seen as punishment for the Pharoah's decree that all Hebrew male infants should be killed as soon as they were born, rather than merely as something horrendous and cruel; 25. God keeps his promises to his people and he is a God of liberation and not of enslavement.

THE JOURNEY TO THE PROMISED LAND BEGINS

2. Assign the students to read Deuteronomy 32:48–52; 34:1–12. Ask:
   - What is the reason given for Moses' death before the Israelites entered the Promised Land? (His disobedience at Meribah.)
   - How old was Moses when he died? (120; explain that Moses probably didn't live that long. Advanced age in the Bible is a literary device to show that God has favored that person. Because Moses was an extraordinary prophet of God, who spoke to God face to face, the author of Deuteronomy had him live to a very old age.)
   - What do you think is the overall message of the Bible passage you just read? (Death is punishment for sin. Life means obeying God.)

3. Quiz the students on the definitions of the following vocabulary terms: civil laws, natural law, religious laws, elders, Hyksos, Jubilee, "murmurings," punitive justice, and restorative justice. Also ask again some or all of the Review Questions from the chapter to help the students prepare for the Chapter Test.

4. **Prayer Service:** Play a recording or lead singing of "Go Down Moses" (lyrics on page 109). Have the students recite the Canticle of Moses (Ex 15:1–18). Divide the class in half with each side alternating between reciting verses. Conclude by leading this final prayer:

   O Lord, you call us by name and we are your people. We believe you have a purpose for us, a wonderful plan of redemption and freedom. Help us always to remember our covenant with you and remain faithful to your commandments. We ask this in union with your Son Jesus, who is the New Moses, and the Holy Spirit, who guides both our days and our nights. Amen.

5. **Homework Assignment:**
   - Study for the Chapter 4 Test.

CHAPTER 4 TEST

Teaching Approaches

1. Allow a brief time for review. Then administer the Chapter 4 Test (online at **avemariapress.com**) Each question is worth four points.
2. For extra credit, consider having the students write the meaning of each of the Ten Commandments.
3. Preview Chapter 5. Or, review some of the lessons from the Catholic Handbook of Faith (pages 259–280 of the Student Text).

Introducing Chapter 5

This chapter focuses on the Biblical books that make up *Deuteronomic History* (i.e., books based on the book of Deuteronomy). These books are Joshua, Judges, 1 and 2 Samuel, 1 and 2 Kings, as well as the book of Ruth. Primarily, the chapter focuses on Joshua and Judges, books that describe Israelite history from the conquest of Jericho to the time of the kings.

During this time in history, Israel consisted of a loose federation of tribes. The book of Joshua portrays a picture of a united Israel—all twelve tribes marching to war in order to conquer various territories in Canaan. However, the book of Judges paints a more realistic picture—a slow period of settlement, marked by individual tribes engaging in warfare.

As the Israelites settled into Canaan, judges or military leaders ruled over the individual tribes. Among these judges were Gideon, Deborah, and Samson. At this time, the Israelites had no king because they looked to Yahweh as their Warrior-King, the One who would protect them from foes and obtain victory for them in battles.

The long account of the "conquest" of Jericho reflects the "miracle warfare" mentality of the Israelites. They believed that if they truly trusted in Yahweh, they did not need to fight. God would fight for them and ensure victory. Eventually, as they encountered many strong enemies among the Canaanites and the Philistines, the Israelites began to put more faith in their own military strength than in Yahweh. The result was that they inevitably lost the battles.

The judges were not just military leaders; they also functioned as prophets, reminding the people to put their trust in Yahweh alone. God told the judge Gideon to go to war with only a handful of men. Deborah prophesized that the victory against Sisera would come through a woman. Samson regained his strength and won a great victory only after he returned to the worship and belief in Yahweh.

While the books of Judges and Joshua are fraught with bloody conflicts and battles, they contain a religious message that echoes throughout the New Testament—fidelity to God ensures victory or success. Trust in one's own prowess is fruitless; in fact, it usually ends in disaster.

In exploring the topic of warfare and peacemaking, the students will see that Yahweh is a God of peace rather than of warfare. The chapter presents the tenants of the "just war" theory proposed by St. Augustine, but also makes a strong case for making peace. Like the ancient Israelites who frequently lapsed back into idolatry, we too are in need of continual conversion. We, too, are called to place our trust firmly and solely in God.

Chapter 5 Outline

Introduction
Deuteronomic history tells Israel's history from the conquest of Palestine to the time of the kings.

Understanding the Events of Settlement
The books of Joshua and Judges describe in several different ways the conquest of Palestine.

Exploits of the Judges
The judges fill the gap in leadership between the time of Joshua and the time of the kings.

Israel at Home In Palestine
With some people already living in Canaan, the former Hebrew slaves form the tribes of Israel.

The Last Days of the Independent Monarchy
The northern kingdom of Israel falls to the Assyrians and shortly afterward Babylon destroys Judah, the southern kingdom.

Further Reflections

Background Notes for the Teacher

Joshua is an important transitional figure between life in Egypt and life in the Promised Land. The name "Joshua" (a variation of the name "Jesus") means "Yahweh is salvation." The Bible depicts Joshua as a perfect military leader who succeeded Moses. Just as Moses led the Israelites out of Egypt by crossing the Red Sea, so Joshua symbolizes a new Moses who led the Israelites across the river Jordan and into the Promised Land. Joshua further symbolizes and prefigures Jesus, the Messiah who leads his people from the slavery of sin to the salvation of life as children of God.

Resources
Music Suggestions: see page 116
Printed Materials: see page 122
Audiovisual Materials: see page 123
Internet Links: see page 125

CHAPTER 5
THE JOURNEY TAKES NEW SHAPE
A People at Home

Relevant Teachings from Church Documents

- The fifth commandment forbids the intentional destruction of human life. Because of the evils and injustices that accompany all war, the Church insistently urges everyone to prayer and to action so that the divine Goodness may free us from the ancient bondage of war (Cf. *GS* 81 §4.) (*CCC*, 2307).
- All citizens and all governments are obliged to work for the avoidance of war. However, "as long as the danger of war persists and there is no international authority with the necessary competence and power, governments cannot be denied the right of lawful self-defense, once all peace efforts have failed" (GS 79 §4) (*CCC*, 2308).
- Because of the evils and injustices that all war brings with it, we must do everything reasonably possible to avoid it (*CCC*, 2327).
- The Church and human reason assert the permanent validity of the moral law during armed conflicts. Practices deliberately contrary to the law of nations and to its universal principles are crimes (*CCC*, 2328).
- At all times and among every people, God has given welcome to whosoever fears Him and does what is right (cf. Acts 10:35). It has pleased God, however, to make men holy and save them not merely as individuals without any mutual bonds, but by making them into a single people, a people which acknowledges Him in truth and serves Him in holiness. He therefore chose the race of Israel as a people unto Himself. With it He set up a covenant. Step by step He taught this people by manifesting in its history both Himself and the decree of His will, and by making it holy unto Himself (Vatican II, *Dogmatic Constitution on the Church*, #9).

Background Notes continued

Throughout the books of Joshua and Judges, we find several important themes. First, the people are to trust in God who continually calls them to conversion and fidelity to the covenant. And second, the Chosen People are entitled to the land that God will give them. We find in the books of Joshua and Judges the same belief in "manifest destiny" that marked American expansion in the days of the western frontier. The people felt they had a right to this land, that God had promised it to them and would help them overcome all obstacles to obtain it. Obtaining the Promised Land was very important to the Israelites' identity as a nation and was at the basis for the unduly bloody scenes depicted in Joshua and Judges.

Advance Preparations

- Choose appropriate lessons to play all or part of some of the suggested videos to help the students learn the stories of Samson, Gideon, and Deborah and the specifics surrounding the battle of Jericho.
- Provide art material for the mural on the conquest of Jericho suggested on page 120 of the TWE.
- Recordings of some of the suggested music can be used as background to play while the students are working individually or in small groups. Also, choose a recording or plan to lead the lyrics for a song that can be part of the class Prayer Service (see page 132 of the TWE).
- If possible, invite a representative of the diocese's social justice commission to present the Church's teaching on peace and the fighting of a just war.

Chapter Objectives

The students will be able to:

- understand why the books of Joshua, Judges, 1 and 2 Samuel, and 1 and 2 Kings are considered "deuteronomic history."
- know the importance of the religious reforms of King Josiah.
- see how God can work with people with imperfections such as Rahab, Samson, Gideon, and Deborah.
- appreciate the religious message behind the conquest of Jericho and many of the battles described in Joshua and Judges.
- discover what archaeology tells us about the conquest of Jericho and other cities throughout Canaan at this time.
- explore the morality or immorality of warfare, including the "miracle warfare" of the ancient Israelites and the "just war" theory of St. Augustine.
- consider how God is calling people today to ongoing penance and conversion

Chapter 5

INTRODUCTION
COMMON PHRASES

Bell-Ringers

1. **Re-teach:** Offer a brief review of some of the main points of Chapter 4 of this text and the book of Exodus. For example, summarize a key teaching from Exodus 3:15–17 as a way to explain who God is by what he does. Point out the following (write on the board):
- God sends his people to advance his mission.
- God is concerned for his people.
- God will lead his people.
- God will provide a home for his people.

Also, stress the importance of the Ten Commandments as a great moral code. If the Chapter 4 Tests are graded, return with comments of your choosing.

2. On the board print the following:
- **Memoirs**
- **Autobiography**
- **Biography**
- **History**

Explain that these words all deal with a review of past events. Ask the students to spend a few minutes writing about a past time in their lives (e.g., something that happened, how they felt about it then, and how they feel about the same event now). Allow students to share what they have written. Then call for a class summary. Ask the students to explain how time and perspective can change our perspective on historical events. Explain that Chapter 5 deals with the section of the Old Testament known as "the Historical Books." These books were written many centuries after the events and were written after many generations of reflections on the events and what they meant.

THE OLD TESTAMENT

Deuteronomic History—The six books of the Bible influenced in their language and theology by the book of Deuteronomy, including Joshua, Judges, 1 and 2 Samuel, and 1 and 2 Kings.

Introduction

The book of Deuteronomy is set in the time just before the arrival of the Israelites in Canaan in about 1250 B.C. This chapter will cover the history of the Israelites from the time they came to Palestine to the beginning of the monarchy around 1050 B.C. This history was not recorded in the form we now have it until the Israelites were exiled in Babylon in 587 B.C., several centuries later. The study will focus on two questions: How is it known that this portion of history was actually recorded during Babylonian captivity? And how are the six historical books of the Old Testament that cover this history related?

The six historical books covered in this chapter included many oral and written stories, all edited into books now known as **Deuteronomic History**. These books are Joshua, Judges, 1 and 2 Samuel, and 1 and 2 Kings. The book of Ruth, which falls between Judges and the first book of Samuel, is more a dramatic story

COMMON PHRASES

One of the main arguments to support the theory that the book of Deuteronomy influenced the other Deuteronomic History books is that common phrases unique to Deuteronomy can be found in the other books. Consider the classic phrase from Deuteronomy about loving or following God with all your "heart and soul," which Jesus quotes as the greatest commandment:

Therefore, you shall love the Lord, your God, *with all your heart, and with all your soul*, and with all your strength (Dt 6:5).

Though the phrase is never found in any other book of the Torah, it is heavily used throughout the book of Deuteronomy—for example, 4:29; 10:12; 11:13; 11:18; 13:4; 26:16; 30:2,6,10. The phrase turns up again in several places outside the book of Deuteronomy, linking those books with Deuteronomy. For example,

In the book of Joshua:
But be very careful to observe the precept and law which Moses, the servant of the Lord, enjoined upon you: love the Lord, your God; follow him faithfully; keep his commandments; remain loyal to him; and serve him *with your whole heart and soul*" (Jos 22:5).

In the first book of Kings:
. . . and the Lord may fulfill the promise he made on my behalf when he said, "If your sons so conduct themselves that they remain faithful to me *with their whole heart and with their whole soul*, you shall always have someone of your line on the throne of Israel" (1 Kgs 2:4).

The phrase is also used in 1 Kings 8:48 and in 2 Kings 23:3 and 23:25. From these examples it is clear that the history books borrowed language, style, and even moral themes from the book of Deuteronomy.

Resources

Music Suggestions

"All the Ends of the Earth" by David Haas and Marty Haugen from *We Have Been Told*, *Celebrate,* or *Gather* (GIA).

"Blest be the Lord" by Dan Schutte from *A Dwelling Place* (OCP [NALR]); *Gather* (GIA); *Breaking Bread* (OCP).

"City of God" by Dan Schutte from *Lord of Light* or *Glory & Praise 3* (OCP [NALR]); *Celebrate* or *Gather* (GIA); *Breaking Bread* (OCP).

"For You Are My God" by John Foley, SJ, from *Neither Silver Nor Gold* or *Glory & Praise 1* (OCP [NALR]); *Breaking Bread* (OCP); *Gather* (GIA).

"Shall We Gather at the River" by Robert Lowry in *Gather* (GIA).

"Shelter Me, O God" by Bob Hurd from *In the Breaking of the Bread* or *Breaking Bread* (OCP); *Gather* (GIA).

"Shepherd Me, O God" by Marty Haugen from *Shepherd Me, O God* or *Gather* (GIA); *Breaking Bread* (OCP).

"We Praise You" by The Dameans from *Glory & Praise 2* (OCP [NALR]); *Gather* (GIA).

"We Will Serve the Lord" by Rory Cooney in *Spirit Song* (OCP).

than a history, although it is traditionally understood to have historical roots. The book of Ruth will also be examined in this chapter.

The term "Deuteronomic History" reflects the influence of a twentieth century German Biblical scholar, Martin Noth, whose thesis was that these six historical books were actually six parts of one long work, in the same way that the Gospel of Luke and the Acts of the Apostles from the New Testament were originally two parts of one written volume. The term "Deuteronomic History" arose because the six books contain both theological perspectives and actual phrases that have their roots in the book of Deuteronomy itself (see "Common Phrases," page 112).

The connection between the book of Deuteronomy and the other six Deuteronomic History books is not simply a question of literary style. There are several religious or theological themes that these books have in common—such as the central importance of the city of Jerusalem, especially the Jerusalem Temple.

In Deuteronomy, there are regulations that are found only there, such as:

- The Temple is the *only* acceptable location for sacrifice on the face of the earth;
- astrology, the worship of stars, is forbidden; and
- celebrating Passover is legally required among *all* the Israelites.

These three regulations in Deuteronomy do not appear in the older collections of the law (in Exodus or in the older parts of Leviticus). Furthermore, they are not actually put into practice until the time of King Josiah (640–609 B.C.), a very late king of Judah (see 2 Kgs 22–24). It is King Josiah who actually legislates these regulations among the Israelite people. He allows sacrifice *only* in Jerusalem at the famous Temple. He forbids star worship and he states that the Passover celebration is to take place each year.

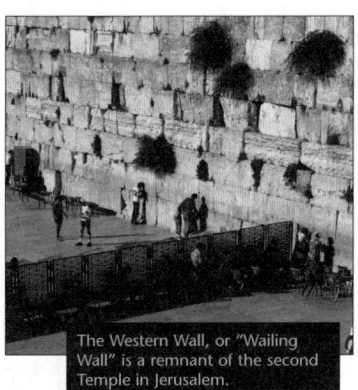

The Western Wall, or "Wailing Wall" is a remnant of the second Temple in Jerusalem.

It is reported in 2 Kings 22:6 that the high priest in King Josiah's reign "found the book of the law in the temple of the Lord." If it is not until 2 Kings 22–24 that we actually have an Israelite king who enacts the unique Law of Deuteronomy (laws not found in the books of Exodus or Leviticus), then it makes sense that the book found in the Temple during Josiah's reign was the book of Deuteronomy—the only part of the laws of Moses that specifically requires the same laws that Josiah passed. This also means that the book of Deuteronomy was added to the Torah very late in history. After this book became influential, writers who were composing later materials were deeply influenced by its style as well as its important collection of laws.

In summary, there seems to be a clear relationship between the book of Deuteronomy and the six books that make up Deuteronomic History. Furthermore, it makes sense that Deuteronomy influenced the writing of the historical books mainly because Deuteronomy had only recently

THE JOURNEY TAKES NEW SHAPE

Teaching Approaches

1. Allow time for the students to read the Introduction and the feature, "Common Phrases" (pages 112–114). Review by asking: "What three laws are found in the book of Deuteronomy and nowhere else in the Pentateuch?" (Offer sacrifice only in the Temple in Jerusalem. Do not worship the stars [astrology]. Celebrate the Passover each year.)

2. Summarize why anyone who studies the Bible can understand that the work of Deuteronomic History was completed after 587 B.C. See "Teaching Approaches" on page 76 of the TWE for example.

3. Share more information about the three unique regulations that are found in Deuteronomy. Use the questions for each regulation as a basis for discussion.

- *Temple sacrifice*: What is a sacrifice? (An offering made to God as an act of worship. After the offering, the sacrifice is consumed or destroyed so that it can't be used for any other purpose.) Why do you think people throughout history have engaged in ritual sacrifice? (Essentially, it is a way to communicate with the deity. Specific reasons might include praise, thanksgiving for a blessing given, to persuade the god to grant a petition, perhaps to express atonement for sin.) Using "Temple Sacrifice" (Overhead 5A online at **avemariapress.com**), discuss the occasions that "required" a Temple sacrifice. Point out that restricting sacrifices to the Temple in Jerusalem was great for the tourist trade in Jerusalem. People were periodically required to journey to Jerusalem.

- *Astrology*: What is astrology? (It is a study of the stars and planets in order to predict the future.) Explain that the use of astrology was widespread in Mesopotamia and among the peoples of Canaan when the Israelites arrived there. Ask: "Why do you think astrology was forbidden by the Israelites?" (Astrology, first of all, was a form of idolatry. It made the sun and stars and planets more important than God. Secondly, astrology was a form of superstition or fatalism. It denied the existence of human free will and the person's responsibility in shaping the future.) Also teach that astrology remains a sinful practice today. Casual acquaintance with astrology (such as occasionally reading one's horoscope) is not necessarily sinful, but placing all your trust in astrology rather than in God is.

- *The Passover*: What is the Passover? (It is a ritual commemoration of deliverance from slavery in Egypt. The angel of death "passed over" the houses of the Israelites and did not kill their firstborn sons, but did kill the Egyptian firstborns.) How did the Israelites celebrate the Passover? (They gathered as a family, slaughtered a lamb, and ate a ritual meal that recalled the Exodus story.)

Chapter 5

4. If time permits, direct the students to begin working on the Journal Assignment, page 114. Distribute Bibles to the students. Have them read and share the passages in small groups.

5. **Homework Assignment**:
   - Write answers to the Review and Reflection questions 1–2, page 114.
   - Complete the Journal Assignment, page 114.
   - Read Joshua 2–6.
   - Read "Understanding the Events of Settlement" through the subsection "Rahab and the Fall of Jericho," pages 115–116.

THE OLD TESTAMENT

HOW WE LOVE OTHERS

Jesus equated love of others with love of God. He also said, "Love your enemies and do good to them" (Lk 6:35). Develop a concrete seven-day plan for "doing good" for those you have not got along with in the past. In this way you will be showing your love for them and for God. Write your plan for the week. Include the names of people you will try to reach out to and what you will try to do. At the end of each day, write a summary of what you were able to accomplish and how and why you adapted your plan.

become well known—when Josiah, through his high priest, "found" it.

This information helps scholars date the Deuteronomic History material. How so? Think of it this way: If you are reading an American history book that claims to be comprehensive, and you do not know when that book was published, how might you decide roughly when the book was written? You would probably look at the *last* event described in the work. If the last event described in the book occurred when President Bill Clinton was in office, you would likely conclude that the book was published shortly after the year 2000 when President Clinton left office.

The last event described at the end of 2 Kings is the beginning of the Babylonian Exile. Thus we can conclude that this long historical sequence of books (which begins with Joshua and ends with 2 Kings) must have been written sometime after 587 B.C. While there is some question as to whether *parts* of Deuteronomic History were written before 587 B.C., few, if anyone who studies the Bible, dispute that the work was completed after 587 B.C.

To summarize:

- ◆ The book of Deuteronomy was "found" during the reign of King Josiah (2 Kgs 2:26).
- ◆ Josiah reigned from 640–609 B.C.
- ◆ Deuteronomic History was written after 587 B.C.

As we pick up the story in the book of Exodus of the Israelites' foray into Palestine, it is important to keep two things in mind. First, all of the records of this experience were written during the same historical period. And second, they were written many years after the incidents they describe actually occurred.

REVIEW & REFLECTION

1. List the six books known as Deuteronomic History. How have scholars been able to determine when they were written?
2. What textual evidence links the six books? What elements of style and theological themes are consistent between the books?

JOURNAL ASSIGNMENT

- Look up and read carefully the seven passages listed on pg. 112 ("Common Phrases") for the occurrence of the phrase "with your whole heart and your whole soul." Write about what it might mean for you to love God and follow his commandments with your "whole heart and whole soul."

Review and Reflection Answers

1. The six books known as Deuteronomic History are Joshua, Judges, 1 and 2 Samuel, 1 and 2 Kings. Scholars looked at the last events recorded in these books and determined that they were probably written in post-exilic times.
2. There are common phrases between the six books and the book of Deuteronomy, most notably the phrase, "with your whole heart and soul." The six books also borrow language, style, and moral themes from the book of Deuteronomy. For example, they uphold the regulations found uniquely in Deuteronomy; that is, offer sacrifices only in the Temple in Jerusalem, do not engage in astrology, and celebrate the Passover each year.

Understanding the Events of Settlement

How did the early settlement of Palestine by the Israelites take place? The story of settlement is told in the books of Joshua and Judges, and there are a couple of points on settlement that are interesting for study. But remember, the words of Joshua and Judges were inspired by God. They are intended to reflect a religious and economically just lesson that he wants to communicate to people of all ages. No matter how the land was settled, there is no doubt that the religion of the God named Yahweh was quite different from the religions of Egypt and Caanan with all of their different gods and goddesses.

The common understanding from the Bible is that the settlement was, at least on some level, a "conquest." According to this traditional view, Joshua was put in charge of the people of Israel after Moses died. Joshua became a military leader and led a militia composed of the young men of the wilderness generation. This Israelite "army" (surely not a very well-equipped one!) attacked the "Promised Land" in military actions that began with the amazing conquest of Jericho. In fact, the book of Joshua opens with a long section (chapters 2–6) about the conquest of Jericho.

Typically, the conquest of Jericho is dated between 1250 and 1200 B.C. Certainly something called "Israel" existed in Palestine by the time Pharaoh Merneptah claimed to have defeated Israel in his inscription of 1207 B.C. It is the earliest reference to "Israel" outside the Bible, and is an important source for dating the formation of Israel, because it tells us that there was, in fact, a people in Canaan called "Israel" by around 1207 B.C.

The description of the siege of Jericho (5:13–6:27) is well-known, especially as a popular subject for children's books and songs. The very lengthy description of this battle at the beginning of the book of Joshua alerts us to the fact that it was considered important as the opening battle for the land. (The entire record of the conquest battles is told in the first twelve chapters of Joshua, nearly half of which is devoted to the battle of Jericho alone.) According to Scripture, Jericho was conquered by means of a miracle of God, and the people only participated in the "cleanup operation" that followed the actual fall of the city. Chapters 12 to 21 of the book of Joshua mainly explain how the land was divided among Israel's tribes, though "a very large part of the land still remains to be conquered" (12:1).

The modern town of Jericho on the West Bank, near to the archaeological site of the ancient city.

Rahab and the Fall of Jericho
Read Joshua 2–6

The prostitute Rahab is a central character in the fall of Jericho. According to the book of Joshua, she risked her life to help the Israelite spies. Certainly, Rahab had little reason to be loyal to Jericho. As a prostitute, she was likely abused by the men of the city and shunned by most of the women. For her assistance, the Israelites spared Rahab and her family when they destroyed the rest of the city.

Rahab is also a symbolic figure in the story of the conquest. The Law of Moses offered equality and social justice on a level to which the native Canaanites were not accustomed

---

Background Information
Priesthood in the Old Testament

In the time of the monarchy in Israel, the king or the head of the household could offer the sacrifice. In post-exilic times, only priests could offer the Temple sacrifices.

Priesthood was an inherited position in the Israelite community. Priests had to come from the tribe of Levi or from the descendants of Aaron. In post-exilic times, there were twenty-four classes of priests in Jerusalem. Some offered sacrifices in the Temple on a rotating weekly basis. Others performed daily sacrifices there. Zechariah, the husband of Mary's cousin Elizabeth, was a Temple priest. The leader of the priests was the high priest. On the Day of Atonement, only the high priest was allowed to enter the Holy of Holies in the Temple and offer sacrifice on behalf of the people.

THE JOURNEY TAKES NEW SHAPE

UNDERSTANDING THE EVENTS OF SETTLEMENT
Rahab and the Fall of Jericho

Bell-Ringer

1. Introduce the exercise "How We Love Others" (page 114). Conduct an experiment. Have the students work in pairs with one person in each pair serving as an observer while the other person walks around the campus greeting people in a friendly way with either a smile or a "hello." The observer should note the reactions to these greetings.

2. Allow time for the students to develop their plans for the "How We Love Others" exercise. Remind them to be specific in their approach to reach out to others.

3. Bring real estate ads for vacant land from several different regions. Have the students examine the ads. Then, ask: If you could choose a place to purchase land and settle, where would it be?

Teaching Approaches

1. Print the term **manifest destiny** on the board. Ask the students to offer their definitions. Point out that in colonial and frontier America, manifest destiny was a philosophy of settlement in which Americans felt "entitled" to settle in certain new territories. Manifest destiny especially marked the development and acquisition of the land west of the Mississippi River and led to the eventual eviction of Native Americans to reservations. Explain that the Israelites also had a strong sense of manifest destiny. They believed God had given them the land of Canaan through Abraham, and that nothing should prevent them from resettling there. They engaged in numerous battles in the belief that God willed them to have the land.

2. Arrange to play all or part of the production from the Standard Video Bible Series on Joshua and Judges (see page 123 of TWE). Ask the students to debate the particular theories of the battle of Jericho, remembering all the while that the Bible teaches important religious truths about the event. Explain that the important message of the story of the battle of Jericho is that God is the one in control of the Israelites' destiny. God acts as both a warrior and king.

3. **Re-teach:** Check the students' comprehension of the homework reading assignment. Ask: "Who was Rahab?" (A prostitute who lived in Jericho who

Chapter 5

helped the Israelites gain entrance to the city. She and her family were spared after the conquest.) Also, discuss the evolution of morality related to war.

4. Distribute newsprint and art materials. Direct the students to retell the story of the conquest of Jericho in a mural. Assign different students to different segments of the mural. Display the finished murals where all can see them.

5. **Homework Assignment**:
   - Read the following sub-sections to "Understanding the Events of the Settlement:" "Comparing Stories of Conquest" and "Peace over War" including the separate features, "Archaeological Evidence" and "Israelite Warfare Traditions."
   - Read 1 Samuel 7–8, detailing the events leading to Israel's request for a king.
   - Write a short biography of Dame Kathleen Kenyon (see page 117).

> **Enrichment:** Research and list some of the statutes of the Geneva conventions and how they apply to fighting a just war. See the link from the American Red Cross website for more information: http://www.redcross.lv/en/conventions.htm#geneva.

Comparing Stories of Conquest
Israelite Warfare Traditions

Bell-Ringers

1. Collect the reports on Dame Kathleen Kenyon. Call on a sampling of students to report their findings to the class. Make sure all the students realize that Kenyon's findings do not corroborate the Biblical account of the fall of Jericho. But they do support evidence that the whole of the Middle East seems to have experienced social and political upheaval around 1200 B.C., and the upheaval was followed by a "dark age" in Palestine marked by sociopolitical fragmentation and decline.

2. Joshua 24 offers a review of the good God has done for the Israelites to this point in their history. Have the students read this chapter and write a brief summary of the main points.

---

under their ancient elitist system of government and society. There were probably many poorly treated Canaanites like Rahab—especially lower-class workers and peasants—who abandoned their old society and joined with the new incoming group under Joshua.

Besides the role of Rahab, the other main issue to consider involving the fall of Jericho is the actual destruction of its famous walls. According to Joshua 6:1–20, God brought down the walls of Jericho following the shouts and marching of the Israelites. The miraculous nature of the story may reflect the religious tradition about warfare in early Israel (see "Israelite Warfare Traditions," pages 118–119).

The message, in this case, is that the miraculous fall of Jericho illustrates how the Israelites should depend on God over their own strength and abilities.

It is also possible that the story highlighted the miraculous nature of the battle in order to emphasize this point: when the Israelites have faith, God takes care of them. Since we know that the story was written at a much later time, perhaps the inspired author felt a particular need to emphasize the importance of trust in God. (One of the major complaints of the prophets of the time of the Babylonian exile, when these stories were recorded, was that the kings of Israel and Judah relied more on alliances with foreign nations than on God for protection against their enemies. This story was perhaps a reminder to the people to trust in God's power and his care for them.)

Comparing Stories of Conquest

A different picture of the settlement of the Israelites in Canaan emerges from the stories in Judges. The book of Judges includes an element of peaceful settlement of the land, in contrast with the more exclusive use of military campaigns detailed in Joshua. The following differences can be found in the two accounts:

- The book of Joshua finishes with the end of the conquest before settlement takes place (see Jos 23 ff.). But the book of Judges suggests that some settlement preceded the battles of conquest!
- An encounter with Jabin, king of Hazor, is described in Joshua 11:1–11 where it is finally said that Hazor was "burned with fire." But in Judges 4:1–5:31, Jabin is mentioned again, Hazor is still in existence, and the city is being fought over once more. It is unclear why the battle is mentioned in both books. Judges may simply be a second, more detailed version of the same battle. Or it may be that the two books have two different accounts of what happened.
- Joshua describes a complete campaign of conquest: "And so the Lord gave Israel all the land he had sworn to their fathers he would give them. Once they had conquered and occupied it, the Lord gave them peace on every side, just as he hard promised their fathers" (Jos 21:43). The book of Judges suggests a much more mixed population of peoples throughout the land, with various pagan peoples existing alongside the Israelites "to this very day."
- There are even differences within the book of Judges. In Judges 4, two tribes engage in the battle of Kishon. In Judges 5 the text says that six tribes were involved!

What is clear is that the books of Joshua and Judges both contain accounts of battles, biographies of soldiers, and details of the conquest of the land of Palestine (particularly the settlement of the twelve tribes). Both books describe God as being actively involved in the military campaigns, although often in highly unconventional battles. When the Israelites are faithful to God and to the covenant, he rewards them with victory. More information on this "literature and theology of warfare" is detailed in the next section.

Background Information

Evolution of Morality Regarding War

During the time of Joshua and the Judges, the common practices among the Israelites and other Near East peoples regarding war was somewhat savage. After victory, the victor often burned down the city and routinely killed all the inhabitants who did not manage to flee. The story of Rahab, written many centuries later after the Israelites had been held as "prisoners of war" in Babylon, shows a change in the Israelites' thinking regarding moral behavior during war. The story describes how Rahab and her family were spared. The Israelites had grown in their awareness that "innocent" people should be protected. Prisoners of war should be treated humanely. Point out that it was only in the twentieth century that most nations accepted the Geneva conventions regarding warfare and the humane treatment of prisoners. Today, countries and individual leaders who violate the Geneva conventions can be tried for war crimes.

THE JOURNEY TAKES NEW SHAPE

The Journey Takes New Shape

ARCHAEOLOGICAL EVIDENCE

While recent archaeological study has not been able to corroborate all of the historical details of the Israelite's conquest of Palestine as recorded in the Bible, archaeologists have reached two main conclusions from that time and place:

1. The whole of the Middle East seems to have experienced social and political upheaval in approximately 1200 B.C.
2. The upheaval was followed, during the opening centuries of the Iron Age, by what amounts to a "dark age" especially in Palestine—dark both in the sense that the ancient world underwent sociopolitical fragmentation and decline, and in that surviving written sources are scarce.[1]

DAME KATHLEEN KENYON

Write a short biography of Dame Kathleen Kenyon, a prominent archaeologist of the twentieth century. Include information about her major archaeological discoveries in the Holy Land. See, for example, the Palestine Exploration Fund at: http://www.pef.org.uk/Pages/Kenyon.htm.

In the Iron Age, a major fortress was erected on the summit of this site to protect Israel's southeastern border. While Amalekites and other nomadic peoples could be troublemakers, Judah's chief enemy in this direction was Edom. This fortress was destroyed by the Edomites at least once.

117

Teaching Approaches

1. Review the story of the fall of Jericho with the students. (The Israelites marched once around the city for six days. On the seventh day they marched around the city seven times, sounding horns. The walls collapsed.) Point out the strong symbolism connecting this story with the first creation story in Genesis. (God creates in six days and then rests on the seventh.) The writer describes the conquest of Jericho as a time of new creation for the Israelites. Also point out the symbolism connecting this story to the Hebrew idea of Jubilee. (The Jubilee year occurs in the seventh sabbatical year, seven times seven. The writer is inferring that the fall of Jericho is a form of justice. The land returns to its original owners, just like in the Jubilee Year.)

2. **Re-teach:** Ask the students to define "Miracle Warfare." (The Israelites believed that God would win battles for them so they did not need huge numbers or weapons.) Why did the theology of "Miracle Warfare" not continue? (The Israelites saw that their stronger neighbors and enemies all had kings. They wanted a king, too. They decided it was smarter to put their trust in military leaders, soldiers, and weapons, instead of God.)

3. Divide the class into two groups. Print the following statements on the board:
    1. **People of faith do not have to take responsibility for their own lives. They need to trust in God who is in charge. Then everything will turn out all right.**
    2. **People of faith realize they have a responsibility to work hard to make their own futures happen. This includes going to war and defending one's family from enemies.**

Chapter 5

4. Have one group develop a list of logical reasons to support statement 1. Have the other group develop a list of logical reasons to support statement 2. After sufficient preparation time, conduct a class debate, giving credence to the positive points in both statements.

5. Explain that people have debated the "morality" of warfare since the beginning of time. The Church at present has two positions regarding war. First, peace is to be maintained and war is to be avoided in most cases. (On the board or overhead, print **pacifist**. Explain that a pacifist is someone who believes all wars are unjust. A true pacifist will refuse to fight. Next, print **conscientious objector**. Explain that a conscientious objector is someone who believes a certain war is unjust and refuses to fight in that particular war. A conscientious objector will, however, fight in a war he or she deems just.) Also, there are some situations that justify going to war. Ask the students to name the conditions under which a war may be justified (the **just war doctrine**). Write these conditions on the board or overhead (see page 120 of the TWE). Briefly discuss a recent war the United States has entered into. Let the students discuss the justification of the war based on the guidelines listed.

THE OLD TESTAMENT

Israelite Warfare Traditions

War was most certainly a major part of the experience of the Hebrew people. Recall that Palestine was in the middle of the main roads that linked Egypt with Mesopotamia. Israel was very familiar with the armies of each civilization, as they marched through Palestine on their way to engage each other. In short, given the location of Palestine, it seems hardly surprising that war is a major subject of the Old Testament.

But location alone does not account for all the warfare described in the Old Testament. The early Israelites were involved in many conflicts with ancient societies that had gods of war. These people believed that their gods went to war with their armies to help in the conflict. Consider the carving of the Assyrian monarch Assurbanipal below. Flying over the head of the mighty Assyrian ruler is an image of Assur, the national god of the empire, with his bow drawn. This carving illustrates the

Assurbanipal

belief that the gods fought *with* the armies of the ancient world. The Israelites had a rather different notion about the connection of Yahweh with warfare. Recall how Moses reassured the people as they prepared to cross the Red Sea:

> Fear not! Stand your ground, and you will see the victory the Lord will win for you today. These Egyptians whom you see today you will never see again. The Lord himself will fight for you; you have only to keep still (Ex 14:13–14).

The unique idea in this passage is that the Lord will actually fight *for* Israel, not merely *with* Israel's warriors. The idea of warfare in earliest Israel was very unusual. It was fought miraculously by God alone, with minimal involvement of the people and sometimes, as with the case with the Egyptian defeat in the Red Sea, with no involvement at all!

In Judges 7, this idea is illustrated again in a very powerful (and somewhat humorous) way. The judge Gideon thinks that he needs a huge army to defeat the Midianites. He starts with nearly 30,000 soldiers. But God tells him to *reduce* his armies. In the end, Gideon is told to go to war against the Midianites with an army composed of just three hundred men carrying horns in one hand and jars and torches in the other (see Jgs 7:20). They don't have a hand free to draw a sword or any other weapon! The point of this unusual story for the Israelites was that wars were won through the power of God, not men.

Also interesting to note are all the exemptions listed in Deuteronomy 20, allowing men to avoid fighting in a war. A man who had just planted a garden, built a house, or become engaged to marry, was to refrain from fighting. Also, those who were afraid were supposed to go home (see Ex 20:8–9). The reason the exemptions are so liberal is again to show that it is only God's power that matters in war. As Moses told the soldiers:

Resources

Printed Materials

"Joshua, The Book of" and "Judges, The Book of" in *The Oxford Companion to the Bible*, ed. by Bruce M. Metzger and Michael D. Coogan. (New York, NY: Oxford University Press, 1993), pp. 384–387, 397–399.

"Joshua" and "Judges" in *Dictionary of the Bible*, ed. by John L. McKenzie, S.J. (New York, NY: Macmillan Publishing Co., Inc., 1965), pp. 457–459, 464–465.

Coogan, Michael David. "Joshua" in *The New Jerome Biblical Commentary*, ed. by Raymond E. Brown, S.S., Joseph A. Fitzmyer, S.J., and Roland E. Murphy, O.Carm. (Englewood Cliffs, NJ: Prentice Hall, 1990), pp. 110–131.

Exum, J. Cheryl. "Judges" in *Harper's Bible Commentary*, ed. by James L. Mays. (San Francisco, CA: Harper & Row Publishers, 1988), pp. 245–261.

Grindel, John A., C.M. "Joshua" in *The Collegeville Bible Commentary*, ed. by Dianne Bergant, C.S.A. and Robert J. Karris, O.F.M. (Collegeville, MN: The Liturgical Press, 1989), pp. 229–247.

Grindel, John A., C.M. "Judges" in *The Collegeville Bible Commentary*, ed. by Dianne Bergant, C.S.A. and Robert J. Karris, O.F.M. (Collegeville, MN: The Liturgical Press, 1989), pp. 248–264.

O'Connor, M. "Judges" in *The New Jerome Biblical Commentary*, ed. by Raymond E. Brown, S.S., Joseph A. Fitzmyer, S.J., and Roland E. Murphy, O.Carm. (Englewood Cliffs, NJ: Prentice Hall, 1990), pp. 132–144.

Rast, Walter E. "Joshua" in *Harper's Bible Commentary*, ed. by James L. Mays. (San Francisco, CA: Harper & Row Publishers, 1988), pp. 235–244.

The Journey Takes New Shape

Hear, O Israel! Today you are going into battle against your enemies. Be not weakhearted or afraid; be neither alarmed nor frightened by them. For it is the Lord, your God, who goes with you to fight for you against your enemies and give you victory (Dt 20:3–4).

This theology of "**Miracle Warfare**" (this concept has been referred to as "Divine Warfare" or "Yahweh War") did not continue. Why not? The reason is explained in the first book of Samuel, when Israel chose a human king.

Read 1 Samuel 7–8

In 1 Samuel 8, the people ask for a king, and Samuel the prophet is disappointed. God is also disappointed, so it seems, because he tells Samuel, "They are rejecting me as their king" (1 Sm 8:7). This passage infers that God is King! An ancient king was mainly a warrior. Rejecting God as their warrior and king meant the Israelites no longer trusted God to protect them by means of miracles. To make matters worse, the rejection of God as king and the request to "be like the other nations" (1 Sm 8:5) occur right after 1 Samuel 7, which tells of yet another miraculous deliverance of the Israelites from the Philistines by God. The request for a king in chapter 8 is doubly ungrateful, given what had just happened.

Another intriguing point from 1 Samuel 8 is all the things that the people will have to face when they get a human king instead of honoring God as their king—mainly taxation and the military draft. The theological point is clear: in the past the Israelites trusted God for deliverance from enemies. Now they want to do it themselves. God tells the Israelites that they will suffer all the financial and social strains of maintaining a military just as the other nations do (1 Sm 8:10–18).

From this time on in Deuteronomic History, the warfare of the Israelites becomes much more conventional in focus. There are only occasional reminders of the days of Miraculous Warfare—typically associated with prophets, especially Elijah and Elisha (see 2 Kgs 6).

In summary, there is a major change in the practice of warfare in Ancient Israel—from the early period of Miracle Warfare to the later period, during the monarchy, of conventional warfare. Throughout Deuteronomic History, there is an impression that some of the authors treated that earlier period as a kind of "golden age" when Israel trusted God more deeply and God responded with miraculous protection. Perhaps the story of the fall of Jericho reflects this same tendency to describe events as if they were "better then because of our greater trust in God." Whatever the case, the Old Testament authors associated conventional warfare with a time when the Israelites rejected God.

Miracle Warfare—The idea, unique to the Israelites, that God will fight, not just *with* them, but *for* them against their enemies.

6. Distribute copies of "The Challenge of Peace" (Handout 5A, page 276 of the TWE) from the document by the United States Catholic bishops. Direct the students to read the handout and then begin working on the Journal Assignment, page 121. Remind the students that they must reference the stories from Joshua and Judges in their argument. They will be asked to share their thoughts at the next class session.

Resources

Audiovisual Materials

A & E Old Testament Collection: Samson and Delilah (New Video Group)—50 minutes

Location footage, rare paintings and artifacts, and interviews with experts help to detail the tragic story of judge Samson and Delilah.

Ancient Tales from a Promised Land: Deborah and the Headbanger/Gideon Gets His Woolly Wet (Ecufilm)—30 minutes

The first part of the video depicts the Israelites asking Deborah for advice. She appoints Barak to lead an army against their enemies. In the second part, Gideon smashes up the Canaanite corn goddess, proving her to be completely powerless against Yahweh.

Ancient Tales from a Promised Land: Gideon's Exploding Pickle Pots/Samson Gets Knotted (Ecufilm)—30 minutes

In the first part of this video, the outnumbered Israelite army uses trickery to frighten the Canaanites into surrendering. In the second part, judge Samson marries a Philistine girl, who gets him into trouble.

Ancient Tales from a Promised Land: Samson Gets a Haircut/Samuel and the Spooky Godbox (Ecufilm)—30 minutes

In the first part of this video, Samson falls in love with Delilah, another Philistine. She betrays him by revealing the reason for his strength. In the second part, the Philistines steal the Ark of the Covenant. Meanwhile, Samuel emerges as leader of the Israelites.

Old Testament: Gideon, the Liberator (Vanguard)—15 minutes

Depicts Gideon and 300 Israelites driving out the invading Midianites.

Standard Video Bible Series: Joshua/Judges (Kerr Associates)

Offers interviews with Christian and Jewish scholars that raise questions about the military victories described in the book of Joshua, the role of women such as Deborah, and what the Joshua/Judges saga has to do with the present-day Middle East.

Chapter 5

7. **Homework Assignment:**
   - Answer the Review and Reflections questions 1–3, page 120. For question 3, list each point of the just war doctrine.
   - Complete the Journal Assignment on page 121.
   - Assign the exercise, "Israel's Climate Changes," (page 125). You may wish to do a comparison of weather (e.g., temperature, rainfall, etc.) between Israel and the region you live in.
   - Read "Exploits of the Judges," (pages 121–124) including the separate features.

THE OLD TESTAMENT

PEACE OVER WAR

It can never be claimed—though some have tried—that the Bible favors warfare over peacemaking. Those who hold to this false argument often cite examples of "Divine Warfare" found in the Old Testament. Their attempt to legitimize war from this argument ignores the teaching of 1 Samuel 8: traditional warfare in the Old Testament came only after the people rejected God as king. War was a result of Israel's unfaithfulness and lack of trust, not Yahweh's desire to conquer other peoples in his name.

The Church has long held to the position that war must be averted: "All citizens and all governments are obliged to work for the avoidance of war" (CCC, 2308). Yet, the Church also acknowledges that there are some situations where military force may be justified. The conditions for legitimate defense by military force are summarized in the "**just war doctrine**," which derives, in part, from the ideas elaborated by St. Augustine. Here are the main points of this doctrine:

- The war must have a "just cause" like self-defense. It must also be called by a legitimate moral authority.
- The aggressor must have inflicted lasting, grave, and certain damage on the attacked nation(s).
- All other means of settling the dispute must be shown to be impractical or ineffective.
- There must be serious prospects for the success of the war.
- Non-combatants are not to be targeted and the use of weapons may not produce evils graver than the evil being perpetrated by the aggressor nation. (The use of modern weapons of mass destruction weighs very heavily in this case (see also, CCC 2307–2317).

Many Catholics throughout history have chosen to avoid war altogether through history and chose a completely non-violent solution (see American bishops' 1983 Pastoral Letter, *The Challenge of Peace: God's Promise and Our Response*). As the bishops' 1983 document states: "There is no notion of a warrior God who will lead the people in an historical victory over its enemies in the New Testament."

REVIEW & REFLECTION

1. Explain some of the differences in the accounts of the settlement of Canaan put forward in the books of Joshua and Judges. What conclusions have archaeologists reached about the time period of the settlement of Canaan by the Israelites?
2. Explain the concept of "Miracle Warfare." Give two examples of battles that were won by "miracles" and explain how the details provided in the story show that the victory was due to God and not to the prowess of Israel's warriors.
3. Give an explanation of the just war doctrine first developed by St. Augustine.

Review and Reflection Answers

1. The book of Joshua describes a united Israel (all twelve tribes) fighting against the Canaanites. The book of Judges describes a slow settlement, in which one or two individual tribes fought for small portions of land. Archaeologists such as Dame Kathleen Kenyon have concluded that Jericho and some of the other cities described in Joshua and Judges were actually deserted by the time the Israelites arrived there.
2. "Miracle Warfare" is a concept that says God is a Warrior and a King. God will fight and win battles for the Israelites. The Israelites do not have to do much, if anything, to procure victory. Two examples of miracle warfare are the conquest of Jericho (the people blew on horns and the walls came tumbling down) and Gideon's victory over the Midianites (instead of taking 32,000 soldiers, Gideon took only 300 men, and God enabled his side to be victorious).
3. The just war doctrine says that war may be justified if the following conditions are met:
   - The war must have a "just cause," such as self-defense against an aggressor.
   - A legitimate moral authority must declare the war.
   - All peaceful means of settling the dispute must have been tried and shown to fail.
   - The aggressor must have inflicted lasting, grave, and certain damage.
   - There must be a serious probability of winning the war.
   - Non-combatants are not to be targets.
   - The use of weapons may not produce evils greater than the evil that already exists.

THE JOURNEY TAKES NEW SHAPE

JOURNAL ASSIGNMENT

- Use the stories of Joshua and Judges to support your own argument for or against the use of warfare to resolve disputes among nations. Be as persuasive as you can.

Exploits of the Judges

The Hebrew word *shofet* was traditionally translated as the English word "**judge**," although the actual role of a "shofet" may be closer to "temporary military leader." The function of the judges as described in the book of Judges included other responsibilities besides military leadership. For example, judges also settled political disputes within their own tribe and between tribes and continually reminded the people to turn to God.

The judges filled the gap in leadership between the time of Joshua (ca 1200 B.C.) and the beginning of the monarchy (ca 1030 B.C.) The judges were leaders who were spiritually selected by God to lead the tribal peoples—though they rarely led *all* of the tribes at the same time. Three of the most well known judges are the following:

- *Deborah*, a woman who successfully called a war in which Israel was victorious, and is heralded in the famous "Song of Deborah" (Judges 5);
- *Gideon*, a man who had serious doubts about God's ability to lead his people; and
- *Samson*, who was considered wise, yet allowed his love for the wrong woman (a Philistine woman named Delilah) to lead him to foolish decisions.

While it is difficult to place dates on the exact time of the judges, a major theme of the judge stories seems to be that there *was* a time when the Israelites were led by God. Whenever God needed assistance, he would spiritually "deputize" a judge for a brief period. Also, when any of these judges was asked to be "king," he or she very dutifully reminded the people that *Yahweh alone was their king*. The concluding chapters of the book of Judges note some of the disintegration of the unity within and among the tribes of Israel, leading to the call for a new form of leadership. The final verse of Judges expresses this: "In those days there was no king in Israel; everyone did what he thought best" (Jgs 21:25).

The following sections briefly detail the stories of the three most famous judges.

Deborah
Read Judges 4–5

Deborah is called both a prophetess and a judge. Her story is a second version of the defeat of the king of Hazor.

After another incident of Israel offending Yahweh, the Israelites found themselves under the reign of the Canaanite Jabin, who reigned in Hazor. The general of his army was Sisera. Deborah summoned the Israelite general Barak and asked him to march on the troops of Sisera. Barak

just war doctrine—Teachings of the Church that define the moral limits of warfare.

judge—In ancient Israel, one who acted as a temporary military leader, as well as arbiter of disputes within and between tribes. Judges were also expected to remind the people of their responsibility to God.

EXPLOITS OF THE JUDGES

Bell-Ringer

1. Divide the class into four groups. Encourage each group to develop a way to summarize the assigned story in a creative way (e.g., choral reading, mime, contemporary role play) to get the religious message across. Provide any necessary supplies (e.g., art supplies for puppets, masks, or other props). Give the following assignment:

- Group 1: Read and summarize Judges 4–5.
- Group 2: Read and summarize Judges 6–8:35.
- Group 3: Read and summarize Judges 13–16.
- Group 4: Read and summarize the book of Ruth.

Allow about 20 to 25 minutes for the class to work on their summaries.

Resources
Internet Links

www.dur.ac.uk/oriental.museum
Tour the Oriental Museum at the University of Durham, England, to view findings from excavations of Jericho, the city conquered by Joshua.

www.carlos.emory.edu/COLLECTION/NEAREAST
Visit the near Eastern exhibit at the Michael C. Carlos Museum in Atlanta, Georgia. The collection includes objects from the ancient site of Jericho.

www.bible.ca/maps
View a high-resolution map of the land of the twelve Israelite tribes in Canaan, from Joshua to Saul (1400–1100 B.C.).

http://research.haifa.ac.il/~hecht/
Visit the Reuben and Edith Hecht Museum at the University of Haifa in Israel. See artifacts from the Late Canaanite Period (1550–1200 B.C.).

www.christiananswers.net/q-abr/abr-a011.html
Slides and discussion of archaeological digs at the site of ancient Jericho. Presents evidence that the city walls really did tumble down in an earthquake.

Chapter 5

Teaching Approaches

1. Call on each group to present its story to the class. Make sure everyone understands the basics of the four stories, as well as their religious message. Review and supplement with the following information as needed:

- The poem of Deborah is one of the oldest pieces in the Bible. The poem recounts Deborah's story, the successful calling of a holy war in which the Israelites were victorious.
- Despite Gideon's objections that he was too weak and unworthy, the angel of the Lord assured Gideon that he would lead the Israelites to victory. God gave him the sign of a fleece (6:36–40) to show that Yahweh would deliver Israel through him.
- The real source of Samson's strength was not his hair, but the spirit of God which enabled him to fight Israel's enemies, the Philistines. Samson's story reveals a strong man who was also flawed and who suffered for his infidelities in much of the same way Israel suffered throughout history.
- Ruth is mentioned in the family tree of Jesus (Mt 1:5). In the Jewish liturgy the book of Ruth is read on the feast of Pentecost. The book describes the loyalty of Ruth, It was likely written after the Babylonian exile when national fervor encouraged intolerance of foreigners, and marriages between Jews and Gentiles were dissolved.

---

responded to Deborah, "If you come with me I will go; if you do not come with me, I will not go" (Jgs 4:8). Deborah consented and also pointed out that God would eventually have Sisera fall under the power of a woman.

The fall occurred when Sisera was retreating from Barak's forces. When he sought to hide in the tent of a friend's wife, Jael, he expected her to help him avoid capture. Instead, she murdered him while he was asleep, driving a peg through his temple down into the ground. Sisera's cowardice in deserting his army and hiding behind a woman was seen as even worse than Jael's disregard for the customs of hospitality, which would ordinarily prohibit the murder of a guest.

The story is accompanied by a poem—the Canticle of Deborah—in which Sisera's fate is further ridiculed and Jael is redeemed:

> Blessed among women be Jael,
>   blessed among tent-dwelling women.
> He asked for water, she gave him milk;
>   in a princely bowl she offered curds.
> With her left hand she reached for a peg,
>   with her right, for the workman's mallet.
> She hammered Sisera, crushed his head;
>   she smashed, stove in his temple
>   (Jgs 5:24–26).

The poem itself is considered to be among the oldest passages in the entire Bible, perhaps written before the time of the Israelite monarchy.

Gideon
Read Judges 6–8:35

Following the time of Deborah, the Israelites again offended the Lord and faced the rule of the Midianites. God raised a young man, Gideon, to lead the people as judge. Gideon protested to the Lord: "How can I save Israel? My family is the meanest [poorest] in Manasseh, and I am the most insignificant in my father's house" (Jgs 6:15). The Lord responded, "I shall be with you, and you will cut Midian down to the last man" (Jgs 6:16).

After Gideon led victory over the Midianites, the people wanted him to be king. He told them: "I will not rule over you, nor shall my son rule over you. The Lord must rule over you" (Jgs 8:23).

However, the story immediately reports that Gideon next asked the people for their gold taken as booty from the latest battle. From the gold, Gideon fashioned an *ephod*, which was likely a golden idol. The story shows how easily even a leader of Israel could be swayed away from God. Later, God brought a curse on Gideon's sons because of Gideon's idolatry.

Samson
Read Judges 13–16

Samson's story begins with a legend of his birth, announced by an angel to his mother who was thought to be barren. (Remember, birth stories occur in the Bible when the person is to play a significant role in the history of Israel.) The woman had her son take the Nazirite vow, described in Numbers 6:5, to set himself apart for the Lord and let his hair grow freely. The Lord said to her:

> As for the son you will conceive and bear, no razor shall touch his head, for this boy is to be consecrated to God from the womb. It is he who will begin the deliverance of Israel from the power of the Philistines (Jgs 13:5).

The legend around Samson was that his strength came from his long hair. Actually, his reliance on God was the source of his strength. Among his legendary feats were these:

- He killed a lion with his bare hands, tearing it "in pieces as one tears a kid [goat]" (Jgs 14:6).
- He fixed torches on the tails of three hundred foxes and set them loose in

the grain fields of the Philistines (Jgs 15:5).
- He killed a thousand men with the "jawbone of an ass" (Jgs 15:15).
- He pushed on two columns of the temple of Dagon, killing himself along with "more than those he had killed during his lifetime" (Jgs 16:30).

Earlier, Samson's fiancée had betrayed him to the Philistines at their wedding feast and then married his best man. The men of Gaza laid an ambush for Samson while he was with a harlot in their city; and then there was Samson's weakness, his foolish love for Delilah. His infidelities caused the loss of his personal strength in the same way Israel's infidelities to the Lord caused a loss of their independence and power as a nation.

The book of Judges provides more evidence of the need for Israel's reliance on Yahweh. When the Israelites are faithful to the covenant, they are supported by the Lord; when they are not, they fall under the rule of oppressors. What the book of Judges does not do, however, is provide much additional detail on the formation of Israel as a people and the development of their religious codes.

LOYALTY

Among her many positive traits, Ruth was loyal to her first husband, his family, and his religion. Write a poem, short essay, or design a piece of artwork that expresses the story and character of Ruth.

levirate marriage—The marriage of a widow to a near relative of her deceased husband. The first male child of a levirate marriage would be considered the legal son of the widow's first husband.

THE BOOK OF RUTH

A glance at the table of contents of the Old Testament will show that the book of Ruth comes immediately after the book of Judges and just prior to 1 and 2 Samuel. This placement was made in later Greek and Latin canons of the Bible, probably because the book contains a genealogy that connects Ruth, a Moabite woman, with the family of King David. The book was most likely written sometime after the Babylonian exile. But the book itself also claims to come from the time of the judges (see Ru 1:1).

The story of Ruth involves a foreign woman's fidelity to the Jewish family of her widowed husband. Ruth follows her mother-in-law, Naomi, back to the land of Judah after the death of her husband, despite Naomi's protests that she ought to return to her father's house and be married again. Once back in Judah, Ruth *is* married again, observing a law detailed in the book of Leviticus that required her to marry her nearest male relative. This was called a **levirate marriage**; it would allow her to bear a son who would be considered her first husband's heir. This law was intended to keep property within the same clan or family by ensuring that there was an heir even if a man died before he had a son. By eventually marrying Boaz, her relative by marriage, Ruth was sealed by covenant to the Israelite family, becoming an ancestor of King David (and of Jesus). Although Ruth was a foreigner, she accepted the God of her Jewish husband and today is honored for her choice.

---

2. Introduce the exercise "Loyalty," page 123. You may wish to divide the class into three groups and assign one of each type of exercise (poem, short essay, or artwork) to the people in each group. Plan to set up a display table for the next class session where these works on Loyalty can be viewed by all.

3. If time permits, have the students begin working individually on the Journal Assignment, page 124. To parallel their profile of biblical courage, have the students locate a contemporary news story of a person who exemplifies courage and compare it to the Old Testament judge they wrote about.

4. **Homework Assignment:**
   - Answer the Review and Reflection questions 1–3, page 124.
   - Complete the Journal Assignment on page 124, if you have not already done so.
   - Read the entire section, "Israel at Home In Palestine" (pages 124–128).
   - The exercise, "Israel's Climate Changes" (page 125) will be due at the next session.

Chapter 5

ISRAEL AT HOME IN PALESTINE

Bell-Ringer

1. Call on students to present their findings to the exercise, "Israel Climate Changes." Arrange for displays on power point, poster board, or other display. The following website offers some details on month to month climate changes, including rainfall and temperature, in various cities of Israel:

www.geographyiq.com/countries/is/Israel_climate_f.htm

THE OLD TESTAMENT

REVIEW & REFLECTION

1. What was the function of the judges in Israel following the settlement of Palestine?
2. What was the traditional response of the judges if the people of Israel asked them to be king?
3. Name the main religious point throughout the book of Judges about the relationship between Israel and God.

JOURNAL ASSIGNMENT

- Read the full account in the book of Judges of one of the three judges: Deborah (Jgs 4–5), Gideon (Jgs 6–8), or Samson (Jgs 13–16). Write a short "profile of courage" of the judge you have chosen.

Israel at Home In Palestine

Returning to the larger question of how Palestine was settled by the Israelites, the answers to two related questions can help shed more light on the issue:

1. Did most of the people who formed the twelve tribes of Israel come to Palestine from Egypt with Moses?
2. Or, were most of these people native to the land, simply changing their religious and political identities upon the arrival of some returning slaves from Egypt?

From archaeological evidence it can be determined that the central hill country of Palestine suddenly grew in population in the early Iron Age, that is, between 1200 and 1000 B.C. In previously uninhabited land, where only about twenty-three villages once existed, archaeologists have identified some 114 new villages from that period.[2] Furthermore, judging from the material remains of many of these villages, their pottery styles are virtually the same as Canaanite cities on the coastal plains.

Everyone agrees that new villages suddenly appeared in the hill country. But where did the people who formed these villages originate? Were they all former slaves from Egypt? Consider for a moment if they were not all former slaves from Egypt.

This position is supported by the book of Judges, which seems to describe slow settlement among other peoples rather than the organized military campaign as described in the book of Joshua. The stories of a slow settlement and the similar pottery and architecture suggest that some of the new villages in the hill country were established by people who had never left Canaan and who had never been slaves in Egypt. Instead, they simply left the larger coastal towns and the Transjordan (land across the Jordan River from Palestine) and settled in the new villages in the hills.

There are a number of reasons why people from the lowlands of Canaan might have relocated to the hillsides. There was general unrest throughout the Ancient Near East in this time. Egyptian authority was weakened, and there were small warring

---

Review and Reflection Answers

1. The judges were temporary military leaders, settling disputes within one tribe or between two or more tribes. Some judges also had the gift of prophecy, reminding the people to turn to God.
2. The judges traditionally replied that they already had a king, Yahweh. God alone was their king.
3. The main points throughout the book of Judges are these: We are to trust in God rather than in our own abilities or strength. We are to be faithful to Yahweh. When Israel is not faithful, the country loses its independence and power; Israel falls under the rule of oppressors. When Israel is faithful to God, God supports them and gives them victory over their enemies.

The Journey Takes New Shape

city-states in the area that is now Syria and Lebanon. Perhaps the people wanted to escape the upheaval in the cities caused by invaders. Also, the groups of "sea peoples" (some of whom were the famous Philistines) arrived from what are today Greek territories, and their arrival may have pushed some of the peasants further into the hills to escape these new warriors.

There is some evidence to indicate that the Philistines and other sea peoples may have come to Canaan because of climatic changes that made their own homelands more difficult to farm. Perhaps the radical climate changes and political pressures in these centuries forced major population shifts, which might have caused many peoples to abandon the Canaanite cities on the coast for an independent existence in the hills. After all, the Bible not only records conflict with the Philistines, but it also points out that they were fearsome warriors. Perhaps the many battles of the book of Joshua and Judges were generally correct memories of conflict, retold much later in simplified and well-ordered terms.

It is also possible that people left the Canaanite city states because life there was oppressive—especially for the poor. Their movement may have been a revolutionary response to their poverty, a deliberate escape to a place where land did not end up in the hands of the few wealthy landowners and kings of the Canaanite cities. The Law of Moses contrasts dramatically with what we know about the older Canaanite religious views. Certainly the stories of the prophets emphasize a great contrast between the injustice and violence of the Canaanites, and the more just and equal sharing of the Mosaic law. This new society would have been appealing to people who were poor and oppressed.

According to the stories that fit more typically under the book of Judges than the book of Joshua, the settlement process was much slower than Joshua's "lightning campaign" and likely took between 200 and 300 years or longer. Certainly there may have been some violence in the lives of the Israelites (raiding parties, trouble with Canaanite cities, conflict with the Philistines) as described in both Joshua and Judges, but these battles may not have been part of a large organized conquest of one people by another. Instead, the formation of a people in the hillsides of

Israel's Climate Changes

Produce a chart that details month-to-month climate changes (including rainfall totals) for at least three different regions (e.g., coastal, mountain, desert) of modern Israel. Further explore the question of how radical differences in the climate might cause people to prefer to live in other regions of the nation other than the coast. Cite other evidence gleaned from news articles and real estate statistics on the subject.

The Sea of Galilee

125

Teaching Approaches

1. **Re-teach:** With the students, go over the four possible reasons that caused people to settle in the hill country of Palestine between 1200 and 1000 B.C.? Some of these reasons are:
   - The need to escape the political unrest and battles taking place in the coastal towns at this time.
   - The need to avoid conflict with the sea peoples who arrived at this time in the coastal towns.
   - The need to escape the oppression the poor experienced in the coastal cities. They looked to the hill country and the more liberal Israelite laws for a better life.

2. Point out that regardless of how the Israelites came to settle in Canaan, the central religious message of the books of Joshua and Judges is that the people are to turn away from false gods and to trust God completely.

Chapter 5

3. Direct the students to the Learn by Doing exercise on page 129. Make this an individual, reflective exercise. Point out that the service that Joshua 24:1–24 calls for is not easy and those who promise themselves to it must fight against human weakness.

THE OLD TESTAMENT

Palestine may have been the result of a combination of the common interests of the arriving former slaves from Egypt and the rural peoples caught between the competing interests of major empires (Egypt and Mesopotamia) and affected by the lesser political ambitions of smaller states and cities. Although almost all scholarship rejects the idea of a huge migration of former slaves from Egypt—certainly not 600,000 as the traditional Biblical number would have it—there is also little doubt that some Hebrew slaves came from Egypt and that Moses was most certainly a historical figure who led and taught them during their wilderness sojourn between Egypt and Palestine. With some people already living in Canaan (e.g., Rahab), these groups organized into a coherent identity—the Tribes of Israel.

The entire process resulting in the formation of a people of Israel settled in Palestine may not have been complete until the start of the monarchy (ca. 1000 B.C.). Under this view, it was only when the Israelites looked back while in exile in Babylon that they were able to write and edit the version of the experience that appears in the books of Joshua and Judges. But why do the books of Joshua and Judges represent the foundation of Israel as a military conquest by people exclusively outside of Canaanite society when evidence suggests that, in reality, people from Canaan joined in the formation of the Israelite people during the course of a slow settlement of the region?

The books of Joshua and Judges were written after the fall and destruction of Jerusalem in 587 B.C. One of the central questions the authors faced was why God allowed this to happen. Was it because the people lacked faith? Remembering the settlement stories as part of an organized conquest may well have been motivated by the religious lessons the authors wished to teach a later generation. Perhaps the laying out of the events in Joshua and Judges was meant to exaggerate the contrast between the loss of faith in the present time (the time of exile), which resulted in catastrophe, and the trust of the people in the earlier era, which resulted in great feats of conquest and glory. It is as if God inspired the authors to say, "Look what we accomplished when we truly trusted Yahweh, rather than our own resources."

The Israelites: People of the Hills

However the Israelites actually settled Palestine, it is clear that the hill country of Palestine was the area that became the homeland for the people of Israel. Israelite social formation began to emerge at the Iron Age (1200–1000 B.C.) and continued to evolve to a monarchy system after 1000 B.C. Other elements of an Israelite government and social structure can be gleaned from both the

Pottery from the Iron Age, 1200-1000 B.C.

126

Background Information

Bet Av

The family unit in Israel was partriarchical, hence the term *Bet Av* or "House of the Father." The criterion for family membership was a blood relationship,

legal ties (marriage or adoption), or geographical proximity. The father was head of the family and chief authority. The father was also expected to be compassionate and loving to his family. (see Ps 103:13; Gn 25:28;37:4;44:20).

The patriarchal blessing carried legal force with regard to the distribution of the estate of the father. He controlled the family property (Nm 26:54–55). The mother occupied a place of honor and authority in spite of her subordination to her husband. At his death she could become the actual and legal head of the household (see 11Kgs 8:16) if there were no sons who were of legal age.

Bible and other historical and archaeological sources.

The basic social unit of a village in Israel was the *Bet Av* ("House of the Father"). This was a patriarchal household of extended family members. There is even strong evidence that the famous "four pillar house" that archaeologists have identified in many early Israelite villages was the basic physical unit of residence for these *Bet Av* units.

The *Bet Avs* were themselves gathered into associations that became known as "clans" (*Mishpachah* in Hebrew). These clans probably arose from two natural needs—agricultural needs for families to help each other with planting and harvest, and military needs for families to help defend each other.

Finally, as the Israelites emerged as a people, so did the traditional "tribes." These tribes were probably originally identified by the geographical regions they occupied, though some of the tribal names may even predate their association with the Israelites. Of course, the Biblical authors wrote from a later perspective suggesting that these "tribes" had their origins in the twelve sons of Jacob.

The village-based tribes were governed by councils of elders—the heads of the various "Houses of the Father." Many Biblical texts explain that day-to-day judgments and general order were maintained by appealing to these elders. The elders made decisions based on traditional laws that were supplemented by the formal religious traditions associated with Moses (whose laws may well have included much of these traditional village laws in the first place). Some anthropologists compare early Israel to villages in developing societies today, some of which have elders who preside over village life.

Early Israelite Religious Practices

The Biblical texts tell us that the early Israelites were influenced by the Canaanites, even in religion. They turned to Baal to help ensure abundant crops and livestock in defiance of the covenant, though they did not entirely abandon Yahweh. While there are clear signs of Canaanite influence throughout the Bible, the Israelites' religion eventually became a distinct tradition, radically different from all the surrounding religious options.

The Israelite religion was revolutionary in its expectations of the people. The life of the people in the hills of Palestine was to be a place to model this new social existence. But more temptations followed, and the worshippers of Yahweh eventually had their strength and moral convictions tested. The time of the kings was one of even greater betrayal of the covenant, until eventually the people were removed from the land and sent into exile.

Bet Av—The basic social unit of the Israelite society, a patriarchal household of immediate and extended family members.

Mishpachah—The Hebrew word for a "clan" that was an association of related *Bet Avs*, gathered together to help with planting and harvesting, and with defense against aggressive neighbors.

THE JOURNEY TAKES NEW SHAPE

4. **Homework Assignment:**
   - Answer the Review and Reflection questions 1–3, page 128.
   - Complete the Journal Assignment on page 128. Make sure that you focus more on familial, social, and cultural structures than on political and economic structures of the time.
   - Read the "Further Reflections" section of the text, pages 128–129.
   - Complete the reflective Learn by Doing exercise, page 129.

Enrichment: Test the pattern of the Israelite's history described above (sin, Yahweh's punishment, sorrow, Israelite's conversion and return to Yahweh) by reading Judges 2:1–4, 3—4 and explaining how this pattern is present in these passages.

Enrichment: Expand on the "How We Love Others" exercise (page 114). Develop more strategies for reaching out to others. Ideas should focus on service oriented activities. For example: visiting with shut-ins, doing chores for neighbors, asking forgiveness from those who have hurt you.

Chapter 5

FURTHER REFLECTIONS

Bell-Ringer

1. Building on the Learn by Doing exercise, lead a discussion on idols. Call on volunteers to share their lists of popular idols that they or their peer group worship. Compile a class list of the most mentioned idols. Discuss possible plans for avoiding the temptation of idolizing the items on the list. Call on the students to present ideas about how they can put God first in their lives.

Teaching Approaches

1. **Re-teach** the homework reading assignment by asking these questions:
   - What is the behavioral pattern that seems to repeat itself through the books of Joshua and Judges? (The people are disloyal to Yahweh. As a result, their enemies oppress them. The people then seek repentance. Yahweh sends a judge to deliver them from the evil they face. When peace is restored, they return to ignoring God and worshipping idols. The cycle then repeats itself.)
   - What does the word "conversion" mean? (Conversion means a radical reorientation of one's life.)
   - How do you think God is calling teens today to conversion? (Accept all reasonable answers.)

2. **Review:** Use the vocabulary words and the Review and Reflection questions to help the students study for the Chapter 5 Test.

3. **Prayer Service:** Play a recording or lead singing of "Blest be the Lord" (see page 116 of the TWE). Call on a student to read Joshua 1:7–9. Then divide the class into two sides. Have them recite the prayer of St. Ignatius (see Called to Prayer, page 129), alternating from line to line. Choose another student to read Ruth 1:16–17. Allow time for shared reflection on both readings. Conclude with another song, for example, "Shelter Me, O God" (see page 116).

4. **Homework Assignment:**
   - Carry out your plan for the exercise, "How We Love Others" (page 114).
   - Study for the Chapter 5 Test.

THE OLD TESTAMENT

REVIEW & REFLECTION

1. List some of the indications that the settlement of Canaan occurred at a slower pace than the conquest stories of the book of Joshua describe.
2. What was the religious lesson that the authors of Joshua and Judges meant to convey with their conquest stories?
3. Describe the social organization of the villages of ancient Israel.

JOURNAL ASSIGNMENT

- How is the social organization of modern America similar to and/or different from that of ancient Israel? What do you think you would have liked or disliked about the *Bet Av* and *Mishpachah* system?

Further Reflections

The stories of the judges are of charismatic leaders who courageously cared for the well-being of the tribes of Israel in the times of crisis.

The book of Judges includes the Deuteronomic cycle of judgment on Israel in these stories. For example, note the pattern of 1) apostasy (abandoning God), 2) oppression by Gentiles, 3) penitence by Israel, and 4) deliverance to freedom in the following passage:

> Because they had thus abandoned him and served Baal and the Ashtaroth, the anger of the Lord flared up against Israel, and he delivered them over to plunderers who despoiled them. He allowed them to fall into the power of their enemies round about whom they were no longer able to withstand. Whatever they undertook, the Lord turned into disaster for them, as in his warning he had sworn he would do, till they were in great distress. . . . Whenever the Lord raised up judges for them, he would be with the judge and save them from the power of their enemies as long as the judge lived; it was thus the Lord took pity on their distressful cries of affliction under their oppressors. But when the judge died, they would relapse and do worse than their fathers, following other gods in service and worship, relinquishing none of their evil practices or stubborn conduct (Jgs 2:13–15, 18–19).

As this passage shows, the problems of the tribe can be traced to disloyalty to Yahweh. Only when the people are oppressed by enemies do they seek repentance. Yahweh responds to their change of heart and sends a judge to deliver them from the evil they face. When peace is restored, however, they return to ignoring God and worshipping idols. Then the cycle repeats itself.

The religious theme found in Joshua and Judges is also found in the New Testament. *Conversion*—a radical reorientation of one's life—is a central element of Christ's preaching. Catholics seek this type of repentance and renewal in the sacrament of

---

Review and Reflection Answers

1. The formation of the people in the hillsides may be the result of a combination of the common interests of the arriving former slaves and the competing interests of the major empires (Egypt and Mesopotamia). Also the lesser ambitions of the smaller states and cities played a role in this formation as well.
2. The authors of Joshua and Judges were trying to remind the people that when they trusted God in the past, life went well for them. When they did not trust God, their enemies triumphed over them.
3. The basic social unit was the *Bet Av,* the House of the Father. This was a patriarchal household of extended family members. The *Bet Avs* were gathered into associations known as clans. Clans in the same geographical region eventually gave rise to tribes, that were probably governed by a council of elders.

Penance. As the *Catechism of the Catholic Church* teaches:

> Conversion is first of all a work of the grace of God who makes our hearts return to him . . . God gives us the strength to begin anew. It is in discovering the greatness of God's love that our heart is shaken by the horror and weight of sin and begins to fear offending God by sin and being separated from him (CCC, 1432).

Like the Israelites before, people today often return to their sinfulness and remain in need of conversion over and over.

Learn By Doing
Read Joshua 24:21–24. In the passage, Joshua asks the people to turn away from false idols and turn to God. Apply the passage to your own life. List at least ten things, people, places, behaviors, and the like that you idolize. For each item, write how idolization of it could become a problem. Write a plan for avoiding this temptation. Finally, write ten specific ways that you can put God first in your life.

Called to Prayer
Lord, I freely yield all my freedom to you.
Take my memory, my intellect, and my entire will.
You have given me everything I am and have;
I give it all back to you to stand under your will alone.
Your love and your grace are enough for me;
I shall ask for nothing more.
— St. Ignatius of Loyola

Notes
1. Calloway, p. 71.
2. See the excellent summary in Ch. 1, "New Understandings of the Israelite Settlement Process," in Robert Gnuse, *No Other Gods*, Sheffield Academic Press: Sheffield, 1997, pp. 23–61.

THE JOURNEY TAKES NEW SHAPE

CHAPTER 5 TEST

Teaching Approaches
1. Distribute the Chapter 5 Test (online at **avemariapress.com**). Allow enough time for the students to complete the entire test. Then collect and grade.

2. If you did not have a chance to complete the Prayer Service from the previous session, allow time after the test to do so.

3. Encourage the students to peruse Chapter 6 in the time they have remaining in the period. Or, review some of the lessons from the Catholic Handbook of Faith (pages 259–280 of the Student Text).

Chapter 5
Parish Religious Education Adaptation

- Use the Chapter 5 Parish Religious Education Adaptation (online at **avemariapress.com**) if you are covering the text material in a parish religious education setting. The two-hour lesson plan offers a youth ministry approach for referencing the material over a shorter amount of time.
- Make sure to assign Chapter 5 for reading along locating the six books of Deuteronomic History found in the Old Testament.

Chapter 5 Test Answers
Part 1: Matching: 1. d; 2. g; 3. b; 4. h; 5. a; 6. c; 7. e; 8. f.
Part 2: True or False: 9. +; 10. 0; 11. +; 12. +; 13. 0; 14. 0; 15. 0.
Part 3: Lists: 16. Joshua; 17. Judges; 18. 1 Samuel; 19. 2 Samuel; 20. 1 Kings; 21. 2 Kings; 22. The Temple is the only place acceptable for making sacrifices; 23. The worship of stars (astrology) is forbidden. 24. Everyone must celebrate the Passover. 25–28. (1) a just cause, (2) the aggressor nation must have already attacked and caused serious harm, (3) war can only be declared by those with proper authority to do so, (4) all peaceful means to resolve the conflict must be proven ineffectual, (5) non-combatants must be protected, (6) there must be legitimate hope of victory and eventual peaceful relations, (7) weapons used in defense must not cause graver evil than those being inflicted by the aggressor nation.
Part 4: Short Fill-ins: 29. "the Lord must rule over you": 30. "with your whole heart and whole soul;" 31. his long hair/his reliance on God; 32. reduce/a horn and a torch.

Introducing Chapter 6

The two books of Samuel, most likely written many centuries after the time of the monarchy, contain numerous warnings about Israel's requesting and then taking on a human king. The Israelites ignored these warnings, however, and insisted that Samuel (a military leader/judge/prophet) anoint someone as king. Samuel selected Saul, who turned out to be a poor choice. His mental instability and disobedience of Yahweh's commands made him unfit to continue as king.

The books of Samuel contain two accounts of how David replaced Saul as king. In the first account, Saul anointed David as king, and David later found a place in Saul's court as a harp player. In the second account, David, a young shepherd, killed the Philistine Goliath and was brought to court by Saul. As king, David was Israel's greatest monarch despite many personal failings. His son Solomon succeeded him as king and was noted both for his wisdom and for his building programs. But even Solomon had his failings: Solomon enslaved many people, including the Israelites themselves, in order to build his palace, the Temple in Jerusalem, and numerous walled cities.

After Solomon, the kingdom was divided into two—Israel with ten tribes in the north and Judah with two tribes in the south. Only the kings of Judah were direct descendants of King David.

Chapter 6 shows how many of the kings of Israel and Judah turned to polytheistic practices in order to bolster their power. Such practices included offerings to idols, astrology, sexual rites involving cult prostitutes, and even human sacrifice. The authors of the books of Samuel and the books of Kings attributed the kings' infidelity to Yahweh as the main reason why both kingdoms were eventually conquered and destroyed by enemies. The Assyrians conquered Israel in 722 B.C. In 539 B.C., the Babylonians conquered the southern kingdom of Judah.

The New Testament shows a vital link between Jesus and the Israelite monarchy. Jesus is a descendant of David. He is the new King of Kings. He rules, not with oppressive power and taxing authority, but with the attitude of a servant. He ushers in God's kingdom of justice and peace for all people, not just the wealthy.

Chapter 6 Outline

Introduction
God considers Israel's request for a king a rejection of him.

Religious Developments During the Monarchy
The Chosen People continued to be tempted to follow other gods while ruled by kings.

The "United" Monarchy: Saul, David, and Solomon
The consolidated monarchy in many ways results from the threats of the Philistines.

The Divided Monarchy
The southern kingdom is called "Judah" with its descendants traceable to King David while the ten tribes of the northern kingdom are called "Israel."

The Last Days of the Independent Monarchy
The northern kingdom falls to the Assyrians in 722 B.C. while Judah manages to evade destruction until the Babylonian Nebachudnezzar destroyed it in 587 B.C. and exiles the Jewish people.

Further Reflections

Chapter Objectives

The students will be able to:
- summarize the plot and religious themes of the books of 1 and 2 Samuel and 1 and 2 Kings.
- learn about the pros and cons of the united monarchy in Israel.
- appreciate the strengths and weaknesses of Israel's first three kings: Saul, David, and Solomon.
- see how the prophets such as Samuel served as a "check and balance" to the king's decisions.
- correlate Israel's success in battle to its fidelity to Yahweh.
- discover how Solomon's greatest accomplishment—the building of the Temple in Jerusalem—was also the reason for the demise of the united kingdom.
- link Jesus, a descendant of David, to the Israelite monarchy and the coming kingdom of God.

Resources

Music Suggestions: see page 136
Printed Materials: see page 139
Audiovisual Materials: see page 140
Internet Links: see page 143

CHAPTER 6

THE MONARCHY
The Journey Takes a New Direction

Background Notes for the Teacher

The first and second books of Samuel were originally one book. When they were divided, they were known as 1 and 2 Kings. Likewise, the present books 1 and 2 Kings were also one book. The first book of Kings continues the family history of David, describes his death and the preparation of Solomon to take over the throne. Solomon's history is told in 1 Kings. The second book of Kings continues the history of the kingdoms through the fall of Israel.

The theology of the books of Samuel and Kings tells us a great deal about the true nature of political authority and power. The king is not the highest ruler of the country; he rules with God's consent. The books of Samuel and Kings remind us that even the king is subject to God's commandments. Samuel, as God's prophet, serves as a source of checks and balances to the king's power. He judges the king in God's name.

The kings of Israel—especially King David—were successful in battle only when they were acting in obedience to Yahweh. But even David was not perfect; he, too, had to pay the consequences of his sins against Yahweh.

The great accomplishment of Solomon—the Temple in Jerusalem—was also partly responsible for the demise of the united kingdom. The tribes in the north resented the assertion that Jerusalem was the only place where Yahweh could be worshiped. They also resented the excessive taxation and enslavement Solomon placed on them in order to build the Temple.

The books of Samuel and Kings teach a great spiritual truth. Our power is not in our own accomplishments, but in our relationship with God. When we obey the commandments and act with justice toward others, God is present both to individuals and to nations.

Relevant Teachings from Church Documents

- Faith in God leads us to turn to him alone as our first origin and our ultimate goal, and neither to prefer anything to him nor to substitute anything for him. (*CCC*, 229)
- *Everyone is called to enter the kingdom.* First announced to the children of Israel, this messianic kingdom is intended to accept men of all nations. (*CCC*, 543)
- The Law, the sign of God's promise and covenant, ought to have governed the hearts and institutions of that people to whom Abraham's faith gave birth. "If you will obey my voice and keep my covenant, . . . you shall be to me a kingdom of priests and a holy nation." (*Ex* 19:5–6; Cf. 1 *Pet* 2:9.) But after David, Israel gave in to the temptation of becoming a kingdom like other nations. The Kingdom, however, the object of the promise made to David, (Cf. 2 *Sam* 7; *Ps* 89; *Lk* 1:32–33.) would be the work of the Holy Spirit; it would belong to the poor according to the Spirit. (*CCC*, 709)
- David is par excellence the king "after God's own heart," the shepherd who prays for his people and prays in their name. His submission to the will of God, his praise, and his repentance, will be a model for the prayer of the people. His prayer, the prayer of God's Anointed, is a faithful adherence to the divine promise and expresses a loving and joyful trust in God, the only King and Lord. (Cf. *2 Sam* 7:18–29.) (*CCC*, 2579)
- Therefore, while we are warned that it profits a man nothing if he gain the whole world and lose himself, the expectation of a new earth must not weaken but rather stimulate our concern for cultivating this one. For here grows the body of a new human family, a body which even now is able to give some kind of foreshadowing of the new age.
- Earthly progress must be carefully distinguished from the growth of Christ's kingdom. Nevertheless, in the extent that the former can contribute to the better ordering of human society, it is of vital concern to the kingdom of God.
- For after we have obeyed the Lord, and in His Spirit nurtured on earth the values of human dignity, brotherhood and freedom, and indeed all the good fruits of our nature and enterprise, we will find them again, but freed of stain, burnished and transfigured. This will be so when Christ hands over to the Father a kingdom eternal and universal: "a kingdom of truth and life, of holiness and grace, of justice, love, and peace." On this earth that kingdom is already present in mystery. When the Lord returns, it will be brought into full flower. (Vatican II, *Pastoral Constitution on the Church in the Modern World*, #39)

CHAPTER 6

INTRODUCTION
The Monarchy: Positives and Negatives

Bell-Ringers

1. **Re-teach:** Remind the students of these four lessons learned from the books of Joshua and Judges (write on board):
- The Israelites promised to love and serve Yahweh.
- The Israelites turned away from Yahweh and worshipped false gods.
- Yahweh then let Israel's enemies conquer them. The Israelites repented and turned back to God for help.
- Yahweh forgave the people and appointed a leader over them.

Call on several students to discuss some specific examples related to each of the above points.

2. Return and comment on the Chapter 5 Test, if they have been graded.

3. Print the word **hero** on the board. Call on a student to be "on the spot." Ask the person to describe his or her concept of a hero and to name people in their lives that they consider to be heroes. Allow several students to take turns being on the spot. Compare and contrast their descriptions of heroes with popular culture's designation of "heroes" who are often famous, physically fit, and good looking. Finally, suggest that the books of Samuel and Kings, discussed in Chapter 6, offer a glimpse of the Israelite's understanding of a hero.

Advance Preparations
- *Optional:* Arrange for a guest speaker to speak of life living under a form of government different from democracy.
- Invite a local business leader, politician, or parish leader to discuss how a person's religious beliefs impact on his or her socioeconomic and political beliefs (see page 152 of the TWE).
- Obtain and preview any videos you wish to use during this chapter. If possible, show one of the videos of archaeological finds dating to the reign of King Solomon. Such findings indicate the extensive range of his building projects, as well as the importance of the Temple in Jerusalem.
- Obtain recordings of music you wish to use for the prayer service at the end of the chapter.
- Make copies of the handouts that are included with Chapter 6 for each student (found on pages 277–280 of the TWE).

THE OLD TESTAMENT

David—The king of the united kingdom of Israel from 1009 to 969 B.C. He conquered the TransJordanian states, gaining control of the major trade routes linking Egypt and Mesopotamia. Jesus was a descendant of David.

Saul—The first king of Israel, anointed by the prophet Samuel. He was never able to fully unite the twelve tribes and organize them into a recognizable nation.

Solomon—David's and Bathsheba's son, the last king of the united monarchy. He was renowned for his wisdom as well as for his wealth and his many large building projects. In addition to the king's palace and numerous walled fortresses throughout Palestine, he also built the Temple of Jerusalem to house the Ark of the Covenant.

Introduction

As mentioned in Chapter 5, Israel's request for a human king had immediate, negative consequences—the most important of which was that Yahweh considered the request a rejection of his kingship over the people. At the same time, the prophet Samuel warned Israel about the eventual, long-term consequences of having a king. Among the things a king would require of the people, Samuel told them:

- Their sons would be assigned to run before his chariot.
- They would be required to be his soldiers.
- They would do his farming and plowing.
- They would make his military and farming equipment.
- Their daughters would be his ointment-makers and cooks.
- Their best produce would be used to feed his officials and profits would be given to his servants.
- Their own servants and work animals would be taken to give service to the king as well.

Samuel concluded, "He will tithe your flocks and you yourselves will become his slaves. When this takes place, you will complain against the king whom you have chosen, but on that day the Lord will not answer" (see 1 Sm 8:17–18).

Still, for all this, the people did not give in. "Not so! There must be a king over us. We too must be like other nations, with a king to rule us and to lead us in warfare and fight our battles" (1 Sm 8:19–20).

Chapter 8 of the first book of Samuel hardly presents a ringing endorsement for an Israelite monarchy. Because King **David**, his predecessor **Saul**, and his son and successor **Solomon** are among the most remembered and revered heroes of the Old Testament, it may be surprising to learn that the monarchy was not an overall positive experience for Israel. That is why it is important to begin a chapter on the Israelite monarchy by remembering the negative consequences that resulted from the people's request for a king and the ways these results were recorded in the Old Testament.

Many Biblical scholars believe that 1 Samuel 8 was not written *before* there were kings, but rather, long *after* the fall of monarchy, as a commentary on what happened. The monarchy was placed in this context in order to send a message to the Jews reading the text many years later: "We should have known better than to do this," and perhaps even, "We are not meant to have any king but Yahweh. We are better off with God alone." Perhaps this was meant to comfort and even guide them during the time of exile.

Also, in reading 1 Samuel 8, note the incident that preceeds Israel's request for a king: the routing of the Philistines in 1 Samuel 7. For twenty years, the Israelites had "turned to the Lord," giving up their foreign gods and worshipping God alone.

Resources
Music Suggestions

"Amazing Grace" by John Newton from *Glory & Praise 1* (OCP [NALR]); *Worship* (GIA); *Breaking Bread* (OCP); *Spirit Song* or *Gather* (GIA).

"Bring Forth the Kingdom" by Marty Haugen in *Gather* (GIA).

"Center of My Life" by Paul Inwood from *Come to Set Us Free* (St. Thomas More); *United as One 2* or *Breaking Bread* (OCP); *Gather* (GIA).

"City of God" by Dan Schutte from *Lord of Light* or *Glory & Praise 3* (OCP [NALR]); *Celebrate* or *Gather* (GIA); *Breaking Bread* (OCP).

"God Has Chosen Me" by Bernadette Farrell in *Gather* (GIA).

"How Lovely is Your Dwelling" by Jean Janzen in *Gather* (GIA).

"Psalm 72" Every Nation on Earth" by Michael Joncas in *Gather* (GIA).

"Psalm 89: For Ever I Will Sing" by Marty Haugen in *Gather* (GIA).

"The King of Love My Shepherd Is" by Henry W. Baker in *Gather* (GIA).

"Thy Kingdom Come" by Rory Cooney in *Gather* (GIA).

THE MONARCHY

Once again, God had miraculously delivered the Israelites from the powerful Philistine army. The request for a king was probably precipitated by Israel's fear of the Philistine armies, yet there is irony in the timing: just after a twenty-year period of faithfulness and a mighty display of God's power to defeat their enemies, the Israelites suddenly didn't trust God's power to protect them. They wanted a king, such as other nations had, to fight their battles. This incident serves only to highlight the religious significance of the stories, that Israel prospers when the people honor the covenant, yet time and again, they turn their backs on Yahweh.

The Monarchy: Positives and Negatives

It is important to read the story of Israel's kings with balance. There were also many positive aspects of the monarchy in Israel's history. For example, Israel became a nation with a strong central leadership, as opposed to a fragmented cluster of clans as during the time of the judges. A holy city was built in Jerusalem. And from the family of King David, a dynasty was formed with an ancestral line that eventually led to the birth of a messiah, or one anointed by God. Jesus Christ is connected in scripture to the Davidic line (see Mt 1:6 and Lk 23:31).

While many positive aspects of the monarchy are explicitly tied to King David, it is equally true that the Scriptures also detail his failings—including his ill-fated affair with a married woman, Bathsheba, when he abused his powers and killed her husband to cover his sin (see 2 Sm 11–12). David's son, Solomon, too, ended his life having compromised his faith in God for the sake of political alliances with nations all around him. The most damaging criticisms of the kings of ancient Israel are from two main sources: the Historical Books (especially 1 and 2 Kings), which complain constantly that the Kings encouraged polytheistic worship, and the prophets, who not only repeat that criticism, but also add that the king's allowed an economic system to develop that rewarded the rich and punished the poor.

The review of King David's reign is largely positive, but it is heavily marked by personal failings. Before these positive aspects are reviewed, read the overwhelming evidence the Old Testament offers that the idea of a monarchy was a failure. Look at the specific accusations leveled against the following kings. Similar evidence can also be cited for the other kings who are not mentioned here:

Criticism of Saul
◆ 1 Samuel 15:1–9

Criticism of David (although accompanied by positive evaluation)
◆ 2 Samuel 11:1–27

Criticism of Solomon
◆ 1 Kings 11;1–10

Criticism of Jeroboam
◆ 1 Kings 14:1–10

Criticism of Ahaz (of Judah)
◆ 2 Kings 16:1–4

Criticism of Baasha
◆ 1 Kings 16:1–6

Criticism of Omri
◆ 1 Kings 16:23–26

Criticism of Joram (of Israel)
◆ 2 Kings 3:1–3

Criticism of Ahaziah
◆ 2 Kings 8:25–27

Criticism of Zechariah (of Israel)
◆ 2 Kings 15:8–10

Criticism of Manasseh
◆ 2 Kings 21:1–16

Criticism of Zedekiah
◆ 2 Kings 24:18–25:7

Teaching Approaches

1. On the board or overhead, print the name **Samuel**. Ask the students to describe the life of Samuel of the Old Testament. (Accept answers such as judge, prophet, military leader, and religious leader.) Explain that because the authors of the books of Samuel considered Samuel to be an important figure in Israel's history, they also included the story of his unusual birth.

2. Assign 1 Samuel:1. When the students have finished reading, ask: How does this story compare to other Old Testament birth stories? (For example, Jacob has two wives. Leah has many sons, while Rachel has none. Finally, she gives birth to Joseph, who becomes Jacob's favorite. Also, in Judges 13, the wife of Manoah is barren. She prays for a son and promises to offer him to God as a Nazirite. She finally gives birth to Samson, a judge of Israel.) Explain that Samuel is a transitional figure, linking the Israelite monarchy to the former authority of the patriarchs and the judges.

3. Explain that Samuel also prefigures Jesus as King of Kings. Compare Hannah's song (1 Sm 2:1–10) with the canticle of Mary (Lk 1:46–55). Have the students read each passage and then write their answers to the following questions (write on the board):
   - **How are the two songs similar?** (Accept all reasonable answers.)
   - **What is the religious message that links the two readings?** (God is a God of justice who is concerned about the oppressed and the poor. God raises up the lowly, chooses unlikely people to carry out his plan of salvation.)

Handout 6A "Criticism of Israel's Kings" Answers

Saul: He disobeyed God after a victory against the Amaleks. God had ordered that Saul kill all the Amaleks and destroy everything in the city (the ban). Saul spared the king Agag, as well as the best sheep, oxen, and lambs.

David: He killed Uriah, one of his soldiers, to cover up his adultery with Uriah's wife Bathsheba.

Solomon: To keep his pagan wives happy, he let them worship their gods and induce others to do the same. He also enslaved his own people in order to complete his many building projects.

Jeroboam: He made strange gods and molten images, and worshiped them rather than Yahweh.

Ahaz: He sacrificed his son to pagan gods. He sacrificed and burned incense to these gods on the high places, on hills, and under every leafy tree.

Baasha: He "caused God's people to sin." Presumably this means that he led or allowed the people to worship false gods.

Omri: He made false gods and molten images and worshiped them rather than Yahweh.

Joram: He continued to worship false gods and molten images.

Ahaziah: He "did evil in the Lord's sight." Presumably he engaged in polytheistic worship.

Zechariah: He "did evil in the Lord's sight." Presumably he engaged in polytheistic worship.

Manesseh: He built altars to false gods, especially to Baal, set up a sacred pole, and served the whole host of heaven.

Zedekiah: He "did evil in the Lord's sight." Presumably he engaged in polytheistic worship.

Chapter 6

4. Assign the Introduction for individual reading. Summarize the text by making the following points:
   - The Israelites' request for a king was particularly offensive because they were rejecting Yahweh as their king. God had just given them victory over the Philistines and they were showing ingratitude.
   - Samuel told the Israelites that there would be negative consequences to having a king. Basically, people would be taxed, and they would become slaves to the king.

5. Assign the text subsection, "The Monarchy: Positives and Negatives" (pages 133–134).

6. Distribute copies of Handout 6A, "Criticism of Israel's Kings" (page 277 of the TWE). Pass out Bibles and have the students work individually or with a partner to complete the assignment. When completed, review the answers from below. Make sure that the students realize that prophets such as Samuel, Nathan, and others, acted as a source of checks and balances to the king. They brought God's judgment (affirmation and condemnation) on the king's actions and decisions. They reminded both the people and the king that the king's power was not absolute. God was the supreme authority in Israel.

7. **Homework Assignment**:
   - Answer the Review and Reflection questions 1–3, page 134. For question 2, refer to the notes for 1 Samuel 7–8 in the *New American Bible*.
   - Complete the Journal Assignment, page 134. Refer to the list of positive and negative reasons for living under a monarchy from pages 133–134. Also, you may wish to cite testimonies from people who have lived under two different political systems.
   - Read the entire section, "Religious Developments During the Monarchy" (pages 134–138).

Enrichment: Research the grievances that the colonists in the New World had against the king of England. How were these grievances similar to those Samuel predicted that the Israelites would have if they chose a human king?

THE OLD TESTAMENT

When these Scripture references are compared with the criticism of the monarchy at its very origin in 1 Samuel 8, the overall message is clear: the Biblical authors writing at a later time considered the monarchy of ancient Israel to be a failure. In Chapter 7, you will read that the more authentic heroes of the Chosen People were actually not the kings of Israel or Judah, but rather the prophets—God's messengers who called the people (including the kings) back to a proper observance of the Law of Moses.

REVIEW & REFLECTION

1. What were the consequences Samuel warned the Israelites about should they choose a king?
2. What is the religious significance of 1 Samuel 7–8?
3. When were the accounts about the monarchy likely written? What message did these accounts give?

JOURNAL ASSIGNMENT

- What do you perceive to be the advantages and disadvantages of living under a monarchy as opposed to a democratic government?

Josiah—The last independent king of Judah, and one of only two kings to receive unmitigated praise in the Old Testament. He initiated religious reforms attempting to purify the worship of Yahweh in the Temple. He was killed in a battle with the Egyptians who then established a puppet government in Jerusalem.

Baal—The Canaanite god of fertility, associated with storms and rain. He was the most prominent of the Canaanite gods and the one most often worshipped by the Israelites.

Religious Developments During the Monarchy

Pagan and polytheistic practices, which appeared throughout the time of the judges, continued to crop up among the Israelites during the time of the kings. The Old Testament offers testimony to this. The investigation into how and when this occurred is best begun at the end of the monarchy, during the reign of King **Josiah** in 640-609 B.C.

According to 2 Kings 22:2, Josiah "pleased the Lord and conducted himself unswervingly just as his ancestor David had done." Josiah was considered a righteous king because of his determination to purify the religion of the state and return it to a faith more devoted to Yahweh. (The previous kings had encouraged polytheistic practices and worship.) Consider, for example, what Josiah had to do in order to purify the Jerusalem Temple.

Read 2 Kings 23: 1–15

This passage reveals much about the state of Israelite religious practice under the monarchy. Canaanite gods and goddesses, like **Baal** and Asherah, are mentioned. The first commandment condemns

134

Review and Reflection Answers

1. The negative consequences of having a king included:
   - Their sons would be assigned to run before the king's chariots.
   - They would be required to be his soldiers.
   - They would do his farming and plowing.
   - They would make his military and farming equipment.
   - Their daughters would be his ointment-makers and cooks.
   - Their best produce would be used to feed his officials, and profits would be given to the king's servants.
   - Their own servants and work animals would be taken to give service to the king as well.
   - The king would tithe their flocks and make the people his slaves.
2. The people showed great ingratitude to God by asking for a king, especially after God has just given them victory over their enemies.
3. The accounts of the monarchy were probably written long after the fall of the monarchy. These accounts were a negative commentary on the monarchy. Basically they said, "We should have known better than to do this."

Ancient statue of Ugarit god Baal

The Monarchy

such idolatry, the worship of false gods. Yahweh is the living God who gives life and intervenes in history (see *CCC*, 2112). There have never been, nor are there now, "other" gods or goddesses.

The passage also alludes to some of the pagan Canaanite practices—offerings made in Temple, images of the gods, and astrological practices (e.g., burning incense to Baal, to the sun, moon, and signs of the Zodiac). It mentions sexual rites associated with pagan religions (e.g., cult prostitutes) and even human sacrifice. Remember, Josiah's reign came at the end of Israel's monarchy. The pagan practices mentioned in this passage developed during the reigns of the preceding kings of Israel. This passage in 2 Kings provides a clear indication of how far the kings of Israel before Josiah had taken Israelite worship into a mix of pagan religions. Josiah had to clean up Solomon's famous Temple.

Recall that the first commandment states that "you shall worship the Lord your God and him only shall you serve." Worship of false gods was the greatest offense against Yahweh for those living at the time of the kings. Superstition is also a violation of the first commandment.

The Old Testament is critical of Israel's kings in many other places as well. The kings are criticized for their excessive spending related to building projects almost as often as they are criticized for encouraging the practices of pagan religions. In fact, only two of Israel's forty-two kings, Hezekiah and Josiah, received unmitigated praise:

> [Hezekiah] pleased the Lord, just as his forefather David had done. It was he who removed the high places, shattered the pillars, and cut down the sacred poles. He smashed the bronze serpent called Nehushtan which Moses had made, because up to that time the Israelites were burning incense to it. He put his trust in the Lord, the God of Israel; and neither before him nor after him was there anyone like him among all the kings of Judah (2 Kgs 18:3–5).

> Before [Josiah] there had been no king who turned to the Lord as he did, with his whole heart, his whole soul, and his whole strength, in accord with the entire law of Moses; nor could any after him compare with him (2 Kgs 23:25).

THE BOOKS OF CHRONICLES

The two books of Chronicles form a unified historical work that represents a fascinating "rethinking" of Israelite history that was written a few hundred years later than the books of Samuel and Kings. The books of Chronicles cover the time span between the reign of Saul and the Exile, roughly the same period as covered in the books of Samuel and the books of Kings. However, the Chronicles omit certain themes from other historical sources and write a report that stresses two religious themes: true worship of Yahweh and the importance of the priests to God's People. This history emphasizes issues of interest to the community well into the period of Persian Rule (539–333 B.C.).

THE MONARCHY

RELIGIOUS DEVELOPMENTS DURING THE MONARCHY

Bell-Ringers

1. If you've arranged for a guest speaker to present information on living under a political system other than a democracy, allow time for him or her to speak at the beginning of class. Connect the presentation to the student's Journal Assignment from page 134.

2. Have the students form groups of four or five. Distribute copies of "Kings of Judah and Israel" (Handout 6B, page 278 of the TWE). Direct the students to look up the Scripture passages cited for the earlier kings and then describe who the kings were and what religious developments took place during their reign according to the cited passage. When the groups have finished, summarize the discussion (see Handout 6B answers, page 141 of the TWE). Form a panel of students to debate this issue: "Who is responsible when the nation's morals decline? The leader or the people?"

Resources

Printed Materials

"Samuel," "Samuel, Books of," "Kings, The Books of" in *The Oxford Companion to the Bible*, ed. by Bruce M. Metzger and Michael D. Coogan. (New York, NY: Oxford University Press, 1993), pp. 673–677, 409–413.

"Samuel," "Samuel, The Books of," "King," and "Kings, Books of" in *Dictionary of the Bible*, ed. by John L. McKenzie, S.J. (New York, NY: Macmillan Publishing Co., Inc., 1965), pp. 767–772, 474–479, 482–484.

Bowes, Paula. "1 and 2 Samuel" in *The Collegeville Bible Commentary*, ed. by Dianne Bergant, C.S.A. and Robert J. Karris, O.F.M. (Collegeville, MN: The Liturgical Press, 1989), pp. 265–295.

Campbell, Antony F., S.J., and James W. Flanagan. "1–2 Samuel" in *The New Jerome Biblical Commentary*, ed. by Raymond E. Brown, S.S., Joseph A. Fitzmyer, S.J., and Roland E. Murphy, O.Carm. (Englewood Cliffs, NJ: Prentice Hall, 1990), pp. 145–159.

Cohn, Robert L. "1 Samuel" in *Harper's Bible Commentary*, ed. by James L. Mays. (San Francisco, CA: Harper & Row Publishers, 1988), pp. 268–286.

Gunn, David M. "2 Samuel" in *Harper's Bible Commentary*, ed. by James L. Mays. (San Francisco, CA: Harper & Row Publishers, 1988), pp. 287–304.

Laffey, R.S.M. "1 and 2 Kings" in *The Collegeville Bible Commentary*, ed. by Dianne Bergant, C.S.A. and Robert J. Karris, O.F.M. (Collegeville, MN: The Liturgical Press, 1989), pp. 296–320.

McCarter, P. Kyle, Jr. "1 Kings" in *Harper's Bible Commentary*, ed. by James L. Mays. (San Francisco, CA: Harper & Row Publishers, 1988), pp. 305–322.

Walsh, Jerome T., and Christopher T. Begg. "1–2 Kings" in *The New Jerome Biblical Commentary*, ed. by Raymond E. Brown, S.S., Joseph A. Fitzmyer, S.J., and Roland E. Murphy, O.Carm. (Englewood Cliffs, NJ: Prentice Hall, 1990), pp. 160–185.

Chapter 6

Teaching Approaches

1. Re-cap the presentation by the guest speaker and connect the discussion on various political systems with information the students found out about during the Journal Assignment on page 134.

2. **Re-teach:** Ask the following questions either orally or in a written quiz to check the student's comprehension of the first part of the homework reading assignment (pages 134–135). Ask:
   - Who was King Josiah? (He was a late king of Judah.)
   - Does the Old Testament treat him favorably or unfavorably? Why? (Favorably, because he instituted the Deuteronomic reforms. He emphasized worship in the Jerusalem Temple alone, he mandated annual observance of the Passover, and he discouraged polytheistic practices.)

3. Read or have the students read 2 Kings 23:1–15. Discuss with the students the need in their own lives to rededicate themselves to God's plan. Have the students note Handout 6B. Only Hezekiah and Josiah out of all the other kings were described positively in the Old Testament.

Resources

Audiovisual Materials

A&E Old Testament Collection: King David (New Video Group)—50 minutes

This production employs rare paintings, interviews, and visits to the Holy Land to tell David's story. We witness his transition from shepherd boy to hero to king.

A&E Old Testament Collection: Solomon and Sheba (New Video Group)—50 minutes

At age twelve, Solomon became king of all Israel. Despite his great wisdom (and many wives), Solomon remained a lonely man until he met Sheba, the mysterious queen.

Ancient Tales from a Promised Land: Saul Rips up His Camel/David Gets a Good Gig (Ecufilm)—30 minutes

In the first part of the production, the prophet Samuel anointed Saul as king, but was later disappointed in Saul's performance. In the second part, a young shepherd named David impressed King Saul.

Ancient Tales from a Promised Land: David and the Hairy Man Mountain/Saul Goes Bonkers (Ecufilm)—30 minutes

The first part of the production retells the story of David and the giant Goliath. The second part tells how David humiliated Saul who vowed to get rid of him.

Ancient Tales from a Promised Land: Saul Bumps into a Witch/David Gets to Number One (Ecufilm)—30 minutes

In the first part of the production, King Saul sought advice from the Witch of Endor. Instead of a good fortune, he learned of his own impending death. In the second part, David became king of the Israelites. Despite his success, he was disturbed by the visions of the prophet Nathan.

David (Vision Video)—200 minutes

As a teenager, David became famous for his victory against Goliath. He became king after Saul and, despite numerous personal faults, became God's faithful follower.

Great Figures of the Bible: Story of David (EcuFilm)—60 minutes

This production presents King David in all his humanity, his passion and greatness as well as his weakness and sinfulness.

Old Testament: Samuel, A Dedicated Man (Vanguard)—15 minutes

This production explores various aspects of the life of the prophet Samuel—his childhood, leadership, life as a teacher of God's word, and his anointing of the first king of Israel.

Standard Video Bible Series: 1 and 2 Samuel—two videos 30 minutes each

These productions make use of animated maps, actual footage from Palestine, and interviews with Bible scholars to help us understand 1 and 2 Samuel. We consider what these Biblical books tell us about modern faith.

The Old Testament

Who Was Tempted to Paganism?

What was the nature of the pagan religion of the Canaanites that is so often condemned in the Bible? Who were the false gods Baal and Asherah so often mentioned? In the past century a great deal more about Canaanite religion has been learned, largely because of one magnificent archaeological discovery—the ruins of **Ugarit**.

Ugarit was an ancient capital city at the center of a small territorial expanse that flourished in the second millennium (2000–1180 B.C.). Evidence suggests that the site was finally abandoned following a major destructive act in 1180 B.C. What makes this archaeological site so very significant is the amount of texts found in it. Most of the texts were written in a local language now known as "Ugaritic." This language closely resembled Hebrew. (In fact, it is often suggested that Hebrew is a dialect of the same language family as Ugaritic.)

Ugarit—An ancient city of the Canaanites which was discovered in 1928. Many texts were found there, from which scholars have learned a great deal about the Canaanite religion.

Among the many different kinds of texts discovered at Ugarit were a number of religious texts that told stories of some of the Canaanite gods and characters known to us from the Bible—most prominently the god Baal. Baal was considered the god of fertility and was often associated with images of storms and rain. (A rain god would have been very important to a largely agricultural society, particularly in the relatively arid climate of Palestine.) Many of the texts in Ugarit portrayed Baal in battle. The two most interesting of these battles are the one between Baal and Yam ("Yammu"), the god of the sea, and the battle between Baal and Mot, the god of death.

The battle between Baal and Yam echoes the better-known story of the Babylonian god Marduk against the Babylonian god of the sea, Tiamat. The Babylonian story contains an account of the creation of human beings. Thus, a large number of people of ancient Mesopotamia and the coastal regions were familiar with a creation epic that included the idea of a great battle between gods—especially the god of the storm versus the god of the sea. The sea often represented chaos to the ancient peoples, so it is possible that the conceptual idea behind this myth was that chaos and disorder were defeated by Baal, and this defeat allowed organized civilization to emerge. Order came from chaos.

The other great battle was the struggle between Baal and Mot. In this battle, Baal is initially defeated and sinks down into the underworld—the world of the

Ruins of the ancient city Ugarit near present day Syria

The Monarchy

dead where Mot is ruler. Baal is there assisted by his wife-sister Anat, and is able to re-engage the battle and rise up out of the underworld in victory over Mot. Some scholars of Ugaritic literature have suggested that the Baal-Mot conflict may actually be tied to regular celebrations of the changing of the seasons. Autumn, when everything is "dying," must be the time of Baal's defeat by Mot. In Ezekiel 8:14, there is a reference to "weeping for Tammuz [Baal]." This may be a "mourning" rite associated with an autumn observance of Baal's descent into the underworld.

When it is spring, and everything is rising into new life again, this is the time when Baal is victorious over Mot and rises into the world of the living. It is possible that the Canaanite/coastal peoples like those at Ugarit actually had certain rituals and rites surrounding this myth that were connected to the changing of the seasons. Spring has invited festivals of fertility in many different societies.

The Ugaritic texts provide insight into why pagan worship was tempting for the Israelites. First, it was the common religion of the area. Many of the people who lived near or even among the Israelites practiced some form of it. Second, it was associated with fertility, and agriculture was obviously the main basis of all ancient economies. What was good for the economy probably seemed absolute and true. Third, and perhaps most importantly, it was a religion that served the establishment. Kings and priests ruled the people according to these religious ideas, which provided stability and an explanation for why things were the way they were. But it was a stability that was often oppressive since these traditional fertility religions typically bolstered the authority of the kings and told the common people that their state in life was determined by the gods.

Estimates are that pagan religion supported a social structure in which as few as five percent of the population (kings, priests, and landowners) ruled over the remainder of the population—mostly landless agricultural peasant workers. These peasant workers were all kept locked in the belief that these "gods" must be kept happy and that the kings must be obeyed.

Consider the famous story of **Jezebel** (1 Kings 21). She was a Canaanite princess who married the Northern Israelite king, Ahab. Hebrew law limited the power of the king so that even he could not

The sea often represented chaos to ancient people.

Jezebel—A Canaanite princess, married to Ahab, one of the kings of the northern kingdom. She orchestrated the murder of Naboth in order to gain his property for her husband.

4. Summarize why pagan or polytheistic worship was tempting for the Israelites (see "Who Was Tempted to Paganism?", pages 136–138):
   - Polytheism was common in the region. Many of the people who lived near or even among the Israelites practiced some form of it. Many Israelites married pagan spouses who continued to practice their religion.
   - Polytheistic worship was associated with fertility, which would have been crucial to an agricultural economy.
   - Polytheism served the establishment. It bolstered the power of kings and kept common people in their places.

Handout 6B "Kings of Judah and Israel" Answers

Rehoboam: The Old Testament criticized the people under his reign. They worshiped pagan gods. As a result, foreigners invaded them and looted the Temple.

Jeroboam: Jeroboam was criticized for starting worship in the North, away from Jerusalem.

Abijam: Abijam was criticized because his heart was not true to God.

Asa: Asa banished male temple prostitutes, destroyed pagan images, and deposed his own mother for idolatry. But he did not remove the pagan places of worship.

Nadab: Nadab continued worship of God in the north and was criticized for doing so. He was killed by Baasha.

Baasha: Baasha continued worship of God in the north and was criticized for doing so.

Elah: Elah was killed during a coup staged while he was drunk.

Zimri: Zimri ruled for only seven days and then committed suicide. He was criticized for doing evil.

Omri: Omri was a powerful ruler who ruled for four generations. He established Samaria as the capital of Israel, accumulated wealth, and expanded boundaries. But he was criticized for false worship.

Ahab: From a religious point of view, Ahab was the worst king of Israel. He allowed his foreign wife to lead him into pagan worship.

Chapter 6

5. Continue the discussion on polytheism among the Israelites. Have the students write or discuss answers to the following questions:
   - Why was polytheism an "establishment religion"? (It supported the political system in which five percent of the population (kings, priests, and landowners) ruled over the remainder of the population. People accepted this way of life because they thought the gods willed it.)
   - In what ways was the Israelite religion an anti-establishment religion? (It fostered social justice and charity, encouraged people to share, take care of one another, and made sure that no one oppressed others. This religion especially encouraged care for the weakest members in society—the orphans, widows, and foreigners.)

6. **Homework Assignment:**
   - Write answers to the Review and Reflection questions 1–3, page 138.
   - Complete the Journal Assignment, page 138. Also, consider how the entire Christian Gospel is "radical" or "risky."
   - Complete the exercise, "Standard of Living," page 140. A good place to begin your research is with the statistics database at the United Nations webpage at www.un.org.
   - Read "The 'United' Monarchy: Saul, David, and Solomon," (pages 139–144).

---

seize whatever land he wanted, but Jezebel the Canaanite thought this was ridiculous and took matters into her own hands. Ahab wanted property that by right belonged to a Israelite peasant named Naboth. Jezebel had Naboth executed and took his land. She was acting as a Canaanite ruler might have. This story illustrates what pagan religion would mean in terms of its social consequences. It contrasts sharply with the stories of the prophet Elijah, living with and saving the lives of a widow and her only son in the name of the one, true, God, Yahweh (see 1 Kings 17).

It is easy to see why Israel clashed so strongly with the societies who honored the ancient pagan and polytheistic religions. The central event of Israelite religion was the liberation of slaves away from the greatest known "king" of the ancient world—the Pharaoh of Egypt. Furthermore, the basis of the religion of Israel was a collection of "laws" that guaranteed that all people shared with one another, took care of one another, and made sure that nobody ruled oppressively over another. Israelites especially offered care for the "widow, the orphan, and the foreigner"—the weakest members of society. The Israelite religion was a revolutionary religion of changing circumstances (it started by ending slavery in Egypt) and maintaining community ties that were not oppressive.

So why were the kings of ancient Israel so deeply tempted to encourage pagan religion in their kingdom? A polytheistic religion with many gods supported the rule of the kings much more strongly than the questioning, radical religion of Yahweh that placed even the highest king under judgment for his behavior. (It was for this reason that American slaveholders never wanted their African slaves to learn to read. Although they wanted their slaves to be "Christian," they feared the slaves might read the Bible and learn about Moses and the release of the Hebrews from slavery.)

REVIEW & REFLECTION

1. List some of the pagan practices that made their way into the Israelite communities during the period of the monarchy.
2. What were the most common complaints made against the kings of Israel and Judah? Which two kings were praised and why?
3. What are two religious themes stressed in 1 and 2 Chronicles?

JOURNAL ASSIGNMENT

- What Bible stories seem radical or dangerous to you, or might seem so if people began to take them seriously? Why are they risky? Who or what could they change?

Enrichment: Create an art project (e.g. collage or drawing) that depicts the many gods (e.g. possessions, fame, power, beauty, astrology, self-help,) that some people falsely worship today. In your project, find a way to superimpose a cross or other symbol of Christianity to show how Christ conquers such beliefs.

Review and Reflection Answers
1. Pagan practices included worshiping in "high places," temple prostitutes, human sacrifice, and worship of gods other than Yahweh (especially Baal).
2. The most common complaints against the kings were their promotion of polytheism and their extensive building projects that taxed and enslaved the people.
3. The two religious themes of the books of Chronicles are true worship of Yahweh and the importance of the priests to God's people.

The "United" Monarchy: Saul, David, and Solomon

The monarchy began under the conditions of both internal and external crisis. At the same time that the tribes of Israel were consolidating, or at least loosely bringing themselves into a sometimes stormy union, the legendary Philistines were coming together to take their share of Palestine.

The social dynamics of 1200–1000 B.C. Palestine included interesting and complex interactions between traditional Canaanite settlements, newly emerging Israelite settlements, and Philistine settlements. The conflicts between the Israelites and Philistines became most severe at times. In the midst of these conflicts, the Israelite tribes determined to organize themselves more effectively against the Philistine threat.

The Philistines threatened in two significant ways. First, they had the ability to fashion weapons with iron, which tribal Israel was not yet capable of doing. Iron was a decided advantage over bronze, not only in weaponry but in agriculture as well. Iron plows, for example, were much sturdier and more effective for farming. Agricultural advantage meant economic advantage. Second, the Philistines' military strength was partly based on their effective self-organization. Tribal Israel, on the other hand, was rather poorly organized. There were clearly times when the Philistines dominated over tribal Israel.

Saul and the Philistines
Read 1 Samuel 9–10

Saul, from the family of Benjamin, was selected the first king of Israel. When the prophet Samuel first caught sight of Saul, the Lord told him: "This is the man of whom I told you; he is to govern my people" (1 Sm 9:17). However, Saul was a deeply troubled leader with an apparently fragile mental state. He failed to establish a centralized government.

During Saul's rule, Israel was probably not an organized entity at all, much less an actual state. He was as much the last of the judges as he was the first king. He "reigned" over a loose-knit organization of tribes and people who were mostly farmers. It has been estimated that the largest settlement in his "kingdom" probably amounted to no more than 100 people. There was no capital city or administrative center.

Saul was essentially a warrior with limited success against the Philistines—especially in the southern Israel hill country where his heartland was located and where the emerging state of Judah would be located. The following description of a battle led by Saul and his son Jonathan provides a clue to the difficulties the Israelites faced in battling the Philistines during the time of Saul:

> Not a single smith was to be found in the whole land of Israel, for the Philistines had said, "Otherwise the Hebrews will make swords or spears." All Israel, therefore, had to go down to the Philistines to sharpen their plowshares, mattocks, axes, and sickles. . . . And so on the day of battle neither sword nor spear could be found in the possession of any of the soldiers with Saul or Jonathan. Only Saul and his son Jonathan had them (1 Sm 13:19–20, 22).

Eventually, Saul's unfaithfulness to Yahweh and the charismatic rise of one of Saul's assistants, David, led to the anointing of Israel's greatest and most well-known king.

David's Rise to Power
Read 1 Samuel 16–17

David was king from approximately 1009–969 B.C. His rise to power is described in differing Biblical accounts. David is first introduced when the prophet Samuel is impressed with one of the older sons of Jesse, though he does not have a clear sense from God that this young man is really the future king. As the story continues, God scolds Samuel for trusting in only outward

---

THE MONARCHY

THE "UNITED" MONARCHY: SAUL, DAVID, AND SOLOMON

Bell-Ringers

1. Complete the "Standard of Living" exercise, page 140, by helping the students decipher information learned from their research. It might be helpful to point out some facts on standards of living from several different nations. To find updated information, conduct an Internet search with the key words: *standard of living* and *worldwide statistics*.

2. As a class, discuss the questions from the Journal Assignment, page 138. Make a list of the Bible stories that the students consider radical or dangerous and focus the discussion on why they think this is so.

Resources
Internet Links

http://hearstmuseum.berkeley.edu
View drinking cups, figurines, statues, mosaics, and bottles from the ancient Mediterranean.

www.eimuseum.co.il/english/main.html
Visit the Eretz-Israel Museum in Tel Aviv. See glass, coins, pottery, and metalworking found in archaeological digs at an ancient Philistine city destroyed by King David's army.

www.bible.ca/maps
View a high-resolution map of the united kingdoms of David and Solomon (1000 B.C.).

http://research.haifa.ac.il/~hecht
This is the home site of the Reuben and Edith Hecht Museum at the University of Haifa in Israel. See artifacts from the Early Israelite Period (1200–1000 B.C.).

www.museum.upenn.edu
Tour the Museum of Archaeology and Anthropology at the University of Pennsylvania. Learn about the times, daily life, economy, and religion of King David's reign during the second Iron Age in Canaan.

Chapter 6

Teaching Approaches

1. Review the threats that the Philistines presented to Israel. Also note how the threat from the Philistines led the Israelites to organize a more centralized government.

2. Read 1 Samuel 9–10. Summarize these main points:
   - Saul was good-looking and tall; he looked like a king.
   - Saul's physical attributes were not enough to make Saul a good leader.
   - Saul had a fragile mental state; he was very jealous of anyone who threatened his authority.
   - Saul failed to establish a central government.

3. Play all or part of a video about the lives and transition of power from Saul to David (e.g., *David*, see page 140 of the TWE).

4. Have the students read 1 Samuel 16–17 (and the text under the subsection, "David's Rise to Power," pages 139–140). Summarize the following points:
   - David was a handsome, young, musician, who was fearless and faithful to God.
   - David was considered a better king than Saul because he was more faithful to God. He was a successful military leader who enforced submission in a large territory.
   - God promised David that his throne would stand firm forever. This would be accomplished through Jesus, a descendant of David. Jesus was the Messiah (see the feature, "The Davidic Line," page 141).

THE OLD TESTAMENT

appearances of the older sons, all of whom God rejects. When Samuel asks Jesse if he has any other sons, Jesse replies,

"There is still the youngest, who is tending the sheep." Samuel said to Jesse, "Send for him; we will not begin the sacrificial banquet until he arrives here." Jesse sent and had the young man brought to them. He was ruddy, a youth handsome to behold and making a splendid appearance. The Lord said, "There—anoint him, for this is he!" Then Samuel, with the horn of oil in hand, anointed him in the midst of his brothers; and from that day on, the spirit of the Lord rushed upon David (1 Sm 16:11–13).

David goes on to succeed Saul eventually as the chosen king of Israel, though the story of how it happens varies. Part of the difficulty is that David's reign as king has to be clearly justified, since he is not of the family of Saul. The first book of Samuel represents Saul as having been rejected for his sin (see 1 Sm 15:1–35), but there are two different traditions about how David came into Saul's employ:
- In the first version, David becomes Saul's "armor-bearer" (1 Sm 16:14–23).
- In the second version, David comes to Saul after the famous incident when he kills the Philistine warrior, Goliath, in a single battle (1 Sm 17). David is then presented to Saul as a conquering hero.

After a series of wars between the relatives of Saul and David and his associates, David finally consolidates his reign. But the path to the throne for David is clearly paved in blood. He systematically eliminates rivals to the throne from the family of Saul; he also engages in military conquests that include not only successful raids against the Philistines, but also successful military campaigns against the political communities across the Jordan River—the peoples of Ammon, Moab, and Edom.

The significance of conquering these Trans-Jordanian states cannot be overemphasized, since this was the path of most of the major trade routes through Palestine, linking Egypt, Phoenicia, and the Mesopotamian Empires. Controlling these trade routes meant David's regime would also control taxes and payment of passage fees. David's regime seems to have become wealthy on precisely these terms.

Ironically, there is very little archaeological evidence of David's kingdom or mention of its existence outside the Bible. There are occasional hints, however. An inscription from a later time period, from the kingdom of Moab, refers to the royalty in Israel as the "House of David." This is the oldest non-Biblical reference to the time of David.

At the very least, David was probably a mobile warrior who enforced his control over a wide range of territory by means of a well-trained private (and probably relatively small) army. It is more accurate to think of David less as a king over a vast kingdom and more as a military leader who enforced submission in a large territory. There was no vast administration or central bureaucracy in Israel—yet.

STANDARD OF LIVING

Research the division of wealth in the nation and the world. What percent of the people control the total income? What is the gross national product? What is the average income for families? What is the poverty level? How many people live at the poverty level? Compare the division of wealth to the division the prophets found unacceptable in Israel and Judah.

140

THE MONARCHY

THE DAVIDIC LINE

The second book of Samuel records a central promise made to David by the Lord:

> It was I who took you from the pasture and from the care of the flock to be commander of my people Israel. I have been with you wherever you went, and I have destroyed all your enemies before you. And I will make you famous like the great ones of the earth. I will fix a place for my people Israel; I will plant them so that they may dwell in their place without further disturbance. Neither shall the wicked continue to afflict them as they did of old, since the time I first appointed judges over my people Israel. I will give you rest from all your enemies. The Lord also reveals to you that he will establish a house for you. And when your time comes and you rest with your ancestors, I will raise up your heir after you, sprung from your loins, and I will make his kingdom firm. . . .Your house and your kingdom shall endure forever before me; your throne shall stand firm forever (2 Sm 7:8–12, 16).

The prophecy is the basis for the Jewish expectation of a Messiah, a son of David, which Jesus would eventually fulfill. The gospels of Matthew and Luke provide genealogies of Jesus that trace his ancestry through David.

Solomon: A Mixed Portrait

More than with his father, David, there is considerable archaeological evidence of King Solomon's role as an administrator of a united kingdom. This makes sense, because Solomon was reputed to be the great builder in the Bible. Solomon not only built up Jerusalem, including an actual palace and the Temple itself, but he also built many other walled cities as military fortresses. Many of these walled fortresses—dated to nearly the exact period of Solomon's rule—have been excavated by archaeologists to lend non-Biblical evidence to his rule.

The Biblical portrait of Solomon is a mixture of positive and negative impressions. Among the positive impressions is the famous story of a king who wisely settles a dispute between two women who both claim an infant as her own (see 1 Kgs 3:16–28). Another is the story of Solomon's response when God tells him to ask for anything he wants and God will grant it to him. Solomon asks God only for the gifts of "an understanding heart to judge your people and to distinguish right from wrong" (1 Kgs 3:9).

God is so impressed with this request that he promises Solomon both wisdom and the wealth that comes with human success. But it is clear that the bright portrait of Solomon dims as he grows older. He apparently engages in a number of political marriages, and

GENEALOGIES OF JESUS

Read the two genealogies of Jesus in the gospels: Matthew 1:1–17 and Luke 3:37–38. Research: Why does Jesus' genealogy in Matthew trace to Abraham and the one in Luke trace to Adam? Why do you think Jesus' genealogy in Luke's gospel is not placed until the third chapter?

141

---

5. Use the notes in the *New American Bible* to complete the separate exercise, "Genealogies of Jesus" (page 141). Point out that neither genealogy is historically accurate, though each is designed to teach a religious point. Matthew, who wrote for a Jewish-Christian audience, emphasized Jesus' connection to Abraham, the founder of the Jewish faith. Luke, who wrote for a Gentile audience, connected Jesus not just to Jewish history, but to the history of all humanity—from Adam. His message was: "Jesus is related to all humans. He is the savior of all."

6. Summarize the text section "Solomon: A Mixed Portrait." Have the students note both positive (e.g., the wisdom of Solomon described in 1 Kings 3:16–28) and negative accomplishments of Solomon (e.g., the building of a palace for himself, the heavy taxation of his people, and the use of his own people as slaves).

Chapter 6

7. Focus the next part of the lesson on the building of Solomon's Temple. Assign the feature, "The Temple of Solomon" and the exercise "Building Solomon's Temple," both on page 143. Distribute copies of Handout 6C, "Solomon's Temple," showing the floor plan of the Temple (page 279 of the TWE). Ask the students to read 1 Kings 6–8, noting the accuracy of the measurements on the handout. You may wish to assign the building of the model Temples as group projects. Allow the students to use whatever building materials are available (clay, plywood, foam board, sugar cubes, Lego blocks, soda cans, etc.) Allow time for the individuals or groups to begin planning their model.

The Old Testament

Ark of the Covenant—The portable shrine built to hold the tablets on which Moses wrote the Law. It was a sign of God's presence to the Israelites. Solomon built the Temple in Jerusalem to house the ark.

Showbread—The twelve loaves of bread presented on the altar every Sabbath as an offering to Yahweh. The priests consumed the bread at the end of every week. (This is also sometimes spelled "shewbread" but the pronunciation does not change.)

the Biblical historians portray this as the source of his downfall—not because civil law did not permit many wives (ancient treaties were often sealed by exchanging royal children in marriage), but because many of these were pagan women whom Solomon allowed to foster polytheistic religious practices among the Israelites.

But there is an even more serious issue blotting Solomon's record—namely how he treated his own people. Even his great building accomplishments are called into question: How could Solomon afford such extravagant projects? An older section from 1 Kings claims that Solomon enslaved foreigners and maintains that he would never enslave or overburden his own people with the tasks of his great building campaigns:

> All the non-Israelite people who remained in the land, descendants of the Amorites, Hittites, Perizzites, Hivites, and Jebusites whose doom the Israelites had been unable to accomplish, Solomon conscripted as forced laborers, as they are to this day. But Solomon enslaved none of the Israelites, for they were his fighting force, his ministers, commanders, adjutants, chariot officers, and charioteers (1 Kgs 9:20–22).

But in another part of the record of Solomon, it states clearly that he certainly *did* force his own people into labor: "King Solomon conscripted thirty thousand workmen from all Israel" (1 Kgs 5:27). From this passage it is not completely clear if the workers were all actual Israelites. However, the proof that they were is most evident in the events that overtake Solomon's son and successor, Rehoboam.

When Rehoboam hears that the Northern Israelite peoples are upset and angry over their years under Solomon, he goes to meet with the elders of the Northern Tribes and find out why they are so upset:

> They said to Rehoboam: "Your father put on us a heavy yoke. If you now lighten the harsh service and the heavy yoke your father imposed on us, we will serve you." "Come back to me in three days," he answered them (1 Kgs 12:3–5).

When the people returned, Rehoboam showed little of his father's reputed wisdom. His answer to the people led directly to the split of the kingdom, into a northern kingdom and southern kingdom. Rehoboam told them:

> "Whereas my father put a heavy yoke on you, I will make it heavier. My father beat you with whips, but I will beat you with scorpions" (1 Kgs 12:11).

These words of Rehoboam make the case against Solomon fairly tight. Solomon enslaved his own people and a large percentage of them resented it. Eventually, a group broke away from the southern kingdom and formed a separate state under a new king, Jeroboam. Usually the final split between the two kingdoms is dated at the death of Solomon, approximately 922 B.C.

THE MONARCHY

THE TEMPLE OF SOLOMON

King David had great concern for the **Ark of the Covenant**, which had been housed in a tent throughout Israel's wanderings in the wilderness. His desire was to build a Temple for the ark. However, the Lord, through the prophet Nathan, said that such a place was unnecessary. "In all my wanderings everywhere among the Israelites, did I ever utter a word to any one of the judges whom I charged to tend my people Israel to ask: Why have you not built me a house of cedar?" (2 Sm 7:7). Nevertheless, David's son, Solomon, proceeded with the plans for a Temple. Chapters six to eight of the first book of Kings describe in detail the building, furnishing, and dedication of the Temple.

Many details of the Temple reflected Canaanite-Phoenician patterns. Its basic floor plan consisted of three parts. Approaching from the east, one walked between two free-standing, bronze-covered pillars into a small vestibule. This opened into the largest of the three rooms, the Holy Place. It was about sixty feet long and contained an incense altar, a table of **Showbread**, and ten candlesticks. Canaanite art of pomegranates, lilies, and palms decorated the walls. The third room, the Holy of Holies, was thirty square feet in measurement. There were no windows. This room housed the ark of the covenant. On both sides of the ark were cherubim. This was the place where Yahweh was believed to be present, enthroned over the ark. Other rooms along the back and side walls were used for storage. The Temple's small size was due in great part to the fact that only priests could enter the building. Worshippers stood in the courtyard *near* the Temple.

Throughout the years of the monarchy, a close connection was maintained between the Temple and the kings. The Temple was destroyed in the Babylonian capture of Jerusalem in 587 B.C. It was rebuilt after the exile (520–515 B.C.). This "second Temple" was destroyed in 70 A.D. by the Romans.

BUILDING SOLOMON'S TEMPLE

Build or draw a model of Solomon's Temple to scale. Read 1 Kings 6; 7:13–51 (note that a cubit equals 1 1/2 feet). Make sure to include the following features: winged creatures, Ark of the Covenant, Holy of Holies, storerooms, the Holy Place, porch, free-standing pillars, and bronze tank. Write a report mentioning at least ten other facts about Solomon's Temple gleaned from the Bible and other resources. Finally, spend some time before the Blessed Sacrament at a Catholic church or chapel. Compare the tabernacle design to the ark of the covenant. Think about how architecture, room size, and decoration makes you *feel* when you stand in that place. Pray for the gift of wisdom in the presence of the Lord.

Model of King Solomon's Temple

8. **Homework Assignment**:
   - Continue to work on the "Building Solomon's Temple" project.
   - Answer the Review and Reflection questions 1–3, page 144.
   - Complete the Journal Assignment on page 144. You may have the students write a prayer for their Church and parish community much as Solomon did in 1 Kings 8:22–65.
   - Read the text section, "The Divided Monarchy," pages 144–148, including the separate feature, "Naboth's Vineyard."

Enrichment: Write a report on the Iron Age, which was in progress in Palestine around the time of King Saul.

Enrichment: Make a chart contrasting the Israelites and Philistines in regard to origin, religion, language, culture, and warfare.

CHAPTER 6

THE DIVIDED MONARCHY

Bell-Ringers

1. If completed, have the students display their models of Solomon's Temple. Or, allow time for them to work on the models in class.

2. Call on volunteers to offer their opinions about why Solomon built his Temple. If they also wrote a prayer as part of the Journal Assignment, call on volunteers to share these as well.

3. If there is a chapel at your school or a church nearby, arrange for a knowledgeable staff person to lead the students on a tour, pointing out its most distinguishing and important features.

THE OLD TESTAMENT

REVIEW & REFLECTION

1. What advantages did the Philistines have over the Israelites during Saul's reign?
2. What were the accomplishments of King David? What were his failings?
3. What was the chief complaint of the people against King Solomon?

JOURNAL ASSIGNMENT

- Why do you think King Solomon built the Temple? Read 1 Kings 8 for clues about what the Temple meant to the Israelites. What does the church building mean to Catholics today?

The Divided Monarchy

Judah—The name of the southern kingdom after the splitting of the monarchy. It included the territory originally belonging to just two of the twelve tribes, Judah and Benjamin.

When Solomon died, Israel divided into two separate kingdoms. The southern kingdom was called **Judah**. It consisted of the traditional territory of two of the original twelve tribes: Benjamin and Judah. The northern kingdom was called "Israel" and was made up of the other ten tribes. The two kingdoms existed side by side for several centuries, ruled by a succession of kings. Both Judah and Israel engaged in several internal struggles during those years as well as fighting battles with outside nations, including the Arameans.

Judah's kings considered themselves the legitimate rulers because their ancestors could be traced to King David. However, the unequal division of the tribes strongly hints that the majority of the people from the former united Israel rejected the kings of Judah because of the abuse of Solomon and the threats of Rehoboam.

The books of 1 and 2 Kings tell details of the divided monarchy. Some kings have several details provided about their reign. Others are mentioned very briefly indeed. The next sections report on some of the highlights of this historical period leading to the sieges of the northern kingdom by the Assyrians in 722–720 B.C. and of the southern kingdom by the Babylonians over a century later.

The Insurrection of Jeroboam

Jeroboam, son of Nebat, led the insurrection against King Rehoboam and founded the northern kingdom of Israel (see 1 Kgs 12:12–33; 2 Chr 11:1–4). There are a number of interesting elements to Jeroboam's story. As King Solomon's officer, he was in charge of forced labor (1 Kgs 11:28). Did he, like Moses, observe the suffering of "his people" and come to be a voice for liberation from the enslavement of Solomon's regime? It is certain that Jeroboam fled Solomon's anger after speaking out against

144

Review and Reflection Answers

1. The Philistines had the ability to fashion weapons from iron; the Israelites did not. The Philistines were also very organized; the Israelites were poorly organized.
2. David engaged in military conquests that included successful raids against the Philistines, the Ammonites, the Moabites, and the Edomites. He probably had a well-trained private army. David's failings included his lust for Bathsheba and consequent killing of her husband Uriah. He did not accomplish major building projects as his son Solomon would later do.
3. The chief complaint of the people against Solomon was that he taxed them too heavily and enslaved them in order to build his many projects.

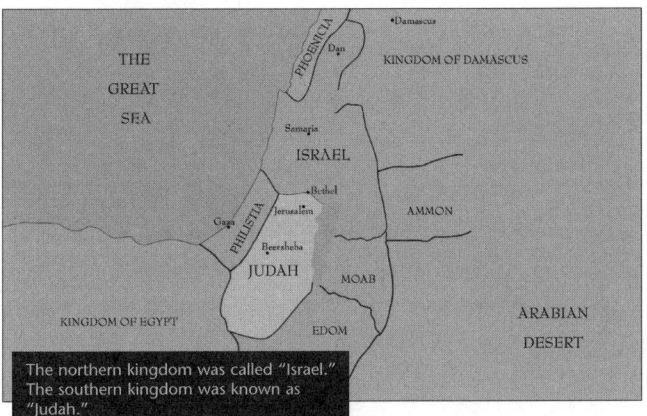

The northern kingdom was called "Israel." The southern kingdom was known as "Judah."

the people's mistreatment. He sought sanctuary in an unlikely place—in the land of Pharaoh Shishak of Egypt (see 1 Kgs 11:40).

Shishak may have accepted Jeroboam as a protected guest because Shishak entertained the thought of reasserting Egyptian dominance in the lands of Canaan lost during the rules of Saul, David, and Solomon. Egyptian records carved on the walls of the Temple of Karnak on the banks of the Nile River (still visible today) verify that Shishak most certainly did engage in military campaigns in Judah and Israel. Egypt probably did re-take control of the region during Shishak's rule. As 1 Kings reports:

In the fifth year of King Rehoboam, Shishak, the king of Egypt, attacked Jerusalem. He took everything, including the treasures of the temple of the Lord and those of the royal palace, as well as all the gold shields made under Solomon (1 Kgs 14:25–26).

What the relationship of Jeroboam was to this campaign is not clear. According to 1 Kings 15:1, Jeroboam continued to rule in the north after the reign of Rehoboam in Judah ended.

Rivalry and Religion in the Northern Kingdom

Read 1 Kings 12:26-33

Jeroboam feared the reunification of Judah and Israel that might possibly arise through continued worship at a single Temple in Jerusalem. In the northern cities of Dan and Bethel, Jeroboam brought gold calves and built temples there. He also appointed priests from among the people living in those areas who were not Levites, the traditional tribe of priests.

Most people living in the north were already disillusioned by the burdens placed on them by Solomon and Rehoboam, so that their loyalties waned before the establishment

THE MONARCHY

Teaching Approaches

1. Remind the students of America's Civil War. Explain that a similar situation developed with the united kingdom of Israel. Partly because of the issue of slavery, the nation split in two, with ten tribes forming the northern kingdom of Israel and two tribes forming the southern kingdom of Judah. Reference the opening text under "The Divided Monarchy."

2. Assign 1 Kings 12:12–32 and 2 Chronicles 11:1–4 to introduce the insurrection of Jeroboam. Explain that Jeroboam's actions of setting up separate worship of God in the north were severely criticized by the Judean editors of the books of Kings and Chronicles. They cite this reason as the cause of the northern kingdom's fall more than 100 before the fall of the kingdom of Judah. Ask students whether they think Jeroboam was right or wrong in rebelling against Rehoboam. (Accept all reasonable answers.)

Chapter 6

3. Note the rivalry of religious beliefs of the Northern Kingdom. Highlight the conflict between the prophet Elijah and the prophets of Baal, the Canaanite god of fertility, in 1 Kings 18. Explain that Ahab was king in the north; he favored the worship of Baal. Elijah was a prophet from the south, who advocated worship of Yahweh alone. Discuss the story as needed. Explain that the important religious lesson of the story is that Elijah was able to convert the people who worshiped Baal to worship only Yahweh.

4. Remind the students that the "establishment religion," polytheism, supported the desires of the rich. This can be seen in policies regarding possession of the land. The Israelite religion, on the other hand, fostered justice in the way land was distributed. Connect that lesson with what happens today in the United States: people have the right to own land until the state has need of it (for example, to build a freeway, a dam, or national park). The government—for the common good—has the right to seize the land from the landowner. But the government must also pay the owner the fair market value for the land.

Neo-Assyrian Empire—a new empire in the Mesopotamian region that eventually conquered the northern kingdom, sending its ruling class into exile in 722 B.C.

Establishment religion—A religion that tends to support the power of the ruling class over the common people. In the case of the Israelite monarchy, it joined Yahweh worship with the worship of other of temples in Dan and Bethel. The sacrificing to golden calves in these temples led to the sin of idolatry (1 Kgs 12:30).

The continued social, political, and religious relationship between Judah and Israel was one of constant conflict—conquest and counter-conquest. These battles with one another were complicated by the involvement of other local regimes and larger empires.

By 900–800 B.C. the rise of the **Neo-Assyrian Empire**, based in the northern Mesopotamian city of Nineveh, caused difficulties for all the regimes in the area of Palestine, Syria, and the coastal port cities of what is today Lebanon. The Assyrian Empire used brute force to dominate the entire region. By 722 B.C., the Assyrian Empire finally conquered all of the northern kingdom.

1 and 2 Kings (and 2 Chronicles) describe the period between 922 and 722 B.C. as a time of corruption of the kings of both Judah and Israel. Though there were many notable achievements of these various kings, the Bible focuses more on the survival and perpetuation of the form of Yahweh worship that:
- was much more consistent with the messages of the prophets, and
- was opposed to the official versions of the religious establishments supported by Israel's and Judah's rulers.

The rivalry between and often within Judah and Israel can be

The foreground of this picture is the area of the discovery of the Dan inscription which mentions the "House of David."

described as a conflict between a form of Yahweh worship that also allowed the worship of other lesser deities in addition to Yahweh, and a more prophetically inspired form of worship that was *exclusively* devoted to Yahweh.

Each of these religious views had strong links to particular socioeconomic ideas about how society ought to be organized. Those who believed Yahweh alone should be worshipped (represented strongly by the prophets) seem to have had a more radical orientation on the Law of Moses. They supported a community where the rich shared with the poor, where social balance was maintained, where justice was practiced, and where land was distributed fairly to all. The other perspective, identified in the Bible as a form of paganism, was more closely identified with the ancient polytheism of the Canaanites and kings and with the landowning classes. In short, this view might be called an **Establishment religion**. Perhaps the most powerful expression of this difference is given in the famous story of Elijah and the prophets of Baal recorded in 1 Kings 18.

Naboth's Vineyard
Read 1 Kings 21

In this story, Jezebel and Ahab abuse their royal powers by expropriating the land of an Israelite peasant by the name of Naboth. There is a miscarriage of justice, and Jezebel is portrayed as the central player in the entire episode. In short, Jezebel, a royal figure with Canaanite roots, is blamed for an open violation of the Mosaic covenant notion of justice and land distribution, and limitations on royal power and privilege. These were limitations that Jezebel refused to acknowledge. The Jezreel Valley where Naboth's vineyard was located became a flash point of conflict for the anti-Canaanite forces of the northern kingdom. For example, 2 Kings 9–10 details Jehu's massacre of the line of Ahab precisely in the same valley.

What this tradition suggests is that these cited battles were not strictly between two groups who merely worshipped differently. The battles reflected a struggle between two rival ways of life—two radically different social, political, and economic policies. The Canaanite religion was the establishment religion. The Yahweh religion of the prophets seemed to have a much more profound sense of social justice and care of the poor and disenfranchised. This is a critically important difference if we are to understand why there was so much animosity between the two rival religious perspectives in the Bible.

A view of Mount Tabor and the Jezreel Valley from the Nazareth ridge

5. Assign the separate feature, "Naboth's Vineyard" and 1 Kings 21. Review by asking the students to identify Jezebel and to name her act of injustice (the seizure of Naboth's vineyard).

6. **Homework Assignment**:
   - Answer the Review and Reflection questions 1–3, page 148.
   - Complete the Journal Assignment on page 148. This assignment requires you to survey the opinions of one or more adults about the impact of their religious beliefs on their political and economic behavior.
   - Complete the project, "Building Solomon's Temple" (page 143).
   - Read "The Last Days of the Independent Monarchy" (pages 148–151).

Enrichment: Write an essay explaining what God was trying to teach his people through the sins and failures of Israel's kings.

Background Information
Symbol of the Bull

In the ancient Near East, the bull was often considered a divine symbol because of its strength and virility. The Fertile Crescent area was sometimes described as the shape of a bull's horns (the two ends of the crescent). The bull was the symbol of the moon god Sin among the Canaanites. In Ugarit, the bull was the symbol of El, the head of the pantheon. In Mesopotamia, the bull represented the god Marduk who was thought to be the Creator. In the northern kingdom of Israel, Yahweh was depicted as standing on top of a bull-shaped pedestal. Because Yahweh was invisible, however, some people came to worship the bull as Yahweh, thus perpetuating idol worship.

CHAPTER 6

THE LAST DAYS OF THE INDEPENDENT MONARCHY

Bell-Ringers

1. Ask the students to express their reflections and findings from the Journal Assignment on page 148. Accept all reasonable answers, provided the students are logical in their arguments. Make sure that the students realize that many religious people tend to favor the poor, but do not necessarily belong to one of the two main political parties.

2. Invite a local business leader, politician, or parish leader to discuss the idea presented in the Journal Assignment which relates religious behavior to political and socioeconomic beliefs.

THE OLD TESTAMENT

REVIEW & REFLECTION

1. What was the root cause of the division of Israel into the northern and southern kingdoms?
2. Why did Jeroboam build alternative temples in Dan and Bethel?
3. What were the differences between the two forms of Yahweh worship that were prevalent during the period of the divided monarchy? What relationship was there between these religious viewpoints and people's socioeconomic views?

JOURNAL ASSIGNMENT

- In thinking about today's society, how can you make generalized connections between people's religious viewpoints and their socioeconomic opinions? Ask your parents or another adult whose opinion you value, what connections they make between their religious beliefs and their political or economic behavior.

The Damascus city gate

The Last Days of the Independent Monarchy

The first great outside threat to the northern kingdom of Israel was the Neo-Assyrian Empire in Mesopotamia. The preface "neo" means "new" and indicates that there were some older empires in this same location. This empire was located in what today is the northern portion of Iraq.

Another threat to Israel came from a rising local power, based in the ancient city of Damascus in Syria. Damascus organized a group of "coalition states" that recognized Damascus as their head. The Assyrians directed a great deal of their fury at keeping the Damascus coalition subservient, though they were not always successful. When Damascus was powerful, the coalition frequently engaged in conflict with the northern kingdom of Israel.

The ongoing tensions between Damascus and Assyria weakened each state and distracted them from attacking Judah and

148

Review and Reflection Answers

1. The root cause of the division was Rehoboam's decision to continue Solomon's policies of heavy taxation and forced labor.
2. Jeroboam didn't want the Israelites in the north to return to Rehoboam's power by going to Jerusalem to worship. So he set up places in the north for them to worship, making periodic trips to Jerusalem unnecessary.
3. In the south, worship focused exclusively on Yahweh. In the north, worship included the worship of additional lesser deities. In the south, people's socioeconomic views tended to favor social justice, especially toward the poor. In the north, people's socioeconomic views tended to favor the establishment, especially the rich who were in power.

THE MONARCHY

Israel. The years between 785 and 730 B.C. were fairly prosperous for both Hebrew states, especially the northern kingdom of Israel. During this time, prophets condemned the fact that this prosperity benefited mainly elite landowners. It was during this period that the prophet Amos decried the lifestyles of the rich:

> They trample the heads of the weak
>   into the dust of the earth,
>   and force the lowly out of the way
>   (Am 2:7).

Assyrians Assert Power

The wealth and success of the northern kingdom leadership began to unravel with the accession of Tiglath-Pileser III (745–727 B.C.) as ruler of Assyria. He revived the military power of Assyria, and began to reassert that power in the west, including the northern kingdom of Israel. His successors, Shalmaneser and Sargon II, crushed a revolt that broke out in that region.

Finally, in 722 B.C., the Assyrians completely devastated the northern kingdom of Israel. As part of their dominance, the Assyrians practiced a military strategy of deportation. The Assyrian conquerors would remove the upper class and elite of the captured society and exile them elsewhere in their vast territories in order to crush any revolt before it even got started.

At the conquest of Israel, the Assyrians carried away a substantial number of the northern elite (most likely the royal family members, military leaders, landowners, and any others who might threaten a revolt) and dispersed them. These exiles are often referred to as the "Ten Lost Tribes of Israel." Although this group is never heard from again in history, the Assyrians certainly did not exile the entire population of the northern kingdom. After all, the Assyrians were interested in resources and taxes. They would certainly have left the majority of the population in place to work the land and provide wealth to the new Assyrian overlords. There is no evidence for the continued life of these exiles.

The Assyrians and Judah

The Old Testament suggests that Hezekiah, the king of the southern kingdom of Judah, escaped Assyrian wrath and was allowed to stay on the throne by actually aligning with the Assyrians. In fact, Hezekiah maintained relations to Assyria as a vassal until a conflict broke out between 705–700 B.C. at the rise of Sargon II. Sargon attacked Jerusalem. In order to survive the long siege, Hezekiah dug the famous tunnel that still exists in Jerusalem. This tunnel allowed water from the Gihon Spring to flow within the walls of Jerusalem, so that the people in the walled city could have fresh water and a chance for survival.

The Assyrian siege of Jerusalem is worth mentioning, precisely because it is one of the rare occasions when an event is covered by more than once source that we can read even today; in this case Sargon's own Assyrian archives *and* the description in 2 Kings 18–20. Both sources agree that the siege was unsuccessful. In 2 Kings 19:35–36, an "angel"

Teaching Approaches

1. Examine the last days of the independent monarchy from the text material and the words of the prophet Amos. Point out: Amos was a prophet in the northern kingdom who criticized the lifestyles of the rich who showed no concern for the poor. Amos told the rich that they would be the first to be exiled as punishment for their sins. When the Assyrians conquered Israel, they deported the leaders and the rich because they were the people most likely to revolt.

2. **Re-teach:** Continue checking the student's comprehension of the homework reading assignment. Ask:
   - When did the Assyrians conquer the northern kingdom? (722 B.C.)
   - What happened when Sargon II came to power? (Sargon's army besieged Jerusalem, but withdrew before really conquering it.)
   - Why did the Assyrians not continue to conquer Jerusalem and the southern kingdom? (King Hezekiah of Judah bribed the new Assyrian king Sennacherib in order to avoid the same fate as the north.)

Background Information

The Prophet Amos

Amos was a shepherd and tree farmer from Tekoa, near Bethlehem. He preached to the northern kingdom around 750 B.C. Amos' message of social justice was that worship of God must show itself in good deeds to the poor and lowly. Amos spoke out against genocide, cruelty, anger, dishonesty, greed, lawlessness, sexual excess, desecration of the dead, rejection of the prophets, robbery violence, selfishness, deceit, injustice, and pride.

Chapter 6

3. Direct the students to read 2 Kings 23:36–25:26. Summarize the Babylonian destruction of Judah. Make the following points:
   - The Babylonians under Nebuchadnezzar defeated Jerusalem in 597 B.C. and set up a puppet government.
   - King Zedekiah was initially loyal to the Babylonians, but eventually sided with the Egyptians and tried to revolt against Babylon.
   - Nebuchadnezzar's forces returned in 587 to destroy Jerusalem and the Temple.

Also point out that the number of Jews taken to Babylon was not very large. According to Jeremiah 52, three deportations totaled 4,600, though this total may have only included adult males. The captives were permitted to live in farming communities, own houses, marry, and raise families. Eventually, the Babylonian captivity served as an opportunity to strengthen and renew the Hebrew faith.

Enrichment: Research information on King Sargon II. List some of the key accomplishments of his reign, especially from an Assyrian point of view.

---

miraculously strikes down the Assyrian soldiers. Assyrian records say that Sargon simply determined that his point of strength had been made, and he broke the siege. In the end, Hezekiah's tribute to Sargon's successor, Sennacherib, the Assyrian king, guaranteed he would remain on the throne in Judah though the northern kingdom had been decimated.

Archaeologists have determined that there was some movement of population to the southern state of Judah from the north

after Israel collapsed. The next century, the eighth century B.C., brought even more changes to the region. Egypt reasserted its independence and the tribes south of Assyria (centered near the ancient city of Babylon) unified to rise and conquer Assyria itself, leaving only Egypt and Babylon with power in the region.

Babylonian Destruction of the Southern Kingdom

Read 2 Kings 23:36–25:26 and 2 Chronicles 2–23

After 722–720 B.C. the northern kingdom of Israel no longer existed as an independent political state. The southern kingdom of Judah continued for another 135 years, although for part of this time it was under the imperial control of Egypt or Babylon. Babylon had asserted independence in one form or another from Assyria from the middle of this turbulent century onward. When the Chaldean tribes of Babylon unified the southern peoples into an imperial power, their ambitions were finally realized. Their young prince Nebuchadnezzar, who finally defeated the last of the Assyrian forces, also conquered the Egyptian forces in two great battles north of Palestine (609 B.C. and 605 B.C.). The way was clear for Nebuchadnezzar to control the land route to Egypt.

The final days of Judah were largely determined by the rivalry between the Egyptian and Babylonian Empires. From 609 to 597 B.C., following the death of King Josiah in a battle with the Egyptians, the royal house in Judah (King Jehoiakim and his son, King Jehoiachin) were really Egyptian puppet rulers. Their government was established in Jerusalem by Pharaoh Necho in order to create a buffer between Egypt and Babylon.

When Nebuchadnezzar defeated Jerusalem in 597 (young King Jehoiachin surrendered), he chose one of the descendants of Josiah to be the figurehead of Babylonian rule in Jerusalem. King Josiah (640–609 B.C.) seems to have been predisposed to an alliance with Babylon. Perhaps that alliance explains Nebuchadnezzar's choice of Mattaniah, whom he renamed "Zedekiah," to rule Jerusalem.

Zedekiah was initially loyal to Babylon, but was eventually persuaded by Egyptian agents, including a false prophet, Hananiah (see Jer 26–29), to attempt a revolt against Babylonian power and join a coalition with Egypt. The results were catastrophic. Nebuchadnezzar's forces returned to Jerusalem in 587 or 586 B.C. and devastated it. The catastrophe of the fall of Judah in 587 B.C. was a major event in the history of God's Chosen People. The years that followed the Exile were marked by a reorientation in the way the Jews kept their part of the covenant with God. The implications of the end of the monarchy will be explored further in Chapter 7.

To summarize the events of this chapter: It is clear that Hebrew fate was largely determined by the ambitions of regional powers in Egypt and Mesopotamia. The reigns of the various kings of the northern and southern kingdoms take place under the shadow of these larger conflicts. From a religious point of view, the stories chronicled in the time of the kings also pointed a finger at the Chosen People themselves for choosing kings for themselves other than Yahweh and for breaking the covenant by worshipping foreign gods.

4. Allow students who have just completed their Solomon's Temple projects to display them.

5. **Homework Assignment**:
   Answer Review Questions 1–3, page 151.
   - Complete the Journal Assignment. There are many contemporary examples of exiles, including the Kurds in Iraq, the Palestinians in Israel, and modern Jews prior to the establishment of the state of Israel. Find news articles to support your answers.
   - Read "Further Reflections" (page 152) in the text.

1. When and to whom did the northern kingdom fall? What happened to the people who were there?
2. When and to whom did the southern kingdom fall? What happened to the people of Judah?
3. What reason did the prophets give for the fall of Israel and Judah?

JOURNAL ASSIGNMENT

- What parallels are there in modern history to the exile of the Jews from Israel and Judah following their conquest by the Assyrians and the Babylonians? How do you think it would feel to be an exile?

Review and Reflection Answers
1. The northern kingdom fell in 722 B.C. to the Assyrians. The military officers, political leaders, and rich landowners were deported to Assyria in order to prevent a rebellion.
2. The southern kingdom fell in 587 B.C. to the Babylonians. Some, but not all, of the people were taken to Babylon in exile.
3. The prophets blamed the kings for the downfall of the two kingdoms. They especially cited the kings' sin of idolatry.

CHAPTER 6

FURTHER REFLECTIONS

Bell-Ringers

1. Ask volunteers to share their insights into the Journal Assignment questions. Set up a bulletin board where students can post news articles that support their answers.

2. Use the vocabulary words listed in the margins of this chapter for a review game. Divide the class into two teams. Call a representative from one team to stand before the class. Ask him or her to spell and define one of the vocabulary terms. Give two points for correct spelling and an additional four points for saying a correct definition. If the person misses, call on a representative from the other team to respond. Correct spelling for this "second chance" merits one point, while a correct definition is worth two points. Continue the game, calling on a representative from the team that did not begin to come forward for round two.

Teaching Approaches

1. Continue the chapter review by going over some or all of the Review and Reflection questions from the chapter. If you wish, continue in the game format described above assigning points for correct answers to the questions.

2. Assign the Learn by Doing exercise and essay. Go over the qualities of David's leadership skills from the passages listed. For example:
   - 1 Sm 16:18—musician, soldier
   - 1 Sm 17:32–51—brave
   - 1 Sm 20:1–17—friend
   - 1 Sm 24—compassionate
   - 2 Sm 5:9–12—powerful
   - 2 Sm 7:18–19—prayerful
   - 2 Sm 8—military expertise
   - 2 Sm 11–12:2–5—weakness, humility
   - 2 Sm 18:19–19:9—mournful

Tell students that they will be called on to share their insights from the exercise at the beginning of the next chapter.

3. **Prayer Service:** Pass out Handout 6D, "Chapter 6 Prayer Service," to each student (page 280 of the TWE). Assign readers for the various parts, including the Scripture reading from 2 Samuel 5:1–3. Divide the class into two sides. Choose an opening and closing song (e.g., "The King of Love My Shepherd Is" and "Thy Kingdom Come,"

THE OLD TESTAMENT

Further Reflections

The prophet Samuel was displeased when the people asked for a king. Samuel felt they did not need a human king because Yahweh was their king. He prayed and the Lord answered,

> Grant the people's every request. It is not you they reject, they are rejecting me as their king. As they have treated me constantly from the day I brought them up from Egypt to this day, deserting me and worshiping strange gods, so do they treat you too (1 Sm 8:7–8).

The monarchy was founded with the naming of Israel's first king, Saul. David, Israel's greatest king, and his son Solomon followed. From the family of David, Jesus was born. Jesus' ancestry to David is traced through his foster father, Joseph (see Mt 1:1–17).

Jesus constantly reminded his disciples of the differences between himself and David, saying his kingdom was "not of this world." Furthermore, Jesus noted the violence so often used to settle differences between nations and said: "Offer no resistance to one who is evil. When someone strikes you on your right cheek, turn the other one to him as well" (Mt 5:39).

The kingdom of God initiated by Jesus is one of servanthood and compassion, not power and domination. Remembering this helps to put the relation of Jesus to David in context: Jesus is a New David, but he is not David. Jesus is a different kind of king for a different kind of kingdom. The earliest Christians, who were all Jews, would have understood this irony.

Jesus Christ (in Greek, "anointed one") is the one whom God the Father anointed with the Holy Spirit and established as priest, prophet, and king. Christians share in the royal office of Christ, drawn in by his death and resurrection. Christ's kingship is different than that of earthly kings. Christ does not serve from a base of force. Rather, he is the humble servant who "did not come to be served but to serve and to give his life as a ransom for many" (Mk 10:45). Christians who reign with Christ the King do so in service, particularly in the service of the poor and suffering. This reign of service is much different from that envisioned by the Israelites who first requested of Samuel a king. As St. Leo the Great wrote:

> What, indeed, is as royal for a soul as to govern the body in obedience to God? (*Sermo* 4, 1:PL 54, 149).

Learn by Doing

There are many types of leaders. The authoritarian leader takes no suggestions and makes all decisions for himself or herself. The non-intrusive leader often lets the group "do its own thing" and offers no concrete help. The consultative leader takes input from everyone in the group, realizing that with more information he or she can make a more informed decision. Look up the following passages. For each, name a quality of King David's leadership skills that are expressed:

- 1 Sm 16:18
- 1 Sm 17:32–51
- 1 Sm 20:1–17
- 1 Sm 24
- 2 Sm 5:9–12
- 2 Sm 7:18–29
- 2 Sm 8
- 2 Sm 11–12:25
- 2 Sm 18:19–19:9

Chapter 6 Parish Religious Education Adaptation

- The Chapter 6 Parish Religious Education Adaptation (pages 14–15 of the TWE) breaks down Chapter 6 for coverage in either a one- or two-hour lesson and is suitable for most parish religious education or youth ministry settings.
- Assign Chapter 6 for reading prior to the first class session. The students are also to complete the assigned Review and Reflection questions from Chapter 5.

Write a short essay describing your ideal leader. How does your profile incorporate Jesus' model of "servant leadership" which leads from humility and compassion rather than power and coercion?

● *Called to Prayer*

Loving God,
    you conquer evil's hold on us
    and bring us to new life through our Lord, Jesus Christ,
    the King of the Universe.
May we never cease to praise
    your glory
    and love you with all of our hearts.
We ask this through Jesus Christ, our Lord,
    who lives and reigns with you and the Holy Spirit
    for ever and ever.
Amen.
    —adapted from Opening Prayer,
    feast of Christ the King

---

see page 136 of the TWE). Play or lead the opening song. Then read these words as an introduction:

> Today as we come together in prayer, we take time to reflect on the meaning of leadership. We recall the examples of Israel's kings, especially King David and King Solomon. We pray for the best qualities of leadership of these kings. We also look to the example of our Lord, Jesus Christ, our leader *par excellence*.

Proceed with the Scripture reading. Continue through the handout. For a concluding prayer, have the students use the "Called to Prayer" on page 157.

4. **Homework Assignment:**
   - Study for Chapter 6 Test.

CHAPTER 6 TEST

Teaching Approaches

1. Allow enough time for the students to work on the Chapter 6 Test (online at **avemariapress.com**). Collect and grade. Note that each question is worth four points. However, you may consider making the essay (question 25) worth ten points, applying the additional points as extra credit.

2. Reserve some time for a closing prayer. If you did not do the Chapter 6 Prayer Service in the previous session, do so now.

3. Refer to the Catholic Handbook for Faith for additional lesson ideas.

Chapter 6 Test Answers

Part 1: Multiple Choice: 1. c; 2. d; 3. e; 4. b; 5. e; 6. d; 7. a; 8. d; 9. e; 10. c.

Part 2: True or False: 11. 0; 12. +; 13. 0; 14. 0; 15. 0 16. +; 17. +; 18. +; 19. +; 20. 0.

Part 3: Short Fill-ins: 21. Ugarit; 22. Saul; 23. Israel/Judah; 24. Jezebel.

Part 4: Short Essay: 25. The two forms are 1) Yahweh worship that allowed the worship of lesser deities in addition to Yahweh, and 2) a more prophetically inspired form of worship devoted exclusively to Yahweh. The first form was the "establishment religion" that was more supportive of the kings and land-owning classes. The second, influenced by the preaching of the prophets, called for a greater degree of economic justice, for the rich to share with the poor, justice to be practiced, land to be fairly distributed.

Introducing Chapter 7

Chapter 7 presents an overview of the role and purpose of prophets in the Old Testament. It also provides brief biographical sketches of some of the prophets of the time period. As the text explains, scholars classify the prophets into two groups: the former prophets and the latter prophets. The former prophets include Moses, Aaron, Deborah, Samuel, Nathan, Elijah, and Elisha. The latter prophets include three major prophets (Isaiah, Jeremiah, and Ezekiel) and twelve minor prophets (Hosea, Joel, Amos, Obadiah, Jonah, Micah, Nahum, Habbakuk, Zephaniah, Haggai, Zechariah, and Malachi). Specifically, this chapter deals with the prophets of the northern kingdom Israel in the ninth and eighth centuries B.C.: Elijah, Elisha, Hosea, and Amos.

The Old Testament prophets took on several roles for God's People. They were called by God to be his messengers, or spiritual warriors. Their purpose was to speak out against social injustices. And they continually called people to repentance and conversion, to return to a right relationship with Yahweh. Though their methods differed, the prophets all spoke the same basic message: Repent and God will save you. Fail to repent, and God will punish you.

Elijah, the father of the prophets, lived during the reign of King Ahab. Elijah opposed the king's wife, Jezebel, who persisted in fostering the worship of Baal. In a famous contest, Elijah challenged Jezebel's priests and publicly proved that Yahweh, not Baal, was the god of rain and fertility. Because Elijah was such an important prophet in Israel's history, the Bible contains the story of his miraculous passing. Rather than dying, he was assumed into heaven on a fiery chariot.

Elisha, the disciple and successor of Elijah, was well known for his miracles that mirrored the feats of Elijah. Elisha was especially remembered for siding with the suffering of the poor and for calling people to exclusive religious devotion to Yahweh.

Amos was a shepherd and tree farmer when God called him to be his messenger. Often known as the prophet of doom and gloom, Amos spoke out against the many sins of Israel: genocide, cruelty, anger, dishonesty, greed, sexual excess, injustice, and pride. He especially condemned the abuses of the wealthy and predicted that, if they didn't change, God would punish them.

Hosea lived out the message he preached. Just as he described the relationship of Yahweh to Israel as a marriage between a man and an unfaithful wife, so Hosea chose to marry Gomer, a prostitute. The book of Hosea described how hurt Hosea was when his wife was unfaithful. Instead of condemning her, however, he took her back and forgave her. Hosea's message is that Israel had been unfaithful to Yahweh by worshiping false gods. But Yahweh truly loved Israel and called her back into a covenant relationship.

Despite the preaching of these prophets, the people of the northern kingdom continued to sin against Yahweh. As a result, they were punished when the Assyrians invaded the country in 722 B.C. and took many of the rich into exile.

Background Notes for the Teacher

A study of the prophets shows that social justice is at the core of the Old Testament's message. God sides with the poor—especially the orphan, the widow, and the alien resident. Furthermore, God judges us, not by our elaborate worship ceremonies but by the way we treat others. Jesus himself confirms the prophets' vision. When the kingdom of God comes, Jesus said, the Son of Man will judge people according to their just and loving treatment of others. God will reward those who give shelter to the homeless, feed the hungry, and care for the sick. Likewise, God will punish those who oppress others.

Chapter 7 Outline

Introduction
The prophets are special messengers from God, following in the tradition of Moses.

Marks of the Prophets
God calls prophets to be spiritual warriors, social revolutionaries, and heirs to the role of Moses.

The Servants, the Prophets
The prophets of the northern kingdom in the eighth and ninth centuries B.C. fulfilled their role as God's servants by continually calling the people back to right relationship with Yahweh.

The Contrasting Styles of the Prophets
Though their methods differ, the message of all prophets is essentially the same: "Repent of your sins and God will save you. Fail to repent and you, and your nation, will be doomed."

Further Reflections

Resources

Music Suggestions: see page 162
Printed Materials: see page 163
Audiovisual Materials: see page 164
Internet Links: see page 165

CHAPTER 7
GOD'S PROPHETS
At the Heart of the Journey

In teaching about the Old Testament prophets, it is important to explain to the students that the prophets were not just spokesmen for their own times. Their message is a universal one, one that applies to all centuries. Like God's Chosen People of the Old Covenant, we are called to be faithful to God's New Covenant in Christ. We are called to love and worship God by treating our neighbor with justice. We, too, are to be prophets in the twenty-first century—applying Biblical principles to modern-day topics such as abortion, the death penalty, genetic research, warfare, poverty, the environment, and so forth.

Advance Preparations
- The students should have separate journals for the Learn by Doing exercise.
- As social justice is an important part of the study of the prophets, you should have on hand a number of recent newspapers, news magazines, and Church documents concerning contemporary social justice topics such as abortion, warfare, the environment, poverty, the rights of workers, and so forth. These resources will especially be needed for the Learn by Doing exercise on page 173.
- *Optional:* Invite a person you consider to fit the definition of a prophet described in the text to speak to the class about how the students can also live out this call (see page 165 of TWE).
- *Optional:* Ask a husband and wife to share with the class their reflections on the books of Hosea and/or Amos and tell how particular passages help them in their faithfulness to the marriage covenant.
- Prepare any handouts and overhead transparencies (found at **avemariapress.com**) you plan to use with the class.
- Obtain and view any videos or Internet resources you wish to include in your lesson plan.
- Obtain a recording of any music you wish to include in your lesson plan.

Relevant Teachings from Church Documents
- Through the prophets God forms his people in the hope of salvation, in the expectation of a new and everlasting Covenant intended for all, to be written on their hearts. (Cf. Is 2:2–4; Jer 31:31–34; Heb 10:16.) The prophets proclaim a radical redemption of the People of God, purification from all their infidelities, a salvation which will include all the nations. (Cf. Ez 36; Is 49:5–6; 53:11.) Above all, the poor and humble of the Lord will bear this hope... (*CCC*, 64)
- Through the prophets, [God] prepared [Israel] to accept the salvation destined for all humanity. (*CCC*, 72)
- In the course of its history, Israel was able to discover that God had only one reason to reveal himself to them, a single motive for choosing them among all people as his special possession: his sheer gratuitous love. And thanks to the prophets Israel understood that it was again out of love that God never stopped saving them and pardoning their unfaithfulness and sins. (*CCC*, 218)
- Giving alms to the poor is a witness to fraternal charity: it is also a work of justice pleasing to God. (*CCC*, 2462)
- It was [God's] strategy that Israel might learn by experience God's ways with humanity and by listening to the voice of God speaking to them through the prophets might gradually understand his ways more fully and more clearly... (Vatican II, *Dogmatic Constitution on Divine Revelation*, #17)
- The movement of return to God, called conversion and repentance, entails sorrow for and abhorrence of sins committed, and a firm purpose of sinning no more in the future. Conversion touches the past and the future and is nourished by hope in God's mercy. (*CCC*, 1490)

Chapter Objectives
The students will be able to:
- associate the Old Testament prophets with the tradition of Moses.
- explore the nature of a prophet's "calling" from God.
- see how the prophets were messengers of God as well as social revolutionaries.
- learn more about the times and message of the prophets Elijah, Elisha, Amos, and Hosea.
- understand how the Old Testament explains the fall of the northern kingdom in religious terms.
- discover how the prophets also prepared people for the coming of a Messiah.
- appreciate their own call to be prophets in the twenty-first century.

CHAPTER 7

INTRODUCTION

Bell-Ringers

1. Print this statement from Chapter 6 on the board: **Jesus is a New David, but he is not David. Jesus is a different kind of King for a different kind of kingdom.** Ask the students to write an explanation of this statement. Look for words like servanthood and compassion in their responses.

2. Return the Chapter 6 Tests to the students if you have graded them. Go over any questions the students may have.

3. Ask several students to share their essays from the Chapter 6, Learn by Doing exercise, relating their description of an ideal leader based on Jesus' model of leadership. As the students read, make a list on the board of adjectives they use to describe their chosen leader.

Teaching Approaches

1. Introduce the meaning of "prophet" in the Old Testament. Explain that a prophet was a person who was raised up by God to tell the people of the will, plans, and warnings of God. Make sure that the students understand that a prophet is not someone who predicts the future. Rather, the Biblical prophets were people who had a personal relationship with God and were able to communicate his perspective to the people. Usually, the content of the prophet's message concerned itself with faithfulness to God's commandments and issues of social justice. Often, a prophet's message was hard to hear because it forced people to change their lives. In addition, the prophets reminded people of God's forgiveness and ongoing love for them. Usually, the message of a prophet is universal. It not only applies to the people of his or her time; it also applies to people today.

2. Assign the Introduction, page 156, for individual reading. Then check for comprehension. Ask:
   - Who was the first prophet in the Bible? (Moses)
   - Why do we call some prophets "former prophets"? (They appeared in the Deuteronomic History books—Joshua, Judges, 1 and 2 Samuel, 1 and 2 Kings.) Point out that the "latter prophets" have separate books in the Old Testament. The prophet probably did not write the book attributed to him. A later editor probably collected the sayings of the prophet and wrote them down in a book that is now part of the Bible.

THE OLD TESTAMENT

nabi—The Hebrew word translated as prophet.

major prophets—Three of the latter prophets, Isaiah, Jeremiah, and Ezekiel, whose books in the Old Testament are quite lengthy

minor prophets—The twelve prophets of the Old Testament whose recorded sayings are much briefer than those of the major prophets: Hosea, Joel, Amos, Obadiah, Jonah, Micah, Nahum, Habbakuk, Zephaniah, Haggai, Zechariah, and Malachi.

Introduction

The prophet is a special kind of messenger from God. Prophets were present through the early and late stages of the Old Testament. In fact, the Hebrew word associated with prophet, *nabi*, is connected first with Moses. Moses was the prophet who heard God's message of liberation and shared it with the people while they were still enslaved in Egypt. Moses' brother, Aaron, was also called a prophet because he spoke for Moses before the Pharaoh.

The prophets are mentioned throughout Deuteronomic History. Samuel, the last of Israel's judges, was also called a prophet. Deborah, another judge, was a "prophetess" (Jgs 4:4). The second book of Samuel mentions the prophet Nathan confronting David about his sinful behavior involving Bathsheba and Uriah, though no other information is told of him. Also included among these "former prophets" are the prominent figures of Elijah and Elisha.

Prophecy became a literary movement, too. The sayings of selected prophets were gathered up and kept, just as the sayings of Jesus were kept by the earliest Christians. Amos (Approx. 740 B.C.) was the earliest prophet whose gathered sayings were written in book form. After Amos, other books were formed from the sayings of different prophets. And then, somewhat mysteriously, the books of prophetic messages ceased in the Old Testament, although the early Christians also had prophets.

The group of "latter prophets" (as opposed to the former prophets who appear in Deuteronomic History) was made up of three **major prophets** (Isaiah, Jeremiah, and Ezekiel) along with a larger group of **minor prophets** (Hosea, Joel, Amos, Obadiah, Jonah, Micah, Nahum, Habbakuk, Zephaniah, Haggai, Zechariah, and Malachi). "Major" and "minor," incidentally, are terms that refer to the size of the book, not to the importance of the prophet or his message.

A main objective of this chapter is to introduce the origins of the prophets. Several ideas will be explored, each one contributing to how the prophets took on a central role with God's Chosen People of the Old Testament. Biographical sketches of four prophets—Elijah, Elisha, Amos, and Hosea—who preached God's justice prior to the fall of the northern kingdom will be offered in this chapter.

Chapter 8 will cover more of the prophets' messages specifically related to the fall of the northern and southern kingdoms and the exile of Israel to Assyria and Judah to Babylon. First, a return to the question of the origins of the prophets.

REVIEW & REFLECTION

1. Explain the difference between "former" and "latter" prophets and between "major" and "minor" prophets. List examples of each.
2. Which prophet was the first to have his sayings collected in a written work? Where does this book appear in the Bible?

Background Information

More on Minor Prophets

Recall that the so-called "minor prophets" are named that only because of the brevity of their written collections. Actually, prophets like Hosea, Amos, Haggai and Zechariah were "major" prophets in their own time. The following list is a the chronological order of when the minor prophets appear in Israelite history:

1. Amos
2. Hosea
3. Micah
4. Zephaniah
5. Nahum
6. Habbakuk
7. Haggai
8. Zechariah
9. Malachi
10. Obadiah
11. Joel
12. Jonah

JOURNAL ASSIGNMENT

- Read from the books of the minor prophets until you find a few verses that seem to you to apply to a current event or situation. Copy the passage and then explain how it applies and what you think the prophet would have to say about that event or situation today.

Marks of the Prophets

Several common marks or roles of the prophets provide clues to their origins.

First, prophets received a call from God and felt compelled to leave their former way of life to follow it. Amos, for example, was a shepherd: "The Lord took me from following the flock, and said to me Go, prophesy to my people Israel" (Am 7:15). This call from God came in different ways. Prophets heard voices, had dreams, saw visions, or received inspiration to share God's message. In some ways, they were like the oracles of other religious traditions (ancient Greek) to whom people went to ask questions about God. However, false prophets are also mentioned in many places throughout the Old Testament, sometimes making it difficult to determine who were the true prophets.

Second, the prophet often spoke messages that were unpopular with the ruling establishment. In response, the king sometimes tried to rid himself of the prophet in the belief that doing so would keep the prophet's dire message from coming true. Needless to say, "killing the messenger" did not, in any way, make the message less true. In general, the message of the prophets was to warn the people to repent for their sins under the penalty of punishment if they failed to do so. More characteristics of the prophets follow.

The Prophets Inherited the Role of Moses

The concept of a person being called by God or his angel to perform a particular task or to play a certain role in the life of the community of Israel is central to the understanding of prophets. The **call narratives** of Isaiah and Jeremiah each follow a similar pattern:

1. The setting is one of mystery or holiness.
2. God initiates the call.
3. The person resists.
4. God reassures the person.
5. God sends the person on a mission.

Read Jeremiah 1:4–10 and Isaiah 6:1–9

This pattern is the same as Moses' call to be God's deliverer of the people of Israel in Egyptian slavery:

> Moses, however, said to the Lord, "If you please, Lord, I have never been eloquent, neither in the past, nor recently, nor now that you have spoken to your servant; but I am slow of speech and tongue." The Lord said to him, "Who gives one man speech and makes another deaf

call narrative—A story that describes a person's initial awareness that God wanted him or her to do something specific. The calls of the prophet have five common elements: there is something mysterious and holy about the encounter, God acts first, the prophet resists, God reassures, and God sends the prophet on his or her mission.

Review and Reflection Answers

1. Former prophets occur in the Deuteronomic History books (Joshua, Judges, 1 and 2 Samuel, and 1 and 2 Kings). Examples of former prophets are Samuel, Deborah, Nathan, Elijah, and Elisha. Latter prophets occur in the prophetic literature of the Bible. Examples of latter prophets are Isaiah, Jeremiah, Ezekiel, Hosea, Joel, Amos, Obadiah, Jonah, Micah, Nahum, Habbakuk, Zephaniah, Haggai, Zechariah, and Malachi. Major prophets are prophets whose writings are long. Major prophets include Isaiah, Jeremiah, and Ezekiel. Minor prophets are prophets whose writings are short. Minor prophets include Hosea, Joel, Amos, Obadiah, Jonah, Micah, Nahum, Habbakuk, Zephaniah, Haggai, Zechariah, and Malachi.
2. Amos was the first prophet to have his sayings collected into a written work. The book appears third among the writings of the minor prophets.

GOD'S PROPHETS

- What is the difference between a major prophet and a minor prophet? (The length of the Biblical book. Major prophets are named for longer books. Minor prophets are named for shorter books.)

3. Peruse the Learn by Doing exercise (page 173) with the students. Explain that every age has its prophets. These prophets speak out on timely issues. The Church's Magisterium has a special call from God to be a prophetic voice today. It publishes many documents, articles, and books to help people apply Biblical principles to modern-day issues.

4. Have the students form small groups to discuss the topics in the Learn by Doing exercise, and to brainstorm additional justice issues. After giving the students sufficient time to work, print the students' ideas on the board or overhead. Add other current issues if you wish.

5. Make available recent newspapers, news magazines, and church documents for the students to look through. Also make available art supplies. Allow time in class for the students to begin to research entries for the journal of contemporary prophetic statements. The students should use separate journals from their regular class journals for this assignment.

6. **Homework Assignment**:
   - Write answers to the Review and Reflection questions 1–2, page 156.
   - Complete the Journal Assignment. As an option, consider designing one of your chosen passages as an art project (e.g., on a matted board for display).
   - Continue to work on the Learn by Doing exercise.
   - Read the text section "Marks of the Prophets" (pages 157-161) including the separate feature "Literary Styles of Hebrew Prophecy."

MARKS OF THE PROPHETS

Bell-Ringers

1. Ask volunteers to read some of the verses they copied from the minor prophets or display their mounted copies of inspirational verses (see the Journal Assignment, page 157). Have the students explain what the passage meant in the prophet's time and what it might mean today.

2. This section talks about what it is like to be "called" by God. Ask the students to discuss this topic prior to delving more deeply into the issue. Ask: "When have you felt called by God?"

Chapter 7

Teaching Approaches

1. Summarize the reading assignment. Focus on the similar pattern of the call narratives of the prophets Isaiah and Jeremiah:
   1. The setting is one of mystery or holiness.
   2. God initiates the call.
   3. The person resists.
   4. God reassures the person.
   5. God sends the person on a mission.

2. Read and review the call narratives of Isaiah (Is 6:1–9) and Jeremiah (Jer 1:4–10). Call on students to name how each narrative fits the pattern described.

3. Next, have the students read Luke 1:26–56 and discuss how Luke uses the same "call narrative" pattern to describe Mary's call to be the Mother of God. Ask: Does this make Mary a prophet? Why or why not? (Accept all reasonable answers.) Then have the students read John 2:1–11. Ask: How does this story about Jesus at the wedding in Cana resemble the pattern of the call narrative? Does this make Jesus a prophet? Why or why not? (Prophecy was a part of Jesus' ministry.)

4. Make sure to emphasize how the role of the prophets changed from the time of judges to the time of kings. The prophets were spiritual leaders and military leaders in the time of judges. During the time of the monarchy, prophets had more of a spiritual role while the kings were the military leaders.

Enrichment: As the students continue to work on the Learn by Doing exercise, ask them to pick out one contemporary justice issue they have discovered. Have them prepare a report on the scope of the problem, what the Church teaches about the issue, and something practical they can do to effect positive change in this area.

THE OLD TESTAMENT

and dumb? Or who gives sight to the one and makes another blind? Is it not I, the Lord? Go, then! It is I who will assist you in speaking and will teach you what you are to say" (Ex 4:10–12).

Like Moses, the prophets Isaiah and Jeremiah protested that they were not good enough to speak for God. It seems that the similarity is intentional. The latter prophets were carrying on the work of Moses. Was Moses the first prophet? Consider this passage from the time of Moses' death:

> Since then no prophet has arisen in Israel like Moses, whom the Lord knew face to face (Dt 34:10).

The prophets usually based their criticism of Israel on the statutes and commandments of Moses; these ethical guidelines were the basis for their denouncing Israelite behavior. All of this suggests a strong connection between Moses the "lawgiver" and the prophets as "law protectors" (insisting that the Law of Moses be obeyed). So, in determining the origins and development of the prophets, the connection with Moses is important. But it is still not the complete picture of the prophets.

The Prophets Were "Spiritual Warriors"

There is textual evidence throughout the Old Testament to support the identification of the judges as prophets also. As mentioned, the judge Deborah, who was a military leader, was directly called a prophet (see Jgs 4:4). Other judges shared the experience of being called by God, or by an angel of God, to their position of leadership. Recall the story of the call of Gideon as he was selected for leadership:

> . . . the *angel of the Lord appeared to him* and said, "The Lord is with you, O champion!" (Jgs 6:12).

Or consider the call of Samson before his birth:

> An angel of the Lord appeared to the woman and said to her, "Though you are barren and have had no children, yet you will conceive and bear a son" (Jgs 13:3).

Compare these calls with the call of Moses at the burning bush:

> There *an angel of the Lord appeared to him* in fire flaming out of a bush. As he looked on, he was surprised to see that the bush, though on fire, was not consumed (Ex 3:2).

The appearance of "an angel of the Lord" at the moment of the call of these judges indicates that, like Moses, the judges, too, were considered prophets. They combined the vocations of prophet (a person summoned by God or his messenger and selected by God to guide his people) and king (someone chosen to be a warrior and to lead the people to military victory). A judge was a "warrior-prophet" in a sense, combining both roles in one vocation.

When the Israelites decided to choose kings of their own, they wanted warriors to fight their battles and lead them to victory over adversaries (recall 1 Sm 8). The kings of Israel were more one-dimensional than the judges. They were warriors without the spiritual dimension that came from being called directly by God.

Did this mean that God stopped "calling on" men and women to speak to the people during the time of the kings? Indeed not. It was during the time of the kings that the prophetic movement became particularly influential and important. Remember, it was the prophet Samuel who identified the king the people had asked for. Although God chose Saul, and then David, to rule as king of Israel, he did not call them directly, nor did his angel appear to them. Instead, God communicated his choice to his prophet, Samuel, and Samuel anointed Saul, and later

• 158

Resources

Music Suggestions

"Change Our Hearts" by Rory Cooney from *Gather* (GIA).

"Hosea" by Gregory Norbet from *Glory & Praise 3* (OCP [NALR]); *Gather* (GIA); and *Breaking Bread* (OCP).

"I Have Loved You" by Michael Joncas from *On Eagle's Wings* or *Glory & Praise 2* (OCP [NALR]); *Gather* (GIA); *Music Issue* or *Breaking Bread* (OCP).

"Let Justice Roll Like a River" by Marty Haugen from *Gather* (GIA).

"Psalm 103: The Lord is Kind and Merciful" by Jeanne Cotter in *Gather* (GIA).

"Psalm 110: The Name of God" by David Haas in *Gather* (GIA).

"Return to God" by Marty Haugen from *Gather* (GIA).

"Seek The Lord" by Roc O'Connor from *Earthen Vessels* or *Glory & Praise 1* (OCP [NALR]); *Breaking Bread* (OCP).

"Seek Ye First" by Karen Lafferty from *Even the Sparrow* (Maranatha! Music); *Breaking Bread* (OCP); *Gather* (GIA).

God's Prophets

David, as a sign to the community of God's choice. One way to describe the prophets during the time of the kings is "demilitarized judges," since warfare became the business of the kings. The prophets then became the "spiritually selected messengers of God."

This idea suggests that prophecy was rooted in the early military leaders of Israel, before the rise of the monarchy under Saul, and later, the House of David. The Old Testament supports the idea that prophets once had a military role in early Israelite society. For example, when a servant of Elisha doubted the prophet's strength, Elisha prayed for the appearance of a "heavenly army":

"O Lord, open his eyes, that he may see." And the Lord opened the eyes of the servant, so that he saw the mountainside filled with horses and fiery chariots around Elisha (2 Kgs 6:17).

Passages like this strongly associate prophets with miraculous acts of warfare. This could be because of the prophets' earlier association with warfare from the time of the judges. In the time of the kings, the prophets retained their connection to the military activities of Israel since they were often consulted about the likelihood of victory prior to battles. Still, there is more to the prophets than this.

The Prophets Were Social Revolutionaries

The Old Testament prophets showed passionate concern for the poor whenever they suffered oppression by the rich. It is hardly accidental, then, that the strongest prophets (e.g., Amos, Jeremiah, Isaiah, and Ezekiel) appeared precisely during the time when there was the worst oppression and mistreatment of the poor. Their testimony on behalf of the poor was forthright, unflinching, and forceful. God would revoke his word from the Israelites:

Because they sell the just man for silver,
 and the poor man for a pair of sandals.
They trample the heads of the weak
 into the dust of the earth,
 and force the lowly out of the way.
Son and father go to the same
  prostitute,
 profaning my holy name.
Upon garments taken in pledge
 they recline beside any altar;
And the wine of those who have been fined
 they drink in the house of their god
  (Am 2:6–8).

Many of the prophets announced that God would judge Israel by a single "measuring stick" of their righteousness—that is, how they treated the weakest members of their society: the widow, the orphan, and the foreigner. The Law of Moses demanded that the people most "at risk" in society be cared for so that they could survive, and live reasonably stable lives, rather than being neglected or taken advantage of by the rich. Isaiah and Jeremiah made very clear what they considered the faults of Israel:

5. Print **social justice** on the board or overhead. Ask the students to suggest definitions for the term. Summarize their answers on the board. Explain that the ancient Israelites believed firmly that every person has dignity and rights because he or she is made in the image of God. The Church today upholds this same vision. Because people are to be respected and have rights, we are to treat each person with justice (fairness).

6. Divide the class into groups of four. Distribute Bibles and Handout 7A, "Social Justice Issues" (page 281 of the TWE) to each students. Each person should be responsible for reading one passage and filling out the corresponding section on the handout. When completed, the students should take turns sharing their summary with their group as everyone then completes the handout. Finally, have the groups read and discuss Matthew 25:31–46 and write about Jesus' response to social justice.

7. Allow time for the students to continue working on their Learn by Doing journals. You may wish to set up a work table in the room where the students can refer to periodicals as they work through these issues. Perhaps they can work at the table as part of independent study time.

8. Note the definition of *oracle* on page 161. Choose one of the prophetic books of Obadiah, Micah, Nahum, Habakkuk, and Zephaniah to reference and have the students find an example of the basic form of an oracle ("Thus says the Lord"). See, for example, Obadiah 1:1.

Resources
Printed Materials

"Prophet, Prophecy" in *Dictionary of the Bible*, ed. by John L. McKenzie, S.J. (New York, NY: Macmillan Publishing Co., Inc., 1965), pp. 694–699.

"Prophets" in *The Oxford Companion to the Bible*, ed. by Bruce M. Metzger and Michael D. Coogan. (New York, NY: Oxford University Press, 1993), pp. 620–623.

Blenkinsopp, Joseph. "Introduction to the Prophetic Books" in *Harper's Bible Commentary*, ed. by James L. Mays. (San Francisco, CA: Harper & Row Publishers, 1988), pp. 530–541.

Collins, John J. "Isaiah" in *The Collegeville Bible Commentary*, ed. by Dianne Bergant, C.S.A. and Robert J. Karris, O.F.M. (Collegeville, MN: The Liturgical Press, 1989), pp. 411–452.

Ellis, Peter F. "Jeremiah" in *The Collegeville Bible Commentary*, ed. by Dianne Bergant, C.S.A. and Robert J. Karris, O.F.M. (Collegeville, MN: The Liturgical Press, 1989), pp. 453–480.

Vawter, Bruce, C.M. "Introduction to Prophetic Literature" in *The New Jerome Biblical Commentary*, ed. by Raymond E. Brown, S.S., Joseph A. Fitzmyer, S.J., and Roland E. Murphy, O.Carm. (Englewood Cliffs, NJ: Prentice Hall, 1990), pp. 186–200.

Chapter 7

9. Provide direction for the "Modern Prophets" exercise, page 161. Encourage freedom in the students' poster designs. For example, socially conscious business people as well as soup kitchen workers can both be advocates for the poor. (You may wish to make this a group project.)

10. **Homework Assignment:**
    - Continue work on the Learn by Doing journal exercise.
    - Write answers to the Review and Reflection questions 1–3, page 162.
    - Complete the Journal Assignment, page 162. If you can name a supporting prophet, do so with supporting evidence.
    - Complete the "Modern Prophets" exercise.
    - Read "The Servants, the Prophets" through the subsection "Elijah" (pages 161–164).

THE OLD TESTAMENT

> Woe to those who enact
>   unjust statues
>   and who write oppressive decrees,
> Depriving the needy of
>   judgment
>   and robbing my people's
>   poor of their rights,
> Making widows their
>   plunder,
>   and orphans their prey!
> What will you do on the day
>   of punishment,
>   when ruin comes from
>   afar? (Is 10:1–3).

Thus says the Lord: Do what is right and just. Rescue the victim from the hand of his oppressor. Do not wrong or oppress the resident alien, the orphan, or the widow, and do not shed innocent blood in this place (Jer 22:3).

Also read Isaiah 1:17, Ezekiel 22:3, 7; Zechariah 7:10; and Malachi 3:5

These passages make it clear that the prophets were concerned about the social and economic practices of their times, especially the oppressive behavior of the rich in both the kingdoms of Judah and Israel. The religious concern of the prophets—to serve Yahweh and no other gods—was always accompanied by their social and political concerns.

When Jesus taught about compassion for the poor (e.g., Mt 25:31–46) he was clearly standing in the prophetic tradition of ancient Israel. Thus, the element of justice is crucial to understanding the prophets. But it is still not the whole picture of the role of the prophets.

messenger formula—The opening words of a prophetic speech, attributing what follows to God, as in "Thus says the Lord . . ." or "The Lord said. . . ."

The Prophets Were Messengers of God

The common understanding that prophets were "messengers of God" gains credence from consistent textual evidence. First, the prophets almost always spoke in the first person, as if God were speaking. They often began their speeches with the famous words: "Thus says the Lord," which means quite literally, "Here is the message from God." This short little bit at the beginning of the speeches is often referred to as the "**messenger formula**." It may have been borrowed from other correspondences in the ancient world, particularly messages sent between kings. For example:

> [Ben-hadad] sent couriers to Ahab, king of Israel, within the city, and said to him, "This is Ben-hadad's message . . . (1 Kgs 20:2–3).

When the prophet says "Thus says God" (in one form or another), it certainly resembles the language of other messengers in the Old Testament. Though prophets began speeches using other formulas as well, the prevalence of the "messenger formula" makes a clear connection between the prophets and other messengers, thus enabling us to identify the prophets as "messengers of God."

In addition, the prophets are often classified as God's servants:

> And though the Lord warned Israel and Judah by every prophet and seer, "Give up your evil ways and keep my commandments and statutes, in

---

Resources

Audiovisual Materials

In the Beginning: Prophets in the Desert (Oblate Media)—30 minutes
Israel's prophets foretell the salvation of God's people through the coming of a Messiah.

Mysteries of the Bible: The Prophets, Soul Catchers (Videos with Values)—50 minutes
We learn about various Old Testament prophets, including Amos, Hosea, and Isaiah.

Old Testament: Joseph/Jeremiah (Ikonographics)—35 minutes
The section on Jeremiah talks about his life, as well as the role of prophets in Israelite history.

The Bible according to Kossoff: Elijah (Films for the Humanities and Sciences)—20 minutes
In this video, the prophet Elijah asks a poor widow for food. Elijah makes sure that she and her son do not run out of flour and oil until the rain comes.

The Old Testament Covenant: A Kingdom Divided—The Early Prophets (De Sales Catholic Video Library)—60 minutes
This video studies the Israelite prophets of the northern and southern kingdom before the conquest of the Babylonians.

accordance with the entire law which I enjoined on your fathers and which I sent you by my servants the prophets," they did not listen (2 Kgs 17:13–14).

From the day that your fathers left the land of Egypt even to this day, I have sent you untiringly all my servants the prophets (Jer 7:25).

By now we have seen that there are reasons to identify the prophets with many different roles. How are we to know which is correct? Are the prophets messengers, law-protectors, advocates for the poor, servants? The answer is: all of the above!

All of these points tell something of the origins and development of the Old Testament prophets. They also make it clear that prophecy was a complex and multi-faceted phenomenon in ancient Israel. The central role of the prophets in the Old Testament is undeniable. While the historical books often condemned the kings of ancient Israel, the prophets were revered, at least by the time their stories were recorded.

While some of the autobiographical material of the prophets may have been recorded by the prophets themselves, the oracles were more likely collected over long period of time by the prophet's disciples. It is important to remember that the prophecy of the writing prophets began as oral speeches first delivered in meetings between the prophets and those who heard them. The settings varied between places such as the court of the Temple (see Jer 7:1–2), a lesser shrine (see Am 7:13), or a city gate (see Jer 17:19). These speeches were only written down years later.

The Servants, the Prophets

The prophets of the ninth and eighth centuries B.C. fulfilled their roles as God's servants by continually calling the people back to right relationship with Yahweh. During this time many Israelites

MODERN PROPHETS
Prophets of the Old Testament were messengers, law-protectors, advocates for the poor, and servants. Find news articles on modern prophets who fit in each of the same categories. Cut out the articles and attach them to a poster. Write a brief explanation for each on why the person fits the particular category.

oracle—A brief, poetic declaration preceded by the messenger formula, "Thus says the Lord," which establishes it reliably as a message from God. Pagan religions also use the word sometimes for the person who delivers the message, as was the case with the famous "oracle of Delphi."

LITERARY STYLES OF HEBREW PROPHECY
The basic literary style of the written prophecies in the Old Testament is an **oracle**. An oracle, in its basic form, is a brief, poetic declaration following the formula establishing it as a message from God: "Thus says the Lord." Most of the books of the latter prophets are collections of oracles that resemble the poetic texts of the books of Psalms and Proverbs. However, only the prophetic books of Obadiah, Micah, Nahum, Habbakuk, and Zephaniah are entirely written in poetic form. The oracles in the book of Ezekiel are contained within autobiographical narratives of the prophet. (Biographical information was not crucial in these works. However, there is usually a superscription that indicates the prophet's family connections and the kings who ruled during the time the oracles were given.)

THE SERVANTS, THE PROPHETS
Elijah

Bell-Ringers
1. Call on volunteers to share their responses to the Journal Assignment. Discuss as needed. Suggest that Martin Luther King, Jr., Nelson Mandela, and Bishop Desmond Tutu as examples of modern prophets if the students fail to mention them.

2. Display the posters from the "Modern Prophets" assignment. Allow five or ten minutes for the students to review the completed work of all the other students.

3. *Optional:* Arrange for a local person you believe fits the definition of "modern prophet" to speak to the class about how students can speak out against injustices with their words and actions.

Resources
Internet Links
www.bible.ca/maps
View high-resolution maps of the divided kingdoms of Israel and Judah (900–722 B.C.) as well as other biblical sites.
http://research.haifa.ac.il/~hecht
Visit the Reuben and Edith Hecht Museum at the University of Haifa in Israel. See artifacts from the Late Israelite Period (1000–586 B.C.).
www.questia.com
Research the Old Testament prophets at the world's largest online library. Read entire books about the various Old Testament prophets.
http://www.biblicalstudies.org.uk/amos.html
Several links are provided with information about the prophet Amos.
http://www.newadvent.org/cathen/08179b.htm
The *Catholic Encyclopedia* site offers detailed background on the book of Isaiah.

CHAPTER 7

Teaching Approaches

1. Follow-up on the Bell Ringer activities. Remind the students of the two main teachings of the prophets (write on board):
   - **There is only one true God and that God is Yahweh.**
   - **The people must renounce sin.**

2. Continue the summary of the text reading assignment. Introduce the prophet Elijah as a prophet during the reigns of Ahab and Ahaziah of Israel. Have the students form groups of three. Assign each person to read and report on one of the following scripture passages about Elijah:
   - 1 Kings 17:1–24
   - 1 Kings 18:1–46
   - 1 Kings 19:1–21

After each person has reported on his or her assigned Scripture (including the moral of the story), have the group choose one passage to depict in a creative way (choral reading, mime, skit, etc.). Allow time for the groups to offer their performances to the rest of the class.

THE OLD TESTAMENT

REVIEW & REFLECTION

1. What are the five marks or roles of the prophets? Briefly explain each.
2. Who was the first prophet? What do all the later prophets have in common with him?
3. What were the main social concerns of the prophets? What religious issues troubled them?

JOURNAL ASSIGNMENT

- Do you think that there are "prophets" in the world today? How would these marks help you recognize a modern prophet or identify a false prophet?

had begun to worship the god Baal (and perhaps other Canaanite gods as well) along with Yahweh.

There were four prophets of this time in the northern kingdom—Elijah, Elisha, Amos, and Hosea—who called the people back to Yahweh. They reminded the people that Yahweh was a jealous God who demanded their loyalty and required justice for others. They continued to teach that:

- *There is only one true God and that God is Yahweh.* The prophets reminded people that God is the creator of heaven and earth. He is the Lord of all nations. They taught that all other gods are without power; in fact, they do not even exist.
- *The people must renounce sin.* The prophets reminded people of the Law of Moses and the covenant demands that they worship God with a commitment to truth and justice.

The servant prophets modeled and announced these messages. They called on the people to take them to heart and to follow their example.

More information on the four prophets of the ninth and eighth centuries B.C. follows.

Elijah

Though there are many stories of Elijah, there is no "book of Elijah." Some Biblical scholars have suggested that perhaps a separate collection of the stories of Elijah, and his famous disciple, Elisha, once existed; this collection was later incorporated into the larger historical work we now know as the six books of Deuteronomic History (Joshua, Judges, 1 and 2 Samuel, and 1 and 2 Kings).

The name *Elijah* means "The Lord is my God." This was the central message of Elijah's mission. Elijah is considered the father of the prophets. He lived in the northern kingdom in the ninth century B.C., under the rule of

The Prophet Elijah

162

Review and Reflection Answers

1. The five marks of the prophets are:
   1. Their call from God. Most prophets perceived a special call from God that caused them to leave their previous way of life in order to live as a prophet.
   2. Their call to be God's spokesperson or messenger. They spoke God's mind to the people, often beginning their message with "Thus says the Lord."
   3. Their duty to protect the law of Moses and God's covenant. They criticized people for sinning against God's law and urged people to return to the covenant.
   4. Their duty to be advocates for the poor. (They were concerned about social justice issues.)
   5. Their duty as servants to call people back to right relationships with God. (They reminded people—by the example of their own lives—of God's great faithfulness and ability to forgive them.)
2. The first prophet was Moses. The later prophets were like Moses in that they reminded people of God's laws and what they had to do in order to live freely as God's chosen people.
3. The prophets were concerned about the sins and selfishness of the wealthy, about the worship of false gods, and about the unjust treatment of the poor. The prophets also taught that people should worship Yahweh alone, not false gods.

King Ahab who married the Phoenician princess, Jezebel. The key to understanding Elijah is understanding the tension in Israel between the worship of Yahweh and the influences of the ancient Canaanite religion. Elijah, in many ways, was a spiritual warrior in a struggle that sometimes became violent.

Read 1 Kings 17–18

Elijah is introduced somewhat suddenly in 1 Kings 17. He is identified as a "Tishbite," but that is all. There is no "call narrative," and there is very little biographical information about his background. He is suddenly thrust into history by his confrontation with Ahab:

> As the Lord, the God of Israel, lives, whom I serve, during these years there shall be no dew or rain except at my word (1 Kgs 17:1).

The announcement was short and shocking: God decreed that there would be no rain. Elijah then fled east across the Jordan River, where he was fed miraculously by ravens. (This story reminds us of the miraculous feeding of the Hebrews in the wilderness after their liberation from Egypt.)

Eventually Elijah was sent to a widow woman in Zarephath near Sidon. Zarephath was north of the kingdom of Israel and was territory where Canaanite worship of Baal was particularly strong. Here, Elijah met a humble woman and her son, who were starving to death and apparently preparing to die even as Elijah arrived. Elijah was able to reassure the widow of God's promise to feed her family for as long as the drought lasted, and, later, to raise her son back to life after he died of an illness. This striking series of events powerfully reminds Christian readers of some of the ministry of Jesus—a comparison, of course, that is not missed by the writers of the Gospels (see Lk 4:25-26).

In 1 Kings 18, at Mount Carmel (near present day Haifa on the northern coast of Israel), there is a dramatic contest between Jezebel's hired priests and priestesses of Baal and Elijah, the sole defender of worship to Yahweh. Recall from Chapter 5 that the Canaanites believed Baal to be the god of rain, produce, and fertility. But Elijah's own life demonstrates that it was Yahweh who was in control. By stopping the rain, Yahweh proved that he alone was the provider of the rain. By feeding the woman and child (and Elijah himself), Yahweh demonstrated that the God of Israel was, in fact, the provider of the produce of the fields. Finally, by healing the child, Yahweh demonstrated that it was the God of Israel who provided human life, not Baal. In the great demonstration described in 1 Kings 18:21–46, Elijah proves that Yahweh is the true God.

Unfortunately for Elijah, Jezebel was angry about the defeat. She threatened his life. So Elijah took refuge at Mount Horeb (Sinai)—the same place where Moses received the laws and encountered Yahweh. This location was fitting, for it was Elijah's mission to restore God's covenant

FINDING GOD'S PRESENCE

God came to Elijah, not in the form of fire or earthquake or strong wind, but in a tiny whispering sound: a still, small voice (1 Kgs 19). The prayer form called *meditation* is a way to find God in such a manner. Use the following process to help you discover God's presence in your life.

- Select a quiet, peaceful place to meditate.
- Choose an outdoor natural scene or a setting with people to meditate on. (Or, if indoors, choose a picture of a natural scene or one with people in it to meditate on.)
- Assume a comfortable position.
- Spend about three to five minutes meditating on what the scene might be telling you about itself. Are there any symbols in it? What message might be communicated to you by the scene?
- Where can you find God in the scene? Imagine that God has a message for you in the scene. What is that message?

After you have finished your meditation, write a short prayer to God thanking him for your time together and with a resolution on how you will be a better disciple of his.

3. Explain to the students that Elijah's importance comes because he reminds the people of Moses and also prefigures Christ. Discuss the similarities between Moses, Elijah, and Jesus, using Overhead 7A ("Parallels between Moses, Elijah, and Jesus", online). Make sure to comment on the miraculous way Elijah is taken up to heaven in a fiery chariot without dying. The story symbolizes his worthiness in God's eyes. This story also prefigures Jesus' ascension into heaven. There is a further connection to the Church's teaching on the assumption of the Virgin Mary into heaven. Also note the commonality between the three in that each makes it of primary importance to learn God's will for their lives.

4. Explain the exercise, "Finding God's Presence" on page 163. Allow time in class for the students to meditate. Play a recording of nature sounds or instrumental music while the students pray.

5. **Homework Assignment**:
   - Continue to work on the Learn by Doing journal exercise.
   - Complete the short prayer of thanksgiving asked for in the "Finding God's Presence" exercise. You will have an opportunity to share this prayer at the prayer service at the end of the chapter.
   - Finish reading the text section, "The Servants, the Prophets" beginning with the subsection "Elisha" pages 164–169 (including the separate feature, ""What Kind of Prostitute Was Gomer?").

Background Information

Summary of Scripture Passages on Elijah

1 Kings 17:1–24. Elijah predicted three years of drought, and his prediction came true. Everyone was starving. Elijah himself was fed by ravens. He came to the house of a widow and her son and persuaded her to feed him. He then provided food for the widow and her son. Later, he raised the boy from the dead.

1 Kings 18:1–46. On Mount Carmel, Elijah challenged the prophets of Baal in a contest to offer sacrifice. The Baal prophets used ritual dance and ecstasy, but Baal was silent. Elijah waited until the end of the day and even doused the sacrifice with water. Suddenly, lightning struck the sacrifice and burned it up. Then it started to rain.

1 Kings 19:1–21. Elijah fled from Jezebel's wrath to Mount Horeb. There he encountered God, not as violence but as gentleness. Elijah later condemned Jezebel for killing Naboth and taking his vineyard.

Chapter 7

Elisha
Amos
Hosea

Bell-Ringers

1. Explain that just as Elijah prefigured Jesus, so too did Elisha prefigure Jesus. Have the students work in pairs. Assign each person to read 2 Kings 4:8-37 and 2 Kings 4:42–44. Then have them compare these passages with Luke 7:11–17 and Mark 6:30–40. Finally, ask the students to discuss the following questions (write on board) with their partners:
   - Why do you think the Gospel writers modeled their stories after the stories of Elisha?
   - What message do you think they were giving us?
   - Do you think the stories really happened? Why or why not? Does that make a difference to your faith?

After allowing sufficient time for discussion, call on volunteers to summarize what was discussed with their partners.

2. To review the section on Elijah, consider showing all or part of a video about him (e.g., *The Bible according to Kossoff: Elijah*).

---

and the pure faith among the people. Elijah met the Lord at Horeb—not in a strong and heavy wind, not in an earthquake, and not in a fire. Rather, "after the fire there was a tiny whispering sound. When he heard this, Elijah hid his face in his cloak and went and stood at the entrance of the cave" (1 Kgs 19:13).

Elijah rightly holds a place among the great prophets of the Old Testament. Elijah, through it all, was a prophet who symbolized the struggle between the religion of Yahweh and the religion of the Canaanites. At the transfiguration of Jesus, Elijah appeared along with Moses. Future generations of Jews thought Elijah was the one would who would announce the coming of peace to the world at the end of time. He was also believed to be the precursor to the Messiah. In fact, when Jesus came to the earth, many thought him to be Elijah, while the New Testament cast John the Baptist in the role of Elijah announcing Jesus as Messiah.

The authors of the Deuteronomic History understood the importance of Elijah. Though there is no miraculous birth story to introduce him, there is a uniquely miraculous story to mark his passing: He is described as being transported to heaven in a whirlwind. Conversing with his successor, Elisha, "a flaming chariot and flaming horses came between them, and Elijah went up to heaven in a whirlwind" (2 Kgs 2:11).

Elisha

The fact that some events in the life of Elisha parallel the life of Elijah demonstrates for the reader of the Bible that Elisha "carries on" the work of Elijah. It also further communicates the idea that the God of Israel continues his powerful work among the people of God through his servants, the prophets. In 2 Kings 2, Elijah literally "throws his mantle" on the back of Elisha; he transfers his cape-like shawl to the shoulders of Elisha to symbolize Elisha's "promotion." Elisha is honored as the successor:

> The guild prophets in Jericho, who were on the other side, saw him and said, "The spirit of Elijah rests on Elisha." They went to meet him, bowing before him (2 Kgs 2:15).

The stories of 2 Kings 4 involving Elisha also resemble the famous miracles of Elijah. Like Elijah, Elisha sides with the suffering of the poor (2 Kgs 4:1–2). Again, the parallels with the Gospels are clear. These early prophets are shown breaking all kinds of social norms and conventions—honoring the poor, women, and people who need help and healing.

The stories of Elijah and Elisha set the stage for the prophetic books that make up a large section of the Old Testament. One can summarize the main concerns of Elijah and Elisha as: social justice and religious devotion to Yahweh. These two issues are always connected. Devotion to Yahweh as taught in the Law of Moses requires a commitment to social justice. These two themes will carry through all of the prophets of the Old Testament.

The Prophet Elisha

Amos

Amos is described as a shepherd and tree farmer from Tekoa, near Bethlehem, in the southern kingdom. His prophetic ministry takes place during the rule of Jeroboam II (786–746 B.C.). Amos is the first prophet for whom there is a separate, recorded collection of sayings. As with the other books of the prophets, the book of Amos was probably collected and recorded by the prophet's disciples. Like Elisha's relationship to Elijah, it seems clear that prophets almost always had disciples with whom they were close and who participated in their itinerate travels and ministry.

Because of his background as a shepherd, Amos is often depicted as coming from working-class origins. However, that assumption depends on the interpretation of Amos 7:14–15, where Amos says to the priest of Bethel:

> I was no prophet, nor have I belonged to a company of prophets; I was a shepherd and dresser of sycamores. The Lord took me from the following flock, and said to me, Go, prophesy to my people Israel.

From the passage it is not clear whether Amos was a hired shepherd or the owner of the land and flocks. One idea is that the first two chapters of the book of Amos indicate that Amos knew too much about international events to be a poor farm laborer. However, Amos could have been well informed and still have been a hired shepherd!

The prophet Amos was perhaps strongest on the issues of social justice. He spoke out against many of the sins of those living in the northern kingdom: genocide, cruelty, anger, dishonesty, greed, lawlessness, sexual excess, desecration of the dead, rejection of the prophets, robbery, violence, selfishness, deceit, injustice, and pride. He also condemned the abuses of the wealthy. He was particularly angry with an abusive lifestyle that extorted work from the poor for very low wages. At times this concern of Amos reaches a spectacular literary flourish. Speaking to the people of Samaria who had been living in luxury, oblivious to their sins and the threat of the Assyrians, Amos said about them:

> Lying upon beds of ivory,
>   stretched comfortably on their couches,
> They eat lambs taken from the flock
>   and calves from the stall!
> Improvising to the music of the harp,
>   like David, they devise their own accompaniment.
> They drink wine from bowls
>   and anoint themselves with the best oils;
> yet they are not made ill by the collapse of Joseph!
> Therefore, now they shall be the first to go into exile,
>   and their wanton revelry shall be done away with (Am 6:4–7).

It is easy to imagine the indulgent parties described in this passage—people wealthy enough to have furniture with inlaid ivory (not native to Palestine, so it must have been imported), to feast on young animals (a luxury that would appall most of the poor), and to drink wine (according to Amos 2:8, this wine was bought with the taxes and fines they imposed on the poor) not from cups, but from *bowls*—abandoning any moderation at all.

Amos was particularly angry at the wealthy for pouring excess money into shows of Temple worship. The rich seemed to justify their oppressive lifestyles by purchasing many animals for Temple sacrifice, and

The Prophet Amos

God's Prophets

Teaching Approaches

1. Summarize the text section on Elisha. Explain that Elisha was originally a farmer whom God called to be a prophet. He lived a long life during the reigns of Ahaziah, Joram, Jehu, Joahaz, and Joash in the northern kingdom. The miracles attributed to him in 2 Kings were given as "proof" that he was God's messenger.

2. Next, review the text section on Amos and the book of Amos. Summarize with the following information with the students:
   - Amos was a prophet in the northern kingdom during a period of peace and prosperity. Normally, peace and prosperity were signs that God was pleased with his people. But Amos had a different message. He was very critical of the status quo, saying that if the people did not start practicing justice toward one another—especially toward the widow, orphan, and foreigner—God would punish them.
   - Amos preached in or near Bethel against the policies of the northern king. (Remember, Bethel was one of the places King Jeroboam chose to be an official sanctuary, or place of worship. He wished to discourage people from going to Jerusalem to worship God.) This made Amos extremely unwelcome and unpopular in Bethel.
   - Amos was convinced that the Israelites did not have any position of privilege when it came to obeying God's laws. Like other nations, if they were unfaithful to the covenant, God would punish them.
   - Amos condemned Israel for its hardheartedness and injustice toward the poor, specifically selling the just man for silver and the poor man for a pair of sandals.
   - Amos believed that everything that happened was God's doing. Nothing happened by chance. God's hand was to be seen in good events as well as bad events.
   - Amos changed the annual harvest celebration called "The Day of the Lord" into a day of judgment in which Israel would be punished. As Amos taught, ritual alone is not enough to worship Yahweh. Yahweh also demands justice in the way we treat others.

Chapter 7

3. Assign the exercise, "Amos and Society's Moral Decline." Allow sufficient time in class for the students to work on the exercise. Then call for volunteers to share their answers (below). Lead to a discussion about how cheating is a form of social injustice.

Answers:
- Amos 5:12—Amos condemned those who oppressed the just, accepted bribes, and turned away the needy at the gate.
- Amos 8:5—Amos condemned cheaters and people who were greedy.
- Amos 2:6–7; 5:11–12; 8:4–6—Amos condemned people who looked down upon, refused to help, or cheated the poor.

The Old Testament

Amos and Society's Moral Decline

Amos viewed a society whose moral backbone was in decline. Not only were the rich land-grabbing from the poor, but other serious issues abounded. Read the following passages and write what issue Amos is speaking out against in each:

- Amos 5:12
- Amos 8:5
- Amos 2:6–7; 5:11–12; 8:4–6

thus made great public shows of their "piety." Amos spoke strongly against this practice:

> I hate, I spurn your feasts,
> I take no pleasure in your solemnities;
> Your cereal offerings I will not accept,
> nor consider your stall-fed peace offerings.
> Away with your noisy songs!
> I will not listen to the melodies of your harps.
> But if you would offer me holocausts,
> then let justice surge like water,
> and goodness like an unfailing stream (Am 5:21–24).

As with other Old Testament prophets, Amos' message was often one of judgment. However, most of the time when prophets preached a warning, the warning itself was intended to keep the dire event from happening. There is some debate about whether or not the prophet Amos had any hope that the people of the northern kingdom would be able to adhere to his words and thus avoid the judgment he predicted. Some scholars are of the opinion that Amos did not believe Israel could possibly comply, hence making him a "prophet of doom":

> Then the LORD said to me:
> The time is ripe to have done with my people Israel;
> I will forgive them no longer.

> The temple songs shall become wailings on that day, says the Lord God.
> Many shall be the corpses, strewn everywhere.—
> Silence! (Am 8:2b–3).

Amos did know that the destruction of the people by God was intended to be instructive, not destructive. Though people persisted in their sinfulness, Amos believed that such behavior could never completely frustrate the plan of God for the salvation of mankind. The closing words of the book of Amos reveal his hope in a future that would bring God's blessings again:

> But I will not destroy the house of Jacob completely . . .
> I will bring about restoration of my people Israel;
> they shall rebuild and inhabit their ruined cities,
> Plant vineyards and drink the wine, set out gardens and eat the fruits
> (Am 9:8b,14).

Hosea

The book of Hosea offers some brief biographical information on the prophet. Hosea was born and prophesied in the northern kingdom. His ministry overlapped that of Amos and probably began in the last years of Jeroboam II. Both prophets seemed to anticipate the fall of Israel to the Assyrian Empire in 722 B.C.

Hosea, however, had quite a different character from Amos. Where Amos was the unrelenting prophet of despair and destruction, Hosea certainly seemed to hold out some hope for Israel. There were other differences between Hosea and Amos as well.

To begin with, Hosea lived a very interesting life! In the opening verses, it is explained that God called Hosea to marry a known prostitute, Gomer. The Lord said to Hosea:

> Go, take a harlot wife and
>   harlot's children,
>   for the land gives itself to
>   **harlotry**, turning away from
>   the LORD (Hos 1:2).

This action was no doubt shocking to the people who knew and listened to Hosea. Yet it makes very clear the fact that Hosea was a prophet who must be both *watched* and *listened to*. In other words, Hosea acted out part of his message in his own life. His first audience—and readers of the book of Hosea—must pay attention to what his strange actions may mean.

Hosea did marry Gomer, and then proceeded to have three children with her—each child named for one of Hosea's controversial ideas. The name of the first child, Jezreel, implied a criticism of the house of King Jehu for the murder of the entire house of Ahab in the valley of Jezreel. Even though Jehu thought he was doing God's will when he murdered all the members of the family of Ahab, Hosea hinted strongly that he went too far, and his bloodshed was an unnecessary brutality. The name would have been understood as a criticism of the royal house of Jehu. (Hosea was obviously unafraid of political comment.)

Hosea then named his second child Lo-ruhama. This translates literally as "she is not pitied." Hosea's message connected with Lo-ruhama was a dire warning:

> The LORD said to him:
>   Give her the name
>   Lo-ruhama;
>   I no longer feel pity for the
>   house of Israel:
>   rather, I abhor them utterly
>   (Hos 1:6).

Finally, Hosea's third child has the most ominous name of the three: Lo-ammi, which means "not my people." The warning attached to this name was most deeply threatening:

> Then the LORD said:
>   Give him the name Lo-ammi,
>   for you are not my people,
>   and I will not be your God
>   (Hos 1:9).

This was the ultimate threat because it was a reversal of God's promise to Israel in the covenant promise made to Moses:

> I will take you as my own people, and you shall have me as your God. You will know that I, the Lord, am your God when I free you from the labor of the Egyptians and bring you into the land which I swore to give to Abraham, Isaac and Jacob (Ex 6:7–8).

harlotry—In the Old Testament, this term refers not only to a woman's illicit sexual behavior, but perhaps even more commonly to the practice of worshipping Canaanite gods along with Yahweh. Jezebel is referred to as a "harlot" in this sense, not because she was ever unfaithful to Ahab.

God's Prophets

4. Explain that Hosea was another prophet in the north, at approximately the same time as Amos. Check the students' comprehension of the homework reading assignment. Ask:
   - How did Hosea mirror the essence of his message in his own life? (He married a prostitute who continued to be unfaithful to him. He compared this situation to the people's relationship to God. They were the prostitute.)

Point out that Hosea used two other metaphors in his teaching. Have the students read and Hosea 2:16–25 and Hosea 11:1–4 to discover what theses metaphors are. (The first is the metaphor of desert as an experience of purification and conversion similar to the Israelites' forty-year sojourn in the Sinai desert. The second metaphor is that of a good and loving parent.)

Background Information

The Marriage Covenant

By an almost 20:1 margin, the Fathers of the Second Vatican Council approved the use of the term *covenant*—not contract—to describe marriage. The document continued:

> Thus a man and a woman, who by the marriage covenant of conjugal love "are no longer two, but one flesh" (Mt 19:6), render mutual help and service to each other through an intimate union of their persons and of their actions. Through this union they experience the meaning of their oneness and attain to it with growing perfection day by day. As a mutual gift of two persons, this intimate union, as well as the good of children, imposes total fidelity on the spouses and argues for an unbreakable oneness between them (*Gaudium et Spes*, 48).

Chapter 7

5. Refer to the separate feature, "What Kind of Prostitute Was Gomer?" (page 169). Explain that we don't know for sure what kind of prostitute Gomer was. She may have been a cult prostitute to the pagan god Baal before her marriage to Hosea. In that case, Hosea knew exactly what the situation was, but perhaps thought Gomer would change. Or, Gomer may have been an ordinary woman when Hosea met and married her, but became unfaithful to him, much like a prostitute. Either way, Gomer broke Hosea's heart. He divorced her, but then God told him to remarry her and establish a covenant relationship with her. Compare this story with the Church's understanding of marriage as a covenant relationship. Just as God will always be faithful to his people, so a husband and wife are called to be faithful to one another.

In the following sections of the book of Hosea, it is clear that the prophet is "acting out" the role of God, and that his controversial marriage symbolizes to God's relationship with Israel. Gomer's unfaithfulness mirrors Israel's desertion of Yahweh in favor of worshipping Baal.

Read Hosea 2

In chapter 2 of Hosea, it appears as if the prophet is angry with his own wife, Gomer, and makes many kinds of threats against her (presumably for adultery on her part). But as the chapter proceeds, the reader learns that it is *really* God's relationship with Israel that is threatened:

> I will punish her for the days of the Baals,
> for whom she burnt incense
> While she decked herself out with her rings and her jewels,
> and, in going after her lovers,
> forgot me, says the LORD (Hos 2:15).

After these words one would expect the prophet to bring final condemnation and judgment. But here the book of Hosea takes a fascinating turn. Just at the moment when one would most expect to hear a word of condemnation and judgment from the prophet, suddenly he assures the reader of God's forgiving compassion:

> So I will allure her;
> I will lead her into the desert
> and speak to her heart (Hos 2:16).

Not only does God speak words of forgiving compassion, the rest of the section reads like a wedding vow as God proposes marriage to his adulterous partner, Israel, as a way to reestablish their relationship:

> I will make a covenant for them on that day,
> with the beasts of the field,
> With the birds of the air,
> and with the things that crawl on the ground....
> I will espouse you to me forever:
> I will espouse you in right and in justice,
> in love and in mercy;
> I will espouse you in fidelity
> and you shall know the Lord (Hos 2:20a; 21–22).

In Hosea 3, God tells the prophet to take Gomer back as his wife. This is symbolic of

Hosea

God's everlasting love for his people: after a period of trial (the dissolution of the kingdom), the people will fully return to their relationship with the Lord. Human passion is compared favorably to God's love

---

Enrichment: Complete the following reading and writing assignment. Answer the following:
- What was Amos's vocation (see Amos 1:1; 7:10–15)?
- What were the signs from God that Israel ignored (see Amos 4:6–11)?
- What was the meaning of Amos's visions of locusts, fire, plumbline, and a basket of ripe fruit (see Amos 7—8)?

for humanity, and this is an important message. The prophet compared the love of God with the two most powerful passions in human existence: the love between a husband and a wife, and the love between a parent and a child (see Hos 11:1–4). This faithfulness and love of Yahweh for his people is the lasting message of the book of Hosea.

Asherah—The Canaanite goddess sometimes called the "Queen of Heaven." She was the consort of Baal and the goddess of fertility.

What Kind of Prostitute Was Gomer?

Who was Gomer? What were her origins? Was she a Hebrew or a foreigner? These are interesting questions which the book of Hosea does not explicitly answer. However, clues are offered. Note the instructions given by God to Hosea at the beginning of chapter 3:

> Give your love to a woman
> beloved of a paramour, an adulteress;
> Even as the Lord loves the people of Israel,
> though they turn to other gods
> and are fond of raisin cakes (Hos 3:1).

These "raisin cakes" were a specific offering for the Canaanite goddess **Asherah**, sometimes called "the Queen of Heaven" by the Canaanites and some heretical Hebrews (see Jer 7:18).

Gomer may have been a Hebrew woman who had become a Canaanite temple prostitute, involved in the sexual rites of Canaanite worship. This would complete the message of Hosea: like Gomer, Israel "prostituted herself" to Canaanite gods. This was surely a startling way of communicating; but then prophets were never known for quiet, unassuming behavior.

Review & Reflection

1. What are the two main concerns of the prophets, Elijah and Elisha?
2. What were Amos's biggest complaints about the behavior of the people?
3. There was more to Hosea's prophecy than what he *said*. What was unique about the way that Hosea revealed God's word to the people?

Journal Assignment

- Skim through the books of Amos and Hosea to find four or five passages that you believe still apply today. Copy them and write a brief explanation of how you think they are relevant to today's society.

God's Prophets

6. **Homework Assignment**:
   - Write answers to the Review and Reflection questions 1–3, page 169.
   - Complete the Journal Assignment, page 169. You will need your Bible to complete this assignment.
   - Continue to work on the Learn by Doing journal exercise. Plan to share some categories and entries with other students in the class period prior to the Chapter 7 Test.
   - Read the text section "The Contrasting Styles in the Prophets" (pages 170–171).

Review and Reflection Answers

1. The main concerns of Elijah and Elisha were (1) social justice and (2) religious devotion to Yahweh.
2. Amos spoke out against the sins of the people: genocide, cruelty, anger, dishonesty, greed, lawlessness, sexual excess, desecration of the dead, rejection of the prophets, robbery, violence, selfishness, deceit, injustice, and pride. He condemned the abuses of the wealthy. He was particularly angry with an abusive lifestyle that extorted work from the poor for very low wages.
3. Hosea actually modeled, or lived, his message in his own life. He married a prostitute to show what the people's relationship with God was like. God was the faithful husband; the people were the prostitute.

Chapter 7

THE CONTRASTING STYLES IN THE PROPHETS

Bell-Ringers

1. Form a panel of students. Ask each person on the panel to share one passage from Amos or Hosea that they believe applies today and to tell why they believe this (from Journal Assignment, page 169). Allow discussion between the panel members and also from the rest of the class.

2. *Optional:* Ask a husband and wife to share with the class their reflections on the message of Hosea and/or Amos and tell how particular passages help them in their faithfulness to the marriage covenant.

Teaching Approaches

1. Emphasize that each of the prophets discussed in Chapter 7 had a personal relationship with God and a unique experience of him. Out of this relationship and experience, they preached a particular message to the people. Use Overhead 7B, "Main Themes of the Prophets" (online at **avemariapress.com**), to review the names of the prophets covered in this chapter along with some of the themes most associated with them.

2. Continue to check student comprehension of the reading assignment. Ask the following questions:
   - What is the main theme we can find in all four prophets? (Repent for your sins, and God will save you. Fail to repent, and you and your nation will be doomed.)
   - What is the secondary theme we can find in all four prophets? (God can bring good even from destruction. Even the people's sinfulness will not cause Yahweh to abandon his covenant with them.)

The Contrasting Styles of the Prophets

God sent prophets to the northern kingdom in the centuries prior to the Assyrian takeover and relocation. If a common theme can be named between the ninth century B.C. prophets (Elijah and Elisha) and the eighth century B.C. prophets (Amos and Hosea) it would be: "Repent of your sins and God will save you. Fail to repent and you and your nation will be doomed." A secondary theme—gleaned especially from Hosea—is that God can bring good even from destruction; even the people's sinfulness will not cause Yahweh to abandon his covenant with the people.

The contrast between these two "writing prophets"—Amos and Hosea—is quite clear. Amos was a nearly unrelenting prophet of judgment and doom, while Hosea portrayed God as a loving, compassionate, and ultimately deeply forgiving God for whom sin was equivalent to the deeply painful betrayal of a loved one.

All the prophets of this time were at once "conservative" and "radical." They were conservative in the sense that they sought to preserve the devotion to Yahweh that required obedience to the Law of Moses; they "conserved" the covenant obligations. At the same time, they often introduced radical new ideas along the way. For example:

- Elijah and Elisha both asserted the basic incompatibility between Canaanite paganism (with its enslavement of the people under a false religion that justified the elite privilege of a few against the economic rights of the many), and true Yahweh worship (which insisted upon a more just division of wealth within the community and the responsibility of all community members to care for one another).
- Amos questioned a luxurious, materialistic lifestyle that depended on the poverty of others despite the great displays of "piety" at the Temple that were possible because of it.
- Hosea taught about God's compassion and forgiveness using human love as a metaphor and example.

The Fall of the Northern Kingdom

From the ninth century to the seventh century (ca. 800–609 B.C.), the Assyrian empire was a brutal military power in the Ancient Near East. By 738 B.C., the Assyrian ruler Tiglath-Pileser III (known by his Babylonian name Pul; see 2 Kgs 15:19) was receiving taxes from the Syrian states Hamath, Tyre, Byblos, and Damascus—and Israel.

Tiglath-Pileser went even further. He oversaw the strengthening of Assyria's central government so that the local Syrian states had little authority in

Tiglath-Pileser III Receiving Homage (detail), 745/727 BC Assyrian

managing their own affairs, even on a local level. Tiglath-Pileser also streamlined the process by which new lands could be incorporated under Assyrian rule. This was the beginning of the end for the northern kingdom of Israel.

King Pekah of Israel invaded the southern kingdom in 734 B.C. to try to force King Ahaz of Judah to join a coalition with Damascus against Assyria. Ahaz had other ideas. Instead, he sent tribute to Tiglath-Pileser and asked for Assyrian help against Israel. The Assyrians easily destroyed the coalition and made Israel a vassal state. When Shalmaneser V succeeded Tiglath-Pileser in 726 B.C., Israel's king, Hoshea, saw a window of opportunity. He sought out Egypt's help. That plan backfired too.

Assyria invaded Israel and captured the city of Samaria in 722 B.C. Many of its upper-class residents and landowners were deported to upper Mesopotamia (see 2 Kgs 17:6).

Though the mass population of Israel was left in the north to continue to work the land for the Assyrians, the kingdom of Israel itself ended in 722 B.C.

Chapter 8 will explore the warnings of the prophets of the southern kingdom, one of whom was a near contemporary to Amos and Hosea—namely, Isaiah. These southern prophets warned about Judah's impending punishment from God: its fall to Babylon, a consequence of their disobedience and betrayal of the covenant with Yahweh.

REVIEW & REFLECTION

1. What is the common theme that unites the four prophets of the northern kingdom?
2. What is the main difference between Amos's and Hosea's prophetic messages?
3. What new ideas did each of the four prophets introduce to the religion of Yahweh?

JOURNAL ASSIGNMENT

- Think about the love relationships in your life—with your parents, grandparents, siblings, cousins, or best friends. What have you learned about God through those relationships?

---

3. Call on volunteers to share examples from their own lives or from the news to show how God can bring good even from destruction.

4. Summarize the subsection, "The Fall of the Northern Kingdom." Have the students speculate as to why King Ahaz sided with the Assyrians rather than with King Pekah in the north? (Perhaps it was self-preservation. Ahaz knew the Assyrians were stronger; they would win. He might have thought that they would deal favorably with the south.)

5. Allow time in class for the students to complete the Learn By Doing exercise (page 173) with contemporary prophetic statements.

6. **Homework Assignment:**
   - Finish working on the Learn by Doing exercise.
   - Write answers to the Review and Reflection questions 1–3, page 171.
   - Complete the Journal Assignment, page 171.
   - Read the Further Reflections section in the text. Make sure to note how Matthew 2:5–6; 15; 17–18; and 23 fulfill the prophecies of the Old Testament prophets.

Review and Reflection Answers

1. The common theme that unites the four prophets of the north is: Repent for your sins, and God will save you. Fail to repent, and you and your nation will be doomed.
2. Amos was a prophet of doom and gloom. He reflected a strict God of justice, anger, and jealousy who was quick to punish the people for their sins. Hosea, on the other hand, reflected a God who loved the people and wished to have a covenant relationship with them. This type of God was forever forgiving and willing to take the people back, despite their sins.
3. Elijah and Elisha pointed out the basic incompatibility between Canaanite paganism and true worship of Yahweh. Amos questioned a luxurious, materialistic lifestyle: that depended on the poverty of others despite the great displays of "piety" by the rich at the Temple were possible because of the poverty of others. Hosea taught about God's compassion and forgiveness using human love as a metaphor and example.

Chapter 7

FURTHER REFLECTIONS

Bell-Ringer

1. Call on students to be "on the spot" in front of the class and share their reflections on some of the love relationships in their lives (see Journal Assignment, page 171). Ask them to express what they have learned about God through those relationships.

Teaching Approaches

1. Allow time for the students to work with a partner and quiz each other using the Review and Reflection questions and vocabulary words from the chapter.

2. Discuss the passages listed in the "Further Reflections" text (Luke 8:22–35; 9:10–17; 7:11–17) related to how Jesus continued the prophets' work. For example, in the feeding of the multitudes Jesus nourished the crowds with both physical food and with the word of God.

3. Determine a way for the students to present their journals from the Learn by Doing exercise so that everyone has a chance to share. For example, the students could pass the journals around in small groups. Or, each student could be allowed one to two minutes to share the most important issues highlighted in the journal. Spend about one-third of the class time on this activity. Collect all the journals for grading.

4. **Prayer Service:** Play a recording or lead singing of "Hosea" (see page 162 of the TWE) or another appropriate song. Pray together the "Called to Prayer" from Hosea 2:21–22 (see page 173). Call on volunteers to pray the prayers they wrote for the "Finding God's Presence" exercise. Conclude with another song, perhaps "I Have Loved You" (see page 162 of the TWE).

5. **Homework Assignment:**
Study for the Chapter 7 Test.

Further Reflections

The prophets were central figures in the Old Testament. Their insistence on exclusive Yahweh worship and real justice for the poor makes them even more truly heroic than the kings. But there is one more dimension to the prophets we have not yet touched upon. In addition to their roles as protectors of the law, military leaders, social reformers, servants, and messengers, the Old Testament prophets prepared the people for the coming of Jesus Christ, the Messiah. Read chapter 2 of Matthew's Gospel (verses 5–6, 15, 17–18, 23) to see how the stories of Jesus' birth fulfill the prophecies of the Old Testament prophets.

The prophetic words of Hosea, Isaiah, and others about the coming Messiah served more than one purpose. In the immediate context of the prophet's own lifetime, they were hopeful messages that looked forward to the end of the difficult times the people of Israel were facing. The Messiah to come was yet another proof that God would not abandon his people. But more than that, in the long run, the prophets' writings and actions prepare us for the kind of Messiah Jesus Christ would be.

Jesus' social concerns place him squarely in the tradition of the Old Testament prophets, a role he willingly adopts. Consider the evidence of the following passage from the gospel of Luke which Jesus reads from the book of Isaiah:

"The Spirit of the Lord is upon me,
    because he has anointed me
        to bring glad tidings to the poor.
He has sent me to proclaim liberty to
    captives
    and recovery of sight to the blind
        to let the oppressed go free,
and to proclaim a year acceptable to the
    Lord" (Lk 4:18–19).

Jesus read these words from the scroll of Isaiah in the synagogue in Nazareth and immediately applied them to himself: "Today this scripture passage is fulfilled in your hearing" (Lk 4:21). He continued by making comparisons between himself and the prophets Elijah and Elisha, making clear his own understanding that he, too, was working in the tradition of the Old Testament prophets.

Like the Old Testament prophets, Jesus affirmed his compassion for the poor and suffering. Comparisons between Jesus, Elijah, and Elisha reveal just how closely connected Jesus is to the Old Testament prophets. Remember the three miracles of Elijah that confirmed God's supremacy over Baal: the three-year drought God announced through Elijah; the miraculous feeding of the widow, her son, and Elijah himself; and the healing of the widow's son. The gospels record miracles that parallel, yet go beyond each of these. *Read the following passages to see how Jesus continued the prophet's work: Luke 8:22–25, Luke 9:10–17, and Luke 7:11–17.*

The Holy Spirit is also associated with both the prophets of the Old Testament and Jesus in the New Testament. Elisha's succession to Elijah is announced in these words: "The spirit of Elijah rests on Elisha" (2 Kgs 2:15)—that is, the same Spirit that inspired and sustained Elijah, the Holy Spirit, is now with Elisha. Prior to Jesus' speech in the synagogue, the gospel reports that "Jesus returned to Galilee in the power of the Spirit" (Lk 4:14). The *Catechism of the Catholic Church* teaches that

> Jesus Christ is the one whom the Father anointed with the Holy Spirit and established as priest, prophet, and king (CCC, 783).

Like Jesus, the whole People of God share in these offices of Christ and are called to live and preach prayer and compassion to all.

God's Prophets

● _Learn by Doing_
  . Prepare a journal with what you consider to be contemporary prophetic statements on the following issues. Develop your own creative design for the journal. Use the issues as separate chapter headings. Include quotations with references from "modern prophets" who speak a message of truth, justice, and compassion about the issue. Besides the issues below, include at least three issues of your own.
  ◆ Abortion
  ◆ Death Penalty
  ◆ Genetic Research
  ◆ Warfare
  ◆ Poverty
  ◆ Environment
  ◆ Immigration
  ◆ Political Refugees
  ◆ Religious Tolerance
  ◆ Racism
  ◆ Political Reform

● _Called to Prayer_
  I will espouse you to me forever:
    I will espouse you in right and in justice,
    in love and in mercy;
  I will espouse you in fidelity,
    and you shall know the LORD.
                                  —Hosea 2:21–22

Notes
1. It is interesting that Amos mentions "beds of ivory" enjoyed by the very rich. Archaeologists have discovered a large hoard of ivory items dated to this time period. Since ivory is a valuable commodity which is not native to Palestine, the discovery would seem to indicate that trade was active during this period and elite Israelites were successfully amassing wealth for themselves through that trade.

GOD'S PROPHETS

CHAPTER 7 TEST

Teaching Approaches

1. Distribute the Chapter 7 Test. There are various points assigned for each item. Note that the two short essays are worth eight points each. Allow the students to use a separate sheet of paper for these essays.

2. In any time remaining, have the students peruse Chapter 8 after their tests have been collected.

3. Assign material from the Catholic Handbook for Faith (pages 259–280 of the Student Text).

Chapter 7 Test Answers
Part 1: Matching: 1. a; 2. f; 3. g; 4. d; 5. c; 6. h; 7. e; 8. b; 9. i.
Part 2: Multiple Choice: 10. a; 11. c; 12. e; 13. b; 14. b; 15. c; 16. a.
Part 3: Short Fill-ins: 17. messenger formula; 18. mouthpiece or spokesperson; 19. harlotry; 20. God's everlasting love and faithfulness to his people; 21. Elisha's taking Elijah's place as prophet.
Part 4: Short Essay: 22. The two themes are social justice and religious devotion. Students should make clear their understanding that, as far as the prophets were concerned, the two went hand in hand. Devotion to Yahweh demanded care for the weakest members of society. Examples will vary. 23. Answers will vary. Be certain answers clearly identify a current injustice, the prophet's condemnation of it, and a consequence that is logically connected to the offense.

Chapter 7
Parish Religious Education Adaptation
- See **avemariapress.com** for a one- to two-hour lesson plan adaptation for Chapter 7 suitable for parish religious education classes. See also pages 14–15 of the TWE for further explanation.
- Assign Chapter 7 for reading prior to the first class session. The students are also to complete the assigned Review and Reflection questions from Chapter 6.

Introducing Chapter 8

Chapter 8 covers some of the events leading to the destruction of Jerusalem by Babylon in 587 B.C., the exile of the people of Judah to Babylon, and their eventual return to Palestine with the help of King Cyrus of Persia. More importantly, the chapter deals with several important prophets of this time: Isaiah of Jerusalem, Micah, Ezekiel, Jeremiah, Deutero-Isaiah, and Third Isaiah. Although the Babylonian conquest of Jerusalem and the destruction of Solomon's Temple was a horrific event in Israelite history, it was also a source of great blessing. During the time of exile, a portion of God's People, known as the "remnant," took the warnings of the prophets to heart and began to recommit themselves to the covenant with Yahweh and the law of Moses.

Before the Exile, the prophets Isaiah and Micah called the people of Judah to true worship of Yahweh. They warned the people that if they didn't return to their covenant with God, he would punish them and the nation. A third prophet, Habakkuk, predicted that the rising political power of Babylon would eventually set its sites on Jerusalem. These prophets were all correct. King Nebuchadnezzar invaded Jerusalem in 597 and took King Jehoiachin and other Israelites into exile to Babylon. Nebuchadnezzar returned ten years later to destroy the city and its Temple. Thousands of Israelites were sent into exile to be slaves for the Babylonians.

The prophet Ezekiel lived and preached among the exiles in Babylon, giving them hope that God would one day reestablish Judah, Jerusalem, and the Temple. The prophet Jeremiah, meanwhile, ministered to the people remaining in Judah. He urged them to cooperate with the Babylonians so that more destruction would not occur. Jeremiah, too, reminded the people of God's faithfulness to the covenant and his desire to establish a new covenant in the future.

Deutero-Isaiah, the name given to the unnamed prophet, foretold the eventual demise of the Babylonians to the Persians. He compared the Israelites to God's Suffering Servant who would be restored to Jerusalem through an anointed "messiah." The prophet was probably speaking about Cyrus, the Persian king who let the Israelites return home. He may also have been prophesying about Jesus as the coming Messiah. Trito-Isaiah or Third Isaiah is even more hopeful. This portion of the book of Isaiah prophesized that Israel would be a light to other nations, attracting all people to God.

When the Israelites returned to Judah, they continued to live as slaves of the Persians. For the next 600 years and more, they would live under foreign rule. During this time, the Jews rebuilt the Temple and other cities throughout Judah. Their prayers were a constant reminder of how their sins had led to their downfall.

Chapter 8 Outline

Introduction
The end of the independent Hebrew states—first Israel, then Judah—present the most significant change in the life of the Chosen People since the time of their formation.

Judah Before the Exile
Two prophets—Isaiah and Micah—emerge in the ninth and eighth centuries B.C. to call the people of Judah to true worship of Yahweh and to warn them of the coming destruction.

The Exile of Judah
The rise of Babylon meant the end of the Assyrian threat to Judah, but it wasn't long before Nebuchadnezzar defeated Jerusalem and established his own government there.

Prophets of the Exile
Ezekiel's prophecy among the exiles in Babylon and Jeremiah's prophecy at home in Jerusalem warn the Jews of the impending destruction of Jerusalem and the Temple.

The Exiles Return to Judah
Despite the purported end of the Exile, the Hebrews, from 587 B.C. through the early Christian period, live under Imperial rulers who control power, wealth, territory, and human resources.

Major Themes of Writing Before, During, and After the Exile
For many of the Jews returning to Palestine after 539 B.C., the most important project is the restoration of the Temple in Jerusalem, which, they feel, is necessary for them to receive God's blessings again.

Further Reflections

Background Notes for the Teacher

The significance of the major and minor writing prophets in the overall message of the Bible cannot be underestimated. As the *Catechism of the Catholic Church* explains,

Through the prophets, God forms his people in the hope of salvation, in the expectation of a new and everlasting Covenant intended for all, to be written on their hearts. The prophets proclaim a radical redemption of the People of God, purification from all their infidelities, a salvation which will include all the nations (*CCC*, 64).

In the prophets, we find the message that God can be found everywhere, even outside the Temple in Jerusalem. Furthermore, God is also present in our times of suffering. Suffering itself has a purpose, even if we don't understand what it is. The prophets showed that suffering helps to strengthen our faith, to purify our attitudes and behaviors. Just as the people are God's Suffering Servant, so the future Messiah will be God's Suffering Servant who redeems us through his pain.

Resources

Music Suggestions: see page 183
Printed Materials: see page 184
Audiovisual Materials: see page 185
Internet Links: see page 187

CHAPTER 8
TURNING POINT IN THE JOURNEY
The Destruction of Judah, Exile, and Return

Background Notes continued

While the prophets pointed out that God's justice necessitated punishment for the sins of the people, they also offered an unshakable hope in God's mercy. God is not only just; he is compassionate and merciful. God restores the exiles to Jerusalem. The *Catechism* teaches:

> Two prophetic lines were to develop, one leading to the expectation of the Messiah, the other pointing to the announcement of a new Spirit. They converge in the small Remnant, the people of the poor, who await in hope the "consolation of Israel" and the "redemption of Jerusalem" (*CCC*, 711).

In presenting the material in this chapter, be sure to point out the connections between the prophets' message and the life of Jesus. Be sure to emphasize the ever-present virtue of hope, especially to students who may be struggling with their everyday problems.

Advance Preparations
- Direct the students to any Internet resources and printed resources (pages 187 and 184, respectively) that will help them research the exercise "Rebuilding Judah" (page 193) that calls for details about the rebuilding campaign when the Jews returned from Babylonian captivity.
- Obtain and preview all media, including music, you may wish to include in your lesson plan.
- Make sure you have adequate and appropriate art supplies on hand for the Learn by Doing project, page 199.

Relevant Teachings from Church Documents
- The forgetting of the Law and the infidelity to the covenant end in death: it is the Exile, apparently the failure of the promises, which is in fact the mysterious fidelity of the Savior God and the beginning of a promised restoration, but according to the Spirit. The People of God had to suffer this purification. (Cf. *Lk* 24:26.) In God's plan, the Exile already stands in the shadow of the Cross, and the Remnant of the poor that returns from the Exile is one of the most transparent prefigurations of the Church. (*CCC*, 710)
- Through the prophets, [God] prepared [Israel] to accept the salvation for all humanity. (*CCC*, 72)
- Through the prophets, God forms his people in the hope of salvation, in the expectation of a new and everlasting Covenant intended for all, to be written on their hearts. The prophets proclaim a radical redemption of the People of God, purification from all their infidelities, a salvation which will include all the nations. (*CCC*, 64)
- Two prophetic lines were to develop, one leading to the expectation of the Messiah, the other pointing to the announcement of a new Spirit. They converge in the small Remnant, the people of the poor, who await in hope the "consolation of Israel" and the "redemption of Jerusalem." (*CCC*, 711)

Chapter Objectives
The students will be able to:
- understand the historical context and basic message of the major and minor writing prophets.
- learn that the book of Isaiah is probably the compilation of three separate prophets: Isaiah of Jerusalem, Deutero-Isaiah, and Third Isaiah.
- visualize the fall of Jerusalem and the life of the Israelites in exile.
- see how many of the prophets, especially Ezekiel, gave the people reason to hope that Israel would one day be restored under equitable and just circumstances.
- receive insight into the nature of prophecy itself and how each of us is also called by God to be prophets today.
- appreciate the importance for the returning exiles to rebuild the Temple and to see that we ourselves are to be God's temple today.
- connect the message of the Old Testament prophets to the coming Messiah, Jesus Christ.

Chapter 8

INTRODUCTION
JUDAH BEFORE THE EXILE

Bell-Ringers

1. On the board or overhead, write these questions:
   - What was the worst thing that ever happened to you or your family?
   - How did God help you get through that time and on to better times?

Have the students answers these questions by either writing them in their journal or discussing them with a partner. When they have had time to answer, take a sampling of student comments. Then tell the class that Chapter 8 deals with one of the worst things that ever happened to the Jewish people—the destruction of Jerusalem and being taken as slaves into exile.

2. Remind the students of the lessons of Chapter 7. To review, call on one or more students to explain the difference between a "major prophet" and "minor prophet." Return the Chapter 7 Tests if you have graded them. Discuss any questions the students may have regarding them.

Teaching Approaches

1. Allow time for the students to individually read the "Introduction" and "Judah before the Exile" text sections on pages 176–179.

2. When they have completed the reading, make sure the students understand that approximately 200 years after the fall of the northern kingdom, the smaller kingdom of Judah was fighting the Assyrians (who had conquered Israel) as well as Egypt from the south. Also point out that the Judeans were so convinced that they were God's people and that he would protect them, they could not fathom the idea that their enemies would triumph over them. In a way, they had a certain false sense of invincibility, that nothing bad would happen to them as it had to the northern kingdom. Compare the Judeans' sense of security with what many Americans felt before December 7, 1941 or September 11, 2001. Prior to those dates, most Americans never dreamed that foreigners would invade their nation and kill so many people.

THE OLD TESTAMENT

Cyrus—The Persian king who allowed some of the Jews to return to Jerusalem after he conquered the Babylonians in 539 B.C. This event is typically understood to mark the end of the Exile, although, in truth, many Jews remained in the Diaspora, never returning to Palestine (which remained, in any case, under the control of the Persians).

Introduction

King Ahaz's decision to align with Assyria may have saved Judah from the same fate as Israel, but it only delayed the end that was to come. This chapter describes some of the events leading to the destruction of Jerusalem, the exile of the kingdom of Judah to Babylon, and the eventual return of many exiles to the land of Palestine with the help of the Persian king, **Cyrus**.

The end of the independent Hebrew states—first Israel, then Judah—presented the most significant change in the life of the Chosen People since the time of their formation during the Exodus. Just how serious was the change that ultimately brought the destruction of Jerusalem and the exile of many of its residents? Old Testament historian, John Bright, offers this perspective:

> When one considers the magnitude of the calamity that overtook her, one marvels that Israel was not sucked down into the vortex of history along with the other little nations of western Asia. . . .[1]

During the time of exile, God's Chosen People finally took the warnings of the prophets to heart and began to recommit themselves to the covenant with Yahweh and the Law of Moses.

Judah Before the Exile

As mentioned before, Judah was a much smaller kingdom than Israel in both land and population. It included the hills around Jerusalem as well as some land in the Negev desert. The people subsisted on farming and sheep herding. They also traded with Egypt and Arabia. Though the kings of Judah were descendants in the Davidic line, the kings of Israel were more charismatic during this time of division.

Solomon's son Rehoboam, who had provoked the wrath of Israel and the division of the kingdom, was succeeded in Judah by his son, Abijah, who ruled from 915–913 B.C. Abijah recaptured part of the northern kingdom, including Bethel, but the territory was hard to hold. The next two

176

Turning Point in the Journey

kings—Asa and Jehoshaphat—continued the skirmishes with Israel, but also attempted some reforms designed to reestablish the covenant with their people. Asa had to quell an Egyptian incursion from the south. While this was happening, Israel was able to move troops within five miles of Jerusalem. Only after Asa aligned with Damascus was he able to secure Jerusalem again (see 1 Kgs 15:16–22). Jehoshaphat (873–849 B.C.) instituted a series of judicial reforms, including a court of appeals. He attempted an alliance with the northern kingdom during the reign of King Ahab of Israel.

Jehoshaphat's successors, however, married into the family of the northern king Ahab and Jezebel and from that point the same problems faced in the northern kingdom—including idolatry and injustice—infected Judah. It was during this time, the ninth and eighth centuries B.C., that two prophets—Isaiah and Micah—emerged.

Isaiah

The New Testament quotes Isaiah more than any other prophetic book. However, the book of Isaiah presents some interesting dilemmas for analysis.

Isaiah of Jerusalem, the prophet for whom the book is named, is said to have started his ministry in the reign of King Uzziah (see Is 1:1). Uzziah died about 740 B.C. The problem with accurate dating occurs with the mention of the Persian emperor Cyrus in Isaiah 45:1. Cyrus defeated Babylon in 539 B.C. It is virtually certain that the same prophet did not begin his career before 740 and then live to see the rise of Cyrus the Persian two centuries later!

This issue along with others has led to the understanding that the book of Isaiah actually contains the work of more than one writer, from more than one time. The book of Isaiah is usually divided as follows:

- *Isaiah 1–39*. These chapters are mostly stories about, and sayings of, the actual prophet Isaiah of Jerusalem for whom the book is named.
- *Isaiah 40–55*. A second, unnamed prophet known as "Second Isaiah" is credited with this portion of the book. Second Isaiah lived at the end of the Babylonian period and the beginning of the Persian period (545–535 B.C.) and likely witnessed the collapse of Babylon to the Persian empire. Examination of the texts and message of Second Isaiah will accompany our study of Judah in exile in Babylon.
- *Isaiah 56–66*. The final chapters are thought to have been collected by disciples of Second Isaiah (called "**Third Isaiah**"), writing from Jerusalem and the Diaspora after the exile. These chapters emphasize the importance of the Temple and invite all nations to join Israel as God's Chosen People.

The first thirty-nine chapters of the book of Isaiah detail the ministry of the prophet in Jerusalem. At the Temple, Isaiah had a vision of

Third Isaiah—The group of disciples of Second Isaiah who are credited with writing chapters 56–66 in the book of Isaiah. They are believed to have been writing from Jerusalem and the Diaspora after the Exile.

---

3. Note the text section "Isaiah" on pages 177–178 and have the students read the material. When completed, summarize these main points.
   - Because the span of history covered in the book of Isaiah is more than 200 years,, biblical scholars understand that Isaiah was written by more than one author.
   - The book of Isaiah is divided as follows: chapters 1–39 deal with Isaiah of Jerusalem; chapters 40–55 deal with Second Isaiah and the collapse of the Babylonian empire to the Persians; chapters 56–66 deal with the time after the exiles have returned to Jerusalem.

4. Share with the students information from "Isaiah of Jerusalem" (Overhead 8A, online). Ask them to take notes as needed. The two questions on the overhead can be used for discussion or as an extra Journal Assignment.

5. Point out the Vineyard Song in Isaiah 5. Have the students work in pairs on the Journal Assignment to read and discuss the Vineyard Song (Is 5:1–7) and the same image in Matthew 21:33–44. Allow sufficient time for the groups to prepare their list of similarities between the two passages (see Background Information, below). Call on volunteers to share their findings. List on the board. Assign the question about the vineyard as a good symbol for the Church as an individual Journal Assignment.

6. Assign the text subsection, "Micah" (page 178). Make sure to note that Matthew 2:6 and John 7:42 are taken from Micah 5:1.

Background Information
The Vineyard Song compared with Matthew 21

The "friend" in the Vineyard Song is Yahweh. The "vineyard" represents the Chosen People. Yahweh has taken great pains and care to cultivate the Israelites into a nation, but to no avail. They continue to be "wild grapes"; they continue to sin. The result: God will destroy the vineyard, the Israelites. Jesus uses the same analogy in Matthew 21 to show that God will take away his favor from the Jews and give it to those who believe in his son, Jesus. There will be a new covenant which will be open to both Jews and Gentiles.

Enrichment: Write answers to these questions: Where was Isaiah when he received his call to prophecy (Is 6:1)? According to Isaiah, what is God's outstanding quality (Is 6:3)? How was Isaiah purified for his task as a prophet of the Lord (Is 6:6–8)?

Chapter 8

7. Point out the exercise "The Prophets and the Advent Liturgy" (page 178). Assign class time for the students to work on the exercise. Use the key below to check the assignment:
   - Jeremiah 33:14–16 is fulfilled in Jesus, the Messiah and eternal priest.
   - Isaiah 40:1–5, 9–11 describes the Lord leading the return of the exiles, just as the Messiah will lead the people away from sin.
   - Isaiah 35:1–6a, 10 speaks of the Lord ransoming people from the control of sin.
   - Isaiah 7:10–14 tells of a virgin who will be with child (Immanuel).

8. **Homework Assignment:**
   - Finish "The Prophets and the Advent Liturgy" exercise.
   - Write answers to the Review and Reflection questions 1–3, page 178.
   - Read the text section "The Exile of Judah," pages 179–182.

The Prophets and the Advent Liturgy

During Advent (and Christmas) many of the readings are taken from the Old Testament prophets, especially Isaiah. Read the following passages from the Sundays in Advent. Write how they refer to the coming of the Messiah and God's kingdom.
Jeremiah 33:14–16
Isaiah 40:1-5, 9–11
Isaiah 35:1–6a, 10
Isaiah 7:10–14

Vineyard Song—An important passage of the book of Isaiah depicting the Chosen People as the vine of God. This image recurs in the New Testament in the words of Jesus and the writings of the apostle Paul.

the Lord in glory. Isaiah was humbled and proclaimed his unworthiness to be God's messenger. The story tells of a seraphim (an angel) touching Isaiah's mouth with an ember from the altar and thus removing his sinfulness.

Then I heard the voice of the Lord saying, "Whom shall I send? Who will go for us?" "Here I am," I said; "send me!"(Is 6:8).

The prophet then foretold to the people their stubbornness, which would eventually lead to the fall of Judah. Isaiah asked the Lord how long this period would be:
Until the cities are desolate, without inhabitants,
Houses, without a man, and the earth is a desolate waste.
Until the Lord removes men far away, and the land is abandoned more and more (Is 6:11–12).

The first thirty-nine chapters of the book of Isaiah include several other notable passages, including the **Vineyard Song** (Is 5) that depicts the Chosen People as the vine of God. This image recurs in the New Testament in the words of Jesus (Mt 21:33–44) and the letters of Paul (Rom 11:23–24).

Micah

Micah was another prophet from the late eighth century B.C. He was a contemporary of Isaiah and also preached in Judah. His warning was traditional: If the people did not return to the Lord and observe the Law of Moses, they would be destroyed.

Micah witnessed the fall of Samaria and the advance of the Assyrians on Jerusalem in 701 B.C. He was the first prophet who preached the eventual fall of Jerusalem:
Therefore, because of you,
   Zion shall be plowed like a field,
   and Jerusalem reduced to rubble,
And the mount of the temple to a forest ridge (Mi 3:12).

Micah's prophesy concerning the birth of the Messiah in Bethlehem (Mi 5:1) is cited in the gospels (Mt 2:6; Jn 7:42).

REVIEW & REFLECTION

1. Who were the major prophets of the southern kingdom before the fall of Jerusalem to Babylon?
2. How can we tell that the book of Isaiah was not written by just one prophet? How is the book of Isaiah divided?
3. What was the message of the prophet Micah? What was special about his prophecy?

Review and Reflection Answers

1. The major prophets of the southern kingdom before the fall of Jerusalem to Babylon were Isaiah of Jerusalem, and Micah.
2. The timeframe covered in the book of Isaiah is over 200 years, longer than the human life span. The book of Isaiah is divided into three major parts. Chapters 1–39 deal with Isaiah of Jerusalem; chapters 40–55 deal with Second Isaiah and the defeat of the Babylonian empire by the Persians; chapters 56–66 deal with Third Isaiah, the time after the exiles have returned to Jerusalem.
3. The message of Micah was this: if you do not return to the Lord and observe the laws of Moses, you will be destroyed. Micah's message was special in that he was the first prophet to predict the fall of Jerusalem itself.

TURNING POINT IN THE JOURNEY

JOURNAL ASSIGNMENT

- Read the Vineyard Song in Isaiah 5, and the parable Jesus told in Matthew 21:33–44 that seems to be based on it. List the parallels between the two. Does the vineyard make a good image for the Church today? Why or why not?

The Exile of Judah

The Assyrians threatened God's Chosen People (and many other nations) for nearly two hundred years; then their power began to wane. In 612 B.C. the Babylonians and Medes overtook the Assyrian capital city of Nineveh. The prophet Nahum spoke of the fall of Nineveh (see Na 2:2–14). Shortly after Nahum, the prophet Habbakuk warned that the Babylonian King Nebuchadnezzar II would not stop with Nineveh and Egypt (captured in 605 B.C.). Babylon would set its sights on Judah, he warned:

Look over the nations and see,
    and be utterly amazed!
For a work is being done in your days
    that you would not have believed,
        were it told.
For see, I am raising Chaldea,
    that bitter and unruly people,
That marches the breadth of the land
    to take dwellings not his own
        (Hb 1:5–6).

The prophet was correct. Nebuchadnezzar's siege of Jerusalem began in 597 B.C. From Nebuchadnezzar's own inscriptions, he "appointed in Jerusalem"... a king of his liking, took heavy booty from it, and brought it into Babylon."[2] The Judean king Jehoiachin, only on the throne for three months, surrendered and was deposed and deported to Babylon.

He wasn't the only one. With him went many other leaders and craftsmen of Jerusalem. According to 2 Kings 24:14, the number of exiles taken at that time was 10,000. Adding 7,000 artisans and 1,000 "smiths" (2 Kgs 24:16), the total reached 18,000. The book of Jeremiah, on the other hand, lists 3,023 persons carried into captivity on this first excursion (Jer 52:28). Even if the smaller number of Jeremiah (3,023) is accepted, it must be multiplied by an average family size, since Nebuchadnezzar's regime was known to carry away whole families.

Nebuchadnezzar did place a king of his own choosing in Jerusalem—Mattaniah, third son of King Josiah, who was renamed "Zedekiah." He was a weak ruler who was never accepted by the Jews. Zedekiah ruled for ten years, until he attempted to revolt against the Babylonians—the very people who put him in power.

Among the more striking archaeological confirmations of Biblical history was the discovery of a "ration list" in the ruins of Babylon—a text that mentions Jehoiachin.[3] The text also provides a postscript on Zedekiah: He eventually fell prey to the promises of Hophra, son of Psammetichus II of Egypt, and withheld tribute to Babylon. In other words, Zedekiah foolishly attempted to assert his independence from Babylonian rule.

In August 587 B.C. Nebuchadnezzar returned to Jerusalem, and the city finally fell. Zedekiah's resistance was crushed, and he was captured. His sons were killed before his eyes, and then his eyes were put out before he was taken "in fetters" to Babylon (see 2 Kgs 25:7).

Evidence of the Destruction

It seems beyond dispute that Jerusalem was treated severely. Archaeological finds show a total cessation of occupation of the towns near Jerusalem. These sites also indicate that vicious battles were fought

THE EXILE OF JUDAH

Bell-Ringers

1. Lead a discussion about occasions when students have been involved in or witnessed a bigger person, group, or team picking on a smaller one. Connect the example with the destruction of Judah by the stronger Babylonians.

2. Print these two events on the board:
- Exodus from Egypt
- Exile to Babylon

Have the students compare and contrast these two events in Israel's history: the first event was exhilarating, the second devastating.

Teaching Approaches

1. Summarize the homework reading assignment. Explain that once Assyria captured the northern kingdom, the Assyrians became an immediate threat to the southern kingdom. The prophet Nahum, from the southern kingdom, predicted that the Assyrians would be defeated at Ninevah. In 612 B.C., Ninevah did fall to the Babylonians and Medes. Nahum, along with the rest of Judah, rejoiced in the fact that Assyria would never bother them again. Nahum's prophecy goes no further. Otherwise, the prophet may have predicted the fall of Judah because of its wickedness. The prophet Habakkuk (605–597) does make the prediction of Judah's fall. He tells the people that the Babylonians will also capture Jerusalem and destroy it.

Resources

Music Suggestions

"Be Not Afraid" by Bob Dufford, S.J. from *Earthen Vessels*, *Glory & Praise 1*, or *Young People's Glory & Praise* (OCP [NALR]); *Celebrate* or *Gather* (GIA); *Breaking Bread* or *Spirit Song* (OCP).

"City of God" by Dan Schutte from *Lord of Light* or *Glory & Praise 3* (OCP [NALR]); *Celebrate* or *Gather* (GIA); *Breaking Bread* or *Spirit Song* (OCP).

"Deep River" (Afro-American Spiritual) in *Lead Me, Guide Me* (GIA).

"Free at Last" (Afro-American Spiritual) in *Lead Me, Guide Me* (GIA).

"Psalm 137: Let My Tongue Be Silent" by Carl Johengen in *Gather* (GIA).

"Save Us, O Lord" by Bob Dufford, SJ, from *Lord of Light* or *Glory & Praise 3* (OCP [NALR]); *Breaking Bread* (OCP).

"Shall We Gather at the River" by Robert Lowry in *Lead Me, Guide Me* or *Gather* (GIA).

"Swing Low, Sweet Chariot" #147 (African-American Spiritual) in *Lead Me, Guide Me* (GIA).

"There is a Balm in Gilead" (African-American Spiritual) from *Worship II* or *Gather* (GIA); *Breaking Bread* (OCP).

Chapter 8

2. Introduce the feeling of vengeance or revenge. Both prophets call on God to take vengeance on their enemies. Ask the students whether or not we should pray that God will destroy our enemies. (Lead the students to realize that Jesus taught us to love our enemies. We are to forgive them because it makes us better people and leaves open the possibility of their conversion.)

3. Continue by outlining the two-staged fall of Jerusalem:
   - In 597 B.C., the Babylonians invaded Jerusalem and took King Jehoiachin into exile.
   - The Babylonians put a puppet king, Zedekiah, on the throne. At first Zedekiah was loyal to Babylon; then he started to negotiate with Egypt to overthrow the Babylonians.
   - When the Babylonians caught wind of the plot, they attacked Jerusalem again in 587 B.C., destroying it completely and taking away more exiles. Zedekiah was killed.

Enrichment: Isaiah had a vision in which he pictured the march of the Babylonians against Jerusalem. Read the vision in Isaiah 10:28–34. Outline the places the prophet mentions on a map.

Enrichment: Read Psalm 146:7–8, Zechariah 9:12, and Isaiah 42:7, 61:1 and summarize the kind of treatment the prisoners received while held in captivity.

THE OLD TESTAMENT

there. Modern archaeologists confirm much of what Kathleen Kenyon discovered in her early twentieth-century digs in certain Jerusalem locations.
. . . [Kenyon's excavations] yielded a picture of ruin and desolation that confronted the first returnees of 539–538. While some people had no doubt continued to live in Jerusalem, the archaeological picture is one of their squatting among the rubble, which increased as the terrace walls . . . collapsed through lack of care and the debris accumulated in impassable piles on the lower slopes. No great change in the condition of the city occurred until the time of Nehemiah's arrival in 445. . . .[4]

It is difficult to estimate the human extent of the crisis. For example, if around 20,000 Jews were previously exiled, how many more residents of Jerusalem and the surrounding area were taken? Higher estimates reach as much as 50,000–60,000. Some estimate those numbers as being almost the entire population of the region. It is important to note, however, that the Bible does not even attempt to determine the numbers of those who fled or were killed.

By combining the archaeological evidence of destruction and difficult times in exile with Scripture references that indicate the emotional response of the Jewish people, the horrific picture of what happened is very clear.

Lamentations—The book of Hebrew poetry written in response to the devastation in Jerusalem by those who remained behind after the conquest of 587.

The following psalm is just one of many passages that reveal the depth of the Jews' sense of despair over the loss of their homeland:

> By the rivers of Babylon
> we sat mourning and weeping
> when we remembered Zion.
> On the poplars of that land
> we hung up our harps.
> There our captors asked us
> for the words of a song;
> Our tormentors, for a joyful song:
> "Sing for us a song of Zion!"
> But how could we sing a song
> of the Lord
> in a foreign land?
> If I forget you, Jerusalem,
> may my right hand wither.
> May my tongue stick to my palate
> if I do not remember you,
> If I do not exalt Jerusalem
> beyond all my delights (Ps 137:1–6).

The entire book of **Lamentations** is a collection of sorrowful poetry that gives us an even better sense of the devastation of the exilic events:

> How lonely she is now,
> the once crowded city!
> Widowed is she
> who was mistress over nations;
> The princess among the provinces
> has been made a toiling slave (Lam 1:1–2).

Resources
Printed Materials

"Exile" in *Dictionary of the Bible*, ed. by John L. McKenzie, S.J. (New York, NY: Macmillan Publishing Co., Inc., 1965), pp. 254–255.

"Kings, Books of" in *Dictionary of the Bible*, ed. by John L. McKenzie, S.J. (New York, NY: Macmillan Publishing Co., Inc., 1965), pp. 482–484.

"Kings, The Books of" in *The Oxford Companion to the Bible*, ed. by Bruce M. Metzger and Michael D. Coogan. (New York, NY: Oxford University Press, 1993), pp. 409–413.

Laffey, R.S.M. "1 and 2 Kings" in *The Collegeville Bible Commentary*, ed. by Dianne Bergant, C.S.A. and Robert J. Karris, O.F.M. (Collegeville, MN: The Liturgical Press, 1989), pp. 296–320.

Long, Burke O. "2 Kings" in *Harper's Bible Commentary*, ed. by James L. Mays. (San Francisco, CA: Harper & Row Publishers, 1988), pp. 323–341.

Walsh, Jerome T., and Christopher T. Begg. "1–2 Kings" in *The New Jerome Biblical Commentary*, ed. by Raymond E. Brown, S.S., Joseph A. Fitzmyer, S.J., and Roland E. Murphy, O.Carm. (Englewood Cliffs, NJ: Prentice Hall, 1990), pp. 160–185.

The Babylonians destroyed the Temple of Solomon. They carried many of the religious implements of worship into exile with the people. The policy of Nebuchadnezzar was to place captured religious implements or statues in the temple of **Marduk**, the main state god, in the city of Babylon in order to symbolize the capture of the people and the defeat of their gods. In the case of the Jews, a capture of Temple vessels served the same purpose. (This practice may underlie the stories of Belshazzar's feast in Daniel 5 and the return of the Temple furnishings in Ezra 1–6.)

There would have been a succession of crises for those Jews who remained in Jerusalem during the Exile. The famous ancient Jewish historian, Josephus, suggested that Nebuchadnezzar was back in Palestine again in 582, probably in reprisal for the murder of Gedaliah, the Jewish governor he left in charge after the siege of 587. The historical evidence, then, suggests a series of traumatic events were experienced by the Jews—whether in exile or back in the land.

Status and Treatment of the Exiles

The book of Lamentations includes poetry of the devastation in Jerusalem by those who apparently remained behind after the conquest of 587. But what about the people who were taken as exiles? We possess very little written information from the Babylonians themselves about how they treated the Jews or any other exile communities. But one inscription of Nebuchadnezzar II reads, in part, as follows, indicating forced labor:

> . . . the whole of the races, people from far places, whom Marduk my Lord delivered to me—I forced them to work on the building of Etemenanki—I imposed on them the brick-basket. . . . [3]

Archaeological surveys of the central flood plain of the Euphrates River—the source of water for the entire agricultural life of the surrounding region—show that there were increases in settlements during the time of

The Babylonian king Nebuchadnezzar placed captured vessels from the Temple in the temple of Marduk.

Marduk—The main state god of the Babylonians during the reign of Nebuchadnezzar. It was to his temple in the city of Babylon that the Temple furnishings and vessels from the Temple of Solomon were carried following the destruction of the Temple and Jerusalem in 587 B.C.

Turning Point in the Journey

4. Call on the students to answer the following questions:
   - What happened to Solomon's Temple and its religious implements? (The Temple was destroyed. the religious implements were carried away to Babylon where they were put in the temple of Marduk.)
   - What was life like for the people in exile? (They were made into slaves, often held in chains.)

5. Read the Journal Assignment (page 182) with the students. Have them meditate quietly on what life must have been like for the Israelites in Babylon. Then allow time in class for them to write their prayers. Tell the students that they will have an opportunity to share these prayers at the next class session.

6. **Homework Assignment:**
   - Complete the Journal Assignment, page 182.
   - Answer the Review and Reflection questions 1–3, page 182.
   - Read "Prophets of the Exile" through the "Ezekiel" subsection (pages 182–187).

Resources

Audiovisual Materials

In the Beginning: Release from Babylon (Oblate Media)—30 minutes
God raises a new king over the Babylonians, who allows the captive Israelites to return to their own country.

In the Beginning: The Exile of Israel (Oblate Media)—30 minutes
Because of their continued sinful choices, the Israelites are conquered by the Babylonians. Many Israelites are taken away in exile.

Old Testament: Ruth—A Faithful Woman (Vanguard)—15 minutes
Ruth, a convert to Judaism, chooses to accompany her mother-in-law Naomi back to Jerusalem. The story shows her great faith, and how God rewards her in the end.

Testament, Bible and History: Chronicles and Kings (Films for the Humanities and Sciences")—52 minutes
John Romer, writer and archaeologist, leads us on a journey of discovery to Jericho, Philistia, and Jerusalem. He discusses the Babylonian invasion of the Judah and the exile of its people.

The Old Testament Covenant: The Babylonian Disaster and the Later Prophets (De Sales Catholic Video Library)—60 minutes
This video discusses the impact of the Babylonian victory over Judah. The prophets of this time remind the Israelites that God remains faithful to his promises. They also call the people to remain faithful to the religion of their ancestors.

CHAPTER 8

PROPHETS OF THE EXILE
Ezekiel

Bell-Ringers

1. Open the class with a prayer. Call on several volunteers to read aloud their prayers as exiles (the Journal Assignment, page 182).

2. As a follow-up, discuss the daily experiences of contemporary people who are exiled from their homes due to war, natural disaster, or politics. Cite examples.

Teaching Approaches

1. Introduce the text section. Explain that during this lesson you will focus on the prophet Ezekiel. In later lessons, details about the prophets Jeremiah and Second Isaiah will be explored.

2. Provide the following information about Ezekiel: He was a priest who was taken into exile with other Israelites. His place of exile was a village named Tel Abib. As a priest in Judah, Ezekiel would have been on rotating duty at the Temple to offer sacrifices to God on behalf of the people. In exile, there was no Temple. There was really no role for Ezekiel to fulfill other than being a slave like the other Israelites. He was not only displaced from his country; he had lost his ministry.

THE OLD TESTAMENT

Babylonian rule. This increase may have been due in part to the influx of deported people from Judah and other conquered peoples.

The Old Testament describes the conditions of exile in very dark terms. Several places mention the exiles being held with chains and bonds (e.g., Na 1:13, 3:10; Is 52:2; and Ps 107:14). The second book of Chronicles reports of the imprisonment of Jehoiakim: "Nebuchadnezzar, king of Babylon, came up against him and bound him with chains to take him to Babylon" (2 Chr 36:6). The book of Lamentations also speaks of sieges and chains after the conquest of Jerusalem:

> He has hemmed me in with no escape
>   and weighed me down with chains;
> Even when I cry out for help,
>   he stops my prayer;
> He has blocked my ways with fitted stones,
>   and turned my paths aside (Lam 3:7–9).

There are frequent descriptions of the exiles as prisoners. The "release of prisoners" is mentioned often, indicating the kind of treatment they received (see Ps 146:7–8; Zec 9:12; Is 42:7, 61:1).

REVIEW & REFLECTION

1. What archaeological evidence is there to support the Biblical story of the conquest and exile of Jerusalem?
2. What happened to King Johiachin? Why did Nebuchadnezzar return to Jerusalem ten years after the original conquest? What became of King Zedekiah?
3. Describe the probable conditions the Jews faced in exile.

JOURNAL ASSIGNMENT

- Imagine that you are among the people conquered by Nebuchadnezzar and taken to Babylon as forced labor. Write a prayer to God, describing a typical day and expressing your feelings.

Judea—The Aramaic name for the place formerly called Judah. It was a name first given after the Babylonian Exile. Though the region varied over the years, it always included the city of Jerusalem.

Prophets of the Exile

Ezekiel and Jeremiah were two prophets whose lives overlapped with the events of the Babylonian Exile, but from two very different perspectives. Ezekiel was deported to the Babylonian heartland where he lived with other exiles from **Judea**. Jeremiah remained behind in Jerusalem until he was taken by force to Egypt by a group of Jews who were sympathetic to assistance being offered by the Egyptians in their attempt to break free from Babylonian rule.

A third important prophet of the Exile will also be covered in this section. Second Isaiah consoled the exiles and wrote of a promised time of peace beyond suffering. He described this time as a new Exodus. The prophet also may

---

Review and Reflection Answers

1. The archaeological evidence in Babylon includes a "ration list" with the name Jehoiachin on it and shows an increase in settlements in the central flood plain of the Euphrates River during the time of the exile. The archaeological evidence in Jerusalem shows a total cessation of occupation of the towns near Jerusalem. These sites also indicate that vicious battles were fought there.
2. King Johiachin was taken in exile to Babylon. He never returned. Nebuchadnezzar returned to Jerusalem ten years later because King Zedekiah, the puppet king he had put in control of Judah, was plotting with the Egyptians to overthrow Babylon. After Nebuchadnezzar reconquered Jerusalem, he made King Zedekiah witness the killing of his sons. Then Zedekiah was blinded and taken in fetters to Babylon.
3. The Jews were most likely treated as criminals and slaves. They were subject to forced labor and were sometimes kept in chains.

have considered Cyrus, the Persian king who liberated the Jews, as God's Messiah.

Ezekiel

Of the sparse information known about Ezekiel, his writings reveal that he was a priest. Although some of the other prophets may have been from priestly families, Ezekiel seems to have been the only prophet who served actively as a priest. Priests were in charge of maintaining the purity of individuals and all of Israel. Part of this task was accomplished by conducting Temple sacrifices. Another part of the priest's ministry was to advise the people on issues of conduct and day-to-day living.

Ezekiel was deported with the first group of exiles in 597 and began his role as a prophet five years later in Babylon; he was the first prophet called to prophesy outside the Holy Land. Ezekiel's "call narrative" describes a vision of cherubim who gave him a scroll containing the word of God, which he was to proclaim to the people. The words "Lamentation and wailing and woe!" were written on the scroll that he was then instructed to eat. This event was the first in a series of bizarre visions and actions Ezekiel experienced through the course of his prophesying (Ez 3:1–4). For example, he shaved, burned, and divided his hair as a sign of the fate of the people of Jerusalem when they were defeated by Nebuchadnezzar for the second time (Ez 6:1–4); and he pantomimed the actions of the exiles (Ez 12:1–20).

The book of Ezekiel is laid out with a clear division of parts:

- *Ezekiel 1–24.* This section—known as "Oracles of Judgment"—warns of Jerusalem's impending doom, sometimes reaching a rather severe level of rhetoric and anger.
- *Ezekiel 33–48.* These "Oracles of Hope" speak of the restoration of Jerusalem after the Exile and culminate in a

Ezekiel's Vision by Raphael

grand vision (Ez 40–48) in which Ezekiel "sees" a hopeful reestablishment of the Israelite state under equitable and just circumstances.

This division leaves a somewhat enigmatic section in Ezekiel 25–32. These chapters may have been added by an editor at a later time, because the subjects of chapters 24 and 33 are precisely the same: the fall of Jerusalem. It seems that these originally connected chapters were split by the insertion of the passages that now make up chapters 25–32.

Ezekiel 25–32 are sometimes called the "Oracles against the Nations," because they contains speeches of judgment directed against foreign nations. Why were these chapters inserted in this part of the book of Ezekiel? It is easy to figure out at least part of the answer. Look at the timing and placement of these speeches: they were placed in the text at the very moment of Jerusalem's destruction by a foreign nation (Babylon). Perhaps they were meant to assure the reader

TURNING POINT IN THE JOURNEY

3. Ask the students to show how the book of Ezekiel is divided into two parts and to explain the difference between the two parts. (Ezekiel 1–24 is known as the "Oracles of Judgment" and warns of Jerusalem's fall. Ezekiel 33–48 contains "Oracles of Hope" which speak of the restoration of Jerusalem after the Exile.)

4. The next subsections introduce the visions of Ezekiel and some of the acts of Ezekiel. It will be important for the students to read from the Biblical text as well as the explanations of these passages from pages 184–187.

Resources

Internet Links

www.bible.ca/maps
View a high-resolution map of successive world kingdoms: Persia, Babylon, and Assyria (900–500 B.C.).

http://research.haifa.ac.il/~hecht
Visit the Reuben and Edith Hecht Museum at the University of Haifa in Israel. See artifacts from the Babylonian Period (586–538 B.C.) and the Persian Period (538–332 B.C.).

www.emuseum.mnsu.edu/prehistory/middle_east
This site connects you to the E Museum at Minnesota State University. Learn about the history of the Fertile Crescent, as well as the archaeological findings from ancient Persia, Assyria, Babylon, and Sumer.

www.providence.edu/dwc/mesopot1.htm
This site contains information and visuals regarding archaeological finds from the period of Babylonian captivity. Includes many links to other relevant websites.

www.otgateway.com/jeremiah.html
Tabor College in Victoria, Australia, offers online resources for studying the book of Jeremiah.

CHAPTER 8

5. Distribute copies of "Ezekiel's Actions" (Handout 8A, page 282 of the TWE) to the students. Have the students form "learning groups" made up of six members. Assign each group only one passage to read and discuss. They should also fill in their charts for their assigned passage. When everyone has finished, have the students move to new "teaching groups" of six students each, with each person representing one of the passages. The teaching group members should then teach their passage to the others while everyone in the group completes the chart (see Handout 8A Answers, page 189).

6. **Application:** Share with the students examples of public and sometimes outrageous symbolic protests in American history. Among these were the burning of bras by women during the '60s as a symbol of women's rights; the burning of the American flag to protest the war in Vietnam; the pouring of blood on buildings at nuclear armament sites to protest nuclear weapons. Call on students to think of additional examples of symbolic or prophetic actions.

THE OLD TESTAMENT

that the evil done to Jerusalem would have its consequences for the perpetrators.

The unique character of the book of Ezekiel is best understood by the series of visions and actions of the prophet.

The Visions of Ezekiel
1. *The Call (Ez 1–2)*

The first vision is really the "call narrative" of Ezekiel; he receives his "commission" as a prophet in the first two chapters. In this vision, Ezekiel sees the throne of God in heaven, accompanied by a series of strange creatures equipped with wheels and wings. The theme appears to be movement: the creatures are moving and the setting for the throne of God is moving. Before his vision is complete, however, Ezekiel is called to be a prophet, even though he is told that the people may well reject his message:

But speak my words to them, whether they heed or resist, for they are rebellious (Ez 2:7).

It was at this point of his commissioning that Ezekiel was handed a scroll covered with writing on the front and back. The Lord, then makes an unusual request:

Son of man, eat what is before you; eat this scroll, then go, speak to the house of Israel (Ez 3:1).

Ezekiel ate the scroll "and it was as sweet as honey" (Ez 3:3). Then, God said:

Son of man, go now to the house of Israel, and speak my words to them (Ez 3:4).

Ezekiel was so overcome with this experience that he sat stunned for seven days.

2. *The Transport to Jerusalem (Ez 8–11)*

In his second great vision, Ezekiel is transported to Jerusalem with other exiles from Babylon. They are stopped on four occasions, each time moving closer and closer to the Temple. At each stop Ezekiel is appalled by what he sees—pagan worship and rituals being performed right up to the steps of the Temple itself.

Keeping in mind that Ezekiel was a priest, this vision of the severity of pagan mixing with the religion of Yahweh must have been particularly distasteful. At the end of his "tour of sin" around the Temple complex, Ezekiel is placed on a hillside overlooking Jerusalem. There he sees something that he couldn't imagine in his worst nightmare: the Spirit of God actually leaves Jerusalem.

And the glory of the Lord rose from the city and took a stand on the mountain which is to the east of the city (Ez 11:23).

Ezekiel was shown two important things in this vision: 1) the extent of the pagan corruption in Jerusalem, and 2) the fact that God was not permanently "locked" to the Temple; his spirit could be found anywhere and everywhere. This second point was very important to exiles who might have believed that when they left Jerusalem, God had been left behind.

3. *The Valley of the Dry Bones (Ez 37)*

In the most well-known vision from the book of Ezekiel, the prophet is set among a valley of bones, a horrific sight. One theory is that this valley was in the midst of a battlefield, and the dry bones represented the fallen of Israel who had died in the battles and destruction of the exilic events themselves. Before his eyes, Ezekiel sees the bones drawn together, filled out with flesh and skin, and restored to life.

Remember, this vision is recorded in the "Oracles of Hope" section. Ezekiel is seeing a vision of the restored Israel. The message from this vision is that restoration is possible. Even the devastation of the destruction brought down on Israel as a result of the conquests of Assyria and Babylon can be overcome in the plan of God.

Background Information

Ezekiel's Actions Follow a Pattern

Many people in Babylon thought Ezekiel was crazy. He was prone to very strange, actions in public. What the book of Ezekiel makes clear is that these actions all follow the same pattern:

- God gives Ezekiel a command to act a certain way.
- Ezekiel carries out the command, usually in a public setting.
- The symbolism of the action is explained.

Turning Point in the Journey

4. The Restored Israel (Ez 40–48)

The entire final section of the book contains a dramatic vision about the restoration of Israel. There are many details about the reconstructed Temple and some elements of the city. But what is particularly interesting is the fact that Ezekiel sees a redistribution of land in this vision. Each of the tribes are to get equal shares of land in the restored Israel. The royal leader will only be given a set amount of land and will no longer oppress the people. This vision describes Ezekiel in the tradition of the earlier prophets, speaking for the rights of the people against the greed of the royal and aristocratic leaders:

> . . . the princes of Israel will no longer oppress my people, but will leave the land to the house of Israel according to their tribes. Thus says the Lord God: Enough, you princes of Israel! Put away violence and oppression, and do what is right and just! Stop evicting my people says the Lord God (Ez 45:8–9).

This vision let the people know that the restored Israel would not go back to its old ways. A new and just Israel was on the horizon.

The Acts of Ezekiel

Some of the actions of Ezekiel give the impression that he was mentally unstable, because of the extreme variations of his personality. For example, examine these seven acts of Ezekiel:

Houses on hillside of Olive Mountain in Jerusalem

1. After his call from the Lord, Ezekiel sits in his own house; unlike many of the prophets who seek out the people to whom God wishes to speak, Ezekiel waits until people come to him. Even then, he speaks only when the Lord opens his mouth (see Ez 3:24–27).
2. Ezekiel builds a model of Jerusalem, complete with battering rams, siege walls, and other weapons of war. He then lies—first on his left side and then on his right side—facing the model. He eats impure food cooked in an impure manner—probably representing the sickness, death, and starvation of the people living under siege conditions (see Ez 4).
3. Ezekiel cuts off his hair, and then divides it into thirds, cutting one part, burning one part, and throwing one part to the wind. This likely represents the fate of the people of Jerusalem in the coming destruction—a third will die by the sword of the invaders, a third will burn in the fire of siege and conquest, and a third will flee as refugees or be

7. Explain that Ezekiel is also known for his visions. Continue with the class divided into the six teaching groups. Assign each group one of the following visions. (It is fine if some groups are assigned the same vision.)
   - Ezekiel 1–2: The Call
   - Ezekiel 8–11: The Transport to Jerusalem
   - Ezekiel 37: The Valley of the Dry Bones
   - Ezekiel 40–48: The Restored Israel

   Tell each group to read and discuss the vision they were assigned. Allow the rest of the class time for the groups to figure out a creative way to present the vision and its meaning to the entire class (e.g., in masks, with a narrator and mime, a skit with props or costumes, puppets, etc.) Tell the students that they will be expected to do their presentation of the vision at the next class session.

8. **Homework Assignment**:
   - With your group, finish working on your presentation of one of the visions of Ezekiel.
   - Read text subsections "Jeremiah," "Second Isaiah," and the feature "Third Isaiah" (pages 187–190).

Handout 8A "Ezekiel's Actions" Answers

Ezekiel 4:1–3 Ezekiel uses a clay model of Jerusalem to show how the city will be attacked.

Ezekiel 4:4–8 Ezekiel reclined on his left side for 390 days, and on his right side for 40 days to symbolize that the siege against Jerusalem would be lengthy.

Ezekiel 4:9–15 Ezekiel fasted as a symbol of the people's hunger and thirst during the siege. They would be lucky to eat bread and drink water without considering whether or not it was clean.

Ezekiel 5:1–12 Ezekiel cut and burned his hair. This action was a symbol of the burning of Jerusalem and the subsequent scattering of the survivors.

Ezekiel 12:1–16 Ezekiel repeatedly packed his bags and acted as if he was leaving the city. This action symbolized that most, if not all, of the people would be taken into exile.

Ezekiel 12:17–20 Ezekiel trembled and shook with fear as he ate. This action symbolized the fear that the Israelites will feel as Jerusalem is attacked, and they are taken into exile.

Chapter 8

Jeremiah
Second Isaiah
THIRD ISAIAH

Bell-Ringers

1. Read Ezekiel 36:24–29 to the class. Note for the students that Yahweh is going to restore the Israelites. Have them point out the sentence that refers to the renewal of the covenant (vs. 26).

2. Call on each group to present its vision of Ezekiel, as well as its meaning. Limit the time of the presentations so that they take up only half to two-thirds of the class time.

THE OLD TESTAMENT

taken as prisoners of war to the "far corners of the earth" (see Ez 5).
4. Ezekiel packs an exile's bag and is seen leaving the city again and again, re-enacting the events of being conquered and exiled by Babylon (see Ez 12).
5. Ezekiel returns to his model of the city of Jerusalem, adding a road approaching it from Babylon. This is likely meant to show that Nebuchadnezzar would return to Jerusalem to destroy it (see Ez 21).
6. When Ezekiel's wife dies suddenly, he does not mourn for her in the customary ways; instead, he puts on his sandals and turban and goes about as usual. When the people question him about it, he tells them that this will be their response, too, when Jerusalem falls—there will be no time for mourning (see Ez 24:15–26).
7. After the vision of dry bones, Ezekiel joins together two sticks marked "Israel" and "Judah" to represent the reunification of the old rival states of the Hebrews (see Ez 37:15–22).

What do these symbolic acts mean? Were these just theatrics meant to impress the importance of his message on the people? Was he, in fact, mentally unstable? A comparison with the poems of the book of Lamentations suggests another idea:

♦ *Compare Ezekiel 3:22–27 and Lamentations 3:7–9*
Ezekiel sits confined in his home with hands tied by cords. Lamentations speaks of a people being hemmed in and bound by chains.

♦ *Compare Ezekiel 4:1–3 and Lamentations 1:11; 2:12; 4:4; 9–10*
The siege of Jerusalem forces some people to eat impure foods, or foods prepared in an impure manner. Lamentations echoes the concern with the ability to feed oneself and one's family properly. (Also see Jer 52:6 and 2 Kgs 25:3.)

♦ *Compare Ezekiel 5:1–17 and Lamentations 1:1; 2:21.*
Ezekiel acts out the tri-fold punishment of Jerusalem—a third of the people burnt in the city, a third dying by the sword, and a third exiled ("strewn to the wind"). Lamentations bemoans the lonely, once crowded city.

♦ *Compare Ezekiel 12 and Lamentations 1:3, 18*
Ezekiel prepares "an exile's baggage" and is led through a hole in a wall to exemplify being taken as a prisoner of war. He is reliving the events of the Exile—first, his own exile to Babylon, and second, his image of events to come when Jerusalem will fall and be utterly destroyed. Lamentations mourns the fate of Judah, finding no place to rest as her people are led into exile.

♦ *Compare Ezekiel 21 and Lamentations 2:21; 5:9*
In Ezekiel, the image of the sword is used to refer to Babylonian forces. In Lamentations the image of the sword is a symbol for foreign rule.

The book of Lamentations expresses in powerful, emotional terms the devastation of the city of Jerusalem, and the profound grief of the people of Judah and Israel. When the book of Ezekiel is read with Lamentations, we realize how deeply Ezekiel suffered from the devastation of the siege he went through in 597 B.C., and the destruction that he and others heard about while in Babylon in 587. His actions, therefore, must be understood, not as the ravings of one afflicted with mental illness, but as the outpouring of an almost overwhelming sense of grief, loss, and pain.

Today we know much more about the psychological impact of warfare and disaster.

Ezekiel is as much a prophet for modern times as he was for the exiles in Babylon. He suffered the same fate as the millions of homeless and refugees fleeing warfare and hunger today who also must deal with the psychological and spiritual impact of a horrific situation. God chose a broken refugee to be a prophet of hope to all who find themselves in a similar situation.

Jeremiah

Jeremiah began his ministry as a prophet during the reign of King Josiah in approximately 626 B.C. He finally disappeared from the pages of history in 587 B.C. Unlike Ezekiel, Jeremiah remained in Jerusalem through all the events of the siege and the exile of the people.

According to Jeremiah, Judah was paying a price for its sins and the best course of action would be to submit to Babylon so that Jerusalem could escape destruction. Jeremiah walked through the streets of Jerusalem with a wooden yoke on his shoulders preaching this message. This course of action was not popular among God's Chosen People, especially among those who wanted to forcibly resist Nebuchadnezzar.

But Jeremiah hoped to avoid the destruction of God's People. He also understood the current political subjugation to Babylonian rule to be God's response to the people's sinfulness. As such, they should not resist it, but should submit to it and repent of their idolatry and their abuse of the poor in their midst, in the hope that God would relent and return them to their previous position. It is possible that if Jerusalem had not tried to revolt against Babylon in 587, the first Temple would have remained standing. As it was, however, the Temple was destroyed along with the whole city of Jerusalem in response to Zedekiah's revolt.

In the "Temple Sermon" of Jeremiah 7, the prophet's full message is clear as he warns that those who oppress refugees, orphans, or widows will not be spared just because they come to the Temple. They must first reform their evil ways.

Read Jeremiah 7

Jeremiah stood in the very Temple area itself, and proclaimed his message. Here are the main points:
- The sacrificial system does not automatically take away the consequences of sin. The sacrifice is invalid if the person intends to sin again.
- Jerusalem is not immune to punishment just because the Temple stands there. God destroyed Shiloh, another famous Temple, and he can destroy Solomon's great Temple as well.
- The sins of pagan worship and oppression of the "alien, orphan and widow" are severely condemned (vs. 6).

Perhaps his most famous point is Jeremiah's bitter attack on the Temple itself as a "den of thieves" in Jeremiah 7:11. These are the very words used by Jesus to condemn the corrupt Temple practices of his day (see Mt 21:13). Anyone who heard Jesus' warnings would have instantly recognized the reference (see other similarities between Jeremiah and Jesus on page 188). Jesus was quoting one of the most radical accusations made by *any* of the prophets, and in Jeremiah, the prophet went on to suggest that the Temple would in fact be destroyed for the sins of the people. Was Jesus implying this too? (The Temple Jesus knew was destroyed in 70 A.D., not long after his ascension to heaven around 33–34.)

The Confessions of Jeremiah

Jeremiah, like Ezekiel, had to struggle with the personal trauma of being a prophet with an unpopular message. A series of "confessions" in the book of Jeremiah describe much of his personal agony.

Turning Point in the Journey

Teaching Approaches

1. Review Ezekiel's message: God's presence (in the Temple and among the people) requires that they act with justice. Each person has the responsibility for keeping the covenant.

2. Summarize the text material on Jeremiah, a prophet living in Jerusalem during the time of the siege. Share the three main points of Jeremiah's Temple Sermon.
   - Coming to the Temple for worship was not enough in itself to please God. The people also had to turn away from sin and injustice.
   - Jerusalem was not immune from God's punishment because the Temple was there.
   - God will punish the people for their injustice against aliens, orphans, and widows.

3. Share more biographical information about Jeremiah as time permits (see Background Information, below).

Background Information

Jeremiah

Jeremiah began his ministry in 627 with the collapse of the Assyrian Empire. After the Babylonians took Jerusalem in 597, King Zedekiah joined forces with the Egyptians to try and rebel against Babylon. Jeremiah warned him not to do this. The Babylonians found out about Zedekiah's betrayal and retaliated by entering Jerusalem again in 587 B.C. and destroying the Temple.

Jeremiah remained behind in Jerusalem with some Jews. They eventually fled to Egypt, against Jeremiah's advice, taking him with them. He died there.

Chapter 8

4. Distribute "Jeremiah's Feelings" (Handout 8B, page 283 of the TWE) and have the students work individually to summarize Jeremiah's feelings described in each passage. When everyone has finished, check the responses (see below). Make the point that Jeremiah was very much like people today. He struggled with doubts, faith, and feelings of abandonment. Even though Jeremiah vented his anger, frustrations, and despair, he was always faithful to working out God's purpose in his life and in the life of the community. Finally, form a panel of four or five students. Use the Discussion Questions at the bottom of the handout as a basis for panel discussion. Also, allow the rest of the class to contribute to the discussion.

5. Share the following information about Second Isaiah:
   - The main message of Second Isaiah is that a servant of God will rise up and save his people.
   - Second (Deutero) Isaiah lived with the exiles in Babylon. He prophesized during the last years of the Babylonian Exile (around 540) and the beginning of the exiles' return under Cyrus (around 538).
   - Chapters 40–55 in the book of Isaiah are attributed to Second Isaiah. The message of these chapters is very hopeful: Ultimately, God is a God of comfort and love. King Cyrus was God's anointed servant, who would defeat the Babylonians and set the Israelites free. Symbolically, God would build a path through the desert, facilitating the people's journey home.

Enrichment: Read the separate feature, "Jeremiah and Jesus," on page 188 and the cited Scripture passages that compare Jeremiah to Jesus. Make a chart and write summaries of each passage.

The Old Testament

Read Jeremiah 8:18–23; 15:10–21; 17:14–18; 18:18–23; 20:7–18

In the final confession, Jeremiah reveals an intimate connection with God and his commitment to preaching his word in spite of derision he receives from those who oppose him:

> Yes, I hear the whisperings of many:
> "Terror on every side!
> Denounce! let us denounce him."
> All those who were my friends
>   are on the watch for any misstep of mine.
> "Perhaps he will be trapped; then we can prevail
>   and take our vengeance on him."
> But the Lord is with me, like a mighty champion:
>   my persecutors will stumble, they will not triumph" (Jer 20:10-11).

Eventually, Jeremiah's enemies did manage to silence him. He was smuggled to Egypt by some Jews who supported Egyptian hopes to bring Judah into an alliance of nations opposed to Babylon. After Jeremiah was taken to Egypt, no further mention of him occurs in the Bible. Presumably he died there, a lonely and unpopular prisoner of Jews who did not agree with his theology or politics.

Jeremiah and Jesus

There are many similarities between the life of the prophet Jeremiah and the life of Jesus. God was active in the lives of each in similar ways at key times. Jeremiah prefigures Jesus in many ways.
- They are rejected by their family members and neighbors (see Jer 12:6; Lk 4:24–29).
- Jeremiah and Jesus each weep over the city of Jerusalem (see Jer 8:23; Lk 19:41).
- The authorities harass both Jeremiah and Jesus over the truth of their message.
- Jesus denounces the corruption of the Temple by quoting the famous phrase of Jeremiah that the Temple had become a "den of thieves" (e.g., Mk 11:17).

Deutero-Isaiah (Second Isaiah)—The disciple of Isaiah who is credited with writing chapters 40–55 of the book of Isaiah. Second Isaiah lived at the end of the Babylonian period and the beginning of the Persian period (545–535 B.C.) and likely witnessed the collapse of Babylon to the Persian Empire.

Second Isaiah

The messages of both Ezekiel and Jeremiah, though dire, hint at new beginnings for Israel. Another prophet of the Exile—Second Isaiah—is someone whose precise identity is unknown to us, but his influence was important in the exilic communities that authored and formed a majority of the Old Testament.

Second Isaiah or "**Deutero-Isaiah**" was a prophet at the time of the Babylonian Exile. The prophet understood that Persia was soon to be the new power of the region and that its more tolerant ruler, Cyrus, would be God's instrument to return the Jews to their homeland. Cyrus, indeed, was a key factor in the end of Babylonian captivity for the

---

Handout 8B "Jeremiah's Feelings" Answers

Jeremiah 12:1–5 Jeremiah lamented that life was unfair. Godless people seemed to succeed and prosper. Jeremiah wished that God would punish them.

Jeremiah 15:10–21 Jeremiah didn't understand why his life was so miserable when he had been faithful to what God asked of him. He complained loudly!

Jeremiah 17:14–18 Jeremiah had been warning people of coming disaster, and all they did was laugh at him. Nothing bad had happened yet. Jeremiah prayed to be proven right.

Jeremiah 18:18–23 Jeremiah was outraged that people were plotting to kill him. He prayed that God would strike down his enemies and stand by him.

Jeremiah 20:7–18 Jeremiah was weary. It seemed that he was always swimming upstream, always banging his head against a wall. He knew that God had rescued other poor people in similar situations, and he prayed that God would rescue him soon.

Jewish exiles, even though the Persians maintained rule over the lands of Palestine and the Jewish people.

The text of Second Isaiah includes four Servant Songs. A messianic figure, known as the "Servant of God" is described as having the mission to bring righteousness to the world. He is opposed, suffers, and is apparently put to death or dies a martyr.

Read Isaiah 42:1–4; 49:1–6; 50:4–9; 52:13–53:12

The Servant Songs are clearly connected with the mission of Jesus. In fact, the New Testament writers use the fourth song to interpret the redeeming nature of Jesus' death:

> But he was pierced for our offenses,
>   crushed for our sins;
> Upon him was the chastisement that
>   makes us whole,
>   by his stripes we were healed
>   (Is 53:5).

It is important to remember that Second Isaiah's words had comfort for the people at the time they were written as well as 500 years later with the coming of Jesus Christ. So, who might the prophet have been referring to as the Suffering Servant at the time these words were written?

The prophet clearly believes that at least one possible identity of the "Suffering Servant" is the Jewish people themselves, due to their experience in exile. They are collectively the "Servant of God" (see Is 41:8-10). If this is the case, then what is their new mission to be? Is it to forget what they have learned in their suffering and to punish the nations that hurt them so badly? Some passages seem to indicate this (see Ps 137:1, 8–9), but Second Isaiah represents another tradition, one that recognizes that suffering has given the people a more peaceful and loving way to view and respond to the rest of the world:

> It is too little, he says, for you to be my
>   servant,
>   to raise up the tribes of Jacob,
>   and restore the survivors of Israel;
> I will make you a light to the nations,
>   that my salvation may reach to the
> ends of the earth (Is 49:6).

The death of Jesus fulfills the Suffering Servant prophecies of Second Isaiah

In this passage, the prophet goes far beyond simply preaching the restoration of Israel. Now, the people of God will be a missionary people, with a "light" to take to all the nations.

While many other identifications of the Suffering Servant have been proposed (e.g., the prophet himself, or another prophet living at that time), the Church is clear in its pronouncement that the Suffering Servant prophecies are fulfilled in Jesus Christ. The *Catechism* teaches:

Turning Point in the Journey

6. Assign each of the Servant Songs listed on page 189 (Is 42:1–4; 49:1–6; 50:4–9; 52:13–53:12) for reading. Shift the focus to Isaiah 53:10–12 which addresses the exaltation of the Messiah. Call on students to name other ways that the Servant Songs clearly connect with the mission of Jesus.

7. Briefly summarize the main message of Third Isaiah. (It is a message of hope; some day God's light will attract all people to God.) As time permits, share more information on Third Isaiah (see below).

Background Information

Third Isaiah

Third Isaiah lived in Judah after the Exile and wrote after the Temple was rebuilt (537–500 B.C.). He was thought to be responsible for chapters 56–66 in the book of Isaiah. At this time, people were pulled by the conflict between Persia's rebuilding campaign and their Jewish identity. They still sinned, acted with avarice and greed, and showed injustice toward the poor. Third Isaiah's main concern was for authentic worship and justice. He said that the suffering experienced in the Exile should make God's People more sensitive to those among them who were suffering. True worship of God meant justice toward one's neighbors.

Chapter 8

8. Introduce the Learn by Doing exercise on page 199. Suggest some possible media—collage, original art, music, short video, slide show, puppet show—for the assignment. Decide if you want the students to work alone on the exercise or in small groups.

9. **Homework Assignment**:
   - Complete the Learn by Doing project, page 199.
   - Answer the Review and Reflection questions 1–3, page 190.
   - Complete the Journal Assignment (page 190) which involves reading the book of Lamentations and applying its message to contemporary world events.
   - Read the text section "The Exiles Return to Judah" (pages 191–194).

The Scriptures had foretold this divine plan of salvation through the putting to death of "the righteous one, my servant" as a mystery of universal redemption, the slavery of sin. Citing a confession of faith that "Christ died for our sins in accordance with the scriptures." In particular, Jesus' redemptive death fulfills Isaiah's prophecy of the suffering Servant (CCC, 601).

THIRD ISAIAH

The final eleven chapters of the book of Isaiah are attributed to "Third Isaiah." The material is a mixture of poetry and prose composed by the disciple(s) of Isaiah shortly after the return from Exile. The message of Third Isaiah is one of hope; it looks forward to a day when God's light will attract all people to God. Some of these passages even prepare the way for Jesus' inclusive message of God's love for *all* people, Jews and Gentiles alike:

> I come to gather nations of every language; they shall come and see my glory. I will set a sign among them; from them I will send fugitives to the nations . . . that have never heard my fame, or seen my glory; and they shall proclaim my glory among the nations.
>
> From one new moon to another,
>   and from one sabbath to another,
> All mankind shall come to worship
>   before me, says the Lord (Is 66:18-19, 23).

REVIEW & REFLECTION

1. Compare and contrast the two major prophets of the exile, Jeremiah and Ezekiel.
2. What was unique about Ezekiel and his call to be one of God's prophets? How were his messages unusual, or unusually delivered? What are some possible explanations for the intensity of his prophetic speech and actions?
3. What was the contribution of Deutero-Isaiah to the messages of the prophets in exile? What new understanding of the exile did this prophet share with the people?

JOURNAL ASSIGNMENT

- Read the book of Lamentations. Think about current events around the world. What people would be very likely to understand the message of Lamentations today? Why?

Review and Reflection Answers

1. Ezekiel was in Babylon during the exile. He prophesied that God would eventually restore the exiles and give them new life. Jeremiah was in Jerusalem during the siege. He prophesied about the coming destruction of Jerusalem, but also about a hope that the people would live God's covenant in their hearts.
2. Ezekiel was the first prophet to speak outside Israel or Judah. His messages were accompanied by bizarre, symbolic actions. His message was passionate because he deeply suffered from the devastation of the siege he went through, and the destruction he and others heard about while they were in exile. His actions and preaching were the outpourings of an almost overwhelming sense of grief, loss, and pain.
3. Deutero-Isaiah talked about a "Servant of God" who would save the people and restore them to Jerusalem. Deutero-Isaiah may have been predicting the actions of the Persian King Cyrus; he may also have been predicting the future messiah, Jesus.

The Exiles Return to Judah

The end of the Neo-Babylonian regime came in 539 B.C. with legendary swiftness. Cyrus the Persian king, after unifying the Persian tribes and defeating the Medes, conquered the city of Babylon. According to classical sources (e.g., the Greek historian, Herodotus), Cyrus was able to conquer the city without violence because the Persians surprised the Babylonians during the celebrations of the New Year—an historical event probably also reflected in the story of Belshazzar's Feast (see Dn 5). According to Second Isaiah, God used Cyrus as an instrument of change.

> Thus says the Lord to his anointed, Cyrus,
> whose right hand I grasp,
> Subduing nations before him,
> and making kings run in his service,
> Opening doors before him and leaving the gates unbarred:
> I will go before you and level the mountains;
> Bronze doors I will shatter, and iron bars I will snap.
> I will give you treasures out of the darkness,
> and riches that have been hidden away,
> That you may know that I am the Lord,
> the God of Israel, who calls you by your name (Is 45:1–3).

The Biblical sources about the early Persian period (e.g., Ezra 1–6) indicate that the Persians were relatively generous in their return of exiles of all nations and races to their homelands, including the Jews. But this generosity can be exaggerated. It was surely not entirely altruistic. The missions led by the Jewish leaders Ezra and Nehemiah back to Palestine, accompanied by former exiles, were probably a calculated Persian imperial policy. An increased military presence was needed on the western flank facing the Greek enemies—particularly after an Egyptian revolt in 460 (sometimes called the "**Inarus Revolt**") in which the Greeks were involved. (This revolt was eventually crushed by the Persian ruler Artaxerxes I in 454—a time very close to the period of Ezra and Nehemiah.)

Part of the exaggeration of Persian benevolence is the idea that the Exile actually ended in 539. Really all that ended was Neo-Babylonian dominance of the Jews and it was quickly replaced by Persian dominance. Although some of the Jews were allowed to return to Jerusalem, not by any means did all of them do so. And their return was not an altruistic policy of returning people to their homeland and restoring their sovereign status. Persian policies were just as powerfully oriented toward gaining material wealth and control of territory as were those of any of the regimes before it. The Persian government was particularly famous for levying all kinds of taxes throughout its

Inarus Revolt—An Egyptian revolt against the Persians in 460 that had Greek support. It may have influenced Cyrus' decision to allow the Jews to return to Palestine and rebuild Jerusalem, as it would have allowed for increased military presence on the western flank of the Persian Empire facing Greece.

TURNING POINT IN THE JOURNEY

THE EXILES RETURN TO JUDAH

Bell-Ringers

1. Display the completed Learn by Doing projects. Allow time for the students to review the projects. While they are doing that, choose three readers to read aloud the suggested Scripture passages: Isaiah 5, Matthew 21:33–44, and Romans 11:23–24.

2. Connected with the Journal Assignment (page 190), call on students to discuss the importance of expressing sorrow when reconfiguring one's life after a wrong.

Teaching Approaches

1. Point out the step-by-step process in which the exiles returned to Judah from Babylon. Use Overhead 8B (online), "The Return of the Exiles." Assign the students to take notes from material as needed. Also, during the presentation share information about the central roles Ezra and Nehemiah played in the return of the exiles (see Background Information, below).

2. Call on one student to be "on the spot." Ask him or her to pretend to be King Cyrus suddenly giving the Jews their freedom and permission to return home. Next, choose others to respond in the name of the Jews to the decree. See Ezra 1 for material.

Background Information

Ezra and Nehemiah

Ezra was an expert on the Torah, which the priests in Babylon developed during the Exile. He witnessed many of the exiles no longer practicing their religion, and he said the reason was that these Jews had married outside their religious community. Ezra denounced such mixed marriages. He was trying to keep the Jewish community from becoming extinct. Ezra emphasized the importance of heredity and pure bloodlines. There was a problem with Ezra's policy: Jews grew in their identity by separation from and discrimination against people of other religions and cultures. The Samaritans, who had intermarried, opposed Ezra and his reforms.

Nehemiah was a layman, the cupbearer of King Artaxerxes I of Persia. Artaxerxes sent Nehemiah to Palestine to rebuild Jerusalem. He did it, despite opposition from the locals, in fifty-two days. Under Nehemiah, the Torah became the official moral guide for the

Chapter 8

3. Assign the research activity "Rebuilding Judah" (page 193). Refer the students to helpful Internet sites. Help the students visualize the rebuilding effort by comparing it to a modern example of rebuilding after the devastation of a hurricane, tornado, earthquake, fire, or other natural disaster.

4. Show all or part of the video *In the Beginning: Release from Babylon* (see page 185 of the TWE) as part of the presentation.

Enrichment: Report on one of the following topics: (1) Cyrus encouraged the Jews to return to Jerusalem (Ez 1:1–14); (2) The request and revenge of the Samaritans (Ez 4:1–24); (3) Completion and dedication of the Temple (Ez 6:14–22).

THE OLD TESTAMENT

post-Exilic—Referring to the time after the return of the exiles to Jerusalem in 539 B.C.

Empire and pressing peoples into forced labor for massive building projects. There was no interest in helping citizens acquire business success or economic independence on their own. In fact, the Persian government referred to all the citizens of the Persian Empire as "slaves." One famous historian of the Persian Empire wrote:

> . . . labor and production in Persia were organized on a huge scale by the central administration in a way that would seem to leave relatively little scope for what we should call modest private enterprise . . . [even] sheep raising was also organized on a large scale. . . ."4

Likewise, the Jewish priest and reformer Ezra pointed out in his public prayer that the Jews were slaves in their own land under the Persians:

> But, see, we today are slaves; and as for the land which you gave our fathers that they might eat its fruits and good things—see, we have become slaves upon it! Its rich produce goes to the kings whom you set over us because of our sins, who rule over our bodies and our cattle as they please. We are in great distress! (Neh 9:36–37).

Long-Term Exile

The prophet Jeremiah foretold of seventy years of exile for the Jews:

> Seventy years these nations shall be enslaved to the king of Babylon; but when the seventy years have elapsed, I will punish the king of Babylon and the nation and the land of the Chaldeans for their guilt, says the Lord (Jer 25:11–12).

However, **post-Exilic** Biblical writers, such as Daniel, imply that the people were still in exile in the Persian period and beyond—to the time of Hellenistic rule beginning under Alexander the Great, who conquered Palestine in 333 B.C. The regimes that followed in Alexander's wake—Hellenistic rulers who were descendents of Alexander's generals—practiced the same kind of economics and politics of material gain. Historian Peter Green describes the Hellenistic rulers who ruled Palestine from 323 (after Alexander died) through 64 (when the Roman Empire ruled Palestine directly) in the following way:

> The main, indeed the overwhelming, motivation that confronts us in these Greek or Macedonian torchbearers of Western culture, throughout the Hellenistic era, is the irresistible twin lure of power and wealth. . . ."5

The point is simply this: the Hebrews from 587 B.C. through the early Christian period lived under Imperial leaders who controlled power, wealth, territory, and human resources. In short, the Hebrew people lived under foreign rule for nearly 600 years before the time of Jesus and continued to live under Roman domination in Palestine for centuries after Jesus as well. These political, economic, and social realities provided the context

Turning Point in the Journey

Turning Point in the Journey

for the time that the Old Testament was brought together as a collection of writings. It is also the context for the entire New Testament.

In summary, what is known about the end of the Babylonian Exile is that the Persians eventually invaded Babylon and allowed at least some of the exiled Jews to return to their homeland. The Persians even sponsored some of the caravans that returned to Judah, complete with some of the holy items from the Temple that were originally captured by the Babylonians. The condition of the land and community found in Judah upon the exiles' return is difficult to assess. It is often presumed that some form of religious life continued in the ruins of the Temple, but there is no direct evidence of it.

Some conflict broke out between those who returned from exile and those who had been left behind in Judah. The prophet Ezekiel rejected the claim that the survivors in Judah had any claim to the land; he says that the new Israel should be formed by the exiles (see Ez 33:23–29). Likewise, Jeremiah saw that no good could come from the people left in Judah under Zedekiah or those who had fled to Egypt. Jeremiah compared the returning exiles and those who remained to good and bad figs:

> The good ones are very good, but the bad ones are very bad, so bad they cannot be eaten (Jer 24:3).

The exiles and former exiles who had remained faithful to Yahweh during the time of captivity are known as God's **remnant**, the remnant spoken of by the prophets, including Isaiah:

> A remnant will return, a remnant of Jacob, to the mighty God (Is 10:21).

REBUILDING JUDAH

Research and report from archaeological resources on the building campaign in Judah when the Jews returned from captivity in Babylon. Include in the report information on the rebuilding of Solomon's Temple, including differences in dimensions between the first and second Temples.

remnant—The exiles and former exiles who remained faithful to Yahweh during the time of captivity and who were expected to restore Jerusalem.

REVIEW & REFLECTION

1. When did the Babylonian regime come to an end? Who assumed power in the area with the end of the Babylonian empire?
2. What improvements were there in the condition and treatment of the exiles under the new regime? What aspects remained unchanged?
3. Who were the leaders of the Jerusalem community after the return from exile? What did they think was important to the community?

5. Homework Assignment

- Complete the "Rebuilding Judah" exercise on page 193.
- Answer the Review and Reflections questions 1–3, page 193.
- Complete the Journal Assignment, page 194. You may be asked to share what you have written with the class.
- Read the text section, "Major Themes of Writing Before, During, and After the Exile" (pages 194–197), including the separate feature, "Jonah: The Reluctant Missionary of Peace."

Review and Reflection Answers

1. The Babylonian regime came to an end in 539 B.C. when the Persians conquered the city of Babylon. The Persians assumed power.
2. A major improvement was that the Persians allowed the Israelite to return to their homeland and practice their religion. What did not change was that the Israelites were still slaves to a foreign power. Persia expected them to do all the rebuilding and to pay taxes.
3. One leader was Ezra. He thought that the people should not marry Gentiles and should return to obeying the Torah. Nehemiah also believed that the people should follow the Torah; he also urged the people to rebuild Jerusalem and the Temple.

Chapter 8

MAJOR THEMES OF WRITING BEFORE, DURING, AND AFTER THE EXILE

Bell-Ringers

1. Form triads and ask the students to share their findings from the "Rebuilding Judah" exercise. Note on the board relevant statistics like estimates on numbers of workers, materials used, and dimensions of the Temple

2. Have the students remain with their triads. Share with the students the statement, "You can never go home again." Ask them to comment on the truth of this based on what they wrote for their Journal Assignment.

JOURNAL ASSIGNMENT

- Think of a time when you looked forward to returning to a place or an activity you had really enjoyed before. Were you able to return? Was it as good as you remembered? Why, or why not? Compare your experience to the experience of the people returning to Jerusalem from exile.

Major Themes of Writing Before, During, and After the Exile

The times of the divided kingdom, the Exile, and its aftermath are arguably the most important studies for anyone who reads and prays with these sacred texts. This period of time produced the greatest amount of the material that makes up the Old Testament. Understanding the cultural, political, and religious practices of the time helps to put these texts into context. Chapter 9 will cover more of the largest section of post-Exilic writings—the Wisdom literature. For now, we will explore some of the major themes of writing during the years surrounding the Exile, including what it was like for the Jews to live under Persian rule.

A Temple-Centered People

Second Isaiah expressed a new hopefulness based on the idea that the Persians would institute a new regime, perhaps less oppressive than the Babylonian empire. But with the reality of life in Babylonian Exile ending and life under Persian rule just beginning, the Jews had a chance to reflect on what directions their life would take as the People of God.

Several questions persisted: Were they meant to return to Palestine and rebuild the Temple in Jerusalem? Or, given that there were still Jews living outside of Palestine even after the end of the Exile, was there any reason the Jews should focus on reclaiming political rule? Should they be more concerned with rededicating themselves to interior spiritual life?

Prophets Haggai and Zechariah sought to encourage the Jews to complete the rebuilding of the Temple. The returning exiles laid the foundation for the Temple in 538 B.C. but enthusiasm quickly waned. In the next years, the people worked on rebuilding their own homes and businesses, and the Temple project remained incomplete. Haggai began a campaign in 520 B.C. to encourage the people to re-start the work. Within months, the project began.

Zechariah's ministry began two months after Haggai's. He, too, encouraged the completion of the Temple. The book of Zechariah records a series of visions he received about work on the Temple and about the future glory of Jerusalem. In Zechariah 9:9–17, the prophet's oracle calls for restoration of Jerusalem led by a Messiah who comes not as a conquering warrior, but in lowliness and peace:

> See, your king shall come to you; a just savior is he, meek, and riding on an ass, on a colt, the foal of an ass (Zec 9:9).

The Temple was, in fact, rebuilt about 520–515 B.C. Neither Haggai or Zechariah recorded its completion. But many of the older people, who had seen the former Temple, were disappointed that the new structure was not as impressive. Upon the laying of its foundation:

Turning Point in the Journey

Many of the priests, Levites, and family heads, the old men who had seen the former house, cried out in sorrow as they watched the foundation of the present house being laid. Many others, however, lifted up their voices in shouts of joy, and no one could distinguish the sound of the joyful shouting from the sound of those who were weeping; for the people raised a mighty clamor which was heard afar off (Ezr 3:12–13).

For some Jews—both young and old—the rebuilding of the Temple was the absolute key to their receiving God's blessing (see Hg 2:15–19). For many, their existence under Persian rule required that their religious identity be complete, even if they were not allowed to be a politically independent entity. The completion of the Temple was key to this.

In the Persian Period (539–333 B.C.), another historical Biblical text was written for the Bible, the two books called first and second Chronicles. A great deal of the material in Chronicles was based on the older historical books of the Bible, namely Joshua, Judges, 1 and 2 Samuel, and 1 and 2 Kings. However, the historical perspective in Chronicles is much different than these other works.

In the Chronicles version, the kings of the Davidic line are praised or condemned, not so much for their military or political success, but rather for their dedication to building projects—especially the building of the Temple and the city of Jerusalem. Chronicles presents a Temple-centered version of prior Hebrew history probably because, for Jews living under Persian (and later, Hellenistic) rule, the Temple was the center of Jewish identity.

Compare the two descriptions of King Asa from the older first book of Kings and the second book of Chronicles from the Persian period. Notice the different emphasis:

From 1 Kings 15:11–13–15
Asa pleased the Lord like his forefather David, banishing the temple prostitutes from the land and removing all idols his father had made. He also deposed his grandmother Maacah from her position as queen mother, because she had made an outrageous object for Asherah. . . . Asa's heart was entirely with the Lord as long as he lived. He brought into the temple of the Lord his father's and his own votive offerings of silver, gold, and various utensils.

From 2 Chronicles 14:1–2, 4–6
Asa did what was good and pleasing to the Lord, his God, removing the heathen altars and the high places, breaking to pieces the sacred pillars, and cutting down the sacred poles. . . . He removed the high places and incense stands from all the cities of Judah, and under him the kingdom had peace. He built fortified cities in Judah, for the land had peace and no war was waged against him during these years because the Lord had given him peace. He said to Judah: "Let us build these cities and surround them with walls, towers, gates and bars. The land is still ours, for we have sought the Lord, our God; we sought him, and he has given us rest on every side." So they built and prospered.

For many Jews living under Persian rule, the building of the Temple and cities was remembered as the most important part of pre-Exilic history. The Temple's centrality to religious identity could also be maintained even for Jews living in the Diaspora. This is one reason why the High Priest, the leader of the Temple administration, rose to become the most important leader of the Jewish people from about 400 B.C. until the time of Jesus. The Temple was indeed the central institution in the life of many Jews after the Exile.

Teaching Approaches

1. Review the text reading by asking the following questions. Call on students to answer without opening their texts.

- Why are the periods of the divided kingdom, the Exile, and the post Exile important to Bible scholars? (These were the time periods when most of the Old Testament was compiled, written, and edited.)
- What was the main message of the prophet Haggai? (He urged the people to rebuild the Temple.)
- What was the main message of the prophet Zechariah? (He also urged the people to rebuild the Temple.)
- How do 1 and 2 Chronicles (written during this time) differ from the earlier historical books (Joshua, Judges, 1 and 2 Samuel, and 1 and 2 Kings)? (Chronicles praised or condemned the Israelite kings based on their dedication to building projects rather than to their devotion to Yahweh).
- Why did 1 and 2 Chronicles have this perspective? (Rebuilding the nation, especially Jerusalem and the Temple, was key to re-establishing the people's identity.)

2. Distribute copies of "Prayer Themes of the Diaspora" (Handout 8C page 284). Have the students form small groups to read the Scripture passages and discuss what the themes meant to the Israelites as well as write a common theme for each set of readings (see answers below).

Handout 8C "Prayer Themes of the Diaspora" Answers

Ezra 9:6–7 We admit and feel shame for the sins of the past.
Nehemiah 9:16–17 We are sorry that our ancestors were obstinate in their sinfulness.
Daniel 9:8 Just as our ancestors sinned, so we have sinned. We feel shame about this.
Baruch 1:15b–17 We admit that we have disobeyed God just like our ancestors did. We are contrite.
Common Theme: We are sorry for our own sins as well as for the sins of our ancestors.
Ezra 9:7–9 Even though God punished us for our sins by making us slaves, God has not abandoned us. He is with us as we try to rebuild Jerusalem.
Nehemiah 9:36–37 Our slavery to foreign kings is just punishment for our sins.
Daniel 9:12 We were warned, but did not change. God was just in destroying Jerusalem and taking it away from us.
Baruch 2:1 God warned us, and then carried out his punishment for our sins.
Common Theme: Even though we have suffered and continue to suffer, it is justice for our sins.
Ezra 9:10–11 The land itself is unclean because of our disobedience to the laws of Moses.
Nehemiah 9:13 God was with us when he spoke on Mount Sinai and gave us the commandments.
Daniel 9:5 God abandoned us because we disobeyed the commandments.
Baruch 1:18 It's our fault we are where we are now. We disobeyed the commandments.
Common Theme: We need to obey the laws of Moses once again; then God will be with us.

Chapter 8

3. Review the basic story line of the book of Jonah. For example, point out the following: God sent Jonah to warn the people of Ninevah to repent. Jonah didn't want to do this because the people of Ninevah were his enemies. He tried to get away from God by ship, but was thrown overboard and swallowed by a whale. The whale spit him out and he arrived in Ninevah where he preached God's word. The people repented, and God did not punish them, much to Jonah's regret.

4. Call on students to answer the following question:
   - What is the religious message of the book of Jonah? (Jonah represents God's People who do not follow his commands. The whale represents the more powerful nations who captured God's People and took them into exile. Like Jonah, the people were to follow God's word and do what he wanted.)

5. **Optional:** Choose several students to do a creative reading of Jonah 1–2. The students you select should take the parts of narrator, sailors, and a group to recite Jonah's prayer of Thanksgiving.

Enrichment: Write a modern version of the Jonah story. In your story, try to teach the same religious lesson as does the book of Jonah.

The Old Testament

Prayer Traditions of the Diaspora

For people living in the Diaspora, history had other lessons to teach. From post-Exilic literature, a tradition of prayers emerged that repeated several of the same themes, including:
- shame associated with the sins of ancestors (see Ezr 9:6–7; Neh 9:16–17; Dn 9:8; Bar 1:15b–17)
- exile or slavery as conditions that were warned about (Ezr 9:7–9; Neh 9:36–37; Dn 9:12; Bar 2:1)
- the importance of the Law of Moses (Ezr 9:10–11; Neh 9:13; Dn 9:5; Bar 1:18)

These samples serve to illustrate the continuity of these themes over a period exceeding hundreds of years of tradition (these books were written over a 400 year period of history), but they also raise questions about why such ideas would be continuous. The answer is that prayers are also reminders for people—reminders not to repeat the sins of the past—especially from the time of the monarchy. Second Isaiah's call for Israel to be the "Servant of God" (see pages 189-190) pointed the way to a new future.

Jonah: The Reluctant Missionary of Peace

It is unfortunate that the book of Jonah has often been written off as a mere child's story. This inspired story actually contains an important theological message. A fuller appreciation of this, however, requires that we place the book in its most likely historical context.

The book of Jonah likely comes from a late historical period, certainly after the destruction of Jerusalem in 587 B.C. Thus, the book derives from the long period of occupation of the land of the Hebrews, but also a time when thousands of Hebrews lived as minorities throughout the Diaspora.

The city of Nineveh was, for a time, the capital of the Neo-Assyrian Empire. Recall that the Assyrians conquered the northern kingdom of Israel in 722 B.C. and deported a group of the upper class from that region. In this story, Jonah is called to deliver his prophetic message to the center of one of the most feared and hated regimes the Hebrews ever faced. (Also, Nineveh is a symbol of the non-Jewish population.)

Any sane Jew feeling himself "called" to the center of the Assyrian Empire would probably hop a boat heading in the opposite direction. And that is exactly what Jonah does. But Jonah soon realizes that there is no escape from the God of the Hebrews. Even the sea monsters are subservient to God.

The heart of the book of Jonah is the psalm of thanksgiving that appears in Jonah 2:3–10. Biblical scholarship has suggested that the psalm is much older than the Book of Jonah and that the story of Jonah was modeled to fit around the psalm, illustrating the meaning (a teaching method that Jewish rabbis came to call a *midrash*).

The references in the psalm to missing the Temple (Jon 2:4), being away from the land, and the allusions to prison (Jon 2:6) all suggest that it dates from the Exile when the people in the Diaspora lamented their fate (cf. Ps 107:10–16; Ps 137; Is 42:7; Lam 3:34). So it seems clear that the book of Jonah derives much of its power and meaning by being read in the Diaspora. This is a major clue to the meaning of the text.

Jonah's news to the king and people of Nineveh has a most interesting result: The king descends from the throne, removes his robe, and all the people fast and mourn. The king also decrees:

> Every man shall turn from his evil way and from the violence he has in hand (Jon 3:8).

In other words, the Assyrians repent of their ways and change their behavior. God recognizes the Assyrian's repentance, and Jonah is furious at God's compassion. It is, of course, the same compassion that earlier saved his own sea-soaked skin. But now that God is showing compassion to an *enemy*, it is too much.

There is no escaping the power of this story: The Book of Jonah is about God's compassion on *all* people, even those who are not Jews. God cares for the well-being and transformation of all. But there is more.

The Book of Jonah is often described as a parable with a double meaning. Jonah, we must remember:
- is called by God.
- rejects the call.
- is sent into darkness.
- is released to a mission.

Does this sound familiar? This pattern is the general historical theme of the Bible, preeminently represented in the books of Joshua, Judges, 1 and 2 Samuel, and 1 and 2 Kings. In fact, some believe that the prophet Jeremiah's famous comments may have originally inspired the book of Jonah:

> He has consumed me, routed me,
> [Nebuchadnezzar, king of Babylon,]
> he has left me as an empty vessel;
> He has swallowed me like a dragon:
> filled his belly with my delights,
> and cast me out (Jer 51:34).

In this parable, *Jonah is Israel*. The people of Israel were called by God, but sinfully rejected the call and listened to their own voices. As punishment, they were sent into exile. If Jonah does represent Israel, what have the people learned from the experience of the exile? The author of Jonah teaches that there is now a radical redefinition of what it means to be the People of God. If this is true, then Jonah is a symbol of Israel herself, missionary to the world and agent of God's salvation. But Jonah is reluctant; sin and rejection of God's laws sent Israel into exile as Jonah was sent into the belly of the big fish.

With Jonah (and Second Isaiah, 49:6), the point is made that *during* the Exile some of the Jews finally came to understand the profound nature of their call from Yahweh. It was the same call that was repeated and taken up so powerfully in the teaching and example of Jesus. Jesus, too, renewed God's call and initiated his kingdom. Jesus told the people: "You are the light of the world" (Mt 5:14).

Turning Point in the Journey

6. Introduce the "Our Call to Prophecy" exercise on page 198. Go over each of the tasks listed in the exercise. Then, brainstorm with the students several situations at school, in the neighborhood, at church, and in the world at large that need improvement. Allow the students to form groups to work on the project in an area of their own choosing.

7. **Homework Assignment:**
   - Continue to work on the "Our Call to Prophecy" exercise. Firm up your plan and be prepared to present what you and your group will do
   - Answer the Review and Reflection questions 1–3, page 198.
   - Complete the Journal Assignment on page 198. (You will have a chance to share your prayer at the prayer service at the end of the chapter.)
   - Read the "Further Reflections" section in the Student Text (pages 198–199).

Chapter 8

FURTHER REFLECTIONS

Bell-Ringer
1. Call on a representative from each group to present its plan of action from the "Our Call to Prophecy" exercise to the class. Spend about two-thirds of the class time on this sharing. Tell the students that they are to carry out their plan and report on it at the beginning of the next chapter.

Teaching Approaches
1. Share the adage "Those who do not know the past are condemned to repeat it" in reviewing the material from the "Further Reflections" text. After we make mistakes, we have a choice. We can choose to keep making the same mistakes, with the same outcomes. Or we can choose to learn from our mistakes and try to change for the better. The Judeans of post-exilic times were choosing to do the latter.

2. Have the students take a practice quiz on some of the vocabulary words highlighted in this chapter. For example, have them write definitions (or sentences using the vocabulary word) for the following words:
   - **Cyrus**
   - **Judea**
   - **Post-exilic**
   - **remnant**
   - **Vineyard Song**

3. Also use the Review and Reflection questions from this chapter to help the students prepare for the Chapter 8 Test.

4. **Prayer Service:** Choose a song to call the students to prayer. For example, "Psalm 137: Let My Tounge Be Silent" by Carol Johengen (see page 183 of the TWE). Have the students recite together the World Peace Prayer (page 199). Choose a student to read Isaiah 2:2–3. Call on students to offer spontaneous prayers of sorrow using or based on the prayers they wrote for the Journal Assignment, page 198. Conclude by playing a recording of or leading singing of "City of God" by Dan Schutte (page 183 of TWE) or another appropriate song.

5. **Homework Assignment:**
   - Study for the Chapter 8 Test.
   - Complete chosen tasks from the "Our Call to Prophecy" exercise.

THE OLD TESTAMENT

OUR CALL TO PROPHECY

Two common elements of the prophets are that they are called by God and that they communicate with God. We are all called by God to a unique ministry based on our God-given talents. Exercise your prophetic ministry by doing the following:
- Reflect on and name situations in your own life, your neighborhood, your school, your Church, and the world that need improvement.
- Before working for change in the areas listed above, name several ways you can change personally to be a better person.
- Choose at least two of the areas and develop a concrete plan for improvement for the issue you named.
- Enact the plan. This may mean asking others to join you in your efforts, contacting agencies, writing letters, or doing some hands-on work (e.g., collecting food for the homeless vs. writing a letter to inquire about what is being done to feed the homeless).
- Write a follow-up piece to your planning and action. Answer the following questions: What was most difficult about this experience? How was the experience similar to that of Old Testament prophets? Also, write a prayer for yourself and the people you served as part of this experience.

REVIEW & REFLECTION

1. When was the Temple rebuilt? What made rebuilding the Temple so important to the people returning to Jerusalem from exile?
2. What is the biggest thematic difference between the history presented in 1 and 2 Kings and that in 1 and 2 Chronicles?
3. What three themes emerge in the prayers of post-Exilic literature?

JOURNAL ASSIGNMENT
- Write you own prayer expressing sorrow or shame for a wrong you have done, awareness of the consequences of that wrong act, and understanding of God's desire for you not to repeat it. (Note: You do not have to mention the wrongdoing by name.)

Further Reflections

The returning Jews from Babylonian Exile longed for the restoration of the monarchy. There was also considerable feeling that the enemies who perpetrated the horrendous series of events on the Jews should be punished. Consider Psalm 137, written from the time of the Exile. The psalm begins by expressing the sadness of the people, but concludes with a call for vengeance:

> Remember Lord, against Edom
> that day at Jerusalem.
> They said: "Level it, level it down to its foundations!"
>
> Fair Babylon, you destroyer,
> happy those who pay you back
> the evil you have done us!
> Happy those who seize your children
> and smash them against a rock! (Ps 137:7–9).

In short, some Jews looked for the restoration of Davidic power and were also seeking vengeance for their defeat.

On the other hand, while some Jews supported a violent restoration of the monarchy and punishment of enemies, the Exile also inspired another type of

---

Review and Reflection Answers
1. The Temple was rebuilt around 520–515 B.C. Rebuilding the Temple was important because it represented God's presence among the people, and the people's desire to return to the law of Moses.
2. The history presented in 1 and 2 Kings praised or condemned the kings of Israel and Judah for their obedience to God. The history presented in 1 and 2 Chronicles praised or condemned the kings for their building projects.
3. The three themes in post-exilic prayers are: shame and sorrow for sins of the past; a recognition that what has happened to the people is just because of their sins; a desire to return to the law of Moses.

thinking among the authors of Scripture. In this view, the Jews were to be a People of God who would reach out to and inspire other nations. Chapter 2 of Isaiah explains how the people will be delivered from war and violence by the coming of a restored world under God, when all nations will stream to the mountain of God:

> In days to come,
> The mountain of the Lord's house
>   shall be established as the highest mountain,
>   and raised above the hills.
> All nations shall stream toward it;
>   many peoples shall come and say:
> "Come, let us climb the Lord's mountain,
>   to the house of the God of Jacob,
> That he may instruct us in his ways,
>   and we may walk in his paths"
> (Is 2:2–3).

For these Jews, the Exile created a new sense of mission. Israel was not merely going back to its old and violent ways. It was going to become a nation recommitted to the covenant and to becoming the People of God, which would eventually be embodied in Jesus Christ.

● *Learn by Doing*
Read the Vineyard Song in Isaiah 5. Visualize the scene described. Also read Matthew 21:33–44 and Romans 11:23–24. Create in whatever media you choose some of the images of God's Chosen People as the vine attached to the Lord.

● *Called to Prayer*
> Lead us
>   from death to life,
>   from falsehood to truth,
>   from despair to hope,
>   from fear to trust.
> Lead us
>   from hate to love,
>   from war to peace.
> Let peace fill our hearts,
>   let peace fill our world,
>   let peace fill our universe. Amen.
>   —World Peace Prayer

Notes
1. John Bright, *History of Israel* (Westminster: Philadelphia, 1981) pp. 345, 347 respectively.
2. 80, "Post-Exilic Palestine: An Archaeological Report," S. S. Weinberg, *Proceedings of the Israel Academy of Sciences and Humanities* 1971(4) 78–97.
3. 46–47, Weissbach, *Das Hauptheiligtum des Marduk in Babylon* (Leipzig, 1938). The translation from Weissbach's German is my own.
4. J. M. Cook, *The Persian Empire* (Shocken: New York, 1983) 89–90.
5. Peter Green, *Alexander to Actium* (University of California Press, 1993) 187.

Chapter 8 Parish Religious Education Adaptation
- Pages 14–15 of the TWE describes several models for adapting the chapters of the Student Text for a parish religious education setting. The Chapter 8 Parish Religious Education Adaptation (online) offers ideas for a one- to two-hour lesson.
- Assign Chapter 8 for reading prior to the first class session. See the Parish Religious Education lesson plan for the assigned questions from Chapter 7.

TURNING POINT IN THE JOURNEY

CHAPTER 8 TEST

Teaching Approaches
1. Distribute the Chapter 8 Test (online at **avemariapress.com**). Remind the students to take their time on the essay (worth 12 points), making sure to answer each of the related questions in detail. Allow the students to use additional paper for the essay, if needed.

2. Preview Chapter 9 after you have collected all of the tests.

Chapter 8 Test Answers
Part 1: True or False: 1. 0; 2. +; 3. +; 4. 0; 5. +; 6. 0; 7. +; 8. 0.

Part 2: Multiple Choice: 9. d; 10. a; 11. b; 12. c; 13. c; 14. d; 15. b; 16. c.

Part 3: Short Fill-ins: 17. Isaiah/Micha; 18. King Johiachin /Babylon/Zedekiah; 19. eat it; 20. dry bones; 21a. the destruction of Jerusalem; 21b. the "Oracle of Hope;" 21c. the "Oracle against the Nations."

Part 4: Short Answer: 22. Ezekiel is transported in the vision from exile to the Temple in Jerusalem, stopping on four occasions, each time closer to the Temple. He sees pagan worship and ritual performed right up to the steps of the Temple. Then he is taken to a hillside overlooking Jerusalem where he sees the Spirit of God leaving the city. Although the vision is horrifying, there is comfort in the knowledge that God is not bound to the city of Jerusalem. The exiled Jews need not fear that they have been separated from God just because they no longer live in Jerusalem.

Introducing Chapter 9

Chapter 9 introduces Biblical "Wisdom literature" especially in the books of Job, Psalms, Proverbs, Ecclesiastes, Song of Songs, Sirach, and Wisdom. One of the purposes of this literature is to help people determine the best way to live their lives. Although the biblical authors borrowed a lot from the Wisdom literature of neighboring countries, there is a core message that remains unique: one's relationship with God is the beginning of all wisdom. Yahweh is the source of all wisdom and understanding.

In general, Wisdom literature uses short, often contrasting statements to express insights into the meaning of the life and the source of happiness. Some statements also give advice about family relationships, friendships, and money management. While many of the wisdom sayings were written by the affluent for the affluent, other wisdom sayings apply to people of all economic strata.

The spirituality found in the Wisdom books differs in emphasis from the spirituality found in other books of the Bible. The Wisdom books focus on creation and God as Creator—a broader concept than Yahweh as the God of the covenant with Abraham, Jacob, and Joseph. Wisdom literature became particularly popular among the Israelites in the post-Exilic period, perhaps due to their need to renew their vocation and identity as God's People.

Also found in Chapter 9 is a brief overview of biblical "apocalyptic literature." Such literature is found primarily in the book of Daniel, although it may also be found in portions of Isaiah, Ezekiel, Zechariah, and Joel. Apocalyptic literature usually uses symbolic language to teach about present issues as if they were in the past or future. The "visions" show what God will do in the future. Their message is that God is still in control, despite historic evidence to the contrary.

Both Wisdom literature and apocalyptic literature in the Bible can teach us to live in the present moment and act as members of God's People. These instructions can be a guide for moral living.

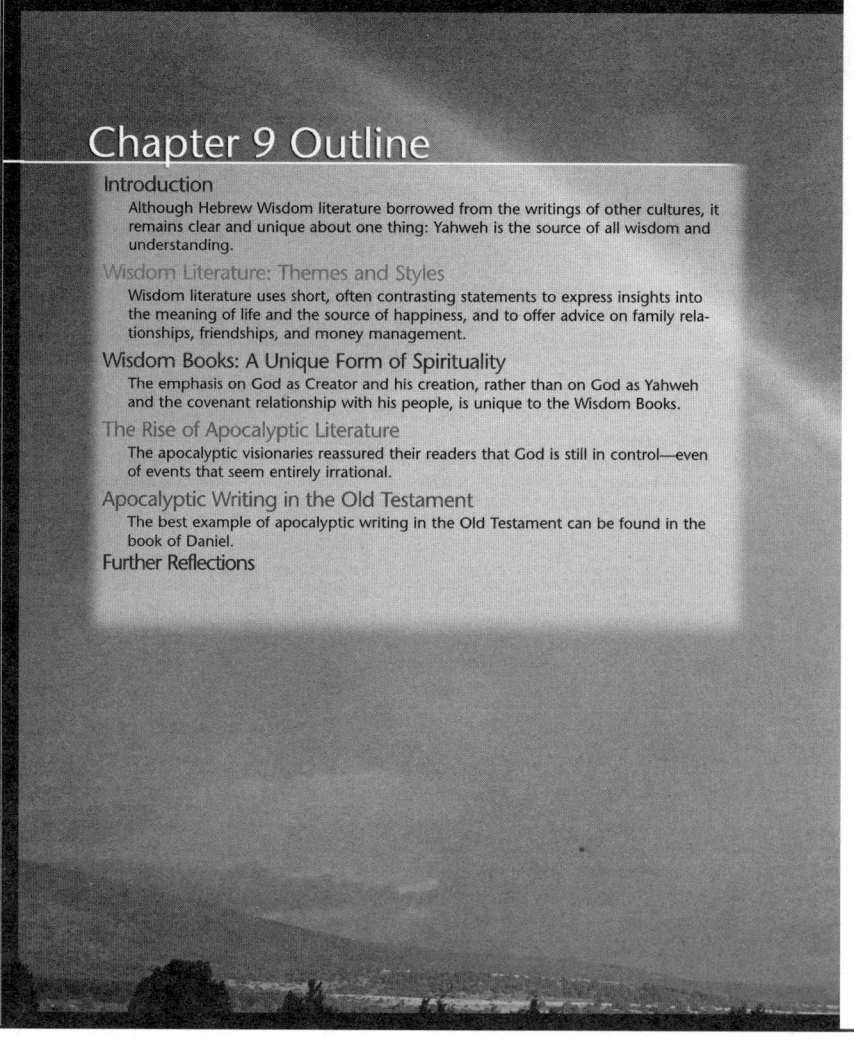

Chapter 9 Outline

Introduction
Although Hebrew Wisdom literature borrowed from the writings of other cultures, it remains clear and unique about one thing: Yahweh is the source of all wisdom and understanding.

Wisdom Literature: Themes and Styles
Wisdom literature uses short, often contrasting statements to express insights into the meaning of life and the source of happiness, and to offer advice on family relationships, friendships, and money management.

Wisdom Books: A Unique Form of Spirituality
The emphasis on God as Creator and his creation, rather than on God as Yahweh and the covenant relationship with his people, is unique to the Wisdom Books.

The Rise of Apocalyptic Literature
The apocalyptic visionaries reassured their readers that God is still in control—even of events that seem entirely irrational.

Apocalyptic Writing in the Old Testament
The best example of apocalyptic writing in the Old Testament can be found in the book of Daniel.

Further Reflections

Background Notes for the Teacher

Some people have difficulty with "real" life. Wisdom literature helps us to find that God is present in all human experience. We find God through our day-to-day challenges, not in addition to them. The Wisdom books repeatedly say—through proverbs, riddles, parables, and metaphors—that God not only creates the world but also sustains it. God is with us in everything we do. God's Spirit helps us to discern meaning and find happiness in the midst of our experiences.

Basically, the Wisdom books deal with human welfare, dignity, virtues, and values. They teach us how to be successful in God's eyes; they show us how to pursue the good. They help us to discern what is right and wrong in each situation of life. They assure us that we will be rewarded for choosing good and punished for choosing evil.

An overview of the Wisdom books shows the following:
- The book of Job primarily deals with the problem of suffering including why bad things happen to good people.
- Psalms is a collection of religious song-poems that are prayers of praise, contrition, and thanksgiving to God.
- Proverbs is a collection of short sayings that give advice about daily living.
- Ecclesiastes points out the vanity of living superficially. What gives meaning to life is our relationship with God.
- The Song of Songs is a group of love poems that uses human love as a symbol of God's relationship with us.
- Wisdom emphasizes traditional Jewish teachings and reinterprets them for people living in a Greek culture.
- Sirach is a collection of proverbs that exhort people to remain faithful to their religious traditions, despite secular pressures.

Resources

Music Suggestions: see page 206
Printed Materials: see page 208
Audiovisual Materials: see page 215
Internet Links: see page 218

CHAPTER 9
A SPIRITUAL JOURNEY:
A Look at Wisdom and Apocalyptic Literature

Background Notes continued

The Wisdom books are intended to be used. The students will be encouraged to turn to these books in the Bible for help when they have their own questions about life and its meaning today.

Apocalyptic literature is a highly symbolic style of writing in which truths are revealed within the framework of a narrative. The primary example of apocalyptic literature in the Old Testament is in the book of Daniel.

Advance Preparations

- Instead of teaching this chapter on a strictly discursive level, aim at teaching the students on an affective level as well. Use the videos on the psalms to help you achieve this goal. Allow time throughout the week for reflection and silence on the "big" life questions the students may be asking themselves. What is the meaning of life? What is my purpose in life? Why do good people suffer and/or die? How do we find happiness?
- Obtain and preview any videos you wish to use during this chapter.
- Obtain recordings of music you wish to use in the chapter prayer service.
- Photocopy the Handouts you will use during your lesson plan.
- Preview the assignments suggested in this chapter, including the Learn by Doing exercise on page 222 which lists making a collage with magazine photos as one assignment option.

Relevant Teachings from Church Documents

- And so we see the Holy Spirit, the principal author of Sacred Scripture, often attributing actions to God without mentioning any secondary causes. This is not a "primitive mode of speech," but a profound way of recalling God's primacy and absolute Lordship over history and the world, (Cf. *Is* 10:5–15; 45:5–7; *Dt* 32:39; *Sir* 11:14.) and so of educating his people to trust in him. The prayer of the Psalms is the great school of this trust. (Cf. *Ps* 22; 32; 35; 103; 138; *et al.*) (*CCC*, 304)
- At the end of time, the Kingdom of God will come in its fullness. (*CCC*, 1060)
- The People of the "poor"—those who, humble and meek, rely solely on their God's mysterious plans, who await the justice, not of men but of the Messiah—are in the end the great achievement of the Holy Spirit's hidden mission during the time of the promises that prepare for Christ's coming. It is this quality of heart, purified and enlightened by the Spirit, which is expressed in the Psalms. (*CCC*, 716)
- In the Psalms David, inspired by the Holy Spirit, is the first prophet of Jewish and Christian prayer. The prayer of Christ, the true Messiah and Son of David, will reveal and fulfill the meaning of this prayer. (*CCC*, 2579)
- The books of the Old Testament provide an understanding of God and humanity and make clear to all how a just and merciful God deals with humankind. These books, even though they contain matters which are imperfect and provisional, nevertheless contain authentic divine teaching. Christians should accept with reverence these writings, which express a lively sense of God, which are a storehouse of sublime teaching on God and of sound wisdom on human life, as well as a wonderful treasury of prayers; in them, too, the mystery of our salvation is implicitly present. (Vatican II, *Dogmatic Constitution on Divine Revelation*, #15)

Chapter Objectives

The students will be able to:

- overview the Wisdom books of the Old Testament—Job, Psalms, Proverbs, Ecclesiastes, Sirach, Wisdom, and Song of Songs.
- discover that true wisdom is centered in one's relationship with God.
- see that faith can grow from reflection on creation and daily relationships as well as through revelation.
- become aware of the themes and styles of writing found in the Wisdom literature.
- understand the nature and meaning of apocalyptic literature found in the Bible.
- relate the Wisdom literature and apocalyptic literature of the Old Testament to the teachings and parables of Jesus.
- apply the message of the Old Testament's wisdom and apocalyptic literature to modern life.

CHAPTER 9

INTRODUCTION
WISDOM LITERATURE: THEMES AND STYLES

Bell-Ringers

1. Return the graded Chapter 8 Tests. Discuss any questions the students may have concerning them.

2. Call on volunteers to report their experiences from the "Our Call to Prophecy" exercise (page 198). Ask the students to share any insights they gained because of the projects, especially what they found most similar to experiences of the Old Testament prophets.

3. On the board or overhead, print **wisdom**. Ask the students to brainstorm a definition for this word. Have a volunteer check the dictionary. Then direct the students to the Journal Assignment on page 203. Have them base their letters to "younger students" on the definition for wisdom discussed in class. Then have the students share their letters with a partner. The partners should comment on how well the letter would speak to a younger person.

THE OLD TESTAMENT

Wisdom literature—Collections of wise sayings, proverbs, and short stories that offer insights into the proper way to live. Hebrew Wisdom literature began to be collected during the Exile and the post-Exilic period.

apocalyptic literature—A highly symbolic style of writing in which hidden truths are revealed within a narrative framework. The revelation is often delivered by an angelic or visionary being.

Introduction

After the Exile, the Persians, and later the Greeks, ruled over the Israelites. Then came Roman domination, which lasted through the life of Christ and after. At this time, two unique literary responses to faith emerged and became refined in the Jewish communities living in the Diaspora—Wisdom literature and apocalyptic literature. Both forms of literature focused on four main themes: God's creation, the natural laws, the future, and the meaning of life itself.

Wisdom literature was a part of many different cultures in the Middle East. These various cultures all had collections of wise sayings, proverbs, and short stories to help people deepen their faith and understand how to live. The Jewish wisdom authors borrowed from the collections of nations such as Egypt, and those peoples likely borrowed from Jewish writings as well for additions to their own collections. In the Old Testament, Wisdom literature includes the books of Job, Psalms, Proverbs, Ecclesiastes, Sirach, and Song of Songs.

While Hebrew tradition borrowed and adapted a great deal from the writings of other cultures, it remained clear and unique about one thing:

> The beginning of wisdom is the fear of the Lord, and knowledge of the Holy One is understanding (Prv 9:10).

According to Hebrew Wisdom literature, people are to reverence God and respect his power. Humans should know that God is the Creator, and we are only the created. The first nine chapters of the book of Wisdom express "fear of the Lord" as the moving force behind a wise person's way of life.

The second form of literature to be examined in this chapter is known as **apocalyptic literature**. The Greek word *apokalypsis* means "revelation" or "unveiling." Apocalyptic literature claims to reveal or uncover the truth. The second half of the book of Daniel is the only example of purely apocalyptic literature in the Old Testament. Portions of Isaiah (24–27), Ezekiel (38–39), Zechariah (1:7–6:8), and Joel (2:1-11; 4:1–21) are other examples of the development in that direction. Between the third century B.C. and the second century A.D. other apocalyptic books—both Jewish and Christian—were written. The Revelation to John in the New Testament is the best known of these.

Eleventh century carving depicting Daniel in the lions den

202

Resources
Music Suggestions

"Center of My Life" by Paul Inwood from *Come to Set us Free* (St. Thomas More); *United as One 2* or *Breaking Bread* (OCP); *Gather* (GIA).

"On Eagle's Wings" by Michael Joncas from *On Eagle's Wings* (OCP [NALR]), *Young People's Glory & Praise Vol. 1.* (OCP [NALR]), *Glory & Praise 2* (OCP [NALR]); *Breaking Bread* or *Spirit Song* (OCP); *Gather* (GIA).

"Only in God" by John Foley, SJ from *Glory & Praise 2nd Ed.* (OCP [NALR]); *Gather* (GIA).

"Psalm 19: Lord, You have the Words" by David Haas from *Gather* (GIA).

"Psalm 25: To You, O Lord" by Marty Haugen from *Gather* (GIA).

"Psalm 27: The Lord Is My Light" by David Haas from *Gather* (GIA).

"Psalm 91: Be with Me, Lord" by Marty Haugen from *With Open Hands, Celebration Series: Psalms for the Church Year, Celebrate, Gather* (GIA).

"Psalm 95: If Today You Hear God's Voice" by David Haas from *Gather* (GIA).

"Psalm 100: We Are God's People" by David Haas from *Celebrate* or *Gather* (GIA).

"Psalm 110: The Name of God" by David Haas in *Gather* (GIA).

"Psalm 122: I Was Glad" by David Haas in *Gather* (GIA).

"Psalm 137: Let My Tongue Be Silent" by Carl Johengen in *Gather* (GIA).

"Sing a New Song" by Dan Schutte from *Breaking Bread* (OCP); *Glory and Praise* (OCP [NALR], and *Gather* (GIA).

"Taste and See" by James Moore in *Gather* (GIA).

"You Are Near" by Dan Schutte from *Neither Silver Nor Gold* (OCP [NALR]), *Glory & Praise 1* (OCP [NALR]), *Young People's Glory & Praise Vol. 1.* (OCP [NALR]), *Breaking Bread* (OCP); *Gather* (GIA).

A Spiritual Journey

A Spiritual Journey

REVIEW & REFLECTION

1. What is Wisdom literature? Give examples of Wisdom literature from the Old Testament.
2. Describe apocalyptic literature and give an example of it from the Old Testament.
3. What is unique about the Wisdom literature of the Bible when compared to the Wisdom literature of Persia, Egypt, or the other cultures that influenced the Hebrew community?

JOURNAL ASSIGNMENT

- Wisdom is a gift of the Holy Spirit. Reflect on how you have grown in wisdom since you were a young child. Write a letter to a younger person explaining what you have learned about life or relationships.

Wisdom Literature: Themes and Styles

The purpose of Wisdom literature is fairly clear. Wisdom literature has to do with gaining what is called in Hebrew, *hokma* (wisdom). The wisdom described is basically moral in character, involving lessons in truth, moderation, prudence, and kindness.

Many people seek guidelines, proverbs, or general principles to help them determine the best way to live their lives. Some may ask an older or more experienced person for his or her opinion of a decision or an idea. Sometimes a favored teacher or coach will impart lasting wisdom through short sentences that are often repeated frequently enough that they are committed to memory.

The Book of Proverbs is precisely that—a collection of short, wise sayings—so it is a good place to begin looking at Wisdom literature. One characteristic of proverbs specifically, and Wisdom literature in general, is how universal they are. The message of any wise saying is usually applicable between cultures across different eras as well. Consider the following two "proverbs":

1. The journey of folly must be traveled a second time.
2. Don't be proud of your knowledge, but consult the ignorant and the wise. The limits of art are not reached; no artist's skills are perfect.

Both of these sayings strike us as quite true and wise, even though the first saying is taken from a modern, twenty-first century African culture, while the second comes from Ancient Egypt and is over 4,000 years old. Both sayings communicate their message perfectly well for today's audience. This is the fascinating thing about wisdom—it seems to apply to anyone, anywhere. Perhaps this is because human nature does not change much from culture to culture or over the centuries. People everywhere seek answers to the meaning of life and want to live it the best way possible. People are still

Teaching Approaches

1. Read or summarize the Introduction. Take some time to allow the students to browse the Scripture references listed in the text and read them from the Bible. This will help them to get an idea of "Wisdom literature" and "apocalyptic literature."

2. Assign the Review and Reflection questions (answers below), page 203, to complete in class. Remind the students to keep a written record of their answers to use as a study guide for the chapter test.

3. Ask the students to read the opening section of "Wisdom Literature: Themes and Styles" (stop at "Wisdom in the Bible"). Then have the students suggest other popular wisdom sayings they are familiar with. Print some of the suggestions on the board.

4. Point out the exercise, "Your Life and Wisdom Literature" (page 204). Have the students begin the assignment, focusing on practical ways these passages apply to their own lives.

5. **Homework Assignment**:
   - Complete the "Your Life and Wisdom Literature" exercise.
   - Read the text sub-section "Wisdom in the Bible" (pages 204–205).
   - Write answers to the Review and Reflection questions 1–2, page 205. For question 1, write your own life questions that relate to the aspects of wisdom.

Enrichment: Locate the Wisdom books in your Bible. Print their names and page numbers in the form of a table of contents on an index card. Use the card as a reference for easy access to these books.

Enrichment: Brainstorm a list of wise sayings which people use today. For example, "A penny saved is a penny earned."

Review and Reflection Answers

1. Wisdom literature includes wise sayings, proverbs, and short stories that help people deepen their faith and understand how to live. Old Testament Wisdom literature is made up of the books of Job, Psalms, Proverbs, Ecclesiastes, Sirach, and Song of Songs.
2. Apocalyptic literature reveals or uncovers a hidden truth. The book of Daniel is the only example of purely apocalyptic literature in the Old Testament. Other examples include portions of Isaiah (24–27), Ezekiel (38–39), Zechariah (1:7–6:8) and Joel (2:1–22; 4:1–21).
3. The Wisdom literature of the Bible is unique in that it cites a personal relationship with God as the source of true wisdom.

Chapter 9

Wisdom in the Bible

Bell-Ringer

1. Divide the class into eight small groups. Assign each group responsibility for one scripture passage from the "Your Life and Wisdom Literature" exercise. Have the groups develop a list of applications to be shared with the class. For example, for Sirach 3:1–16 (duties for parents), students might mention how, as adults, they may have to care for their parents. When a list has been made, divide the groups again so that each passage is represented by a person in a new teaching group. Instruct those "teachers" to share their applications for their particular passage.

THE OLD TESTAMENT

YOUR LIFE AND WISDOM LITERATURE

Consider this exercise. Ask yourself what you think about when you are on your own time—when your mind is free from thoughts about work, school, or activities. Where does your mind go in its wandering? Probably to things like money, your goals in life, relationships, and the meaning of life. These are precisely the things that the Wisdom Books of the Old Testament—Job, Psalms, Proverbs, Ecclesiastes, Song of Songs, Sirach (Ecclesiasticus), and Wisdom—address. The subject of Wisdom literature is life itself! Read the following passages from the book of Sirach. For each passage, write one way you will apply it to your life or how you will make a greater effort to follow it in your life:

- Sirach 2 (duties to God)
- Sirach 3:1–16 (duties to parents)
- Sirach 4:20–21 (sincerity and justice)
- Sirach 5:11–6:1 (sincerity in speech)
- Sirach 6:5–17 (true friendship)
- Sirach 17:19–27 (return to God)
- Sirach 19:5–16 (proper use of speech)
- Sirach 23:7–15 (proper use of the tongue)

made happy or unhappy in the same ways. They want to know why they are here, what the point of life is, what will bring them the most happiness, how best to get along with other people, and what will be the most meaningful work for them to do with their lives. Wisdom offers insights into just these sorts of perennial questions.

It should hardly come as a surprise then that some of the same wisdom sayings from the book of Proverbs appear in ancient Egyptian writings. Although the Hebrew authors needed to resist any encroachment of foreign religion in their worship of Yahweh, they were more willing to exchange insights into less explicitly theological questions with their foreign neighbors. The early American statesman, Benjamin Franklin, followed similar principles. Franklin was fascinated with short, wise sayings and collected a number of them to pass on to his friends. Many of them are still familiar today, for example:

- Early to bed, early to rise, makes a man healthy, wealthy and wise.
- A penny saved is a penny earned.

These sayings, too, could apply to anyone, anywhere, at any time.

The Wisdom Books (listed in the sidebar at left) share styles as well as the themes we have been discussing. One popular writing style contrasts the behaviors of a wise person with those of a foolish person. Here are some examples from the book of Proverbs:

A wise son makes his father glad,
  but a foolish son is a grief to his mother (Prv 10:1).

Wisdom builds her house,
  but Folly tears hers down with her own hands (Prv 14:1).

A wise son makes his father glad,
  but a fool of a man despises his mother (Prv 15:20).

Jesus taught using this same formula:

Everyone who listens to these words of mine and acts on them will be like a wise man who built his house on rock. . . . And everyone who listens to these words of mine but does not act on them will be like a fool who built his house on sand (Mt 7:24, 26).

Wisdom in the Bible

The wisdom movement originated outside Israel in neighboring nations, where it typically revolved around a sage who operated within the organized government and was supported by its leaders. A *sage* is defined as a person venerated for his or her experience, judgment, and wisdom. The second book of Samuel describes a "gifted woman of Tekoa" who was sought out for her advice (2 Sm 14:2). However, most sages identified in the Old Testament seem to have been the "wise counselors" of other nations,

204

Resources
Printed Materials

"Wisdom, Wisdom Literature and" "Wisdom of Solomon" in *Dictionary of the Bible*, ed. by John L. McKenzie, S.J. (New York, NY: Macmillan Publishing Co., Inc., 1965), pp. 929–933.

"Wisdom," "Wisdom Literature," and "Wisdom of Solomon" in *The Oxford Companion to the Bible*, ed. by Bruce M. Metzger and Michael D. Coogan. (New York, NY: Oxford University Press, 1993), pp. 800–805.

Boadt, Lawrence E., C.S.P. "Introduction to Wisdom Literature" in *The Collegeville Bible Commentary,* ed. by Dianne Bergant, C.S.A. and Robert J. Karris, O.F.M. (Collegeville, MN: The Liturgical Press, 1989), pp. 634–643.

Collins, John J. "Old Testament Apocalypticism and Eschatology" in *The New Jerome Biblical Comm*entary, ed. by Raymond E. Brown, S.S., Joseph A. Fitzmyer, S.J., and Roland E. Murphy, O.Carm. (Englewood Cliffs, NJ: Prentice Hall, 1990), pp. 298–304.

Murphy, Roland E., O.Carm. "Introduction to Wisdom Literature" in *The New Jerome Biblical Comm*entary, ed. by Raymond E. Brown, S.S., Joseph A. Fitzmyer, S.J., and Roland E. Murphy, O.Carm. (Englewood Cliffs, NJ: Prentice Hall, 1990), pp. 447–452.

Reese, James M. "Wisdom of Solomon" in *Harper's Bible Commentary*, ed. by James L. Mays. (San Francisco, CA: Harper & Row Publishers, 1988), pp. 820–835.

and they are generally not well thought of by the Old Testament authors. For example:

> Utter fools are the princes
> of Zoan!
> the wisest of Pharaoh's
> advisers give stupid
> counsel (Is 19:11).

I will make [Babylon's] princes and her wise men drunk, her governors, her prefects, and her warriors, so that they sleep an eternal sleep, never to awaken, says the King whose name is the Lord of hosts (Jer 51:57).

Sages are rarely mentioned in Israel itself, so it's uncertain who the authors of the Biblical wisdom sayings might have been. It may be that the authors of Wisdom literature in the Bible were been men with experience and wealth in ancient Israel. Consider this example from Proverbs:

> He is in a bad way who becomes surety [takes on a loan] for another,
> but he who hates giving pledges is safe (Prv 11:15).

Obviously, poor people would not have to worry about whether or not they should accept another person's debt. No one making such a loan would consider their pledge to be worth much in the first place.

Also, note this passage from the book of Sirach:

> Seek not from the Lord
> authority,
> nor from the king a
> place of honor.

This passage advises people to remain humble before a powerful person who might be easily offended. Only the wealthy would be in a position to meet royalty on any regular basis. Passages such as these are the basis for the supposition that the upper class authored much of Wisdom literature.

Some wisdom sayings, however, deal with issues and use images that come from the simpler life of the majority of the people—family concerns, reputation, and images taken from the experience of agriculture, farming, and herding. This makes it more likely that the wisdom sayings in the Bible were collected from all levels of society.

Relief from the Egyptian chapel of Pta'h-hotep

REVIEW & REFLECTION

1. What is the purpose of Wisdom literature? What questions does it try to answer?
2. Describe a common style of wisdom writing found in Proverbs. Where else in the Bible can you find this style?

A SPIRITUAL JOURNEY

Teaching Approaches

1. Keep the students in their teaching groups to work on the first Journal Assignment, page 206. Allow sufficient time for the students to work as a group to write examples of proverbs. Then call for class sharing. Ask representatives from each group to read the selected proverbs and tell how they might be applied by teens today.

2. Allow time in class for the students to work individually on the second Journal Assignment. You may wish to provide art media so that the students can print their favorite proverbs creatively and display them around the classroom.

3. **Homework Assignment**:
   - Read "Wisdom Books: A Unique Form of Spirituality" through the sub-section "Job" in the text. (pages 206–208)
   - Read the book of Job from the Bible.
   - In your journal, write answers to the questions from "Christian Views of Suffering" (page 208).

Review and Reflection Answers

1. The purpose of Wisdom literature is to teach people wisdom involving truth, moderation, prudence, and kindness.
2. A common style of writing in Proverbs is to contrast the behaviors of a wise person with those of a foolish person. Jesus uses this same formula in Matthew 7:24, 36.

Chapter 9

WISDOM BOOKS: A UNIQUE FORM OF SPIRITUALITY
Job

Bell-Ringer
1. Have the students meet with a partner to discuss the journal answers from "Christians View of Suffering." Call on volunteers to offer short summaries on each question for the entire class.

2. Call on several students to form a panel and address this query: Describe a time when your suffering had a positive effect in your life.

Teaching Approaches
1. Make the following points to introduce the lesson and to review the opening section of the homework reading:
- Solomon probably did not write the Wisdom books, even though they are often attributed to him.
- Most of the Wisdom books were written after the Exile.
- The Wisdom books were popular for several reasons: (1) Wisdom literature was popular in other cultures, and the Jews wanted to collect their own texts of wise sayings. (2) General wisdom sayings were something the Jews had in common with other cultures. (3) Wisdom literature was a comfort to people living under foreign rule. (4) Wisdom literature helped to train young people in the ways of the Jewish faith.

2. Briefly summarize the story of Job: Job is a rich man, a friend of God, who loses everything. Although he suffers greatly and doesn't understand why God has sent him so much pain and misfortune, he remains faithful to God. In the end, God restores everything he lost.

Enrichment: The book of Job reads like a play. Rewrite the prologue (Job 1–2) in play form. Choose classmates to take on the roles. Plan to enact it for the rest of the class.

JOURNAL ASSIGNMENT
- Spend a few minutes thinking about your friends and about friendship in general. Write two or three short sentences (your own proverbs), using the contrasting style described in the text, that express your views on friendship. (Perhaps describe how a friend should be chosen or what you must do to be a good friend.)
- Look through the book of Proverbs for a few minutes. Are there any proverbs there that you are familiar with? Write them down. Then find a few more that you think would help you live better. Write them down, too.

Wisdom Books: A Unique Form of Spirituality

Wisdom literature in the Old Testament is a unique form of spirituality. Except in the later book of Sirach, the central themes and characters of the Old Testament (the Exodus, the Patriarchs, Yahweh's presence in history, and the Law of Moses) scarcely appear in Biblical Wisdom literature.

This is surprising. These teachings and people were essential to the religious identity of the Jews. It would seem logical, then, that these central teachings and characters—especially the Law of Moses—would find a prominent place in Wisdom literature with its teachings about the meaning of life and how to live. But for the most part, they do not. Instead, Hebrew Wisdom literature focuses more on God as Creator and on creation itself. Readers discover who God is by studying what he has made. The tough questions presented by God to Job are an example of this:

> Where were you when I founded the earth?
> Tell me, if you have understanding.
> Who determined its size; do you know?
> Who stretched out the measuring line for it?
> Into what were its pedestals sunk, and who laid the cornerstone,
> While the morning stars sang in chorus and all the sons of God shouted for joy? (Jb 38:4–7).

Everything about God's identity in this passage centers on God as Creator rather than as Yahweh, the God of the Patriarchs, the Chosen People, and the Mosaic covenant. Wisdom literature describes God by what he has made; it is descriptive, rational, and objective. This is a different form of spirituality than that found in the writings of the prophets, which tend to be more emotive and charismatic.

The spirituality of wisdom—knowing God by what he has made—is actually very similar to the faith of those today who seek God through their discoveries as physicists, astronomers, biologists, or mathematicians. Their studies give them a more profound sense of the work and accomplishments of God. Modern science is very similar to Hebrew Wisdom literature in that it, too, is rational and based on observation. The very presence of Wisdom literature in the Bible suggests that faith can come from rationality and careful study as well as through revelation.

Is all Hebrew Wisdom literature from the post-Exilic era of Biblical history? This is likely so, although some part of the Proverbs may be from as early as the time of the kings. It is traditional to assign much of Wisdom literature to King Solomon, but this is mainly because Solomon was known as a wise king (see 1 Kgs 3). Solomon certainly did not write all of the Wisdom literature, or even all of the book of Wisdom which is sometimes called the "Wisdom of Solomon."

Many suggestions have been made to explain why Wisdom literature became popular in the post-Exilic Diaspora. They include:
- The Jews were impressed with the wisdom teachings in other cultures and were inspired to collect their own texts of wise sayings and stories.
- Based in human realities, Wisdom literature could be shared with people of other cultures. It was an area of common ground between Jews and foreigners.
- Wisdom sayings were comforting to a minority people living under foreign rule. They reminded the Jews of how to live a good and prosperous life and of their status as God's Chosen People.
- The Diaspora was seen as a threat to the Jewish community. Parents were concerned about their children remaining grounded in their faith and staying out of trouble. It has been suggested that as urban areas formed after the time of Alexander the Great (323 B.C.), a delinquent element of teens was also present (see, for example, Proverbs 1:10–15). Wisdom literature was intended to train young people.

King Solomon

Wisdom literature was another response of the Jews to the challenges of living as a minority people in the ancient world. The next sections briefly examine the wisdom books of the Old Testament. The book of Psalms is covered in more depth on pages 211–214.

Job

The author of Job is unknown, but the book itself was probably written between 500–400 B.C. Though there are some similarities to the text of Job and Egyptian and Babylonian literature of the time, the work is highly unique.

The standard belief of the time was that a good person would be rewarded with good health, material wealth, and general good fortune (see, for example, Psalm 37). But human experience then, as now, was sometimes contrary to this. Bad things did happen to good people. The book of Job

3. Ask several questions about the book of Job to check the student's comprehension. For example,
   - Does Job solve the mystery of suffering? (No)
   - What is Satan's bet with God? (Satan bets that Job will curse God when he is forced to suffer.)
   - How do Job's friends explain his suffering? (They believe Job is suffering because he is a sinner. Or, they also suggest that Job is suffering because he is a good man and God sends trials to those he loves.)
   - What enables Job to accept his suffering and deal with it? (His faith in God's goodness and God's love for him.)

Make sure the students realize that it is alright to complain to God about our suffering. It is also alright to ask why and to seek answers. God does not inflict the suffering on us. If we are open to God's presence in our suffering, God will help us handle it and grow from the experience.

4. **Homework Assignment**:
   - Read the text sub-sections "Proverbs," "Ecclesiastes," "Song of Songs," "Wisdom," and "Sirach" (pages 208–210).
   - Begin work on the Learn by Doing Exercise, page 222. Look for magazine photos that best represent each page.

Background Information

More on Suffering

God doesn't cause our suffering. Instead, God is with us when we suffer. God has empathy with us because Jesus, who is both God and human, really suffered. When we suffer, we always have a choice about our attitude and behavior. We can make life miserable for ourselves and everyone else. Or we can use the suffering as an opportunity to grow closer to the God who suffered on a cross for us.

See the *Catechism of the Catholic Church* (e.g. 385) for more explanation for why there is suffering.

CHAPTER 9

**Proverbs
Ecclesiastes
Song of Songs,
Wisdom
Sirach**

Bell-Ringer

1. Distribute Handout 9A (page 285 of the TWE), "Egyptian Proverbs." Read the directions. You may wish to have the students work in groups to compare the two versions of proverbs with a partner. Allow time for them to work and discuss. Then call volunteers to note the main similarities and differences as well as ways each proverb applies to people today.

Teaching Approaches

1. Continue the summary of the Bell Ringer exercise. Explain to the students that proverbs do not command us to do something; rather, they persuade us to act in a certain way. Their purpose is not to command or bully; rather, their purpose is to educate. In ancient Israel, there may have been a professional class of teachers who were appointed to teach young men the arts of diplomacy. However, among most families, the parents (both mothers and fathers) taught their children to be wise and to live virtuously.

2. Use "Wisdom and Virtue" (Overhead 9A online at **avemaripress.com**) to explain further the connection between wisdom and personal virtue. Call on a student to be "on the spot" for the discussion questions. Ask one or more of the questions of the student who is to respond before the whole class. Then choose other students to be on the spot and to respond to the same question.

THE OLD TESTAMENT

CHRISTIAN VIEWS OF SUFFERING

Read the following quotations on suffering of famous saints and answer each related question in your journal.

> God measures out affliction to our need.
> —St. John Chrysostom

Do you believe that God only gives you the amount of suffering that you can reasonably handle? Explain.

> There is no such thing as bad weather. All weather is good because it is God's.
> —St. Teresa of Avila

How do you find good in suffering?

> Whenever anything disagreeable or displeasing happens to you, remember Christ crucified and be silent.
> —St. John of the Cross

What is the lesson that Christ teaches you about the meaning of suffering?

rejects the simplistic belief that good is rewarded and evil is punished. Job does not so much solve the problem of the suffering of the innocents as it ponders it, lives with it, and explores it.

The faithful Job, a wealthy man with a large, loving family and many possessions, loses everything: first his possessions, then his family, and finally his own health. He does not understand why any of this has happened, but rejects the conventional wisdom of his friends that he must have sinned in some way. He rejects as well the idea that God sends trials to those he loves, and he finally cries out to God for an explanation. Although God does not explain himself to Job, choosing instead to remind Job of his perogative as the Creator of all, the face-to-face encounter is enough to console Job and restore his trust in God. His faith has been strengthened and deepened by his suffering and his experience of God. The story has a happy ending with Job being restored to health and prosperity and having more children, but it is, by this point, anti-climactic and to a large degree beside the point.

Proverbs

The book of Proverbs was collected as the best of the Israelite wisdom tradition, probably in the fifth century B.C. Some of the proverbs may well date back to the time of Solomon. Other proverbs come from unknown times and places.

The proverbs teach three types of wisdom: knowledge of God's created world, the skill of making right choices, and the art of living before God. Some proverbs are also secular, with little or no religious implications. As introduced on page 204, most of the proverbs teach by comparison. "The fear of the Lord is the beginning of wisdom" (Prv 1:7) is the main teaching of the text. Wisdom is also known as the "firstborn" of God:

> The Lord begot me, the
> firstborn of his ways,
> the forerunner of his
> prodigies of long ago
> (Prv 8:22).

Ecclesiastes

The title of the book is the Greek translation of the Hebrew word *Qohelet*, meaning "someone who calls an assembly." The title refers to someone like a preacher or teacher who presides over a meeting, but not to an actual historical person. Ecclesiastes is a loose collection of proverbs, laments, poems, and rhetorical questions. Qohelet may simply refer to "a gatherer," that is a person who gathered or assembled all these sayings. It was written about the third century B.C.

The book is concerned with the value of human life. Hard work does not guarantee happiness, for it is often marred by suffering. Riches and pleasures will not bring happiness nor guarantee long life. Talents and skills generally result in the stress of competition with others for praise and honor, which even if won is fleeting. A major theme of the book is the vanity of all things. People cannot find happiness and answers to the mysteries of life without God. The author eventually recognizes that

> there is nothing better than to be glad and to do well during life. For every man, moreover, to eat and drink and enjoy the fruit of all his labor is a gift of God. I recognized that whatever God does will endure forever; there is no adding to it, or taking from it. Thus has God done that he may be revered (Eccl 3:12–14).

Song of Songs

Though the Song of Songs has been attributed to Solomon, its language and style reveal that it was written after the Babylonian Exile. It is a collection of love poems. The title itself is a Hebrew way of saying "the greatest of songs."

The love poems express the alternating views of two lovers describing each other in very erotic language. From a Jewish point of view, the poems refer to the love between Yahweh and Israel. Catholics have interpreted the Song of Songs as an allegory describing Christ's love for the Church. Song of Songs is also a joyful celebration of the love between a husband and wife in a marriage blessed by God, and as such is read during the Liturgy of the Word at wedding Masses.

Wisdom

The complete title of this book is "Wisdom of Solomon," although the author actually was a Jew living in Alexandria in Egypt. The book was written in Greek and reveals a **Hellenistic** influence, though the author was also deeply versed in the Hebrew scriptures.

The book of Wisdom was the last book of the Old Testament to be written, some time in the middle of the first century B.C. It has been divided into three main sections:

- The Book of Eschatology (1:1–6:21). This section speaks of the reward of justice. While human destiny is in God's hands, the choices made by a person can make a difference.
- Praise of Wisdom (6:22–11:1). Wisdom is personified as the spirit of God. The author reviews Israel's history to show how God's wisdom was present through all times.
- God's Special Providence during the Exodus (11:2–19:22). This section

Hellenistic—Relating to the culture, history, or language of Greece after the death of Alexander the Great in 323 B.C.

---

3. Summarize the text section on Ecclesiastes. Because of one of its famous passages—"Everything in life is vanity," or illusion—the book is often thought to be pessimistic. Explain that the book is really saying the same thing as Psalm 127:1, "Unless the Lord build the house, they labor in vain who build." We must let God be a part of everything we do, or our efforts are futile. It is also important to see life as God sees it—in totality as a "big picture." Then direct the students to read Ecclesiastes 3:1–8. Ask them to explain, in their own words, what they think this passage means.

4. Summarize the text section on the Song of Songs. The main truth of the book is that God has blessed and created our sexual nature. Sexual love between a man and a woman within marriage is good, not evil. It symbolizes the love Christ has for us as members of the Church. Read Song of Songs 4:1–16 aloud to the class. Ask the students to list images from the passage which they find most appealing. Print them on the board.

> **Enrichment:** Read Wisdom 2:23–3:12. Write answers to the following questions: What was God's original intent for people? How did death enter human history? What will happen to the souls of the just?

> **Enrichment:** Rewrite Ecclesiastes 3:1–9 using contemporary images. Or, use magazine photos or original artwork to illustrate each of these verses.

> **Enrichment:** Read Song of Songs 2:8–10, 14, 16; 8:6–7. Write how these would make appropriate readings for a wedding Mass.

Background Information

Vanity of Vanities

The second verse of the book of Ecclesiastes sets out its main theme: "Vanity of vanities, says Qoheleth, vanity of vanities! All things are vanity!" (Eccl 1:2).

The Hebrew word for vanity translates as "breath, mist, vapor, or thin air." It refers to things that vanish. Vanity is anything that is insubstantial or fleeting. The author concludes that much of what we consider important is meaningless and leads only to death. God has given us life, so we should live it fully in the present, remembering that everything we do on earth will ultimately fade away.

Chapter 9

5. Review the text subsections on Wisdom and Sirach together by explaining that both Wisdom and Sirach were probably written sometime in the first century B.C. Alexander had conquered Palestine and introduced Greek culture to the people there. Biblical authors at this time who lived in Alexandria wrote in Greek, because this language was forced on the people. The Catholic version of the Bible includes the books of Wisdom and Sirach, whereas the Jewish and Protestant canons do not include these books. The authors of Wisdom and Sirach set out to re-emphasize traditional Hebrew teachings. They urged the Israelites, despite the pressures and influence of Greek culture, to remain faithful to their covenant with Yahweh.

6. *Optional:* If any students have prepared a play from Job 1–2, allow them to perform it now in front of the class.

7. **Homework Assignment**:
   - Write answers to the Review and Reflection questions 1–3, page 210.
   - Complete the Journal Assignment on page 210. Think of a practical example to add to the discussion on the meaning of suffering. For example, an athlete puts in months of painful exercise and training in order to achieve a worthwhile goal.
   - Continue working on the Learn by Doing exercise, finding ways to illustrate several passages of wisdom literature.
   - Read the separate feature "An Inward Journey: The Book of Psalms" (pages 211–215).

---

focuses on two main ideas related to the Exodus: 1) the sufferings of the Egyptians were due to their own sins and 2) the evils that affected all the enemies of Israel were a part of God's salvation offered to his Chosen People.

Sirach (Ecclesiasticus)

The book of Sirach is unique among wisdom books because the author is identified: Jesus, son of Eleazar, son of Sirach. He was likely a sage who lived in Jerusalem and who had great love for the law, priesthood, Temple, and worship. The book, which contains numerous sayings, laments, psalms of praise, and moral maxims was written in Hebrew in the second century B.C. The book has also been called *Liber Ecclesiasticus*, meaning "Church Book" because it was used extensively by the early Church in the formation of catechumens and in the instruction to the faithful. It is the longest, and most widely cited, of the writings included in the Latin Christian Bible not found in Hebrew scriptures.

Sirach is similar to the book of Proverbs in style, but it is better organized, with proverbs addressing similar topics grouped together. In fact, it has been considered an updated Proverbs for the later challenges facing Israel.

REVIEW & REFLECTION

1. What is the most striking difference between the spirituality of the wisdom books and that of the rest of the Old Testament?
2. When were the wisdom books written? List some of the reasons Wisdom literature was popular at that time.
3. List the six books (other than Psalms) that comprise the Wisdom literature of the Old Testament, and briefly describe each.

JOURNAL ASSIGNMENT

- How would you comfort a friend who was suffering? Why do you think bad things happen to good people? What good can come from suffering?

Review and Reflection Answers

1. The spirituality of most of the Old Testament focuses on Yahweh and his covenant with the patriarchs, Moses, and the Chosen People. Additionally, the spirituality of the Wisdom books focuses on God as the Creator, who can be known through creation and ordinary daily experiences.
2. The wisdom books were written after the Exile, perhaps between the fourth and first centuries B.C. Wisdom literature was popular for the following reasons:
   - Because of the influence of neighboring cultures, the Jews were inspired to collect their own wisdom sayings.
   - Because it was based on human realities rather than religion, Wisdom literature could be shared by the Jews with people of other cultures. It was a common meeting ground.
   - Wisdom sayings were comforting. They reminded the Jews of how to live a good and prosperous life as God's Chosen People. Parents used Wisdom literature to train young people in their faith and to help them stay out of trouble.
3. In addition to Psalms, the books that comprise the Wisdom literature of the Old Testament are Job, Proverbs, Ecclesiates, Wisdom, Sirach, and Song of Songs. Job deals with the question of human suffering, especially the suffering of good people. Proverbs is a collection of short sayings that deal with virtuous living in day-to-day relationships. Ecclesiastes reminds people that life is vanity unless it is grounded in God. Wisdom and Sirach contain wise sayings to help people remain faithful to their religious traditions despite social pressure to conform to the dominating culture. Song of Songs compares human love to the love God has for his people.

AN INWARD JOURNEY: THE BOOK OF PSALMS

More than any other part of the Old Testament, the psalms present an inward journey of worship and prayer that prepares Christians for the coming of Jesus and his proclamation of God's kingdom.

Psalms is derived from a Greek word that comes from the name of a stringed instrument called a "psalter," a kind of harp. The book of Psalms actually refers to "songs to be sung with a psalter." The Hebrew word for the book of Psalms is *Tehillim*, which means, "praises."

Literary Styles of the Psalms

The overall literary style of the psalms is poetry. Understanding Hebrew poetry requires understanding the poetic style called "**parallelism**" in the verses of the psalms. There are two types of parallelism. The first type refers to the practice of restating the same thought. The second kind of parallelism alternates between opposing thoughts (e.g. light and dark, night and day).

Psalm 2 offers an example of a parallel verse form that simply repeats the same thought in different words:

> Why do the nations protest
> and the peoples grumble in vain? (Ps 2:1)

The parallel thoughts are easy to read. *Nations* equates with *people* and *rage* is parallel to *grumble in vain*.

An example of parallelism that contrasts opposing thoughts is Psalm 1:

> For the Lord watches over the way of the just
> but the way of the wicked leads to ruin (Ps 1:6).

Note the difference. In the Bible, "the way" is a common term for "manner of living" or moral conduct. The "way of the just" is approved by the Lord, while the "way of the wicked" is not permitted to continue.

Finally, another literary style of the psalms has the lines of a verse building up or advancing a thought, almost like a stair-step:

> They are like a tree
>   planted near streams of water,
>   that yields its fruit in season;
>   It's leaves never wither;
>   whatever they do prospers (Ps 1:3).

It is important in reading Biblical poetry—including prophetic poetry, but especially the poetry of the Psalms—to pay attention to the relationship between the lines in different verses. Noting the different types of parallelism or the building of lines within a verse can assist a reader in determining the meaning of the verse and the entire psalm.

parallelism—A characteristic common to Hebrew poetry in which two lines express the same or opposite thoughts, one right after the other.

A Spiritual Journey

AN INWARD JOURNEY: THE BOOK OF PSALMS

Bell-Ringer

1. Begin a discussion based on the Journal Assignment (page 210). Brainstorm with the students some of the ways that teenagers suffer. For example (print on board):
   - **divorce of parents**
   - **breakup with girlfriend/boyfriend**
   - **subject of rumors or gossip**
   - **disappointments over not making a team or getting into a college**

2. Have the students form small groups. Ask each group to develop a short skit which introduces a teen's suffering followed by a way that his or her peers can offer consolation.

Resources

Audiovisual Materials

Catholic Update Video: Teach Us to Pray—Praying the Psalms (St. Anthony Messenger Press)—31 minutes
David Haas, a contemporary Church musician, explains how the Psalms inspire him to write music. Then he offers a video reflection for prayer.

Greatest Adventure: Daniel (Ecufilm)—30 minutes
Two twentieth-century children time-travel to the days of the prophet Daniel.

Praying the Psalms (Corpus Video)—21 minutes
Sr. Joan Chittister, O.S.B., discusses how to apply the Psalms to one's own life. She gives the historical context of the Psalms, why they were written, and how they challenge us today.

Psalms, Vol. I (Cokesbury)—80 minutes
This video consists of four study sessions on the Psalms with Dr. Maxie Dunnam. Session 1 focuses on Psalms 30 and 34. Session 2 covers Psalms 4 and 11. Session 3 centers on Psalms 10 and 27. Session 4 deals with Psalm 56.

Psalms, Vol. II (Cokesbury)—80 minutes
Dr. Maxie Dunnam presents three sessions on the Psalms. Session 1 focuses on Psalm 137. Session 2 zeroes in on Psalms 24 and 127. Session 6 concentrates on Psalm 23.

Psalms (Treehaus)—5 videos, 30 minutes each
These videos visualize psalm readings with live-action shots of people and places throughout the world. Good for short devotionals. *Psalms of Hope* includes Psalms 139, 62, 116, 27, 65, 23, and 121. *Psalms of Joy* includes Psalms 100, 104, 96 and 8. *Psalms of Love* includes Psalms 145, 91, 19, 34, and 63.*Psalms of Praise* includes Psalms 145, 103, 67, 146 and 148. *Psalms of Thanksgiving* includes Psalms 84, 11, 107 and 29.

Chapter 9

Teaching Approaches

1. Introduce the book of Psalms, the subject of this lesson. For example, point out that the book of Psalms was compiled in post-exilic times, but many of the religious hymns were created during the time of the monarchy and during the exile itself. About half of the psalms are attributed to King David, though he may have had little to do with their composition. Have the students examine their Bibles and note how the group of 150 psalms is arranged in imitation of the Pentateuch: 1–41; 42–73; 74–89; 90–106; 107–150.

2. Ask the students to explain the three types of literary styles found in the psalms. (One type of parallelism restates the same thought over two lines. Another type of parallelism alternates between opposing thoughts, and a third literary style has the lines of a verse building up or advancing a thought, almost like a stair-step.) Next, have the students find an example of each style in the book of Psalms and share their examples with the class.

Origins of the Psalms

The evolution of the psalms over a long period of time is clear to anyone who reads the references to David in the first few dozen psalms, but then reads the references to the Babylonian Exile—hundreds of years after the time of David—in Psalm 137. In fact, many who have studied the Psalms suggest that originally there were five "books" of the Psalms (that perhaps coincided with the five books of the Pentateuch). The five original books were:

Book 1: Chapters 1–41
Book 2: Chapters 42–72
Book 3: Chapters 73–89
Book 4: Chapters 90–106
Book 5: Chapters 107–150

The evidence that these books were originally separate is twofold:
1. The final chapters of each book (i.e. 41, 72, 89, 106, and 150) each include a doxology that ends with "Amen. Amen." This would have been a conclusion that appeared at the end of each separate book.
2. There is one "doublet" or repeated passage in the book of Psalms. Psalm 14 and Psalm 53 are the same. In other Biblical research, doublets are evidence that two different text versions have been brought together, creating some duplication of material.

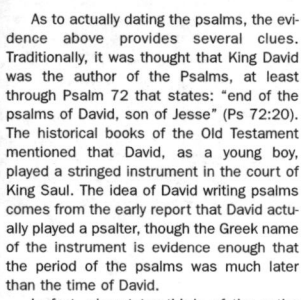

As to actually dating the psalms, the evidence above provides several clues. Traditionally, it was thought that King David was the author of the Psalms, at least through Psalm 72 that states: "end of the psalms of David, son of Jesse" (Ps 72:20). The historical books of the Old Testament mentioned that David, as a young boy, played a stringed instrument in the court of King Saul. The idea of David writing psalms comes from the early report that David actually played a psalter, though the Greek name of the instrument is evidence enough that the period of the psalms was much later than the time of David.

In fact, almost two-thirds of the entire book of Psalms are believed to come from the period of the second Temple, that is, after 520 B.C. but before 333 B.C. The correct dates for most psalms are hard to determine exactly. Those that mention historical events are easier. Again, Psalm 137 is the easiest example because it mentions a historical event—the Babylonian Exile. It is certain that Psalm 137

Background Information

Liturgy of the Hours

The Liturgy of the Hours, or divine office, is a response to the words of St. Paul to "pray constantly" (see 1 Thes 5:17). Besides psalms, the Liturgy of the Hours contains hymns, scripture passages, responses, intercessory prayers, canticles, and other spiritual writings. The Liturgy of the Hours is part of the Church's official, public prayer. It is recited seven times over the course of twenty-four hours and recalls Christ's saving actions. It also prolongs the Eucharist and makes holy the entire day. (See also *CCC* 1174–1178; 1196.)

can be no *older* than 587 B.C. The historical Psalms 105 and 106 must have been written after the last events mentioned in their poetic lines. The historical survey of Psalms 105–106 includes references to the destruction of Jerusalem and the Babylonian Exile. For example:

> So the Lord grew angry with his people,
>   abhorred his own heritage;
> He handed them over to the nations,
>   and their adversaries ruled them.
> Their enemies oppressed them,
>   kept them under subjection (Ps 106:40–42).

Psalm 29 may be the oldest psalm in the Bible because its poetry is considered very similar in style to Canaanite poetry of an earlier era. In Psalm 29, Yahweh is depicted as a storm God with thunder and lightning as his weapons. For example:

> The voice of the Lord strikes with fiery flame;
>   the voice of the Lord rocks the desert,
>   the Lord rocks the desert of Kadesh (Ps 29:7–9).

Psalms about the Temple (e.g., Ps 65:5, 68:30), obviously, cannot come from David, because the first Temple was built by his son, Solomon. Furthermore, it is not always clear which Temple is being talked about—Solomon's Temple or the second Temple built around 520–515 B.C.

Different Kinds of Psalms

However the book of Psalms came together, there is agreement that many different kinds of psalms make up the overall collection. Not all the psalms seem to have been written for the same occasion or purpose. There are four main categories of psalms as follows:

1. Psalms of Lament (sorrow over tragedies)

The psalms of lament come in two types, individual and communal. That is, the speaker in the psalm is either a single person or the entire Hebrew community. They are psalms requesting God's help and protection in dealing with a variety of needs. Many of these psalms conclude with a few lines of thanksgiving and praise for God's response to the appeal for help.
- Psalm 3 (military threat)
- Psalm 10 (legal problems or grievances from fellow Israelites)
- Psalm 38 (personal illness)
- Psalm 44 (communal laments for groups to sing)

2. Psalms of Praise and Thanksgiving

Psalms in this category focus on praising God. They often begin with an invitation to join in the praise and continue with a list of reasons for praise and thanksgiving to God.
- Psalm 19
- Psalm 33

3. Remind the students of the ways the psalms are used in the Church's liturgy. Read the responsorial psalm from the previous or upcoming Sunday Mass. Have the students point out its literary styles. Inform the students that another place the Church uses the psalms is in its morning and evening prayer. This form of liturgy is known as the Liturgy of the Hours or Divine Office. Members of religious communities are required to pray the Liturgy of the Hours each day. Many lay people in parishes pray these psalms as well.

4. If time permits, show one of the suggested videos on the psalms (see page 215 of the TWE). Or, play a musical selection of a psalm. Provide lyrics for the students to sing along.

5. Ask: What are the four main categories of Psalms? (Psalms of Lament, Psalms of Praise and Thanksgiving, Psalms of Instruction, Wisdom, or History, and Liturgical Psalms) Next, distribute "Kinds of Psalms" (Handout 9B, page 286 of the TWE). Have the students work in groups of three or four and complete the handout. When the groups are finished, invite class sharing. Use the answers provided below to check their responses.

Handout 9B "Kinds of Psalms" Answers

1. Psalms of Lament. These psalms speak of personal sorrow over tragedies and communal sorrow. Many of these psalms also ask for God's help.
   - Psalm 3 deals with a military threat.
   - Psalm 10 covers legal problems and grievances from fellow Israelites.
   - Psalm 38 speaks of personal illness.
   - Psalm 44 is a communal lament for groups to sing.
2. Psalms of Praise and Thanksgiving. These psalms either praise God directly or give reasons to praise and thank God.
   - Psalm 19 praises and thanks God for creation and for his law.
   - Psalm 33 praises and thanks God for creation and for leading the nation to victory in battles.
3. Psalms of Instruction. These psalms are either wisdom psalms or historical psalms.
   - Psalm 104 is a wisdom psalm that instructs us to be virtuous.
   - Psalm 105–106 is a historical psalm that reviews what God has done throughout the history of Israel, from Abraham and Jacob to the Exodus.
4. Liturgical Psalms. These psalms were intended for use during liturgical celebrations.
   - Psalm 24 was likely sung by pilgrims while traveling to the Temple.
   - Psalm 100 was perhaps sung by worshippers who entered the Temple courts.

Chapter 9

6. If time permits, direct the students to begin working on the Journal Assignment, page 215. Provide hymnals for students to use as a resource. However, they should begin the assignment by looking through the psalms in their Bibles.

7. **Homework Assignment:**
   - Complete the Journal Assignment.
   - Answer Review and Reflection questions 1–3, page 218. Cite examples with your response to question 3.
   - Continue working on the Learn by Doing exercise.
   - Read the text section, "The Rise of Apocalyptic Literature" (pages 215–217).

Enrichment: Several psalms follow a definite pattern. The first part is an invitation to praise God; the second part gives the reason for the psalm; the third part is a repetition of the first part. Chart the following psalms according to this threefold pattern: Psalms 32, 46, 94, 95, and 102.

---

historical psalm—A psalm recounting events from the history of Israel such as the covenant with the Patriarchs, the Exodus, or the settling of the Promised Land.

3. *Psalms of Instruction*
   These psalms can be divided into two types. The wisdom psalms share the same themes as the Wisdom literature that has been discussed throughout this chapter. The **historical psalms** retell portions of the history of the Chosen People.
   - Psalm 1 (wisdom psalm)
   - Psalm 104 (wisdom psalm)
   - Psalms 105–106 (historical psalms)

4. *Liturgical Psalms*
   Some psalms were intended for use during Temple celebrations. They often reveal a dialogue structure and may have been written to be sung by two choirs or by a cantor with the congregation responding.
   - Psalm 24 (perhaps to be sung while traveling to the Temple)

How were the psalms used? Some, such as the liturgical psalms, were used for worship in the Temple. Other psalms were used for religious festivals outside of the Temple. There is no description in the Bible of exactly how the psalms were used in Temple services, but it is presumed that choirs sang some of them (see Ps 68:27). All but thirty-four of the psalms have titles or musical directions. These addendums were added much later than the text of the psalms themselves.

Obviously not all the psalms were intended for Temple singing. It would be hard to imagine an occasion for singing the historical psalms, such as Psalms 105–106, unless students sang them as a way to recall the history of Israel. That would be especially valuable for Hebrew children growing up in the Diaspora where songs would be an effective way to maintain identity and to provide a connection with their religious and spiritual traditions.

Other psalms seem to have been used for entirely different occasions. *Read Psalm 35, a lament psalm.* The psalm is an appeal to God for help. But help against whom? Verses 1–3 describes the threat of an enemy. However, verses 11–14 refer to "unjust witnesses" that have risen up and spoken against the psalmist, repaying "evil for good." It may be that the help requested from God in Psalm 35 is to settle an argument between two groups of Israelites. In cases like this, where the argument is with fellow Israelites, the dispute would have been brought to the Temple where the two parties would have appealed to the priests. The priests in turn would instruct them to seek God's vindication to settle the dispute, which may have been over money, debts, business, or marriage contracts. It is not certain how the psalm might have fit into the process of seeking a judgment from the priests, but it does seem to be connected to that process.

Part of the continuing appeal of the book of Psalms is that these songs to the Lord help modern readers "hear the hearts" of the Israelites despite the great differences of time and culture that separate them. The psalms help to engage readers and praying people of all generations in the most intimate moments of pain, praise, joy, and sorrow of the ancient Hebrews. Jesus, himself, turned to the comfort of one of the lament psalms at the moment of his death:

Resources
Internet Links

www.usccb.org/nab/bible/wisdom.htm
The United States Catholic Bishops offer a brief introduction to the Wisdom books of the Old Testament with related links.

www.otgateway.com
Tabor College in Victoria, Australia, offers online resources for studying Wisdom literature in the Bible, the book of Psalms, and apocalyptic literature. Type in the book of the Bible you wish to study in the search engine of the website.

http://religion.rutgers.edu/vri/tanakh.html
Rutgers University sponsors a website with links to many resources for studying the Old Testament, including Wisdom and apocalyptic literature.

My God, my God, why have you abandoned me,
    Why so far from my call for help,
        from my cries of anguish?
(Ps 22:2).

It is important to note here that the psalm Jesus chose ends in triumph just as Jesus' pain was ultimately vindicated in his resurrection—the triumph over the Cross and over death. The psalms are expressions of the deepest human pain and highest human joys. When we are feeling such joy that we are speechless or such deep pain that we don't know what to say, the words of the psalms can become our words, too.

REVIEW & REFLECTION

1. What are the two forms of "parallelism" that can be found in the poetry of the Psalms? Find two examples of each.
2. What evidence is there that the book of Psalms was originally five separate books?
3. List and describe the four different types of psalms. Find an example of each.

JOURNAL ASSIGNMENT

- Many of the psalms have been rewritten into songs that we sing at Mass today. Skim through the book of psalms looking for words and phrases that you recognize from songs you have heard at Mass. Make a list of at least four songs you know that are based on the psalms and identify the psalm from which the song is taken. Indicate whether the words have been largely rewritten or taken nearly word for word from the psalm.

The Rise of Apocalyptic Literature

Apocalyptic literature has some things in common with the Wisdom literature, including the time period in which some of these books were written. Two different answers to the same question—How can God's Chosen People live under foreign rule?—were provided by these styles of literature. Wisdom literature primarily looked back to the teachings of creation and the experience of God to determine the proper course of action. Apocalyptic literature looked forward to what God was *about to do* in history.

For some Jews, comfort came in teaching that the world was rational, that it had been created by a God who planned everything to the smallest detail. This cool, sober, and rational approach to life was well represented by Wisdom literature. For others, however, life under Persian, Greek, and Roman rule seemed out of control. The apocalyptic visionaries reassured their readers that God was still in control—even of events that seemed entirely irrational.

A SPIRITUAL JOURNEY

THE RISE OF APOCALYPTIC LITERATURE

Bell-Ringers

1. Conduct a class discussion of the Journal Assignment, page 215. If time permits, play a tape or CD of a liturgical song based on a psalm that has been sung recently in your parish. Also, if any students have written their own song lyrics, have them make copies and share them with the class.

2. Direct the students' attention to the Journal Assignment on page 217. Explain that they will all be completing the assignment based on one of these categories: Psalms, Proverbs, Job, Sirach, Ecclesiastes, Song of Songs, and Wisdom. Encourage the students to summarize the background on the book they chose (e.g., authorship, year written, audience, thematic focus).

Teaching Approaches

1. Note the style of apocalyptic literature by re-reading the three selections from Zephaniah, Enoch, and Daniel. Make sure to emphasize that only the third passage from the book of Daniel is in the Old Testament. Note the definitions and characteristics of apocalyptic literature on pages 216–217 of the text.

2. Ask the following questions to summarize the text reading in more detail. Ask the students to write the questions and answers. Then call on volunteers to share their responses.
- **What does the word "apocalypse" mean?** (Apocalypse means "revelation.")
- **What three characteristics define apocalyptic literature?** (1) It has a narrative framework; it tells as story. (2) The revelation is given by an otherworldly being to a human recipient. (3) The revelation discloses an ultimate reality that exists at the current time, but which also involves another supernatural world.)

Review and Reflection Answers

1. The first type of parallelism repeats the same thought, using different words. The second type of parallelism contrasts opposites. Accept all reasonable examples.
2. First, the final chapters of each book (41, 72, 89, 106, and 150) include a doxology that ends with "Amen." This would have been a conclusion that appeared at the end of each separate book. Second, there is one "doublet" or repeated passage in the book of Psalms. Psalm 14 and Psalm 53 are the same.
3. The four types of psalms are: Psalms of Lament, Psalms of Praise and Thanksgiving, Psalms of Instruction, and Liturgical Psalms. Accept all reasonable examples.

Chapter 9

3. Use "Apocalyptic Literature" (Overhead 9B online at **avemariapress.com**) in tandem with the following presentation notes.

Apocalyptic literature is characterized by:
- *heavy use of symbolism and images.* Apocalyptic writers often talk "in code" to hide the true meaning of what they are saying from political authorities who might punish them. The story may tell of horned beasts and the sea. The beasts represent foreign nations. The sea may represent chaos or war. The danger with writing "in code" is that it can be easily misinterpreted.
- *angels and demons.* Apocalyptic literature often uses the supernatural in its stories. The angels and demons are not to be interpreted literally. Instead, they add a sense of mystery and they dramatize divine control over human events.
- *pseudonymity.* The author of Daniel lives in the second century B.C. but writes about much older events. This technique allows the author two advantages. First, he can make statements about the present and camouflage them as events taking place in the past. He can also make "predictions" from the later time period that have already come to pass by his era. These "predictions of the future" foster hope and inspire right conduct in the readers.
- *determinism.* In apocalyptic stories, the whole of history is confined to a certain time period, such as seventy weeks or years. This device calls people to take control and to make good decisions in times of crisis because (a) what they decide matters, and (b) they must act soon before the world ends.
- *predictions of the end.* Many apocalyptic writings set a date for the "end of the world." This device encouraged people to stand firm in their faith during persecution. If they thought relief was coming soon, it was easier to keep going.

Make sure the students realize that apocalyptic literature is not about predicting the future or the date of the "end of the world." Instead, apocalyptic literature uses symbolic language to comment on the present political situation under the guise of past events.

Defining Apocalyptic Literature

Read the following passages:

A Spirit took me and brought me up into the fifth heaven. And I saw angels who are called "lords," and the diadem was set upon them in the Holy Spirit, and the throne of each of them was sevenfold more brilliant than the light of the rising sun . . . and they were dwelling in the temples of salvation and singing hymns to the ineffable most high God. . . . Truly, I, Zephaniah, saw these things in my vision. . . .

And Enoch, the blessed and righteous man of the Lord took up his parable while his eyes were open and he saw, and said, This is a holy vision from the heavens which the angels showed me: and I heard from them everything and I understood. I look not for this generation, but for the distant one that is coming . . . and I took up with a parable saying, The God of the universe, the Holy Great One, will come forth from his dwelling, and from there he will march upon Mount Sinai and appear in his camp emerging from heaven. . . .

In the first year of King Belshazzar of Babylon, Daniel had a dream as he lay in bed, and was terrified by the visions of his mind. Then he wrote down the dream; the account began: In the vision I saw during the night, suddenly the four winds of heaven stirred up the great sea, from which emerged four immense beasts, each different from the others. The first was like a lion, but with eagle's wings. While I watched, the wings were plucked; it was raised from the ground to stand on two feet like a man, and given a human mind. The second was like a bear; it was raised up on one side, and among the teeth in its mouth were three tusks. It was given the order, "Up, devour much flesh." After this I looked up and saw another beast, like a leopard; on its back were four wings like those of a bird, and it had four heads. . . .

The first passage above is from a book known as the "Apocalypse of Zephaniah." The second passage is from the book of Enoch. Neither book is in the Bible. However, the third passage is from the book of Daniel (7:1–6). All three are examples of apocalyptic literature.

Although there are not very many examples of apocalyptic literature in the Bible—only Daniel 7–12 and the Revelation to John in the New Testament are fully developed examples—it was clearly a very popular form of literature for many nations and cultures of the day. Many of these books have survived to help us study and compare with those apocalyptic writings that *are* in the Bible.

Recall that *apocalypse* means "revelation." Apocalyptic literature is a "literature of revelation." In more detail,
- Apocalypse is a literature of revelation within a narrative framework. It tells a story.
- The revelation is given by an otherworldly being to a human recipient.
- The revelation discloses an ultimate reality that exists at the current time, but which also involves another supernatural world.[1]

There are two main models of apocalyptic writing from among the dozens of examples known. The first involves otherworldly journeys. The second is known as "historic symbolic," that is, it uses symbols to represent people, places, and historical events. This second type of apocalyptic literature is used in the Bible. However, it is worth noting that the apocalyptic journey (where the author "visits" levels of heaven or hell) is a style that was also well known by Biblical authors (see 2 Cor 12:2).

Enrichment: Read Daniel 7:1–28. List at least six images that can be classified as symbolic. From a Bible commentary, identify the meaning of the images you identified as symbolic.

Enrichment: Read Daniel 12:1–4. What is unique about this passage to the Old Testament? (It is the first place in the Hebrew scriptures that a personal resurrection from the dead is affirmed.)

A Spiritual Journey

Specific characteristics of the historic symbolic style of apocalyptic literature are:

- The writings are written in a style emphasizing spiritual and social turmoil. Things are not right in the world, and the writer expresses a great sense of unrest.
- There is often a sense of urgency in the writing. The changes that are coming in the world (or the entire cosmos!) are coming very soon.
- History as understood by humans is coming to an end.
- Beyond the coming catastrophes is a new paradise (The book of Revelation speaks of a "new heaven and a new earth").
- In most cases, the apocalyptic writing features a mediator—some heavenly being (e.g., the angel Gabriel in the book of Daniel) who explains the bizarre visions and images that the "seer" is reporting in the book.
- Typically, the apocalyptic literature describes visions populated by strange and alarming beasts—multi-headed dragons and animals that combine features from different species (e.g., winged leopards, etc.).
- Many images are consistent across different apocalyptic works (which is why a reader of Daniel 7–12 will recognize some of the images that turn up in the book of Revelation, as well as in apocalyptic books outside the Bible).
- The literature is typically written under a pseudonym or pen name, probably because it is usually controversial political writing that is critical of present regimes and governments. It would be dangerous for the author to be identified. Also, symbols are used in the subject of the writing as well. For example, the book of Revelation refers to the Roman Empire as "the Beast."

Most of these characteristics are typical of the apocalyptic writings both within and outside of the Bible. It is important to be aware that apocalyptic is a literary style with *many* examples.

Apocalyptic Writing in the Old Testament

The book of Daniel is the only pure source of apocalyptic writing of the Old

REVIEW & REFLECTION

1. Where does apocalyptic literature appear in the Bible?
2. List three characteristics of apocalyptic literature and describe the two most common models of apocalyptic writing. Which one of the two appears in the Old Testament?

JOURNAL ASSIGNMENT

- Read the descriptions of the wisdom books again (beginning on page 206) and skim through them in your Bible before choosing one to explore in more depth. What drew you to the book you chose? Identify two or three favorite passages and explain their meaning and the significance they have for you.

---

4. Answer any questions the students may have involving the text sections covered. Also, allow the students time to read the Scripture passages referenced in the text and make notes on these to help prepare them for the Chapter 9 Test.

5. **Homework Assignment**:
   - Near completion of the Learn by Doing exercise, page 222.
   - Write answers for the Review and Reflection questions 1–2, page 217.
   - Read the text section "Apocalyptic Writing in the Old Testament" (pages 217–221).

APOCALYPTIC WRITING IN THE OLD TESTAMENT

Bell-Ringer

1. Divide the class into triads. Assign the exercise, "Daniel's Visions (page 219)." Allow time for the students to read Daniel 2 and Daniel 7, and then answer the questions in the exercise. When the groups have finished, lead a class discussion of the findings. Explain that Daniel 2 and Daniel 7 both talk about four empires: Babylonian, Median, Persian, and Hellenistic. In Daniel 2 the symbols for these empires are: the gold head of a statue (Babylonia); the silver chest and arms of the statue (Media); the bronze belly and thighs of the same statue (Persia); and the iron legs and feet of the statue (Greece). In Daniel 7 the symbols for these are a lion with eagle's wings (Babylonia); a bear with tusks (Media); a leopard with four wings and four heads (Persia); a beast with eleven horns and iron teeth (Greece). Both visions mean that four successive kingdoms will rule over the Israelites but in the end, all of these will be crushed by a Messiah or Son of Man.

Review and Reflection Answers

1. Apocalyptic literature appears in the Book of Daniel in the Old Testament and in the Revelation to John in the New Testament.
2. The three characteristics of apocalyptic literature are: (1) It tells a story. (2) The revelation is given by an otherworldly being to a human recipient. (3) The revelation discloses an ultimate reality that exists at the current time, but which also involves another supernatural world. The two most common models of apocalyptic writing are: the involvement of otherworldly journeys, and the use of symbols to represent people, places, and historical events. The second model is used in the Bible.

Chapter 9

Teaching Approaches

1. Direct the student's attention to the Journal Assignment, page 221. Distribute art materials (e.g., color pencils and paper) and have the students draw their pictures of apocalyptic beasts that represent something in the modern world. When the students have finished working, display the pictures for all to see. Ask individual students to "explain" what their beasts mean. *Option:* Have the students create masks (e.g., using paper bags) to represent the beasts.

2. Point out the similarities between Daniel and the patriarch Joseph in that they both interpret dreams for kings. Daniel is also like the wise Solomon, who determined which woman was the rightful mother of a baby. Assign the story about the virtue of Susanna in Daniel 13. Lead a class discussion of how justice won out in the end. Point out also how the story also contrasts the moral intent of the southern kingdom versus the northern kingdom (see Dn 13:57).

THE OLD TESTAMENT

Testament. However, the prophets Isaiah, Ezekiel, Joel, and Zechariah do employ the apocalyptic style in certain places, suggesting that apocalyptic draws on prophetic themes as well.

For example, the book of Joel employs apocalyptic imagery in a number of places. Joel sees in a terrible plague of locusts that ravages the land a sign of God's impending judgment on the people. He also describes a vision of the future when all the nations will gather in the Valley of Jehoshaphat to face God's judgment. The book of Joel has a very eschatological tone that is common to apocalyptic literature. **Eschatology** refers to a study of the "last things" such as death, judgment, immortality, heaven and hell, and the like.

The first part of the book of Zechariah (1:1–6:8) contains apocalyptic visions of such varied things as four horsemen, a lamp stand, a flying scroll, a flying bushel basket, and four chariots. All of these visions were intended to promote the rebuilding of the Temple and to encourage the people after the disruption and devastation of the Exile.

It is the book of Daniel that is the main example of apocalyptic literature in the Old Testament. Chapters 7 to 12 contain apocalyptic visions of the future. When Jesus is called before the Sanhedrin (the Jewish court), he evokes the words of Daniel in speaking of the coming of the Son of Man on the clouds of heaven:

> Then Jesus answered, "I am; and 'you will see the Son of Man seated at the right hand of the Power and coming with the clouds of heaven'" (Mk 14:62; see also Dn 7:13).

More information about the narrative and apocalyptic nature of Daniel follows.

Daniel

In the Hebrew scriptures, the book of Daniel is classified with the Writings. These books include Wisdom literature and the psalms. The Catholic canon includes Daniel with the prophetic books. While it does contain prophecy, the book of Daniel also contains history and, of course, apocalyptic literature.

The book of Daniel has three main divisions:

- Daniel 1–6. This part includes six stories about a young Jewish boy, Daniel. Along with his friends, Daniel remains faithful to Yahweh under the reigns of King Nebuchadnezzar II and the Persian kings. These stories probably originated in the Persian era, but were retold during the persecution of the Jews by Antiochus IV (see Chapter 10).
- Daniel 7–12. This section contains four symbolic visions that center on the "heavenly battle" with Israel's enemies, especially Antiochus IV (see below).
- Daniel 13–14. Three other stories found only in the

eschatology—A study of the "last things," such as death, judgment, immortality, heaven and hell, and the like.

Septuagint (not considered inspired by Jews and Protestants) end the book. In one of the stories, Daniel saves a young maiden named Susanna.

The middle section of Daniel was written in approximately 164 B.C. by an anonymous author. The story is told as if it had occurred four centuries earlier. This was done for one reason: doing so allowed the author to take on the role of the prophet and discuss the difficulties facing the people during the time of Antiochus IV without fear of persecution. By using symbols and giving the story a supposedly historical context, the author could speak more freely than the oppressive government would normally allow.

The visions of Daniel 7–12 seem to repeat elements in the dream of Nebuchadnezzar in Daniel 2. In Daniel 7:1–28, the prophet sees four beasts coming from the sea. The beasts signify the Babylonian Empire, the kingdom of the Medes, the Persian Empire, and the empire of Alexander. The message of these visions is that pagan kingdoms grow progressively worse, reaching their climax in the "little horn" that represents Antiochus (Dn 7:8). The people are destined to suffer under him for a period of apparently three and a half years. Relief will come only when God himself intervenes.

Why did apocalyptic writing appeal so much to Jews in the centuries prior to, during, and immediately after Jesus' life on earth? Most likely, the apocalyptic books arose in circumstances of oppression—when the social and political policies of the Persian, Greek, or Roman rulers became especially brutal. In such circumstances, the Jews literally cried out to God and had visions from God of hopeful reassurance that he was with them. The highly symbolic nature of the writing protected the authors—as well as the readers—from persecution, since the

DANIEL'S VISIONS

The first of Daniel's visions in Daniel 7 repeats a good deal of the dream of Nebuchadnezzar in Daniel 2. Do the following: 1) Identify the four empires symbolized in both Daniel 2 and Daniel 7. 2) Name the images used to symbolize the empires in Daniel 2. 3) Name the beasts used to symbolize the empires in Daniel 7.

An artist's version of the four beasts depicted in Daniel 7:1–28

3. Note the separate feature, "Hidden Books of the Bible?" (page 220). Use the following questions to further understand the material:
   - Why were some books of apocalyptic literature accepted into the canon of Scripture whereas other apocalyptic books were not? (Those who were rejected were not considered to be inspired by the Holy Spirit. They were either forgeries, strange, or rejected by the earliest Christians.)
   - Why do historians consider the non-biblical apocalyptic books important? (They show what was important and what some Jews and Christians were thinking about in various times of history.)

Mention the similarity between apocalyptic writing and the Spirituals sung by African slaves in early nineteenth-century America. The spirituals used "encoded" language and images from the Exodus to speak of their own hope for liberation.

Chapter 9

4. **Homework Assignment**:
   - Answer the Review and Reflection questions 1–3, page 220.
   - Read the "Further Reflections" text section, page 221.
   - Complete the Learn by Doing exercise.

Enrichment: Write a short essay contrasting the religious beliefs of the Greeks with those of the Jews in the second century B.C.

Enrichment: Cite passages in the book of Daniel that offer consolation to human suffering.

THE OLD TESTAMENT

language would be difficult to decipher by those outside the cultural context of the author and his intended audience.

Consider the mood and thinking surrounding apocalyptic literature. The times were bad and the Jews held on to the belief that God was going to bring about immediate change. This is one of the central messages of apocalyptic visions: God is in control. What seems awful and unpredictable is *not* outside of God's control.

HIDDEN BOOKS OF THE BIBLE?

What about the other apocalyptic writings of the period? Why are they not included in the Bible? This is an easy question to answer. These "other" apocalyptic writings are not in the Bible because they were not accepted by the Church Fathers as having been inspired by the Holy Spirit. Thus, they have no place in sacred Scripture.

Usually, the particulars of the decision were easy—many of these books were clearly forgeries or just plain strange, and were rejected by the earliest Christians. Other books were read and enjoyed, but not considered central to the purpose of the Old Testament, to reveal the coming of the Savior, Jesus Christ. (The book of Enoch is cited in Jude 1:14, for example. It was read but still not considered central.)

Even though these books are not part of sacred Scripture, they are very useful to historians. These books² are helpful indicators of what was important and what some Jews and Christians were thinking about in various times of Hebrew and Christian history.

REVIEW & REFLECTION

1. In what Old Testament books do examples of apocalyptic writing occur?
2. Why did the author of the book of Daniel, who lived in the second century B.C., write as if the character Daniel had lived during the reign of Nebuchadnezzar?
3. Explain the appeal of apocalyptic writing during the time that Israel was ruled by the Babylonian, Persian, and Roman empires.

Review and Reflection Answers

1. Apocalyptic writing occurs throughout the book of Daniel and in portions of Isaiah, Ezekiel, Joel, and Zechariah.
2. The author of Daniel did so to make truthful criticisms and comments about the political leaders of his day without being punished for saying these things.
3. Apocalyptic books arose in circumstances of oppression when the social and political policies of the Persian, Greek, or Roman rulers became especially brutal. The highly symbolic nature of apocalyptic writing protected the authors from persecution since the language would be difficult to decipher by those outside the cultural context of the author and his intended audience.

Journal Assignment

- Search through the apocalyptic material in the Bible and try to visualize one of the "beasts" described. Write how this beast might symbolize someone or something in the modern world.

Further Reflections

Hebrew Wisdom literature was part of a larger cultural phenomenon of the ancient Near East. Great "pearls of wisdom" were collected as short maxims and shared among cultures. Hebrew wisdom was influenced by the wisdom sayings of Egypt and Mesopotamia in particular.

Wisdom writings were based on tradition. Their subject matter was taken from looking back at the gleaned experience of the Hebrews and other peoples to answer current questions and problems of the day. The value of wisdom is best summarized at the opening of the book of Proverbs:

> That men may appreciate wisdom and discipline,
> may understand words of intelligence;
> May receive training in wise conduct in what is right, just and honest;
> That resourcefulness may be imparted to the simple,
> to the young man knowledge and discretion.
> A wise man by hearing them will advance in learning,
> an intelligent man will gain sound guidance,
> That he may comprehend proverb and parable,
> the words of the wise and their riddles.
> The fear of the Lord is the beginning of knowledge;
> wisdom and instruction fools despise (Prv 1:2–7).

Apocalyptic writing was another popular style of the time. One modern understanding of apocalyptic literature is that it is intended to predict the future through the use of secret codes and hidden messages. This is not accurate. By the very fact that God revealed himself so perfectly and clearly in Jesus Christ, it is obvious that hiding messages in secret codes is not God's style. Christian faith understands that God seeks to be known, not hiding in codes or secrets.

Jesus himself warned against trying to predict future events:

> Asked by the Pharisees when the kingdom of God would come, he said in reply, "The coming of the kingdom of God cannot be observed, and no one will announce, 'Look, here it is,' or, 'There it is.' For behold, the kingdom of God is among you" (Lk 17:20–21).

Both Wisdom literature and apocalyptic literature teach people to live in the present and to behave as members of God's Chosen People. Whether looking backward or forward, these Scripture styles are instructions for living in God's world—now and for all time to come.

FURTHER REFLECTIONS

Bell-Ringers

1. Form a panel of students. Ask the panel to reflect on the importance of wisdom and to cite personal examples that support their comments. Note similarities between the students' examples and the summary of wisdom from Proverbs 1:2–7. Also, ask the panel to address the question of why it is important not to try and predict future events, especially the end of time based on Jesus' words in Luke 17:20–21.

2. Call on the students to share their words and collages from the Learn by Doing exercise. Collect the students' work for grading.

Teaching Approaches

1. Have the students work with partners or in small groups to create a crossword puzzle or other word game using the vocabulary words and Review and Reflection questions highlighted in Chapter 9. Make copies of the completed work as necessary. Then have the students exchange the puzzles and complete them as part of their study review for the Chapter 9 Test.

Chapter 9

2. Refer to the "the end of the world" as discussed in the "Further Reflections" text. Point out that various people throughout the centuries have tried to predict the date of the end of the world. Many movies have dealt with apocalyptic themes and "signs" that the end is approaching. Remind the students of what Jesus said—that no one really knows the time or the hour. What is important is that we live each moment in union with God. If we have a personal relationship with Christ, then the kingdom of God is really within us. Our awareness of God's presence within us will be so strong that we should have no fear of the future. We live in God's love, and that is enough for us. Such trust brings the wisdom and peace talked about in both the wisdom books and the apocalyptic books of the Bible.

3. **Prayer Service:** Play a recording or lead singing of "You Are Near" (see page 206 of the TWE). Choose a reader to read Sirach 1:1–11. Next, have the students recite together the Thomas Merton prayer from page 222. Choose another song as a closing, for example "On Eagle's Wings" (see page 206 of the TWE).

4. **Homework Assignment:**
   - Study for the Chapter 9 Test.

Learn by Doing

Wisdom has many different meanings in the Old Testament. Look up the following passages. Do one of the following: 1) Paraphrase in your own words the meaning of wisdom described in each passage or 2) Make a collage with magazine photos that represent the meaning of wisdom in each passage. Print the words of the passage near the photo that goes with it.

- Proverbs 24:14
- Job 12:12
- Proverbs 31:1
- Sirach 39:5
- Sirach 51:23
- Proverbs 1:7
- Wisdom 7:14b
- Proverbs 8:13
- Proverbs 4:1
- Ecclesiastes 2:13

Called to Prayer

My Lord God,
I have no idea where I am going.
I do not see the road ahead of me.
I cannot know for certain where it will end.
Nor do I really know myself,
and the fact that I think that I am following your will
does not mean that I am actually doing so.
But I believe that the desire to please you
does in fact please you.
And I hope I have that desire in all that I am doing.
I hope that I will never do anything apart from that desire.
And I know that if I do this,
you will lead me by the right road
though I may know nothing about it.
Therefore I will trust you always
though I may seem to be lost in the shadow of death.
I will not fear, for you are ever with me,
and you will never leave me to face my perils alone.
　　　　　　　　　—Thomas Merton

Notes

1. Professor John Collins has written many works on Apocalyptic literature. Some of this material is drawn from his masterful commentary on Daniel published for the *Hermeneia Commentary Series*. (Fortress Press, 1994)
2. One excellent translation of these apocalyptic texts not found in the Bible is: *The Old Testament Pseudepigrapha: Apocalyptic Literature and Testaments* (Old Testament Pseudepigraphia, Vol 1) edited by James H. Charlesworth, New York: Doubleday, 1983.

A Spiritual Journey

Chapter 9 Parish Religious Education Adaptation

- Note the Chapter 9 Parish Religious Education Adaptation online at **avemariapress.com**. Preview the lesson plan to be aware of media and other supplies you will need. Pages 14–15 offer suggestions for scheduling one- or two-hour lessons.
- Assign Chapter 9 for reading prior to the first class session and assigned Review and Reflection questions from Chapter 8 (see the Parish Religious Education Adaptation).

A Spiritual Journey

CHAPTER 9 TEST

Teaching Approaches

1. Allow time for the Chapter 9 Test (online at **avemariapress.com**). Note the varied point values for each section of questions.

2. Use some of the suggestions for games on page 225 of the TWE to cover some of the material in the Catholic Handbook for Faith, pages 259–280.

3. If there is time, allow the students to peruse Chapter 10 in their texts.

Chapter 9 Test Answers

Part 1: True or False: 1. +; 2. 0; 3. 0; 4. +; 5. 0; 6. 0; 7. +; 8. +; 9. +; 10. 0; 11. 0.

Part 2: Multiple Choice: 12. b; 13. d; 14. c; 15. d; 16. a; 17. d; 18. b.

Part 3: Short Fill-ins: 19. Proverbs, Sirach, Job, Ecclesiastes, Song of Songs, and Wisdom; 20. (1) Psalm of Lament: requests for God's help and protection (2) Psalm of Praise/ Thanksgiving: the praise of God is their entire focus (3) Psalms of Instruction: retelling the history of the Chosen People or expressing the themes of wisdom literature generally (4) Liturgical Psalms: intended for use during Temple celebrations; 21. The apocalyptic journey, in which the author "visits" different levels of heaven or hell, and the "historic symbolic," in which symbols are used to represent known people, places and historical events. The latter is used in the Bible. 22. (Parallelism is a poetic verse form in which two lines either restate the same thought in different words or alternate between contrasting ideas. In both cases, the grammatical structure of the two lines is identical or nearly so. Examples of the two styles will vary.

Part 4: Short Answer: 23. Wisdom literature is focused on God as Creator and on creation itself. It doesn't really dwell on God's actions in freeing the Hebrews from slavery, establishing the Promised Land, or on the law of Moses and the covenant between God and his people. Wisdom literature describes God through what he has made; it is more descriptive, more rational, more objective than the descriptions in the rest of the Old Testament. It suggests that faith can come from rationality and study as well as from revelation.

Introducing Chapter 10

Chapter 10 covers the last 600 years of Israel's history before the birth of Christ and on into Jewish history through modern times. In the years before Christ, the Jews lived under successive foreign rule: the Babylonians, the Persians, the Greeks, and the Romans. Stories from this time period—from the books of Daniel, Tobit, Esther, and Judith—contain messages about how the Jews were to survive under foreign rule. Some stories tell the Jews to cooperate with civil authorities while remaining faithful to prayer and obedience to God's law. The story of Judith urges the Jews to resist injustice proactively.

After Alexander the Great conquered Palestine, the Jews were under tremendous pressure to adopt Greek culture and religion. Some Jews, seeking survival, chose to do this. Other more conservative Jews chose to resist foreign authority (either actively or passively) and persist in their practice of traditional Judaism. Among the latter group of Jews were the Maccabees, a family that led a revolt against the Greeks in order to gain control of the Temple in Jerusalem.

The chapter debates the pros and cons of each response to foreign rule. Was it better for the Jews to resist foreign rule or was it better for them to cooperate? The second book of Maccabees records examples of Jews who tried to live in peace with their rulers but remained faithful to the laws of Moses. Such Jews "spiritually" resisted the Greeks to the point of martyrdom. Jesus himself exemplifies this latter response.

The Jews lived as a displaced people after Jesus' life on earth. In 70 A.D. the third Temple was destroyed by the Romans. From then on, the Jews adapted their religion in the Diaspora. The rabbis took on a central function. The final section looks at Jewish history and worship through the founding of the state of Israel in 1948.

Chapter 10 Outline

Introduction
  The Jews lived under foreign rule from six centuries before Christ until the mid twentieth century.
How God's People Lived Under Foreign Rule
  Jews resisted foreign rule both peacefully and with military resistance.
Tracing Jewish History Prior to the Maccabean Revolt
  Hellenization in many forms influenced the years before Roman domination in Palestine.
From the Maccabees to Roman Control
  The Maccabees led a revolt that retook control of the Temple and restored Jewish religious practice.
Cooperation or Resistance: What Was the Best Course for the Jews?
  There were pros and cons for the Jews in all ways of dealing with foreign domination.
What Happened to the Jews?
  The Jews survive for centuries as a people displaced from the Holy Land.
Further Reflections

Background Notes for the Teacher

In order to fully understand the New Testament, it is important to have a solid background in Old Testament study. The final chapter prepares students for the social and political milieu in which Jesus lived. For one thing, it helps them understand the conflict between the Sadducees and the Pharisees and how these groups of Jews arose.

The Sadducees were originally an aristocratic group of wealthy Jerusalem Jews. They observed the strict letter of the Torah and all the regulations for Temple sacrifices. These practices were the most important observances in Jewish life. They denied the doctrine of an afterlife or resurrection of the dead. The Pharisees emphasized study and interpretation of the Law. They also placed a strong emphasis on pious religious rites in the home, such as washings and prayers before meals. While Jesus had conflicts with both groups, he was most likely raised within the Pharisaic tradition of Jewish faith and practice.

Many of Jesus' followers hoped that he would lead a political rebellion against the Romans. Jesus, however, advocated a more "passive aggressive" stance: cooperating with the Roman authorities while remaining faithful to traditional Jewish religion. Students who study the Old Testament often wonder what happened to the Jews after Jesus' time. Beyond the Jewish religion, Jerusalem and the Temple became one based in synagogue

Resources

Music Suggestions: see page 230
Printed Materials: see page 235
Audiovisual Materials: see page 236
Internet Links: see page 237

CHAPTER 10
THE JOURNEY LEADS TO THE TIME OF JESUS AND BEYOND

Relevant Teachings from Church Documents
- Such holy women as Sarah, Rebecca, Rachel, Miriam, Deborah, Hanna, Judith, and Esther kept alive the hope of Israel's salvation. (*CCC*, 64)
- ... When she delves into her own mystery, the Church, the People of God in the New Covenant, discovers her link with the Jewish People, (Cf. *NA* 4.) "the first to hear the Word of God" (*Roman Missal*, Good Friday 13: General Intercessions, VI). The Jewish faith, unlike other non-Christian religions, is already a response to God's revelation in the Old Covenant. To the Jews "belong the sonship, the glory, the covenants, the giving of the law, the worship, and the promises; to them belong the patriarchs, and of their race, according to the flesh, is the Christ" (*Rom* 9:4–5), for the gifts and the call of God are irrevocable" (*Rom* 11:29). (*CCC*, 839)
- In the Old Testament God reveals himself to us as the liberator of the oppressed and the defender of the poor, demanding from man faith in him and justice towards man's neighbor. It is only in the observance of the duties of justice that God is truly recognized as the liberator of the oppressed. (1971 Synod of Bishops, *Justice in the World*, Chapter 2)
- Special attention needs to be given to catechesis in relation to the Jewish religion. Indeed "when she delves into her own mystery, the Church, the People of God in the New Covenant, discovers her links with the Jewish People, the first to hear the word of God."

Background Notes continued

worship. The Jews were almost completely separated from the Holy Land until the founding of the state of Israel after World War II.

Both the Old Testament and the New Testament call Christians today to live in peace and to approach enemies with kindness. Christian kindness toward non-believers purifies the non-believers and brings them to faith in Christ.

Advance Preparations
- Obtain and preview any videos you wish to use during this chapter.
- Obtain recordings of music you wish to use in the chapter prayer service.
- Photocopy the handouts you will use with your lesson plan.
- Arrange for a guest speakers who are Jewish to speak to the class on topics of worship, politics, and society in the modern world and issues specifically related to pages 244–247 (see pages 241 and 246 of the TWE).
- Schedule a visit to a local synagogue to help the students complete the Learn By Doing Activity.

Chapter Objectives
The students will be able to:
- get an overview of the history and political situation in Palestine during the 600 years preceding Jesus.
- see how the spiritual messages of Daniel 1–6, Tobit, Judith, and Esther helped the people deal with foreign rule while remaining faithful to the laws of Moses.
- understand that the Jews themselves were divided about how to respond to foreign rule and whether they should cooperate or resist.
- learn about the revolt led by the Maccabees and the miracle behind the feast of Hanukkah.
- learn about the Septuagint in the development of the canon of the Bible.
- understand more about Jewish worship and feast days.
- find out what happened to the Jews from the destruction of the Temple up to modern times.

- "Religious instruction, catechesis, and preaching should not form only towards objectivity, justice and tolerance but also in understanding and dialogue. Both of our traditions are too closely related to be able to ignore each other. It is necessary to encourage a reciprocal consciousness at all levels." In particular, the objective of catechesis should be to overcome every form of anti-Semitism. (*General Directory for Catechesis*, 199)

Chapter 10

INTRODUCTION
HOW GOD'S PEOPLE LIVED UNDER FOREIGN RULE

Bell-Ringers

1. Return and review the graded Chapter 9 Test. Answer any questions the students continue to have about the Chapter 9 material.

2. Direct the students' attention to the Journal Assignment on page 229. After the students reflect and write their responses, form small groups to discuss the situations and questions. After allowing the groups sufficient time to share, call on volunteers to mention several situations when they had to make a difficult choice that involved their faith.

Teaching Approaches

1. Have the students read the Introduction and "How God's People Lived under Foreign Rule" to the section on Daniel 1–6 on pages 227. Review the material by covering the following points:
- The foreign countries that ruled over Palestine during this 600-year history before the birth of Christ were the Babylonians, Persians, Greeks (including the Ptolemies and Seleucids), and the Romans.
- The Jews responded to being ruled by foreigners by being divided among themselves. Some wanted to throw off foreign rule completely in order to return to their own monarchy. Other Jews sought to cooperate with foreign rulers in an effort to survive.
- The books of the Bible covered in this chapter were written during the Greek occupation of Palestine. These books include Daniel 1–6, Judith, Esther, and Tobit.

2. Divide the class into four groups. Assign each group to one of these categories: Daniel 1–6, Judith, Esther, and Tobit. Have each person read his or her assigned book in the Bible, along with the corresponding section in the text. Then ask the individuals to summarize the reading using these questions (print on the board):
- **What happens in this book? What are the main stories? (Be prepared to summarize the main storyline for the class.)**
- **What does the book tell us about daily life in the Diaspora?**
- **What is the spiritual message of the book?**
- **How does the book urge Jews to live and act under foreign rule?**

Allow the rest of the remaining class time for the students to work on the assignment. Tell them that you will be calling on them to present their findings at the next class section.

THE OLD TESTAMENT

Introduction

From about six centuries before the time of Christ and extending to his life and beyond, the Jews lived under a succession of foreign rulers. Not until the establishment of the state of Israel following World War II did the Jews regain control of their own governance in their own land. Living dispersed from the land (the Diaspora) and under foreign control in the Holy Land, was the reality of Jewish experience from the time of the Babylonian Empire (587 B.C.) onward. After the Babylonians, the Jews lived in Palestine under a succession of rulers to the early Christian era. These included:

Alexander the Great

- The Persian Empire (539–333 B.C.)
  - Alexander the Great and the Hellenistic (Greek) Rulers (see below) that followed his death (323–64 B.C.):
    - The Ptolmies who ruled Palestine from Egypt (323–200 B.C.)
    - The Seleucids who ruled Palestine from Babylon and the East (200–64 B.C.)
  - The Roman Empire (64 B.C. to the early Christian centuries)

Very few Biblical books actually claim to have been written during the Persian Period. But we know that some material *was* written in this time, although it seems that the Persian Period was given over more to the organization of the writings that make up a great deal of the Old Testament, rather than to writing much new material. When Ezra visited Jerusalem around 450 B.C. he referred to "scrolls of the Law" (see Neh 8:1–4). These scrolls were the beginning of the Bible that was already taking shape. But there would be an important change in the life of the Hebrews with the coming of the Greeks under Alexander the Great. Stories from the books of Daniel (chapters 7–12), Tobit, and Esther reveal what life was like in the Diaspora and in Palestine during this period.

This chapter presents an overview of the years prior to the birth of Christ and the last books of the Old Testament authored during this period as well as some historical perspective on what happened to the Jewish people to the present time.

How God's People Lived Under Foreign Rule

The Old Testament reflects different ways the Jews chose to survive while ruled by foreigners. There were some occasions when Jews served as advisers to foreign rulers and were able to function peacefully under foreign kings or regional governors. Stories from the books of Daniel (1–6), Tobit, and Esther suggest that there were dangers in being a minority people. If the people remained faithful to Yahweh, however, survival was possible.

Some Jews held a much more nationalistic perspective of the situation. These Jews wanted to throw off foreign rule completely in order to return to their own monarchy or some other form of self-rule and government. Biblical books such as 1 Maccabees and Judith reflect a more "proactive" stance for reclaiming Jewish independence. But Daniel and Tobit represent a more nonviolent resistance to a foreign power and foreign religious influence.

The differing views on how the Jews ought to approach foreign rule during this time are important because this same issue surfaces among Jews living at the time of Jesus—even among his own disciples. (Jesus clearly favored the peaceful resistance of

226

Resources
Music Suggestions

"Healer of Our Every Ill" by Marty Haugen from *Gather* (GIA).

"I Lift Up My Soul" by Tim Manion from *Glory & Praise 1* (OCP [NALR]) or *Breaking Bread* (OCP).

"Let There Be Peace on Earth" by Sy Miller and Jill Jackson from *Young People's Glory & Praise Vol. 1.* (OCP [NALR]); *Breaking Bread* (OCP); *Lead Me, Guide Me* or *Gather* (GIA).

"Psalm 91: Be with Me, Lord" by Marty Haugen from *With Open Hands, Celebration Series: Psalms for the Church Year, Celebrate, Gather* (GIA).

"Shelter Me, O God" by Bob Hurd from *In the Breaking of the Bread* or *Breaking Bread* (OCP); *Gather* (GIA).

"Song of the Chosen" by Rory Cooney in *Gather* (GIA).

"Though the Mountains May Fall" by Dan Schutte, from *Earthen Vessels, Glory & Praise 1, Young People's Glory & Praise* (OCP [NALR]), *Celebrate* or *Gather* (GIA); *Breaking Bread* (OCP).

"We Praise You" by The Dameans from *Glory & Praise 2* (OCP [NALR]); *Gather* (GIA).

Daniel over the more forceful, even violent, resistance of the Maccabees and Judith.) In tracing the issue, it is helpful to consider what the Biblical stories in the books of Daniel (1–6), Tobit, Esther, and Judith reveal about the conditions faced by the Jews while living under foreign rule.

Daniel 1–6

Recall that the book of Daniel is divided into three sections (see pages 218–219) and was finished between the years of 167 and 164 B.C., though it is set in the royal household during the Babylonian Exile four hundred years earlier. The stories in chapters 1 to 6 are built around Daniel, a young Hebrew taken into the Babylonian king's service where he distinguishes himself by his interpretation of dreams and prophecy. Daniel and his companions very carefully observe Jewish laws in spite of opposition from others in the royal court. For example, in chapter 1, rather than eating the king's food and wine (which has not been prepared according to the Law), Daniel and his friends eat only vegetables and water for ten days to prove that by obeying God's laws they will be even healthier than the others in the court.

In chapter 6, Daniel refuses to worship pagan idols and disobeys the order of the king not to address petitions to God for thirty days. He continues to pray in his room three times a day until the men who have promoted the order of the king (expressly to be able to punish Daniel) catch him in the act. Though the king hates to punish his faithful servant, he is bound by the law he has signed. Before casting Daniel into the lions' den, the king says to him: "May your God, whom you serve so constantly, save you" (Dn 6:17).

God sends an angel to keep the lions' mouths closed so that Daniel will not be hurt. The message of this story, as with the others in chapters 1 to 6, is that cooperation with civil authorities combined with faithful prayer and obedience to God's law will protect the Jews and allow them to survive and even thrive under foreign rule.

Tobit

The book of Tobit is written as a religious novel. It is a deuterocanonical book from the second or third century B.C. In 1955, fragments of the book in its original language (Aramaic) were found near the Dead Sea. As with the stories in Daniel 1–6, Tobit emphasizes the benefits of traditional forms of Jewish piety—prayer, fasting, and almsgiving. Its message is that God will never abandon his people as long as they remain faithful to him.

Tobit is set at the time of the fall of the northern kingdom to the Assyrians. It is actually two stories. The characters—Tobit, his wife Anna, and their son Tobiah—are deported to Nineveh. Their story takes place there. Tobit suffers several trials, including blindness from cataracts.

In another city some miles away, a young woman, Sarah, also experiences misfortune. All seven of the men she has married have died on her wedding night at the hands of a jealous demon. The stories come together when Tobiah marries Sarah, survives the wedding night under the protection of the angel Gabriel, defeats the demon, and returns home with Sarah to help his father regain his sight. These tales contain some striking insights about living as a faithful minority in a foreign land.

In chapter 13, Tobit praises God in a joyful prayer. It, too, reminds the Jews of the need to remain faithful in spite of hardships:

> He scourged you for your iniquities,
>   but will again have mercy on you all.
> He will gather you from all the
>   Gentiles
>   among whom you have been
>   scattered.
> When you turn back to him with all
>   your heart,

THE JOURNEY LEADS TO THE TIME OF JESUS AND BEYOND

3. **Homework Assignment**:
   - Complete the group work and answer the questions for your assigned Old Testament book.
   - Read the text sub-sections "Daniel 1–6," "Tobit," "Esther," and "Judith" in the text.

Daniel 1–6
Tobit
Esther
Judith

Bell-Ringers

1. Allow five or ten minutes for the students to confer in their groups and finalize their answers to the questions about their assigned Biblical book or passage.

2. Play a recording of a song with reflective lyrics (e.g., "Psalm 91: Be with Me, Lord") and allow time for quiet reflection.

Teaching Approaches

1. Have the students form groups of four, with each group having one person who represents one of the assigned Scripture passages. Ask the students to take turns summarizing their presentations of Daniel 1–6, Tobit, Esther, and Judith to each other using the summary questions from page 230 of the TWE.

2. Allow about twenty-five minutes for discussion. Then summarize each of the readings using the following information. Encourage the students to take notes.

Daniel 1–6. In Chapter 1, Daniel and his companions receive a Chaldean education in addition to their Hebrew heritage. In Chapter 2, God helps Daniel interpret the king's dream. Daniel shows respect for the Gentile king, and reminds him that the king, like all humans, must be subject to God's will. In Chapter 3, Daniel and friends refuse to worship the king's statue, even at the threat of death. Daniel also continues to pray as a Hebrew, even though it has been forbidden. Daniel is eventually thrown into the lions' den, but is miraculously saved from being eaten. The point of Daniel 1–6 is that God is in control and will remain faithful to his loved ones. God's People can remain faithful to Yahweh regardless of the political system in which they find themselves.

Chapter 10

Tobit. This book is a religious novel. It interweaves the stories of three people—Tobit, Sarah, and Tobiah. All three are good people, yet suffer undeservedly. All three pray, and God answers their prayers. The Jews in the Diaspora read Tobit and were comforted in knowing that God was with them in their own suffering. Like Tobit, Sarah, and Tobiah, they are encouraged to move from despair to prayer.

Esther. This book explains the background of Purim, one of the Jewish feasts of the year. The word *Purim* means "lots." In the book of Esther, a Jewish courtier named Mordecai comes to work for the Persian emperor. The emperor notices Mordecai's niece Esther, and falls in love with her beauty. Haman, another Persian official, hates the Jews and plots to kill them by drawing lots to see which Jews should be killed. Esther reveals to the emperor that she is Jewish; he rescinds his decree to kill the Jews and, instead, kills Haman. Today the Jewish people celebrate the feast of Purim around the first of March.

Judith. The name *Judith* means "Jewish woman." In the book of Judith, the widow Judith represents all Jewish women who have helped to save Israel from the hands of its enemies. In the story, the Israelites cower in fear before Holofernes, the commander of Nebuchadnezzar's armies. Judith, with God's help, takes matters into her own hands. She seduces Holofernes and then beheads him. The religious message is that God will deliver the Jews, but not always through the people or events they had come to expect.

3. **Homework Assignments:**
   - Answer the Review and Reflection questions 1–3, page 229. Use your notes from the class presentations to help you answer these questions.
   - Read "Tracing Jewish History prior to the Maccabean Revolt," including the subsections "Under Persian Rule," "The Beginning of Hellenization," "The Rule of the Ptolemies," "Seleucid Rule," and "Antiochus IV and the Impending Revolt" and the separate feature "The Septuagent" (pages 229–235).

Enrichment: Read one or more of the following stories from the book of Daniel and write the main religious lesson for each story: Daniel and the refusal to eat food (Dn 1:1–21); the fiery furnace (Dn 3:1–56); Daniel in the lions' den (Dn 6:2–25).

---

to do what is right before him,
Then he will turn back to you,
and no longer hide his face from
you (Tb 13:5–6).

The religious message is that the virtue of God's people will triumph over the sinfulness of their oppressors and their own sinfulness.

Esther

The book of Esther is another example of a story whose message says it is better for the Jews to negotiate with foreign kings and function religiously under foreign rule than to oppose them with military force or other forms of extreme nationalism. The story is set in Persia during the reign of Ahasuerus (or Xerxes I). Esther, a beautiful Jewish maiden, is chosen to replace the former queen of Persia. Meanwhile, Ahasuerus, because of the influence of a power-hungry assistant named Haman, has decreed that all Jews should be obliterated. Haman targets the Jews for destruction because Mordecai, Esther's uncle, refuses to kneel in worship to him.

Esther persuades the king to reverse the decision (see Est 6–8). The king—because of his love for Esther—spares the Jews, and Haman is hanged instead. The Jews celebrate this triumph with a great feast (see Est 9). The feast is the origin of the Jewish spring festival *Purim*, which means "lots" (referring to the lot that Haman drew to determine the day to slaughter the Jews).

The message of Esther is much the same as the one in the book of Daniel: Cooperation with the civil rulers and refusal to compromise in religious matters, combined with the traditional elements of Jewish faith—prayer, fasting, and almsgiving—will ensure God's protection. There is another similarity between the two stories. In both stories, it is not ultimately the king whom the Jews have to fear; it is the unscrupulous, jealous, or power-hungry men who surround the king that threaten the Jews' survival.

Esther is also unique because it exists in two forms—a Hebrew edition and a longer Greek edition. The Greek text is not simply added to the end of the Hebrew text; it is interspersed within it. In the *New American Bible*, the added text appears in chapters A through F, which interrupt the numbered chapters of the Hebrew story.

Judith

The book of Judith tells another story with a different message about what the Jews must do to survive life in the Diaspora under foreign rule. The story introduces a fictional woman named Judith ("Jewish woman") in chapter 8, after King Nebuchadnezzar's general, Holofernes, has besieged the Jews for thirty-four days and cut off their water supply rather than attack them directly and risk the loss of his soldiers. As the people perish, the Jews consider surrendering. Judith chides the Jews for their inaction and promises that Yahweh will save his people through her.

Faithfulness to Yahweh, as in the other stories described above, was paramount in the protection of the Jews living in the Diaspora. But Judith does more than resist passively. After praying, she actively stands up for her faith on behalf of God's People. She disguises herself, enters the enemy camp, and beheads Holofernes (see Jdt 13:4–10). This type of proactive response is interspersed in the historical events related to the Jews living under foreign rule in the centuries prior to the birth of Christ.

THE JOURNEY LEADS TO THE TIME OF JESUS AND BEYOND

REVIEW & REFLECTION

1. Explain the two options of the Jewish people in their relationship with the foreign powers that rule over them. Which option is endorsed by Jesus?
2. What do the books of Esther and Daniel have in common?
3. In what ways is the message of Judith different from that of Esther? In what ways is it similar?

JOURNAL ASSIGNMENT

- Have you ever faced a time when you had to choose between what your faith required and what a coach, teacher, or other authority wanted you to do? Perhaps you had game that would make it difficult for you to attend Mass on Sunday. Or you went to a pizza party on a Friday night during Lent—and all the pizzas had pepperoni! How did you resolve the conflict? Would you make the same choice today? What would you do?

Tracing Jewish History Prior to the Maccabean Revolt

The history that led up to the Maccabean Revolt and the events that occurred right up to the time of direct Roman rule in 63 B.C. are complex. It is important to understand some of the historic events of this time period. They provide an important backdrop to events immediately preceding the time of Jesus.

Under Persian Rule

The Persian Period lasted over 200 years, from the time of Cyrus's conquest of Babylon in 539 until the arrival of Alexander the Great in 333 B.C. Little is known about what daily life was like under the Persians. The most significant sources are the Biblical books of Ezra and Nehemiah, and these short works do not report the general conditions of living under the Persian Empire. At least part of the oral tradition that formed the stories of Daniel 1–6 may reflect conditions in the Persian Period, but it is difficult to be certain.

The Persians controlled vast amounts of land extending from Egypt in the West to the Indus River in the East. Palestine was part of a large Persian province known as "Beyond the River." The Jews did have a fair amount of religious and personal freedom, although they were without political rights. The official Persian religion was **Zoroastrianism**, a religion that held that the universe was caught in a constant struggle

Zoroastrianism—The official religion of the Persian Empire, which understood the universe to be caught in a constant struggle between light and darkness. Jewish belief in angels and in Satan's influence can be traced to the influence of this foreign religion.

229

TRACING JEWISH HISTORY PRIOR TO THE MACCABEAN REVOLT

Bell-Ringers

1. This section focuses on how the Jews were affected living under the political and cultural rule of other nations. To begin, make a comparison with how there are pockets or areas in the United States that were influenced by the previous rule and culture of other nations. For example, California and Arizona show the influence of the Mexican government. The thirteen original colonies show the influence of British culture and government. Louisiana, especially New Orleans, shows French influence. Call on volunteers to share examples of this influence (e.g., architecture, cooking styles, language differences, and so forth.) Then explain that the Jews in post-exilic Palestine were also influenced by the foreign powers that ruled over them.

2. Ask the students to summarize what foreign rulers influenced Jewish history and culture from the return from Exile to the birth of Christ. Write this summary on the board. (The Persian Period, ending in 333 B.C.; the Greek Period, beginning with Alexander's conquest of Palestine and continuing with the rule of two of his officers, Ptolemy and Seleucus.)

Review and Reflection Answers

1. The Jews had two options in their relationship with the foreign powers that ruled over them: They could openly resist, or they could cooperate.
2. Both Esther and Daniel urged the Jews to cooperate with the civil rulers while refusing to compromise in religious matters. Traditional elements of Jewish faith—prayer, fasting, and almsgiving—will ensure God's protection.
3. In both books, women saved God's people from foreign rulers or intrigue. While Esther urges the Jews to cooperate with foreign rulers, Judith urged the people to take action by resisting. Both books stressed the importance of being faithful to Yahweh.

Chapter 10

Teaching Approaches

1. Play the entire video, *Religious Diversity in America* (see page 236 of the TWE).

2. Call on students to help summarize the subsection "Under Persian Rule" and explain what life was like under the Persians. Add details to the discussion by using references from the Background Information below.

THE OLD TESTAMENT

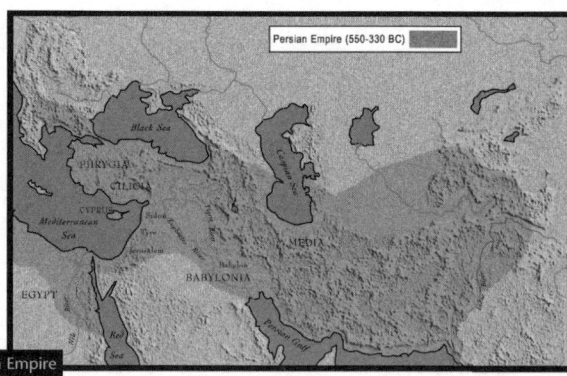

The Persian Empire

koine—The common Greek language introduced in Palestine by Alexander the Great in 333 B.C. It is the language of the Septuagint and remained the common language of Palestine until Latin replaced it in A.D. 500.

Septuagint—The oldest, complete edition of the Old Testament. It is a Greek translation of earlier Hebrew texts, probably written in Alexandria during the time of Ptolemaic rule over Palestine. The word itself, *Septuagint*, is Latin for "seventy" which refers to the traditional story that seventy scholars from the Holy Land were brought to Alexandria to accomplish the translation.

between light and darkness. The influence of this religion on the Jews can be seen in their growing belief in angels and in the larger role assigned to Satan, the fallen angel. By the second century B.C., the books of Daniel and 2 Maccabees clearly stated these beliefs.

The Beginning of Hellenization

The famous general Alexander the Great brought sweeping changes to the region. His time of campaigns was a short nine years (334–323 B.C.) but he conquered massive amounts of territory: Asia Minor in 334 B.C.; Phoenicia, Palestine, and Egypt by 333–332 B.C; the crushing defeat of the Persian army and the ensuing capture of Babylon, Susa, and Persepolis by 331 B.C. One legend

of Alexander tells that when he reached northern India and realized there were no more lands to conquer, he wept.

Alexander introduced Greek ideals, language, learning, dress, and customs to the people whose lands he controlled. Greek athletic contests became popular, and the common Greek language, *koine*, became the official language of the Near East. (The process of imposing Greek culture on conquered civilizations is called Hellenization.) Greek remained the common language of the Middle East until A.D. 500 when it was supplanted by Latin. The *Septuagint* translation of the Hebrew scriptures and the entire New Testament were written in Greek. As a result of the extent of Alexander's Empire and the success of his policy of Hellenization, all of Western

230

Background Information

The Persian Era

The census of Jews at this time in Palestine seemed to be around 50,000. Among these Jews were two groups: those who had returned from Exile in Babylon and those who had either never left Palestine or had returned before 538 B.C. We know that Nehemiah was governor for a time, and Ezra was a priest. The two introduced reforms based on Deuteronomy that included the divorce of Jewish men from Gentile wives, a return to the laws of the Pentateuch, and a rebuilding of the Temple. From that time on, priests and Levites were in charge of Temple worship services. While rebuilding the Temple helped to solidify and define Jewish identity under foreign rule, it also served to divide the Jewish people. The Samaritans rejected the concept that God could only be worshiped in the Temple in Jerusalem. Eventually, they built their own temple on Mount Gerizim, leading to increased hatred between Samaritans and other Jews.

The Persians let the Jews worship according to their own customs. But the Persian religion of Zoroastrianism also influenced Judaism. Zoroastrianism is the religion founded by Zarathushtra, an Iranian-speaking prophet, in the second century B.C. In Zoroastrianism, God is known as Ahura Mazda, or Lord Wisdom. An evil spirit who is always destructive opposes him. Sometimes the evil spirit is called Satan. Satan is a heavenly "accuser" whose function is to question and to test the sincerity of human virtue. He sends sickness, natural catastrophes, and evil to people in order to test their faith.

The Journey Leads to the Time of Jesus and Beyond

culture retains the influence of Greek thought, learning, values, and ideals to this day.

The principle Biblical sources describing Hellenistic influence on the Jews are the first and second books of Maccabees. The first book of Maccabees was written to describe events from the Jewish revolt in 167 down to the period of John Hyrcanus (134–104 B.C), the first ruler of the brief Jewish dynasty known as the Hasmoneans. The second book of Maccabees focuses mostly on the events of the revolt itself, but has a more pious tone than 1 Maccabees. The Jewish historian Josephus, who lived during the time of Christ, provides more information about this period. However, his sources are sometimes called into question.

Upon his death at the young age of thirty-three, Alexander's vast empire was divided among his generals. Although there were periods of cooperation between them, there were many incidents in which one general would dispute with another to try to reestablish control of a larger territory.

The two generals that had the most affect on the Jews were Ptolemy, who ruled in Egypt, and Seleucus of the Seleucid family, who ruled from Syria and controlled large parts of Alexander's eastern empire (Mesopotamia and the Northern Palestine/Lebanon territories). Once again, geography became destiny. The struggles between these two ruling dynasties over the little strip of land that was Palestine determined the fate of the Jews for the next few centuries.

The Rule of the Ptolemies

The **Ptolemies**, rulers in the dynasty that descended from Alexander's general, Ptolemy, controlled Palestine from about 320–200 B.C. The Ptolemies were known for retaining strong, centralized economic control of their territories and laying heavy taxes on the occupied people. However, the Ptolemies also allowed religious autonomy and apparently made no outright efforts to impose Hellenization on the Jews. Despite this, whether forced or not, the Jews themselves divided into factions over the issue of Greek influence. One group began to adopt Greek customs—games, plays, athletics, and philosophy. The other group was staunchly opposed to Greek assimilation and remained strictly loyal to Jewish practices and customs. Of course Greek culture inevitably had some influence even on the traditional factions.

The Egyptian city of Alexandria also came under the rule of the Ptolemies. Alexandria was a great seaboard city—the "Jewel of the Mediterranean"—and an important cultural and economic center. One of the most important developments under the Ptolemies was the construction and maintenance of the great Library of Alexandria.

The Jews in Palestine were free to immigrate to Alexandria. A Jewish community began to grow there as many Jews settled in Alexandria to take advantage of its

Ptolemies—The dynasty descending from Ptolemy I, a general under Alexander the Great, that ruled Egypt and Palestine from 320 to 200 B.C. when they lost control of the land to the Syrian Empire.

3. Use the following review questions to summarize the subsection "The Beginning of Hellenization."
   - Who was Alexander the Great? (He was a Greek general who conquered most of Asia Minor. He introduced Greek ideals, language, learning, dress, and customs to the peoples there. Greek became the official language.)
   - How did the Greek language influence the development of the Bible? (During the Hellenistic age, books or parts of books in the Bible were written in Greek.)
   - What is the Septuagint? (It was a Greek translation of the Hebrew Scriptures and the entire New Testament. This version of the Bible, which contains seventy books, was the oldest known form of the Bible before the Dead Sea Scrolls were discovered.)
   - What Greek generals succeeded Alexander in controlling Palestine? (Ptolemy led the Greeks in Egypt. Seleucus led the Greeks in Asia. Both generals fought one another for control of Palestine.)

Resources
Printed Materials

"Maccabee" and "Macabees, Books of" in *Dictionary of the Bible*, ed. by John L. McKenzie, S.J. (New York, NY: Macmillan Publishing Co., Inc., 1965), pp. 529–532.

"Maccabees, The Books of" in *The Oxford Companion to the Bible*, ed. by Bruce M. Metzger and Michael D. Coogan. (New York, NY: Oxford University Press, 1993), pp. 475–482.

Collins, John J. "3 Maccabees" in *Harper's Bible Commentary*, ed. by James L. Mays. (San Francisco, CA: Harper & Row Publishers, 1988), pp. 916–921.

McEleney, Neil J., C.S.P. "1–2 Maccabees" in *The New Jerome Biblical Commentary*, ed. by Raymond E. Brown, S.S., Joseph A. Fitzmyer, S.J., and Roland E. Murphy, O.Carm. (Englewood Cliffs, NJ: Prentice Hall, 1990), pp. 421–446.

Schiffman, Lawrence H. "1 Maccabees" and "2 Maccabees" in *Harper's Bible Commentary*, ed. by James L. Mays. (San Francisco, CA: Harper & Row Publishers, 1988), pp. 875–915.

Spilly, Alphonse P., C. PP.S. "1 Maccabees" and "2 Maccabees" in *The Collegeville Bible Commentary*, ed. by Dianne Bergant, C.S.A. and Robert J. Karris, O.F.M. (Collegeville, MN: The Liturgical Press, 1989), pp. 370–410.

Stowers, Stanley K. "4 Maccabees" in *Harper's Bible Commentary*, ed. by James L. Mays. (San Francisco, CA: Harper & Row Publishers, 1988), pp. 922–934.

Wright, Addison G., Roland E. Murphy, O.Carm., and Joseph A. Fitzmyer, S.J. "A History of Israel" in *The New Jerome Biblical Commentary*, ed. by Raymond E. Brown, S.S., Joseph A. Fitzmyer, S.J., and Roland E. Murphy, O.Carm. (Englewood Cliffs, NJ: Prentice Hall, 1990), pp. 1219–1252.

Chapter 10

4. Explore some of these issues more deeply. For example, have the students read the separate feature "The Septuagint" (page 232). Also, assign the "Investigating the Dead Sea Scrolls" exercise on page 233.

5. Summarize the text sections on the periods of the Ptolemies and Seleucids through Antiochus IV. Highlight the bitter rule of Antiochus IV. Point out that he banned the practice of traditional Jewish religion. He forbade study of the Law, observance of the Sabbath, circumcision of male children, and Temple sacrifice unless it was pagan sacrifice.)

The Old Testament

cultural and economic opportunities. The Alexandrian Jewish community would remain an important center of Jewish culture in the Diaspora for centuries after this. It is likely that the book of Wisdom originated in Alexandria around 100 B.C. Most likely, the great task of translating the Hebrew scriptures into Greek was also undertaken in Alexandria. (See "The Septuagint," below).

The Septuagint

The *Septuagint* (Latin for "seventy") is the term used to refer to the Greek translation of the Hebrew scriptures. It is often indicated by simply using the Roman numeral LXX. Until the discovery of the **Dead Sea Scrolls**, the Greek versions of the Old Testament were the oldest actual manuscripts available for doing textual analysis of the Bible in ancient languages. They are still the oldest complete editions of the Bible.

The legend of the Septuagint appears in a book known as the "Letter to Aristeas." This work says that the Ptolemies were deeply disturbed to find that the Library of Alexandria did not include the great writings of the Jews. So they brought seventy-two Hebrew elders (six from each tribe) to Egypt and commissioned them to translate the Bible into Greek. (These seventy-two translators are where the Septuagint gets its name.) The translators divided into teams, and when they were finished, a miracle had occurred. Each of their translations was exactly the same! Though a delightful story, the only verifiable truth to the tale was that the Septuagint was produced in Egypt in the time of the Ptolemaic rule over Palestine.

In actuality, the writing of the Septuagint does not appear to have been a well-organized effort. There are indications of many different translators at work on the various books. There were clearly multiple attempts to translate similar passages. The resulting earliest work—known as the "Old Greek"—was itself often criticized and re-translated by others.

There are some interesting curiosities about the Greek versions of the scriptures. For example, material that was written at a later period—closer to the time of the Septuagint translation—was added to a number of older books. The book of Esther, for example, grew to almost twice the size of the Hebrew version. Daniel picked up a number of new chapters. Whole books, such as Sirach, Tobit, Judith, and the Maccabean literature, were all eventually made a part of this collection. This expanded collection of books became for Christians the "Old Testament."

These additional books and passages are what makes the "Catholic Bible" different from the "Protestant Bible." It is not that Catholics "added" these additional books; rather, Martin Luther and the Protestants removed them in the sixteenth century. Today these books that are unique to the Greek versions of the Old Testament are known as the "deuterocanonical" or "apocryphal" books.

Dead Sea Scrolls—Ancient scrolls containing the oldest known manuscripts of the books of the Old Testament in Hebrew. They were discovered in caves near Qumran on the Dead Sea between 1947 and 1953.

Resources

Audiovisual Materials

Enigma of the Dead Sea Scrolls (Vision Video)—50 minutes
An introduction and examination of the key issues related to the Dead Sea Scrolls.

In Search of the Holy Temple (Vision Video)—25 minutes
Computer animation shows the Temple of Jerusalem as it was 2,000 years ago. Since the days of King Solomon, the Temple in Jerusalem symbolized God's covenant with the Jewish people. Six hundred years after its construction, the Temple was the scene of a Jewish revolt against legions of Roman soldiers. We learn why Rome was determined to prevail, and what happened to the Temple.

Judaism: The Religion of a People (EcuFilm)—25 minutes
The video traces the development and practice of Judaism from its earliest beginnings to the present day. Topics discussed include: the Torah, Jewish practices, the Holocaust, Judaism in the Middle East, the State of Israel, and Judaism in America.

Religious Diversity in America (Oblate Media)—23 minutes
A short introduction to several religious traditions present in the United States today. The video defines religious terminology such as pluralism, polytheism, monotheism, and exclusivity, and explores the basic tenets of Judaism, Islam, Christianity, Hinduism, and Buddhism.

Religions of the World: Judaism (Social Studies School Service)—50 minutes
In addition to tracing the history of Judaism, the video examines sacred texts and various Jewish holidays. It also explores the two centers of Jewish life: the synagogue and the home.

The Journey Leads to the Time of Jesus and Beyond

Seleucid Rule

The Seleucid rulers, who based their part of the old Alexandrian Empire in Babylon and the Eastern cities, also ruled over much of Syria. In approximately 200 B.C., these rulers drove out the Egyptian-based Ptolemies and came into power in Palestine under the leadership of Antiochus III. While the Jews hailed the Seleucids as liberators at first, Jewish life under Seleucid rule deteriorated rapidly. The Roman Empire was also increasingly becoming a strong and forbidding presence in the region. It was during this time that historical events began to get complicated.

There was considerable internal turmoil among the Jewish community in Palestine early in the reign of the Seleucids over the issue of control of large sums of Temple funds. The Temple acted as the most secure "bank," for the Jews in this region, and thus considerable sums of money were accumulated in Temple treasuries. This made the Temple and its administrators prime targets of the Seleucid rulers. (Temples of most religions throughout the region served as the local "bank," so they were nearly always prime targets for outside conquerors who often went to the temple, first, when they invaded a city.)

Inevitably, a struggle broke out among Jewish factions over who would be the High Priest and thus earn the right to negotiate financial and trade deals with the Seleucids. There were other key administrative positions for Jews to seek as well—such as the right to collect taxes. A tax collector's reward was to keep whatever he collected beyond the obligations to the government. Obviously, the potential for abuse under such a system was very great.

These internal debates were made worse by the fact that a growing faction of Jews continued to be more Hellenized in attitude, practice, and outlook. Accompanying this, these Jews became less and less scrupulous about the observation of traditional Jewish practice and rites. Such Hellenistic attitudes inevitably drew a reaction from more traditional Jews. After all, the Jewish people had lived under pagan imperial control since 587 B.C. They had no real ruler, and did not control their land, so their traditions and faith were the centerpieces of their existence. This placed the Temple at the center of the political and religious controversies of both groups of Jews.

INVESTIGATING THE DEAD SEA SCROLLS

Research and report on the relationship of the Dead Sea Scrolls to the Old Testament. Include controversies surrounding the scrolls, especially over their translation and publication. Also add information on the Church's response to the finding of the Dead Sea Scrolls. Finally, make a list of the five web sites you found most valuable in researching this topic.

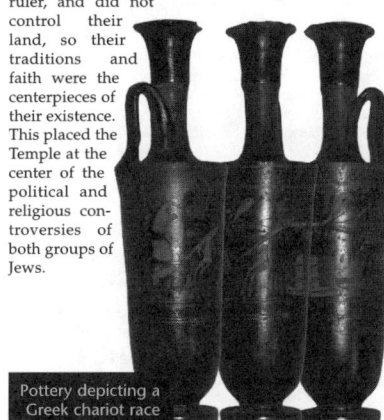

Pottery depicting a Greek chariot race

6. Form a panel with five or six students to discuss this situation: Imagine that a foreign power took control of the United States and banished the right of religious freedom. The government refused to let you attend church, pray with others, baptize your children, receive any of the sacraments, or teach your children about Catholicism. Ask these questions:
   - How do you think you would react?
   - Would you openly rebel?
   - Would you silently rebel by continuing to be a Catholic in private? Or would you acquiesce to what the government has ruled?

Allow sufficient time for the panel to discuss the issue. Also allow comments from the rest of the "audience" (students). Follow up by explaining that this was the situation the Jews found themselves in under Antiochus. They were back in Palestine and they had rebuilt the Temple, but they could not live or worship as God's People.

Resources
Internet Links

www.americancatholic.org/Newsletters/SFS/an0901.asp
This article from Scripture From Scratch focuses on chapters 7–12 of the book of Daniel.

www.time.com/time/international/1995/951127/archaeology.html
Read a 1995 *Time Magazine* article about the archaeological discovery of the tomb of the Maccabees.

http://home.comcast.net/~dboals1/m-east.html
A history/social studies website for teachers with links to many sites from the Ancient Near East, including information and images of artifacts from the archaeological dig at Yodefat from the time of the Maccabees.

www.fas.harvard.edu/~semitic
View the Semitic Museum at the Harvard College Library to see artifacts from ancient Jewish culture.

www.jewishmuseum.org
Examine objects of Jewish culture from ancient and modern times at the Jewish Museum in New York City.

www.imj.org.il
Survey wedding costumes, spice boxes, Torah scroll cases, mezuzah cases, and other artifacts of Judaica and Jewish Ethnography from the Israel Museum of Jerusalem. One exhibit "Envisioning the Temple" presents ancient scrolls, stones, and symbols of the Temple in Jerusalem.

www.templeinstitute.org/main.html
View ancient Temple vessels and archaeological findings at the Temple Institute in Jerusalem.

Chapter 10

7. **Homework Assignment:**
   - Write answers to the Review and Reflection questions 1–5, page 235.
   - Complete the Journal Assignment, page 235. Relate the entry to some of the issues brought up in the class discussion.
   - Complete the "Investigating the Dead Sea Scrolls" exercise.
   - Read "From the Maccabees to Roman Control" (pages 235–241).

Antiochus IV and the Impending Revolt

The Temple debates led to two opposing Jewish factions confronting each other: the Hellenized Jews and the more traditional group. The confrontation came to the forefront when a wealthy Jewish family (the house of Tobiah), who had created their financial dynasty from their business dealings with the Hellenistic administration, attempted to remove Onias III as High Priest. The more traditionalist Jewish families considered Onias to be the legitimate head of the Temple.

Both Jewish factions appealed to the Seleucids for support. But the Seleucid family at the time was also unstable. Antiochus III died and was followed by Seleucus IV. But Seleucus IV was soon killed, probably by the one who then assumed the throne, the infamous Antiochus IV, who called himself "Epiphanes" ("God is with us"). In order to consolidate his power, Antiochus IV acted quickly in dealing with the Jews. When Onias came to Antioch to appeal for his rightful role as the High Priest, Antiochus IV imprisoned him, and appointed his brother Jason as the High Priest, most likely because he had been bribed by Jason and his supporters. Jason was sympathetic to the Hellenized Jews.

Modern day Alexandria

Three years later a powerful family called the Tobiads outbid Jason, and the disastrous Menelaus was made High Priest. Menelaus further enraged the more traditional Jews by his support of Greek traditions. He even cooperated with Antiochus IV in the construction of Greek shrines in Jerusalem and the looting of the Temple.

Antiochus IV was as zealous about Hellenization as Alexander the Great had been. Believing that the Jews were the cause of many of his problems (including his unsuccessful efforts to take control of Egypt), he virtually banned the practice of traditional Jewish religion. He forbade study of the Law, observance of the Sabbath, circumcision of male children, and Temple sacrifice (unless it was pagan sacrifice).

It is likely that Antiochus IV was acting under the advice of some of his Hellenized Jewish supporters, who wanted to gain a permanent advantage over the traditionalist Jews. In fact, among the Jews who were attracted to Greek culture, Antiochus IV's policies met with little or no resistance. Among these "modernist" Jews, Greek dress and participation in the gymnasium were popular. (Some of these Jewish males even had surgery to reverse their circumcisions in order to avoid embarrassment when participating in athletics in the nude!) Those who participated in athletics at the gymnasium had to recognize the Greek gods who were the gymnasium's patrons. Worship of false gods was the greatest abomination to traditional Jews.

The policies instituted by Antiochus IV were certainly brutal in their own right. But it is important to understand that some of Anitochus IV's mandates were instituted in response to the internal conflict among the Jews that Antiochus was determined to use to his own advantage.

Background Information

From the Ptolemies to Antiochus IV

The Ptolemies ruled over Palestine from 300 to 200 B.C. It was during this time that the Hebrew Scriptures were translated into Greek. In Jerusalem, the Jewish community was led by the high priest, who was both a civil and religious authority, and a council of elders.

In 200 B.C. the Seleucid king Antiochus III defeated the troops of Ptolemy V. From that time on, the Seleucids ruled over Palestine. Antiochus III was generous with the Jews, allowing Temple worship to continue. His son, Seleucus IV, took power. He was killed by an army general named Heliodorus, who allowed Antiochus IV access to the throne. Antiochus IV enforced Greek language and customs on the people of Palestine. He also taxed them heavily to finance his building campaign. Antiochus was sometimes called "The Mad Man." Under Antiochus, the High Priest and Temple staff became vulnerable because they controlled Temple finances and Antiochus was always in need of more money. Certain Jews became hated tax collectors among the Israelite people

THE JOURNEY LEADS TO THE TIME OF JESUS AND BEYOND

FROM THE MACCABEES TO ROMAN CONTROL

Bell-Ringers

1. Choose a recent political debate (national or local) that aroused strong but differing opinions among Americans (e.g., a presidential campaign, foreign policy, whether or not to go to war, taxation issues, environmental issues, the death penalty, etc.) Call on a student to be "on the spot" and present his or her opinion on the issue. Next, ask a student with a differing view to be on the spot. After allowing sufficient time for discussion, explain that even though people hold different beliefs and views, they are still all Americans. The same was true of the Jews in first and second-century Palestine. They held different beliefs and views about how to live under foreign rule, but they were all still Jews.

2. Play part of the video *Enigma of the Dead Sea Scrolls* (see page 237 of the TWE). The video runs for 50 minutes.

REVIEW & REFLECTION

1. What influence did the time spent under the control of the Persians have on Jewish faith?
2. Describe the process of Hellenization. Why do you think Alexander the Great would have insisted on Hellenization in the lands he conquered?
3. Explain the importance of the Jewish community in Alexandria. What brought them there? What were they able to achieve?
4. Who were the Seleucids and when and how did they come to power in Palestine?
5. What was the source of internal division within the Jewish community in Jerusalem? How did this affect the relationship between the Jewish community and the Seleucid ruler, Antiochus IV?

JOURNAL ASSIGNMENT

- How was the division between Hellenistic Jews and traditional Jews like the arguments between today's opposing political parties and viewpoints? Give examples.

From the Maccabees to Roman Control

The conditions of internal conflict and resentment over the barbarous mandates of Antiochus IV were soon to reach their boiling points. Antiochus certainly did not understand the uncompromising nature of Jewish monotheism, the belief in Yahweh alone. As Jewish resistance to his policies mounted, Antiochus enacted sterner measures. When Antiochus suffered the humiliating forced withdrawal of his troops from Egypt at the order of the Romans near 167 B.C., he blamed the Jews. He then unleashed his army on the Jews in Jerusalem and issued an edict forbidding the practice of Judaism in all traditional forms. Jews were even forced to eat foods forbidden by the Law.

Read 2 Maccabees 6:18–7:42

The final offense came when an altar to Zeus was erected in the Temple in Jerusalem and unclean swine's flesh was sacrificed on it. Jews considered this act to be an "abomination of desolation" that defiled the entire Temple. The first book of Maccabees describes some of the desperation of the traditional Jews' situation:

> ... the king erected the horrible abomination upon the altar of holocausts, and in the surrounding cities of Judah they built pagan altars. They also burnt incense at the doors of houses and in the streets. Any scrolls of the law which they found they tore up and burnt. Whoever was found with a scroll of the covenant, and whoever observed the law, was condemned to death by royal decree. So they used their power against Israel, against those who were

---

Review and Reflection Answers

1. The Persian religion, Zoroastrianism, introduced angels and demons (specifically Satan) to the Jewish religion.
2. After the Greeks gained control of Palestine, they introduced Greek ideals, language, learning, dress, and customs to the people there. This process was called Hellenization. Alexander probably used Hellenization as a way to enforce his authority over the peoples he conquered.
3. The Jewish community in Alexandria was an important center of Jewish culture in the Diaspora. It is likely that this community translated the Hebrew Scriptures into Greek and wrote the book of Wisdom.
4. The Seleucids were rulers from the line of Seleucus, one of Alexander's generals. They came to power in Palestine in 200 B.C. when the Seleucid king Antiochus III defeated the troops of Ptolemy V.
5. The Jewish community in Jerusalem was divided into the Hellenized Jews and the more traditional group. The confrontation came when the Hellenized family of Tobiah attempted to remove Onias III as High Priest. The traditional Jews protested, believing Onias was the rightful high priest. When Antiochus IV came to power, he imprisoned Onias III and appointed his brother Jason as High Priest. Jason was eventually replaced by Menelaus, another Greek sympathizer. Menelaus cooperated with Antiochus IV in the construction of Greek shrines in Jerusalem and the looting of the Temple.

CHAPTER 10

Teaching Approaches

1. Assign 2 Maccabees 6. Summarize the text, making the following points:
   - Antiochus IV desecrated the Temple in Jerusalem by turning it into a brothel honoring Zeus.
   - Antiochus forced Jews to renounce their religion and to eat pork, an unclean food.
   - Eleazar was a ninety-year-old Jew who refused to eat pork or meat that had been offered to Greek gods. He was courageous in standing up for his beliefs, even though it meant torture and death.

   Ask the students: What can you learn from Eleazar to help you combat social and peer pressures?

2. Introduce Judas Maccabeus from the text subsection and from 1 Maccabees 4:36–59, the attack of the Temple. Explain that Judas was one of the sons of Mattathias Maccabees, a local priest who refused the order to sacrifice to Greek gods. He killed the king's officer who came to his village to enforce it. Mattathias called other Jews to join him in revolting against the Greeks. When Mattathias died, Judas led the revolt.

---

hasidim—A Hebrew word meaning "loyal ones." It refers to a group who supported the Maccabees in the military effort against Antiochus IV. They also were probably the core members of the later group known as the Essenes.

Pharisees—A group of Jews whose response to foreign rule was one of cultural and religious separatism. They valued adherence to the Law, and exhibited great respect for teachers and interpreters of the Torah. They were responsible for the introduction of rabbis and synagogues into the cultural life of the Jews.

Essenes—A group of Jews whose resistance to foreign influence took them to the extreme position of living in entirely separate communities in the desert around the Dead Sea. It is probable that they were the ones who hid the Dead Sea Scrolls, which were not discovered until the middle of the twentieth century.

caught, each month, in the cities. . . . But many in Israel were determined and resolved in the hearts not to eat anything unclean; they preferred to die rather than to be defiled with unclean food or to profane the holy covenant; and they did die. Terrible affliction was upon Israel (1 Mc 1:54–58, 62–63).

Judas Maccabeus

In the village of Modein, north of Jerusalem, a revolt against the Seleucid powers broke out, led by Mattathias and his sons. Mattathias, a local priest of the family later known as the Hasmoneans, refused the order to sacrifice to Greek gods and killed the king's officer who came to his village to enforce it. Mattathias called all Jews who were loyal to their faith to resist and fight against Antiochus. Support came from a group known as the **hasidim** ("loyal ones"). This group was probably the forerunners of both the **Pharisees** and **Essenes**, later Jewish sects with similarly resistant positions against Hellenistic influences.

When Mattathias died shortly after the revolt began, leadership passed to one of his five sons, Judas, who turned out to be a brilliant military strategist. Judas was called "Maccabeus" which may be translated as "the Hammer." A series of victories by Judas Maccabeus against local military forces led to revolutionary control of the Temple in Jerusalem in December 164 B.C., three years to the month from the time that the Temple was profaned.

After the Temple's purification and rededication, the Jews offered sacrifices there again. This event is still commemorated by Jews in the celebration of "Hanukkah," the Festival of Lights. According to Jewish tradition, a miracle occurred at the rededication of the Temple. The lamp, which was supposed to burn in the Holy of Holies, was fueled with a special oil. But when the Maccabees had purified the Temple and were ready to rededicate it, they found only enough oil to fuel the lamp for one day. Despite this, the lamp remained lit throughout the days of celebration, until more could be made. Today's menorah has nine candles. One is used for lighting the other eight, the number of days the oil miraculously lasted during the Maccabees' celebration of the rededication of the Temple.

Read 1 Maccabees 4:36–59

Even though the Temple was liberated and some elements of traditional Jewish practice were restored, the conflict between the Maccabees and the central Seleucid administration continued to rage on. Judas eventually sent a delegation to Rome in order to secure a treaty (see 1 Mc 8:17–32). This may be an indication that Judas had more than religious motivations in mind; he was now acting like an independent statesman and may have had nationalist aspirations. When Judas was killed in battle in 160 B.C., the open military element of the revolt ended. But the leadership that the revolt had created in the Maccabean family—the descendents of Mattathias known as the Hasmoneans—remained a permanent element in the political life of Palestine from 160 until the Romans determined to rule Palestine directly in 63 B.C.

The Maccabees

After Judas died, his brother Jonathan led the Jews for seventeen years. He was the first of several rulers who oversaw a return of a certain level of Jewish independence to Palestine after centuries of subjection to Persian and Greek rule.

Jewish independence was not yet complete. The Seleucid government still influenced Jewish leaders. Two pretenders to the Selueucid throne—Alexander Balas and Demetrius—sought Jonathan's support. Jonathan chose to support Demetrius. He was rewarded with the title of High Priest and allowed to assemble an army. When Jonathan was killed, Simon, the last surviving son of Mattathias, took over as High Priest. In 141 B.C. Simon's forces overthrew the remaining Syrian fortifications and proclaimed the long awaited Jewish independence, winning decrees of independence from both the Syrians and Rome (see 1 Mc 13–16):

> Thus in the year one hundred and seventy, the yoke of the Gentiles was removed from Israel, and the people began to write in their records and contracts, "In the first year of Simon, high priest, governor, and leader of the Jews" (1 Mc 13:41–42).

Though the Maccabees were not of the Davidic line, some officials and Jews decreed that Simon would be their permanent leader and high priest "until a true prophet arises" (1 Mc 14:42). This may have angered some more traditional Jews and seems to have lead to the development of the Essene movement, a sect that lived in the desert and survived until the second century A.D.

Simon did establish a period of peaceful rule until he was assassinated by his son-in-law in 134 B.C. He was succeeded by his son, John Hyrcanus, who is considered the first ruler of an independent Judea in the **Hasmonean Dynasty**.

Hasmonean Dynasty

John Hyrcanus ruled until 128 B.C. Although Judea had official declarations of independence from both Syria and Rome, for all practical purposes, John Hycranus was a puppet king to these larger empires, much as Zedekiah was in 587 B.C. John Hyrcanus began a campaign to expand Jewish territories, eventually nearly replicating the land Israel held at the time of King David. His forces subdued the Edomites, causing the males to be circumcised and forcing all to obey the Law. (This forced conversion of the Edomites, or Idumeans, would come back to haunt the Jews in the person of Herod, who was an Idumean and

Hasmonean Dynasty—Descendants of the Maccabees who ruled in Judea after the ousting of the last of the Syrians in 141 B.C. until the establishment of Roman authority in 63 B.C. John Hyrcanus was the first ruler in this dynasty and ruled until 128 B.C.

THE JOURNEY LEADS TO THE TIME OF JESUS AND BEYOND

3. Distribute copies of "Traditional Customs of Hanukkah," (Handout 10A page 287 of the TWE) and explain the traditional customs of Hanukkah described at the top of the page. Provide an answer to the first activity questions (when Hanukkah will occur in the coming year). As an option for the second activity, invite a Jewish person to class to explain some of his or her family practices of the holiday.

4. Summarize the text subsections "The Maccabees," "Hasmonean Dynasty," and "Roman Rule". Begin by printing the highlighted vocabulary words from these sub-sections on the board. Ask the students to write a sentence explaining the term and how it fits into the context of the material they read:

   Hasmonean Dynasty—descendants of the Maccabees who ruled in Judea after the ousting of the last of the Syrians in 141 B.C. until the establishment of Roman authority in 63 B.C.. John Hyrcanus was the first ruler in this dynasty and ruled until 128 B.C.

   Rabbi—the local leader of a community's synagogue, respected for his piety and knowledge of the Law. This is a position that came into being with the establishment of the synagogues by the Pharisees.

   Sadducees—originally an aristocratic group of wealthy Jews in Jerusalem who favored strict adherence to the letter of the Torah and regarded Temple worship as essential to Jewish life. They denied such doctrines as the resurrection and the existence of angels because those subjects cannot be found in the Torah.

   synagogue—a meeting place for study and prayer introduced by the Pharisees to foster study of the Law and adherence to the covenant code.

Chapter 10

5. Continue with a review of the material. Divide the class into two teams. Award two points to a team whose representative can answer a question on the first try. Award one point to a team that can answer a missed question after consulting among themselves. Continue alternating the order for each round.
   - What happened after Judas Maccebeus died? (His brother Jonathan took over. When Jonathan was killed, the last brother, Simon, became High Priest and governor.)
   - How did the Jewish people receive Simon? (Some supported him and said he was their permanent leader. Others, such as the Essenes, rejected him and moved to the desert to get away from him.)
   - Who were the Hasmoneans? (They were rulers in Palestine following the death of Simon. The first Hasmonean ruler was Simon's son John Hyrcanus.)
   - How did the Hasmoneans relate to the Greeks? (They cooperated with the Greeks and aided them in their nationalistic goals.)
   - Which group of Jews supported the Hasmonean ruler Alexander Janneus? (The Sadducees, a group of wealthy Jews in Jerusalem.)
   - Which group of Jews openly opposed the Hasmonean ruler Alexander Janneus? (The Pharisees.)
   - How did the Sadducees and the Pharisees differ in their interpretation of Judaism? (The Sadducees did not believe in an afterlife or resurrection from the dead. They observed a strict practice of Torah laws and regulations and Temple sacrifices. The Pharisees believed in an afterlife. They emphasized study and interpretation of the Law. They also placed a strong emphasis on pious religious rites in the home. Eventually, they introduced two new institutions into Jewish religious practice: the synagogue and the rabbi.)
   - To which group did Jesus belong? (The Pharisees)
   - Who were the Essenes? (They were a religious group that moved to the desert. They studied the Old Testament and may have been the ones who left the Dead Sea Scrolls.)

Sadducees—Originally an aristocratic group of wealthy Jews in Jerusalem who favored strict adherence to the letter of the Torah and regarded Temple worship as essential to Jewish life. They denied such doctrines as the resurrection and the existence of angels because those subjects cannot be found in the Torah.

synagogue—A meeting place for study and prayer introduced by the Pharisees to foster study of the Law and adherence to the covenant code.

Rabbi—The local leader of a community's synagogue, respected for his piety and knowledge of the Law. This is a position that came into being with the establishment of the synagogues by the Pharisees.

a hated ruler over the Jews a century later.) John Hyrcanus led the destruction of the Samaritan temple at Mount Gerizim. He also renewed the treaty that Judas Maccabeus had made with the Roman senate.

The Hasmonean kings following John Hyrcanus were equally involved in political gains and nationalism. His successors sanctioned even more moral decay within Judaism, acting like the political and economic modernists they initially defeated. The Hasmoneans cooperated with Greek leaders, and they often assisted the Seleucid dynasty in battle as a loyal ally. Nationalism, it seems, once again created circumstances of compromise.

Internally, the Jewish population was reacting to these political and religious measures in different ways. The reactions led to the development of Jewish sects that remained active through Jesus' time. The **Sadducees** were originally an aristocratic group of wealthy Jerusalem Jews who viewed the strict letter of the Torah and the Temple sacrifices to be the most important institutions in Jewish life. They denied the doctrine of an afterlife or resurrection of the dead because these teachings were not found in the Torah. The Sadducees were supporters of the Hasmonean king Alexander Janneus, and Alexander responded by favoring their status.

The Pharisees (from the term "parash" for "separate") rivaled the Sadducees. They openly opposed the religious and political policies of Alexander Janneus for which they paid a severe price. Alexander had several hundred Pharisees executed by crucifixion because of their opposition. Alexander's wife, Salome, however, reconciled with the Pharisees during her reign as queen and allowed them to have the dominant hand in determining local policy.

The Pharisees established much of their identity during this time, an identity that would be prevalent in New Testament times. The particular emphasis of the Pharisees was on study and interpretation of the Law. The Pharisees exhibited a great respect for their learned teachers and preserved the written commentaries of these teachers with a reverence almost equal to that which they accorded the older Scriptures themselves. The Pharisees also placed a strong emphasis on pious religious rites in the home—for example, washings and prayers before meals. The Pharisees eventually introduced two new institutions into Jewish religious practice: a local meeting place designed for prayer and study known as the **synagogue** and a local leader who was revered for his piety and learning, eventually called a **rabbi**. Jesus himself was most likely raised within the Pharisaic tradition of Jewish faith and practice. St. Paul and other early Christians certainly came from that background, as well.

As mentioned on page 236, a group known as the Essenes reacted to the internal bickering and secularism within Jerusalem by withdrawing from Jerusalem com-

The Journey Leads to the Time of Jesus and Beyond

pletely. The Essenes went to the desert around the Dead Sea, bringing copies of most of the books that would later be made into the Old Testament. They also wrote and studied bizarre apocalyptic books about the coming devastation they believed would place them back in authority in Palestine—a great battle between "The Sons of Darkness" and "The Sons of Light." This desert community is usually considered responsible for hiding the scriptures, which were only discovered again between 1947 and 1953, in the caves by the Dead Sea.

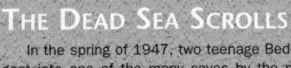

RESURRECTION OF THE DEAD

The second book of Maccabees is one of the first places in the Scripture with explicit references to the resurrection of the dead. Read the following passages from 2 Maccabees with references to the resurrection of the dead:

- 2 Maccabees 7:9–11
- 2 Maccabees 7:23–24
- 2 Maccabees 12:41–46

Trace the idea of resurrection of the dead in the Old Testament using the notes and cross references in your Bible. Also use a Bible concordance to find out more information on the topic.

Finally, write a short essay detailing your own belief in the resurrection. How does your belief center on Jesus? Also, touch on some specifics of how you view life after you die and rise.

THE DEAD SEA SCROLLS

In the spring of 1947, two teenage Bedouin boys chased a young goat into one of the many caves by the shore of the Dead Sea in Palestine. When one of the boys threw a rock into the cave to try to scare the young goat back out, he heard the sound of shattering pottery. When they checked to see what made the noise, the boys found eight earthenware jars containing parchment scrolls. Eventually scrolls and fragments of scrolls containing writings in Hebrew and Aramaic of the Hebrew scriptures, Biblical commentaries, and other writings were found in eleven caves in the area. The scrolls were sold several times to antique dealers before four of the scrolls eventually came into the hands of the Patriarch of Jerusalem. It was at that point that the scrolls began to make international news.

These scrolls are known as the *Dead Sea Scrolls* or *Qumran Scrolls* because they were found near the ruins of a settlement close to Qumran on the shore of the Dead Sea. The Dead Sea Scrolls were the single most important archaeological discovery of the twentieth century (although *many* other important discoveries occurred during that period). They are important because the scrolls contain at least part of every single book of the Hebrew Bible (except Esther). Some of the books were almost entirely complete (e.g., Isaiah), while others are only partially intact. The Dead Sea Scrolls provide Hebrew manuscripts of the Old Testament over one thousand years older than any Hebrew manuscript previously possessed. Biblical scholars are now able to check the previously known Hebrew versions against pieces and manuscripts so much older. The reliability of the Hebrew texts have been improved dramatically.

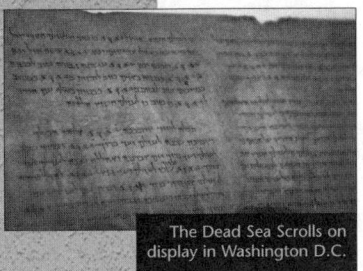

The Dead Sea Scrolls on display in Washington D.C.

---

6. Assign the "Resurrection of the Dead" exercise on page 239. Explain to the students that they will be asked to share some or all of their essays at the next class session.

7. Answer any questions the students have on the Dead Sea Scrolls from the text and video (*Enigma of the Dead Sea Scrolls*) if you were able to show it. Also, refer the students to Luke 4:16–22. Point out that the kind of scroll that Jesus read from in the Nazareth synagogue may be similar to the Dead Sea Scrolls.

Background Information

Resurrection of the Dead

Catholics believe in the resurrection of the body, the resurrection of all the dead (both those who merit reward and those who merit punishment, and the existence of heaven, hell, and purgatory.

The most important quality of the resurrected body is immortality; those who have been raised will never die again. St. Paul lists other characteristics of the resurrected body: imperishable, glorious, powerful, and spiritual.

As to the resurrection of the dead, those who have done good and merit eternal reward will spend eternal life in union with God. Those who die separated from God and who deserve punishment will either spend time in purgatory being cleansed of their sins or in hell. Hell is eternal separation from God.

CHAPTER 10

8. **Homework Assignment**:
   - Finish the "Resurrection of the Dead" assignment, including the essay on your personal beliefs about the resurrection.
   - Write answers to the Review and Reflection questions 1–3, page 241.
   - Complete the Journal Assignment, page 241. You may wish to choose a current issue and comment on it (e.g., public funding at Catholic hospitals, Catholics running for political office).
   - Read the text section "Cooperation or Resistance: What Was the Best Course for the Jews?" (pages 241–244)

Enrichment: Read of the martyrdom of the mother and her sons from 2 Maccabees 7. Rewrite the story using eight modern incidents of courage or martyrdom.

Enrichment: Read 2 Maccabees 15:11–16. Explain how this passage refers to the power of saints in heaven to offer intercession for those on earth. Also, read 2 Maccabees 12:39–46. Explain how these passages show the power of the living to offer prayers and sacrifices for the dead. How have these beliefs been incorporated into Catholic life?

THE OLD TESTAMENT

Dead Sea Scrolls continued

Almost equally important for modern historical research are the dozens of previously undiscovered Scripture commentaries that were found. These commentaries were written by the Essenes, who left Jerusalem during the Hasmonean period, probably in protest against the corruption they experienced there and who probably stored scrolls in the caves in the first place. Their bitter writings directed against the corrupt Hebrews and their leaders back in Jerusalem were often violent, although there is no evidence that the Essenes took violent action against the Hasmoneans. They considered themselves to be the "Sons of Light" who would soon engage in spiritual (and perhaps actual?) battle against the "Sons of Darkness." These Essene documents help to explain the different ways that Jews thought about their faith in this period and how influential apocalyptic thinking was on some of these groups.

Almost all of the Dead Sea materials have now been translated into English in excellent editions with good notes. Only small pieces remain to be translated—a difficult task as some pieces have only a few letters on them.[1]

Roman Rule

The Hasmoneans continued to bicker internally. Salome (76–67 B.C.) appointed her elder son Hycranus II high priest. After Salome's death, Hyrcanus and his younger brother Aristobulus II fought over power. Aristobulus became king and high priest, although Hyrcanus continued to plot for those positions. All of this chaos opened the door for the Romans, the major military power of the region, to intervene in Palestine in 63 B.C.

The Roman general Pompey stripped the Hasmoneans of their power. Palestine was made part of the Roman province of Syria. Pompey separated the civil and religious powers in Judea, appointing his own high priest in Jerusalem and setting up a puppet king who had to answer to Rome. The Jews remained under Roman control until the seventh century A.D. when the Moslem invasions began.

Rome originally ruled Jerusalem, Palestine, and Syria through a governor, Scaurus, leaving religious authority to the high priest, who was influenced by Antipater of Idumaea, a region south of Palestine. Antipater and Hyrcanus II played politics and Rome gave Antipater the title of procurator of Judea while Hyrcanus was named *ethnarch* ("ruler of the people") in addition to being high priest.

In 37 B.C. one of Antipater's sons, Herod, became king of Judea. He was aided by the Roman Octavius, who became the Emperor Augustus of Rome. One of Herod's ten wives was a Hasmonean, but Herod himself had no blood ties to King David. He was a brutal ruler both within and outside of his own family, but he was noted for his building projects in and around Jerusalem. To gain some support from his subjects, he ordered the restoration of the second Temple (originally built in 515 B.C.). The project was not finished until A.D. 63, seven years before the Romans destroyed the Temple once again.

It was during the last days of Herod, while Augustus was emperor (see Lk 2:1), that Jesus, a descendant of King David, was born. Jesus' birth occurred in Bethlehem, where his foster father Joseph had gone to enroll in a government census.

Background Information
More on Hanukkah

According to Jewish law, any holy place, including the Temple, that had been profaned had to be rededicated or consecrated. (The same is true in Catholic Church law today.) After Judas Maccabeus recaptured the Temple, it had to be re-dedicated. During the rededication of the Temple in Jerusalem, a miracle occurred, giving rise to the eight-day holiday Jews celebrate today as Hanukkah. The Jews sang Psalm 30 at the rededication of the Temple. Ironically, the story of Judas Maccabeus is not included in the Hebrew Bible. (But it is in the Septuagint.) Thus, Hanukkah is considered to be a non-biblical feast by the Jews. (See 1 Mc 4:56–59 for more on the origins of Hanukkah.)

THE JOURNEY LEADS TO THE TIME OF JESUS AND BEYOND

REVIEW & REFLECTION

1. What were the offenses of Antiochus IV that led to the Maccabean revolt?
2. What unfortunate characteristic did the kings of the Hasmonean dynasty have in common with the kings of the Judean and Israelite monarchies?
3. Why are the Dead Sea Scrolls so valuable?

JOURNAL ASSIGNMENT

- Explain your opinion on the division between church and state. What do you think would be the ideal relationship between the two?

Cooperation or Resistance: What Was the Best Course for the Jews?

Into the time of Jesus and beyond, the Jews lived under foreign rule. After surveying the centuries before Christ from the time of the Exile to the first century B.C., it is interesting to consider which was the better response of the Jews to foreign rulers. Was it better for them to cooperate with the rulers in the hope of maintaining some semblance of religious and cultural life? Or was it better to resist to the point of military action in the hope of regaining independence? Or was there even another way? As the New Testament teaches, these questions were also important to Jesus' disciples.

This section examines some of the pros and cons surrounding these possible responses to this issue.

Cooperation with Foreign Rule

Cooperating with the foreign empire, to the point of adopting the conqueror's values, lifestyle, and even religious views, was the choice of the modernists or Hellenists. Defiance of the occupying powers and refusal to accept any political or cultural, let alone religious, influence was the choice of other groups. Many of these latter groups, such as the Essenes, eventually found it necessary to remove themselves from the larger community and live in isolation. Between these two extremes lies a whole spectrum of views. For example, even the Hasmonean rulers, who overthrew the Seleucids and restored the Temple, adopted some elements of Greek culture. Decorated Hasmonean minted coins and Hasmonean architecture, for example, reflected a strong classical Greek influence.

We have no literature that represents the position of total compromise—that is, Jewish writings about Jews who totally abandoned their faith in order to embrace Hellenistic religion and culture. It is likely that such apologetics were written, but were not kept by those who tended to support one of the resisting factions.

Political and Military Resistance

Political and military resistance to foreign rule was clearly the view advocated by the

---

COOPERATION OR RESISTANCE: WHAT WAS THE BEST COURSE FOR THE JEWS?

Bell-Ringers

1. List the issues the students cited from their Journal Assignments on the board. For example, tax credits for parents whose children attend religious schools. For each issue listed, conduct a brief discussion allowing students to speak to both sides of the issue.

2. Have the students meet in pairs and either exchange their essays on their belief in the resurrection (see page 239), or highlight their main beliefs for their partner. Randomly choose three our four essays. Read them to the class without naming the authors. Allow a chance for the students to comment.

Review and Reflection Answers

1. Antiochus IV forbade the Jews from practicing their religion. For example, he forbade them to honor the Sabbath, he forced them to eat pork and other unclean food, and he defiled the Temple by turning it into a brothel in honor of Zeus.
2. They were involved in political gains and nationalism. They sanctioned moral decay, acting like the political and economic modernists they had defeated. They cooperated with Greek leaders and compromised their religious values.
3. The Dead Sea Scrolls are so valuable because they provide us with a version of the Hebrew Scriptures in their original languages. This version is much older than the previous source, the Greek translation known as the Septuagint.

CHAPTER 10

Teaching Approaches

1. Print the word **martyr** on the board. Explain that a martyr is someone who dies for what he or she believes. Martyrdom is an act of faith. Death is not the end for people who are faithful to God. Such people are rewarded with eternal life. Share the fact that belief in an afterlife is a late concept in the Old Testament (e.g., 2 Mcc 7, the martyrdom of the woman and her seven sons).

2. Point out that Jesus' response to foreign rule was spiritual resistance. Jesus told his disciples to turn the other cheek, love their enemies, and not to seek revenge. Review the text including Scripture quotes from the text section, "Spiritual Resistance."

3. Distribute "Dorothy Day and Pacifism" (Handout 10B page 288 of the TWE). Share a summary of Day's life using the dates listed on the outline. Have the students read Day's quotations on pacifism. Ask them to write a paragraph reacting to at least one quotation. Allow the students the chance to share their reactions with a partner.

Zealots—A term used to describe many Jewish sects, active during New Testament times, who favored military resistance to Roman authority. Their belief in the coming of the Messiah was strongly linked to their desire for Jewish independence.

Maccabean revolt and the Hasmonean rulers who benefited from the Maccabees' success. Also included in this view were those who sought to establish the Temple as a recognized authority among the Jewish people and those who struggled with the ruling powers over the question of who would be the high priest.

Revenge for centuries of exile and foreign rule was of high priority to writers and supporters of the Maccabean movement. For example, Mattathias, the instigator of the revolt, said:

> Judas Maccabeus, a warrior from his youth, shall be the leader of your army and direct the war against the nations. You shall also gather about you all who observe the law, and you shall avenge the wrongs of your people. Pay back the Gentiles what they deserve, and observe the precepts of the law (1 Mc 2:66–68).

In battle, Judas referred in prayer to the original monarchy and traditions of warfare in ancient Israel:

> Blessed are you, O Savior of Israel, who broke the rush of the mighty one by the hand of your servant David and delivered the camp of the Philistines into the hand of Jonathan, the son of Saul, and his armor-bearer. Give this army into the hands of your people Israel; make them ashamed of their troops and their calvary (1 Mc 4:30b–32).

The military option was certainly one that was available, and exercised, by some Jewish groups. Whether this philosophy was in any way related to the **Zealots**, a group of Jewish sects in New Testament times, is debatable. These militants' belief in the coming of a messiah was intimately connected with their desire to recover Jewish independence as a nation. They did not act as an organized military, but instead were more like political terrorists who killed foreigners, and even Jews, who were against their cause.

In any case, the military option as one to maintain Jewish identity and faith was certainly not the only option available.

Spiritual Resistance

Another way of responding to foreign rule was to focus on maintaining a strong religious commitment in spite of the political challenges. The philosophy was to resist Hellenist and other secular ideas whenever threatened with them. Jews prefered death over defilement, as did the martyrs of the second book of Maccabees (see 2 Mc 6:18–7:42), in the hope that God would witness their suffering and rescue them.

In this tradition, peacefulness was admired, and *spiritual resistance* rather than violent resistance was praised—even if it resulted in martyrdom. This tradition was clearly influenced by Isaiah:

> In the days to come
> the mountain of the
> Lord's house

shall be established as the highest of the mountains,
and shall be raised above the hills;
all nations shall stream to it.
Many peoples shall come and say,
"Come let us go up to the mountain of the Lord,
to the house of the God of Jacob;
that he may teach us his ways
and that we may walk in his paths."
For out of Zion shall go forth instruction,
and the word of the Lord from Jerusalem.
He shall judge between the nations,
and shall arbitrate for many people;
they shall beat their swords into plowshares,
and their spears into pruning hooks;
national shall not lift up sword against nation,
neither shall they learn war any more (Is 2:2–4 NRSV).

Recall, also, that the book of Jonah told of the possibility of new life for former enemies who repented of their violence. The stories of Daniel 1–6 are also examples of peaceful and effective resistance. For example,

Shadrach, Meshach, and Abednego answered King Nebuchadnezzar, "There is no need for us to defend ourselves before you in this matter. If our God, whom we serve, can save us from the white-hot furnace and from your hands, O king, may he save us! But even if he will not, know, O king, that we will not serve your god or worship the golden statue which you set up" (Dn 3:16–18).

Similar passages representing the tradition of spiritual resistance are offered in much of Wisdom literature. For example:

When the ways of the people please the Lord,
he causes even their enemies to be at peace with them
(Prv 16:7 NRSV).

One who is slow to anger is better than the mighty,
and one whose temper is controlled than one who captures a city
(Prv 16:32 NRSV).

Though the entire spectrum of resistance to foreign rulers could be found among the Jews in the first century A.D., Jesus himself seemed to adopt the path of spiritual resistance. In the Sermon on the Mount, he offered an alternative justice from the Law of Moses that limited retribution to an "eye for an eye." In the following passage, read how Jesus affirms the wisdom tradition of peace of the Law of Moses, and St. Paul echoes him:

Jesus' Sermon on the Mount
"You have heard that it was said, 'An eye for an eye and a tooth for a tooth.' But I say to you, offer no resistance to one who is evil. . . . You have heard that it was said, 'You shall love your neighbor and hate your enemy.' But I say to you, love your enemies, and pray for those who persecute you" (Mt 5:38–39, 43–44).

St. Paul's Letter to the Romans
Bless those who persecute [you], bless and do not curse them. . . . If possible, on your part, live at peace with all (Rom 12:14, 18).

The Journey Leads to the Time of Jesus and Beyond

4. Read the "Dorothy Day and Nonviolence" exercise (page 244). Remind the students that for each idea they must write an application for their own lives.

5. **Homework Assignment**:
   - Complete the "Dorothy Day and Nonviolence" exercise. Come to the next class period with at least two practical suggestions for peaceful living that can be applied to your own life and shared with others.
   - Answer the Review and Reflection questions 1–2, page 244.
   - Complete the Journal Assignment on page 244. Think about a general list of dos and don'ts for a Catholic on Sundays.
   - Read "What Happened to the Jews?" (pages 244–247).

Enrichment: Write a report on a favorite saint you pray to for intercession.

Background Information
Violence vs. Non-Violence

The Church does not oppose all uses of violence in dealing with conflicts. However, it does teach violence must be the last resort to solving any conflict. The Church's just-war tradition provides guidelines for situations which violence can be used. For example, the war must have a "just cause" (e.g., self-defense). It also must be called by a legitimate authority, it must be fought for the right intention, the probability of success must be weighed against the loss of human life, and all ethical standards for fighting the war must be maintained.

Again, violence is always the last option. Rather, the preferred option is non-violence—handling conflicts through peaceful communication, negotiation, and compromise. Violence, once begun, always escalates. More and more teenagers each year are killed in incidents of violence.

Being a person of peace is the first step in fostering a peaceful world. Pope Paul VI's famous words on the subject were, "If you wish peace, defend life." This means respecting and loving the lives of those around you, especially the poor in spirit described by Jesus in the Sermon on the Mount.

Chapter 10

WHAT HAPPENED TO THE JEWS?

Bell-Ringers

1. Provide one large sheet of poster paper (or butcher paper) along with art supplies to make a banner. Choose one or two students to give the poster a title for the peacemaking suggestions they thought of. During the class period, call students in groups of two or three to print one of their peacemaking suggestions on the banner. When completed, hang the banner in front of the class. Point randomly to selected peacemaking ideas. Call on the student who wrote the idea to explain it in more detail to the class.

2. Allow some time for sharing on appropriate ways for Christians to spend their Sundays (see Journal Assignment, page 244). Then ask the class for ten reasons why teens go to Mass, along with ten other reasons that teens give for not going to Mass on Sundays. Print on the board and offer comments.

THE OLD TESTAMENT

DOROTHY DAY AND NONVIOLENCE

Dorothy Day was a Catholic layperson of the twentieth century. She was founder of the Catholic Worker Movement that served the poor. She was also opposed to war and promoted nonviolence throughout her life. Read more about Dorothy Day (see, for example, http://www.cjd.org). Find at least ten suggestions for peaceful living from Dorothy's life and the Catholic Worker Movement that can be applied to your own life. Tell how you will apply each of the ideas.

Dorothy Day

REVIEW & REFLECTION

1. Describe three possible positions on the spectrum of responses to the rule of foreign powers, in general, and the process of Hellenization, in particular.
2. What response did Jesus propose to the issue of foreign domination?

JOURNAL ASSIGNMENT

- How can you apply Jesus' teaching to the times in your life when your faith and your secular responsibilities conflict? For example, the Church teaches that Sunday should be a day of rest and prayer, when *unnecessary* work should be avoided. Should you ask your boss not to schedule you to work on Sundays? Should you attempt to complete your homework and studying on Saturdays rather than leaving them for Sunday night even if it means missing out on some good times with your friends?

What Happened to the Jews?

When the Romans destroyed the Temple in A.D. 70 the Jews had the choice of disappearing into the pages of history, or reinterpreting their religious practice without the Temple. The Sadducee and Essene sects disappeared and the rabbis came into prominence as spiritual leaders of Judaism, the descendents of the Pharisees.

The rabbis began to rework Temple rituals for practice outside of the Temple. Many rabbinical schools emerged, with several interpretations of how Jews should practice their religion. Over the next few centuries, a collection of rabbinical teachings called the **Talmud** were created. One set of these commentaries, called the Jerusalem Talmud, was complied in Palestine in the fourth century. The other, the Babylonian Talmud, was compiled in the Babylonian area in the sixth century. These held the highest authoritative writing after the Torah.

244

Review and Reflection Answers

1. The three possible responses were: cooperation with foreign rule, political and military resistance, and spiritual resistance.
2. Jesus did not advocate political and military resistance, but he did seem to advocate spiritual resistance. He affirmed the wisdom tradition of peace.

During the Medieval Period (ca A.D. 638–1783) the Diaspora spread farther and farther away from Palestine. Jews moved to all regions of Europe, Asia, the Arabian Peninsula, and North Africa. There was a resurgence of written commentaries on the Bible and Talmuds in this period. Many prominent rabbinic scholars wrote commentaries on the Bible and Talmud that most Jews learn at a young age and study to this day.

Synagogue Worship

With the destruction of the Temple, Jews looked for other ways to pray and worship. Some Jews maintained that righteous deeds of individuals were equivalent to Temple sacrifices. Others equated the three daily periods of prayer with three daily animal sacrifices in the Temple. The synagogue became the place for Jews to worship in community.

Synagogues are constructed with a gathering space for men, women, and children, and a central chamber for the reading of the Torah and for prayer. (In Orthodox synagogues today, there is separate seating for men and women.) The Torah is kept in a large cupboard that symbolizes the Ark of the Covenant on the eastern wall. The people face the east, not only facing the Ark, but also facing toward Jerusalem.

The synagogue really has three functions: It is a House of Prayer where Jews can address God; it is a House of Study where Jews can study the Torah; and it is a House of Assembly where Jews are able to meet socially.

Jews in the Modern Era

The Age of Enlightenment began the modern era for the Jews (1738 to present). During this time, the Jews achieved social and economic equality alongside their Christian neighbors in Europe. In Germany, Reform Judaism advocated full integration where the Jews lived. This belief extended to the United States. In the United States, Conservative Judaism reacted against Reform Judaism, only modifying Jewish practice in a limited way. Orthodox Judaism is the most traditional wing of Judaism. Its members strictly follow the Torah. In the 1930s, Reconstructionist Judaism developed from Conservative Judaism. It understood Judaism as a culture, not a religion, and did not hold faith in an all-powerful God.

Also, in the late nineteenth century, Zionism, or Jewish nationalism, began as a movement to return the Jews to their homeland in Palestine. After the murder of about six million Jews by the Nazi Germans in the 1930s and 1940s, the worldwide community responded to the goals of Zionism and, with the help of the United Nations, established the State of Israel in 1948.

Originally, Jerusalem remained divided under the rule of Jordan and Israel. The Six Day War in 1967 brought the city under the control of Israel. This war, and the entire return of the Jews to Palestine, has caused the region, and the world, much tension that has yet to be resolved, but it is clear that any resolution must honor the needs and aspirations of Palestinians (both Muslim and Christian) and Jews.

Talmud—A collection of rabbinical teachings collected after the destruction of the Jerusalem Temple in A.D. 70.

245

Teaching Approaches

1. The text offers a brief overview of Jewish history in the years following Jesus' resurrection up to the present. Review the text by printing the following questions on the board and asking the students to write their answers:

- **Why did the rabbis become spiritual leaders of Judaism after 70 A.D.?** (With the Temple destroyed, the rituals needed to be reworked for practice outside of the Temple.)
- **What is the Talmud?** (The Talmud is a set of commentaries on how Jews should practice their religion.)
- **What are the three functions of the synagogue?** (It is a House of Prayer, a House of Study, and a House of Assembly.)
- **What is meant by the Age of Enlightenment?** (It is the time from the eighteenth century to the present when Jews achieved social and economic equality alongside their Christian neighbors.)
- **Define Zionism.** (Zionism is the Jewish nationalistic movement that led to a return of the Jews to their homeland, and the founding of the State of Israel.)

Chapter 10

2. Show a selection of a video (e.g., *Religions of the World: Judaism*) that covers Jewish holidays and feasts. Use this to enrich the separate feature, "Sacred Times."

3. Invite a Jewish person to speak to the class about some of the issues presented in this section (e.g., the Talmud, synagogue worship, Age of Enlightenment, and Zionism).

4. **Homework Assignment**:
   - Answer Review and Reflection questions 1–3, page 247.
   - Complete the Journal Assignment, page 247. You can react to a presentation you have heard in class or refer to a person you know on your own.
   - Read "Further Reflections" (page 247) and "Epilogue" (page 249–254) in the text.
   - Visit a synagogue if your class was not able to take a field trip there. Complete the Learn by Doing assignment.

THE OLD TESTAMENT

SACRED TIMES

While Christians have taken on Sunday as the day of worship, the Jewish Sabbath, called *Shabbat* ("cease and desist") is celebrated from sunset Friday until sunset Saturday. The Shabbat is a reminder to Jews that God rested from the work of creation on the seventh day and they should also.

Friday evening is the Shabbat dinner. Observant Jews attend synagogue services and study the Torah, but do not work at this holiest of time. Sabbath ends at sunset Saturday. A brief ceremony called *Havdalah*, consisting of a lighted candle, a blessing of wine, and a box of spices to take the aroma of the Sabbath into the week, concludes the Shabbat.

While the Shabbat is a weekly event, there are other Jewish sacred times celebrated annually. The major Jewish festivals are divided into two main cycles: the *Tishri* cycle in the fall and the *Nisan* cycle in the spring. The names derive from the first month in each cycle.

Tishri begins in September or October and contains *Rosh Hashanah* (the Jewish New Year) and *Yom Kippur*, the "Day of Atonement." Besides marking the creation of mankind, Jews believe Rosh Hashanah is the day God judges individuals for his or her actions of the previous year. Yom Kippur is the holiest day of the year for Jews. It is a day when Jews ask forgiveness for both communal and personal sins; a person goes directly to the person he or she has offended, if possible, asking forgiveness.

Sukkot, the Feast of Booths or Tabernacles, begins five days after Yom Kippur and lasts for eight days. Sukkot commemorates the forty years the Jews spent in the desert when they had to protect themselves by constructing huts, or booths. This festival reminds Jews that God alone is their great protector.

Pesach is the major feast of the Nisan cycle. It is more commonly known as Passover. It celebrates the Hebrews' freedom from Egyptian slavery. *Shavuot* is celebrated fifty days after the first day of Passover. It was originally a harvest festival celebrating the first of the wheat harvest. It was during this festival that the Holy Spirit descended on the apostles at *Pentecost*, which means "fifty days."

Hanukkah ("Festival of Lights") marks the miracle of the lamp when the Temple was rededicated in the days of the Maccabees. It was not a major Jewish festival until many Jewish parents felt it was important to celebrate it during the time when Christians celebrate Christmas, especially in the United States.

Purim ("Feast of Lots") celebrates the victory of Jews over the Persian "prime minister", Haman, in the fifth century B.C. "Lots" refers to the lots Haman randomly drew to determine the day on which he would slaughter the Jews (see the book of Esther).

The Journey Leads to the Time of Jesus and Beyond

REVIEW & REFLECTION

1. How did Jewish rabbis adapt their religion after the destruction of the Temple in A.D. 70?
2. Name the three functions of a Synagogue.
3. What were the circumstances around the founding of the state of Israel in 1948?

JOURNAL ASSIGNMENT

- Share an experience of meeting and knowing a Jewish person. Describe his or her religious practice and faith as you know and understand it.

Further Reflections

The study of the Old Testament for this course is nearly completed. Needless to say, the development of the Old Testament canon took many years. None of the authors of the sacred books could have imagined that what they were writing at the time would be used by generation after generation for thousands of years to come. Recall, too, that though the prophets knew they were being used as "mouthpieces" for God, their written prophecies were not recorded until years later.

At the time of King Josiah's reform just before the Babylonian Exile, books of the Law of Moses were found and used as the basis for reform. This was the first time the Jews considered their writings to be sacred and God's inspired Word. From 621 B.C. to about 400 B.C. the writings surrounding the Law of Moses grew and eventually became the Torah.

The Deuteronomic History became a historical record of the Jews. Some of the prophetic books also came on the scene. By 200 B.C. these books of the prophets were considered part of sacred scripture. In the last stages of history prior to the birth of Christ, the Wisdom literature and other post-Exilic books developed. The disputes over the canonicity of some of these books have been covered, but in any case the number of books in the Old Testament had filled out, as determined by the Church.

The early Church made constant use of the Old Testament, looking in its pages for how the Old Covenant prefigured the work of salvation only accomplished in the fullness of time in the person of Jesus Christ, God's incarnate Son.

The opening of the letter to the Hebrews describes the climax of God's revelation, which comes with the presence of Jesus Christ:

> In times past, God spoke in partial and various ways to our ancestors through the prophets; in these last days, he spoke to us through a son, whom he made heir of all things and through whom he created the universe,
> who is the refulgence of his glory,
> the very imprint of his being,
> and who sustains all things by his mighty word.
> When he had accomplished purification from sins,
> he took his seat at the right hand of the Majesty on high
> as far superior to the angels
> as the name he has inherited is more excellent than theirs
> (Heb 1:1–4).

FURTHER REFLECTIONS

Bell-Ringers

1. Call on students to share what they learned from a Jewish person about Jewish religious practice and faith.

2. Set up a display where the students can show off their photos or sketches of holy items in a Jewish synagogue. Allow time for all of the class to visit the displays.

Teaching Approaches

1. Divide the class into small groups of four students each. Have each group devise games to help the class review the material from Chapter 10 (e.g., crossword puzzles, hangman, word searches). Allow about fifteen minutes for the games to be developed and then another ten to fifteen minutes for them to be played and shared. (Arrange to photocopy any games that need to be distributed to individual students.)

2. **Prayer Service:** Choose and play a recording or lead the singing of an appropriate song (e.g., "Though the Mountains May Fall"). Allow the opportunity for spontaneous petitions for fellow classmates and their needs. Conclude by having the students recite Psalm 23 (page 248). Divide the class in half. Have the students alternate from side to side praying each verse aloud.

3. **Homework Assignment:**
Study for the Chapter 10 Test.

Review and Reflection Answers

1. The Jewish rabbis founded several rabbinical schools which interpreted how Jews should practice their religion. Written commentaries were called the Talmud. Rabbis also helped Judaism to adapt to a religion practiced in the synagogue, not in the Temple.
2. The three functions of the synagogue were as a House of Prayer, a House of Study, and a House of Assembly.
3. The modern state of Israel was founded in response to the goals of Zionism and with the help of the United Nations after World War II.

Chapter 10 Parish Religious Education Adaptation

- The Chapter 10 Parish Religious Education Adaptation (online) is a lesson plan for the final chapter of the text and abridged for one- to two-hour sessions. One of the suggestions for the lesson is that students work together to create a collage of memories of their Old Testament study. Preview and plan to provide for appropriate media supplies.
- Assign Chapter 10 for reading prior to the first class session and assigned Review and Reflection questions from Chapter 9 (see lesson plan online).

Chapter 10

Chapter 10 Test

Teaching Approaches

1. If there is time prior to distributing the Chapter 10 Test, allow for review. Have the students work in pairs to quiz each other using the Chapter 10 Review and Reflection questions and vocabulary words as study guides.

2. Assign the Chapter 10 Test. Make sure the all the students' texts are closed. Collect and grade the tests when the students have completed them.

Chapter 10 Test Answers

Part 1: Matching: 1. c; 2. e; 3. a; 4. d; 5. f; 6. b.

Part 2: Multiple Choice: 7. e; 8. b; 9. b; 10. d; 11. a; 12. c; 13. d; 14. e; 15. e; 16. b.

Part 3: Definitions: 17. The Essenes were a group of Jews whose resistance to foreign influence took them to the extreme position of living in entirely separate communities in the desert around the Dead Sea. They were probably the people who hid the Dead Sea Scrolls; 18. Hasidim refers to a group of particularly observant Jews who supported the Maccabees in the military effort against Antiochus IV. They were the forerunners of the Essenes and the Pharisees. 19. The rulers of the Hasmonean Dynasty were descendants of the Maccabees. They ruled in Judea after the last of the Syrians were ousted. Although they were officially independent of Syria and Rome, they were in many ways puppet kings of these larger empires. 20. The Pharisees were a group of Jews who favored cultural and religious separatism in response to the occupation of Palestine by the Syrians and, later, by the Romans. They valued adherence to the law, had great respect for teachers and interpreters of the Torah and introduced rabbis and synagogues to the cultural life of the Jews. Jesus was probably raised within the Pharasaic tradition. 21. The Ptolemies were descendants of Ptolemy I, one of Alexander the Great's generals. They ruled Egypt and Palestine from the time of Alexander the Great until the Seleucids removed them from Palestine in 200 B.C. Their rule in Egypt continued until the middle of the first century B.C. 22. The Sadducees were a group of aristocratic, wealthy Jews who favored strict adherence to the letter of the Torah and believed Temple worship was essential to Jewish life. Their struggles with the Pharisees were often over such issues as the possibility of resurrection and the existence of angels. The Sadducees denited the resurrection and angels.

Part 4: Short Answer: 23. One response was to assimilate the new culture completely, abandoning the Jewish way of life and rejecting Yahweh. Another response was to cooperate with the civil authority of the occupying power while persisting in religious devotion to Yahweh. Following this approach, a Jewish person would obey laws and follow cultural custom unless they were in direct opposition to the Jewish faith. This was a non-violent approach, emphasizing prayer and faith in God's protection to the point of being willing to be martyred for one's beliefs. The last response similarly relied on traditional Jewish practices of prayer, fasting and almsgiving but also accepted the necessity of violent resistance in the face of religious persecution. These people expected God's intervention to reestablish Jewish sovereignty. Jesus supported the second of these options. 24. According to the "Letter to Aristeas," the Ptolemies of Egypt were unhappy that their great library in Alexandria had none of the writings of the Jewish people. They gathered seventy-two Hebrew elders, six from each tribe, to translate the Old Testament into Greek. The elders were divided into teams each working separately on their own translation. When all were finished, the translations were all identical. The only part of the legend that can be verified is that the Greek translation of the books of the Old Testament was produced in Egypt during the rule of the Ptolemies over Palestine.

THE OLD TESTAMENT

Learn by Doing

Arrange a visit to a Jewish synagogue. Ask a rabbi or member of the community to point out and explain some of these objects to you:
- The Torah
- A Tallith
- The Holy Ark
- The Siddur
- The Menorah

Either take a photo or draw a sketch of each item and other religious items at the synagogue. Write a caption explaining each of the items you have depicted or photographed.

Called to Prayer

The Lord is my shepherd; I shall not want.
    In verdant pastures he gives me repose;
Beside restful waters he leads me;
    he refreshes my soul.
He guides me in right paths
    for his name's sake.
Even though I walk in the dark valley
    I fear no evil; for you are at my side
With your rod and your staff
    that give me courage.

You spread the table before me
    in the sight of my foes;
You anoint my head with oil;
    my cup overflows.
Only goodness and kindness follow me
    all the days of my life;
And I shall dwell in the house of the Lord
    for years to come.
—Psalm 23

Notes

1. Among the most authoritative translations available is the following: *The Dead Sea Scrolls Translated: The Qumran Texts in English* (Second Edition), ed. Florentino Garcia Martinez (Trans. Wilfred Watson), E.J. Brill/Eerdmans (Grand Rapids, New York), 1996.

Epilogue

Epilogue
Why Should Catholics Know the Old Testament?

This question is important for reflection, although many Catholics today might answer: "We really *don't* need to know the Old Testament very well. After all, Jesus is the most important person in the Bible, and we learn about him in the *New* Testament, not the Old Testament."

The *Catechism of the Catholic Church* teaches that this answer is hardly accurate:

> Christians . . . read the Old Testament in the light of Christ crucified and risen. Such typological reading discloses the inexhaustible content of the Old Testament; but it must not make us forget that *the Old Testament retains its own intrinsic value as Revelation* reaffirmed by the Lord himself. Besides, the New Testament has to be read in the light of the Old. Early Christian catechesis made constant use of the Old Testament. As an old saying put it, the New Testament lies hidden in the Old and the Old Testament is unveiled in the New (CCC, 129; emphasis added).

In other words, understanding Christ and the mysteries of our faith can be more fully accomplished by understanding the text and nuances of the sacred pages of the Old Testament. Several examples help to illustrate how this is so.

Understanding Jesus' Cleansing of the Temple

Jesus' "cleansing" of the Temple is described in all four Gospels. Recall Mark's version of the episode:

> They came to Jerusalem, and on entering the temple area he began to drive out those selling and buying there. He overturned the tables of the money changers and the seats of those who were selling doves. He did not permit anyone to carry anything through the temple area. Then he taught them saying, "Is it not written:
> 'My house shall be called a house of prayer for all peoples'?
> But you have made it a den of thieves."
> The chief priests and the scribes came to hear of it and were seeking a way to put him to death, yet they feared him because the whole crowd was astonished at his teaching. When evening came, they went out of the city (Mk 11:15–19).

It was obviously a shocking display! Imagine the reaction of the crowds. Do you think the reaction of the people who originally witnessed the incident was different from how you, as a modern Catholic, react to reading the story? Unless you know your Old Testament better than many modern Catholics, the people of Jerusalem would most certainly have reacted differently from you in several ways.

First, the people milling around the Temple grounds would not have been totally shocked by what Jesus did. After all, these Jewish people knew well the stories of prophets such as Jeremiah, who often made similar public displays. Jeremiah, for instance, once went about carrying a wooden yoke across his shoulders:

> Thus the Lord said to me: Make for yourself bands and yoke bars and put them over your shoulder (Jer 27:2).

Likewise, the prophet Ezekiel often engaged in public displays that both shocked and instructed, such as the time he shaved himself, then burned part of his hair as a symbol of coming destruction:

> As for you, son of man, take a sharp sword and use it like a barber's razor, passing it over your head and beard. Then take a set of scales and divide the hair you have cut.

Introducing the Epilogue

Understanding Christ and the mysteries of our faith can be more fully accomplished by understanding the text and nuances of the sacred pages of the Old Testament. The students will understand this by looking at three examples from the New Testament that can only be explained fully with study of the Old Testament.

Background Notes for the Teacher

The Gospel stories of Jesus "cleansing" the Temple and reading from the scroll of Isaiah are enriched by Old Testament study. Jesus acted as a prophet in both stories. He predicted the destruction of the Temple because of the sins of the people. He also said that the Temple should be a place for all people who want to be part of the People of God, not only the Jews.

Chapter Objectives

The students will be able to:
- appreciate the importance of Old Testament study in understanding the New Testament.
- be motivated to continue studying the Bible on their own or in their parish.

Relevant Teachings from Church Documents

- The unity of the two Testaments proceeds from the unity of God's plan and his Revelation. The Old Testament prepares for the New and the New Testament fulfills the Old; the two shed light on each other; both are true Word of God. (*CCC*, 140)

Resources

Music Suggestion: see page 254
Printed Material: see page 256
Audiovisual Material: see page 257
Internet Links: see page 258

Epilogue

Bell-Ringer

1. Print the question **Why should a Catholic know the Old Testament?** on the board. Ask the students to write down their responses. Then call on volunteers to share. Make sure that the discussion brings out (1) that the Old Testament is a way to know Jesus and (2) provides added insight into the New Testament.

THE OLD TESTAMENT

Burn a third in the fire, within the city, when the days of your siege are completed; place another third around the city and strike it with the sword; the final third strew in the wind, and pursue it with the sword (Ez 5:1–3).

Given their knowledge of these stories and other dramatic stories involving the prophets, the people around the Temple would probably not have been totally shocked by what they witnessed. Instead, they probably would have stepped to a safe distance, and then *watched and listened!* A student of the Old Testament today would likely react the same way.

Second, the gospel reports that the Temple officials (chief priests and scribes) became so upset with what Jesus had done, that they were "looking for a way to put him to death." But why? Again, someone with little background in the Old Testament would probably think, "Because Jesus caused such a commotion—he made a mess in the Temple. That must be what upset the officials."

But think about that kind of reasoning. Tables can be set back in place and animals can be rounded up. After about forty minutes or so, it was probably "business as usual" in the Temple square. Why seek to kill someone for what amounts to a mere half hour's inconvenience? More likely, the Temple officials were so upset because they knew their Hebrew scriptures. What did the Temple officials hear that modern readers sometimes miss?

Jesus referred to the Temple as both a "house of prayer" and a "den of thieves." Take a deeper look at each reference. Jesus was actually quoting two prophets. Jeremiah stood in precisely the same place where Jesus was standing about six hundred years before. In Jeremiah's famous "Temple Sermon" (see Jer 7), he blasted the sins and corruption of the people who thought that offering sacrifices could "cover over" their immoral behavior—their social injustice toward the widow and the orphans who needed help:

Are you to steal and murder, commit adultery and perjury, burn incense to Baal, go after strange gods that you know not, and yet come to stand before me in this house which bears my name and say: "We are safe; we can commit all these abominations again"? (Jer 7:9–10).

Jeremiah added shockingly:

Has this house which bears my name become in your eyes a *den of thieves*? (Jer 7:11; emphasis added).

At the end of this sermon, Jeremiah stated clearly that the Temple where he was standing was to be destroyed because of the sins of the people. God, he said, would treat "this house" just as he treated Shiloh, an even older shrine that was destroyed by the Assyrians. And, of course, Jeremiah was quite correct: Nebuchadnezzar came and destroyed the Temple.

With this information as background, it becomes clear that the Temple officials were reacting strongly because Jesus referred to the Temple and its officials as a "den of thieves." Not only was Jesus implying that the Temple officials were just as corrupt as those in the time of Jeremiah, but Jesus was also implying that the current Temple was going to be destroyed. And, like Jeremiah before him, Jesus was also quite correct. The Romans destroyed the Temple during the Roman wars against the Jews in A.D. 70—barely one generation after the death and resurrection of Jesus.

Remember, the Temple was the source of both authority and money for these Temple officials. The Temple was also the center of collaboration with the hated Roman occupying forces and the center of the economically corrupt administration that routinely defrauded the Jewish people. The chief or high priest was the closest thing that the Jewish people had to a leader in the Roman period. When Jesus

250

Resources

Music Suggestion

"To You, O God, I Lift Up My Soul" by Bob Hurd from *Alleluia! Give The Glory, Spirit Song,* or *Breaking Bread* (OCP).

Epilogue

implied that the Temple officials were corrupt, *and* that the Temple was going to be destroyed, the Temple officials knew that they could not tolerate this from a prophet whom some of the crowd already considered even greater than Jeremiah!

But that was not all. A third piece of information gleaned from reading and knowing the Old Testament relates to Jesus' use of another surprising phrase as well. Read this passage attributed to Deutero-Isaiah:

> Let not the foreigner say,
>   when he would join himself to the Lord,
> "The Lord will surely exclude me
>   from his people." . . .
> And the foreigners who join
>   themselves to the Lord,
>   ministering to him,
> Loving the name of the Lord,
>   and becoming his servants—
> All who keep the sabbath free from
>   profanation
>   and hold to my covenant,
> Them I will bring to my holy mountain
>   and make joyful in my *house of prayer*;
> Their holocausts and sacrifices
>   will be acceptable on my altar,
> For my house shall be called a *house of prayer* for all peoples.
> Thus says the Lord God,
>   who gathers the dispersed of Israel:
> Others will I gather to him
>   besides those already gathered
>
> (Is 56:3, 6–8; emphasis added).

According to the prophet, God has compassion for *all* people, Jews and Gentiles alike and he is ready to receive non-Jews into the company of the People of God. Deutero-Isaiah announced that God will welcome "foreigners" and then the Temple of God will be a "house of prayer for all peoples." This is, of course, the same language Jesus used.

Only with this understanding of the Old Testament can we really understand what Jesus was saying in this passage. Jesus said that the Temple was corrupt, like Jeremiah did. Jesus implied that the Temple would be destroyed, also as Jeremiah had. Finally, Jesus said that the Temple *should* be a place for *all* peoples who want to be part of the People of God, not only the Jews—just like the book of Isaiah said!

This was too much for the Temple officials to handle. Not only was Jesus threatening the livelihood of the Temple officials and calling them corrupt, Jesus was *also* saying that God loved the Gentiles as he loved the Jews and was willing to welcome them into the Temple to worship. By these words, Jesus was threatening everything that these Temple officials believed in: exclusivity as a religion, along with authority and economic rights of dominance over the Jewish people. This "cleansing of the Temple" passage really points to Jesus as a *Prophetic Messiah*.

This point is only as clear to us today as it was to the first listeners if we know and understand the related passages in the Old Testament.

The Rejection of Jesus at Nazareth

Another example that can help us to understand why knowing the Old Testament is important to understanding the New Testament occurs at the beginning of Jesus' public ministry, as recorded in the gospel of Luke. The passage in Luke 4:14–30 tells us that Jesus went to his home synagogue and read the Scriptures publicly.

Read Luke 4:14–30

What happened in this episode? Jesus read a very popular passage from the book of Isaiah. (Incidentally, notice how important the Prophetic book of Isaiah is in the New Testament!) When he finished the passage, he sat down (the typical sign that a teacher was

Teaching Approaches

1. Review the Epilogue material by asking the following questions:

- Why does Jesus refer to the Temple as a house of prayer and den of thieves? (By referring to the Temple as a "house of prayer" and a "den of thieves," Jesus was saying several things. First, the Temple would be destroyed because of the sins of the people. The Temple officials in Jesus' time were just as corrupt as those in the time of Jeremiah. Also, Jesus words reveal that the Temple should be a place for all faith-filled people, not just the Jews. God loved the Gentiles as he loved the Jews and was willing to welcome them into the Temple to worship.)

- According to Jesus, how will God treat the captives and oppressed? (Jesus says that God will rescue all captives and oppressed people, including the poor. It won't matter if they are Gentile or Jew. God cares for Gentiles as much as he does for Jews. God is a God of all the poor, and not just those who attend synagogue worship.

- What is the meaning of "heap burning coals upon his head" in Paul's letter to the Romans? (In the Old Testament, God used a burning coal to purify the prophet Isaiah. St. Paul refers to this Old Testament story to say that the kindness of a Christian to a non-believer would purify the non-believer, that is, bring him to Christ.)

Epilogue

2. Review the suggestions for continuing personal Bible study "Your Next Step" (pages 253–254). Ask each student to write a three-step plan. Call on volunteers to share all or part of their plans.

The Old Testament

about ready to speak) and said to the congregation, "Today this scripture passage is fulfilled in your hearing" (Lk 4:21).

The passage says that "all spoke highly of him and were amazed at the gracious words that came from his mouth" (Lk 4:22). And, why not? Jesus had just read one of the most powerful promises recorded in Scripture: God would liberate his people. What did the people listening to Jesus think? Well, obviously, they thought that *they* were "the poor" to whom the Spirit of God would bring "glad tidings." They also likely thought of themselves as the "captives" and the "oppressed."

But Jesus surprises them. With his next few words Jesus makes it clear that he is not referring to those in the synagogue as the captives, blind, and oppressed spoken of in the book of Isaiah. Rather, he reminds them of the prophets Elijah and Elisha who healed *foreign* people, not Jews. The people listening to Jesus realized what he was implying: God cares for Gentiles as much as he does for Jews. This kind of talk was too much for those who heard Jesus; they rose to try to kill him, but Jesus miraculously escaped from them.

In this episode, Jesus referred directly to the Old Testament traditions of these prophets, so that his hearers would understand what he meant. Many Jews resented Jesus' message, but many accepted it. Some probably sympathized with Jesus' message, even if they were not sure who Jesus was. Today, even if they do not agree with Christians on who Jesus is, many modern Jews accept that Jesus was an important reformer. Christians, too, should display the same willingness to learn from Judaism.

Understanding the Duties of a Christian According to St. Paul

In St. Paul's letter to the Romans, he addresses a way for Christians to live in peacefulness: "Bless those who persecute [you], bless and do not curse them" (Rom 12:14). Paul continues,

Have the same regard for one another; do not be haughty but associate with the lowly; do not be wise in your own estimation. Do not repay anyone evil for evil; be concerned for what is noble in the sight of all. If possible, on your part, live at peace with all (Rom 12:16–18).

There is little doubt that this strong teaching is reflective of the words and actions of Jesus. However, Paul then quotes a proverb:

Rather, "if your enemy is hungry, feed him; if he is thirsty, give him something to drink; for by so doing you will heap burning coals upon his head." Do not be conquered by evil but conquer evil with good (Rom 12:20–21).

Re-read the prior passage. What does "heap burning coals upon his head" mean? What could this mean? Some have suggested that St. Paul was saying something like: "Let God do the dirty work. You be nice, and God will get your enemies in the end." Another view is that the best revenge is simply to treat one's enemies well. But is this really *consistent* with what St. Paul has written? He finishes this section by writing, "Do not be conquered by evil . . ." so he clearly presumes that his advice is positive, not negative. What does he *really* mean?

Paul's original readers of the letter to the Romans—mostly Jewish Christians—would have been able to put these words into context with what they learned from the Hebrew scriptures. They would have recalled how the prophet Isaiah was made pure when God touched his mouth with a burning coal (see Is 6:6–7). For the prophet Isaiah, the symbol of the ember or coal from the altar actually removed his sin. It was a coal from the altar of sacrifice, which was how ancient Israelites offered sacrifice to cleanse themselves from the stain of sin. So, St. Paul's reference to "heaping burning coals" on an enemy's head most likely referred to a means of purification. The kindness of a Christian to a non-believer

---

Resources
Printed Material

The New Jerome Biblical Commentary, ed. by Raymond Brown, S.S., Joseph A. Fitzmyer S.J., and Roland E. Murphy, O.Carm. (Englewood Cliffs, NJ: Prenetice Hall, 1989)

Epilogue

would purify the non-believer, that is, bring him to Christ.

Again, understanding the Old Testament helps today's reader turn a troubling image into a profound idea.

The Absolute Need for the Old Testament for Today's Catholics

The three examples discussed in the preceding sections help to prove the value of studying the Old Testament. The New Testament contains the eternal truth of God's plan for humanity. But the Church in its wisdom has accepted the *entire* Bible—Old *and* New Testament. There is so much more to learn and appreciate about your Christian faith by continuing your journey through the Old Testament. Consider how different your view of Jesus would be if you did not know anything about the Prophets. Consider how different your view of Jesus would be if you did not know about the kings of Ancient Israel, and the idea of God's promised "Messiah."

Consider how different your view of one of the final words of Jesus, "My God, My God, Why have you forsaken me?" would be if you did not know that Jesus was quoting Psalm 22, which really is a great psalm of triumph that finally alludes to resurrection:

> For dominion is the Lord's
>> and he rules the nations.
> To him alone shall bow down
>> all who sleep in the earth;
> Before him shall bend
>> all who go down into the dust
>> (Ps 22:29–30).

In summary, without the Old Testament, Catholics cannot fully and completely understand all that God has to say to us in the Sacred Scriptures. If you had a seven-page letter from your parents or a friend, would you want to throw away the first five pages of that letter and only read the last two? How much more do we want to hear everything that God intends for us to hear?

You may be at the end of your journey through this textbook, but you are just getting into your stride for the journey through the Bible!

Your Next Step

Hopefully, many of you have decided that Bible study is both interesting and even exciting. You may wish to know how to continue with your Bible study journey now that this course is concluding. Here are three suggestions to help you take your next step:

1. Buy a Bible for yourself.

The treasured "family Bible" in your home should not count as your own Bible. You need a personal copy of the Bible so that you can write notes all over the pages.

Some students think that writing in the Bible is somehow being "disrespectful," but that is silly. Writing notes means that you are studying and thinking. As you read your Bible, mark passages that are especially interesting or put question marks next to passages that you have questions about. There is nothing better than a Bible filled with notes and with pages that are heavily used. It means that a person is really taking Bible study seriously.

2. Join a Bible study at your parish.

Your parish youth ministry or religious education program may offer such a study. You may also be able to participate in an adult Bible study program at your parish. Be careful here. Some Bible studies are lead by well-meaning people with very little training or background in Scripture study or in the teachings of the Church. If you find this to be true, ask your high school teachers or pastor for advice. You can even call the religion department of the nearest Catholic college or

Resources

Audiovisual Material

The Old Testament Covenant: Judaism—The Movement from Politics to Faith (De Sales Catholic Video Library)—60 minutes
This video talks about the Jews' continual challenge of being faithful to God despite political oppression.

Epilogue

university for information on how to further your study of the Bible.

3. Buy or borrow some extra resources to help you study the Bible.

If you are really serious about continuing to study the Bible, think about acquiring some study books to help you along the way. Three really good books to put in your personal Bible study library are:

- A one-volume Bible Commentary like the *New Jerome Biblical Commentary*. In this book, Catholic Bible scholars have provided all kinds of fascinating information about each passage of the Bible. It is good to read the commentary as you read your Bible. Take notes, and write in the commentary, too.
- A Bible Dictionary. You may need to look up words or names that you are not sure about. There are many excellent Bible dictionaries, such as the *HarperCollins Bible Dictionary* or the *Eerdmans Bible Dictionary*. Make sure it is the most recent edition available as these books are updated regularly.
- A Bible atlas (e.g., the *Collegeville Atlas of the Bible*). An atlas will help you to locate places where Biblical events happened. A good Bible atlas will give you maps for each major time period to show you how settlements changed, how empires changed, and how trade routes became more important.

Good luck! See you in Bible class!

Resources

Internet Links

http://christianity-links.com/Pastoral_Resources_Youth_Ministry.html
Provides links to Catholic youth ministry, including Bible study.

www.ymnetwork.net/2004/scripture.htm
Offers links to the United States Catholic Bishop's site with listings of the daily readings and the New American Bible online among other youth links.

RESOURCES

RESOURCES

CATHOLIC HANDBOOK FOR FAITH (pages 259–280 of the Student Text)

Contents

Beliefs
- Apostles' Creed
- Gifts of the Holy Spirit
- Fruits of the Holy Spirit
- The Symbol of Chalcedon

God and Jesus
- Attributes of God
- The Holy Trinity
- Faith in One God
- Famous Quotations about Jesus Christ

Scripture and Tradition
- Books of the Bible with Abbreviations
- How to Locate a Scripture Passage

Church
- Timeline of Church History
- Marks of the Church
- The Apostles and Their Emblems
- The Pope
- Recent Popes
- Fathers of the Church
- Doctors of the Church
- Ecumenical Councils
- The Ten Commandments
- The Beatitudes
- Cardinal Virtues
- Theological Virtues
- Corporal (Bodily) Works of Mercy
- Spiritual Works of Mercy
- Precepts of the Church
- Catholic Social Teaching: Major Themes
- Sin

Liturgy and Sacraments
- Church Year
- Holy Days of Obligation in the United States
- The Seven Sacraments
- How to Go to Confession
- Order of Mass
- Three Degrees of the Sacrament of Orders

Mary and the Saints
- Mother of God
- Marian Feasts Throughout the Year
- Canonization of Saints
- Patron Saints

Devotions
- The Mysteries of the Rosary
- How to Pray the Rosary
- Stations of the Cross
- Novenas
- Liturgy of the Hours
- The Divine Praises

Prayers
- The Sign of the Cross
- Our Father
- Glory Be
- Hail Mary
- Memorare
- Hail, Holy Queen
- The Angelus
- Regina Caeli
- Grace At Meals
- Guardian Angel Prayer
- Prayer for the Faithful Departed
- Morning Offering
- Act of Faith
- Act of Hope
- Act of Love

Catholic Handbook for Faith

General Introduction

Study of the Old Testament is an important first step to understanding the New Testament. In addition to providing the social, political, and moral context in which Jesus spoke and acted, the Old Testament gives us insight into the Church itself. Just as the ancient Hebrews learned that their relationship with God was to be integrated in all aspects of their lives, so Church members today realize the importance of praying always and striving to live fully in love of God and love of neighbor.

Our identity as baptized Catholics links us to a centuries-old tradition of spirituality and worship that began with the ancient Israelites and continued through Jesus and his apostles. We have preserved the Judeo-Christian tradition in a body of beliefs, prayers, devotions, and practices that have come to be known as Catholicism. Throughout this course, you may find that the text stimulates students to ask certain questions about Catholic practice today. This Catholic Handbook for Faith is designed to give you easy-to-find answers to these questions. It is meant to be a supplemental resource that may be used whenever needed.

Teaching Approaches

Instead of just telling the students to memorize certain prayers or dates, there are a number of creative ways that you could use to help the students learn the Handbook material. Among such suggestions are the following:

- **Crossword Puzzles.** Assign the material to be learned and direct the students to make up crossword puzzles with clues. Then have them exchange puzzles with a partner and work to answer them.
- **Individual or Team Games.** Drill the students on certain material in the Handbook by having them play a TV game show based on *Hollywood Squares* or *Jeopardy*. Divide the students into teams to make up questions/answers about the Handbook material that are presented to "contestants."
- **Reflection Essays or Journal Entries.** Have the students reflect and write about their understanding of a single passage from a creed or prayer such as the Apostles' Creed or the Our Father. You may also wish to have the students write about how they might put the passage into practice in daily life.
- **Pop Quizzes.** Give the students a short, objective pop quiz regarding certain material in the Handbook. Use one of the following formats: fill in the blanks, complete the sentences, or matching.
- **Artistic Creations.** Have the students draw/paint a picture or mural that expresses one part of a creed or prayer. You may also wish to have the students draw symbols for certain patron saints. Have the students explain to the class why the Church chose this symbol for the saint.
- **Creative Writing.** Have the students rewrite a creed or prayer in their own words, as a poem, rap, song, or choral reading.
- **Small Group Discussions.** Have the students form small groups to discuss what a certain creed or prayer means to them.
- **Slide Shows.** Have the students put together a slide show to illustrate a certain creed or prayer.
- **Puppet Shows, Skits, or Mime.** Have students retell main events in the life of a saint through homemade puppets, small-group skits, or mime.
- **Research.** Send the students to the Internet or library to find out about the history and origin of a certain creed or prayer.
- **Music.** Have the students compose (or learn) and sing a musical version of a certain prayer, belief, or creed.

Whatever teaching method you use, try to make the learning process interesting and meaningful rather than a dull routine. Help the students internalize the values and beliefs found in this Handbook as a basis for the rest of their lives as Catholics.

Name _____ Date _____

OLD TESTAMENT THEMES

Reading the Old Testament is not like reading any ordinary book. Yes, we need to read the words and sentences. But more than a literal reading of the text, we need to read it with faith. This means we reflect on the underlying message of the text: the message of truth God is wishing to communicate to us. Here are some main themes found in the Bible. Keep these in mind as you study particular stories or events in the Old Testament.

- God created a good world.
- God has blessed human life.
- Humanity has a tendency to sin.
- God is a God of mercy.
- God keeps promises.
- The covenant binds God to Israel.
- The Law expresses Israel's bond to God.
- Worship is praise and thanksgiving.
- Religious life is life in community.
- God directs all of human history.

As the introduction to the *New American Bible* explains, these themes can be applied to our own lives today in the following ways:

- All things in our life must flow from faith.
- Our prayer and our daily life must be one.
- We must respect God's holiness.
- We must imitate God's holiness.
- Holiness must be translated into compassion.
- Life is a journey that requires trust in God.
- We are people of the land. (We must take the environment seriously.)
- Faith is a family affair.
- Prayer must fill our lives.

HANDOUT 1A

Name _____   Date _____

COMPARING TRANSLATIONS OF PSALM 13

New Revised Standard Version
Psalm 13
1 How long, O LORD? Will you forget me forever?
  How long will you hide your face from me?
2 How long must I bear pain in my soul,
  and have sorrow in my heart all day long?
  How long shall my enemy be exalted over me?

3 Consider and answer me, O LORD my God!
  Give light to my eyes, or I will sleep the sleep of death,
4 and my enemy will say, "I have prevailed";
  my foes will rejoice because I am shaken.

5 But I trusted in your steadfast love;
  my heart shall rejoice in your salvation.
6 I will sing to the LORD,
  because he has dealt bountifully with me.

New American Bible
Psalm 13
2 How long, LORD? Will you utterly forget me?
  How long will you hide your face from me?
3 How long must I carry sorrow in my soul,
  grief in my heart day after day?
II   How long will my enemy triumph over me?
4 Look upon me, answer me, LORD, my God!
  Give light to my eyes lest I sleep in death,
5 Lest my enemy say, "I have prevailed,"
III   lest my foes rejoice at my downfall.
6 I trust in your faithfulness.
  Grant my heart joy in your help.
  That I may sing of the LORD,
  "How good our God has been to me!"

Revised English Bible
Psalm 13
1 How LONG, LORD, will you leave me forgotten,
  how long hide your face from me?
2 How long must I suffer anguish in my soul,
  grief in my heart day after day?
  How long will my enemy lord it over me?

3 Look now, LORD my God, and answer me.
  Give light to my eyes lest I sleep the sleep of death,
4 lest my enemy say, 'I have overthrown him,'
  and my adversaries rejoice at my downfall.
5 As for me, I trust in your unfailing love;
  my heart will rejoice when I am brought to safety.
6 I shall sing to the LORD, for he has granted all my desire.

New Jerusalem Bible
Psalm 13
1 How long, Yahweh, will you forget me? For ever?
  How long will you turn away your face from me?
2 How long must I nurse rebellion in my soul,
  sorrow in my heart day and night?
  How long is the enemy to domineer over me?
3 Look down, answer me, Yahweh my God!
  Give light to my eyes or I shall fall into the sleep of death.

4 Or my foe will boast, "I have overpowered him,"
  and my enemy have the joy of seeing me stumble.
5 As for me, I trust in your faithful love, Yahweh.
  Let my heart delight in your saving help,
  let me sing to Yahweh for his generosity to me,
  let me sing to the name of Yahweh the Most High!

Good News Bible
Psalm 13
  How much longer will you forget me, LORD?
    Forever?
  How much longer will you hide yourself from me?
2 How long must I endure trouble?
  How long will sorrow fill my heart day and night?
  How long will my enemies triumph over me?

3 Look at me, O LORD my God, and answer me.
  Restore my strength; don't let me die.
4 Don't let my enemies say, "We have defeated him."
  Don't let them gloat over my downfall.

5 I rely on your constant love;
  I will be glad, because you will rescue me.
6 I will sing to you, O LORD, because you have been good to me.

HANDOUT 1B

Name _____ Date _____

Secret Codes

During World War II, both sides used secret codes to communicate information and military plans to their troops. The Germans used an intricate computer-like machine known as *Enigma*, which changed the codes daily. The Americans used Navajo "code talkers" to exchange information in the ancient Navajo language. Here are three other codes. Use one of these codes (or develop a code of your own) to translate a favorite Old Testament passage.

Code Based on the Greek Language

A	B	C	D	E	F	G	H	I	J	K	L	M
Α	Β	Χ	Δ	Ε	Φ	Γ	Η	Ι	ϑ	Κ	Λ	Μ

N	O	P	Q	R	S	T	U	V	W	X	Y	Z
Ν	Ο	Π	Θ	Ρ	Σ	ς	Υ	ς	Ω	Ξ	Ψ	Ζ

Code Based on Numbers

A	B	C	D	E	F	G	H	I	J	K	L	M
5	7	9	4	6	8	1	3	2	0	13	12	11

N	O	P	Q	R	S	T	U	V	W	X	Y	Z
15	16	17	14	13	18	26	24	25	23	22	21	20

Code Based on Pictograms

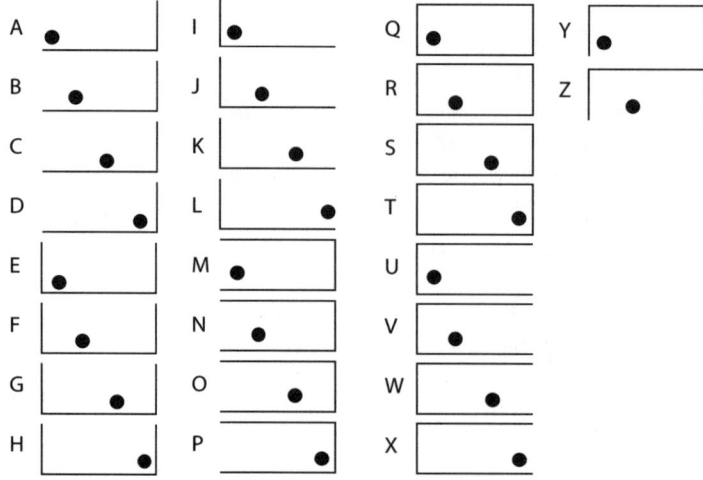

HANDOUT 2A

Name _____   Date _____

ARCHAEOLOGICAL TIME PERIODS AND THE OLD TESTAMENT

NAME	PERIOD	
Hellenistic (Greek)	332–64 B.C.	330–Alexander the Great enters Palestine. 167—revolt of the Maccabees. 63—Pompey's invasion of Palestine. Molded glass vessels, Greek frescoes.
Babylonian and Persian	539–332 B.C.	Coins, figurines, underwater archaeological artifacts. 27 papyrus scrolls found in the caves of Wadi ed-Daliyeh (Aramaic legal documents). The Israelites return to Canaan.
Iron (Late)	900–539 B.C.	Divided kingdom—Israel and Judah. Babylonian exile (539 B.C.)
Iron (Early)	1200–900 B.C.	Transition from bronze to iron tools. The Philistines settled in Canaan and built cities. Age of the Judges in Israel The Monarchy (Saul, David, Solomon)
Bronze (Late)	1550–1200 B.C.	Moses and the Exodus event Israelite settlement of Canaan.
Bronze (Middle)	2000–1550 B.C.	An urban period in Palestine: town planning, city walls, new ceramic forms, a simplified alphabet, and international trade. Ugaritic language = similar to biblical Hebrew. Age of Patriarchs: Abraham, Isaac, Jacob, Joseph.
Bronze (Early)	3200–2000 B.C.	Writing was invented about 3200 B.C. in Iran and at Warka. Stones, copper, and bronze were used for tools and weapons. Jericho was a walled city that flourished from 2900–2300 B.C. Main artifacts are pottery. Age of pyramids in Egypt.
Chalcolithic	4500–3200 B.C.	Hieroglyphics in Egypt. Stones and copper were used for tools and weapons. Ivory and bone were carved. Evidence of metal working and flint tool production. Clay statues, probably used in religious rituals.
Neolithic (Late)	4700–4500 B.C.	Stones were used for tools and weapons.
Neolithic (Pottery)	6000–4700 B.C.	Stones were used for tools and weapons. Pottery was first used.
Neolithic (Pre-pottery)	8000–6000 B.C.	Stones were used for tools and weapons. Extensive use of wheat and barley. Homes had rectangular rooms.
Mesolithic	18,000–8000 B.C.	Stones were used for tools and weapons. Animals were domesticated. People became farmers and herders.
Paleolithic (Upper)	45,000–18,000 B.C.	Stones and flints were used for tools and weapons. People were predominately hunters and food-gatherers.

HANDOUT 2B

Name _____ Date _____

TYPES OF LITERATURE IN THE OLD TESTAMENT

LITERATURE TYPE	EXAMPLE
Poetry	
Work Song	Numbers 21:17–18
Harvest Song	Judges 9:27; 21:21
Marriage and Love Songs	Song of Songs 4:1–10; 5:10–16
Song of Victory	1 Samuel 18:6–7
The Lament (individual and political)	2 Samuel 1:19–27
The Mocking Song	Isaiah 14:4–21
	Book of Psalms
Poetic Stories	
Saga	Genesis 3:13–15
Legend	Joshua 5:13–6:27
Parable	2 Samuel 12:1–4
Anecdote	Judges 15:1–7
Historical Literature	
Recording of History	1 Kings 9:10–28
Speeches	1 Samuel 12
Letters	Jeremiah 29:4–23
Prophetic Literature	Isaiah
Wisdom Literature	Proverbs
Laws	
Ten Commandments	Exodus 20:1–17
Priestly Laws	Leviticus
The Holiness Code	Leviticus 17–27
Deuteronomic Code	Deuteronomy 12–26

HANDOUT 2C

Name _____   Date _____

CATEGORIZING THE OLD TESTAMENT BOOKS

Pentateuch
- Genesis
- Exodus
- Leviticus
- Numbers
- Deuteronomy

Historical Books
- Joshua
- Judges
- Ruth
- 1 Samuel
- 2 Samuel
- 1 Kings
- 2 Kings
- 1 Chronicles
- 2 Chronicles
- Ezra
- Nehemiah
- Tobit
- Judith
- Esther
- 1 Maccabees
- 2 Maccabees

Wisdom Books
- Job
- Psalms
- Proverbs
- Ecclesiastes
- Song of Songs
- Wisdom
- Sirach

Prophetic Books
- Isaiah
- Jeremiah
- Lamentations
- Baruch
- Ezekiel
- Daniel
- Hosea
- Joel
- Amos
- Obadiah
- Jonah
- Micah
- Nahum
- Habakkuk
- Zephaniah
- Haggai
- Zechariah
- Malachi

HANDOUT 2D

Name _____   Date _____

CHAPTER 2 REVIEW PUZZLE

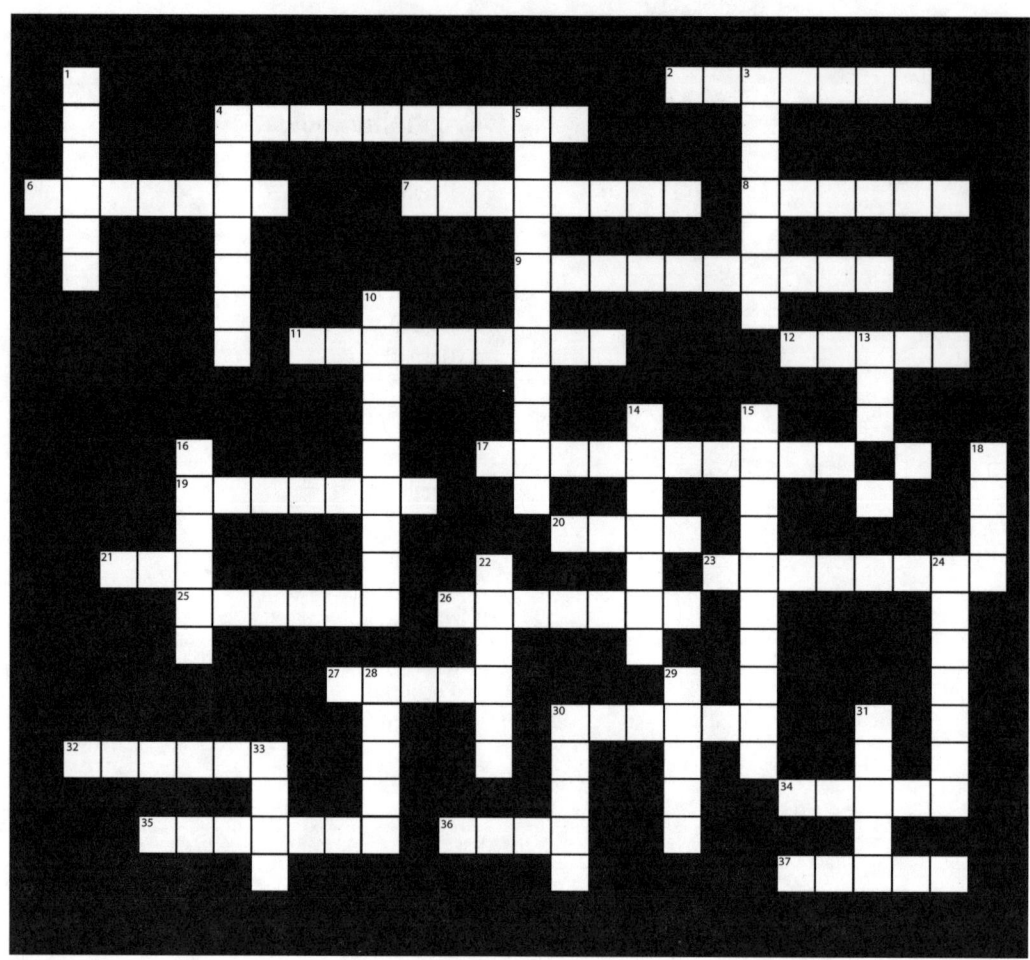

DOWN

1. Suffering servant prophet
3. people who copied scripture
4. person who proclaimed God's message
5. Civilization north and east of Canaan
10. Evidence of ancient life
13. King who mad Jerusalem the capital
14. King who built the Temple
15. A blending of two or more religions
16. Israelite name for God
18. First king of the Israelites
22. Ancient name for land of Palestine
24. Consort of El
28. Civilization south and west of Canaan
29. Religious poem/song
30. Where the Israelites settled in Canaan
31. He freed the Israelites from Babylon
33. A literary style in the Bible

ACROSS

2. Ancient stone inn three languages
4. Earliest form of writing
6. Found in apocalyptic writing
7. Jews living away from Jerusalem
8. Northern kingdom after end of monarchy
9. First five books of Bible
11. Stele that tells of Israel's defeat
12. Southern kingdom after end of monarchy
17. Ancient writing in Egypt
19. First patriarch of Israel
20. First writing prophet
21. Main focus of Pentateuch
23. "history" about the origins of the earth
25. Main event of the Old Testament
26. Place of exile
27. Ancient inscription from Moab
30. Egyptian name for foreign invaders
32. Job and Proverbs, i.e.
34. Another name for the Pentateuch
35. "In_____"; how the Bible should be studied
36. Canaanite rain god
37. Prophet who spoke of God as a lover

HANDOUT 2E

Name _____ Date _____

THE VALUE OF STORIES

As a group, agree on one current movie, television show, and popular book of fiction that provides insight into people your own age. If a future historian came across these media what might they learn about your generation? Would this portrait be true or not? Choose one person to summarize your group's discussion in each area.

MEDIA TYPE	TITLE	WHAT IT SAYS ABOUT MOST PEOPLE'S LIFESTYLE	WHAT IT SAYS ABOUT MOST PEOPLE'S CHARACTER AND VALUES	WHAT IT SAYS ABOUT MOST PEOPLE'S UNDERSTANDING OF GOD AND RELIGION
Movie				
TV Show				
Fiction Book				

HANDOUT 3A

Name _____ Date _____

THE SABBATH OR SHABBAT

Jews celebrate the Shabbat from sundown Friday to sundown Saturday. They spend this twenty-four hour period in rest, joy, and prayer. Here are some of the rules or customs that Jews observe on the Sabbath:

1. Many Jewish families prepare for the Sabbath by cleaning the house, cooking a special meal, bathing, and dressing in nice clothes.

2. Some Jews attend synagogue services on Friday night or Saturday morning.

3. Families eat a festive meal on Friday night. A tablecloth adorns the table. The mother of the family lights candles to announce the beginning of the Sabbath. There is a blessing of family members, the reading of Bible passages, and the singing of songs.

4. Many Jews change the pace of their week on the Sabbath. They refrain from work. They take longer to eat. They walk slower. They try to be more patient in listening. They spend time in spiritual reading. (*Note*: Biblical prohibitions included thirty-nine types of work, including the following: lighting a fire, clapping the hands, jumping, slapping the thigh, or walking more than 3,000 feet.)

5. Jewish spouses make time for one another on Friday evening.

6. Many Jews practice hospitality; they invite guests or strangers to the community to celebrate the Shabbat with them.

7. Some Jews reach out to others by visiting the sick, the shut-in, and the elderly on Saturday.

8. No funerals are permitted on the Shabbat.

9. At the end of the Sabbath, there is a special ceremony, called the havdalah. The family says good-bye to the Sabbath with the taste of wine, the fragrance of spices, and the light of a braided candle.

> Remember to keep holy the sabbath day. Six days you may labor and do all your work, but the seventh day is the sabbath of the Lord, your God. No work may be done then either by you, or your son or daughter, or your male or female slave, or your beast, or by the alien who lives with you. In six days the Lord made the heavens and the earth, the sea and all that is in them; but on the seventh day he rested. That is why the Lord has blessed the sabbath day and made it holy.
>
> (EXODUS 20:8–11)

> Then he said to them, "The sabbath was made for man, not man for the sabbath. That is why the Son of Man is lord even of the sabbath."
>
> (MARK 2:27–28)

- What are some ways you and your family can make Sunday—the Christian day for worship and rest—a day of rest, joy, and prayer?

HANDOUT 3B

Name _____ Date _____

THE FAITH OF ABRAHAM

Read each passage and write a short summary. Check whether the passage describes trust in God or doubt. Be prepared to explain your answer.

PASSAGE	SUMMARY	TRUST	DOUBT
Genesis 12:1–9			
Genesis 12:10–20			
Genesis 13:1–8			
Genesis 14:1–24			
Genesis 15:1–21			
Genesis 16:1–14			
Genesis 17:1–27			
Genesis 18:1–15			
Genesis 18:16–33			
Genesis 20:1–18			
Genesis 21:1–20			
Genesis 21:21–33			
Genesis 22:1–14			
Genesis 23:1–20			

HANDOUT 3C

Name _____ Date_____

BIBLICAL BIRTH STORIES

Isaac (Genesis 18:1–15; 21:1–21)
Summary:

Jacob and Esau (Genesis 25:19–34)
Summary:

Joseph (Genesis 30:1–24)
Summary:

Samson (Judges 13:1–25)
Summary:

Samuel (1 Samuel 1–2:11)
Summary:

How are these stories similar to the story of Moses' birth (Exodus 2:1–10)? How are they different?

HANDOUT 4A

Name _____ Date _____

THE PLAGUES AGAINST EGYPT

Fill in the following chart. Identify the number and order of plagues found in these three Bible sources.

EXODUS 7:8–13:16	PSALMS 78:40–55	PSALMS 105:23–38

HANDOUT 4B

Name _____ Date _____

SEDER FOOD SYMBOLS

The Greens (Karpas)	Although any green vegetable may be used, the most popular Seder greens are celery, parsley, or lettuce. The greens represent spring and rebirth—the rebirth of the Israelites after their slavery in Egypt.
Shank bone (Zeroa)	The shank bone symbolizes the Passover sacrifice brought to the Temple in Jerusalem by Jews. Any meat or poultry may be used at the Seder, but the most popular is a roasted lamb chop or a chicken/turkey neck. The bone is not eaten, since ritual sacrifice is not allowed in the absence of the Temple.
Bitter Herbs (Maror)	These herbs, usually horseradish or romaine lettuce, symbolize the bitterness of slavery. During the Seder, the herbs are dipped into salt water and then eaten.
Bitter Herbs (Chazeret)	Many Jews include a second bitter herb, or chazeret, at the seder, stemming from Numbers 9:11, which refers to "herbs" in the plural. The bitter herbs are eaten with matzah as a sandwich during the Seder meal.
Roasted Egg (Beitzah)	Eggs are traditionally a symbol of mourning in Judaism. The seder egg symbolizes the loss of the Temple and the hope that it will be rebuilt. Some Jews eat the egg dipped in saltwater toward the beginning of the meal.
Fruit and Nuts (Haroseth)	This mixture is symbolic of the mortar used by slaves. Most American Jews make the haroseth with apples, walnuts, sweet red wine, and cinnamon. At the Seder, the bitter herbs are dipped into the haroseth to dull their bitterness.
The Four Cups	During the meal, Jews drink four cups of wine (one at a time). They also leave a full cup of wine on the table for the prophet Elijah, who supposedly is also present during the seder.
Unleavened Bread (Matzah)	Matzah is flat, unleavened bread (flour and water) that symbolizes the unleavened bread the Israelites ate at the first Passover. Matzah is also called the "bread of affliction." At the seder there are three pieces of matzah, symbolic of the three categories of Jews that remain from ancient times: the priests, the Levites, and the Israelites.
Salt Water	This symbolizes the tears of the Jewish slaves in Egypt. The salt water also represents the tears of joy the Israelites shed when they were freed from slavery.

HANDOUT 4C

Name _____ **Date** _____

COMPARING ANCIENT ISRAELITE LAWS

1. In the Covenant Code, read Exodus 21:1–11. Compare this to passages from the Deuteronomic Code (Dt. 15:12–18; 23:15–16) on the same subject.

2. Read and compare the Deuteronomy passages (10:17–18, 24:19–21; 27:19) with those of the prophets (Isaiah 1:17; Jeremiah 7:6–7; 22:3; Ezekiel 22:7; Zechariah 7:10; Malachi 3:5). How are they alike? How are they different?

HANDOUT 4D

Name _____ Date _____

THE CHALLENGE OF PEACE

The following are excerpts from the 1983 document "The Challenge of Peace: God's Promise and Our Response." Think about your response to these statements and incorporate them when possible in your written response to the Journal Assignment, page 121.

Military Service: All those who enter the military service in loyalty to their country should look upon themselves as the custodians of the security and freedom of their fellow countrymen; and when they carry out their duty properly, they are contributing to the maintenance of peace. (p. iv)

Conscientious Objection: It seems just that laws should make humane provision for the case of conscientious objectors who refuse to carry arms, provided they accept some other form of community service. (p. iv)

Non-violence: We cannot but express our admiration for all who forego the use of violence to vindicate their rights and resort to other means of defense which are available to weaker parties, provided it can be done without harm to the rights and duties of others and of the community. (pp. iv–v)

Nuclear War: We do not perceive any situation in which the deliberate initiation of nuclear war, on however restricted a scale, can be morally justified. (p. v) Good ends (defending one's country, protecting freedom, etc.) cannot justify immoral means (the use of weapons which kill indiscriminately and threaten whole societies). (p. vii)

Peace: At the center of the Church's teaching on peace and at the center of all Catholic social teaching are the transcendence of God and the dignity of the human person. The human person is the clearest reflection of God's presence in the world; all of the Church's work in pursuit of both justice and peace is designed to protect and promote the dignity of every person. For each person not only reflects God, but is the expression of God's creative work and the meaning of Christ's redemptive ministry. Christians approach the problem of war and peace with fear and reverence. God is the Lord of life, and so each human life is sacred; modern warfare threatens the obliteration of human life on a previously unimaginable scale. (#15) We are called to be a Church at the service of peace, precisely because peace is one manifestation of God's word and work in our midst. (#27)

The Old Testament:
On War: God is often seen as the one who leads the Hebrews in battle, protects them from their enemies, makes them victorious over other armies. The metaphor of warrior...enabled [the people] to express their conviction about God's involvement in their lives;...they had a God who would protect them even in the face of overwhelming obstacles. (#31)

On Peace: Peace is always seen as a gift from God and as fruit of God's saving activity.... True peace implied a restoration of the right order not just among peoples, but within all of creation. (#32)

Fidelity to the Covenant: If Israel obeyed God's laws, God would dwell among them... God would strengthen the people against those who opposed them and would give peace in the land. (#33)

Hope for the Future: God's people clung tenaciously to hope in the promise of an eschatological time when, in the fullness of salvation, peace and justice would embrace and all creation would be secure from harm. (#38)

HANDOUT 5A

Name _____ Date _____

CRITICISM OF ISRAEL'S KINGS

Read each passage. Answer how each King sinned against Yahweh.

King	Scripture	How did he sin against Yahweh?
Saul	1 Sm 15:1–9	
David	2 Sm 11:1–27	
Solomon	1 Kgs 11:1–10	
Jeroboam	1 Kgs 14:1–10	
Baasha	1 Kgs 16:1–6	
Omri	1 Kgs 16:23–26	
Joram	2 Kgs 3:1–3	
Ahaziah	2 Kgs 8:25–27	
Zechariah	2 Kgs 15:8–10	
Ahaz	2 Kgs 16:1–4	
Manesseh	2 Kgs 21:1–16	
Zedekiah	2 Kgs 24:18–25:7	

HANDOUT 6A

Name _____ Date _____

KINGS OF JUDAH AND ISRAEL

This chart lists the kings of Judah and Israel. Read the scripture passages for the earlier kings. What religious developments took place during their reigns?

Judah (Southern Kingdom)		Israel (Northern Kingdom)	
Years	King	Years	King
922 B.C.	Rehoboam (1 Kgs 14:21–31)	922 B.C.	Jeroboam I (1 Kgs 12:25–14:20)
915	Abijam (1 Kgs 15:1–8)		
913	Asa (1 Kgs 15:9–24)		
		901	Nadab (1 Kgs 15:25–32)
		900	Baasha (1 Kgs 15:33–16:7)
		877	Elah (1 Kgs 16:8–14)
		876	Zimri (1 Kgs 16:15–20)
		876	Omri, Tibni (1 Kgs 16:21–28)
873	Jehosaphat		
		869	Ahab (1 Kgs 16:29–34)
		850	Ahaziah
849	Jehoram	849	Joram
842	Ahaziah	842	Jehu
842	Athaliah		
837	Jehoash		
		815	Jehoahaz
		801	Joash
800	Amaziah	786	Jeroboam II
783	Azariah (Uzziah)		
		746	Zechariah
		745	Shallum
		745	Menahem
742	Jotham		
		738	Pekahiah
		737	Pekah
735	Ahaz	732	Hoshea
		721	Fall of Samaria
715	Hezekiah		
687	Manesseh		
642	Amon		
640	Josiah		
609	Jehoahaz		
609	Jehoiakim		
598	Jehoiachin		
597	Zedekiah		
587	Fall of Jerusalem		

HANDOUT 6B

Name _____   Date _____

Solomon's Temple

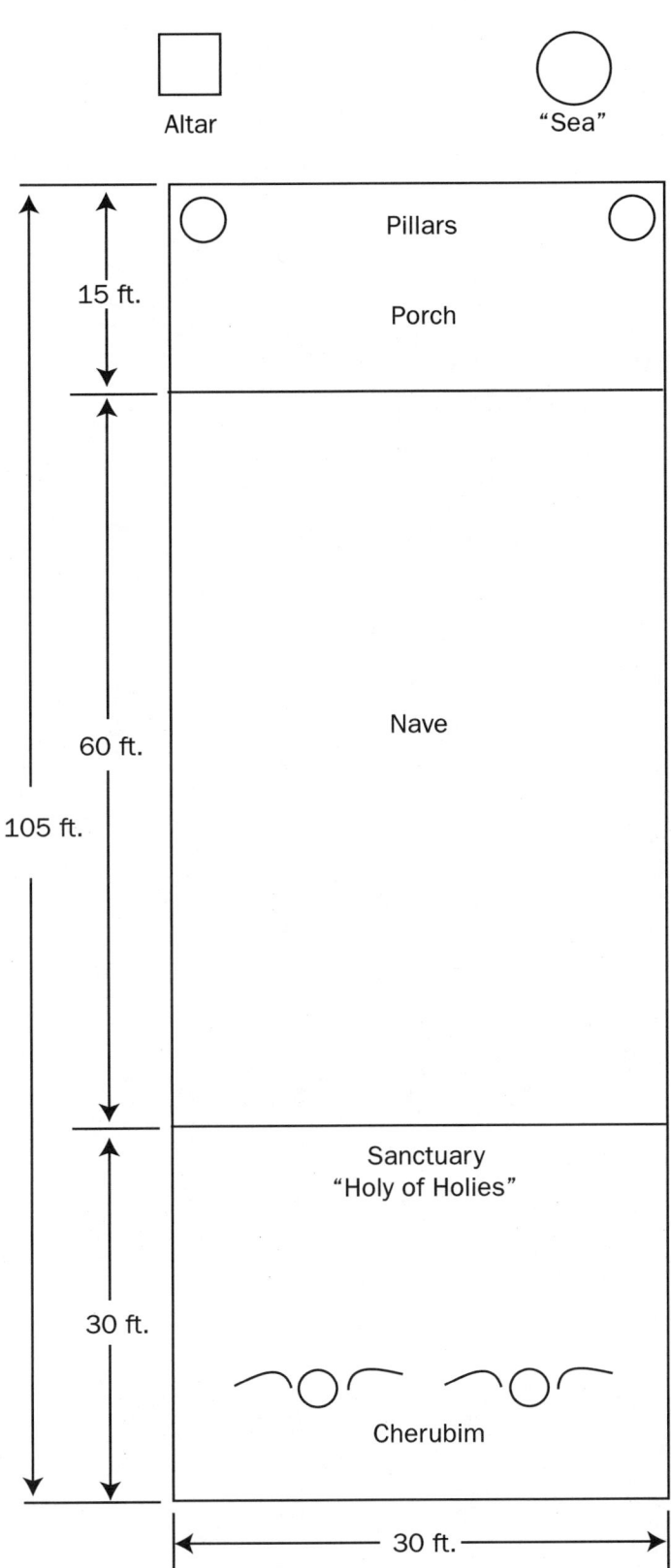

Read 1 Kings 6–8. Note the relative accuracy of the measurements listed here.

Note: There is little reliable information about the arrangement. This diagram shows the main elements.

HANDOUT 6C

Name _____ Date _____

CHAPTER 6 PRAYER SERVICE

Scripture Reading
Reader 1: *Read from 2 Samuel 5:1–3.*

Prayer Response
All:	Blessed is he who inherits the kingdom of David our father.
Side 1:	The Lord is my shepherd; I shall not want, In verdant pastures he gives me repose.
Side 2:	Beside restful waters he leads me; he refreshes my soul.
Side 1:	He guides me in right paths for his name's sake.
All:	Blessed is he who inherits the kingdom of David our father.
Side 2:	You spread the table before me in the sight of my foes;
Side 1:	You anoint my head with oil; my cup overflows.
All:	Blessed is he who inherits the kingdom of David our father.
Side 2:	Only goodness and kindness follow me all the days of my life;
Side 1:	And I shall dwell in the house of the Lord for years to come.
All:	Blessed is he who inherits the kingdom of David our father.

Prayer Intentions
Reader 2: For world leaders, that they may promote policies of justice and human dignity,
All: Lord, hear our prayer.
Reader 3: For our bishops and priests, that they may be people of prayer and wisdom,
All: Lord, hear our prayer.
Reader 4: For leaders in our country, that they may serve the needs of the poor as well as the rich,
All: Lord, hear our prayer.
Reader 5: For the student leaders in our school, that they may influence others for the good,
All: Lord, hear our prayer.
Reader 6: For each of us, that we may cultivate the qualities of good leadership,
All: Lord, hear our prayer.
Reader 6: For our own intentions, (spontaneous petitions)
All: Lord, hear our prayer.

Closing Prayer
All: Loving God,
   you conquer evil's hold on us
   and bring us to new life through our Lord, Jesus Christ,
   the King of the Universe.
May we never cease to praise
   your glory
   and love you with all of our hearts.
We ask this through Jesus Christ, our Lord,
   who lives and reigns with you and the Holy Spirit
   for ever and ever.
Amen.
   —adapted from Opening Prayer, feast of Christ the King

HANDOUT 6D

Name _____ Date _____

SOCIAL JUSTICE ISSUES

According to the Old Testament prophets, love for God equated with love for neighbor. To "love your neighbor" means treating others with justice, fairness, and mercy. Print each passage in the first column. Write a summary that explains the meaning of the passage in the second column.

Passage	Summary
Isaiah 1:17	
Ezekiel 22:3, 7	
Zechariah 7:10	
Malachi 3:5	

Read Matthew 25:31-46. What does Jesus say is our responsibility to social justice?

HANDOUT 7A

Name _____ Date _____

Ezekiel's Actions

Read each passage. Write how Ezekiel's actions follow a pattern: God gives a command, Ezekiel carries it out, and the symbolism is explained.

Action Passage	Pattern		
	1. God tells Ezekiel what to do	2. Ezekiel does the action	3. Symbolism of the action
Ezekiel 4:1–3			
Ezekiel 4:4–8			
Ezekiel 4:9–15			
Ezekiel 5:1–12			
Ezekiel 12:1–16			
Ezekiel 12:17–20			

HANDOUT 8A

Name _____   Date _____

JEREMIAH'S FEELINGS

Jeremiah wanted to be well-liked among his peers, but God had other plans for him. God kept telling Jeremiah to preach a message that the people didn't want to hear. Read the following passages from the book of Jeremiah, and summarize how Jeremiah felt in each of them.

Confessions of Jeremiah	How did Jeremiah feel?
Jeremiah 12:1–5	
Jeremiah 15:10–21	
Jeremiah 17:14–18	
Jeremiah 18:18–23	
Jeremiah 20:7–18	

Discussion Questions
1. How important is it to you to be popular?
2. What are some examples of times that being a Catholic today might cause other teens to reject or ridicule you?
3. Do you think being a Catholic is "worth it" even though it may make you unpopular? Explain.

HANDOUT 8B

Name _____ Date _____

PRAYER THEMES OF THE DIASPORA

The prayers of the exiles and former exiles reveal several common themes experienced and expressed by God's People in that era. Read and summarize each example, then write a common theme for each set of readings.

Scripture Passage	Summary
Ezra 9:6–7	
Nehemiah 9:16–17	
Daniel 9:8	
Baruch 1:15b–17	
Common Theme:	
Ezra 9:7–9	
Nehemiah 9:36–37	
Daniel 9:12	
Baruch 2:1	
Common Theme:	
Ezra 9:10–11	
Nehemiah 9:13	
Daniel 9:5	
Baruch 1:18	
Common Theme:	

HANDOUT 8C

Name _____   Date _____

EGYPTIAN PROVERBS

The Old Testament Wisdom authors sometimes borrowed from ancient Egyptian sources. One such source was the Teachings of Ptah-Hotep (2575–2134 B.C.). Read some of Ptah-Hotep's teachings here and compare them with the book of Proverbs. How are they the same? How are they different? How does the advice apply to people today?

50–60 (Compare with Proverbs 2:1–5 and 19:20.)	85–95 (Compare with Proverbs 11:21 and 17:13.)	120–42 (Compare with Proverbs 23:1–3)

My students, in all things, be intelligent, not arrogant,
    Be wise, not over-confident.
Seek advice from the powerless,
    As well as from the powerful.
No one ever reaches one's full potential.
    There is always more to learn.
Wisdom hides like emeralds,
    But it can always be uncovered . . .
    . . . in a poor man,
    . . . in a young woman grinding grain.
	If you become a ruler, do what is right,
	    Stay above reproach.
	Be just in your decisions,
	    Never ignoring the law.
	Injustice brings punishment,
	    Injustice brings all your work to nothing.
	Injustice brings success for a moment,
	    Justice brings success for two generations.
		If you work for someone else,
		    Take what your master offers.
		Do not look about with envy,
		    Do not always hope for more.
		Stand humbly until your master speaks to you,
		    Speak only when spoken to.
		Laugh when your master laughs,
		    Try to please your master in every thing.
		But remember this,
		    No one knows what is in another's heart.
		When masters are at the table,
		    They may seem to dispense favors as they see fit,
		    . . . to favor those who are useful,
		    . . . to favor those who think as they do.
		The wise soul is guided by the divine assembly,
		    Therefore, do not complain about their choices.

147–60 (Compare with Proverbs 25:13.)	**278–96 (Compare with Proverbs 6:23–29 and 7:24–27.)**	**328–34 (Compare with Proverbs 12:4 and 31:1–31.)**

If you become a messenger for the powerful,
    Be completely reliable on every assignment.
Carry out your orders to the letter.
    Withhold nothing.
    Forget nothing.
    Forge nothing.
    Repeat nothing.
    Embellish nothing.
Do not make harsh language worse.
    Vulgarity turns the mighty into enemies.
	If you become the father of a household or are a houseguest,
	    Stay away from the women of the house.
	Keep your mind on business, your eyes off pretty faces.
	    Foolish dreams become casualties of unwise actions.
	Escape love sickness and lust,
	    And succeed in everything else you do.
		If you become a landowner, establish a household,
		    Be faithful to your wife.
		Feed her, clothe her, make her happy.
		    And she will provide you with an heir.
		Do not sue her in court,
		    But do not let her dominate you.
		To judge a woman's moods
		    Is to read a woman's eyes.
		A wife who shares her husband's wealth
		    Is a wife who is faithful to her husband.

From Victor Matthews and Don C. Benjamin, *Old Testament Parallels: Laws and Stories from the Ancient Near East. 2nd Ed.* (New York, NY: Paulist Press, 1997), pp. 266–269 passim.

HANDOUT 9A

Name _____ Date _____

Kinds of Psalms

Summarize the psalms listed in each category. Then give a definition of each kind of psalm, using your own words.

1. Psalms of Lament:

Psalm 3	
Psalm 10	
Psalm 38	
Psalm 44	

2. Psalms of Praise and Thanksgiving:

Psalm 19	
Psalm 33	

3. Psalms of Instruction:

Psalm 1	
Psalm 105–6	

4. Liturgical Psalms:

Psalm 24	
Psalm 100	

HANDOUT 9B

Name _____   Date _____

Traditional Customs of Hanukkah

Another name for Hanukkah is "Festival of Lights." This name comes from the lighting of an eight-branch candleholder called a *hanukiyah*. On each day of Hanukkah, the family lights a new candle, until all eight are lit on the last night. The candles are tall enough to burn for at least thirty minutes. While the candles are burning, family members are to refrain from work. No mourning or fasting is allowed during the eight days of Hanukkah. Most families exchange gifts during the eight days.

Hanukkah Game

A favorite game of children to play on Hanukkah is Driedel. Here is how to play the game:
Each player starts with an equal number of coins, nuts, raisins, or candies. Each player puts one of these into the middle, or kitty. One person at a time spins the driedel. The driedel is like a four-sided die with Hebrew letters instead of numbers.

 (nun) means the player does nothing.

 (gimmel) means the player gets everything in the kitty.

 (hay) means the player takes half the kitty (or half plus one if there is an odd number in the kitty).

 (shin) means the player must add something to the kitty.

When nothing is left in the middle, everyone must add something. When a player is out of coins, nuts, raisins, or candies, he or she is out of the game. When one person has won everything from the other players, the game is over.

Hanukkah Menu

The Hanukkah menu often includes foods fried in oil (as a reminder of the miracle of the oil). Among the Hanukkah foods are potato latkes (a kind of pancake) and doughnuts. Here is a sample Hanukkah menu:

Butternut Squash Soup
Israeli Salad (cucumbers, tomatoes, scallion, green peppers)
Pan-Glazed Applies with Old-Fashioned Potato Latkes or Cauliflower Pancakes
Broiled Ginger Salmon
Jelly Doughnuts
Ice Cream with Chocolate Sauce
Rosettes (a flaky pastry)
Fresh Fruit: Mandarin oranges

Activities

1. Find out when Hanukkah will be celebrated this year. When does it begin? When does it end?
2. Interview a Jewish friend about how he or she celebrates Hanukkah.

HANDOUT 10A

Name _____ Date _____

DOROTHY DAY AND PACIFISM

Dorothy Day Timeline

1897	Born in Brooklyn, New York.
1917	Went to jail for demonstrating for women's suffrage outside the White House.
1927	Gave birth to a daughter. Became Catholic.
1933	Founded the Catholic Worker Movement with Peter Maurin.
1935	Established a house of hospitality in New York City to assist the needy and downtrodden.
1936	Declared that she and *The Catholic Worker* newspaper were pacifist in response to the Spanish Civil War.
1940s	Took a pacifist stand during World War II.
1950s	Led protests against compulsory air-raid drills in New York, saying they fostered a "war mentality."
1952	Published her autobiography, *The Long Loneliness*.
1960s	Was jailed for protesting the Viet Nam War.
1965	Influenced the bishops of Vatican II to include conscientious objection as a valid Christian response to war.
1973	Went to jail for protesting alongside Caesar Chavez and the United Farm Workers.
1980	Died.

Dorothy Day Quotations on Pacifism

- "Followers of Christ should not kill their brothers and sisters. . . . We believe that Christ went beyond natural ethics and the Old Dispensation in this matter of force and war and taught nonviolence as a way of life."

- "We do not have faith in God if we depend upon the Atom Bomb."

- (After the attack on Pearl Harbor, 1941) "We are still pacifists. Our manifesto is the Sermon on the Mount. . . . Speaking for our conscientious objectors, we will not participate in armed warfare or in making munitions, or buy government bonds to promote it. It has become too late in human history to tolerate wars which none can win. . . . All wars are, by their very nature, evil and destructive."

HANDOUT 10B